# Informatik—Fachberichte

Informatik Fachberichte 109

Herausgegeben von W. Brauer
Im Auftrag der Gesellschaft für Informatik (GI)

# Simulationstechnik

3. Symposium Simulationstechnik
Bad Münster a. St.-Ebernburg
24.-26. September 1985
Proceedings

Herausgegeben von Dietmar P. F. Möller

Springer-Verlag
Berlin Heidelberg New York Tokyo

**Herausgeber**
Dietmar P. F. Möller
Physiologisches Institut
Johannes Gutenberg Universität
Saarstr. 21, 6500 Mainz

CR Subject Classifications (1984): 8.1

ISBN-13:978-3-540-15700-7     e-ISBN-13:978-3-642-70640-0
DOI.10/1007:978-3-642-70640-0

VORWORT


Das "3. Symposium Simulationstechnik" fand vom  23. bis 26. September
1985 auf der Ebernburg in Bad Münster am Stein-Ebernburg statt. Diese
Tagung setzte die Reihe einer vom Fachausschuß 4.5 Simulation ( ASIM )
in der GI ( Gesellschaft für Informatik ) ins Leben gerufenen Tagungen
fort, die 1982 mit dem "1. Symposium Simulationstechnik" in Erlangen
begann, 1983 internationalen Charakter trug als "First European Simulation Congress", durchgeführt in Aachen, und 1983 in Wien  mit dem
"2. Symposium Simulationstechnik" fortgesetzt wurde.
Die Beiträge des "3. Symposium Simulationstechnik" wurden von einem internationalen Programmkomitee ( W. Ameling, RWTH Aachen; I. Bausch-Gall,
München; F. Breitenecker, TU-Wien; K.H. Fasol, Ruhr Univ. Bochum; H. Fuss,
GMD Bonn; J. Halin, ETH Zürich; W. Kleinert, TU Wien; D. P. F. Möller,
Univ. Mainz; H. J. Munser, Dornier GmbH Friedrichshafen; D. Popović,
Univ. Bremen; H. Rake, RWTH Aachen; B. Schmidt, Univ. Erlangen ) sorg-
fältig ausgewählt und spiegeln den aktuellen Stand der Simulation in
Theorie und Praxis wieder.

Um der großen Bedeutung der Simulation in den Anwendungsbereichen gerecht
zu werden, wurde nicht die übliche Einteilung der Beiträge in Methodologie, Software, Hardware und Anwendungen vorgenommen, sondern nach Anwen-
dungsgruppen klassifiziert, wie folgt:

    Modellbildungs- und Softwaremethodik
    Simulationshardware
    Simulationssprachen und Simulationssoftware
    Echtzeitsimulatiom
    Mathematische Verfahren
    Parameteridentifikation
    Simulation in Biologie und Medizin
    Schaltkreissimulation
    Simulation in technischen Anwendungen
    Simulation in der Fertigungstechnik
    Simulation in betriebwirtschaftlichen Anwendungen


Fünf Hauptvorträge mit den ThemenkreisenModellbildung, Diagnoseverfahren,
Echtzeitsimulation, Biokybernetik, Parameteridentifikation arbeiteten
auch prospektive Aspekte der Simulation heraus.

Als "Vorprogramm" zur Tagung wurde am Montag, den 23.9.,nachmittags,das
Tutorium "State of the art of today simulation computers" durchgeführt.
Die Referenten kamen von bedeutenden Computerherstellern bzw. Anwendern,

nämlich EAI ( USA ), M.A.N. ( D ) und CDC (USA ).

Das wissenschaftliche Programm wurde  mit Podiusdiskussionen und Rund-
tischgesprächen zur Echtzeitsimulation ( Organisation: I. Bausch-Gall,
München ) und Leistungsbewertung von Simulationssoftware ( Organisation:
B. Schmidt, Univ. Erlangen ) abgerundet.

Darüber hinaus wurden drei "Senior Lectures" gehalten.

Als gesellschaftliches Rahmenprogramm sorgten der Empfang im Kurhaus
von Bad Münster am Stein-Ebernburg am 23.9. - gesponsert von der Firma
CDC -, der Ebernburger Ritterschmauß am 24.9. - gesponsert von der
Firma EAI - und der Winzerschmauß in der historischen Schloßgaststätte
Schwarze Katze - gesponsert von Rapid Data Ltd. und Dr. Städtler Unter-
nehmensberatung - für ein geselliges Beisammensein.

Abschließend möchte ich allen danken, die zum Gelingen dieser Tagung
beigetragen haben:
- den Autoren und Vortragenden für ihre Beiträge und Zusammenarbeit
- den Teilnehmern, die die Tagung zu einem Forum hohen Niveaus werden
  ließen
- den Sponsoren, den Firmen Control Data Corporation, Electronic
  Associates Incorporation, Mitchel & Gauthier ( Rapid Data Ltd. )
  und Dr. Städtler Unternehmensberatung
- dem Springer Verlag für die gute Zusammenarbeit
- meiner Frau und meiner Tochter für das mir entgegengebrachte Verständnis.

Mainz, im Sommer 1985                    Dietmar P. F. Möller

INHALTSVERZEICHNIS


Seite

<u>TUTORIAL</u> "STATE OF THE ART OF TODAY SIMULATION COMPUTERS"

Z. V. Ilic    ( USA - EAI, West Long Branch, N.J. )

SIMSTAR$^{TM}$ the search for an optimal simulation tool          3

R. Trier    ( D - M.A.N., Nürnberg )
Der Simulationsrechner in der M.A.N. Werk Nürnberg - Konfiguration, Betriebserfahrung und Folgerungen          14

W. R. Ray    ( USA - CDC, Minneapolis, M.N. )
CYBERPLUS, a high performance parallel processing system
for simulation applications          23


<u>HAUPTVORTRÄGE</u>

M. Mansour, A. Altmann    ( CH - ETH Zürich )
Modellbildung dynamischer Systeme - eine Übersicht          37

R. Lunderstädt    ( D - Univ. der Bundeswehr, Hamburg )
Grundlagen und Anwendungen von Diagnoseverfahren          50

W. D. Hass    ( D - Lufthansa, Frankfurt )
Anforderungen an Echtzeitsimulationssysteme für Ausbildung und Training von Verkehrsflugzeugführern          64

M. Buse, J. Werner    ( D - Ruhr Univ. Bochum )
Das thermoregulatorische System des Menschen: 3-D
Simulation auf einem Vektorrechner          65

K. Diekmann    ( D - Ruhr Univ. Bochum )
Experimentelle Modellbildung zur digitalen Simulation          74


<u>SENIOR LECTURE</u>

W. Ameling    ( D - RWTH Aachen )
Methoden und Aspekte zur Planung und Analyse technischer
Systeme          87

B. Schmidt    ( D - Univ. Erlangen )
Was tut man, wenn man simuliert? Versuch einer Begriffsbestimmung          104

Seite

B. Schneider   ( D - Med. Hochschule Hannover )
Modelle für die medizinische Diagnostik                    112


MODELLBILDUNGS- UND SOFTWAREMETHODIK

P. Winkler   ( D - PSI GmbH, Berlin )
Ein Beispiel für Modellierung und Simulation mit
Petrinetz-Modellen                                         129

A. Schöne   ( D - Univ. Bremen )
Ein-Marken-Petrinetze und synchrone Schaltwerke            136

H. Fuss   ( D - GMD, Bonn )
Zur Simulation von Zufall und Verläßlichkeit               141

K. Küspert   ( D - IBM Deutschland, Heidelberg )
Quantitative Bewertung fehlertoleranter Hashtabellen-
Implementierungen in Datenbanksystemen durch Simulations-
reihen                                                     147

K. Kohel, U. Maschtera   ( A - Univ. Linz )
Assoziation bei der Modellierung diskreter Simulationssysteme: Ein Konzept und Überlegungen zu seiner Implementierung                                                    152

U. Maschtera   ( A - Univ. Linz )
Aggregation von Prozessen im Rahmen der konzeptionellen
Modellierung diskreter Simulationssysteme                  157

K. H. Sturm   ( D - VDP, Berlin )
Requirements im Kontext eines Simulationsmodells           162


SIMULATIONSHARDWARE

F. Regen, M. Behrens, W. Ameling   ( D - RWTH Aachen )
Simulation unterschiedlicher Verbindungsnetze im M5PS
Multiprozessorsystem - Modellierung                        171

M. Behrens, F. Regen, W. Ameling   ( D - RWTH Aachen )
Simulation unterschiedlicher Verbindungsnetze im M5PS
Multiprozessorsystem - Lastfälle, Strategien und Simu-
lationsergebnisse                                          177

Seite

R. P. Liedtke   ( D - Forschungszentrum Informatik )
Simulation eines Datenbankrechners für die Prozeßdatenverarbeitung                                                   183


SIMULATIONSSPRACHEN UND SIMULATIONSSOFTWARE

W. A. Havranek   ( UK - Rapid Data Ltd, Worthing )
Update on ACSL                                                    191

I. Bausch-Gall   ( D - München )
Kopplung spezieller Simulationsprogramme mit Simulationssprachen als Modellierungshilfe für kontinuierliche Systeme       196

H. Braun   ( D - Univ. Karlsruhe )
SIDAS II, ein Programmpaket zur modularen blockorientierten
Simulation dynamischer Systeme                                    202

D. Matko, M. Šega, B. Zupančič, R. Karba ( YU - Univ.
                                        Ljubljana )
A compiler for control systems simulation                         211

R. Schaback   ( D - Univ. Göttingen )
Interaktive graphische Simulation kontinuierlicher Systeme        215

P. Eschenbacher   ( D - Univ. Erlangen )
Entwurf einer Allgemeinen Modellbeschreibungssprache              220

K.-J. Langer   ( D - Univ. Erlangen )
Das Simulationssystem SIMPLEX II: Ein Experimentiersystem
mit Allgemeiner Modellbeschreibungssprache                        230

S. Nagel   ( D - Univ. Erlangen )
Transactionsorientierte Modelle mit beschränkten
Warteräumen in GPSS-FORTRAN                                       235

R. K. Bell   ( D - Uttenreuth )
Die Bedienstation in SPIRO                                        241

W. Tettweiler   ( D - Krailling )
MAPLIS - Matrixorientierte Simulation als Fortsetzung der
Statistik in den Sozialwissenschaften                            248

Seite

ECHTZEITSIMULATION

R. Kodweiß   ( D - Dornier GmbH, Friedrichshafen )
Software Konzept für Echtzeit-Simulation                                    251

H. J. Munser   ( D - Dornier GmbH, Friedrichshafen )
Computer assisted procedure Trainer ( CAPT ), ein neues
Ausbildungsmittel  zur Pilotenschulung                                      254

G. Schütz   ( D - Lufthansa, Frankfurt )
Anforderungen an das Datenpaket zum Design und Betrieb
von Flugzeugsimulatoren für      Ausbildung  und
Training von Cockpitbesatzungen                                             255

D.  Shorrock   ( USA - Rediffusion Simulation Inc. )
Computer generated images for aircraft simulators                          264

J. L. Bentz  ( USA - McDonnel Douglas Electr. Comp. )
Multiview$^{TM}$ Display                                                      265


MATHEMATISCHE VERFAHREN

H. J. Halin, K. Tichy   ( CH - ETH Zürich )
Konzepte neuer Algorithmen zur Integration steifer
und hochfrequenter Probleme                                                 269

H. J. Halin, S. A. R. Hepner, H. P. Geering   ( CH - ETH
                                                 Zürich )
Über die Vorteile semianalytischer Methoden zur Lösung
von "Optimal Control Problems"  dargestellt an einem
Beispiel aus der Robotik                                                    271

F. Breitenecker   ( A - TU Wien )
Simulation des Linear-Quadratischen Regelungsproblemes                     273

M. Gräff   ( A - TU Wien )
Simulation des Nachbeulverhaltens achsensymmetrischer
Kugelschalen                                                               279

Seite

<u>PARAMETERIDENTIFIKATION</u>

K. Diekmann   ( D - Ruhr Univ. Bochum )
Selbsttätige Fehlererkennung und Modellanpassung bei
der Simulation                                                  285

K. J. Krechel-Mohr, I. Molnar   ( D - Polch
                                  H - Budapest )
Ein universelles Optimierungsmodul zur Lösung von
Entscheidungsproblemen in der Simulation                        290

W. Renn, H. M. Frauer, R. Maulbetsch, M. Eggstein
                                ( D - Univ. Tübingen )
Der Einfluß des statistischen Modells für den Meßprozeß auf die Auswahl des Verfahrens der Paremeter-
schätzung                                                       297

J. Schlöder, A. Conrads, T. Frank   ( D - Univ. Bonn )
Neuere Verfahren zur Parameteridentifizierung dargestellt
am Beispiel der Modellierung von Rübenwachstum                  304


<u>SIMULATION IN BIOLOGIE UND MEDIZIN</u>

O. Richter   ( D - Univ. Bonn )
Simulation von Ökosystemen                                      311

W. Gabriel   ( D - Max Planck Institut, Plön )
Simulation komplexer Populationsdynamik                         318

L. Galke   ( D - Remscheid )
Computersimulation in der Verhaltensbiologie                    325

Ch. Giersch   ( D - Univ. Düsseldorf )
Simulation biochemischer Prozesse in der Pflanzenphysiologie: Dynamik und Regulation der photosynthetischen $CO_2$-Fixierung im Calvin-Zyklus                       331

O. Hoffmann   ( D - Univ. Gießen )
Simulation zentraler Regulationsstörungen bei intrakranieller Drucksteigerung                                         336

H. Pösinger   ( A - TU Graz )
Ein Programmsystem zur Simulation des Kreislaufsystems
und zur Identifikation von Kreislaufparametern                  341

Seite

D.P.F.Möller, V.Pohl, T.Sikora, E.Hennig   ( D - Univ. Mainz
                                             D - Univ. Bremen
                                             D - FU Berlin )
Simulation eines ungeregelten pulsatilen Modelles des
Herzkreislaufsystems                                            346

B. A. Gottwald   ( D - Univ. Freiburg )
Zur Modellierung zeitverzögerter biologischer Prozesse          350

A. Gilg   ( D - Siemens AG, München )
Simulationen an einem zeitabhängigen Modell des Gegenstromsystems der Niere                                          355

D. P. F. Möller   ( D - Univ. Mainz )
Computersimulation der renalen Hämodynamik                      366

R.Karba, A.Mrhar, F.Kozjek, M.Atanasijević, D.Matko
                              ( YU - Univ. Ljubljana )
Specific cases of drugs multiple dosing using analog-
hybrid simulation                                               371


SCHALTKREISSIMULATION

F. Egger   ( D - Siemens AG, München )
SMILE: Multi-Level-Simulator für den Entwurf logischer
Schaltungen                                                     379

K. Fischer, W. Hahn   ( D - Univ. Passau )
MUSIC: Ein Höchstleistungsrechner für die Simulation
digitaler Systeme                                               385

F. Mündemann, W. Hahn   ( D - Univ. der Bundeswehr, Neubiberg
                          D - Univ. Passau )
Algorithmische Spezifikation von MOSFET's  für
Mixed-Design-Level Simulation                                   392

D. Tavangarian   ( D - Univ. Frankfurt )
Simulation digitaler integrierter Schaltungen                   397

P. Jedele, H. Khakzar   ( D - SEL, Stuttgart, FH Esslingen )
Analyse nichtlinearer frequenzabhängiger Übertragungssysteme
mit Volterra-Reihen und dem Simulationsprogramm SPICE           404

Seite

## SIMULATION IN TECHNISCHEN ANWENDUNGEN

M. R. Heller   ( D - CDC, München )
Vehicle crashworthiness simulation - The role of
supercomputers                                                    415

K.-H. Senger   ( D - DFVLR, Oberpfaffenhofen )
Einsatz von MKS-Formalismen zur KFZ-Simulation                   427

M.Kaczmarek, J.Pietrowsky, B. Woyńska   ( PL - TH Poznań )
Simulationsmodelle für die Untersuchung des Verkehrsablaufes im Straßennetz                                            433

G.Voß, J.Kwaśnikowsky   ( D - Univ. Hannover, PL - TH Poznań )
Zur Glaubwürdigkeit eines Simulationsmodelles für
Eisenbahnfahrten                                                 438

H.-D.Engelmann, H.-H.Erdmann   ( D - Univ. Dortmund )
Simulation als Hilfe zur optimalen Prozeßfindung                 443

W. Wiening, H. Rake   ( D - RWTH Aachen )
Digitale Simulation der Dynamik großer Kreuzstromwärmeübertrager                                                       448

H. B. Keller   ( D - Kernforschungszentrum Karlsruhe )
Unterstützung der Prozeßführung im nuklear-chemischen
Bereich durch den Einsatz der Simulationstechnik                 453

H. Stahl   ( D - Univ. Erlangen )
Modellbildung im Turbinen- und Generatorbereich einer
Kraftwerksanlage                                                 459

M.Atanasijević, R.Karba, F.Bremšak   ( YU - Univ. Ljubljana )
Semibatch distillation modelling and control design             464

J.Čretnik, S.Strmčnik, B.Zupančič   ( YU - Univ. Ljubljana )
A model for combustion of fuel in the boiler                     469

K. Amborski, M. Kociécki   ( PL - TU Warschau )
Die Anwendung des Simulators GPSS-FORTRAN zur Simulation
eines Container-Terminals                                        474

H. Gülich, M. Köhne   ( D - Univ. Siegen )
Modellbildung und Simulation von Abwasserreinigungsanlagen                                                            479

Seite

SIMULATION IN DER FERTIGUNGSTECHNIK

F. Letters    ( D -  Stuttgart )
Die Simulation unterstützt die Montageplanung    483

M. Soliman, G. Reinicke    ( D - Univ. Hannover )
Simulation: Schlüssel zur Optimierung der Betriebs-
mittelspezifischen Aktivitäten im Betrieb    493

J. Sowa    ( D - Translift GmbH, Grenzach-Wyhlen )
Das integrierte Materialfluß-Simulationssystem TRANSIM    500

A. Teriete (D - Fraunhofer-Institut, Dortmund )
Dialogorientierte Simulation von automatisierten
Materialfluß-Systemen    511

A. Reinhardt    ( D - GH Kassel )
Realzeitsteuerung mit dem graphisch-interaktiven
Simulator SIMFLEX/2    512

O. Kapliński    ( PL - TU Poznań )
Die Ausnutzung der Simulationstechnik zur Untersuchung
und die Steuerung der Zuverlässigkeit von Produktionsprozessen im Bauwesen    517


SIMULATION IN DER BETRIEBSWIRTSCHAFTLICHEN ANWENDUNG

W. Ettl    ( A - TU Wien )
Auswirkungen von Modellverbesserungen bei stochastischen
Systemen    525

W. Ettl    ( A - TU Wien )
Finanzielle Auswirkungen von Änderungen eines Pensionssystems auf eine Pensionskasse    531


ANSCHRIFTEN DER AUTOREN/VORTRAGENDEN    537

# TUTORIAL


# STATE OF THE ART OF TODAY SIMULATION COMPUTERS

SIMSTAR™
THE SEARCH FOR
AN OPTIMAL SIMULATION TOOL

Zoran V. Ilic
Electronic Associates, Inc.
West Long Branch, N.J. 07764/USA

## ABSTRACT



Simulation is an essential part of product development and research, because it has proven to reduce total project costs. At the same time, simulation also reduces the development time and helps produce products with more balanced features (price/performance, safety, etc...) for specific market segments.

Faced with a well-defined simulation task(s), one of the first steps required for a simulation engineer is to specify at least an adequate simulation tool for its execution. Over the years, the number of computer-based simulation systems has grown and simulation tasks have become more numerous and more demanding, reflecting a continuous increase in the complexity of engineering systems.

Evaluating different simulation alternatives takes time and money. To enable a preselection of available alternatives, the general characteristics of commercially available simulation tools are given and compared to the general characteristics of SIMSTAR$^{tm}$, EAI's new simulation multiprocessor. The features of SIMSTAR and some of its unique values are illustrated.

## 1. INTRODUCTION

We address ourselves to simulationists, simulation engineers whose jobs seem to be getting more complex despite numerous technological advances within computer-based simulation systems.

If nothing else, the problems being solved today are becoming more complex and the apparent choice of simulation systems much greater. Given a simulation task, the first step is to specify and/or find an adequate simulation tool. How simple if the necessary tool is found in-house and is available. How relatively simple, also, if this tool has been previously used to the point that a simulationist knows from experience how to obtain cost-effective solutions. From this point on, a simulationist can concentrate fully on the execution of the requested task(s). For some simulation tasks, a search for an optimal tool might have to extend beyond available in-house computing facilities. What follows is a review of features of systems currently used for simulation, presented in parallel with features of EAI's product.

## 2. COMPUTER-BASED SYSTEMS CURRENTLY USED FOR SIMULATION

Today, one can find examples of practically every type of computer made being used for simulation : from microcomputers to supercomputers ; from general-purpose computers to special-purpose computers ; from simulation-oriented to nonsimulation-task specific ; from digital and analog to hybrid ; from standalone to "attached" or peripheral processors ; from array processors to an array of processors ; from single-instruction multiple data to multiple-instruction/ multiple data structured systems ; from simple (classical) architecture computers to Real-Time and Multi-processor types of architectures.

The above list is mostly a testament to the evolution of digital computers whose progress today, as yesterday, is mostly due to the pressures coming from the users involved in applications not directly involved with simulation.

### 2.1. Supercomputers

The extreme needs of large-scale high-speed simulations for nuclear, seismic, weather and oil research applications directly influenced development of supercomputers (first as large pipelined standalone array processors, more recently as vector and vector-scalar processors). (5, 7)

Unfortunately, due to their price, they are out of reach for most simulationists. This is not to say that they are not producing cost-effective solutions.

Supercomputers are seldom bought to be used in the real time simulation environment. When they are, the real time problems are not allowed to take 100 % of computer time in order to ensure decent response time to non-RT users connected to the same systems. It is the numerous non-RT users who usually support the operating costs of a supercomputer. Large enough RT problems can severely diminish a response time to other "simultaneous" users. Once a supercomputer has grown older, the maintenance costs grow exorbitantly high to maintain a required MTBF. Simply, supercomputers are not made for the RT environment, with or without hardware-in-the-loop requirements. They certainly can be adapted (by creating special S/W or H/W or both) for special tasks. However, acquiring them to be used for what they are not designed for should be questioned.

## 2.2. Hybrid Computers

Specifically developed for simulation, these affordable machines maintained their price/performance advantage for complex simulations. When the original hybrid computers were developed, the digital computer speed was such that they could only be used for the setup/checkout and simple start/stop mode control purposes (today's equivalent of downloading, debugging and start/stop operations done on host computers in conjunction with attached peripheral processors). For high-speed "digital" operations (needed to solve combinatorial and sequential Boolean equations in parallel), a separate logic section was provided. This was the first level of hybridization of analog machines. Later, hybrid computers included a fast A/D and D/A interface and a miniscientific computer allowing problem partitioning between the two for an optimum speed/accuracy solution. The analog and logic section required manual patching. In later models, scaling was software supported.

### 2.2.1 SIMSTAR - A Hybrid Multiprocessor

The latest generation of hybrid simulation systems (SIMSTAR) contains an imbedded 32-bit supermini (DAP) with Real-Time oriented architecture. A Parallel Logic Processor is included in solving Boolean equations and for an accurate real-time base, a superfast, intelligent A/D and D/A data communications processor, and an analog processor based on macro-oriented hardware primitives. Both shared memory and high-speed data links exist for communicating with a potential host computer. Both "patching" and scaling of the analog/logic processors are automatic. At the highest programming level, the whole multiprocessing system is programmable from a single language.

### 2.3 General Purpose Computers

From microcomputers to superminis and large Electronic Data Processing (EDP) machines ("mainframes"), these machines are understood and used by most simulationists. The smaller general-purpose machines can be very cost-effective to the point that they may be dedicated to a simgle simulation task. Larger ones are seldom bought specifically for simulation, and are often used by several departments for widely different applications. Individual micros can be effectively used only for very small simulation tasks. In a network, micros can be used for larger general-purpose simulation. When in a special multiple microprocessor system, they are usually dedicated to a single application without general-purpose system software.

Minis have started and now superminis are continuing to replace EDP machines for some rather demanding "number crunching" applications. Those minis which offer Real-Time architecture coupled with excellent speed characteristics, can be used for demanding simulations, i.e., both as a general-purpose and high-speed simulation machines. It was an EDP machine for which IBM developed and attached a first array processor many years ago. This resulted in improved performance for a specific computation task of matrix inversions. Today, arithmetic coprocessors are added to microcomputers to enhance their performance. Minis and superminis are offered with integral floating point processors, and both main and disk cache units exist to minimize the effect of CPU/memory communication bottlenecks. Some superminis can, optionally, accept another CPU to split computer-bound and I/O-bound tasks in a multistream environment. Today's language compilers for general-purpose machines are of the optimizing kind, producing object code which can hardly be surpassed by anyone's hand coding for most applications.

Minis and superminis are the most popular "hosts" for array processors. A new generation of a host computer might outperform a combination of the older generation host coupled to an array processor. Caution : a task which is not greatly suited to the array processor might run slower on a host/array processor combination than the same application running totally within the host computer (1).

The versatility of general-purpose computers, as their name implies, as well as their ease of use, coupled with their frequent performance enhancements (even before counting the add-ons which can selectively increase their performance), make them the likeliest simulation computer candidates for all but the very large scale and smaller than large scale, but extremely speed demanding or very special simulation tasks.

It is worth noting that earlier speed improvements of general-purpose processors were largely due to the advancements in component technology. More recently, speed increases are largely due to the novel architecture employed both within and "nearby" general-purpose computers. The level of "intelligence" and speed of attached and I/O processors, the architecture of peripheral processors themselves, as well as implementation of pure hardware solutions for often-used software functions, are all adding to the speed capability of simulation systems based on general-purpose machines.

For comparative purposes, note that in the continuous domain of analog computers, many elemental "functions" are of much higher level than found in the Arithmetic Processing unit of a general-purpose computer (e.g., "INTEGRATE" is an elemental function of analog computers) and all of them operate synchronously and in parallel, passing to each other (where necessary) their results <u>simultaneously</u> while computing. In general, a large number of digital processors operating in parallel cannot begin to match the price/performance of the analog processor due to the delays in intermediate results.

### 2.3.1. <u>Parallel Computation in a Purely Digital Domain</u>

In a multiprocessor environment, the need for communication between the computational units is dictated by equation expressed data dependencies, i.e., by the problem's natural data flow. The communication paths are specific and different for each simulation problem.

This need for interprocessor communication severely reduces the price/performance effectivity of purely digital systems, i.e., when all processors operate in a purely digital domain.

So far, interprocessor communication has proven to be the problem of purely digital systems, especially when used for high-speed simulation of continuous systems in a general-purpose simulation environment. The speed improvement realized (over the speed of a uni-processor system) is usually just a fraction of the theoretical one expected of N processors tied in parallel. The problem revolves around both hardware (H/W) and/or software (S/W) overheads. The pure H/W solutions maximize a price penalty, while pure S/W solutions maximize a time penalty of a solution. There are really no "pure" H/W or S/W solutions, since all practical H/W solutions include a certain amount of S/W overhead, and all S/W solutions need H/W to run on.

A common memory H/W solution does not allow individual processors a truly parallel access to data, needing additional H/W and/or S/W to more or less intelligently serialize the access to memory for all read and write functions. This includes resolving a problem arising when one processor needs a data value before another had time to compute and store it.

Another H/W solution is a "crossbar" switch permitting a simultaneous communication between all processors. The H/W overhead (a price) of the full crossbar interconnect can exceed the price of N processors even for systems where N is small and wordlength less than 32 bits. As such, the crossbar scheme is unthinkable for systems with hundreds of processors or more (e.g., for "Data-Flow" machines).

Going for a partial crossbar increases the S/W overhead (overall solution time) since "transport" of variables has to be scheduled across the interconnect.

Reducing the number of processors in order to minimize the number of switches (full crossbar needs NXN of them), calls for more costly individual processors and leads us back towards a uniprocessor solution. Artificially increasing their power by (e.g.) using a lower level integration algorithm may easily lead to increased dynamic errors in computation.

In the extreme, going for a realizable linear or a ring bus, while significantly reducing the H/W overhead, will inevitably result in the least performing system.

2.4 <u>Special-Purpose Digital Computers</u>

Most of the available special-purpose computers are array and vector processors attachable to minis, superminis and EDP-type of machines. None of them are specifically built for simulation, yet they can be programmed to perform a variety of simulation tasks, to at least partially off-load the host computer.

The only simulation-oriented special-purpose processor is the AD-10, which started as a function generator many years ago (6). Later on, it was expanded with an integration processor. The integration is done within a much wider word, but like its function generator, the integration unit within AD-10 does not perform floating point computations.

For most array processors, the software overhead to transfer data, programs, or control through the host/array processor interface may prove to be too much for an advantageous utilization of the host/Array processor system. The software overhead further increases if it has to handle word format conversions between the two (1). This software overhead effectively precludes utilizing a host for on-line and cooperative computation on the same problem, i.e., a la hybrid.

An efficient compiler for array processors is a must, otherwise an array processor program - unless hand coded in assembly - will result in a slower executing program, thereby defeating the array processor's original purpose. Note that compiler effi-ciency is very much problem dependent (10).

Writing the assembly language code for array processors is much harder than for conventional General-Purpose Computers (GPC) (even when not trying to write an optimal code). The programming word is much wider and one has to synchronize many operations running in parallel within the array processor.

Regardless of how it is programmed, the array processor is most effecient when processing vectors, i.e., when employed to execute highly repetitive arithmetic operations. Also, vectors have to be rather long (not typical of many simulation programs) if the host/array processor combination is to be more cost-effective than a general-purpose computer executing the same algorithm.

Debugging an array processor program requires a simulator (running on the host) or, in its absence, the array processor itself. For successful debugging, a timing diagram for the very low level operations, even for the "synchronous" array processors, might be necessary.

Tying multiple array processors to work on different parts of a larger simulation program is like tying together any other digital processors (special-purpose or general-purpose). When considering <u>practical</u> simulation problems, they simply do not divide nicely into equal (computationally speaking) and independent parts. As a result, one cannot expect, of the multiple array processors system, a materiali-zation of the theoretical improvement in processing speed. Also, to be able to use them in a multiple arrangement might require availability of special software (2).

3. <u>SHOULD YOU CONSIDER A SIMSTAR</u> ?

During the preliminary review of potential candidates, all simulation tools, especially those which are specifically built for general-purpose simulation, should be considered. From the technical point of view, the characteristics of the defined simulation task(s) with its execution environment are primary determinants of a subset of "likely candidates" out of the universe of available simulation tools. The specifics of "execution environment" (i.e., a requirement for integrated and direct analog input/output capability, etc...) might further reduce the number of "likely candidates."

The characteristics of the process to be simulated are less influential, but some of them can <u>definitively</u> help to point in the right direction in a search for the proper simulation tool. Having a budgetary estimate, based on providing a minimum of information requested by the manufacturers, would provide "ball park" prices for the "likely candidates." In the process of providing information necessary for budgetary estimates, a simulationist would learn potentially important facts of considered systems. In the same process, the manufacturer would obtain a basic idea as to the application(s) considered for the system, thereby helping to provide a more appropriate or more appropriately configured system. You should expect different levels of information to be needed by different manufacturers.

3.1. <u>Consider SIMSTAR if...</u>

Three nonexhaustive and nonordered lists are presented to provide a basis for an informed decision to include SIMSTAR in the set of "likely candidates." You <u>should</u> consider SIMSTAR if you find a match (one or more) between the items listed here, and elements itemized on your own list of Simulation Task(s) Characteristics, Simulation Process Characteristics and Desirable Simulation Tool Technical Characteristics.

3.1.1. <u>Simulation Task(s) Characteristics</u>

- High-speed simulation
- Simulation requiring direct interaction between the user and the simulation
- Real-Time (RT) or Faster than Real-Time (FRT) simulations
- Control system design evaluation and testing
- High-frequency and/or on-line multiple channel signal processing
- Optimization/Monte Carlo studies
- Hardware-In-The-Loop (HIL) simulations
- Split domain simulations

3.1.2. <u>Simulation Process Characteristics</u>

- Complex, highly nonlinear dynamic process
- Presence of first or higher order discontinuities
- Highly stiff
- Fast or slow processes (extremely fast processes might have to be solved slower than RT)
- Process describable by highly coupled sets of ordinary differential, algebraic and Boolean equations

3.1.3. <u>Desirable Simulation Tool Technical Characteristics</u>

- Cost effective

° General-purpose

° Easy to learn and use

° RT oriented system (hardware <u>and</u> software)

° 32 to 64 bits of numerical resolution

° Five digit accuracy for analog processor

° Easily synchronizable with real-time

° Easily interfacable with external hardware

° High level programmable from a single source program

° Direct analog input/output capability

° Genuinely parallel processing

° Highly integrated simulation system

° Modularly expandable

° Capability to provide an incremental computing power <u>proportional</u> to the reasonably small incremental funds, where "small" means 1-2 per cent or less of the system price

° Highly reliable

° Availability of both <u>fast</u> (to assert a readiness level) and exhaustive (to detect and isolate the presence of both hard and soft failures to, at least, the board level)

° Easily maintainable and with remote diagnostic capability

° High degree of self-testing, self-adjusting and self-maintenance

° High throughput and independent from CPU, the Analog/Digital and Digital/ Analog Data Conversion Interface

° Availability of a compiler whose inefficiency <u>will not extend</u> to program execution time

° For multiprocessors, automatic resource allocation at least within each processor and automatic generation of interprocessor communication routines

° For fixed point processors, software for automatic scaling with override capability

° Highly interactive system, allowing both direct and indirect (via keyboard) interaction between the modeler/simulationist and a simulation

° Built-in and automatic data acquisition hardware and software

° Slow degradation of accuracy when trying to simulate the same problem at higher speeds

° Excellent price/performance ratio for intended applications.

## 3.2. <u>SIMSTAR : Definition and Application</u>

SIMSTAR is a new <u>simulation</u> multiprocessor from Electronic Associates, Inc.. Its design features <u>reflect the</u> needs of engineers for a cost-effective simulation tool for use in high-speed simulation of dynamic systems.

SIMSTAR is an integrated multiprocessor allowing for easy distribution of simulation tasks. Its major processors are a general-purpose 32-bit supermini designed for real-time applications, coupled with a continuous processor with hundreds of unifunctional and multifunctional continuous processing units. A data conversion processor is used for communication between the numeric and analog worlds, both within the SIMSTAR and in connection with the outside world. Continuous units operate and communicate totally in parallel through the programmable switch matrix. The required communication topology is automatically deduced from the high level problem statement equations. SIMSTAR also contains a parallel logic unit dedicated to solving Boolean equations, and which is also used as the heart of the multiprocessor synchronizing process.

SIMSTAR can be used as a standalone system, or as an attached processor. When attached, its host may be used as one of the processors sharing the total computational load while simultaneously serving other, batch oriented, users.

SIMSTAR is a unique nonhomogeneous multiprocessor, successfully combining a linear computation technology of the analog domain with purely digital processing of a numeric domain, a "hybrid" with the best genes of classical hybrid computers executed in the latest software, hardware and system technologies. Its architectural, programming and technological details are given in References (8), (9) and (4), respectively.

SIMSTAR can be used to solve faster, more accurately and much more conveniently, all simulation tasks currently requiring and/or running on classical hybrid systems. They are generically itemized in Section 3.1.1.. A given simulation task might call for some specific simulation tool feature. Some of SIMSTAR's features are listed in Section 3.1.3..

An example of extremely stiff and nonlinear problems requiring SIMSTAR is in simulation of solid-state switching devices in electrical applications. Rectifiers, inverters, power supplies, high voltage and direct current systems are all characterized by discontinuities, particularly in voltage waveforms. Thus, the frequency circuit analysis programs are usually too slow, inefficient and use up large quantities of computer time for a single solution. Similar inefficiencies are to be found when performing, in a purely numeric domain, AC analysis by simulation of circuits going into IC, LSI and VLSI chip designs.

SIMSTAR offers a computational capability which readily handles the discontinuous operation of switched circuits, via continuous solution of the electrical circuit equations, augmented by parallel logical operation of the switching functions. Thus, real-time, hardware-in-the-loop simulations are possible, affording a two-order of magnitude improvement above all-digital techniques.

Another example is from the control area. Digitally based control systems require thorough testing in order to validate their full operation, i.e., check out all control algorithm's program paths.

This calls for a split domain simulation (a control algorithm is to be simulated on SIMSTAR's numeric processor, while the process is simulated on SIMSTAR's analog processor). The extensive testing is greatly facilitated by SIMSTAR's enormous speed. Providing much faster than real time simulation speed, a true picture of the degree of robustness of the tested controller emerges from SIMSTAR solutions.

## 4. CONSEQUENCES OF USING INADEQUATE SIMULATION TOOLS

In many ways a simulation tool can be inadequate to the task at hand. For example, using a tool which is too slow can result in :

°    Suboptimal design

°    Not fully tested system

°    Unusable (too late) results

°    Costly and less reliable products

°    Need to develop a multiplicity of simpler mathematical models

Consider that a control engineer had to resort to Linear Optimal Control on account of the slow simulation tool. As a result, his solution contains too many feedback loops (from nearly all states). Even if all sensors did exist, and even if all states were accessible and measurable, the unnecessarily added complexity will diminish product reliability and increase its price and maintenance costs.

Another common consequence (so common that it is taken for granted) of not having an adequately fast simulation tool for complex models, is the added cost of extra effort and time needed to develop and test a multiplicity of simpler models which can run fast enough. Including a verification and validation of all lower level models, it might easily take as much to develop these, as it took to develop a single complex model. One just cannot go into the complex model "code" and start deleting the terms and/or "commenting out" active program statements. The development of lower level models, just like the development of a complex model starts at the level of mathematical equations. The slow code of the complex model, once validated, can be used for validation of the simpler models.

## 5. BENCHMARKING LIKELY CANDIDATES

One should not underestimate that very strong and totally nontechnical reasons might heavily influence a final choice of the system, often resulting in a "selection" of far-from-optimal simulation tools. A non-optimal tool will produce nonoptimal results, under the same conditions.

In between other things, the simulationist will, by the nature of experience, influence the solution. Also influential are the degree of knowledge of the problem to be simulated, understanding of the simulation task(s) at hand, and knowledge of the simulation tool. How much time is given to produce simulation results is another very influential factor in the quality of simulation results, especially when having to rely on a slow simulation tool.

Left to make the next step of choosing one system out of the set of "likely candidates," one might have to consider "benchmarking". A benchmark should be one or more programs representative of problem(s) to be solved. The configuration of benchmark machines should be at least close to the one being considered. The feature indices should be objectively measurable. If one's own benchmark cannot be provided, one may use vendor supplied benchmarks. Very few common benchmarks exist. Those that do, might not be typical of your work. One should study benchmark source programs to understand what exactly is being measured. "Whetstone" benchmark is currently a popular program replacing a Gibson Mix for measuring computing power (speed) of numeric processors for scientific applications. It claims to be "typical" since it executes the same high-level language features with the same repetition as found in the sample of almost a thousand small scientific programs. Note that this mix does not include I/O and operating system calls (3).

The program is put in a loop, to execute it enough times until an accurate measur em ent of the duration of a single iteration can be computed. An inverse of this figure is then computed indicating how many Whetstone programs can be executed in a unit of time. This measure of speed can be used for relative comparison of several systems. Since this is a high level program (e.g., written in FORTRAN), the efficiency with which the compiler utilizes the available hardware, is automatically included in the reported figure.

A word of caution : your particular problem with its own mix of high-level instructions might not run twice as fast on machine X versus Y, even though the Whetstone program did.

Note, also, that if your particular problem uses different language compilers than those used for running of the Whetstone program, you cannot expect the same relative results. As a matter of fact, the results might show no difference at all.

CONCLUSIONS

Faced with a defined simulation task(s), a simulationist is expected to specify an adequate, if not optimal, simulation tool for its execution. The adequate tool might not exist in-house and one has to preselect a few "likely candidates" from the outside, based on the defined simulation task(s) and the basic knowledge of the available tools. The set of "likely candidates" is subjected to performance measurements based on benchmark, trying to objectively assess the adequacy of their performance for the task at hand. Basic features of SIMSTAR are given to help in the preselection process. A few SIMSTAR application examples are given. The serious consequences of not using a fast enough simulation tool are discussed using a few examples.

ACKNOWLEDGEMENTS

The author is grateful to his colleagues, Dr. L. Michaels and Mr. J.P. Landauer for their constructive suggestions and many valuable discussions.

REFERENCES

1. R. Bernhard, GIANTS IN SMALL PACKAGES,
   IEEE SPECTRUM, February 82, pp. 39-43

2. J. F. Burns, GREATER THROUGHPUT WITH MULTIPLE ARRAY PROCESSORS,
   Computer Design, September 81, pp. 207-211

3. H. J. Curnow and B. A. Whichmann, A SYNTHETIC BENCHMARK,
   Computer Journal, V. 19, 1976

4. R. W. Embley, THE TECHNOLOGY BEHIND SIMSTAR, AN ALL NEW SIMULATION
              MULTIPROCESSOR,
   1984 Summer Computer Simulation Conference, Boston, Massachusetts, USA

5. H. O. Holingue, A CHACUN SON SUPERORDINATEUR,
   Temps Réel, June 21, 1984, pp. 22-27

6. W. Karplus, PERIPHERAL PROCESSORS FOR HIGH-SPEED SIMULATION,
   Simulation, November 1977, pp. 143-153

7. E. W. Kozdrowski, SUPERCOMPUTERS FOR THE EIGHTIES,
   Digital Design, May 1983, pp. 94-103

8. J. P. Landauer, <u>SIMSTAR - AN ATTACHED MULTIPROCESSOR FOR DYNAMIC SYSTEM ENGINEERING</u>,
   1983 Summer Computer Simulation Conference, Vancouver, British Columbia, Canada

9. J. P. Landauer, <u>THE SIMSTAR MULTIPROCESSOR PROGRAMMING ENVIRONMENT AS APPLIED TO A LAND VEHICLE SIMULATION</u>
   1984 Summer Computer Simulation Conference, Boston, Massachusetts, USA

10. S. Martin, <u>PROGRAMMABLE ARRAY PROCESSORS CRUNCH NUMBERS EFFORTLESSLY</u>,
    EDN, February 20, 1980, pp. 107-115

SMSTM3(I)

# Der Simulationsrechner in der M.A.N. Werk Nürnberg -
## Konfiguration, Betriebserfahrung und Folgerungen

Reinhold Trier, Nürnberg

Zusammenfassung. Aus der Systematik bei der Simulation dynamischer Systeme werden wichtige Gesichtspunkte - die Aufstellung des Simulationsmodells, der Simulationsrechner und die Darstellung der Ergebnisse - herausgegriffen und genauer
betrachtet. Daraus werden Folgerungen für die Hardware und die Software eines
Simulationsrechners abgeleitet, auch unter Berücksichtigung von Echtzeitanforderungen. Das Rechenzentrum für dynamische Systeme der M.A.N. Werk Nürnberg wird
beschrieben und die Betriebserfahrungen werden anhand eines Beispiels erläutert.

Summary. Important points in the systematic procedure for the simulation of
dynamical systems, which are the formulation of the simulation model, the simulation computer and the representation of the simulation results, are in-
vestigated. From these points, the consequences in the hardware and software of
a simulation computer are derived, also regarding real time applications. The
computer centre for dynamical systems of M.A.N.-Werk Nürnberg is described and
the operating experiences are explained with the help of an example.

## 1 Einführung

Der Unternehmensbereich Maschinen- und Anlagenbau der M.A.N. hat in Werk Nürnberg ein Rechenzentrum für dynamische Systeme, das von der Gruppe "Dynamische
Systeme und Mikroprozessoren" betreut wird. Die Gruppe gehört organisatorisch
zur Zentralabteilung "Organisation und Datenverarbeitung" und hat somit gegenüber anderen Abteilungen eine dienstleistende Funktion. Im RZ für dynamische
Systeme werden Simulationen und damit zusammenhängende technische Berechnungen
durchgeführt. Daneben betreibt die Gruppe Entwicklungen von Steuer- und Automatisierungsgeräten und betreut die dafür notwendigen Einrichtungen.

## 2 Die Simulation dynamischer Systeme in M.A.N. Werk Nürnberg

### 2.1 Simulation - systematisch betrachtet

In Abb. 1 ist in ausführlicher Form dargestellt, welche Wege bei der Durchführung
einer dynamischen Simulation beschritten werden können.

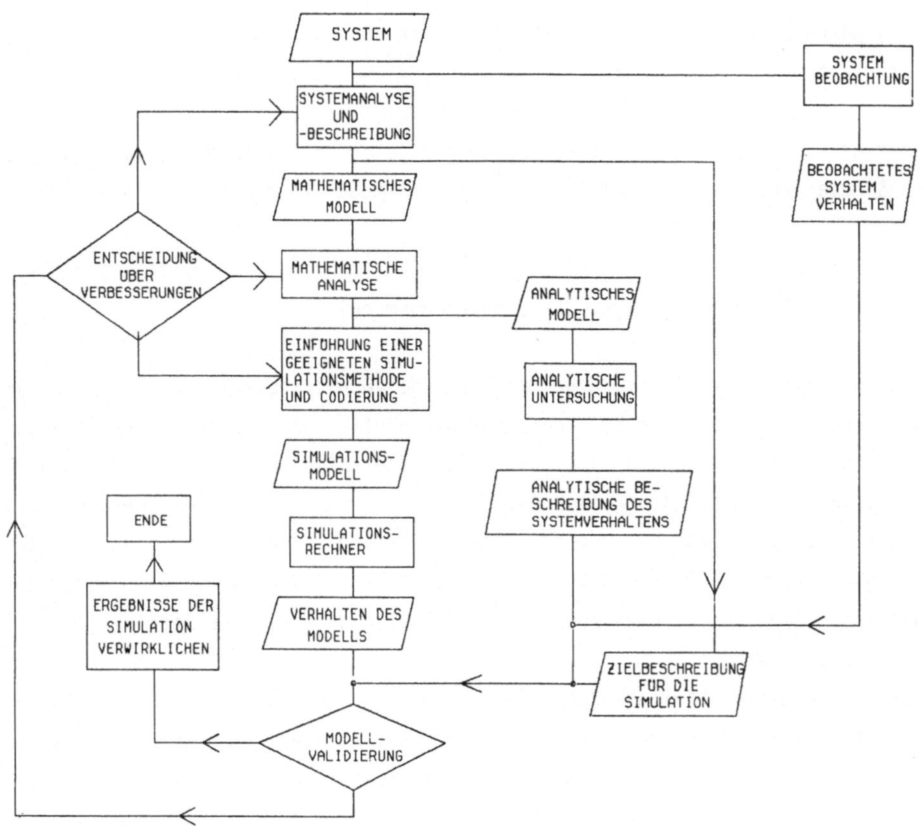



Abb. 1 Untersuchung eines Systems mit Hilfe der Simulation

Ausgangspunkt ist das zu untersuchende System. Von ihm wird einerseits mit Hilfe einer Systemanalyse und einer mathematischen Beschreibung ein mathematisches Modell aufgestellt, andererseits wird - wenn das möglich ist - eine System-Beobachtung durchgeführt, deren Ergebnis später zu Vergleichszwecken dienen soll.
Als nächstes müssen Methoden gefunden werden, um die Gleichungen des mathematischen Modells numerisch zu lösen. Außerdem wird in einfachen Fällen - manchmal nur punktweise - eine analytische Lösung des Gleichungssystems durchgeführt.

Insbesondere ist dies bei linearen oder linearisierbaren kleineren Systemen mit Hilfe der Fourier-Transformation im Bildbereich möglich.
Nach der Einführung der Lösungsmethode und der Codierung kann das so entstandene Simulations-Modell einer Rechenmaschine zum Lösen übergeben werden.
Das am Simulationsrechner erkennbare Verhalten des Modells muß so weit wie möglich mit den Ergebnissen einer analytischen Untersuchung und der Systembeobachtung verglichen werden. Man nennt diesen Vorgang die Validierung des Modells.

Nach der Validierung können die eigentlichen Schlüsse aus der Simulations-Untersuchung gezogen werden, die sich schließlich in der Auslegung des realen Systems niederschlagen sollen.

Von der hier dargestellten Vorgehensweise ist jetzt vor allem der Zusammenhang zwischen Simulationsmodell, Simulationsrechner und Modellverhalten von Bedeutung.


## 2.1.1    Die Arbeitsgrundlage: Das Simulationsmodell

Das mathematische Modell ist in den meisten Fällen nicht direkt lösbar, weder analytisch noch numerisch. Man betrachte nur den häufigen Fall einer instationären Rohrströmung: sie wird durch eine partielle Differentialgleichung mit den unabhängigen Variablen Ort und Zeit beschrieben. Soll sie numerisch gelöst werden, so ist erst einmal zu entscheiden, ob durch Diskretisierung beider unabhängiger Variablen ein Lösungsgitter aus Ort/Zeitpunkten geschaffen wird oder ob die Gleichung zunächst mit Hilfe finiter Differenzen in ein System gewöhnlicher Differentialgleichungen zerlegt wird.
Spätestens an dieser Stelle werden die Überlegungen auch durch das Handwerkszeug beinflußt, das zur Weiterverarbeitung des Modells zur Verfügung steht. Das aufbereitete mathematische Modell, mit dessen Hilfe letztlich die Simulation durchgeführt wird, also das Simulationsmodell, muß ja direkt von vorhandener Hard- und Software weiterverarbeitet werden können.

Auf der Softwareseite ist die Simulationssprache ein wichtiges Hilfsmittel. Als Simulationssprache wird eine höhere Programmiersprache bezeichnet, die es erlaubt, auf möglichst einfache Weise Simulationsmodelle aus mathematischen Modellen zu entwickeln. Einige dieser Sprachen sind nicht (nur) für den frei programmierbaren Digitalrechner, sondern auch zur Programmierung spezieller "Simulations-Hardware" geschaffen.


## 2.1.2    Der Simulationsrechner

Der Simulationsrechner ist gleichsam eine Versuchsanordnung in der Hand desjenigen, der die Simulation durchführt.
Nicht jede elektronische Rechenanlage ist gleich gut als Simulationsrechner geeignet. Die interaktive Arbeitsweise und das Experimentieren mit dem Simulationsmodell - ob nun programmiert oder von Hand gesteuert - erfordern eine hohe Ausführungsgeschwindigkeit. Hinzu kommt in vielen Fällen noch die Bedingung, daß die Simulation in Echtzeit ablaufen soll.

Simulationsmodelle sind aber, bedingt durch eine Vielzahl gekoppelter Differential-
und algebraischer Gleichungen, im allgemeinen sehr rechenintensive Aufgaben für
einen Computer. Aus diesen Gründen wurde bis vor etwa 15 Jahren der Digitalrechner
als ziemlich ungeeignetes Instrument für die dynamische Simulation betrachtet und
ausschließlich elektronischen Analog- bzw. Hybridenrechnern der Vorzug gegeben.
Erst durch die hohen Rechengeschwindigkeiten der heutigen Digitalrechner sind die
Antwortzeiten in diesem Bereich kurz genug. Trotzdem gibt es mehrere Gründe, daß
auch heute noch in vielen Fällen der "normale", frei programmierbare Digitalrechner für die dynamische Simulation nicht ausreicht und durch spezielle Hardware ergänzt wird. Bei solcher spezieller Hardware zur Unterstützung der dynamischen Simulation an einer elektronischen Rechenanlage handelt es sich um

- Hybridrechner (parallele, analoge Verarbeitung der kontinuierlich veränderli-
  chen Daten und digitale, parallele Logik, Beispiele: EAI 581,681,2000)

- Feldrechner (Array-Prozessoren) (Parallele digitale Verarbeitung ausgewählter,
  gleichartiger Rechenoperationen)

- Digitale Parallelprozessoren (Gleichzeitige digitale Verarbeitung verschiedener Programmteile und Synchronisation zu vorgegebenen Zeitschritten, Beispiele: Applied Dynamics AD 10, Delft Parallel Processor DPP)

- Hybride Parallelprozessoren (Parallele digitale und analoge Verarbeitung mit
  digital microprogrammierten Prozessoren, Beispiel: EAI SIMSTAR)

Diese verschiedenen Spezialwerkzeuge haben eines gemeinsam: die Schnittstelle zum
Benutzer wird von einem frei programmierbaren Digitalrechner gebildet, die oben
beschriebenen Anlagenteile sind Ergänzungen (Abb. 2).

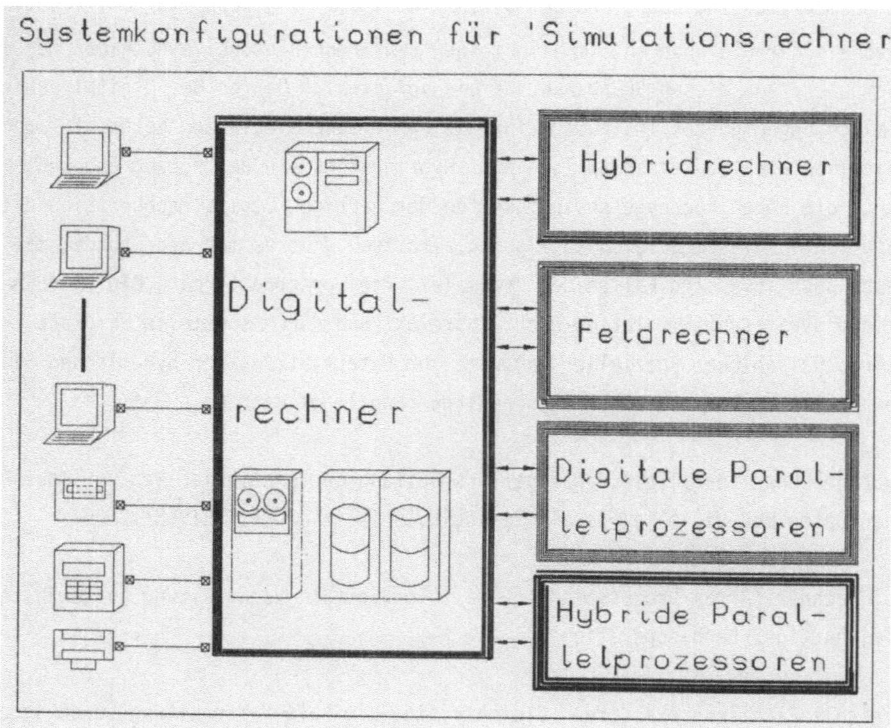


Abb. 2: Zur Verdeutlichung des Begriffes "Simulationsrechner"


## 2.1.3 Die Darstellung des Modellverhaltens

Ein weiterer wichtiger Punkt für die Eignung einer elektronischen Rechenanlage als Simulationsrechner ist die Graphik. Das Modellverhalten ist in Form von Zahlenreihen nichtssagend, eine graphische Ausgabe muß vorhanden sein - und zwar möglichst in interaktiver Form.

Für die meisten Auslegungs- und Optimierungsaufgaben, die mit Hilfe der Simulation durchgeführt werden, ist die Anwendung eines mathematischen Optimierungsverfahrens unwirtschaftlich. Der Aufwand zur Formulierung und Codierung aller Kriterien und Nebenbedingungen für eine Optimierung ist meist erheblich größer, als sich - sprichwörtlich - ein Bild von den wesentlichen Vorgängen zu machen und dementsprechend die weiteren Schritte vorzunehmen.

## 2.2 Der Simulationsrechner in der M.A.N. Werk Nürnberg

### 2.2.1 Beschreibung der Hardware

Im RZ für dynamische Systeme der M.A.N. hat der Simulationsrechner die in Abb. 3
gezeigte Konfiguration.

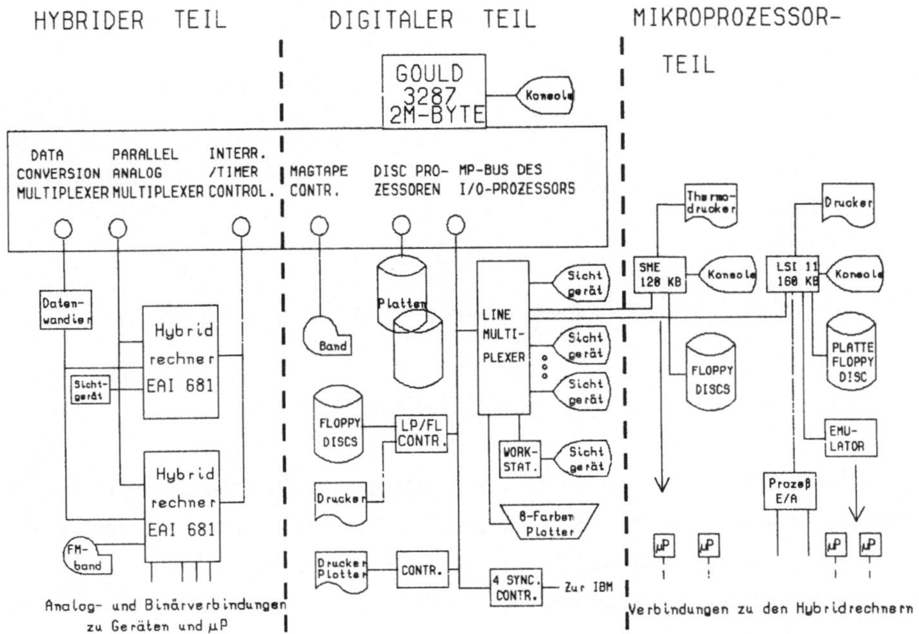



Abb. 3: Rechnerkonfiguration im RZ für dynamische Systeme der M.A.N.

Die Hardware dieses Rechenzentrums besteht aus einem Supermini GOULD 32/87 und zwei
Hybridrechnern EAI 681. Mit Hilfe eines Interfaces EAI HYSHARE können diese Komponenten zu einem hybriden Rechensystem zusammengefaßt werden. Der Rechner Gould Concept 32/87 ist mit 2 MByte Hauptspeicher, 32 KByte Cache-Speicher und 500 MByte
Massenspeicher ausgerüstet. Er hat eine Rechenkapazität von etwa 3,7 MIPS. Derzeit
sind acht Sichtgeräte und drei andere Rechner mit ihm verbunden.
Die Hybridrechner haben zusammen 60 Integratoren, 120 digitale Koeffizienten-Ein-
heiten und multivariable Funktionsgeneratoren.

### 2.2.2 Ein Beispiel

Ein Beispiel ist die Optimierung der Nockenform von Einlaß- oder Auslaßventilen in
Dieselmotoren durch Simulation (Abb. 4).

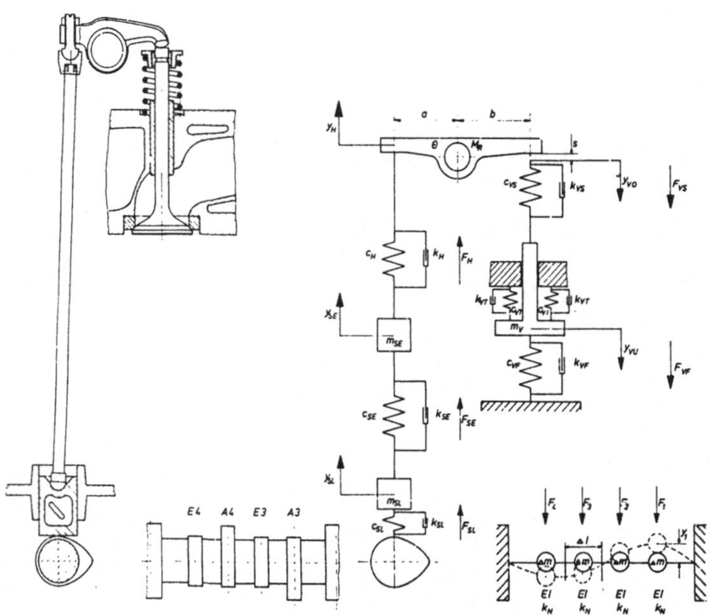

Abb. 4: Graphische Darstellung des Ventiltrieb-Modells

Ein dynamisches System, das aus Ventil, Ventiltrieb und Nockenwelle besteht, wird simuliert, um die günstigste Form des Nockens zu bestimmen. Dabei ist Voraussetzung, daß in kurzer Zeit möglichst viel Gas durch das Ventil strömen soll und daß für die Schmierung besondere Bedingungen eingehalten werden müssen. Vor allem aber müssen die Verläufe der Kraft und der Geschwindigkeit an kritischen Stellen so gestaltet werden, daß die hoch beanspruchte mechanische Anordnung eine möglichst große Lebensdauer hat.

Der Verläufe haben die typische Form der Kurven in Abb. 5. Es ist leicht zu erkennen, wie wenig anschaulich in diesen Fällen eine Darstellung in Form von Zahlenreihen wäre und welcher Aufwand andererseits notwendig wäre, um eine Strategie für eine automatische Optimierung einzuführen. Aus den sofort zur Verfügung stehenden Bildern kann jedoch der Ingenieur schließen, welche Veränderungen in der Nockenform vorgenommen werden müssen, um Verbesserung zu erreichen.

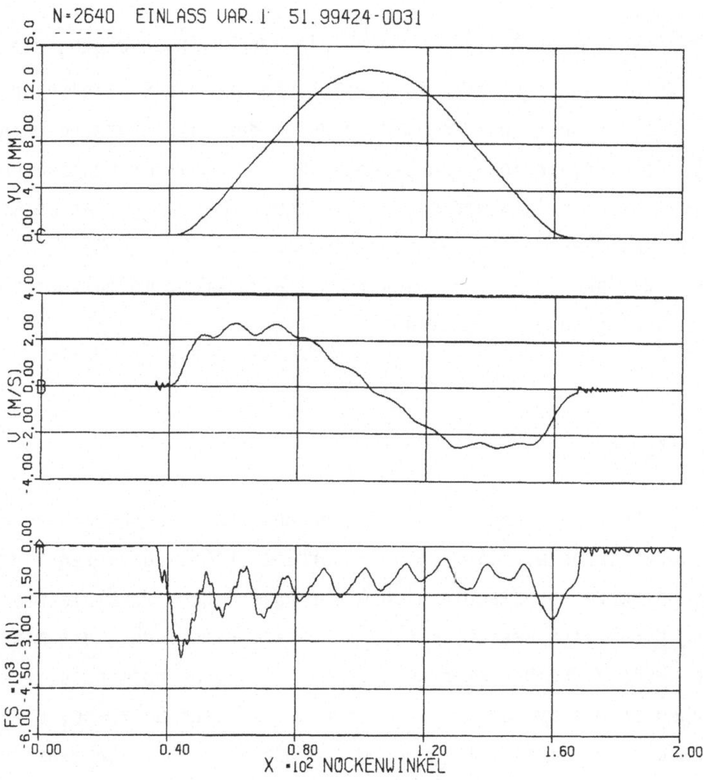



Abb. 5: Ventilerhebung, -geschwindigkeit und -kraft eines Dieselmotors

Als die in Bild 3 gezeigte Rechenanlage noch mit einem erheblichen kleineren und
langsameren Digitalrechner versehen war, wurde die Simulation des Ventiltriebes
ausschließlich hybrid durchgeführt. Es ergab sich dabei wegen der hochgradigen
Nichtlinearität und der Steifigkeit des Systems eine Rechenzeit von ca. 2 Sekunden für einen typischen Rechenfall. Jetzt wird auf der Basis des selben Gleichungssystems (Simulationssprachen ECSSL hybrid, ACSL digital) die Simulation
vorwiegend digital durchgeführt. Die dafür notwendige Rechenzeit von über 60 Sekunden für den oben erwähnten Fall tritt bei der interaktiven Arbeitsweise sehr
störend in Erscheinung. Sie wird aber in Kauf genommen, da andererseits die Rüst-
zeit des Rechners und die Umstellung des Modells auf Neukonstruktionen gegenüber
der hybriden Variante erheblich kleiner ist. Nur in Fällen, in denen bei geringen
Geometrieänderungen eine Vielzahl von Optimierungen notwendig ist, wird nach wie
vor hybrid gerechnet.

Diese Vorgehensweise ist auch typisch für viele andere Anwendungen, aber sie trifft dort nicht zu, wo die analoge Variablendarstellung und die Echtzeiteigenschaften des Hybridrechners gebraucht werden. Gerade durch den Mikroprozessor-Einsatz und die damit verbundene Entwicklung von Steuer- und Automatisierungsgeräten ist für den hybriden Teil des Simulationsrechners ein neues Aufgabengebiet entstanden. Er bildet gleichsam das "Fenster" einer Echtzeitsimulation nach außen, hin zu Geräten und Komponenten, die analog Signale wieder digitalisieren, weiterverarbeiten und unter Umständen analog ausgeben sollen.


## 3  Schlußbemerkungen

Als Simulationsrechner kann man also Digitalrechner hoher Rechengeschwindigkeit bezeichnen, die durch besondere Einrichtungen ergänzt sind. Zu diesen Einrichtungen gehört erstens Hardware zur Beschleunigung der numerischen Rechenleistung, meist durch Anwendung paralleler Rechentechnik. Dabei ist numerisch nicht mit digital gleichzusetzen. Hybride Komponenten werden vor allem dann notwendig, wenn auch Echtzeitanforderungen an das System gestellt werden. Zweitens Software, die dem Anwender in verschiedener Hinsicht entgegenkommt: einerseits durch Vereinfachung seiner simulationsspezifischen Aufgaben, andererseits durch Einbeziehung seiner speziellen Hardware. Drittens muß der Simulationsrechner unbedingt über gute und interaktive Möglichkeiten zur graphischen Ausgabe verfügen.

CYBERPLUS, a high performance parallel processing system for
simulation applications

W.A. Ray

Director Parallel Processing
Control Data Corporation
Minneapolis, Minnesota, USA


## Introduction

Parallel Processing is an old methodology, and is now becoming part
of the design of new applications. The evolution of VLSI technology
and the parallel processing software has provided a base technology
for commercial organizations to introduce high parallel processing
into the marketplace.

Parallel Processing is not a revolutionary concept, but a very simple
fundamental way of doing computations. Parallel Processing is defined
as the ability for the application user to have more than one processor
working on the same job task at the same time. In some communities it
is called multi processing, in other communities it is called parallel
processing and in other communities it is called multi parallel processing. One of the problems that has confronted application designers
over the last N years is the inability of the computer manufacturer to
deliver the performance of computing systems to match the needs of the
scientists. Let us look at the history of computing power.

During the last 30 years, there have been a number of significant
changes of capability and each change initiated a need to improve or
extend the computer technology. As an example, the first computer was
designed to generate tables for scientists. Once completed, it became
evident that the computer could be used to solve the reàl problem and
the need for tables was no longer the goal of scientists.

During the last 30 years, the distinct change of capability were:

> GENERATION OF TABLES FOR SCIENTISTS
> ASSEMBLERS FOR DIGITAL COMPUTERS
> HIGH LEVEL LANGUAGES (FORTRAN)
> MULTIPROGRAMMING COMPUTER SYSTEMS
> INTERACTIVE JOB PROCESSING
> SUPERCOMPUTERS - VECTOR PROCESSING
> PERSONAL COMPUTER - WORK STATIONS

Each of the above provided the application designer, significant tools to solve larger problems yet each of the capabilities forced the application designer to subset the problem, change the mission to fit the computer architecture or change the science to accomodate the computer system limitations.

With the additional capability, the size and scope of the application task also increased to exceed the performance capability of the computer system. If the new computer increased the performance of the application by a factor of 4, within weeks, the scientist increased the scope by factor greater than 4.

The 6600 introduced by Control Data in 1962 set a new standard for computer performance systems that are now called Supercomputers. The term Supercomputer is a relatively new term in the computer industry but in reality the Supercomputer is the fastest machine known in any instance of time. No matter how powerful it is, it is still one order of magnitude less capable than what is required by the applications user. The 6600 broke the computation barrier where in the early 50's the speed of the machine had been reduced to a cycle time of 2 microseconds. Each computation required two or more machine cycles to execute an instruction. The Control Data 6600 improved the performance of the machine by a factor of 20 and its cycle time was reduced to 100 nanoseconds.

During the next 20 years, from 1964 to the present time, we have seen
the cycle time of machine go down. The following chart addresses the
performance of the machines based upon machine cycle times.

| IBM 7094 | 2000 | nanoseconds |
| CDC 6600 | 100 | nanoseconds |
| CDC 7600 | 27.5 | nanoseconds |
| CDC 205 | 20 | nanoseconds |
| CDC 990 | 16 | nanoseconds |
| CRI XMP | 9.5 | nanoseconds |

Hardware designers have been able to reduce the number of cycles to
perform an instruction and overlap instructions to further increase the
performance of a processor.

So in the last twenty years, we have seen the machines power increase
by only a factor of 10 yet the applications require the computer
performance to improve by a factor of 100 or a factor of 1000 to
handle the total application that is needed to be solved.

The last three Computer Systems integrate vector hardware that greatly
increased the potential compute power of their system. Unfortunately
most applications can not use the vector hardware 100% of the time. In
order to better utilize the vector performance, the vector computers
require the applications designer or programmer to change the code or
the algorithm. Vectorizing Fortran compilers have made significant
progress but the percent of vectorizing is still aslong way from a 90%
vectorization of application codes.

If we look to the future of hardware components, the market is seeing
machines with a cycle time of 6 nanoseconds, 4 nanoseconds, but nobody
has really said we will go into the picoseconds. If we continue down
the path of performance based upon pure cycle time, we would need a
computer with a machine cycle time of 50 to 100 picoseconds in order
to solve the problem of the future. The goal of most component engineering is to be able to deliver a 1 nanosecond machine before the end of

the 1980's. That is still the factor of 10 to 20 times slower than the needs of the user.

How will Parallel Processing address the user requirement? Parallel Processing is an old technology and old methodology.

The first computers were Parallel Processing machines, but did not have the tools or the software to allow the user to use and exploit the parallel capability of the hardware. Thus computers went to the serial, serial instruction, the Von Neumann type architecture. The problem with Parallel Processing is the lack of tools, the lack of systems that will allow the user to develop the decomposition of application code for a Parallel Processing System. What is needed is the ability to link together in a very efficient manner a number of processors to do the total application.

The problem facing the Parallel Processing developer is what is the granulatory required by applications. Most computer scientists, feel that there is only one granulatory and that is at the hardware level, but there is a second measure of granulatory that is the applications and what is nutural to the application. If the granulatory, or the hardware performance is low that application will need to break the code, the application, the algorithm into thousands of processors. The application may not contain adequate breaks in the computational structure to achieve a 95% degree of parallelism in order to achieve the performance level needed by the application. The ability to stay on the linear curve of the performance is almost impossible for large numbers of processors (100). Many theoretical examples have shown that a thousand processor system executing a task with a 90% level of parallelism would provide the performance of a five processor system. This is less than .5% of the total peak performance of the parallel processor system.

A Parallel Processing System containing high performance processors (the high level granulatory) requires an interconnection architecture that allows the application to transmit data at the speed of an individual processor in the system.

A Parallel Processing System requires at least two of the following
capabilities in order for the applications to use the parallel
hardware:

1. High Level Languages
2. Software to control execution and
   synchronization
3. Tools to measure parallel bottlenecks
4. Parallel library routines
5. Algorithms for parallel structures

The high level language requirement is the ability to take the present
applications code and have the compiler automatically generate the
parallel code to be run in the parallel processing system. The problem
to date is that the largest percentage of code in existance is in
Fortran. This language does not have the advanced constructs that are
needed to do effective parallel processing. Pascal and Ada are examples
of languages that would allow for effective utilization of a parallel
operating environment.

The software that is required to do parallel processing must provide a
high level ease of use that would allow the application to have control
over individual processing elements within the system. The user needs
to be able to initiate a task, status the task and have software to
provide the necessary task synchronization to support the data transfer
between processors in the system. Software is also needed to provide
path and trace flow since the problem of debugging complex parallel
systems is an order of magnitude more difficult than the present
application verification process.

In the area of tools, the parallel processing application developer
will need a powerful performance measurement and analysis capability
in order to determine the bottlenecks in a parallel application.

An application will require the same library capability that presently
exist on conventional machines. This parallel library must contain a
dynamic capability that will expand to use all of the resources that
are assigned to a given application.

## The CYBERPLUS

The CYBERPLUS is a High Performance Parallel Processing System
offered by Control Data Corporation and provides a capability for
large scale simulations that are not available with other uni-
processor systems or systems containing special purpose array or
attached processors.

The CYBERPLUS Parallel Processing System is a high performance
parallel computing system which allows the user to increase the scope
and size of the simulation by adding additional high performance
CYBERPLUS processors. A CYBERPLUS system is an integration of a Cyber
180 Series Computer and one or more CYBERPLUS Processors. A single
CYBERPLUS processor is capable of providing up to 700 MIPS (Million
Instructions Per Seconds) plus 100 MFLOPS (Million Floating Point
Operations Per Second). The CYBERPLUS software allows the simulation
user to configure the performance of 1 to 64 CYBERPLUS Processors all
operating in parallel on a single simulation.

The CYBERPLUS system contains a unique ring interconnection
architecture which allows for very high speed interchange of data and
control information between individual CYBERPLUS processors. A ring
group contains two 16 bit data rings and a single 64 bit data ring
which interconnects 2 to 16 CYBERPLUS Processors. A Control Data Cyber
180 Computer can support up to 18 ring groups, thus a maximum CYBERPLUS
system could contain up to 289 independent processors. Each CYBERPLUS
ring group connects to the Cyber 180 via a Cyber channel and a high
speed direct memory interconnection.

The CYBERPLUS Processor has a 20 nanosecond instruction cycle time
and because of its unique instruction processing architecture is
capable of initiating up to 15 parallel functions every machine cycle.
The functional units are interconnected by a crossbar connection that
allows output from one functional unit to be transferred to any or all
of the functional units in the machine cycle. With the addition of the
floating point unit, the CYBERPLUS processor is able to provide up
to 65 MFLOPS in 64 bit floating point bit format or 103 MFLOPS in 32
bit floating point format. This MFLOPS performance is in addition to

the CYBERPLUS base processors performance. The floating point unit
adds 3 additional functional units (add/subtract, multiply, divide/
square root) that operate in parallel with the base processors 15
functional units.

The structure of the CYBERPLUS Processor is built around a very long
instruction word. An instruction word contains 240 bits and is read
from a high speed bipolar memory every machine cycle. The 240 bit
instruction word provides the capability of dynamically reconfiguring
the 18 parallel functions every machine cycle. Because of its instruction architecture, the machine provides for a very high performance
engine plus it allows the user to think of the machine as either a
data flow or a data flow like computer system. The architecture of
the instruction handling in a CYBERPLUS Processor has many of the
properties of both an SIMD and MIMD machine architectures.

The memory system of the CYBERPLUS contains four independent bi-polar
16 bit data memories, each memory can read or write 16 bits of data
in one machine cycle. A 512K - 64 bit bi-polar memory can deliver
three 64 bits of data every machine cycle.

As an example of the parallel instructions, let's assume you wanted
to solve an equation where the variables on the right hand side are
using the 16 bit data memory and the variable N is stored in the
64 bit memory:

$$N(I) = J(I) + K(I) + L(I) * M(I)$$

for I = I to LIMIT. The CYBERPLUS instruction flow would be as follows
for the loop initialization and 4 CYBERPLUS instructions.

```
I                        Initialize loop
J, K, L, M               fetch 4 values
J + K,     L * M         add, multiply
Add, Increment loop add
N, Test                  store, test loop to 2
```

Thus, the loop can be executed in 4 CYBERPLUS machine cycles due to the
hardware's ability to perform parallel initiation of the independent

functional units.

The equivalent performance can be achieved using 32 bit floating
point assuming the 32 bit data would be packed in the 64 bit memory
word. The loop would be increased to seven cycles to perform the
calculations in 64 bit floating point format.

A Matrix Multiply of a 400 x 400 matrix takes 6.25 seconds on a single
CYBERPLUS Processor using the 64 bit functional units and less than
3.5 seconds using the 32 bit functional units.

The CYBERPLUS Processor is connected to other processors by dual 16 bit
ring architecture. This dual ring allows for very high speed transfer
of data and control information between all processors on the ring.
The total ring bandwidth is a function of the number of CYBERPLUS
processors since each Processor can be reading and writing a data packet
every machine cycle. To move a 16 bit data packet between adjacent
processors takes 20 nanoseconds, but because of the ring architecture
structure each of the rings can have n packets of data moving around
each ring simultaneously. If the ring consisted of 10 CYBERPLUS
Processors, the bandwidth of each of the dual rings would be 8000
MBITS of data.

MINIMUM HARDWARE INTERCONNECTION

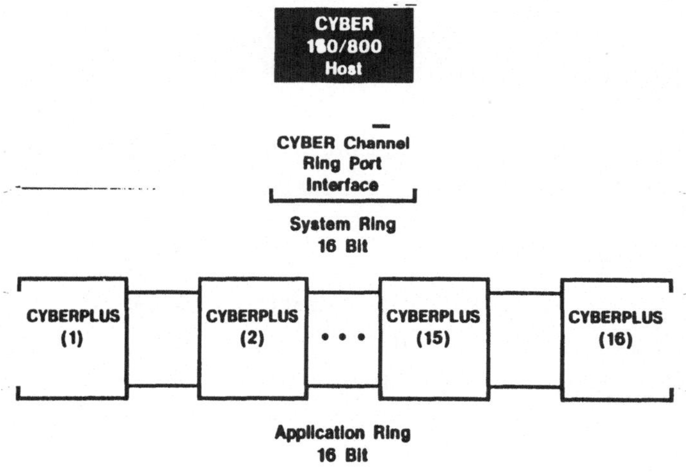

A Cyber 180 Computer can support up to 18 Ring Groups and each Ring Group supports 1 to 16 CYBERPLUS High Performance Processors. The Cyber 180 Computer supports tapes, disks, special devices and communications hardware.

In addition to the small ring architecture, there is a high speed memory interconnection which allows a CYBERPLUS processor to move data and any other processor within its ring group at a sustained speed of one 64 bit word every 20 nanoseconds. The CYBERPLUS Processor can be configured to move data between a CYBERPLUS processor and the Cyber 180 computer at the sustained rate of one 64 bit word every 80 nanoseconds or a transfer rate of 800 MBITS. This allows the user to have the full range of capability of the standard Cyber 180 operating system, and its associated compilers, assemblers, and data management. The Cyber Communications capability allow the installation to connect the CYBERPLUS System to other computer systems via the networks facilities within the Cyber Operating System.

HARDWARE INTERCONNECT

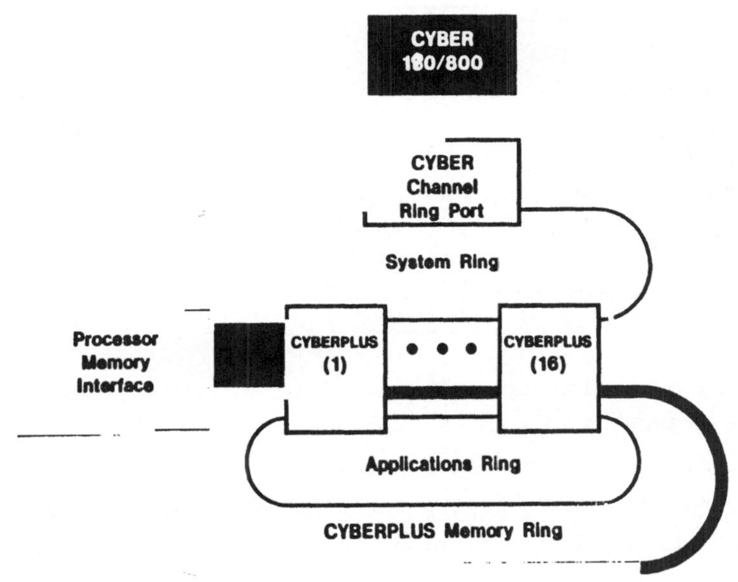


CYBERPLUS Software
In order to do simulation applications, the user needs the ability to

bring into execution the additional CYBERPLUS processors at the given
job step. The simulation user needs to move the code to a CYBERPLUS
Processor, have the processor execute the code and go about executing
other parallel computations in the Cyber 180 or initiating additional
CYBERPLUS Processors.

The software architecture allows the Cyber job, the initiator of the
CYBERPLUS tasks, to have full control of four CYBERPLUS Ring Groups
that have been configured in the total configuration. Thus a user can
have control of up to 64 CYBERPLUS Processors. Using a one single
CYBERPLUS processor system, the Cyber Processor would obtain data
sets, process elements of the data set, then move the data to a
computational process that will be executed by the CYBERPLUS Processor.
This can be achieved in parallel. The Cyber then has the option to
process additional data, to post process previous data or the true
case of a parallel processing system allow the application to monitor
what is happening in the CYBERPLUS.

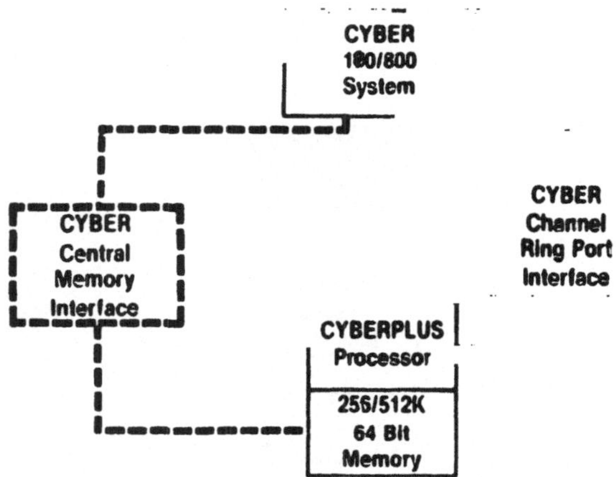


This monitoring operation uses a hardware capability and does not
interrupt the CYBERPLUS due to the options built into the CYBERPLUS
hardware system. Thus a user could obtain the immediate results from
a simulation and use these results for other decision making processes.
This decision making process could be the initiation of another
CYBERPLUS processor, the initiation of another simulation activity
with partial results from a CYBERPLUS or allow the user to abort the
process within the CYBERPLUS because we have reached a boundry
condition or a condition that no longer is valid to the simulation.

Thus the user can start to handle parallel simulation activities and
not be forced to do the operation in the classic discrete simulation.

Carrying this one step further, the ring architecture will allow for
processors to interchange data such that the user could configure the
system to have two simulations going on simultaneously but each of
them are transmitting data on a continuous basis between the
CYBERPLUS processors in order to simulate a large physical system.
Each simulation could then be extended to multiple CYBERPLUS processors
to execute each of the initial simulation tasks as the size of the
simulation is increased.

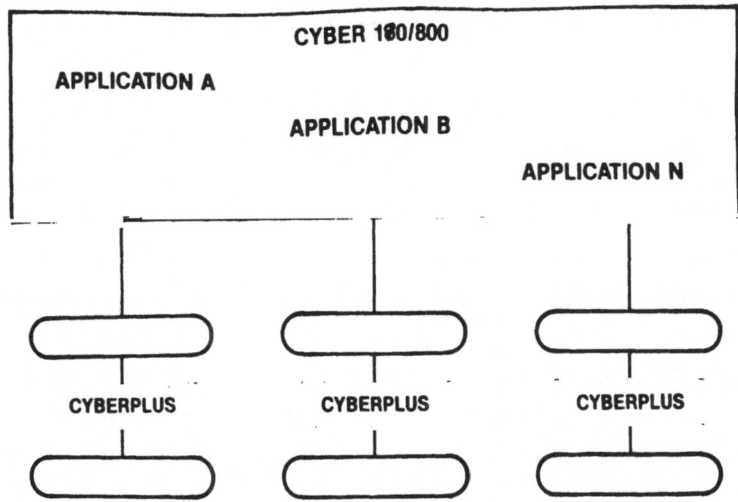


One of the problems facing large simulation systems, is the ability to
provide the user, the output in a manner that can support user needs.
The simulation needs of the future requires a very high sophisticated
computer graphic system not just color but color to the nth degree
such that the user could initiate the simulation, start to look at
critical events, critical operations, boundary conditions, alarms, etc
and be able to change the simulation. One or more of the CYBERPLUS
processors in the high performance simulation system would have the
function of developing the graphic representation. The graphic
representation would use the parallel hardware and software architecture and provide the simulation model the capability to be built
dynamically. The simulation user would then be able to monitor and
understand what is happening in the simulation rather than looking
at just the final results.

The CYBERPLUS Software consists of a Cross Fortran ANSI 77 Compiler, a Cross Assembler Debug facilities, a Ring Group Simulator and the user software to initiate and control the full capability of the CYBERPLUS hardware architecture.

## Summary

Parallel Processing offers the applications user the ability to achieve a quantum jump in the size and scope of applications. Parallel Processing Systems are appearing in the marketplace in an increasing number and will provide experimental systems for computer scientists to develop the parallel processing tools for parallel processing applications.

The software is, the re-evaluation of the present computer algorithms and a development of a parallel algorithm to perform the computational structures. Initial evaluation has indicated that a parallel algorithm could provide an order of magnitude improvement in processing speed compared to the present uni-processor algorithm.

With the CYBERPLUS high performance processor, the ring interconnection architecture and the software to link together computational elements, the CYBERPLUS system offers a unique opportunity for simulation. Not the simulation of the present physical models, but simulation of the total process. The CYBERPLUS offers simulation capability to do the simulation defined by the total as opposed to how we have been forced to do it with respect to present computer architectures.

## References

(1) Maritime Simulation, Proceedings of the First Intercontinental Symposium, Munich, June 1985, p. 9-14, p. 24-29 Springer-Verlag, ISBN 3-540-15620-8

(2) Sumer Simulation Meeting's Proceedings, Boston, July 1984, p. 207-210. ISBN, 0-444-87541-7

HAUPTVORTRÄGE

# Modellbildung dynamischer Systeme - eine Uebersicht

M. Mansour und A. Altmann, Zürich

Zusammenfassung. In dieser Arbeit wird eine Uebersicht über die Methoden der Modellierung dynamischer Systeme gegeben. In erster Linie werden die Methoden endlicher
Bilanzräume, die Lagrange-Methode und die Methode der Bonddiagramme mit der Strukturalgebra besprochen. Es zeigt sich, dass die erste Methode für einfache Systeme genügt.
Für komplexere Systeme kann die Lagrange-Methode verwendet werden. Für komplexere interdisziplinäre Systeme ist die Methode der Bonddiagramme am besten geeignet.

Summary. In this article, a survey of methods for modelling dynamic systems is given.
The method of finite balances, the Lagrange method and the method of bond diagrams in
connection with the algebra of structural numbers are discussed. One can see that the
first method is sufficient for simple systems while the Lagrange method can be used
for more complex systems. The method of bond diagrams in connection with the algebra
of structural numbers is most suitable for complex interdisciplinary systems.

## 1. Einführung [1], [2]

Für die Untersuchung von dynamischen Systemen braucht man ein mathematisches Modell,
welches in bezug auf die Untersuchungsziele das Verhalten des dynamischen Systems wiedergibt. Der Modellierung des Verhaltens liegt die Tatsache zugrunde, dass unter bestimmten Bedingungen Systeme, die,völlig verschieden in ihrer Form, Struktur und der
physikalischen Natur der sich in ihnen abspielenden Vorgänge, gleiches Verhalten haben
können. Als Beispiel betrachten wir die translatorische Bewegung einer Masse mit Feder
und Reibung. Es ist einfach zu beweisen, dass ein elektrisches Netz, bestehend aus
einem Widerstand, einer Induktivität und einem Kondensator in Serie geschaltet, dasselbe Verhalten aufweist wie das erwähnte mechanische System. Beide Systeme haben dasselbe mathematische Modell, nämlich eine Differentialgleichung 2. Ordnung, deren Lösung das Verhalten sowohl vom elektrischen als auch vom mechanischen System wiedergibt. Man kann die Situation wie in Bild 1 darstellen:

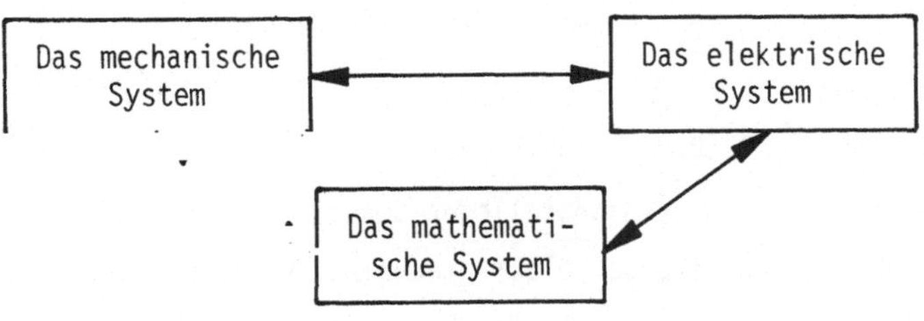



Bild 1:    Das Originalsystem und seine Modelle

Das Verhalten des einen Systems ist bestimmt durch das Verhalten von einem der anderen zwei. Natürlich darf man den approximativen Charakter der Sache nicht aus den Augen verlieren.

Das mathematische Modell besteht im allgemeinen aus einer Reihe abstrakter, mathematischer Objekte (reelle und komplexe Zahlen, Vektoren, Matrizen, usw.) zusammen mit einer Menge wohldefinierter Verknüpfungsoperationen. Dynamische Systeme lassen sich durch Differential- und/oder Differenzengleichungen darstellen. Die Lösung dieser Gleichungen gibt - unter gewisser Bedingung und mit bestimmter Genauigkeit - das Verhalten des physikalischen Systems wieder.

Das mathematische Modell wird bestimmt durch theoretische Prozessanalyse oder durch experimentelle Methoden. In den meisten Fällen ergänzen sich beide Wege und tragen gemeinsam zur Entwicklung einer genügend genauen Modellbeschreibung bei. Bild 2 zeigt die Mischung der theoretischen und experimentellen Methoden. Aus Platzgründen wird auf die Behandlung von experimentellen Methoden verzichtet.

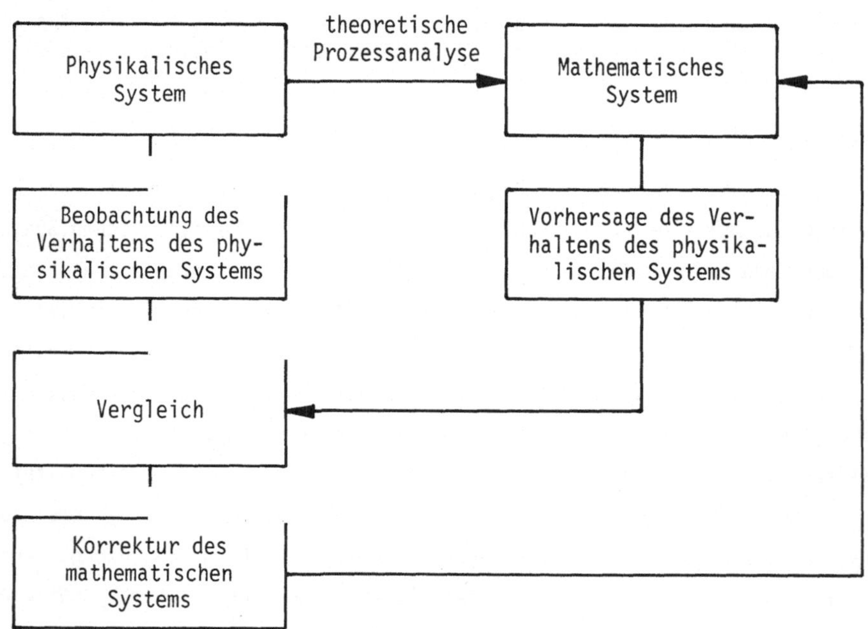


Bild 2:    Modellbildung

## Gewinnung dynamischer Modelle durch theoretische Prozessanalyse

Hier werden mit Hilfe naturwissenschaftlicher Gesetze, z.B. der Erhaltungssätze, der Extremalprinzipien, der Gesetze der Elektrotechnik, Mechanik, Hydraulik, Thermodynamik, usw. die Gleichungen aufgestellt. Die Elemente, aus denen das dynamische Modell besteht, werden als Speicher, Koppler, Wandler und Verbraucher von Energie klassifiziert. Als Beispiel für Speicher seien Massen, Federn, Kondensatoren und Induktivitä-

ten erwähnt. Ideale Hebezüge, ideale Getriebe und ideale Transformatoren sind Koppler.
Bild 3 zeigt die Beziehung zwischen den Grössen dynamischer Systeme:

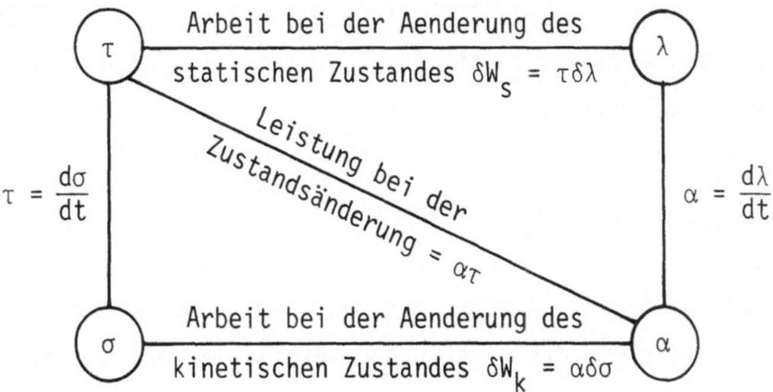


Bild 3:    Beziehungen zwischen den allgemeinen Grössen dynamischer Systeme.

$\tau$ = Kraft bei mechanischen Translationssystemen
= Drehmoment bei mechanischen Rotationssystemen
= Strom bei elektrischen Systemen

$\lambda$ = Verschiebung bei mechanischen Translationssystemen
= Winkelverschiebung bei mechanischen Rotationssystemen
= Induktionsfluss bei. elektrischen Systemen

$\alpha$ = Geschwindigkeit bei mechanischen Translationssystemen
= Winkelgeschwindigkeit bei mechanischen Rotationssystemen
= Spannung bei elektrischen Systemen

$\sigma$ = Impuls bei mechanischen Translationssystemen
= Drehimpuls bei mechanischen Rotationssystemen
= Ladung bei elektrischen Systemen

## Formen dynamischer Modelle

1. Parametrische Modelle:  Für lineare, kontinuierliche Systeme oder nichtlineare,
   kontinuierliche Systeme, die um einen Arbeitspunkt linearisiert sind, kann man
   eine Darstellung in Form eines Systems von Differentialgleichungen 1. Ordnung erhalten. Im besonders wichtigen Fall mit skalarem Ein- und Ausgangssignal lautet
   dann die Darstellung:

$$\underline{\dot{x}} = A\underline{x} + \underline{b}u$$
$$y = \underline{c}^T\underline{x}$$
(1)

wo        $\underline{x}$ = Zustandsvektor

u,y = Ein- bzw. Ausgangssignal;  T bedeutet transponiert

Aufgabe der Identifikation ist, die Elemente der Matrix A und die Vektoren $\underline{b}$ und $\underline{c}$
zu bestimmen. Einige dieser Parameter können durch die theoretische Systemanalyse
bestimmt werden. Für lineare diskrete Systeme gilt:

40

$$\underline{x}(k+1) = A\underline{x}(k) + \underline{b}u(k)$$
$$y(k) = \underline{c}^T\underline{x}(k) \tag{2}$$

Eine andere Beschreibung ist die Darstellung mit Hilfe von Uebertragungsfunktionen
für skalares Ein- und Ausgangssignal und Uebertragungsmatrizen für Mehrgrössensysteme. Im skalaren Fall gilt:

$$G(s) = \frac{y(s)}{u(s)} = \frac{b_{n-1}s^{n-1} + \ldots + b_1 s + b_0}{s^n + a_{n-1}s^{n-1} + \ldots + a_1 s + a_0} \tag{3}$$

Diese Darstellung ist im sog. Bildbereich, und man erhält sie durch Anwendung der
Laplace-Transformation. Für diskrete Systeme erhält man entsprechend:

$$G(z) = \frac{b_{n-1}z^{n-1} + \ldots + b_1 z + b_0}{z^n + a_{n-1}z^{n-1} + \ldots + a_1 z + a_0} \tag{4}$$

durch Anwendung der z-Transformation. Die Formeln (1) oder (3) kann man zurückführen auf eine einzige skalare Differentialgleichung der Form

$$\frac{d^n y}{dt^n} + a_{n-1}\frac{d^{n-1}y}{dt^{n-1}} + \ldots + a_1 \frac{dy}{dt} + a_0 y$$
$$= b_{n-1}\frac{d^{n-1}u}{dt^{n-1}} + \ldots + b_1 \frac{du}{dt} + b_0 u \tag{5}$$

Für Mehrgrössensysteme wird Gleichung (1) wie folgt aussehen:

$$\dot{\underline{x}} = A\underline{x} + B\underline{u}$$
$$y = C\underline{x} \tag{6}$$

wobei B, C Matrizen sind. G(s) in (3) wird zu einer Uebertragungsmatrix, deren
Elemente Uebertragungsfunktionen sind.

Eine weitere Beschreibung der Mehrgrössensysteme ist mit Polynommatrizen

$$P(s)\underline{z} = Q(s)\underline{u}$$
$$\underline{y} = R(s)\underline{z} \tag{7}$$

wobei P(s), Q(s) und R(s) Polynommatrizen sind, und s ein Differentiationsoperator
ist. $\underline{z}$ ist ein partieller Zustandsvektor.

Eine Darstellung für ein System kann mit speziellen Algorithmen in eine andere Darstellung zurückgeführt werden.


2. <u>Nichtparametrische Modelle</u>:  Nichtparametrische Modelle erhält man durch Reaktion
des Systems auf Standard-Eingangssignale, wie Dirac-Stoss, Einheitssprung oder pe-
riodische Eingangssignale.

Die nichtparametrischen Modelle können auch als Zwischenstufe zur Gewinnung von parametrischen Modellen dienen. Es existieren in der Literatur verschiedene Methoden, um parametrische Modelle anhand von gemessener Stossantwort, Schrittantwort oder Frequenzgang zu bestimmen.

## 2. Methoden endlicher Bilanzräume

Lässt sich ein System in geeigneter Weise in Elemente aufteilen, deren Verhalten aber zunächst nicht bekannt sind, dann muss dieses Verhalten mit Hilfe naturwissenschaftlicher Gesetze ermittelt werden, z.B. die Erhaltungssätze der Energie, Masse und Impulse in einem abgeschlossenen endlichen Volumen. Die mathematischen Modelle, die dabei entstehen, sind gewöhnliche Differentialgleichungen, die im linearen Fall einer gebrochenen, rationalen Uebertragungsfunktion entsprechen.

Beispiel:

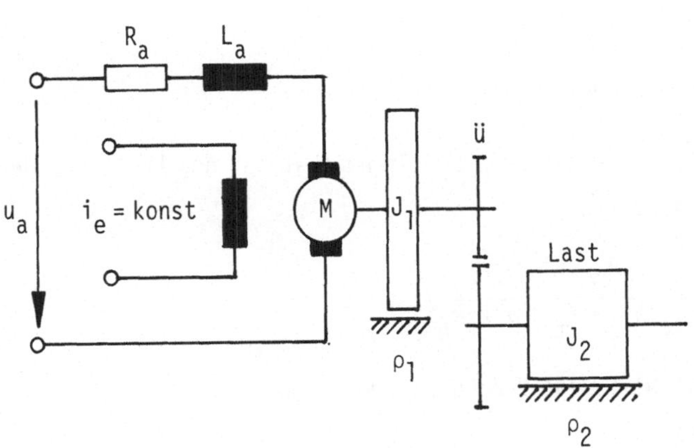


Bild 4:    Elektromechanisches System

M = Stellmotor (Gleichstrommotor mit konstanter Erregung ($i_e$ = konst.); $J_1, \rho_1$ = Trägheitsmoment, Reibungskoeffizient des Läufers; ü = Uebersetzungsverhältnis des Getriebes; $J_2, \rho_2$ = Last-Kenngrössen; Stellmotor: $u_i = k_1\omega$; $u_i$ = Gegeninduktionsspannung; $M_e$ = erzeugtes Drehmoment = $M_1$; $M_e = k_2 i_a$; $i_a$ = Ankerstrom.

Die Spannungsgleichung des Ankerkreises lautet

$$u_a = R_a i_a + L_a \frac{di_a}{dt} + u_i \tag{8}$$

$$u_i = k_1 \dot{\alpha}_1 = k_1 \omega_1 \tag{9}$$

Die Gleichung des mechanischen Teils lautet

$$\text{Erzeugtes Drehmoment} = k_2 i_a = (J_1 + ü^2 J_2)\dot{\omega}_1 + (\rho_1 + ü^2 \rho_2)\omega_1 \tag{10}$$

Die Gleichungen (8)...(10) können umgeformt werden zu

$$\frac{di_a}{dt} = -\frac{R_a}{L_a}\, i_a - \frac{k_1}{L_a}\, \omega_1 + \frac{1}{L_a}\, u_a \tag{11}$$

$$\frac{d\omega}{dt} = \frac{k_2}{J}\, i_a - \frac{\rho}{J}\, \omega_1 \tag{12}$$

oder

$$\begin{bmatrix} \dot{i}_a \\[2ex] \dot{\omega}_1 \end{bmatrix} = \begin{bmatrix} -\tau_e & -\dfrac{k_1}{L_a} \\[2ex] \dfrac{k_2}{J} & -\tau_m \end{bmatrix} \begin{bmatrix} i_a \\[2ex] \omega_1 \end{bmatrix} + \begin{bmatrix} \dfrac{1}{L_a} \\[2ex] 0 \end{bmatrix} u_a \tag{13}$$

wobei

$$J = J_1 + \ddot{u}^2 J_2 \,, \qquad \rho = \rho_1 + \ddot{u}^2 \rho_2$$

$$\frac{R_a}{L_a} = \tau_e = \text{elektrische Zeitkonstante}$$

$$\frac{\rho}{J} = \tau_m = \text{mechanische Zeitkonstante}$$

Die Uebertragungsfunktion zwischen $\alpha_2$ (Drehwinkel bei der Last) und der Eingangsspannung $u_a$ ist gegeben durch

$$\frac{\alpha_2}{u_a} = \frac{\ddot{u} k_2}{R_a \rho s (1 + \tau_e s)(1 + \tau_m s) + k_1 k_2 s} \tag{14}$$

Das System kann mit Hilfe von Blockdiagrammen oder Signalflussdiagrammen wie in Bild 5 dargestellt werden:

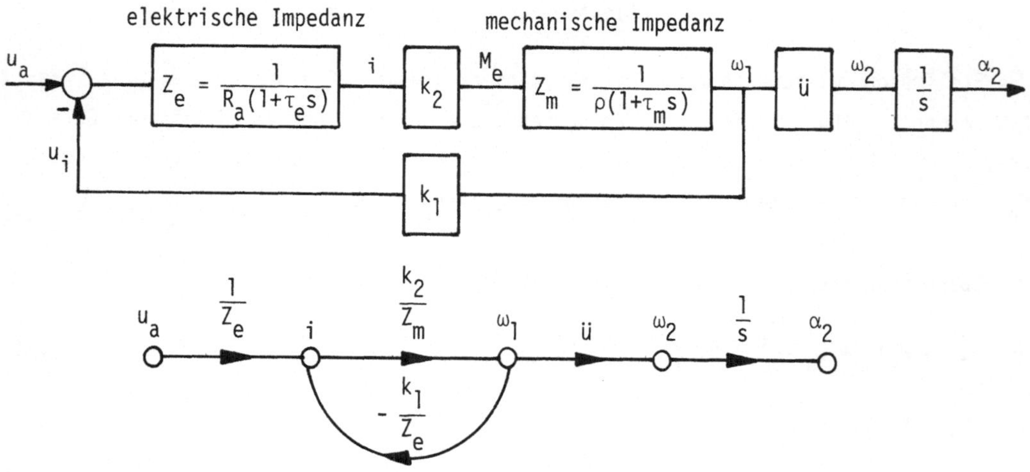


Bild 5:   Blockdiagramm und Signalflussdiagramm des Systems in Bild 4.

## 3. Methoden infinitesimaler Bilanzräume

In vielen Fällen ist es nicht möglich, das System in konzentrierte Elemente aufzuteilen, die feste Eigenschaften haben. Als Beispiel sei die elektrische Leitung erwähnt, wo sich Strom und Spannung entlang der Leitung kontinuierlich ändern. Hier werden die Erhaltungssätze auf infinitesimale kleine Bereiche angewandt. Dabei resultieren partielle Differentialgleichungen, die durch eine grosse Anzahl von gewöhnlichen Differentialgleichungen approximiert werden können, falls man trotzdem die Aufteilung in eine endliche Zahl von Elementen vornimmt.

## 4. Lagrange-Methode

Mit der Lagrange-Zustandsfunktion und der Lagrange-Gleichung [3] erhält man das mathematische Modell des Systems. Eine Wahl der Zustandsgrössen ermöglicht die Beschreibung des Systems mit Zustandsvariablen, d.h. mit Differentialgleichungen 1. Ordnung. Die Methode von Lagrange ist eine allgemeine Methode, die auf verschiedene Systeme (mechanische, elektrische, elektromechanische, thermische, akkustische, usw.) angewandt werden kann.

Die Zustandsfunktion von Lagrange $L(\underline{q},\underline{\dot{q}})$ ist definiert als die Differenz zwischen der kinetischen Energie $U(\underline{q},\underline{\dot{q}})$ und der potentiellen Energie $V(\underline{q})$. $\underline{q}$ und $\underline{\dot{q}}$ sind die verallgemeinerten Koordinaten und Geschwindigkeiten.

Die kinetische Energie $U(\underline{q},\underline{\dot{q}}) = \int_0^{\dot{q}} \underline{p}^T(\underline{q},\underline{\dot{q}})d\underline{\dot{q}} = \int_0^{\dot{q}} \sum_{i=1}^{N} p_i(\underline{q},\underline{\dot{q}})d\dot{q}_i$, wobei $\underline{p}(\underline{q},\underline{\dot{q}})$ das Momentum darstellt und N die Anzahl verallgemeinerter Koordinaten.

Die potentielle Energie $V(\underline{q}) = \int_0^{q} \underline{f}^T(\underline{q})d\underline{q} = \int_0^{q} \sum_{i=1}^{N} f_i(\underline{q})d q_i$, wobei $\underline{f}(\underline{q})$ die potentielle Kraft darstellt. Die zwei Integrationen für U und V müssen wegunabhängig sein. Der einfachste Weg der Integration für die kinetische Energie ist, am Anfang $\dot{q}_1$ mit allen anderen $\dot{q}_i = $ Null zu integrieren, dann entlang $\dot{q}_2$ mit $\dot{q}_1 = $ konstant und die restlichen $\dot{q}_i = $ Null usw. zu integrieren, bis der Punkt $\underline{\dot{q}}$ erreicht ist, d.h.

$$U(\underline{q},\underline{\dot{q}}) = \int_0^{\dot{q}_1} p_1(\underline{q},\dot{q}_1,0..0)d\dot{q}_1 + \int_0^{\dot{q}_2} p_2(\underline{q},\dot{q}_1,\dot{q}_2,0..0)d\dot{q}_2 +...+ \int_0^{\dot{q}_N} p_N(\underline{q},\dot{q}_1,...,\dot{q}_N)d\dot{q}_N \tag{15}$$

Die Bedingung, dass dieses Integral unabhängig vom Integrationsweg sein muss, ist gegeben durch

$$\frac{\partial p_i(\underline{q},\underline{\dot{q}})}{\partial \dot{q}_j} = \frac{\partial p_j(\underline{q},\underline{\dot{q}})}{\partial \dot{q}_i} \qquad\qquad i,j = 1,...,N \tag{16}$$

Die potentielle Energie ist gegeben durch

$$V(\underline{q}) = \int_0^{\underline{q}} \underline{f}^T(\underline{q})d\underline{q} = \int_0^{q_1} f_1(q_1,0..0)dq_1 + \int_0^{q_2} f_2(q_1,q_2,0..0)dq_2 + ... + \int_0^{q_N} f_N(q_1,q_2,...,q_N)dq_N \quad (17)$$

mit der Bedingung

$$\frac{\partial f_i(\underline{q})}{\partial q_j} = \frac{\partial f_j(q)}{\partial q_i} \quad (18)$$

Die Zustandsfunktion von Lagrange ist definiert als

$$L(\underline{q},\dot{\underline{q}}) = U(\underline{q},\dot{\underline{q}}) - V(\underline{q}) \quad (19)$$

Die Tabelle 1 zeigt die verallgemeinerten Koordinaten und Geschwindigkeiten, die Energien, das verallgemeinerte Moment und die potentielle Kraft für verschiedene Systeme:

| System-Typ | verallg. Koordin. $q$ | verallg. Geschwindigk. $\dot{q}$ | kinet. Energie $U$ | pot. Energie $V$ | verallg. Momentum $p$ | pot. Kraft $f$ |
|---|---|---|---|---|---|---|
| mechanische Translation | Position $x$ | Geschwindigk. $\dot{x} = v$ | $\frac{1}{2}M\dot{x}^2$ | $\frac{1}{2}Kx^2$ | Momentum $M\dot{x}$ | Kraft $Kx$ |
| mechanische Rotation | Winkel-Position $\theta$ | Winkelge-schwindigkeit $\dot{\theta} = \omega$ | $\frac{1}{2}J\dot{\theta}^2$ | $\frac{1}{2}K\theta^2$ | Drehmoment $J\dot{\theta}$ | Drehmoment $K\theta$ |
| elektr., Serie | Ladung $q$ | Strom $\dot{q} = i$ | $\frac{1}{2}L\dot{q}^2$ | $\frac{1}{2C}q^2$ | Flussver-kettung $L\dot{q}$ | Spannung $1/C\, q$ |
| elektr., parallel | Fluss-verkett. $\lambda$ | Spannung $\dot{\lambda} = v$ | $\frac{1}{2}C\dot{\lambda}^2$ | $\frac{1}{2L}\lambda^2$ | Ladung $C\dot{\lambda}$ | Strom $1/L\, \lambda$ |

Tabelle 1:    Verallgemeinerte Koordinaten technischer Systeme.

## Die Lagrange-Gleichung

Ausgehend vom 1. Newton'schen Gesetz können wir die Lagrange-Gleichung ableiten:

$$\frac{d}{dt}\frac{\partial U(\underline{q},\dot{\underline{q}})}{\partial \dot{q}_i} - \frac{\partial U(\underline{q},\dot{\underline{q}})}{\partial q_i} = Q_i \qquad Q_i = \text{Kraft} \quad (20)$$

$$Q_i = -f_i - D_i + F_i \quad (21)$$

Hier ist $f_i$ die potentielle Kraft, $D_i$ die Dämpfungskraft und $F_i$ die externe Kraft. $f_i$ kann von der potentiellen Energie erhalten werden

$$f_i = \frac{\partial V(\underline{q})}{\partial q_i} \quad (22)$$

Die Dämpfungskraft $D_i$ enthält die Kraft aller Dissipationselemente, assoziiert mit den

$q_i$ Koordinaten. Falls wir nun die viskose Dämpfung betrachten, ist $D_i = \beta_i \dot{q}_i$. $\beta_i$ ist der Dämpfungskoeffizient.

$$D_i = \frac{\partial \mathcal{D}(\dot{q})}{\partial \dot{q}_i} \tag{23}$$

$$\mathcal{D}(q) = \text{Rayleigh-Dissipationsfunktion} = \frac{1}{2} \sum_{j=1}^{N} \beta_j \dot{q}_j^2 \quad . \tag{24}$$

Wenn $V(q)$ und $\mathcal{D}(q)$ in die Lagrange-Gleichung eingesetzt werden, erhalten wir

$$\frac{d}{dt} \frac{\partial U(\underline{q},\dot{\underline{q}})}{\partial \dot{q}_i} - \frac{\partial U(\underline{q},\dot{\underline{q}})}{\partial q_i} + \frac{\partial V(\underline{q})}{\partial q_i} + \frac{\partial \mathcal{D}(\dot{\underline{q}})}{\partial \dot{q}_i} = F_i \qquad i = 1,2,\ldots,N \tag{25}$$

Durch die Definition der Lagrange-Funktion

$$\frac{d}{dt} \frac{\partial L(\underline{q},\dot{\underline{q}})}{\partial \dot{q}_i} - \frac{\partial L(\underline{q},\dot{\underline{q}})}{\partial q_i} + \frac{\partial \mathcal{D}(\dot{\underline{q}})}{\partial \dot{q}_i} = F_i \tag{26}$$

Zur Anwendung der Lagrange-Gleichung müssen zuerst die verallgemeinerten Koordinaten gewählt werden. Diese müssen unabhängig und ohne Beschränkung sein. Die Anzahl verallgemeinerter Koordinaten $N$ ist gegeben durch $N = N_u - N_c$, wobei $N_u$ die Anzahl Speicherelemente und $N_c$ die Anzahl holonomische Relationen zwischen den Koordinaten dieser Speicherelemente darstellen. $N$ gibt uns die Anzahl Freiheitsgrade des Systems.

Beispiel:

Für das Beispiel in Bild 4 gelten die verallgemeinerten Koordinaten $q_1$ = Ladung $q$, $q_2 = \alpha_1$.

$$U(\underline{q},\dot{\underline{q}}) = \frac{1}{2} L_a i_a^2 + \frac{1}{2} (J_1 + \ddot{u}^2 J_2) \dot{\alpha}_1^2 \tag{27}$$

potentielle Energie $V(\underline{q}) = 0$ \hfill (28)

$$\mathcal{D}(\dot{\underline{q}}) = \frac{1}{2} \beta_1 \dot{q}_1^2 + \frac{1}{2} \beta_2 \dot{q}_2^2$$

$$= \frac{1}{2} R_a i_a^2 + \frac{1}{2} (\rho_1 + \ddot{u}^2 \rho_2) \dot{\alpha}_1^2 \tag{29}$$

$$F_1 = u_a - k_1 \dot{\alpha}_1 \qquad\qquad F_2 = M_e = k_2 i_a \tag{30}$$

$$L = \frac{1}{2} L_a i_a^2 + \frac{1}{2} (J_1 + \ddot{u}^2 J_2) \dot{\alpha}_1^2$$

$$L_a \frac{d i_a}{dt} + R_a i_a = u_a - k_1 \dot{\alpha}_1 \tag{31}$$

$$(J_1 + \ddot{u}^2 J_2) \ddot{\alpha}_1 + (\rho_1 + \ddot{u}^2 \rho_2) \dot{\alpha}_1 = k_2 i_a \tag{32}$$

Die Uebertragungsfunktion ist gegeben durch Gleichung (14).

## 5. Modellierung mit Bonddiagrammen

Bonddiagramme [4] sind Diagramme zur einheitlichen Darstellung von Energieflüssen zwischen den Teilsystemen und Elementen, aus denen man sich ein gegebenes technisches System (Bild 4) zusammengesetzt vorstellen kann (Bild 6).

$$\text{elektrisches Netz} \xrightarrow[i_a]{u_a} \text{Stellmotor} \xrightarrow[\omega_1]{M_1} \text{Getriebe} \xrightarrow[\omega_2]{M_2} \text{Last}$$

Bild 6:   Wort-Bonddiagramm des elektromechanischen Systems aus Bild 1.
$i_a$ = Ankerstrom, $M_1,M_2$ = Drehmomente, $\omega_1,\omega_2$ = Winkelgeschwindigkeit.

Die Teilsysteme des elektromechanischen Systems aus Bild 4 sind in Bild 6 durch entsprechende Bezeichnungen (Wort-Bonddiagramm) dargestellt und durch Linien verbunden, welche die Energie-Austauschstellen zwischen den Teilsystemen symbolisieren (= Bindungen, engl.: bonds → Bonddiagramm).
Trotz der Verschiedenartigkeit (elektrisch, mechanisch) der Teilsysteme des gemischttechnischen Systems in Bild 4, hat das Wort-Bonddiagramm in Bild 6 eine einheitliche Darstellungsform. Die gebietsunabhängige Einheitlichkeit der Darstellung und Modellierung auch gemischttechnischer Systeme ist eine allgemeine vorteilhafte Eigenschaft der Bonddiagramme; sie beruht darauf, dass eine Bindung in allgemeiner Form, d.h. unabhängig vom jeweiligen speziellen Anwendungsgebiet, immer den Austausch einer Momentanleistung $P(t)$ repräsentiert, die ein Produkt der allgemeinen Leistungsvariablen $e(t)$ (Spannungsvariable) und $f(t)$ (Flussvariable) ist (Bild 7).

$$\xrightarrow[f]{e} \qquad P(t) = e(t) \cdot f(t)$$

Bild 7:   Allgemeine Bindung mit Leistungsvariablen $e$ und $f$, Momentanleistung $P(t)$ und Bezugsrichtung des positiven Energieflusses.

In Tabelle 2 sind die Spannungsvariablen und Flussvariablen aus verschiedenen technischen Bereichen zusammengestellt.
Die Verfeinerung von Wort-Bonddiagrammen wie in Bild 6 führt zu einer Darstellung der Teilsysteme durch die allgemeinen Bonddiagramm-Elemente in Tabelle 3.

In den charakteristischen Beziehungen für Speicherelemente kommen die verallgemeinerte Verschiebung $q$ und der verallgemeinerte Impuls $p$ vor (Tabelle 3). Diese Grössen ergeben sich durch Integration von $f$ bzw. $e$ über die Zeit $t$ (vgl. die allgemeine Form der Beziehungen) und drücken somit die Speicherfunktion dieser Bonddiagramm-Elemente aus.

|  | e-Variable | f-Variable | Leistung |
|---|---|---|---|
| elektrische Systemteile: $\dfrac{e}{f}$ | el. Spannung u [V] | el. Strom i [A] | $u \cdot i$ |
| mechanische Translation: $\dfrac{F}{v}$ | Kraft F [N] | Translationsgeschwindigk. $v$ [ms$^{-1}$] = $\dot{x}$ | $F \cdot v$ |
| mechanische Rotation: $\dfrac{M}{\omega}$ | Drehmoment M [Nm] | Winkelgeschwindigkeit $\omega$ [rad s$^{-1}$] = $\dot{\alpha}$ | $M \cdot \omega$ |
| Hydraulik: $\dfrac{p}{q}$ | Druckdiff. p [Nm$^{-2}$] | Volumenstrom $q$ [m$^3$s$^{-1}$] = $\dot{V}$ | $p \cdot q$ |
| Akkustik: $\dfrac{p}{q}$ | Schalldruck p [Nm$^{-2}$] | Volumengeschwindigkeit $q$ [m$^3$s$^{-1}$] = $\dot{V}$ | $p \cdot q$ |
| Thermodynamik: $\dfrac{T}{\dot{S}}$ | absolute Temperatur: T [K] | Entropiestrom S [WK$^{-1}$] = $\dot{Q}/T$ (Q=Wärmemenge) | $T \cdot S$ |
| chemische Systemteile: $\dfrac{\mu}{\dot{N}}$ | chem. Pot.: $\mu$ [J·mol$^{-1}$] (= Arbeit pro mol Teilchen) | Molstrom $\dot{N}$ [mol·s$^{-1}$] (= Teilchenstrom) | $\mu \cdot \dot{N}$ |

Tabelle 2:   Leistungsvariablen gemischttechnischer Systeme

Die Verknüpfungselemente in der Tabelle 3 dienen der Verknüpfung einzelner Bonddiagrammelemente zu einem Bonddiagramm; sie repräsentieren allgemeine physikalische Gesetzmässigkeiten, wie z.B. die Kirchhoff'schen Gesetze, dynamisches Kräftegleichgewicht, Kontinuitätsbedingungen für Volumenströme, usw.

Bild 8 zeigt ein Bonddiagramm für das elektromechanische System in Bild 4, wie es ausgehend vom Wort-Bonddiagramm in Bild 6 entwickelt werden kann:

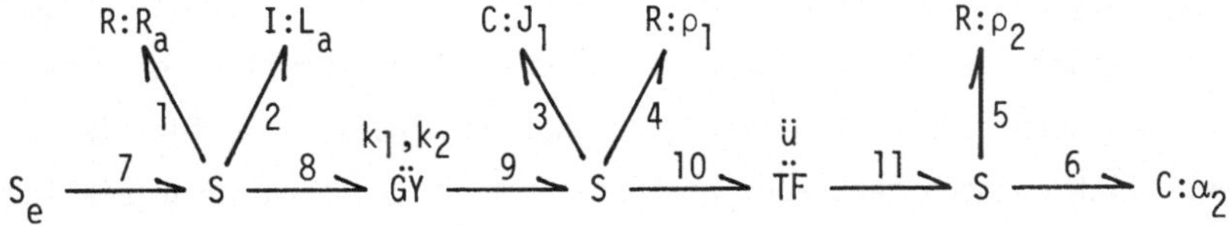


Bild 8:   Bonddiagramm des elektromechanischen Systems aus Bild 4.

| Elemente-funktion | Element | Bonddiagramm-Element | Charakteristische Beziehung: allgemein | linear |
|---|---|---|---|---|
| Speicher-elemente | Kapazitäts-element | $\xrightarrow[f]{e}$ C | $\int\limits^{t} f\,dt = q = \Phi_C(e)$ | $q = C \cdot e$ |
| | Trägheits-element | $\xrightarrow[f]{e}$ I | $\int\limits^{t} e\,dt = p = \Phi_I(f)$ | $p = I \cdot f$ |
| dissipat. Element | Widerstands-element | $\xrightarrow[f]{e}$ R | $e = \Phi_R(f)$ | $e = R \cdot f$ |
| Quellen-elemente | Spannungs-quelle | $S_e \longrightarrow$ | $e = \text{konstant}$ | |
| | Flussquelle | $S_f \longrightarrow$ | $f = \text{konstant}$ | |
| Energie-umsetzer-elemente | Transforma-torelement | $\xrightarrow[f_1]{e_1}\ \overset{\lambda}{TF}\ \xleftarrow[f_2]{e_2}$ | $\lambda$: Uebersetzungs-verhältnis $\ e_1 = \lambda e_2$ $\ e_2 = \lambda e_1$ | |
| | Gyrator-element | $\xrightarrow[f_1]{e_1}\ \overset{m}{GY}\ \xleftarrow[f_2]{e_2}$ | $m$: Umsetzungs-verhältnis $\ e_1 = mf_2$ $\ e_2 = mf_1$ | |
| Verknüp-fungs-element | Parallel-verknüpfung | $\xrightarrow[f_1]{e_1}\ P\ \xleftarrow[f_2]{e_2}$ $\quad e_3\big\vert f_3$ | $e_1 = e_2 = e_3$ $\sum\limits_i P_i(t) = 0$ $f_1 + f_2 + f_3 = 0$ | |
| | Serie-Verknüpfung | $\xrightarrow[f_1]{e_1}\ S\ \xleftarrow[f_2]{e_2}$ $\quad e_3\big\vert f_3$ | $f_1 = f_2 = f_3$ $e_1 + e_2 + e_3 = 0$ | |

Tabelle 3:    Allgemeine Bonddiagramm-Elemente

Das mathematische Modell, z.B. in Form des Uebertragungsverhältnisses $x/u = G(s)$ (x: Systemausgangsgrösse, u: Systemeingangsgrösse; $s := d/dt$), für ein dynamisches System kann mit einer für die Topologie der Bonddiagramme entwickelten Strukturalgebra leicht abgeleitet werden. Die Strukturalgebra hat den Zweck, alle für die Bestimmung von $G(s)$ gewöhnlich notwendigen, rechenintensiven Matrizenoperationen wie Inversion und Mulitplikation, durch einfache Mengenoperationen zu ersetzen. Die erwähnte Strukturalgebra ist auf der Basis der Theorie der Strukturzahlen [5] für die spezielle Topologie der Bonddiagramme entwickelt worden [6].

## 6.  Schlussbemerkungen

Die drei, hier besprochenen Methoden, nämlich die Methode der endlichen Bilanzräume, die Lagrange-Methode und die Methode der Bonddiagramme mit der Strukturalgebra, sind Methoden, die abhängig von der Komplexität des dynamischen Systems angewandt werden. Für einfache Systeme genügt die erste Methode. Für komplexere Systeme kann man die Lagrange-Methode verwenden und für komplexere interdisziplinäre Systeme ist die Methode der Bonddiagramme geeignet.

## Literatur

[1]  M. Mansour: Mathematische Modellbildung. Schweiz. Maschinenmarkt, 10(1978)26-29.

[2]  A.G.J. MacFarlane: Analyse technischer Systeme. Bibliogr. Institut, 1967.

[3]  D.G. Schulz/J.L. Melsa: State Functions and linear Control Systems. McGraw-Hill, 1967.

[4]  D. Karnopp/R. Rosenberg: System Dynamics: a unified approach. John Wiley, 1975.

[5]  S. Bellert: Topological Analysis and Synthesis of Linear Systems. Journal of the Franklin Institute, 274(1962)425-443.

[6]  A. Altmann: Interdisziplinäre Systemanalyse: Eine Strukturalgebra der Bonddiagramme. Springer-Verlag, 1982.

## Grundlagen und Anwendungen
## von Diagnoseverfahren

Reinhart Lunderstädt, Hamburg

Zusammenfassung. In der vorliegenden Arbeit wird ein Überblick über modellbezogene Diagnoseverfahren gegeben. Ausgehend von der Problemformulierung anhand einer typischen Meßkette erfolgt zunächst die Diagnose bei stationärem Systemverhalten. Dabei wird sowohl der Fall mit stochastischen als auch der mit systematischen Meßfehlern behandelt und auf beider Unterschiede und Gemeinsamkeiten hingewiesen. Aus dem rekursiven Schätzalgorithmus für stationäres Systemverhalten wird dann ein entsprechender Algorithmus für instationäres Systemverhalten hergeleitet, der beim Vorliegen gewisser statistischer Eigenschaften ein diskretes KALMANfilter darstellt.


Summary: In this paper a survey is given on model-related diagnosis procedures. Basing on the formulation of problems from a typical measuring chain the first step is the diagnosis in case of stationary system conditions. Thereby both the case with stochastical errors and the one with systematical errors in measurement is dealt with and their different and common properties are pointed out. From the recursive estimation algorithm for stationary system conditions then a corresponding algorithm for non-stationary system conditions is derived, representing a discrete Kalmanfilter in case of certain statistical properties.


## 1. Einführung

Insbesondere bei technischen Großsystemen ist man bestrebt, durch eine geeignete Fehlererkennung sowohl die Sicherheit zu erhöhen als auch über die dadurch gegebene höhere Verfügbarkeit die Kosten des laufenden Betriebes zu senken. Beinhaltet die Fehlererkennung über eine Ja-/Nein-Entscheidung hinaus auch die Ermittlung der Fehlergröße und des Fehlerortes, so spricht man von (Fehler-)Diagnose. Diese wird u. a. erreicht durch eine Vorhersage der Lebensdauer von wichtigen Funktionselementen bzw. der Angabe des jeweiligen Status dieser Elemente. Genau dann kann nämlich eine Wartung nach Bedarf (maintenance on condition) durchgeführt werden, die ein kostenmäßiges Optimum bedeutet. Die geschilderte Aufgabe ist nicht leicht und in ihrer Allgemeinheit auch nicht lösbar. Sie erfordert einerseits eine genaue Kenntnis des mathematischen Modells des zu diagnostizierenden Systems, verbunden mit einem hohen mathematischen Aufwand für die Vorhersage, und andererseits exakte Informationen über beispielsweise das Werkstoffverhalten von Bauelementen in Grenzbereichen und deren Zuverlässigkeit in Abhängigkeit von der Beanspruchungsgröße und Beanspruchungsdauer. Da in vielen Fällen die Durchführung einer Diagnose Eingriffe in das zu diagnostizierende System erforderlich macht, als Konsequenz der Diagnose derartige Eingriffe aber auf jeden Fall erfolgen, ist eine Rechnersimulation vorab meist zwingend, um die Diagnosealgorithmen zu testen und ihre Leistungsfähigkeit sicherzustellen.

Eine Reihe von Anwendungen und Beispielen zur (Fehler-)Diagnose findet sich in [1]. Hierin ist auch eine Arbeit von ISERMANN enthalten [2], in der eine systemtheoretische Charakterisierung verschiedener Diagnoseverfahren durchgeführt wird. Von besonderer Bedeutung sind dabei die modellbezogenen Diagnoseverfahren, bei denen aus der Kenntnis von Meßgrößen $y_j$; $j=1,\ldots,m$ nichtmeßbare Größen wie Zustandsvariable $x_i$; $i=1,\ldots,n$, Parameter $\Theta_k$; $k=1,\ldots,r$ und/oder besondere Kennfunktionen $K_l=f_l(\underline{y},\underline{x},\underline{\Theta})$; $l=1,\ldots s$ ermittelt werden. Hierzu zeigt Bild 1 eine typische Meßkette der modernen Automatisierungstechnik. Sie besteht aus einem dynamischen System (Prozeß), einer

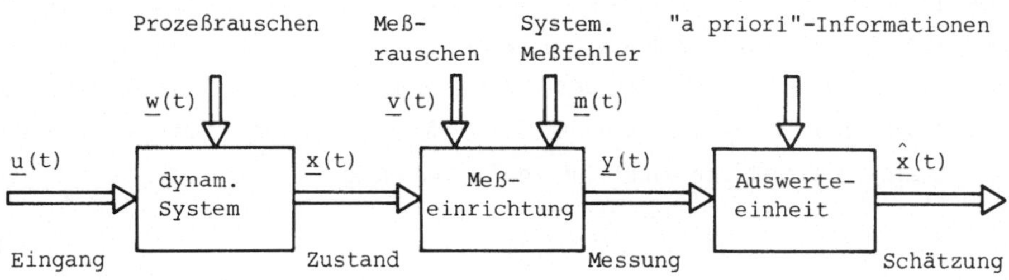


<u>Bild 1:</u> Blockschaltbild einer typischen Meßkette.

Meßeinrichtung und einer Auswerteeinheit. Das dynamische System (Meßobjekt) verfügt über den deterministischen Eingangsvektor $\underline{u}(t)$ (Stell-/Steuergrößen) und den Ausgangsvektor $\underline{x}(t)$ (Zustandsgrößen). Im System ist ein Prozeßrauschen $\underline{w}(t)$ zugelassen. Damit handelt es sich bei $\underline{x}(t)$ um einen Vektor mit stochastischen Zustandsgrößen. Der Vektor $\underline{x}(t)$ wird durch die Meßeinrichtung erfaßt. Sie liefert damit den Vektor $\underline{y}(t)$ der Meßgrößen. Da die Dimensionen von $\underline{x}(t)$ und $\underline{y}(t)$ im allgemeinen verschieden sind und in der Meßeinrichtung zudem sowohl ein Meßrauschen $\underline{v}(t)$ als auch ein Vektor systematischer Meßfehler $\underline{m}(t)$ (bias, offset) auftreten, kann $\underline{x}(t)$ nicht unmittelbar aus $\underline{y}(t)$ ermittelt werden. Es schließt sich deshalb an die Meßeinrichtung eine Auswerteeinheit (Rechner) an, die über geeignete mathematische Verfahren eine bestmögliche Schätzung $\hat{\underline{x}}(t)$ für den Zustandsvektor $\underline{x}(t)$ liefert. Diese Schätzung ist umso besser, je genauer das dynamische System und die Meßeinrichtung mathematisch modelliert werden können und je umfassender die Kenntnisse über $\underline{w}(t)$, $\underline{v}(t)$ und $\underline{m}(t)$ sind, d. h. je mehr "a priori"-Informationen der Auswerteeinheit zur Verfügung gestellt werden können. Über die Bestimmung von $\hat{\underline{x}}(t)$ hinaus ist die Auswerteeinheit in der Regel auch in der Lage, Modellparameter des Prozesses und/oder der Meßeinrichtung $\Theta_k$; $k=1,\ldots,r$

zu ermitteln und (daraus abgeleitete) Kennfunktionen $K_l = f_l(\underline{y}, \underline{x}, \underline{\Theta})$; $l=1,\ldots,s$ zu berechnen. Die Auswerteeinheit (Rechner) erfüllt also genau die Aufgaben, die an eine modellbezogene Diagnose gestellt werden.


## 2. Diagnose für stationäres Systemverhalten

Die weiteren Überlegungen konzentrieren sich zunächst auf stationäre bzw. quasistationäre Vorgänge, wobei unter Quasistationärität "kleine" zeitliche Änderungen in der Meßkette im Vergleich zu ihren dominanten Zeitkonstanten verstanden werden.

Ist in Bild 1 ab einer bestimmten Zeit $t > t_s$ der Eingangsvektor $\underline{u}(t > t_s)$ des dynamischen Systems konstant und handelt es sich bei den Komponenten von $\underline{w}(t)$ um Realisierungen eines stationären stochastischen Prozesses mit $E[\underline{w}(t)] = \underline{0}$, dann wird bei vorausgesetzter Stabilität des dynamischen Systems dessen Ausgang $\underline{\bar{x}}(t > t_s)$ konstant, wenn $\underline{\bar{x}}(t)$ der zu $\underline{x}(t)$ gehörige Vektor der Mittelwerte der Zustandsgrößen ist. Diese Situation liege im weiteren vor, so daß es nach Bild 1 genügt, nunmehr nur die Teilkette mit $\underline{\bar{x}}(t > t_s)$ als Eingang und $\underline{\hat{x}}(t > t_s)$ als Ausgang zu betrachten. Die mathematische Modellierung beschränkt sich damit auf die Meßeinrichtung allein. Setzt man für diese sowohl Stabilität als auch Stationärität bzw. Quasistationärität voraus, dann ergibt sich zunächst der nichtlineare Zusammenhang

$$\underline{y}(t > t_s) = \underline{h}[\underline{\bar{x}}(t > t_s), \underline{v}(t), \underline{m}(t > t_s)]. \tag{1}$$

Nimmt man nun weiter an, daß die Realisierungen der Komponenten von $\underline{v}(t)$ zu einem stationären stochastischen Prozess mit $E[\underline{v}(t)] = \underline{0}$ gehören und diese obendrein geeignet beschränkt sind, dann ist (1) linearisierbar und kann in der Form

$$\underline{y} = \underline{C} \cdot \underline{x} + \underline{D} \cdot \underline{v}(t) + \underline{H} \cdot \underline{m} \tag{2}$$

angegeben werden. Hierbei sind jetzt $\underline{y}$ der $(m,1)$-dimensionale Meßvektor und $\underline{x}$ der $(n,1)$-dimensionale Zustandsvektor; $\underline{C}$ ist die $(m,n)$-dimensionale Meßmatrix. Das Argument $(t > t_s)$ ist jetzt weggelassen und beim Zustand ist auch nicht mehr zwischen $\underline{x}$ und $\underline{\bar{x}}$ unterschieden worden. Die Gewichtsmatrizen $\underline{D}$ und $\underline{H}$ besitzen Diagonalform und sind $(m,m)$-dimensional. Im Prinzip kann man diese auch weglassen, da über $\underline{v}^* = \underline{D} \cdot \underline{v}$ und $\underline{m}^* = \underline{H} \cdot \underline{m}$ alternativ transformierte Vektoren $\underline{v}^*$ und $\underline{m}^*$ benutzt werden können. Die Ermittlung von Parametern $\Theta_k$ und/oder Kennfunktionen $K_l$ ist im übrigen in (2) mitmodelliert, da diese formal zu Zustandsgrößen deklariert werden können und somit als in $\underline{C}$ und $\underline{x}$ mitenthalten angesehen werden können.

Im weiteren besteht nun die Aufgabe, $\underline{x}$ aus $\underline{y}$ zu ermitteln. Das Diagnoseproblem sei so formuliert, da $\underline{x}$ auch als Abweichung gegenüber einem Nominalzustand aufgefaßt werden kann, der fehlerfrei ist ($\underline{x} = \underline{0}$) und $\underline{x}$ folglich dann unmittelbar das Ergebnis der Diagnose darstellt.

## 2.1 Stochastische Meßfehler

Der Einfluß der stochastischen $\underline{v}(t)$ und der systematischen Meßfehler $\underline{m}$ soll getrennt untersucht werden. Im Falle ausschließlich stochastischer Meßfehler lautet die Meßgleichung dann

$$\underline{y} = \underline{C} \cdot \underline{x} + \underline{v}^* \;\;;\;\; \underline{v}^* = \underline{D} \cdot \underline{v} \;\;. \tag{3}$$

Eine allgemeine Form der Schätzung von $\underline{x}$ durch $\hat{\underline{x}}$ und damit der Diagnose folgt nun aus

$$\hat{\underline{x}} = \underline{b} + [\underline{B} + \underline{C}^T \cdot \underline{A} \cdot \underline{C}]^{-1} \cdot \underline{C}^T \cdot \underline{A} \cdot (\underline{y} - \underline{C} \cdot \underline{b}) \;\;, \tag{4}$$

wobei $\dim(\underline{y}) \geq \dim(\underline{x})$ vorausgesetzt worden ist und lediglich ein einziger Meßvektor $\underline{y}$ zugrundeliegt, die Schätzung der Gl. (4) also über einen sogenannten "snapshot" erfolgt.

Je nach der Wahl des Vektors $\underline{b}$ sowie der Matrizen $\underline{A}$ und $\underline{B}$ ergeben sich aus (4) unterschiedliche, in der Literatur bekannte, Schätzverfahren [3]-[5]. Ist beispielsweise $\underline{b} = \underline{0}$ und $\underline{B} = \underline{0}$, so erhält man mit $\underline{A} = \underline{G} = \text{diag}(g_{jj})$; $j = 1, \ldots, m$ die Schätzung

$$\hat{\underline{x}} = (\underline{C}^T \cdot \underline{G} \cdot \underline{C})^{-1} \cdot \underline{C}^T \cdot \underline{G} \cdot \underline{y} \;\;, \tag{5}$$

also das Ergebnis der gewichteten Methode der Minimierung nach den kleinsten Fehlerquadraten (WLS), die für $\underline{G} = g \cdot \underline{I}$, $g = \text{const.}$ in ihren ungewichteten Sonderfall übergeht. Der durch (5) beschriebene Schätzer ist sehr einfach. Er hat zudem den Vorteil, daß über den Rauschvektor $\underline{v}^*$ außer der Mittelwertfreiheit seiner Komponenten sonst nichts bekannt zu sein braucht. Ist allerdings zusätzlich bekannt, daß die Realisierungen der Komponenten von $\underline{v}^*$ normalverteilt sind, dann erhält man mit $\underline{G} = \underline{R}^{-1}$ aus (5) den Maximum-Likelihood-Schätzer (MLS), wobei $\underline{R}$ die zu $\underline{v}^*$ gehörige Kovarianzmatrix ist. Der (WLS)- und der (MLS)-Schätzer unterscheiden sich also formal nur in der unterschiedlichen Wahl ihrer Gewichtsmatrix $\underline{G}$.

Der Fall mit nur einem einzigen Meßvektor $\underline{y}$ ist selten. Vielmehr liegen in der Regel infolge einer zeitdiskreten Abtastung mehrere Meßvektoren $\underline{y}_i$; $i = 1, \ldots, r$ vor. Nimmt man an, daß sich die in der Meßmatrix $\underline{C}$ festgelegten Modelleigenschaften während der Abtastung von $i = 1$ bis $i = r$ nicht verändern - Stationärität ist ausdrücklich vorausgesetzt - dann führen die Meßvektoren $\underline{y}_i$ zu der Schätzung

$$\hat{\underline{x}} = \frac{1}{r} \cdot (\underline{C}^T \cdot \underline{G} \cdot \underline{C})^{-1} \cdot \underline{C}^T \cdot \underline{G} \cdot \sum_{i=1}^{r} \underline{y}_i \;\;. \tag{6}$$

Es ist dies die nichtrekursive Formulierung des (WLS)- bzw. (MLS)-Schätzers, die besonders anschaulich verdeutlicht, daß diese Schätzverfahren eine Mittelwertbildung beinhalten mit einer unterschiedlichen Gewichtung der einzelnen Meßkanäle.

Ausgehend von Gl. (4) wurden bisher mit $\underline{b} = \underline{0}$ und $\underline{B} = \underline{0}$ lediglich Schätzalgorithmen betrachtet, die über keine a priori Informationen verfügen. Ist mit $\underline{b}=\hat{\underline{x}}_0$ beispielsweise eine Ausgangsnäherung für $\underline{x}$ bzw. $\hat{\underline{x}}$ vorhanden und ist mit $\underline{B}=\underline{M}$ eine Gewichtsmatrix zur Gewichtung des Fehlers zwischen $\hat{\underline{x}}$ und $\hat{\underline{x}}_0$ gegeben, dann wird durch

$$\hat{\underline{x}} = \hat{\underline{x}}_0 + (\underline{M}+\underline{C}^T\cdot\underline{G}\cdot\underline{C})^{-1}\cdot\underline{C}^T\cdot\underline{G}\cdot(\underline{y}-\underline{C}\cdot\hat{\underline{x}}_0) \tag{7}$$

eine Schätzung nach der <u>erweiterten</u> gewichteten Methode der Minimierung nach den kleinsten Fehlerquadraten (EWLS) beschrieben [3],[7]. Außer der Forderung nach Mittelwertfreiheit der Komponenten von $\underline{v}^*$ werden auch zur Anwendung von Gl. (7) sonst keine Bedingungen erhoben. Ist allerdings darüber hinaus bekannt, daß $\underline{v}^*$ und $\underline{x}$ normalverteilt sind und liegt mit $\underline{b}=\bar{\underline{x}}$ der Mittelwert von $\underline{x}$ vor, dann geht mit $\underline{M}=\underline{P}^{-1}$ und $\underline{G}=\underline{R}^{-1}$ der (EWLS)-Schätzer der Gl. (7) in den Bayes-Schätzer (BS)

$$\hat{\underline{x}} = \bar{\underline{x}} + (\underline{P}^{-1}+\underline{C}^T\cdot\underline{R}^{-1}\cdot\underline{C})^{-1}\cdot\underline{C}^T\cdot\underline{R}^{-1}\cdot(\underline{y}-\underline{C}\cdot\bar{\underline{x}}) \tag{8}$$

über. Bei diesem ist - wie zuvor beim (MLS)-Schätzer - $\underline{R}$ die Kovarianzmatrix von $\underline{v}^*$ und $\underline{P}$ die Kovarianzmatrix des Schätzfehlers in $\underline{x}$. Es ist zu erwarten, daß Schätzer vom Typ der Gln (7) und (8) zu leistungsfähigeren Ergebnissen führen als sie über Gl. (5) erreicht werden können, sofern mit $\hat{\underline{x}}_0$ und $\underline{M}$ bzw. $\bar{\underline{x}}$ und $\underline{P}$ geeignete a priori Informationen eingebracht werden.

Selbstverständlich ist es auch bei den Gln (7) und (8) so, daß in der Regel mehrere Meßvektoren $\underline{y}_i$, $i=1,\ldots,r$ zur Ermittlung von $\hat{\underline{x}}$ zur Verfügung stehen. Setzt man wieder voraus, daß sich die Modelleigenschaften während der Erzeugung der $\underline{y}_i$ nicht verändern, die Meßmatrix $\underline{C}$ also konstant ist, dann geht für diesen Fall Gl. (7) in

$$\hat{\underline{x}} = (\tfrac{1}{r}\cdot\underline{M}+\underline{C}^T\cdot\underline{G}\cdot\underline{C})^{-1}\cdot(\tfrac{1}{r}\cdot\underline{M}\cdot\hat{\underline{x}}_0 + \tfrac{1}{r}\cdot\underline{C}^T\cdot\underline{G}\cdot\sum_{i=1}^{r}\underline{y}_i) \tag{9}$$

über [7]. In Analogie zu Gl. (6) ist dies die nichtrekursive Darstellung des (EWLS)-Schätzers bzw. für $\hat{\underline{x}}_0=\bar{\underline{x}}$ und $\underline{M}=\underline{P}^{-1}$ die des (BS)-Schätzers. Aus Gl. (9) wird besonders anschaulich deutlich, daß die Bedeutung des (EWLS)- bzw. (BS)-Schätzers im Vergleich zum (WLS)- und (MLS)-Schätzer bei kleinen Werten von r liegt. Für große Werte von r wird nämlich

$$\tfrac{1}{r}\cdot\underline{M} \ll \underline{C}^T\cdot\underline{G}\cdot\underline{C} ,$$

$$\tag{10}$$

$$\tfrac{1}{r}\cdot\underline{M}\cdot\hat{\underline{x}}_0 \ll \underline{C}^T\cdot\underline{G}\cdot\bar{\underline{y}} ,$$

wenn $\bar{\underline{y}}$ der Vektor der Mittelwerte $\bar{y}_j$; $j=1,\ldots,m$ aus den Einzelmessungen $y_{ij}$ ist, d. h. Gl. (9) ist im Grenzfall $r\to\infty$ mit Gl. (6) identisch. Da es sich bei (6) um einen erwartungstreuen und konsistenten Algorithmus handelt, sind diese Eigenschaften für (9) damit gleich mitaufgezeigt.

Die bisher angegebenen Schätzalgorithmen unterscheiden sich durchweg allein in den zur Verfügung stehenden a priori Informationen. Dies betrifft sowohl den Meßvektor $\underline{y}$ als auch den Zustandsvektor $\underline{x}$. Insofern ist Gl. (4) in der Tat eine allgemeine Darstellung für die Zustandsschätzer bei stationärem Systemverhalten. Unterschiede und Gemeinsamkeiten sind deshalb nochmals in Tab. 1 zusammengefaßt [6], wobei mit f(·) - wie in der Literatur üblich - die jeweiligen Verteilungsfunktionen bezeichnet sind.

| Bezeichnung des Schätzers | Kurzzeichen | Algorithmus | Mittelwerte $E(\underline{x})$ | Gewichtung von $\hat{\underline{x}}_0$ | Kovarianzmatrix $\underline{P}$ | $f(\underline{x})$ beliebig | $f(\underline{x})$ normalverteilt | Mittelwerte $E(\underline{v}^*) = \underline{0}$ | Gewichtung der $\underline{y}_j$ | Kovarianzmatrix $\underline{R}$ | $f(\underline{y})$ beliebig | $f(\underline{y})$ normalverteilt | $\underline{x}$ und $\underline{v}^*$ unabhängig $E(\underline{x} \cdot \underline{y}^T) = \underline{0}$ | Bemerkung |
|---|---|---|---|---|---|---|---|---|---|---|---|---|---|---|
| Least-Squares-Schätzer | LS | $\hat{\underline{x}} = (\underline{C}^T \cdot \underline{C})^{-1} \cdot \underline{C}^T \cdot \underline{y}$ (I) | | | | ● | | ● | | | ● | | | $\underline{G} = \underline{I}$ |
| Weighted-Least-Squares-Schätzer | WLS | $\hat{\underline{x}} = (\underline{C}^T \cdot \underline{G} \cdot \underline{C})^{-1} \cdot \underline{C}^T \cdot \underline{y}$ (II) | | | | ● | | ● | ● | | ● | | | $\underline{G} \mathrel{\hat{=}} \underline{R}^{-1}$ |
| Gauss-Markov-Schätzer | GMS | $\hat{\underline{x}} = (\underline{C}^T \cdot \underline{R}^{-1} \cdot \underline{C})^{-1} \cdot \underline{C}^T \cdot \underline{R}^{-1} \cdot \underline{y}$ | | | | ● | | ● | ● | ● | ● | | | $\underline{R}^{-1} \mathrel{\hat{=}} \underline{G}$ |
| Maximum-Likelihood-Schätzer | MLS | | | | | ● | | ● | ● | ● | | ● | | |
| Erweiterter-Weighted-Least-Squares-Sch. | EWLS | $\hat{\underline{x}} = \hat{\underline{x}}_0 + (\underline{M} + \underline{C}^T \cdot \underline{G} \cdot \underline{C})^{-1} \cdot \underline{C}^T \cdot \underline{G} \cdot (\underline{y} - \underline{C} \cdot \hat{\underline{x}}_0)$ (III) | | ● | | ● | | ● | ● | | ● | | | $\underline{G} \mathrel{\hat{=}} \underline{R}^{-1}$<br>$\underline{M} \mathrel{\hat{=}} \underline{P}^{-1}$ |
| Minimal-Varianz-Schätzer | MVS | $\hat{\underline{x}} = \bar{\underline{x}} + (\underline{P}^{-1} + \underline{C}^T \cdot \underline{R}^{-1} \cdot \underline{C})^{-1} \cdot \underline{C}^T \cdot \underline{R}^{-1} \cdot (\underline{y} - \underline{C} \cdot \bar{\underline{x}})$ | ● | ● | ● | ● | | ● | ● | ● | ● | | ● | $\underline{R}^{-1} \mathrel{\hat{=}} \underline{G}$<br>$\underline{P}^{-1} \mathrel{\hat{=}} \underline{M}$ |
| Bayes-Schätzer | BS | | ● | ● | ● | | ● | ● | ● | ● | | ● | ● | $\bar{\underline{x}} \mathrel{\hat{=}} \hat{\underline{x}}_0$ |

Tab. 1: Zustandsschätzer und ihre a priori Informationen.

Die in den Gln (6) und (9) angegebenen Algorithmen sind durchweg <u>nichtrekursiv</u>, d. h. die Zustandsschätzung erfolgt nicht zum Zeitpunkt $t_i$ des Anfallens der einzelnen Meßvektoren $\underline{y}_i$; i=1,...,r, sondern erst zum Zeitpunkt $t_r$ des Eintreffens der letzten Messung $\underline{y}_r$. Mitunter ist man daran interessiert, die Schätzung mit der Messung zu begleiten, d. h. zu jedem Meßvektor $\underline{y}_i$ eine Schätzung $\hat{\underline{x}}_i$ vorzunehmen. Hierfür eignen sich <u>rekursive</u> Algorithmen, die im vorliegenden Fall der stationären dynamischen Modelle als Sonderfälle der bekannten KALMANfilter aufgefaßt werden können [3], [12]. Die rekursiven Algorithmen lassen sich aus den hier angegebenen nichtrekursiven Algorithmen in einfacher Weise durch einen Übergang von r auf r+1 Messungen herleiten [3], [6], [7]. Man erhält für den Gleichungstyp (III) der Tab. 1 dann

$$\hat{\underline{x}}_{r+1} = \hat{\underline{x}}_r + \underline{K}_{r+1} \cdot (\underline{y}_{r+1} - \underline{C} \cdot \hat{\underline{x}}_r) \, , \tag{11a}$$

$$\underline{K}_{r+1} = \underline{P}_r \cdot \underline{C}^T \cdot (\underline{R} + \underline{C} \cdot \underline{P}_r \cdot \underline{C}^T)^{-1} \, , \tag{11b}$$

$$\underline{P}_{r+1} = (\underline{I} - \underline{K}_r \cdot \underline{C}) \cdot \underline{P}_r \, , \tag{11c}$$

$$r = 0, 1, 2, \ldots \, .$$

Hierbei sind $\underline{C}$ und $\underline{R}$ als unabhängig von r angenommen worden, was den bisherigen Voraussetzungen nach Stationärität entspricht.

Der Algorithmus (11) beinhaltet die Gleichungstypen (I) bis (III) der nichtrekursiven Darstellung. Die Unterschiede liegen in den Anfangsbedingungen $\hat{\underline{x}}_0$ und $\underline{P}_0$ für r=0 sowie - wie zuvor - in den statistischen Voraussetzungen für $\underline{R}$ und $\underline{P}$ und die Verteilungen $f(\underline{x})$ und $f(\underline{y})$ [6].

| Bezeichnung | | Bedingungen |
|---|---|---|
| Least-Squares-Schätzer | LS | $\hat{\underline{x}}_0 = \underline{0},\quad \underline{P}_0 \to \infty,\quad \underline{R} = \underline{I},\quad f(\underline{x})$ und $f(\underline{y})$ beliebig |
| Weighted-Least-Squares-Schätzer | WLS | $\hat{\underline{x}}_0 = \underline{0},\quad \underline{P}_0 \to \infty,\quad \underline{R} = \underline{G}^{-1},\quad f(\underline{x})$ und $f(\underline{y})$ beliebig |
| Gauss-Markov-Schätzer | GMS | $\hat{\underline{x}}_0 = \underline{0},\quad \underline{P}_0 \to \infty,\quad \underline{R} = \underline{R},\quad f(\underline{x})$ und $f(\underline{y})$ beliebig |
| Maximum-Likelihood-Schätzer | MLS | $\hat{\underline{x}}_0 = \underline{0},\quad \underline{P}_0 \to \infty,\quad \underline{R} = \underline{R},\quad f(\underline{x})$ beliebig, $f(\underline{y})$ normalverteilt |
| Erweiterter-Weighted-Least-Squares-Sch. | EWLS | $\hat{\underline{x}}_0 = \hat{\underline{x}}_0,\quad \underline{P}_0 = \underline{M}^{-1},\quad \underline{R} = \underline{G}^{-1},\quad f(\underline{x})$ und $f(\underline{y})$ beliebig |
| Minimaler-Varianz-Schätzer | MVS | $\hat{\underline{x}}_0 = \bar{\underline{x}},\quad \underline{P}_0 = \underline{P},\quad \underline{R} = \underline{R},\quad f(\underline{x})$ und $f(\underline{y})$ beliebig |
| Bayes-Schätzer | BS | $\hat{\underline{x}}_0 = \bar{\underline{x}},\quad \underline{P}_0 = \underline{P},\quad \underline{R} = \underline{R},\quad f(\underline{x})$ und $f(\underline{y})$ normalverteilt |

<u>Tab. 2</u>: Verschiedene rekursive Schätzalgorithmen.


## 2.2 Systematische Meßfehler

Sind bei einer Diagnose in der Meßeinrichtung nur systematische, d. h. deterministische und damit reproduzierbare Meßfehler vorhanden, so lautet die Meßgleichung

$$\underline{y} = \underline{C} \cdot \underline{x} + \underline{m}^* \; ; \quad \underline{m}^* = \underline{H} \cdot \underline{m}. \tag{12}$$

Die Ermittlung von $\underline{x}$ aus (12) ist nun i. a. wesentlich schwieriger als beim Auftreten stochastischer Meßfehler. Dies liegt daran, daß Schätzalgorithmen (Filterverfahren) in der im vorigen Abschnitt beschriebenen Form nicht unmittelbar herangezogen werden können, um $\underline{x}$ zu bestimmen bzw. über $\hat{\underline{x}}$ zu schätzen. Historisch gesehen standen deshalb hier auch meist Hardwarelösungen im Vordergrund, indem über mehrere Sensoren eine <u>technische</u> Redundanz erzeugt wurde und beispielsweise über Zwei- aus Dreischaltungen defekte Sensoren kompensiert wurden. Diese Vorgehensweise ist aufwendig und teuer. Sie kommt für viele Anwendungen u. a. auch aus Gewichts- aber auch aus Kostengründen nur in besonderen Ausnahmefällen (z. B. Kernkraftwerke) in Frage. Diesbezüglich günstiger sind Verfahren der <u>analytischen</u> Redundanz, bei denen Sensorfehler softwaremäßig über geeignete Detektionsalgorithmen bestimmt werden. Eine umfassende Übersicht hierzu findet sich in [8]. Demnach sind beim heutigen Stand der Wissenschaft drei verschiedene Vorgehensweisen üblich, systematische Sensorfehler zu detektieren und zwar mit Hilfe von fehlersensitiven Filtern, Mehrfach-Hypothesen-Filtern und inno-

vativen Filtern. Bei den fehlersensitiven Filtern hat sich die Methode der Zustandsvektorerweiterung besonders bewährt. Sie ist geeignet zur Ermittlung sowohl von Mo-
delldefekten als auch von systematischen Sensorfehlern. Sie hat gegenüber anderen Methoden den Vorteil, auch schleichende Fehler zu erkennen, wie sie beispielsweise in
Form von Alterungen auftreten. Nachteil ist, daß die Fehlerbestimmung zu Lasten der
Beobachtbarkeit erfolgt. Die Mehrfach-Hypothesen-Filter basieren durchweg auf Bänken
von Filtern bzw. Beobachtern. Das Filter, das einen Fehler detektieren soll, wird bezüglich dieses Fehlers in Relation zu den übrigen Filtern besonders sensibilisiert.
In einer Entscheidungslogik werden dann die Ergebnisse der unter unterschiedlichen
Hypothesen durchgeführten Schätzungen bewertet. Dies kann beispielsweise über die zu
den Schätzern gehörenden Residuen geschehen [9]. Die grundsätzlich leistungsfähige
Methode erfordert einen hohen Softwareaufwand und hat den Nachteil, daß nur Sensorfehler erkannt werden, die während der Datenerfassung eintreten. A priori Fehler
werden nicht erkannt. Den gleichen Nachteil haben auch die innovativen Filter, die
zudem auch nur auf sprungförmige Fehler ansprechen. Hinsichtlich ihres Aufwandes
sind sie allerdings günstiger als die Mehrfach-Hypothesen-Filter. Bei dem Einsatz in-
novativer Filter erfolgt die Fehlererkennung mit Hilfe statistischer Tests, wobei
sich die Heranziehung eines verallgemeinerten Likelihood-Verhältnisses als nützlich
erwiesen hat [10].

Die zu den fehlersensitiven Filtern gehörende Methode der Zustandsvektorerweiterung
hat gewisse formale Bezüge zu den Zustandsschätzern in Abschnitt 2.1. Dies wird
deutlich, wenn man (12) in der Form

$$\underline{y} = [\underline{C} : \underline{H}] \cdot \begin{bmatrix} \underline{x} \\ \cdots \\ \underline{m} \end{bmatrix} \tag{13}$$

schreibt. Der neue Zustandsvektor $\underline{\tilde{x}} = [\underline{x}^T : \underline{m}^T]^T$ ist jetzt $(n+m,1)$-dimensional, entsprechend ist die neue Meßmatrix von der Dimension $(m,n+m)$. Das Gleichungssystem (13)
ist also unterbestimmt. Im Sinne eines (WLS)-Algorithmus folgt somit

$$\underline{x} = \underline{C}^T \cdot (\underline{C} \cdot \underline{C}^T + \underline{H}^2)^{-1} \cdot \underline{y} \; ,$$

$$\underline{m} = \underline{H} \cdot (\underline{C} \cdot \underline{C}^T + \underline{H}^2)^{-1} \cdot \underline{y} \; . \tag{14}$$

Setzt man die zweite Gl. (14) in (13) wieder ein, dann läßt sich der Zustandsvektor
$\underline{x}$ auch in der Form

$$\underline{x} = (\underline{C}^T \cdot \underline{C})^{-1} \cdot \underline{C}^T \cdot [\underline{I} - \underline{H}^2 \cdot (\underline{C} \cdot \underline{C}^T + \underline{H}^2)^{-1}] \cdot \underline{y} \tag{15}$$

angeben.

Liegt der wichtige Fall vor, daß nicht in allen Meßgrößen systematische Fehler vorhanden sind, dann interessiert vor allem die Situation, bei der die Anzahl der Zu-

standsgrößen und die der systematischen Meßfehler die Anzahl der Meßgrößen nicht übersteigt. Modelliert man dies über

$$\underline{y} = [\underline{C} \,\vdots\, \underline{H}] \cdot \begin{bmatrix} \underline{x} \\ \cdots \\ \underline{\widetilde{m}} \end{bmatrix} \quad , \tag{16}$$

dann ist jetzt $\underline{\widetilde{m}}$ der $(p,1)$-dimensionale Fehlervektor, und $\underline{H}$ ist eine $(m,p)$-dimensionale Gewichtsmatrix. Wie vorausgesetzt, gilt $p \leq m-n$. Sind weniger als $p$ zulässige Sensorfehler vorhanden, dann verfügt $\underline{H}$ in den entsprechenden Spalten über Nullvektoren. Definiert man die $(m,m)$-dimensionale Hilfsmatrix

$$\underline{\Delta} = \underline{I} - \underline{H} \cdot (\underline{H}^T \cdot \underline{H})^{-1} \cdot \underline{H}^T \quad , \tag{17a}$$

so folgt aus (16) sofort

$$\underline{\widetilde{m}} = (\underline{H}^T \cdot \underline{H})^{-1} \cdot \underline{H}^T \cdot [\underline{I} - \underline{C} \cdot (\underline{C}^T \cdot \underline{\Delta} \cdot \underline{C})^{-1} \cdot \underline{C}^T \cdot \underline{\Delta}] \cdot \underline{y} \quad . \tag{17}$$

Setzt man dies in Analogie zu (15) wieder in (16) ein, dann folgt

$$\underline{x} = (\underline{C}^T \cdot \underline{C})^{-1} \cdot \underline{C}^T \cdot (\underline{I} - \underline{H} \cdot \underline{\widetilde{m}}) \cdot \underline{y} \quad , \tag{18}$$

mit $\underline{\widetilde{m}}$ nach (17).

## 2.3 Zusammenfassung

Der Einfluß stochastischer und systematischer Meßfehler wurde hier im Hinblick auf eine Schätzung bzw. direkte Berechnung der Zustandsgrößen $x_i$; $i=1,..,n$ getrennt behandelt. Selbstverständlich lassen sich die Ergebnisse der Abschnitte 2.1 und 2.2 auch kombinieren und damit stochastische und systematische Meßfehler gleichzeitig detektieren und somit auch kompensieren [11]. Im Sinne eines (WLS)-Algorithmus wäre beispielsweise in Gl. (15) bzw. Gl. (18) $\underline{y}$ lediglich durch

$$\frac{1}{r} \cdot \sum_{i=1}^{r} \underline{y}_i$$

zu ersetzen.


## 3. Diagnose für instationäres Systemverhalten

Auch im Falle einer instationären Dynamik des zu diagnostizierenden Prozesses ist die Diagnose in der Regel nur dann erfolgversprechend, wenn sowohl das dynamische System als auch die Meßeinrichtung durch lineare Modelle beschrieben werden können. Unterstellt man dies, so ergibt sich beispielsweise durch Linearisierung um einen Arbeitspunkt für den Prozess

$$\underline{x}[(k+1)\cdot T] = \underline{\Phi}(T)\cdot\underline{x}(k\cdot T) + \underline{\tilde{B}}(T)\cdot\underline{u}(k\cdot T) + \underline{w}^*(k\cdot T), \qquad k = 0,1,\ldots \ . \tag{19a}$$

Hierbei ist $\underline{x}$ der $(n,1)$-dimensionale Zustandsvektor, $\underline{u}$ der $(r,1)$-dimensionale Steuervektor und $\underline{w}^*$ das $(n,1)$-dimensionale Prozessrauschen. Im Sinne einer Rechnerauswertung ist (19a) als Differenzengleichung geschrieben mit T als Abtastzeit. Demnach ist die Koeffizientenmatrix $\underline{\Phi}(T)$ identisch mit der Transitionsmatrix des zu (19a) gehörenden kontinuierlichen Systems und $\underline{\tilde{B}}(T)$ ist die Steuermatrix. Da $\underline{\Phi}$ und $\underline{\tilde{B}}$ als von k unabhängig angenommen sind, ist das durch (19a) repräsentierte System zeitinvariant.

Als Meßgleichung kann auch hier (2) herangezogen werden, wobei in Konsequenz zu (19a) die Darstellung

$$\underline{y}(k\cdot T) = \underline{C}\cdot\underline{x}(k\cdot T) + \underline{D}\cdot\underline{v}(k\cdot T) + \underline{H}\cdot\underline{m} \tag{19b}$$

gewählt wird  mit konstanten Matrizen $\underline{C}$, $\underline{D}$ und $\underline{H}$; ansonsten behalten alle Größen ihre schon zuvor in Abschnitt 2 dargelegte Bedeutung. Setzt man voraus, daß vorrangig stochastische Einflüsse infolge von $\underline{w}^*$ und $\underline{v}^* = \underline{D}\cdot\underline{v}$ für die Diagnose maßgebend sind, so ist in (19b) $\underline{m} \equiv \underline{0}$. Setzt man weiter voraus, daß sich die Diagnose ausschließlich auf den Zustandsvektor $\underline{x}$ erstreckt und daß infolge der zugelassenen Instationärität nur rekursive Schätzalgorithmen von Bedeutung sind, dann kann (11) sofort auf den hier vorliegenden Fall erweitert werden, sofern die zusätzlich erforderlichen Extrapolationsgleichungen für den Zustand und die Fehlerkovarianzmatrix eingefügt werden. Man erhält so den Algorithmus [12]

$$\underline{\hat{x}}_{k+1} = \underline{\hat{x}}^*_{k+1} + \underline{K}_{k+1}\cdot(\underline{y}_{k+1} - \underline{C}\cdot\underline{\hat{x}}^*_{k+1}) \ ,$$

$$\underline{\hat{x}}^*_{k+1} = \underline{\Phi}(T)\cdot\underline{\hat{x}}_k + \underline{\tilde{B}}(T)\cdot\underline{u}_k,$$

$$\underline{P}^*_{k+1} = \underline{\Phi}(T)\cdot\underline{P}_k\cdot\underline{\Phi}^T(T) + \underline{Q}, \tag{20}$$

$$\underline{K}_{k+1} = \underline{P}^*_{k+1}\cdot\underline{C}^T\cdot(\underline{C}\cdot\underline{P}^*_{k+1}\cdot\underline{C}^T + \underline{R})^{-1},$$

$$\underline{P}_{k+1} = (\underline{I} - \underline{K}_{k+1}\cdot\underline{C})\cdot\underline{P}^*_{k+1}, \qquad k = 0,1,\ldots \ ,$$

wobei für $(k+1)\cdot T$ verkürzend $k+1$ gesetzt ist. Zu (20) gehören noch die Anfangsbedingungen

$$\underline{\hat{x}}_0 = E(\underline{x}_0),$$

$$\underline{P}_0 = E[(\underline{\hat{x}}_0 - \underline{x}_0)\cdot(\underline{\hat{x}}_0 - \underline{x}_0)^T] \tag{20a}$$

und $\underline{Q}$ ist die zu $\underline{w}^*$ gehörige Kovarianzmatrix. Sind in (19) die Realisierungen von $\underline{w}^*$ und $\underline{v}$ bzw. $\underline{v}^*$ normalverteilte weiße Rauschprozesse mit $E[\underline{w}^*(k\cdot T)] = E[\underline{v}^*(k\cdot T)] = \underline{0}$ und sind $\underline{w}^*$ und $\underline{v}^*$ nicht miteinander und auch nicht mit $\underline{x}_0$ korreliert, so stellt (20) ein diskretes KALMANfilter dar. Für $\underline{\Phi}(T) \equiv \underline{I}$ und $\underline{u}_k \equiv 0$ sowie $\underline{Q} \equiv \underline{0}$ als Bedingung für eine stationäre Dynamik folgt aus (20)

$$\hat{\underline{x}}^*_{k+1} = \hat{\underline{x}}_k \quad ; \quad \underline{P}^*_{k+1} = \underline{P}_k$$

d. h. die Extrapolationsgleichungen sind identisch erfüllt und (20) geht in (11) über. Damit ist eine formale Übereinstimmung der Schätzalgorithmen für die stationäre und die instationäre Dynamik erreicht.

Treten im Fall des instationären Systemverhaltens auch systematische Meßfehler $\underline{m} \neq \underline{0}$ auf, dann gelten die phänomenologischen Ausführungen in Abschnitt 2.2 auch hier unverändert. Insbesondere läßt sich die Methode der Zustandsvektorerweiterung auch auf den dynamischen Fall unmittelbar übertragen und auch die parallele Detektion stochastischer und deterministischer Fehlereinflüsse ist über entsprechend zu erweiternde Gln (20) unmittelbar möglich.

Erstreckt sich die Diagnose nicht oder nicht nur auf den Zustandsvektor $\underline{x}$ in (19), sondern beispielsweise auch auf Elemente in der Systemmatrix $\underline{\Phi}$ und der Steuermatrix $\underline{\tilde{B}}$ und/oder der Meßmatrix $\underline{C}$, so liegt zusätzlich zur Zustandsschätzung noch ein sogenanntes Parameterproblem vor. Dieses kann im Sinne von Abschnitt 2, dann allerdings in der Regel als zeitvariantes Problem, gelöst werden. Mit der Wahl geeigneter Zustandsgrößen für die gesuchten Parameter kann folglich auch das Parameterproblem mit in (20) eingebettet werden.


## 4. Anwendungen

Die konkrete Anwendung von Diagnoseverfahren auf technische Großsysteme steht erst am Anfang ihrer Entwicklung. Dies liegt zum einen in der Schwierigkeit der Modellbildung begründet und zum anderen in der rechnerorientierten Aufbereitung der Diagnosealgorithmen einschließlich der Rechner- und Rechenkapazität bei Echtzeitaufgaben.

Eine Reihe von Anwendungen insbesondere für niedrig dimensionierte Systeme findet sich in [1]. Ein interessantes Beispiel zur analytischen Redundanz ist in [9] aufgeführt. Dort wird auf der Basis von Mehrfach-Hypothesen-Filtern eine Fehlerdetektion der Instrumentierung eines Teils des Dampfkreislaufes in einem Kernkraftwerk durchgeführt. Das zugrundeliegende System besteht immerhin aus drei Zustandsgrößen $x_i$; $i=1,\ldots,3$ und aus fünf Meßgrößen $y_j$; $j=1,\ldots,5$, so daß für die fünf Sensoren $y_j$ eine Bank aus fünf KALMANfiltern notwendig ist, die in Echtzeit abgearbeitet wird. Die erzielten Ergebnisse sind ermutigend.

Relativ weit fortgeschritten sind Diagnoseverfahren in der zivilen Luftfahrt, zumindest was die Diagnose an den Turboflugtriebwerken anbetrifft. Vor allem URBAN hat auf diesem Gebiet richtungsweisend gearbeitet. Eine gewisse Zusammenfassung seiner

Arbeiten findet sich in [13]. Eine Fortsetzung und Erweiterung hierzu ist in [6] enthalten, wo insbesondere auch das Problem der analytischen Redundanz in die Diagnose miteinbezogen worden ist. Eine Anwendung der Triebwerksdiagnose auch auf den militärischen Bereich ist in [7] und [11] gegeben, wobei die Unterschiede zu [6] und [13] im wesentlichen im andersartigen Aufbau der Triebwerke liegen, aber teilweise auch methodischer Art sind. Folgt man beispielsweise den Überlegungen in [11], dann läßt sich ein Zweiwellenflugtriebwerk durch ein stationäres Modell mit 12 Zustandsgrößen $x_i$; $i=1,\ldots,12$ und 16 Meßgrößen $y_j$; $j=1,\ldots,16$ beschreiben, wobei die Zustandsgrößen so gewählt sind, daß jeweils ein oder zwei Zustände eine Baugruppe des Triebwerks (Verdichter, Turbine, Brennkammer, etc.) vollständig diagnostizieren. Ein Ergebnis hierzu zeigt Bild 2, in dem die Abweichungen $\Delta x_i$; $i=1,\ldots,12$ der 12 Zustandsgrößen von ihren fehlerfreien Nominalwerten $x_i$; $i=1,\ldots,12$ aufgetragen sind und dies für drei verschiedene Lastfälle, um die die Triebwerksgleichungen linearisiert wurden. Das Resultat der Diagnose ist, daß im Zustand $x_1$ (Massendurchsatz des Niederdruckverdichters) gegenüber dem Nominalzustand eine Verschlechterung von ca. 2 % eingetreten ist. Da im übrigen für alle drei Lastfälle im Mittel das gleiche Ergebnis erhalten wird, kann auf eine hohe Genauigkeit des mathematischen Modells einschließlich der Diagnose geschlossen werden.

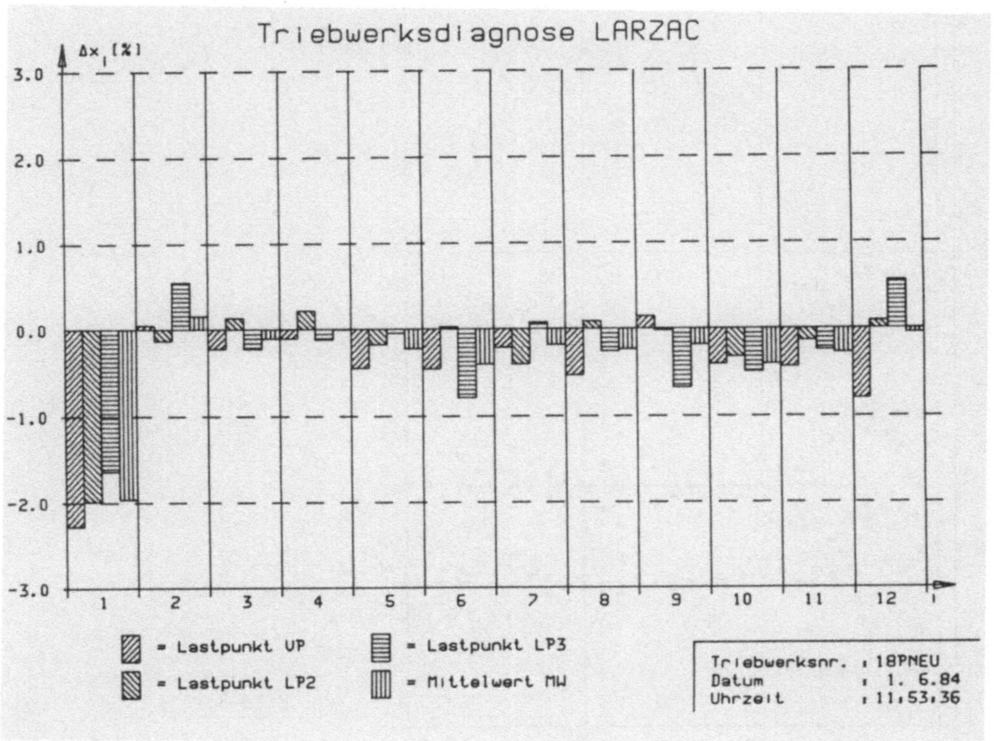


Bild 2: Diagnose eines Fehlers im Zustand 1 eines Turboflugtriebwerks.

Am Beispiel aus Bild 2 zeigt die unterschiedliche Qualität der Schätzalgorithmen Bild 3. Hier ist aufgetragen über die Anzahl r der zur Verfügung stehenden Meßvektoren $\underline{y}_j$; $j=1,\ldots,r$ das Fehlermaß

$$e = \sqrt{\frac{1}{12}\cdot\sum_{i=1}^{12} [\Delta x_i(r)-\Delta x_{i,0}]^2} \quad , \tag{21}$$

das ein Bewertungskriterium für die Konvergenzgeschwindigkeit der Zustandsschätzer darstellt. Es ist dabei $\Delta x_i(r)$ der aktuelle Zustand und $\Delta x_{i,0}$ der Sollzustand. Für die 16 Sensoren wurde die konstante Standardabweichung von $\sigma = 0,1$ bzw. $\sigma = 0,01$, d. h. 10 bzw. 1 % zugrundegelegt. Alternativ wurde ein (WLS)- und ein (EWLS)-Algorithmus genutzt. Das Ergebnis der Diagnose macht deutlich, daß zum einen - wie im Abschnitt 2.1 angeführt - der (EWLS)-Algorithmus wesentlich leistungsfähiger als der (WLS)-Algorithmus ist und diese Leistungsfähigkeit sich für kleines r besonders bemerkbar macht und zum anderen für größere Werte von $\sigma$ doch sehr viele Meßvektoren $\underline{y}_j$ benötigt werden, um den Wert $e(r\to\infty)$ zu erreichen. Durch den Einsatz eines (BS)-Schätzers kann dieses Verhalten erheblich verbessert werden, was auf die dann einzubringenden a priori Informationen zurückzuführen ist.

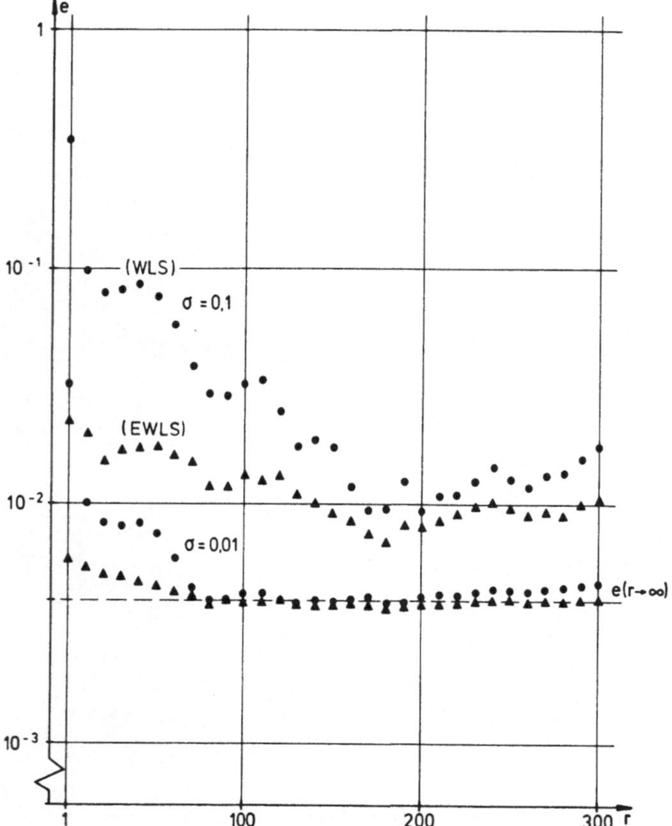



**Bild 3:**

Vergleich zwischen (WLS)- und (EWLS)-Algorithmus.

Literatur


[1]  Barschdorff, D. (Herausgeber):
     Verfahren und Systeme zur technischen Fehlerdiagnose.
     GMR-Bericht 1 zum Aussprachetag "Diagnosesysteme",
     2.-3. April, Langen 1984.

[2]  Isermann, R.:
     Diagnosemethoden mit Modellbildung.
     In [1].

[3]  Sage, A.P.; Melsa, J.L.:
     Estimation Theory with Applications to Communications and Control.
     Mc Graw-Hill Book Comp., New York 1971.

[4]  Mendel, J.M.:
     Discrete Techniques of Parameter Estimation.
     Marcel Dekker, New York 1973.

[5]  Sorenson, H.W.:
     Parameter Estimation.
     Marcel Dekker, New York 1980.

[6]  Roesnick, M.:
     Eine systemtheoretische Lösung des Fehlerdiagnoseproblems am
     Beispiel eines Flugtriebwerkes.
     Dissertation, Fachbereich Maschinenbau der
     Hochschule der Bundeswehr Hamburg, 1984.

[7]  Fiedler, K.; Lunderstädt, R.:
     Diagnoseverfahren für LARZAC-Triebwerk.
     2. Teilbericht (Abschlußbericht)
     Hochschule der Bundeswehr Hamburg, 1983.

[8]  Willsky, A.S.:
     A Survey of Design Methods for Failure Detection on Dynamic Systems.
     Automatica, Vol. 12, S. 601-611, 1976.

[9]  Tylee, J.L.:
     On-Line Failure Detection in Nuclear Power Plant Instrumentation.
     IEEE Transactions on Automatic Control,
     Vol. AC-28, No. 3, S. 406-415, 1983.

[10] Willsky, A.S.; Jones, H.L.:
     A Generalized Likelihood Ratio Approach to State Estimation
     in Linear Systems Subject to Abrupt Changes.
     Proceedings IEEE Conference on Decision and Control,
     S. 846-853, Phoenix, 1974.

[11] Fiedler, K.; Lunderstädt, R.:
     Zur systemtheoretischen Diagnose von Strahltriebwerken.
     Bei der Zeitschrift "Regelungstechnik" zur Veröffentlichung angenommen.

[12] Gelb, A.:
     Applied Optimal Estimation.
     The M.I.T. Press, Cambridge, Mass. 1974.

[13] Urban, L.A.:
     Gas Path Analysis - A Tool For Engine Condition Monitoring.
     33rd Annual International Air Safety Seminar, Flight Safety Foundation Inc.,
     Christchurch, New Zealand, 1980.

# ANFORDERUNGEN  AN  ECHTZEITSIMULATIONSSYSTEME  FÜR  AUSBILDUNG  UND  TRAINING  VON  VERKEHRSFLUGZEUGFÜHRERN

W. D. Hass, Lufthansa Frankfurt

( Vortrag wird während der ASIM Tagung verteilt )

# DAS THERMOREGULATORISCHE SYSTEM DES MENSCHEN:

## 3-D SIMULATION AUF EINEM VEKTORRECHNER

M.Buse, J.Werner, Bochum

**Zusammenfassung.** Im Rahmen der Untersuchung des thermoregulatorischen Systems des Menschen sollen auf der Grundlage der Bio-Heat-Transfer' Gleichung und der Wärmebilanz auf der Haut, Temperaturprofile für den menschlichen Körper berechnet werden. Thermisch wirksame Inhomogenitäten der Wärmeleitfähigkeit, der Wärmeproduktion und der kapillaren Gewebedurchblutung werden auf der Grundlage eines 3 - dimensionalen digitalen Atlas des menschlichen Körpers berücksichtigt. Unterschiedliche Reglermodelle mit zentralen und lokalen Verarbeitungsstrategien werden simuliert und die Temperaturprofile verglichen. Die Lösung des skizzierten Problems wurde auf dem Vektorrechner CYBER 205 mit Hilfe eines ADI Verfahrens programmiert. Das Lösungsverfahren und erste Ergebnisse werden vorgestellt.

**Summary.** For investigation of the human thermoregulatory system the bio-heat-transfer equation' and the heat balance at the skin of the human body are solved and temperature profiles for the human body are calulated. Inhomogeneities of heat-conductivity, heat-production und capillary bloodflow are important system parameters and are considered on the basis of a three dimensional digital database of the human body. Central and decentral controller structures are simulated and resulting temperature profiles are compared with each other. Calculations were done by a FORTRAN program on Cyber 205 vectorcomputer using alternating direction implicit procedure. First results will be presented.

## 1.Einführung

Ein Modell des autonomen thermoregulatorischen Systems (Bild 1) unterscheidet vier funktionelle Einheiten, zunächst das passive System, zweitens eine über den gesamten Körper inhomogen verteilte Rezeptorpopulation, zur Erfassung der jeweiligen Temperaturen bzw. des thermischen Status, drittens, die zentrale und/oder dezentrale Informationsverarbeitung und viertens, die Effektorsysteme Vasomotorik, Respiration, Metabolismus und Evaporation. Störgrößen des Systems sind die Umgebungsparameter Temperatur, Feuchte und Windgeschwindigkeit, sowie der Stoffwechsel des arbeitenden Menschen.
Experimentelle Befunde (Werner, Reents 1980) warfen die Frage auf, inwieweit zur Erklärung der beobachteten Phänomene nicht nur die Anatomie und Inhomogenität des menschlichen Körpers zu berücksichtigen

sind, sondern auch verteilte Reglerkonzepte, mit zentralen und dezentralen Rezeptorpopulationen und Effektoransteuerungsmöglichkeiten angenommen werden müssen. Eine experimentelle Untersuchung dieses Systems gelangt allerdings schnell an ethische Grenzen, so daß der Einsatz von Simulationsverfahren helfen soll, die vorgeschlagenen Reglerkonzepte zu überprüfen und nach der Auswertung möglicherweise weitere gezielte Experimente zu initiieren.

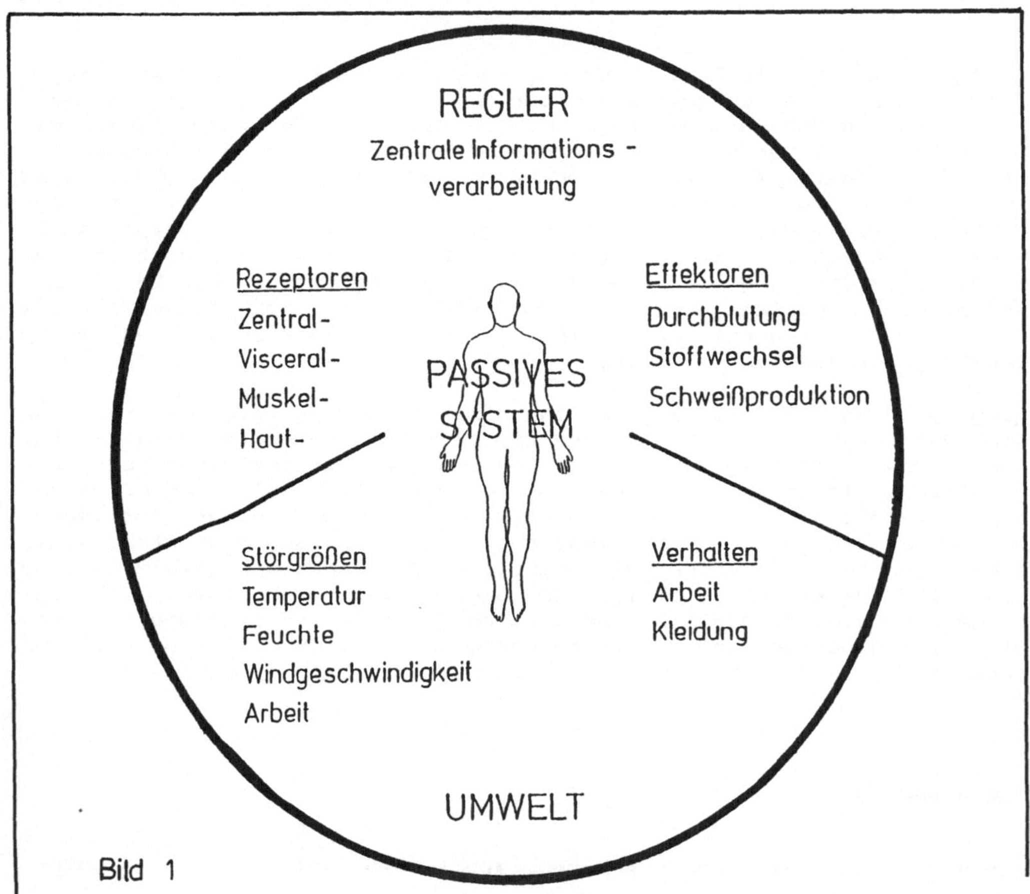


Bild 1

## 2. Das mathematische Modell

Das hier dargestellte Simulationsvorhaben stellt folgende Bedingungen an die Beschreibung des passiven Systems:

• möglichst genaue Nachbildung der makroskopischen Anatomie des menschlichen Körpers,

• Berücksichtigung der Gewebeabhänigkeit der Parameter: Wärmeleitfähigkeit, Basalstoffwechsel und Basaldurchblutung, sowie der Dichte und der Wärmekapazität (bei transienten Untersuchungen).

• Berücksichtigung der Orts- und Zeitabhängigkeit von Temperatur, Stoffwechsel und Durchblutung.

• Berücksichtigung der physiologisch nachgewiesenen Beziehungen zwischen Temperatur und Stoffwechsel ($Q_{10}$) und zwischen Stoffwechsel, Atemminutenvolumen und Durchblutung ($O_2$-Versorung).


## 2.1.Die Gleichungen des Passiven Systems

Der Wärmetransport durch Wärmeleitung und kapillare Blutströmung wird durch die Bio-Heat-Transfer Gleichung (1) beschrieben. Der Wärmeverlust von der Haut ergibt sich als Summe der Einzelverluste durch Konvektion, Konduktion, Strahlung und Verdunstung (Gl 2); die Verluste durch Respiration sind proportional zum respiratorischen Volumen und zur Differenz im Wärmeinhalt zwischen aus- und eingeatmeter Luft (Gl 3). Mathematisch ist dieses Problem damit als dreidimensionales, zeitabhängiges Anfangs-Randwertproblem mit nichtlinearer Randbedingung charakterisiert.

$$\rho(\xi)c(\xi)\,\frac{\partial T}{\partial t} = \mathrm{div}(\lambda(\xi)\mathrm{grad}(T))+M(\xi,t)-h_B(T_B-T) \tag{1}$$

$$-\lambda(\xi)\,\frac{\partial T}{\partial n} = Q_{rad} + Q_{konv} + Q_{eva} \tag{2}$$

$$Q_{res} = AMV\,(r_a c_a(T_{res}-T_a) + \Delta h_v \Delta \rho_{H_2O}) \tag{3}$$

$$\mathrm{mit}\ T := T(\xi,t),\ T_B := T_B(\xi,t)$$

Zur Berücksichtigung der geometrischen und anatomischen Verhältnisse im menschlichen Körper erstellten wir einen digitalen Atlas, der die Identifikation der einzelnen Punkte des Temperaturfeldes mit den zugehörigen Gewebeparametern ermöglicht (Kelterbaum et.al. 1977). Der menschliche Körper wurde zu diesem Zweck auf ein dreidimensionales Rechteckgitter abgebildet, wobei jeder elementare Kubus als homogen angenommen wird. Wir wählten eine Auflösung von 1 cm am Rumpf und 0.5 cm an den Extremitäten und am Kopf. Sie führt zu einem Umfang der Datenbasis von 400 000 Elementen.

## 2.2. Die Reglergleichungen

Die Gleichungen für die drei Effektorsysteme Stoffwechsel, Evaporation und Hautddurchblutung werden durch Matrixgleichungen beschrieben, die eine beliebige lineare Verknüfung von Effektor- und Rezeptorort zulassen:

$$Y_{ij} = A_{(ik)j} \cdot Z_{kj}. \tag{4}$$

Hierbei bezeichnen j das Effektorsystem, i den Effektorort und k den Rezeptorort. Als Reglerinput sind sowohl Temperaturen, als auch ihre zeitliche Änderungen vorgesehen.

## 3. ADI - Verfahren

Die Gleichungen des passiven Systems werden im Wechsel mit den Regler-gleichungen durch ein finite Differenzen Verfahren, speziell durch eine Modifikation eines Alternierende-Richtungen-Verfahrens, wie es bereits 1956 von Douglas und Rachford vorgeschlagen wurde, gelöst.
Dieses Verfahren ist aus zwei Gründen vorteilhaft:
1. Für dieses implizite Verfahren ist bekannt, daß die zugehörige Differenzengleichung für alle $\Delta x, \Delta y, \Delta z$ und $\Delta t$ im homogenen, regulären Fall konvergiert.
2. Da bei diesem Verfahren eine Gleichung mit drei impliziten Rich-tungen in drei Gleichungen mit je einer impliziten Richtung aufge-spalten wird , erhält man drei Tridiagonalsysteme, die leicht durch Standardverfahren lösbar sind.

$$s_{ijk}T^{*}_{i-1jk} + T^{*}_{ijk} + t_{ijk}T^{*}_{i+1jk} = w_{ijk}(T^{n},T^{r}) \tag{5}$$

$$s_{ijk}T^{**}_{ij-1k} + T^{**}_{ijk} + t_{ijk}T^{**}_{ij+1k} = w^{*}_{ijk}(T^{n},T^{r},T^{*}) \tag{6}$$

$$s_{ijk}T^{r+1}_{ijk-1} + T^{r+1}_{ijk} + t_{ijk}T^{r+1}_{ijk+1} =$$

$$w^{**}_{ijk}(T^{n},T^{r},T^{*},T^{**}) \tag{7}$$

Die Lösungen $T^{*}$, $T^{**}$ und $T^{r+1}$ der Tridiagonalsysteme stellen Schätzun-gen der Lösung dar. Die Systeme werden iterativ so oft gelöst $(r:=r+1)$, bis der numerische Fehler der Lösung kleiner als 0.5% der Gesamtwärmeproduktion ist. Im vorliegenden Fall wird diese Fehler-schranke bereits nach 1 bis 2 Durchläufen unterschritten. Für die Koeffizienten s,t,w gilt:

$$s_{ijk} = - a_{i+1jk}/e_{ijk} \qquad (8)$$

$$t_{ijk} = - a_{ijk}/e_{ijk} \qquad (9)$$

$$w_{ijk} = (v_{ijk} + \tau T^r{}_{ijk} + d2T^r y + d2T^r z) \qquad (10a)$$

$$w^*{}_{ijk} = (v_{ijk} + \tau T^r{}_{ijk} + d2T^* x + d2T^r z) \qquad (10b)$$

$$w^{**}{}_{ijk} = (v_{ijk} + \tau T^r{}_{ijk} + d2T^* x + d2T^{**} y) \qquad (10c)$$

$$\text{mit } a_{ijk} = \Delta x (\lambda_{ijk} + \lambda_{i-1jk})/2 \qquad (11)$$

$$e_{ijk} = d_{ijk} + a_{i+1jk} + a_{ijk} \qquad (12)$$

$$d_{ijk} = \frac{\Delta x^3}{\Delta t} c_{ijk}\rho_{ijk} \qquad (13)$$

$$v_{ijk} = d_{ijk}T^n{}_{ijk} + M_{ijk}\Delta x^3 \qquad (14)$$

und $d2T^r y$, $d2T^r z$, $d2T^* x$ und $d2T^{**} y$ bezeichnen die 2.partiellen Ableitungen des jeweiligen Temperaturfeldes im Punkt ijk.


## 4.Programmierung des Vektorrechner

Die Programmierung des Lösungsverfahrens auf der Bochumer CYBER 205
Installation stellt einige besondere Anforderungen, die zum einen auf
die Hard- und Software des Vektorrechners, und zum anderen auf die
Besonderheiten der Bochumer Installation zurückzuführen sind.
"The CYBER 205 ia a virtual memory machine. The program space is
limited only by the available disk space"; "An efficient program uses
its data in such a way as to minimize paging for data access. It also
uses appropriate page size for its data (large or small
pages)."(Reference Manual, 1983). Da das oben beschriebene Problem
mit 10 Feldern a 400000 Elementen die Speicherkapazität (512 kW) des
Rechners um ein mehrfaches übersteigt, besteht ein großer Teil der
Programmierarbeit in der Auseinandersetzung mit diesen harmlos klin-
genden Sätzen. Übersteigt in einem Programmabschnitt der Umfang der
definierten Felder den zur Verfügung stehenden Arbeitsspeicher, hängt
der jeweils aktuelle Paging Aufwand ganz wesentlich von der Umgebung
des Programms in der Maschine ab.
Zur Ausnutzung der Leistungsfähigkeit dieser Maschine muß der Benutzer
den Algorithmus in möglichst langen Vektoren formulieren. Die Umstellung von strukturierter <u>sequentieller</u> Programmierung auf strukturierte
<u>vektorielle</u> Programmierung fällt schwer, zumal dies in der, die struk-
turiert Programmierung nicht unterstützenden Sprache, FORTRAN getan
werden muß. Vektorrechner spezifische Erweiterungen von FORTRAN 77
geben dem Benutzer einige Hilfsmittel, die von der Vektorarithmetik
geforderte sequentielle Anordnung der Feldelemente auch bei mehrdimen-

sionalen Gebieten mit unregelmäßiger Berandung zu erreichen.

Der Bochumer Rechner wurde als Forschungsrechner für das Land NRW angeschafft, und muß seine Anschaffung durch hohe Auslastungszahlen rechtfertigen. Der geringe Speicherausbau in Bochum macht hohe CPU-Auslastungen nur für ganz spezielle Probleme mit geringem Input-/Output- und hohem Arithmetikaufwand möglich. Hohe Benutzerzahlen, closed-shop Betrieb und geringe Benutzerunterstützung erschweren eine effiziente Programmierung und Entwicklungsarbeit. Dennoch muß gesagt werden, daß eine Lösung des Problems ohne diesen Rechner nicht möglich gewesen wäre.


## 5.Ergebnisse

Durch Segmentierung und Komprimierung der Datenbasis konnte mit Hilfe von Indexvektoren eine effiziente Vektorisierung des Lösungsalgorithmus erreicht werden. In Abhängigkeit von Segment und Raumrichtung liegt die mittlere Systemlänge für ein Tridiagonalsystem zwischen 10 und 100 Elementen. Mit Hilfe der von Lambiotte (1975) vorgeschlagenen gekoppelten Lösung dieser unabhängigen Tridiagonalsysteme werden Vektorlängen von ca. 30000 Elementen erreicht. Für die Randelemente und die Ansatzelemente zwischen den Segmenten, liegt die Vektorlänge zwischen 300 und 2000 Elementen. Mit Hilfe von Bitvektoren werden diese Felder komprimiert und die berechnete Koeffizienten expandiert. Zur Reduktion des E/A Transportes wird die Datenbasis in binärcodierter Form zur Verfügung gestellt. Die zur Lösung der Gleichungen 1-3 benötigten CPU-Zeiten und die erreichte CPU Auslastung (CPU/STU) sind in Tabelle 1 dargestellt.

|  | Einzelsegmente | Gesamtatlas |
|---|---|---|
| CPU/STU | 0.96 | 0.69 |
| CPU/$\Delta$t | 3.9 | 23.6 |

Tabelle 1: Rechenzeitbedarf und CPU Auslastung in den Simulationsläufen ($\Delta$t = 600 s)

In verschiedenen Simulationsläufen wurde der Einfluß der Parametervаriationen und der Durchblutung getestet. Einige der Ergebnisse sind in den Bildern 2 bis 4 dargestellt.

• Die Ortsabhängigkeit der Wärmeleitzahl führt zu beachtlichen Temperaturunterschieden zwischen homogenem und inhomogenem Fall in der Muskulatur (ca. 1°C Bild 2).

• Bild 3 zeigt axiale Temperaturprofile des Kopfes für homogene und inhomogene Stoffwechselverteilung ohne Durchblutung. Stoffwechselwerte wie sie in der Literatur für das Gehirn beschrieben werden, führen ohne Durchblutung zu unphysiologisch hohen Temperaturen von über 45°C.

• Die hohe Bedeutung der Durchblutung für die Isothermie im Körperinnern wird nochmals in Bild 4 dargestellt. Zum Vergleich wurden achsiale Profile des Kopfes abgebildet, die für inhomogene Stoffwechselverteilung mit und ohne Durchblutung berechnet wurden.

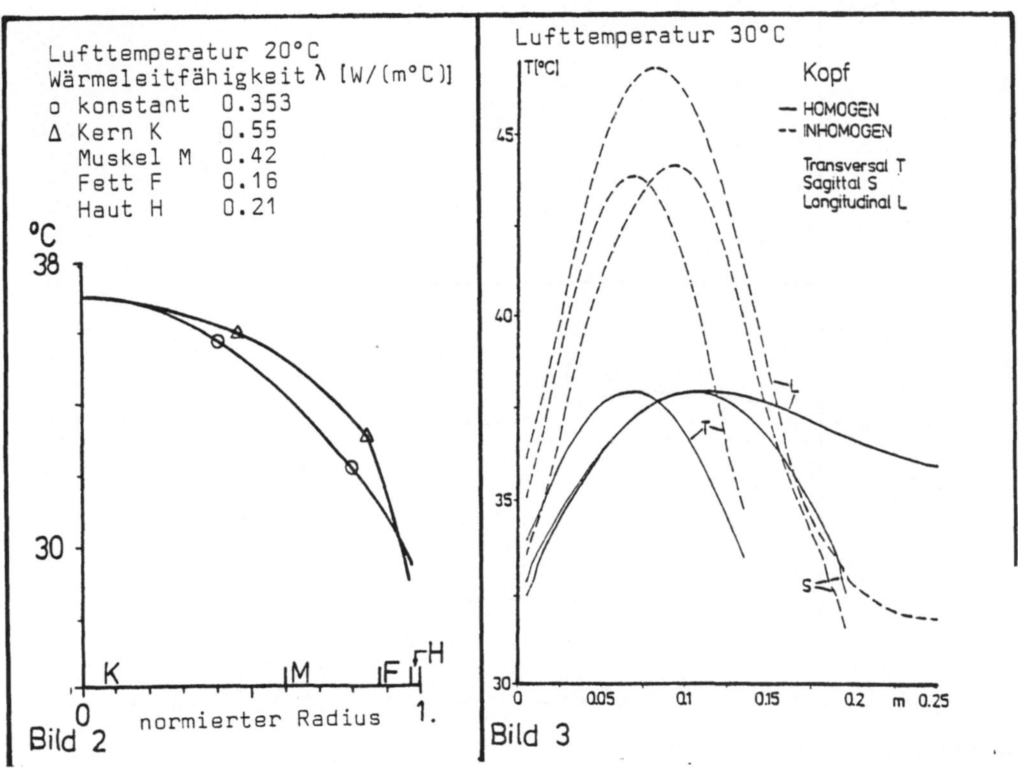

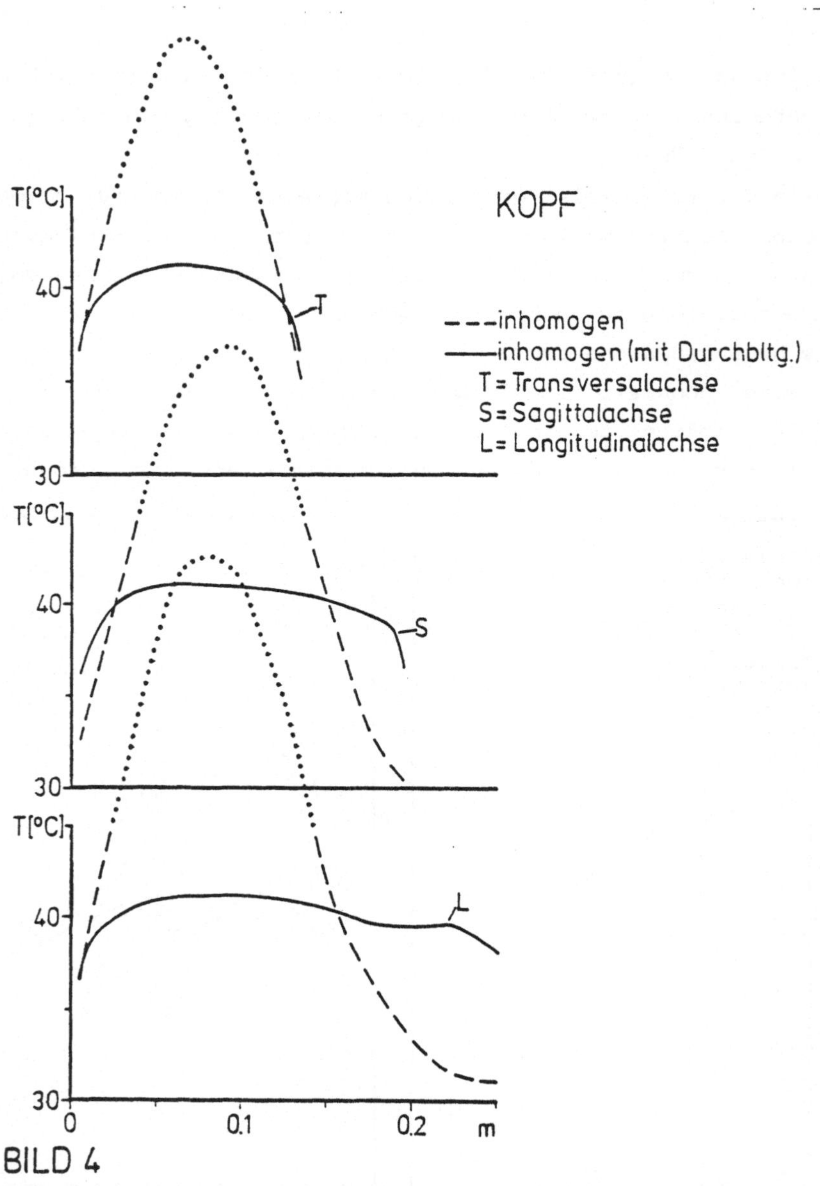


BILD 4

## Formelzeichen und Indizes

| | | |
|---|---|---|
| $\xi$ | Ortskoordinate $\xi = (x,y,z)$ | [m] |
| $t$ | Zeit | [s] |
| $\rho$ | Dichte | [$kg/m^3$] |
| $c$ | spez. Wärmekapazität | [$J/(kg\,^{o}C)$] |
| $\lambda$ | Wärmeleitfähigkeit | [$W/(m\,^{o}C)$] |
| $T$ | Temperatur | [$^{o}C$] |
| $M$ | Stoffwechsel | [$W/m^3$] |
| $h$ | Wärmeübergangszahl | [$W/(m^2\,^{o}C)$] |

| | | | |
|---|---|---|---|
| AMV | Atemminutenvolumen | | [l/min] |
| $\Delta h_v$ | Verdampfungsenthalphie | | [J/(kgPa)] |
| $\Delta \rho_{H_2O}$ | Dichtedifferenz ein- und ausgeatmeter Luft | | [kg/m$^3$] |
| Q | Wärmestromdichte | | [W/m$^2$] |
| n | Normalenvektor | $\tau$ | Konvergenzbeschleuniger |
| rad | Strahlung | B | Blut |
| res | Respiration | a | Umgebung |
| eva | Verdunstung | | |

## Literatur

Buse,M.;Werner,J. Heat Balance of the Human Body: Influence of Variations of Locally Distributed Parameters, J.theor.Biol.,114(1985), 34-51.

CDC VSOS Version 2, Reference Volume 60459410 (1983), Control Data Corporation.

Douglas,J.J. Rachford,H.H. On the Numerical Solution of Heat Conduction Problems in two and three Space Variables, Trans.AMS 82 (1956),421-439.

Kelterbaum,J. Werner,J. Schön,H. Makroskopische Topographie des menschlichen Körpers: Gewinnung der Rohdaten und deren EDV- gerechte Aufarbeitung in einer Datenbank, EDV in Medizin und Biologie 4/1977.

Lambiotte,J.J. The Solution of Linear Systems of Equations on a Vector Computer. Ph.D.Dissertation, University of Virginia, 1975

Werner,J. Reents,T. A Contribution to the Topography of Temperature Regulation in Man, Eur.J.Appl.Physiol 45, 87-94 (1980)

Werner,J. Regelung der menschlichen Körpertemperatur Berlin,New-York, W.de Gruyter, 1984.

# EXPERIMENTELLE MODELLBILDUNG ZUR DIGITALEN SIMULATION


K.Diekmann, Bochum



Zusammenfassung. Die Modellbildung ist eine notwendige Voraussetzung
für Simulationsaufgaben. Ist eine theoretische Modellbildung nicht möglich, so muß das Modell durch eine experimentelle Analyse geschätzt
werden. In dieser Arbeit werden verschiedene Verfahren zur experimentellen Modellbildung vorgestellt, welche sich besonders für die Verwendung in digitalen on-line Simulationen eignen.

Summary: The model design is a neccessary prerequisite for simulation
tasks. If it is impossible to find a model by  theoretical studies, it
must be estimated by an experimental analysis. In this paper different
methods for the experimental analysis are presented. They can specially be used in connection with digital on-line simulations.



## 1. Problemstellung

Mit Hilfe von Simulationen soll das Verhalten des realen Prozesses als
Reaktion auf bestimmte Ereignisse und Zustände wiedergegeben werden.
Aus Kosten- oder Sicherheitsgründen wird die Reaktion nicht am Prozeß
selbst, sondern an einem Modell erprobt. Wird die Simulation an einem
Rechner (analog oder digital) durchgeführt, so wird die Reaktion berechnet. Dazu benötigt man ein mathematisches Modell, welches die physikalischen Eigenschaften des Prozesses in Simulationsgleichungen zu-
sammenfaßt. Die physikalischen Eigenschaften können am besten durch
eine theoretische Modellbildung erfaßt werden, da hierbei alle Einflüsse in ihrer Art und Größe berücksichtigt werden können.

Werden komplexere Prozesse untersucht, führt dies jedoch häufig zu
einem nicht gerechtfertigten Aufwand für die Modellbildung. Auch ist
es oftmals nicht möglich, alle Einflüße quantitativ zu berechnen, wenn
z.B. die physikalischen Zusammenhänge nicht vollständig bekannt sind
oder anlagenspezifische Kenngrößen auftreten. Dann muß das mathematische Modell anhand eines Experiments erstellt werden. In diesem Vortrag sollen verschiedene Verfahren für die experimentelle Modellbildung vorgestellt werden, ohne dabei eine Wertung vorzunehmen, denn die
Art der durchführbaren Experimente kann für die verschiedenen Prozeß-
arten sehr unterschiedlich sein. So wird z.B. der Betreiber einer
unproblematischen Produktionsanlage alle Arten von Testsignalen und

Betriebszuständen zulassen, während von einem chemischen oder medizinischen Vorgang vielleicht nur eine einzige, nicht beeinflußbare Reaktionskurve für die Analyse vorliegt.

Gleichgültig welche Art von experimenteller Modellbildung gewählt wird, ist die Experimentdurchführung und -auswertung für fast alle Verfahren mit der gleichen Problematik behaftet. Informationen über das Prozeßverhalten erhält man allein durch die gemessenen Betriebssignale. Das mathematische Modell kann also nur die Eigenschaften des Prozesses wiedergeben, die aus den Signalen rekonstruierbar sind. Es können nur Prozeßzustände erkannt werden, die während des Experiments auftraten. Experimentell erstellte Modelle sind daher immer mit einem Gültigkeitsbereich bzw. mit der Angabe über die Art des Experiments zu versehen.

## 2. Übersicht und Einordnung experimenteller Analyseverfahren

Um eine Einordnung experimenteller Analyseverfahren zu ermöglichen, sei zunächst eine Grobrasterung angegeben:

| | |
|---|---|
| deterministische Eingangssignale | – stochastische Eingangssignale |
| nichtparametrische Modelle | – parametrische Modelle |
| Zustandsraumdarstellung | – Übertragungsfunktionen |
| kontinuierlich | – diskret |
| off-line | – on-line |

Ist es möglich, daß System durch ein <u>deterministisches Testsignal</u>(z.B. Sprung, Impuls, Sinus, etc.) zu erregen, so können die Systemeigenschaften sehr gut aus der Systemreaktion auf diese Signale hin identifiziert werden. Eine besondere Bedeutung haben hier die Verfahren zur Analyse aus der Sprungantwort gewonnen: Kupfmüller-Approximation, Strejc-App., Verfahren n.Schwarze, Prony-Verfahren. Die Auswertung von Sprungantworten und Gewichtsfunktionen ist besonders geeignet für chemische, ökologische oder medizinische Prozesse. Mit Hilfe eines modifizierbaren Sinus-Signals ist die Aufnahme eines Frequenzgangs möglich, aus dem dann nach verschiedenen Verfahren eine mathematische Beschreibungsfunktion gewonnen werden kann.

In vielen realen Prozessen wird der Anlagenbetreiber jedoch keine Aufschaltung von Testsignalen erlauben. Die Analyse muß dann mit <u>stochastischen Betriebssignalen</u> erfolgen. Hier muß dann der Analytiker entscheiden, ob er ein parametrisches oder nichtparametrisches Modell wünscht. Die <u>nichtparametrischen Modelle</u> geben in sehr anschaulicher, graphischer Weise den Zusammenhang der Ein- und Ausgangssignale in statistischem Sinne wieder. Korrelationsfunktionen werden in der Praxis sehr häufig zur Erkennung von Prozeß- oder Materialveränderungen eingesetzt. Korrelationsfunktionen als Systembeschreibungen wurden ausführlich von Rajbman [3] zusammengestellt. Aussagen über die Signalart liefert die spektrale Leistungsdichte, aus der dann leicht auf den Frequenzgang geschlossen werden kann. Ausführliche Beschreibungen der deterministischen und der nichtparametrischen Analyseverfahren finden sich in den Büchern von Unbehauen [1,2].

Die wesentlichen parametrischen Beschreibungsformen in der Automatisierungstechnik sind die Übertragungsfunktion und die Zustandsraumdarstellung. Letztere findet sehr häufig Anwendung in der Reglersynthese und der analogen und digitalen Simulationstechnik. Die dabei jedoch meist nicht meßbaren Zustandsgrößen sind ein großer Nachteil während der Analyse, denn dann müssen neben den unbekannten Parametern auch die unbekannten Zustandsgrößen bestimmt werden. Dieses nichtlineare Problem ist z.B. mit Hilfe des erweiterten Kalman-Filters lösbar.

Die Analyse vereinfacht sich erheblich, wenn der Zusammenhang zwischen Ein- und Ausgangssignalen mit Übertragungsfunktionen beschrieben wird. Die Ermittlung kontinuierlicher Übertragungsfunktionen geschieht meist durch Auswertung der o.a. Analyseverfahren. Häufige Anwendung findet dabei die Modellbildung anhand des Frequenzgangs: Frequenzkennlinien-Verfahren, Verfahren von Unbehauen. Kontinuierliche Beschreibungsfunktionen eignen sich für die analoge Simulation.

Die Bedeutung von diskreten Beschreibungsfunktionen leitet sich aus folgender Tatsache ab: Die Entwicklung der Prozeßrechentechnik führte in den vergangenen Jahren zu einem vermehrten Einsatz von digitalen Simulationsverfahren in der industriellen Praxis. Aufgrund der gesunkenen Hard- und Software-Kosten ist es durchaus effizient, dem Bedienungspersonal auch komplexere Simulationspakete als Überwachungs- und Entscheidungshilfen für eine optimierte Prozeßführung zu Verfügung zu stellen. Dadurch erhält die Simulationstechnik einen völlig neuen Stellenwert, obgleich ihr die Anerkennung aufgrund der meist impliziten Anwendung fehlt. Für die Modellbildung ist es nun wichtig, experimentelle Analyseverfahren für die digitale Simulation zu entwickeln.

Während die analoge Simulationstechnik fast ausnahmslos im off-line Betrieb arbeitet und für Fallstudien verwendet wird, entwickeln sich für die digitale Simulationstechnik im on-line Betrieb neue wichtige Aufgabengebiete. So werden durch Parallel- Simulationen kritische Prozeßzustände vorhergesagt oder Optimaleinstellkurven vorgegeben. Solche on-line Simulationen stellen hohe Anforderungen an die Simulationstechnik, beweisen aber ihre Effizienz bei der Anwendung in der industriellen Praxis.

Eine der wesentlichsten Anforderungen an die on-line Simulationen ist ein ständig aktualisiertes Prozeßmodell. Mit Hilfe des Prozeßrechners muß daher eine ständige Analyse oder Identifikation des Prozeßverhaltens anhand der gemessenen Ein- und Ausgangssignale des Prozesses durchgeführt werden. Das Ergebnis einer derartigen Prozeßidentifika-

tion ist i.a. ein mathematisches Modell, das den Prozeßhinreichend genau bezüglich seines statischen und dynamischen Verhaltens beschreibt.
Im folgenden sollen nun einige wichtige Identifikationsverfahren
vorgestellt werden.


## 3. Parameterschätzverfahren für lineare Eingrößensysteme

Ziel der Identifikation ist die Erstellung eines Modells in Form einer
mathematischen Beschreibungsfunktion, welches alle wesentlichen Prozeß-
eigenschaften nachbilden kann. Um Prozeß- und Modellverhalten vergleichen zu können, ordnet man sie parallel zueinander an, gemäß Bild 1.,
und erregt sie mit den gleichen Eingangssignalen.

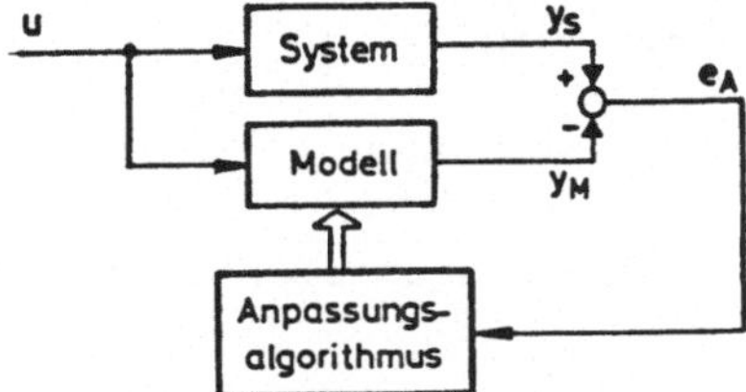


__Bild 1.__  Modellanordnung für die Identifikation


Anhand des Fehlers $e_A$ zwischen dem gemessenen Systemausgang $y_S$ und dem
simulierten Modellausgang $y_m$ läßt sich überprüfen, ob die System- und
Modelleigenschaften übereinstimmen. Ist der Fehler klein, so ist das
Ziel der Modellbildung erreicht. Ist dies nicht der Fall, so müssen
über einen Anpassungsalgorithmus die Parameter des Modells solange
verändert werden, bis der Fehler minimal wird. Aus dieser Zielsetzung
lassen sich folgende drei Aufgaben formulieren:
1) Wahl der Modellform und der Modellordnung
2) Wahl eines Gütekriteriums zur objektiven Beurteilung der  Schätzergebnisse
3) Numerische Minimierung des Gütefunktionals


## 3.1 Wahl der Modellform und der Modellordnung

Die Verwendung digital arbeitender Rechner erfordert eine diskrete Beschreibungsform. Das Äquivalent zu den kontinuierlichen Differentialgleichungen ist hierbei die Differenzengleichung in der Form

$$y(k) + a_1 y(k-1) + \ldots a_n y(k-n) = b_1 u(k-1) + \ldots + b_n u(k-n) \qquad (1)$$

Diese diskrete Darstellung erhält man aus der kontinuierlichen Form
durch eine Umformung über die z-Transformation. Diese liefert für die
kontinuierliche Übertragungsfunktion mit einem Halteglied nullter Ordnung die diskrete Übertragungsfunktion

$$G(z) = \frac{B(z^{-1})}{A(z^{-1})} = \frac{b_1 z^{-1} + \ldots + b_n z^{-n}}{1 + a_1 z^{-1} + \ldots a_n z^{-n}} \qquad (2)$$

Dies ist die einfachste Modellbeschreibung für ein ungestörtes System. Die Aufgabe der Modellbildung besteht nun darin, die unbekannten Koeffizienten $a_i$ und $b_i$ und die Modellordnung n zu bestimmen.

Die Annahme, daß der Prozeß ohne überlagerte Störungen arbeitet, ist in realen Anlagen selten erfüllt. Man führt daher eine dem Ausgangssignal überlagerte Störung R(z) ein, gemäß Bild 2., welche durch Filterung aus einem weißen Rauschsignal $\varepsilon$ entstanden ist.

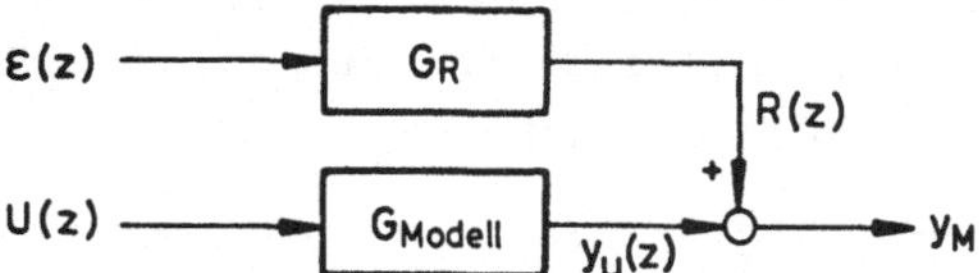


__Bild 2.__  Modellaufbau bei überlagerten Störungen

Für das Störfilter können folgende Übertragungsfunktionen angenommen werden:

Einfaches Modell $\qquad\qquad G_R = 1$

1. Erweitertes Modell $\qquad G_R = 1/D(z^{-1})$

2. Erweitertes Modell $\qquad G_R = C(z^{-1})$

3. Erweitertes Modell $\qquad G_R = C(z^{-1})/D(z^{-1})$

Die Identifikationsaufgabe erweitert sich hier durch die zusätzliche Bestimmung der Koeffizienten des Störfilters.

## 3.2. Wahl des Gütefunktionals

Es wurde bereits oben erwähnt, daß der Ausgangsfehler $e_A$ ein Maß für die Güte der Modellbildung sein kann. Die Minimierung des Fehlers

$$E_A(z) = Y_S(z) - \hat{Y}_m(z) = Y_S(z) - \frac{B(z^{-1})}{A(z^{-1})} \cdot U(z) \qquad (3)$$

würde jedoch aufgrund der gebrochen rationalen Funktion zu einem nichtlinearen Schätzproblem führen. Man multipliziert daher Gl.(3) mit dem Nennerpolynom $A(z^{-1})$ und definiert einen neuen Gleichungsfehler zu

$$E(z) = A(z^{-1}) \cdot Y_S(z) - B(z^{-1}) \cdot U(z) \qquad (4)$$

Der Gleichungsfehler läßt sich im abgeglichenen Zustand durch Filterung auf weißes Rauschen zurückführen und kann wie folgt dargestellt werden:

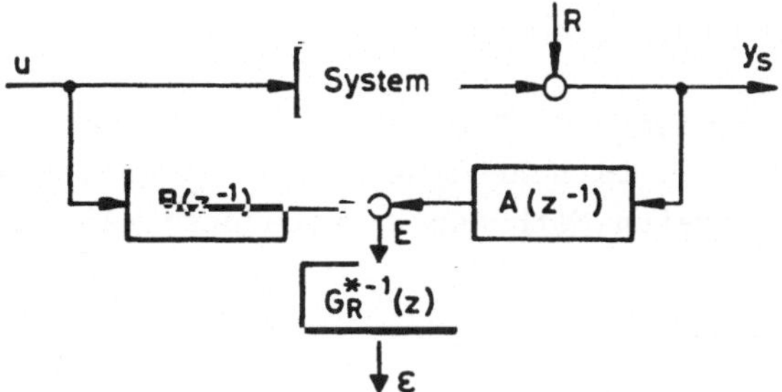



**Bild 3.** Darstellung des Gleichungsfehlers

Die entsprechende Differenzengleichung zu Gl.(4) (ungestört) lautet

$$e(k) = y_S(k) - \left[ -\sum_{\nu=1}^{n} a_\nu \, y_S(k-\nu) + \sum_{\nu=1}^{n} b_\nu \, u(k-\nu) \right] \qquad (5)$$

bzw. in vektorieller Schreibweise mit den Abkürzungen

$$\underline{m}^T = \left[ -y_S(k-1) \; ..-y_S(k-n) \; u(k-1) \; ... \; u(k-n) \right] \qquad (6)$$

$$\underline{p}^T = \left[ \quad a_1 \; ... \quad a_n \quad b_1 \; ... \quad b_n \; \right] \qquad (7)$$

$$e(k) = y_S(k) - \underline{m}^T(k)\underline{p} \qquad (8)$$

Verwendet man für die Modellbildung nicht nur den aktuellen, sondern insgesamt N Meßwerte und kennzeichnet dies in der vektoriellen Schreibweise mit $\underline{e}$, $\underline{y}$ und $\underline{M}$, erhält man die N Fehlergleichungen

$$\underline{e}(N) = \underline{y}(N) - \underline{M}^T(N)\underline{p} \qquad (9)$$

Bereits Gauss erkannte, daß es für Optimierungsaufgaben sinnvoller ist, den qaudratischen Fehler zu betrachten. Als Gütekriterium erhält man somit abschließend

$$V_N(\underline{p}) = \frac{1}{2} \underline{e}^T(N) \cdot \underline{e}(N) = \frac{1}{2} \sum_{k=1}^{N} e^2(k) \qquad (10)$$

Die Minimierung dieser Verlustfunktion durch Veränderung der Parameter kann prinzipiell auf zwei Arten gelöst werden:

1) Im Minimum ist die Steigung dieser Verlustfunktion in Abhängigkeit von den Parametern Null. Leitet man die Verlustfunktion nach den Parametern ab und setzt sie zu Null, kann man eine direkte Lösung für die Parameter berechnen.
2) Man sucht die Lösung über eine der klassischen Optimierungsverfahren. Dabei werden meist der Funktionswert und die Gradienten des Funktionals berechnet und anhand von geeigneten Suchschrittverfahren in iterativer Form der Satz von Parametern ausgewählt, der die Minimierung erzielt. Diese Lösung wird als indirekt bezeichnet.

## 3.3. Numerische Berechnung der Parameter

In den letzten 20 Jahren wurden eine Vielzahl von Schätzverfahren entwickelt, über die ausführlich in Lehrbüchern [4,5,6] berichtet wurde. Hier sollen nur die bekanntesten Methoden kurz dargestellt werden.

### Verfahren mit direkter Lösung

Werden zur Lösung N Fehlergleichungen in geschlossener Form verwendet, so erhält man mit den in der Matrix $\underline{M}$ zusammengefaßten Meßwerten der Ein- und Ausgangsgrößen die nicht rekursive Schätzgleichung

$$\hat{\underline{p}} = \left[ \underline{M}^T(N) \cdot \underline{M}(N) \right]^{-1} \underline{M}^T(N) \underline{y} \qquad (11)$$

Für die Lösung des Schätzwertproblems ist somit allein die Messung der Systemein- und Ausgangsgrößen erforderlich. Die berechneten Parameter sind aus der Menge aller Parameter diejenigen, die den Zusammenhang zwischen den Ein- und Ausgangssignalen am besten wiedergibt. Die Nachteile dieser geschlossenen Lösung über N Meßwerte sind
- hoher Speicherplatzbedarf,
- Invertierung eines Matrixproduktes und
- zeitvariante Prozesse können nicht erfaßt werden.

Um diese Nachteile zu umgehen, ist es sinnvoll einen rekursiven Schätzalgorithmus zu entwickeln, der, von einem Zeitpunkt k ausgehend, durch Auswertung der aktuellen Meßwerte eine Parameterschätzverbesserung zum Zeitpunkt k+1 ermöglicht. In allgemeiner Form läßt sich die rekursive Schätzgleichung wie folgt angeben:

$$\hat{\underline{p}}(k+1) \quad = \quad \hat{\underline{p}}(k) \quad + \quad \underline{q}(k+1) \quad \cdot e(k+1) \qquad (12)$$
neuer Schätzwert=alter Schätzwert+Korrekturvektor·Fehler

mit

$$\underline{q}(k+1) = \underline{P}(k) \, \underline{w}(k+1) \left[ 1 + \underline{m}^T(k+1) \cdot \underline{P}(k) \cdot \underline{w}(k+1) \right]^{-1}$$

$$\underline{P}(k+1) = \frac{1}{\rho} \left[ \underline{P}(k) - \underline{q}(k+1) \cdot \underline{m}^T(k+1) \cdot \underline{P}(k) \right]$$

$$e(k+1) = y_S(k+1) - \underline{m}^T(k+1) \cdot \hat{\underline{p}}(k)$$

In diesen Gleichungen bezeichnet man $\underline{P}$ als die Kovarianzmatrix, $\underline{w}$ als Hilfsvektor und $\rho$ als konstanten Wichtungsfaktor. Der Aufbau des Meßwertvektors $\underline{m}$, des Hilfsvektors $\underline{w}$ und des Parametervektors $\hat{\underline{p}}$ ist für die wichtigsten Verfahren in der Tabelle 1 zusammengestellt. Die Meßwertmatrizen $\underline{M}$ in der nicht rekursiven Schätzgleichung werden analog aufgebaut. Die für die Instrumentelle Variablen Methode zusätzlich benötigte Hilfsgröße $y_H$ wird über ein Hilfsmodell bestimmt [5]. In der Tabelle 1 bedeuten die Abkürzungen für die Verfahren: LS = Least-Squares Methode, 1.(2.,3.)EM = 1.(2.,3.) Erweitertes Matrizen Modell , IV = Instrumentelle Variablen Methode.

| | | |
|---|---|---|
| LS | $\underline{m}^T = [-y(k-1)..-y(k-n)u(k-1)..u(k-n)]$ <br> $\underline{p}^T = [\quad a_1 \quad .. \quad a_n \quad b_1 \quad .. \quad b_n \quad ]$ | $\underline{w}=\underline{m}$ |
| 1.EM | $\underline{m}^T = [-y(k-1)..-y(k-n)u(k-1)..u(k-n)-e(k-1)..-e(k-n)]$ <br> $\underline{p}^T = [\quad a_1 \quad .. \quad a_n \quad b_1 \quad .. \quad b_n \quad d_1 \quad .. \quad d_n \quad ]$ | $\underline{w}=\underline{m}$ |
| 2.EM | $\underline{m}^T = [-y(k-1)..-y(k-n)u(k-1)..u(k-n)\ \varepsilon(k-1)..\ \varepsilon(k-n)]$ <br> $\underline{p}^T = [\quad a_1 \quad .. \quad a_n \quad b_1 \quad .. \quad b_n \quad c_1 \quad .. \quad c_n \quad ]$ | $\underline{w}=\underline{m}$ |
| 3.EM | $\underline{m}^T = [-y(k-1)..-y(k-n)u(k-1)..u(k-n)-\varepsilon(k-1)..\ \varepsilon(k-n)-e(k-1)..-e(k-n)]$ <br> $\underline{p}^T = [\quad a_1 \quad .. \quad a_n \quad b_1 \quad .. \quad b_n \quad c_1 \quad .. \quad c_n \quad d_1 \quad .. \quad d_n \quad ]$ | $\underline{w}=\underline{m}$ |
| IV | $\underline{m}^T = [-y(k-1)..-y(k-n)u(k-1)..u(k-n)]$ <br> $\underline{p}^T = [\quad a_1 \quad .. \quad a_n \quad b_1 \quad .. \quad b_n \quad ]$ <br> $\underline{w}^T = [-y_H(k-1)..-y_H(k-n)u(k-1)..u(k-n)]$ | |

Tabelle 1   Aufbau der Vektoren für verschiedene Schätzverfahren

## Indirekte Lösung

Das leistungsfähigste Verfahren mit indirekter Lösung ist die Maximum-Likelihood Methode. Sie versucht in mehreren Iterationsschritten den Parametersatz solange zu verbessern, bis eine Minimierung der Verlustfunktion eintritt. Aufgrund der für die Iteration notwendigen Rechenzeit ist dieses Verfahren nur in der nicht rekursiven Form sinnvoll. Die besten Ergebnisse werden erzielt, wenn als Optimierungsverfahren die Newton-Raphson oder die Davidon-Fletcher-Powell Methode verwandt werden. Aufgrund des Umfangs ist eine Darstellung der Verfahren hier nicht möglich. Es wird auf die Literatur [4,5] verwiesen.

## 4. Beispiele für die praktische Anwendung

Die praktische Anwendung soll anhand zweier Beispiele gezeigt werden.
### Beispiel 1: Einfaches System
Ein System wird durch eine Sprungfunktion erregt. Die Sprungantwort kann ohne Störungen gemessen werden. Es liegen keine Vorkenntnisse über das System vor. Die Ein- und Ausgangssignale sind in Bild 4. dargestellt.
Anhand der Sprungantwort wird eine für die Identifikation günstige Abtastzeit von T=2.5sec festgelegt. Mit Hilfe eines Strukturprüfverfahrens [7] wird als wahrscheinlichste Ordnung n=2 ermittelt. Da keine Störungen vorliegen, kann die rekursive Least-Squares Methode angewandt werden, die mit dem 3.Meßwert beginnt und den Startwert $\underline{p}(2)=\underline{0}$ verwendet. Bild 4. zeigt das on-line simulierte Modellausgangssignal im Vergleich zu dem gemessenen Prozeßausgangssignal. Eine grobe Annäherung beider Signale wird nach 5 Meßwerten (3 Schätzungen) erreicht. Nach etwa 10 Meßwerten geht der Gleichungsfehler e gegen Null. Auch der Verlauf der Parameter konvergiert nach dem 10.Meßwert gegen die

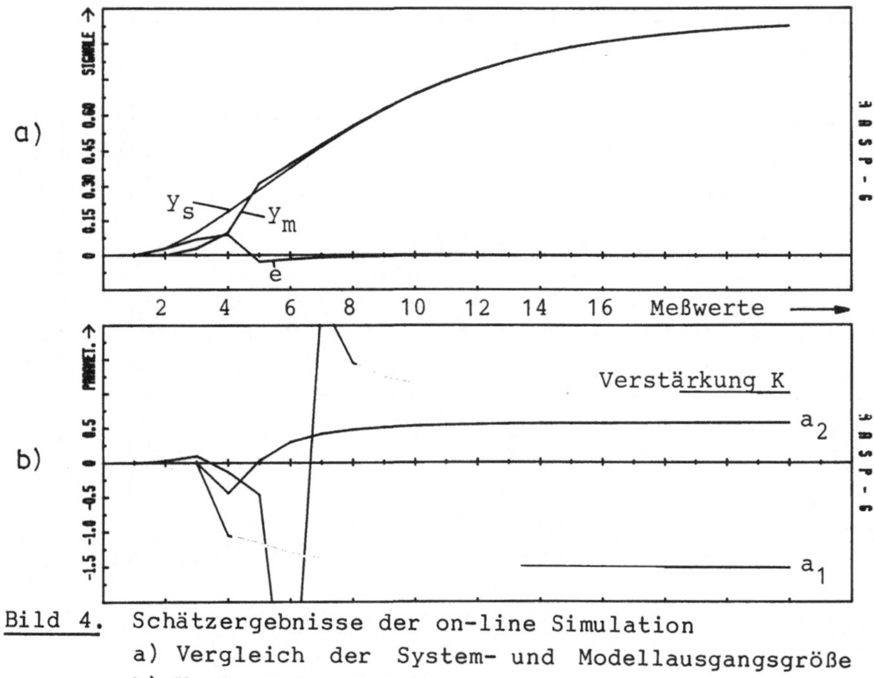


**Bild 4.** Schätzergebnisse der on-line Simulation
  a) Vergleich der System- und Modellausgangsgröße
  b) Verlauf der Modellparameterschätzung

wahren Prozeßparameter.

## Beispiel 2: Komplexes Hochofensystem

Dieses Beispiel wurde ausgesucht, um die Leistungsfähigkeit der experimentellen Modellbildung und der damit verbundenen Simulationstechnik aufzuzeigen. In der Vergangenheit wurde in sehr umfangreichen Untersuchungen versucht, eine theoretische Modellbildung für ein Teilgebiet des Hochofen zu erstellen. Diese Modelle sind sehr komplex, erfüllen ihren Zweck aber leider nur sehr ungenügend. Die Aufgabe der experimentellen Modellbildung bestand nun darin, ein Modell zu bestimmen, mit dem per Simulation die zukünftigen Werte des Silizium-Gehalts im Roheisen berechnet werden können. Dies soll dem Bedienungspersonal ermöglichen, zwischen den Roheisenabstichen Maßnahmen zur Verbesserung des Si-Gehaltes ergreifen zu können.

Solche Maßnahmen können kurzfristig ergriffen werden, wenn die Windgrößen verändert werden. Langfristige Maßnahmen sollten in die Modellbildung nicht einfließen, da diese für das Bedienungspersonal keine Steuerungsmöglichkeiten bieten. Es wurde ein Mehrgrößenmodell mit 5 Eingangsgrößen und 1 Ausgangsgröße angenommen. In den Meßwerten sind Störungen unbekannter Größe und Art enthalten. Daher wurde für die Modellbildung die Instrumentelle-Variablen Methode verwandt. Die Parameterschätzung mußte rekursiv erfolgen, da sich die Parameter durch äußere Ereignisse (Planstillstand, Stauchen) während der Meßwerterfassung verändern. Die Abtastzeit ist durch die Probenentnahme während der Abstiche vorgegeben, die Ordnungen der Teilübertragungsfunktionen wurden wiederum mit Strukturprüfverfahren abgeschätzt [8].

Die Parameterschätzung für dieses modifizierte Instrumentellen-Varia-
blen Verfahren für Mehrgrößensysteme beginnt erst relativ spät. In
Bild 6. wurde daher auf die Anfangsphase verzichtet. Das Bild zeigt
den Verlauf von simulierten und gemessenen Silizium-Gehalt, wobei be-

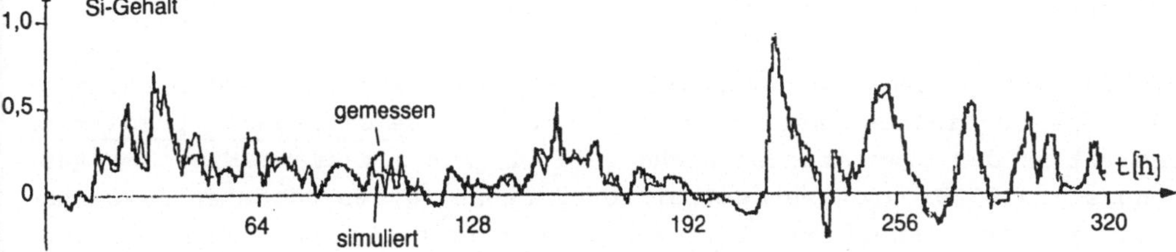


**Bild 6.** Verlauf des simulierten und des gemessenen Si-Gehalts

tont werden muß, daß die Simulationsgrößen dem Betriebspersonal immer
eine Abstichperiode vorher angezeigt werden können, so daß auf Abweichungen reagiert werden kann.


## 5. Digitale on-line Simulationstechnik

Aufgrund der Leistungsfähigkeit moderner Parameterschätzverfahren ist
die Grundvoraussetzung für eine digitale on-line Simulation, nämlich
ein ständig aktualisiertes Prozeßmodell, gegeben. Ähnlich wie bei adaptiven Reglern, die von der gleichen Grundvoraussetzung ausgehen, ist
es nun notwendig, den Anwendern die Vorteile der digitale Simulationstechnik aufzuzeigen. Dabei stehen zwei Anwendungsbereiche im Vordergrund:
- die Simulationstechnik für Kontrollzwecke und
- die Simulationstechnik zur Prozeßvorhersage.

Bei der Simulationstechnik für Kontrollzwecke erfolgt die Simulation
völlig parallel zum Prozeßbetrieb mit einem Vergleichsmodell . Im aktuellen Zeitpunkt wird durch den Vergleich von Prozeß- und Modellverhalten festgestellt, ob Prozeßveränderungen aufgetreten sind. Es können für das dynamische und das statische Verhalten Prozeßveränderungen
in ihrer Größe und ihrer Richtung bestimmt werden. Mit Hilfe eines
modifizierten Parameterschätzverfahrens[9] ist dies sogar dann möglich,
wenn den Meßwerten starke Störungen überlagert sind [10] . Der
Prozeßbetreiber kann anhand der Veränderungsgrößen Fehler in der Anlage oder der Betriebsführung feststellen und entsprechend frühzeitig
reagieren. Diese Fehlererkennung kann teilweise wesentlich schneller
arbeiten als eine optische Kontrolle durch den Menschen ( z.B.Lecker-
kennung in Fernleitungen). Selbstverständlich kann nach der Fehlererkennung eine Modelladaption durchgeführt werden.


Einsatzorte für die Simulationstechnik zur Prozeßvorhersage können
alle Systeme sein, die in verantwortlichem Sinne von Menschen geregelt
oder gesteuert werden. Durch die Simulationstechnik sollen dem Men-

schen Entscheidungs- und Beurteilungshilfen für die Systemführung zu Verfügung gestellt werden, in dem ihm für jede mögliche Aktion die Systemreaktion vorhergesagt wird. Kennt er das zukünftige Prozeßverhalten, so kann er mit optimalen Steuergrößen reagieren, welche er wiederum anhand von Simulationen auswählen kann.

Die Vorhersage des Prozeßverhaltens ist als one-step-ahead prediction oder als continuous prediction möglich. Die one-step-ahead prediction benutzt in der Simulationsgleichung Gl.(1) nur gemessene Ein- und Ausgangssignale. Dadurch werden bei der Berechnung des nächsten Ausgangssignals alle bisherigen Störungen berücksichtigt, was zu einer sehr guten Vorhersage führt. Die Vorhersage für jeweils einen Abtastschritt ist aber nur dann sinnvoll, wenn zwischen den Abtastzeitpunkten genügend Zeit für Reaktionen durch den Menschen besteht( z.B. Hochofen). Die Simulation zur Vorhersage von kritischen Betriebszuständen kann auch für Kontrollzwecke verwendet werden.

Bei der continuous prediction werden in rekursiver Form die folgenden Ausgangssignale bei Vorgabe eines Eingangsignals beliebig weit in die Zukunft berechnet. Der Anwender kann durch einen Vergleich der Systemreaktionen für verschiedene Eingangssignale seine optimale Steuergröße auswählen. Ist das System ferner unterschiedlich konfigurierbar, so kann mit verschiedenen Modellen der günstigste Prozeßzustand ermittelt werden(Zuschaltung von Systemkomponenten, Verbundbetrieb). Aufgrund der sehr schnellen Rechenzeit eröffnet sich für die Simulationstechnik zur Prozeßvorhersage ein weites Anwendungsfeld.

## Literatur


1. Unbehauen, H., Regelungstechnik I, Vieweg-Verlag, Braunschweig,1982
2. Unbehauen, H., Regelungstechnik III, Vieweg-Verlag, Braunschw.,1985
3. Rajbman, N.S., Identification of industrial processes,North-Holland Publ.Comp., Amsterdam, 1980
4. Unbehauen, H., et al., Parameterschätzverfahren zur Systemidentifikation, Oldenbourg-Verlag, München, 1974
5. Isermann, R., Prozeßidentifikation, Springer, Berlin 1974
6. Eykhoff, P.(Ed.),Trends and Progress in System Identification, Pergamon Press, Oxford, 1981
7. Diekmann, K., Unbehauen,H., Test for determining the order of canonical models, IFAC-Symp."Theory and Appl.of Digital Control", Neu Dehli, 1982
8. Diekmann, K., Unbehauen,H., Application of MIMO-Identification to a blast furnace, IFAC-Symp."Identification and System Parameter Estimation", Washington 1982
9. Astroem, K.,Mayne,D.Q., A new algorithm for recursive estimation of controlled ARMA processes, ibid
10.Diekmann, K., Appl. of parameter estimation methods to time variant systems, IFAC-Symp."Digital Computer Applications", Wien,1985

# SENIOR LECTURE

# Methoden und Aspekte zur Planung und Analyse technischer Systeme

Ameling, W. / Aachen

**Zusammenfassung**: Simulationsuntersuchungen werden immer dann durchgeführt, wenn die analytische Berechnung von Modellen zu keiner geschlossenen Lösung führt. Die Simulation hat den Vorteil, daß man ziemlich nah an der Realität modellieren kann. Dies führt einerseits zu einem besseren Systemverständnis und andererseits können die Aussagen und Auswirkungen einzelner Veränderungen, die sich bei der Optimierung der Modellparameter ergeben, leicht überprüft werden. Die Vielfalt möglicher Kombinationen der Parameter zeigt aber u. U. auch widerstrebende Gesichtspunkte. So sind die Wünsche nach möglichst geringer Wartezeit in einem Bedienungssystem nicht mit möglichst geringen Kosten vereinbar. Die Simulation erlaubt jedoch immer, den Einfluß einzelner Größen abzuschätzen und zu beurteilen. Eine Verbesserung der Zielgröße bei Erfüllung der Nebenbedingungen stellt dann ein gewünschtes Ergebnis, ein Quasi-Optimum dar. Im Rahmen dieses Beitrages werden Werkzeuge für die Simulation kontinuierlicher und diskreter Vorgänge vorgestellt und ihre Einsatzmöglichkeiten dargestellt. Diese Werkzeuge verringern den Modellerstellungsaufwand erheblich, und sie ermöglichen die leichte Modifizierbarkeit der Modelle. Beispielsweise können Modellkomponenten leicht hinzugefügt, weggenommen, ausgewechselt oder umgruppiert werden. Dies wird an einem Beispiel gezeigt.

**Summary**: Simulation is a tool which is often used when analytical modelling does not yield a closed solution. Its capability of modeling very close to reality leads to a better understanding of the system, and it allows to study the effects of parameter changes. The diversity of possible parameter combinations often reveals conflicting factors. For example, the minimization of waiting times in a server system is inconsistent with the minimization of costs. However, simulation always allows to assess the influence of a single quantity. An improvement of the target quantity under fulfillment of the marginal conditions is then a desired result, a quasi-optimum. In this article, we present tools for the simulation of continuous and discontinuous processes along with an outline of their applications. These tools reduce the expenditure for model generation considerably, and they allow easy modification, which will be shown in an example.

## 1. Einleitung

In vielen Wissenschaftsbereichen wurden in den letzten Jahrzehnten durch die Entwicklung unterschiedlicher Rechnertypen auch für den Einsatz der Simulation als Untersuchungsverfahren bei der Planung und Analyse technischer Systeme ganz erhebliche Fortschritte erreicht. Die mathematische Beschreibung dynamischer Prozesse führt auf Systeme von Differentialgleichungen, die sich praktisch nie in geschlossener Form integrieren lassen. Ihre Lösungen werden deshalb hauptsächlich auf den verschiedensten Rechnertypen ermittelt.

Zur Kennzeichnung eines Systems wollen wir folgende Festlegung treffen:

> Ein System ist eine Verbindung von Teilen oder Ereignissen, die in natürlicher Weise physikalisch vorgegeben sind oder durch den Menschen geschaffen werden.

Man kann deshalb für technische Systeme auch wie folgt sagen:

> Ein System ist eine Anordnung und Verbindung materieller Einzelglieder, die Wirkungen und Gegenwirkungen unter dem Einfluß eigenen Verhaltens und

äußerer Erregungen erfahren.

Ein technisches System ist deshalb ein System, welches technische Einrichtungen zur Erfüllung eines bestimmten Zweckes enthält. Dieser besteht häufig darin, eine oder mehrere unabhängige Veränderliche am Eingang eines Systems in eine oder mehrere abhängige Veränderliche am Ausgang des Systems in vorgeschriebener oder gewünschter Weise umzuformen. Das Systemverhalten wird dann durch die physikalischen Gesetzmäßigkeiten und die Einflußgrößen der Systemkomponenten bestimmt.

Bei allen planenden und forschenden Arbeiten in den Bereichen der Wissenschaft und Technik ist die Untersuchung und Beschreibung des Verhaltens von Systemen von allergrößtem Interesse.

Das Verhalten zahlreicher technischer und physikalischer Systeme wird durch physikalische Gesetze beschrieben. Diese Gesetze verdeutlichen, daß beobachtbare Ausgangsgrößen als Funktion unabhängiger Eingangsgrößen angesehen werden können. Als mathematische Zusammenhänge ergeben sich lineare oder nichtlineare Gleichungen bzw. Differentialgleichungen.

Vielfach ist auch eine Darstellung in Blockdiagrammen oder Signalflußdiagrammen üblich, wobei in den Diagrammen die Zusammenhänge zwischen Ursache und Wirkung anschaulich dargestellt werden. Hat man aufgrund von Beobachtungen und Messungen als Ergebnis der Untersuchungen eines Systems die mathematische Beschreibung des Systemverhaltens gewonnen, so hat man damit bereits das "mathematische Modell" des Systems erhalten. Die Modellierung und darauf aufbauend die Simulation sind heute die wichtigsten Verfahren von Systemuntersuchungen. Systemsimulation setzt die Anfertigung von Simulationsmodellen voraus, denn die Nachahmung des Ablaufs soll nicht am System selbst sondern am Modell vollzogen werden.

Der Begriff Modell hat sowohl die Bedeutung Abbild als auch Repräsentation des Originalsystems. Da Modelle vielfach nur unter Einschränkungen auf bestimmte Operationen dem Original zugeordnet werden, werden auch nicht alle Eigenschaften des Originals repräsentiert. Vorteil ist jedoch, daß die Untersuchung des Modells vielfach einfacher, schneller, gefahrloser und systematischer durchgeführt werden kann als die Untersuchung des realen Systems. Das Modell kann sowohl ein materielles System als auch eine rein mathematische Beschreibung des Systemverhaltens (mathematisches Modell) sein.

Eine ganz zentrale Bedeutung haben deshalb heute die verschiedenen Verfahren der Modellbehandlung. Diejenigen Verfahren zur Systemuntersuchung werden als Simulation bezeichnet, bei denen nicht das Verhalten des Systems selbst, sondern das Verhalten gegenständlicher oder abstrakter Modelle tatsächlicher Systeme oder auch abstrakter hypothetischer Systeme untersucht wird. Die Güte der Simulation hängt deshalb letztlich von der Güte des Modells ab.

Ein ingenieurmäßiger Ansatz bei der Beschreibung komplexer Systeme besteht in einer geschickten Aufteilung in Teilsysteme, wobei jedes einzelne Teilsystem durch mathematische Beziehungen beschrieben wird.

Das Problem der Systemsimulation und damit der Teilsystemsimulation hängt nun in starker Weise mit der Möglichkeit der Parallelverarbeitung zusammen. Ist man in der Lage, alle Teilsysteme zu simulieren, dann beschreibt das Modell auch das Verhalten des gesamten Systems. Wir erkennen somit: Die Parallelität von Aktionen in den Teilsystemen und der Teilsysteme untereinander kann deshalb bestmöglich durch parallelorientierte Einrichtungen, zum Beispiel Komponenten, Recheneinheiten oder aber durch Parallelarbeit unterstützende Rechnerstrukturen erreicht werden.

Ein deterministisches System (Bild 1) wird durch die Gleichungen

$$X_i = f_i(U_1 \ldots U_m; \quad Z_1 \ldots Z_p) \quad i = 1,\ldots,n; \quad \nu = 1,\ldots,m; \quad \mu = 1,\ldots,p$$

beschrieben.

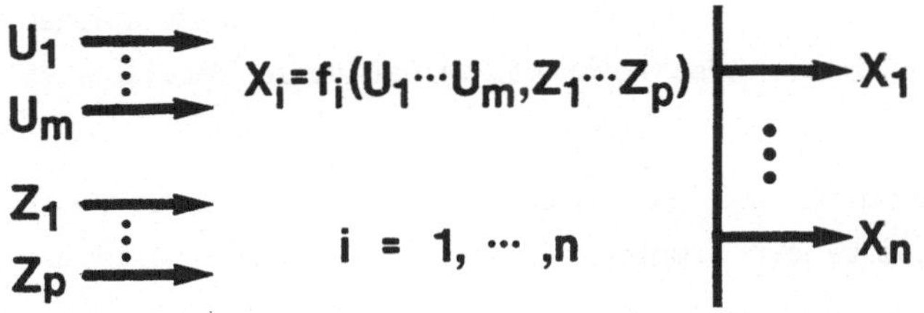

$$U_1 \xrightarrow{\quad} \atop \vdots$$
$$U_m \xrightarrow{\quad}$$

$$X_i = f_i(U_1 \cdots U_m, Z_1 \cdots Z_p) \longrightarrow X_1$$

$$Z_1 \xrightarrow{\quad} \atop \vdots$$
$$Z_p \xrightarrow{\quad} \qquad i = 1, \cdots, n \longrightarrow X_n$$

Hierin bedeuten:
$X_i$ = Ausgangsgrößen
$U_\nu$ = Führungsgrößen
$Z_\mu$ = Störgrößen
$f_i$ = Transformationsregeln

<u>Bild 1</u>:  Modell eines deterministischen Systems

Das Systemverhalten und damit auch das Verhalten des Modells ist darauf zu überprüfen, welche zulässigen Eingangsveränderlichen und Prozeßparameter zu den zugelassenen Werten der Ausgangsveränderlichen gehören. Hier unterscheiden wir im wesentlichen zwischen den linearen und nichtlinearen Systemen. Das lineare System ist durch Proportionalität zwischen Ein- und Ausgangsgröße gekennzeichnet und bringt den Vorteil der Anwendung des Superpositionsprinzips.

Mathematisch gesehen werden lineare Systeme durch gewöhnliche lineare DGL oder lineare partielle DGL beschrieben.

Charakteristikum linearer Systeme ist die Übertragungsfunktion (Quotient zweier Laplace-Transformierter):

$$G(s) = \frac{\mathcal{L}\{\text{Ausgangszeitfunktion}\}}{\mathcal{L}\{\text{Eingangszeitfunktion}\}} = f_b(s) \ .$$

Viele Systeme sind jedoch nichtlinear und es können nur bestimmte Fälle durch Linearisieren der nichtlinearen Glieder einer Behandlung nach den Methoden der linearen Systeme zugänglich gemacht werden.

Führen wir jetzt die Analyse des Systemverhaltens durch, so haben wir folgende
Möglichkeiten:

o analytische Berechnung und Auswertung

o experimentelle Behandlung am Modell (Ähnlichkeitsgesetze usw.)

o Simulation des mathematischen Modells mit Hilfe von Rechnern.

Die letzte Methode ist bei umfangreichen Systemen in der Regel die zeit- und kostengünstigste Methode, insbesondere bei dynamischen Problemen.

Als technische Möglichkeiten zur Simulation dynamischer Systeme stehen uns jetzt
folgende Rechnertypen zur Verfügung:

o Analogrechner

o Digitalrechner

o Hybridrechner

o Digitale Integrieranlagen

o Parallelrechner

Beim Analogrechner, bei der digitalen Integrieranlage und bei Mehrprozessoranlagen
entsprechen den Teilsystemen Komponenten des Rechners, wobei volle Parallelität
gegeben ist.

Elektronische Analogrechner, verfügbar seit den frühen fünfziger Jahren erwiesen
sich stets als nützliche Instrumente zur Simulation kontinuierlicher Modelle und
Prozesse. Der elektronische Analogrechner wurde überall dort eingesetzt, wo physikalische Modelle durch Differentialgleichungssysteme beschrieben werden konnten. Für
einen echten Parallelbetrieb stehen spezialisierte Rechenelemente (Integratoren,
Summierer, Multiplizierer, Funktionsgeneratoren) zur Verfügung. Diese erlauben hohe
Simulationsgeschwindigkeiten bei geringen Kosten.

Da der Digitalrechner grundsätzlich nur zu diskreten Zeitpunkten das Systemverhalten
berechnet, können bei Einprozessoranlagen leicht Simulationszeit und Echtzeit auseinanderfallen und ein Echtzeitbetrieb ist dann vielfach nicht möglich. Auch hier
fordert der Echtzeitbetrieb eine Parallelverarbeitung.

Die Begrenzung des Analogrechners hinsichtlich Genauigkeit einerseits und die Vorteile des Digitalrechners andererseits führten zu sogenannten Hybridrechnern, in
denen die Vorteile beider Rechnertypen voll zum Tragen kommen.

Hybridrechnersysteme werden deshalb eingesetzt, um iterative Rechnungen, Parameter-
Optimierungen, Monte-Carlo-Studien, adaptive oder lernende Steuerstrategien usw.
studieren zu können. Die Klasse der lösbaren zeitrestriktiven Probleme wurde mit dem
Hybridrechner deutlich reduziert, dennoch bleiben aber die Begrenzungen und Nachteile, die sowohl der Analogrechner als auch der Digitalrechner in Form des Einprozessorsystems mit sich bringen.

Besonders in Anwendungen, in denen repetierende Vorgänge schnell bei hoher Genauigkeit ausgeführt werden müssen, erweist sich die digitale Integrieranlage (DDA = Digital Differential Analyzer) als Multiprozessoranlage als ein sehr angemessener Rechnertyp.

Die Fortschritte der Technologie der letzten Jahre hat die Diskussion über parallele Strukturen nach dem Prinzip des DDA neu belebt. Als Rechenelemente kommen heute Mikroprozessoren in Frage. Letztlich geht der Trend zu Rechnerstrukturen, die ein hohes Maß an Parallelität der Ausführung besitzen, damit möglichst auch Echtzeitbedingungen erfüllt werden können.

Für die Simulation von Systemen oder Teilsystemen auf Rechnern ist heute eine Vielzahl von Werkzeugen (im wesentlichen Programmierungswerkzeuge) und Simulationssprachen verfügbar, die für die Simulation sowohl kontinuierlicher Prozesse als auch diskreter Prozesse eingesetzt werden. Merkmal fast aller Simulationssprachen ist die Blockorientierung.

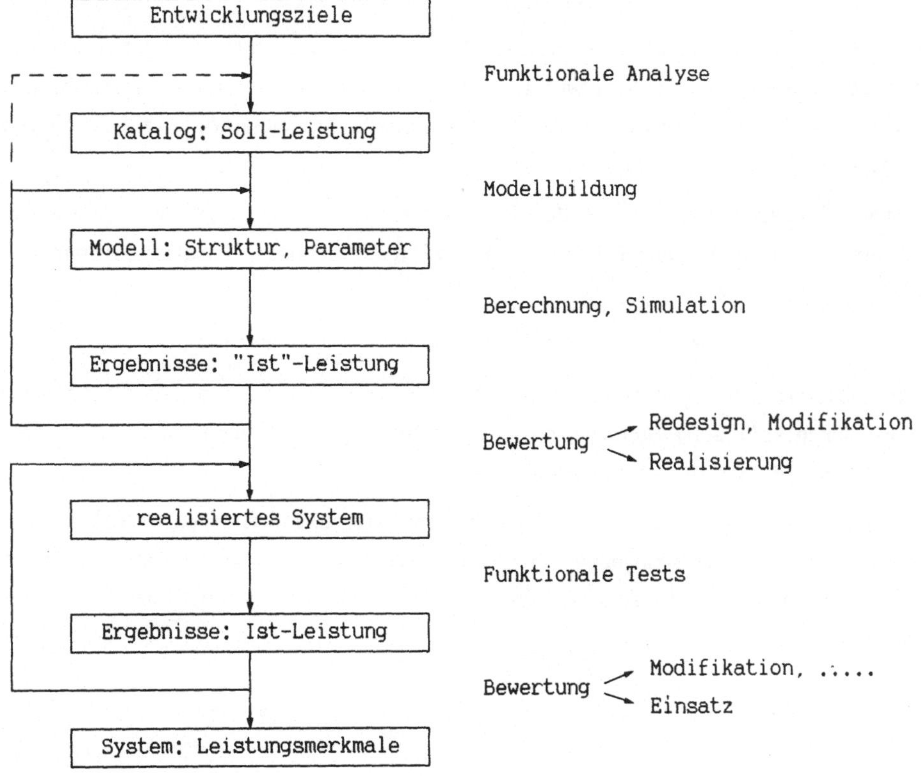


<u>Bild 2</u>: Phasen bei Planung und Analyse eines technischen Systems

Im Bild 2 sind die verschiedenen Phasen bei der Planung und Analyse technischer Systeme skizziert.

Eine Reihe von Vorarbeiten sind erforderlich, hierzu zählen insbesondere:

o Zerlegung des Problems in Teilprobleme oder einzelne Aufgaben.

o Verkettung der Teilsysteme

o Kommunikation zwischen den Teilsystemen

o Klärung der Zeitbedingungen

o Kombination von analytischer Berechnung und Simulation

o Auswahl oder Einstellung der Programmierwerkzeuge und Hilfsmittel

o Auswahl der Simulationssprache

o Rechnerauswahl und Abschätzung des Rechenzeitbedarfs

o Festlegung der Eingriffsmöglichkeiten und Änderung der Modellparameter
   während der Simulation (Mensch-Maschine-Beteiligung)

Wegen der Bedeutung und der Besonderheiten werden im Folgenden die Simulation kontinuierlicher und diskreter Systeme kurz dargestellt und anschließend ein Beispiel zur diskreten Simulation vorgestellt.


<u>2. Simulation kontinuierlicher Systeme.</u>

Ein erster Schritt zu einer allgemeinen Simulation wurde mit der Entwicklung des elektronischen Analogrechners getan. Die Systemgrößen des gegebenen Systems werden durch analoge Größen, in der Regel sich ändernde Spannungen, als Lösungen von Differentialgleichungen dargestellt.

Betrachten wir das mathematische Modell eines physikalischen Systems, so kann sehr einfach aus dem mathematischen Modell das Analogrechnermodell konstruiert werden.

Standardelemente sind: Integratoren, Addierer, Konstantenmultiplizierer, Multiplizierer, Verzögerungsgeneratoren, Funktionsgeneratoren und Servos.

Die Verschaltung der Recheneinheiten ist dann unmittelbar aus der Differentialgleichung durch Auflösung nach der höchsten Ableitung und Anwendung der Methode der fortgesetzten Integration abzuleiten.

In Bild 3 ist das Blockdiagramm zur Lösung einer allgemeinen linearen Differentialgleichung n-ter Ordnung angegeben. Die Parallelität von n-Integratoren und weiteren Analogrechnerelementen ist ersichtlich und wird durch die Verkopplung der Elemente erreicht.

$$\frac{d^n y}{dx^n} = -a_{n-1}(x) \cdot \frac{d^{n-1} y}{dx^{n-1}} - \ldots -a_1(x) \cdot \frac{dy}{dx} - a_0(x) \cdot y + F$$

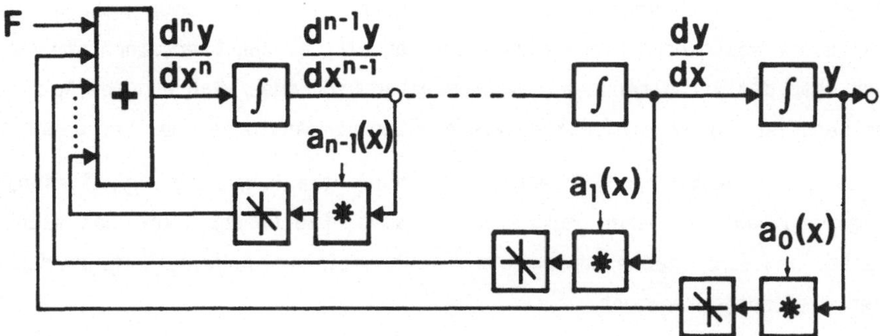

**Bild 3**: Blockdiagramm zur Lösung einer allgemeinen Differentialgleichung n-ter Ordnung

Es lag nahe, die beim Analogreichner erreichbare Genauigkeit durch den Einsatz des Digitalrechners zu verbessern. Um das Zeitproblem zu kompensieren, werden Hybridrechner eingesetzt.

Ein Digitalrechner hat in der Regel nur eine einzige arithmetische Einheit. Aus diesem Grunde müssen in ihm alle Operationen sequentiell ausgeführt werden.

Die Effektivität einer Simulation auf einem Digitalrechner ist für den Benutzer in starkem Maße von den zur Verfügung stehenden Programmierhilfen abhängig. In dieser Hinsicht sind in den vergangenen Jahren enorme Anstrengungen unternommen worden, um wichtige Anwendungsgebiete adäquat durch Simulationssprachen zu unterstützen.

Digitale Simulationssprachen werden im wesentlichen bestimmt durch zwei voneinander verschiedene Aufgabengebiete:

1) Simulation von parallelen, mehr oder weniger kontinuierlichen Prozessen
2) Simulation von diskreten, seriellen Prozessen

In beiden Fällen findet eine Methode der ingenieurmäßigen Betrachtung von Systemen und ihre Analyse durch ein Aufbrechen in Teilsysteme ihren Niederschlag. Einzelnen Funktionen werden Blöcke zugeordnet. Diese Blöcke sind dann Konstrukte einer blockorientierten Sprache.

Eine blockorientierte oder funktional orientierte Betrachtungsweise ist sowohl bei der diskreten Simulation als auch bei kontinuierlichen Systemen anzutreffen.

Nachdem die Konfiguration eingelesen worden ist, wird mit Hilfe eines Sortieralgorithmus festgestellt, welches Element mit der höchsten Ordnung den zugrundeliegenden Differentialgleichungen entspricht. Bei dem Element mit der höchsten Ordnung wird mit der Rechnung begonnen und die Ergebnisse intervallweise den nachfolgenden nachrangigen Elementen übergeben. Ein neuer Rechenschritt darf erst dann ausgeführt werden, wenn die niedrigste Stufe ihre Ergebnisse der Stufe mit der höchsten Ordnung bereitgestellt hat.

Die Ergebnisse eines jeden Iterationsschrittes können aufgelistet oder aber auch gezeichnet werden. Abhängig von der Anzahl der Iterationsdurchgänge, die der Simulationszeit weitgehend proportional ist, erhält der Benutzer einen anschaulichen Überblick über das Verhalten des programmierten Prozesses. Während des Rechnerlaufs kann der Benutzer direkt eingreifen, wie er dies vom Analogrechner her gewöhnt ist.

Bei der Simulationssprache CSMP wird die symbolische Benennung von Blöcken, deren Ein-/Ausgangsgrößen und deren Parametern erlaubt. Die Beschreibung hat sich derart vereinfacht, daß eine starke Analogie zum mathematischen Modell, d. h. zu den mathematischen Gleichungen besteht.

Grundelemente blockorientierter Simulationssprachen sind:

1. Ein Satz vordefinierter funktionaler Blöcke, in denen alle Operationselemente eines Analogrechners als Untermenge enthalten sind.
2. Strukturaussagen zur Beschreibung des zu simulierenden Systems (Funktionale Blöcke lassen sich zur spezifischen Systemstruktur verbinden).
3. Parameteraussagen zur Festlegung der numerischen Werte von Systemparametern (z. B. übertragungsparameter von Blöcken oder Anfangswerte von Integratoren).
4. Bearbeitungsaussagen zur Steuerung der übersetzung, der Simulationsausführung und der Ergebnisausgabe.

Verfügt die Simulationssprache noch über die Eigenschaft, daß der Benutzer besondere, für seine Anwendung typische Funktionen definieren und hinzufügen kann, die in bestimmten Anwendungen verlangt werden, dann expandiert diese Simulationssprache zu einem Werkzeug einer allgemeinen Simulation.

Dies ist z. B. bei CSSL-IV der Fall, die dem Benutzer einen sehr hohen Komfort bietet. Dadurch, daß dem Benutzer eine Reihe von Werkzeugen zur Verfügung gestellt werden, wird die Analyse dynamischer Systeme oder physikalischer Phänomene sehr erleichtert. Auch die Datenerfassung, Darstellung und Ausgabe wird so unterstützt, daß der Benutzer mit minimalen Kenntnissen des Rechnersystems selbst auskommt. Durch die leichte Erlernbarkeit der Simulationssprachen ist der Verbreitungsgrad sehr hoch und der Einsatz auf den unterschiedlichsten Rechnertypen möglich.

Die Idee von Selfridge (1955), ein Verfahren zur Lösung von Differentialgleichungssystemen in einer Sprache zu beschreiben, die sich stark an das beim Programmieren des Analogrechners benutzte Blockdiagramm anschloß, setzte sich durch. Eine solche Sprache sollte dynamische Probleme genauso einfach wie für den Analogrechner beschreiben und zur Lösung auf dem Digitalrechner führen. Bis heute sind mehr als 50 verschiedene Programmsysteme (Simulationssprachen) entstanden, die die Simulation dynamischer Systeme auf dem Digitalrechner gestatten.

Der erste Normungsversuch wurde bereits 1967 unternommen, wobei die Simulationssprache CSSL (Continuous System Simulation Language) von einem Komitee definiert wurde. Die Definition ist sehr allgemein gehalten und läßt viele Punkte offen.

Durch derartige Simulationssprachen werden heute praktisch alle Vorteile eines Analogrechners bis auf die Geschwindigkeit erreicht, sodaß die Echtzeitsimulation größerer Systeme heute immer noch auf Hybridrechnersysteme ausweichen muß. Eine schnelle, rein digitale Lösung von Differentialgleichungssystemen stellt dann noch der DDA dar, bei dem die Komponenten des Analogrechners (Integrator, Summierer, Multiplizierer usw.) durch entsprechende digitale Komponenten dargestellt werden und eine volle Parallelität erreicht werden kann. Ausführungen und theoretischer Hintergrund sind ausführlich in /4/ dargestellt.

Bei der Simulationssprche CSSL (heute teils als Version IV angeboten), steht die Benutzerfreundlichkeit im Vordergrund. Sie hat als Ziel, sowohl Ingenieure und Wissenschaftler bei der Analyse mathematischer Modelle zu unterstützen als auch zu erlauben, den Einfluß des dynamischen Verhaltens physikalischer Phänomene abzuschätzen. Durch die zur Verfügungstellung eines Satzes von Werkzeugen werden die Simulationsvorbereitungen erheblich reduziert. Gleichzeitig werden die benötigten Daten gespeichert und stehen zur Darstellung zur Verfügung. Hierbei sind nur geringe Kenntnisse des Rechnersystems erforderlich. CSSL IV beinhaltet:

      o eine Modell-Beschreibungssprache,

      o den Übersetzer,

      o eine Software-Unterstützungsbibiliothek,

      o den Laufzeitmonitor und

      o ein Betriebssystem-Interface.

Die Modellbeschreibungssprache basiert auf dem CSSL-Standard und erlaubt dem Benutzer, sein Modell unter Verwendung einer leicht handzuhabenden mathematischen Notation in Gleichungsform zu beschreiben. Dem Übersetzer wird das so beschriebene Modell in einen korrekten Satz von FORTRAN 77 - Programmen übersetzt. Große Unterstützung bedeutet für den Benutzer die Software-Unterstützungsbibliothek, die eine Vielzahl überprüfter und ausgereifter Programme für die normale Auswertung, Datensammlung und Datenpräsentation enthält. Durch den Laufzeitmonitor wird es dem Benutzer ermöglicht, in die Simulation einzugreifen, Parameter zu verändern usw. Letztlich sorgt das Betriebssystem-Interface dafür, den Benutzer von den notwendigen aber lästigen Details der Ablaufkontrolle zu befreien. Da CSSL IV alle Verbesserungen der Vorgängerversionen enthält und auf Rechnern der verschiedensten Hersteller lauffähig ist, wird auch dem auf Digitalrechnern nicht besonders erfahrenen Ingenieur die Simulation sehr erleichtert. Da die Übertragungsfunktion $G(s)$ als Quotient zweier Laplacetransformierter für die Regelungstechnik und Nachrichtentechnik von besonders großer Bedeutung ist, akzeptiert CSSL IV eine Vielzahl von Übertragungsfunktionen direkt und erzeugt selbständig die entsprechenden Differentialgleichungen. Eine spätere Rücktransformation in den Zeitbereich kann entfallen, da dies durch CSSL IV automatisch geschieht.

## 3. Simulation diskreter Systeme

Im Gegensatz zur Simulation kontinuierlicher Systeme, bei der Zustandsänderungen im System stetige Funktionen sind, treten bei der Simulation diskreter Systeme die Zustandsänderungen nur zu bestimmten Zeitpunkten auf oder werden nur zu bestimmten Zeitpunkten betrachtet.

Die Qualität des Modells und die Qualität der Simulationsergebnisse sind sehr von der Modellbeschreibungsmethode abhängig. Um ein System im Digitalrechner darstellen zu können, muß zunächst von einer speziellen Bedeutung der Systemkomponenten abgesehen werden, denn nur so ist es wieder möglich, eine begrenzte Anzahl allgemeiner Modellbausteine zu definieren, die sich relativ einfach als Programmelemente darstellen lassen. Für die Simulation von Zustandsänderungen im System muß eine detaillierte Beschreibung des Systems (in der Regel als Netzwerk zur Stukturierung) durchgeführt werden. Mit dem Werkzeug Oscar /3/ wurde ein Konzept vorgestellt, welches zur Beschreibung und Berechnung von Netzwerken mit Warteschlangen herangezogen werden kann.

Ein solches Netzwerk, das sich mit der Warteschlangentheorie exakt berechnen läßt, kann wie folgt durch die Art des Netzwerks, die Eigenschaften der Quellen und Server und deren Übergangswahrscheinlichkeiten beschrieben werden.

Dabei kann das Netzwerk offen, geschlossen oder gemischt sein. Bei den Quellen interessieren die Ausstoßraten und als Eigenschaften der Server sind vor allem die Bedienzeiten und die Bedienstrategien von Wichtigkeit.

Als aussagekräftige Netzwerkgrößen sind dann die Auslastung, die mittleren Warteschlangenlängen, die Antwortzeiten und die Durchsätze anzusehen. In vielen Fällen wird die Berechnung der Mittelwerte und der Momente höherer Ordnung durch speziell modifizierte Algorithmen möglich. Durch Simulation ist die Ermittlung der Kenngößen stets möglich.

Bei dem bereits zitierten System Oscar (für welches an meinem Institut wichtige Algorithmen entwickelt wurden) ist der Bearbeitungsgang wie folgt:

       o Beschreibung des Netzwerks im interaktiven Betrieb

       o Bildung eines "lauffähigen" (Teil)-Netzwerks

       o algorithmische Berechnung dieses Netzwerks.

Für das Warteschlangennetzwerk sind dann folgende Angaben erforderlich: Knoten (Server, Service-Center), Kunden (Jobs, Aufträge), Ketten und Klassen von Jobs, Quellen und Senken von Jobs.

Von einer Zustandsänderung des Systems wird bereits gesprochen, wenn sich der Zustand nur an einer einzigen Komponente verändert. Im einzelnen werden Verkehrswege benutzt, Bedienungsstationen belegt oder freigegeben, Warteschlangen verlängert oder verkürzt, Verkehrseinheiten (Transactions) auf den Verkehrswegen bewegt, an den

Bedienungsstationen bedient, bearbeitet oder verarbeitet, in Lagern gespeichert, in Warteschlangen aufgehalten und an Verkehrsleitstellen blockiert, umgeleitet oder weitergeleitet. Auch Ortsveränderungen gelten als Zustandsänderungen des Systems!

Für die Simulation dieser Zustandsänderungen haben die Transaktionen die beiden wichtigen Funktionen zu erfüllen:

> o Auslösen der Zustandsänderungen
>
> o Versorgen der verschiedenen Programmelemente mit aktuellen Informationen.

Um nur ein Beispiel für die Vielzahl von heute verwendeten Strategien anzugeben, seien die schon "klassischen" Bedienstrategien BCMP 1975 in Warteschlangen angegeben.

> o FCFS (first come first served)
> Bedienung von jeweils einem Job gemäß seiner Ankunftsreihenfolge
> o LCFS (last come first served)
> Bedienung des zuletzt eingetroffenen Jobs
> o PS (processor sharing)
> Sämtliche Jobs im Server werden "quasi gleichzeitig" bedient
> o MSn (multiple server with n servers)
> Den n zuerst angekommenen Jobs werden Server zugeteilt und die übrigen befinden sich in der Warteschlange

Eine Verallgemeinerung der Bedienstarategien erfolgte durch Chandy und Martin im Jahre 1983 wie folgt:

> o WEIRDP (a weird, parameterized discipline)
> Dem ersten Job in der Warteschlange wird der p-te Anteil des Servers zugeteilt und den übrigen der (1-p)-Teil
> o LBPSn (last batch processor sharing with n servers)
> Der Server wird zwischen den n zuletzt angekommenen Jobs geteilt

Für die Bedienzeiten in den Servern wird angenommen, daß diese zufällig sind, ihre Verteilungsdichte-Funktion jedoch rationale Laplace-Transformierte besitzen. Da sich die durch rationale Funktionen vorgegebenen Funktionen im Sinne von Chebyshev beliebig genau approximieren lassen (Padé-Approximation), ist als Folge fast jede Verteilung erlaubt (Ausnahme Server, deren Bedienstrategien gewisse Voraussetzungen nicht erfüllen (z.B. FCFS). Diese Server müssen Bedienzeiten mit Exponentialverteilung besitzen. Eine Berechnung ist nur durch Simulation oder approximative Verfahren möglich).

Für die Berechnung der verschiedenen Netzkenngrößen sind ausschließlich die Mittelwerte der Verteilungen relevant. Diese können konstant oder zustandsabhängig sein.

Eine weitere Aufteilung der Jobs in Klassen und Ketten kann wie folgt erfolgen:

> o Jede Klasse von Jobs hat in jedem Server ihre eigene Bedienzeitverteilung

o Jede Klasse von Jobs hat ihre eigenen (konstanten) übergangswahrscheinlichkeiten von Server zu Server, wobei die Klasse gewechselt werden kann.
(In manchen Simulationssprachen (z.B. PAWS) nicht vorgesehen. In FORCASD
möglich).

o Jeder Kette gehören Jobs aus einer oder mehreren Klassen an. Diese Jobs
können nur einige Server besuchen.

Hierbei gilt als Definition für offene, geschlossene oder gemischte Netzwerke:

- "Offene" Netzwerke: Die Anzahl der Jobs sämtlicher Ketten ist variabel (offene
Ketten)

- "Geschlossene" Netzwerke: Die Anzahl der Jobs sämtlicher Ketten ist konstant
(geschlossene Ketten)

- "Gemischte" Netzwerke: Einige Ketten sind offen und einige geschlossen.

Als Vorassetzungen für die Quellen und Senken von Jobs offener Ketten soll gelten:

Die Ausstoßraten der Quellen sind Poisson-verteilt. Die Mittelwerte können konstant
oder zustandsabhängig sein. Hieraus folgt: Die Ströme der Jobs innerhalb des Netzwerkes sind ebenfalls Poisson-verteilt. Bezüglich der Senken gibt es keine Voraussetzungen.

Unter den gemachten Voraussetzungen und der Bedingung, daß jeder erlaubte Netzzustand in einer endlichen Anzahl von Schritten (Zustandsänderungen) aus jedem anderen
erlaubten Netzzustand erreicht werden kann, läßt sich die Wahrscheinlichkeit eines
Zustands S in folgender Form darstellen (Produktform):

$$P(S) = C \cdot d(S) \cdot g_1(y_1) \cdot g_2(y_2) \cdot \ldots \cdot g_N(y_N),$$

wobei der Vektor $y_i$ die Population des Servers i angibt, die Funktion d(S) vom
Gesamtzustand des Netzwerks abhängt und C die Normierungskonstante darstellt.

Als charakteristische Kenngrößen eines Netzes lassen sich dann ermitteln:

- Auslastung eines Servers: Wahrscheinlichkeit,daß mindestens ein Job
bedient wird (bezogen auf einfache Server).

- Mittlere Warteschlangenlänge eines Servers:Die mittlere Anzahl der Jobs,
die im Server bedient werden oder auf Bedienung warten

- Antwortzeit: Mittlere Aufenthaltszeit (Wartezeit + Verarbeitungszeit) der
Jobs im Server

- Durchsatz der Jobs in einem Server: Anzahl der Jobs, die pro Zeiteinheit
den Server besuchen

Diese Kenngrößen können sowohl für die einzelnen Kundenklassen getrennt, als auch
für alle Kundenklassen zusammen, die den Server besuchen, berechnet werden.

Als Algorithmen zur exakten Berechnung von Warteschlangennetzwerken sind zu nennen:

1. Offene Netzwerke
    "BCMP", "ABCMP" = BCMP beschleunigt, duch analytische Lösungen bzw. Auf-

teilung des Gesamtnetzwerkes in mehrere Teilnetzwerke.

2. Geschlossene Netzwerke, Ergebnisse nur für einen Server

"NCA" für Netzwerke mit einer Kette

"NCAM" für Netzwerke mit mehreren Ketten

3. Geschlossene Netzwerke, Ergebnisse für alle Server

"MVA", "TCA"

Hierbei bedeuten die Abkürzungen:

BCMP    = Algorithmus basierend auf dem Artikel von Baskett, Chandy, Muntz, Palacios

ABCMP   = Accelerated BCMP

NCA     = Normalizing convolution Algorithm

NCAM    = NCA Multichain

MVA     = Mean Value Analysis

TCA     = Tree Convolution Algorithm

An meinem Institut hat sich der Simulator FORCASD /5/, zu dem auf diesem Kongress von meinen Mitarbeitern die Beiträge /7/ und /8/ vorliegen, sehr bewährt. FORCASD ist ein auf Auswertungsnetzen basierendes Programmsystem zur Simulation diskreter Systeme, das im Philips Forschungslaboratorium Hamburg mit dem Ziel entwickelt wurde, ein Hilfsmittel zu schaffen, das Unterstützung auf den Gebieten Systementwurf und Leistungsbewertung bietet.

Insbesondere unterstützt FORCASD die Darstellung von parallelen Prozessen und deren Synchronisation, von Datenflüssen, von datenabhängigem Routing und von Verzögerungs- und Ausführungszeiten. Da außerdem die Darstellung auf verschiedenen Abstraktions- ebenen möglich ist, erfüllt dieses Werkzeug in großem Maße unsere Erwartungen.

Auswertungsnetze sind Petrinetze mit interpretierten Token und tokenabhängigem oder von sonstigen Daten abhängigem Routing mit beliebig komplexen Transitionsprozeduren. Im wesentlichen bestehen Auswertungsnetze aus Token, Stellen und Transitionen. Token stellen die dynamischen Modellobjekte und deren Attribute dar. Stellen sind Speicher für *genau einen* Token und bilden die Verbindungsknoten zwischen den Transitionen. Die Transitionen repräsentieren die permanenten Modellobjekte, d.h. die Orte im Netz, an denen die System-Aktivitäten ausgeführt werden, Tokenattribute geändert werden, die Flußrichtungen von Token bestimmt werden, Zeiten verbraucht werden, syn- chronisiert wird, Token erzeugt werden, usw.

Eine Transition (TRN entsprechend Bild 4) wird beschrieben durch ein Tran- sitionsschema zur Beschreibung der Art der Transition, eine Transitionsprozedur zur Veränderung der Tokenattribute, eine Transitionszeit zur Darstellung der Ausfüh- rungszeiten von System Aktivitäten und eine Entscheidungsprozedur, die im Falle von sogenannten Konflikttransitionen die Flußrichtung in Abhängigkeit von irgendwelchen Daten, z.B. von Tokenattributen bestimmt.

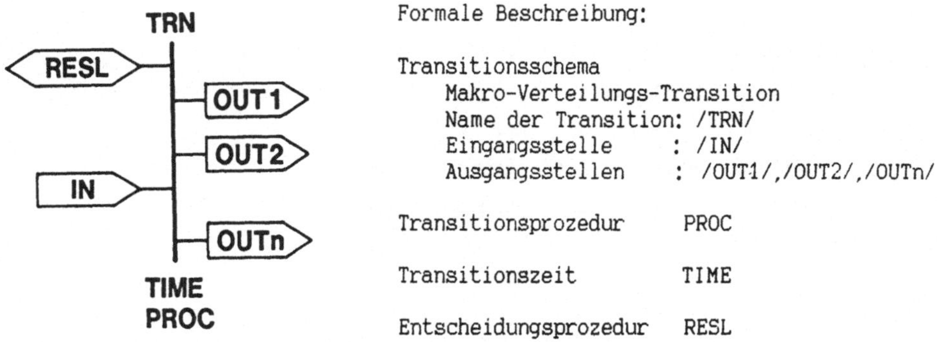



<u>Bild 4</u>: Grafische Darstellung und formale Beschreibung einer
        Makro-Verteilungs-Transition

Will man beispielsweise ein Terminal-System modellieren, so stellt man in einem
ersten Abstraktionsschritt fest, daß das System in zwei unabhängige Arten von funktionalen Blöcken zerlegt werden kann, Prozessor und Terminal.

Der Prozessor bearbeitet Jobs, die durch eine Terminalnummer (von wo sie gestartet
wurden), eine Rechenzeitanforderung und eine bestimmte Priorität gekennzeichnet
sind. Dazu führt der Prozessor eine Reihe von Aktivitäten aus, wie z.B.:

   o Entscheidung, welcher Job bearbeitet wird,

   o Einordnen der ankommenden Aufträge in eine Warteschlange,

   o Ausführen eines Auftrags,

   o Rückmeldung an das Terminal, wenn ein Auftrag fertiggestellt wurde

   o usw.

Das Terminal erzeugt, wenn ein Auftrag zu Ende bearbeitet wurde, nach einer zufälligen Wartezeit einen neuen Job. Das gesamte System ist beschreibbar durch eine Menge
von Aktivitäten (Transitionen), eine Menge von Token (dynamische Modellobjekte) und
ein Netzwerk.

Die Vorteile des Boxkonzeptes (aufteilung in Komponenten) sind:

   o Eine Box ist in einem Modell mehrfach verwendbar.

   o Eine Box ist wiederverwendbar in anderen Modellen.

   o Man kann verschiedene Abstraktionsebenen modellieren.

   o Das Modell läßt sich schrittweise verfeinern.

Weitere Einzelheiten sind in der Literatur /5/ ausführlich dargestellt.

Unsere Erfahrungen mit FORCASD bei der Untersuchung von Mehrprozessorsystemen und
gekoppelten Teilsystemen haben gezeigt, daß es ein äußerst flexibles Werkzeug darstellt, dessen Güte und Genauigkeit sich mit in Echtzeit aufgenommenen Meßwerten als
sehr hoch ergab (einige % Fehler).


## 4. Anwendungsbeispiel zur diskreten Simulation

Als ein Anwendungsbeispiel soll ein überschaubares System vorgestellt werden, bei dem die Überlegenheit der Simulation unter Verwendung des TCA - Algorithmus (Tree convolution Algorithm) voll zum Tragen kommt. Das Werkzeug ist das Programmsystem Oscar.

Gegeben sind drei Rechnersysteme (Kette 1, 2 und 3) bestehend jeweils aus einem Rechner (Knoten 2, 5, 8) einem Plattenspeicher (Knoten 3, 6, 9) und mehreren Terminals (Knoten 1, 4, 7). Jedem Benutzer (Auftrag) kann ein Terminal zugewiesen werden.

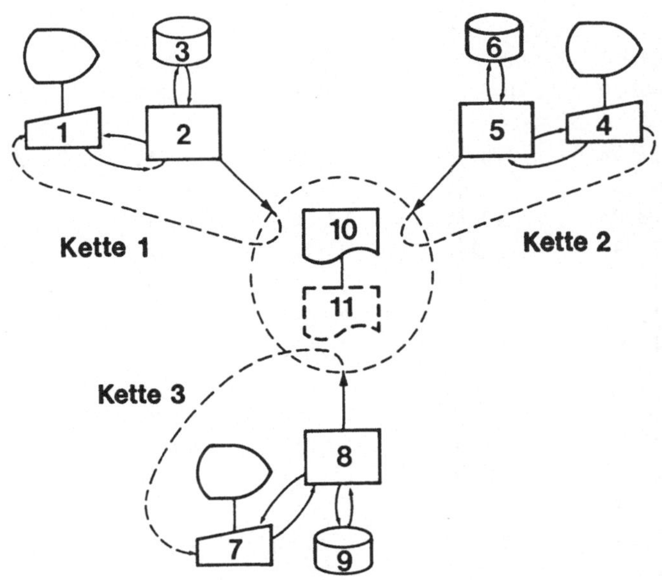


<u>Mittlere Bedienzeiten</u>

| | | |
|---|---|---|
| 1:term1 (IS) $\mu_1= 5$ | 4:term2 (IS) $\mu_4= 6$ | 7:term3 (IS) $\mu_7= 4$ |
| 2:cpu1 (PS) $\mu_2=20$ | 5:cpu2 (PS) $\mu_5=18$ | 8:cpu3 (PS) $\mu_8= 9$ |
| 3:disk1 (FCFS) $\mu_3=10$ | 6:disk2 (FCFS) $\mu_6= 8$ | 9:disk3 (FCFS) $\mu_9=11$ |
| 10:lp (FCFS) $\mu_{10}=25$ | | |

<u>Bild 5</u>: Simulationsbeispiel: 3 Rechnersysteme mit gemeinsamem Druckerzentrum.

Alle Rechner teilen sich ein Druckerzentrum (Knoten 10 und 11). Jeder Rechner bearbeitet eine konstante Anzahl von Aufträgen (geschlossene Ketten).

Die Durchsatzraten im Druckerzentrum sollen als Funktion der Anzahl der Aufträge und der Eigenschaften des Druckerzentrums ermittelt werden. Außerdem sollen die Auslastungen der Rechner berechnet werden.

Folgende Fälle werden untersucht:

a. Das Druckerzentrum besteht aus einem langsamen Drucker.
b. Das Druckerzentrum besteht aus zwei langsamen Druckern, die sich jeweils die Aufträge nach einem festen Schema aufteilen. Es kann also vorkommen, daß ein Drucker

einen Auftrag bearbeitet und ein weiterer Auftrag auf Bearbeitung an diesem Drucker wartet, obwohl der zweite Drucker frei ist.

c. Wie b., nur daß die Aufträge beliebig aufgeteilt werden und kein Drucker untätig ist, während auf den anderen Aufträge warten.

d. Das Druckerzentrum besteht aus einem Drucker, der doppelt so schnell ist wie ein langsamer Typ aus a., b. oder c.

Bezüglich der Anzahl N der Aufträge pro Rechnersystem wird angenommen, daß jeweils 3, 4, oder 5 Aufträge in jeder Kette quasi gleichzeitig bearbeitet werden.Die erzielten Simulationsergebnisse sind im Bild 6 dargestellt.

| | 1 LP l $\mu=25.0$ | 2 LP l $\mu=25.0$ | 2 LP (MS2) l $\mu=25.0$ | 1 LP s $\mu=12.5$ | |
|---|---|---|---|---|---|
| U2 | 56.5% | 78.3% | 84.4% | 85.1% | $\underline{N}=(3,3,3)$ |
| U5 | 47.0% | 71.0% | 79.1% | 80.0% | |
| U8 | 28.0% | 48.7% | 58.6% | 60.3% | |
| $DT \cdot 10^{-2}$ | 3.99 | 6.25 | 7.14 | 7.27 | |
| $D1 \cdot 10^{-2}$ | 1.13 | 1.57 | 1.69 | 1.70 | |
| $D2 \cdot 10^{-2}$ | 1.31 | 1.97 | 2.20 | 2.22 | |
| $D3 \cdot 10^{-2}$ | 1.55 | 2.71 | 3.25 | 3.35 | |
| U2 | 58.2% | 84.0% | 88.9% | 89.2% | $\underline{N}=(4,4,4)$ |
| U5 | 47.5% | 76.4% | 83.3% | 83.7% | |
| U8 | 27.3% | 52.7% | 62.3% | 63.2% | |
| $DT \cdot 10^{-2}$ | 4.00 | 6.73 | 7.56 | 7.62 | |
| $D1 \cdot 10^{-2}$ | 1.16 | 1.68 | 1.78 | 1.78 | |
| $D2 \cdot 10^{-2}$ | 1.32 | 2.12 | 2.31 | 2.33 | |
| $D3 \cdot 10^{-2}$ | 1.51 | 2.93 | 3.47 | 3.51 | |
| U2 | 59.4% | 87.5% | 91.4% | 91.5% | $\underline{N}=(5,5,5)$ |
| U5 | 47.8% | 79.8% | 85.6% | 85.8% | |
| U8 | 26.7% | 55.0% | 64.0% | 64.4% | |
| $DT \cdot 10^{-2}$ | 4.00 | 7.02 | 7.76 | 7.79 | |
| $D1 \cdot 10^{-2}$ | 1.19 | 1.75 | 1.83 | 1.83 | |
| $D2 \cdot 10^{-2}$ | 1.33 | 2.22 | 2.38 | 2.38 | |
| $D3 \cdot 10^{-2}$ | 1.48 | 3.05 | 3.55 | 3.58 | |

<u>Bild 6</u>: Ergebnis des Beispiels nach Bild 5

Eine kurze Interpretation der Ergebnisse ergibt folgende Aussagen:

Bei steigender Anzahl der Aufträge pro Rechnersystem steigen sowohl die Auslastungen der Rechner (U 2, U 5 und U 8) als auch die Durchsatzraten der Aufträge durch das Druckerzentrum (DT = Gesamtdurchsatzrate, D1, D2 und D3 Durchsatzraten der Aufträge stammend aus den Rechnersystemen 1, 2 und 3).

Ähnlich der Verbesserung der Qualitäten des Druckerzentrums wie in b., c. und d.

beschrieben, steigen ebenfalls die untersuchten Kenngrößen. Bemerkenswert ist, daß ein doppelt so schneller Drucker geringfügig bessere Ergebnisse liefert, als zwei langsame. Der Grund hierfür: Falls zwei oder mehr Aufträge im Druckerzentrum sind, werden sie von zwei langsamen Druckern genauso schnell bedient wie von einem doppelt so schnellen. Ist jedoch nur ein Auftrag im Druckerzentrum (die Wahrscheinlichkeit dieses Ereignisses ist ziemlich gering), so wird er vom schnellen Drucker schneller bedient.

## Literatur


/1/ Ameling, W.
*Parallelprocessor solutions for a certain class of optimization strategies*
Parallel Computers – Parallel Mathematics, IMACS SYMPOSIUM, pp.243-246, 1972

/2/ Ameling W.
*Planung und Entwicklung einer programmierbaren digitalen Integrieranlage*
Forschungsbericht des Landes NRW: Nr. 2607, Westdeutscher Verlag GmbH, Opladen, 1976

/3/ Lemer, E.; Laurent M.; Mourges M.
*Oscar – A queuing network resolution package*
Proceedings of the "First European Simulation Congress ESC83"

/4/ Baskett, F.; Chandy, K. M.; Muntz, R. R.; Palacios, F. G.
*Open, closed and mixed networks of queues with different classes of customers*
J. ACM 22, 2 (April 1975); pp.248-260

/5/ Dahmen, N.
*FORCASD – An Evaluation Net Oriented Program System for Modelling and Simulation*
Proceedings of the "First European Simulation Congress ESC83"; Springer-Verlag; pp.267-272

/6/ Ameling, W.
*Parallelism in Computer Architecture*
Proceedings 10th IMACS WORLD CONGRESS; Montreal; 1982

/7/ Behrens, M.; Regen, F.; Ameling, W.
*Simulation unterschiedlicher Verbindungsnetze im MSPS Multiprozessorsystem – Lastfälle, Strategien und Simulationsergebnisse*
Zur Veröffentlichung vorgesehen im 3. Symposium Simulationstechnik, ASIM 85

/8/ Regen, F.; Behrens, M.; Ameling, W.
*Simulation unterschiedlicher Verbindungsnetze im MSPS Multiprozessorsystem – Modellierung*
Zur Veröffentlichung vorgesehen im 3. Symposium Simulationstechnik, ASIM 85

## "Was tut man, wenn man simuliert?"
## Versuch einer Begriffsbestimmung

B. Schmidt, Erlangen

**Zusammenfassung:** Der Begriff "Simulation" wird in sehr unterschiedlichem Zusammenhang mit jeweils wechselnder Bedeutung gebraucht. Es wird versucht, eine eindeutige Begriffsbestimmung zu geben, die auf systemtheoretischen Überlegungen beruht.

**Summary:** The concept "simulation" is used in widely varying contexts with respectively alternating meaning.
An attempt will be made to provide a clear definition founded on system-theoretical thought.

## 1  Systemanalyse und Modellaufbau

Der Erkenntnisgegenstand tritt der wissenschaftlichen Untersuchung zunächst als Menge unstrukturierter Ausgangsdaten entgegen. Hierzu gehören Beobachtungen und Meßergebnisse.
Es ist die Aufgabe der Wissenschaft, die zunächst gegebenen Ausgangsdaten zu interpretieren und zu erklären, indem ein abstraktes Modell entworfen wird.

Ein abstraktes Modell besteht aus gedachten Objekten mit gedachten Merkmalen und einer gedachten Struktur. Es stellt in anschaulicher Betrachtungsweise das Bild des realen Systems im menschlichen Bewußtsein dar.
Ein abstraktes Modell wird mit Hilfe von Sprache repräsentiert. Die Dynamik wird hierbei z. B. mit Hilfe von Differentialgleichungen beschrieben.

Aussagen über das Verhalten des abstrakten Modells sind auf zwei grundsätzlich verschiedene Weisen möglich. Man unterscheidet das analytische Verfahren und die reale Modellierung. Die reale Modellierung soll Simulation genannt werden.

Wird das abstrakte Modell mit Hilfe einer formalen Sprache dargestellt, so ist es möglich, neue Aussagen über das Verhalten des abstrakten Modells mit Hilfe der Ableitungsregeln zu gewinnen, die in der Sprache definiert sind. Das bedeutet, daß man neue, allgemeine Aussagen beweisen kann. Es handelt sich hier um das analytische Verfahren.
In der Regel wird das Verhalten des abstrakten Modells durch mathematische Gleichungen beschrieben. Das analytische Verfahren bedeutet in diesem Fall, die Berechnung dieser Gleichungen. Hierher gehört z. B. die analytische Lösung von Differentialgleichungen.

Bild 1 zeigt den wissenschaftlichen Erkenntnisprozeß in der Übersicht. Eine ausführliche Darstellung, die auch Einzelheiten berücksichtigt findet man in /1/.

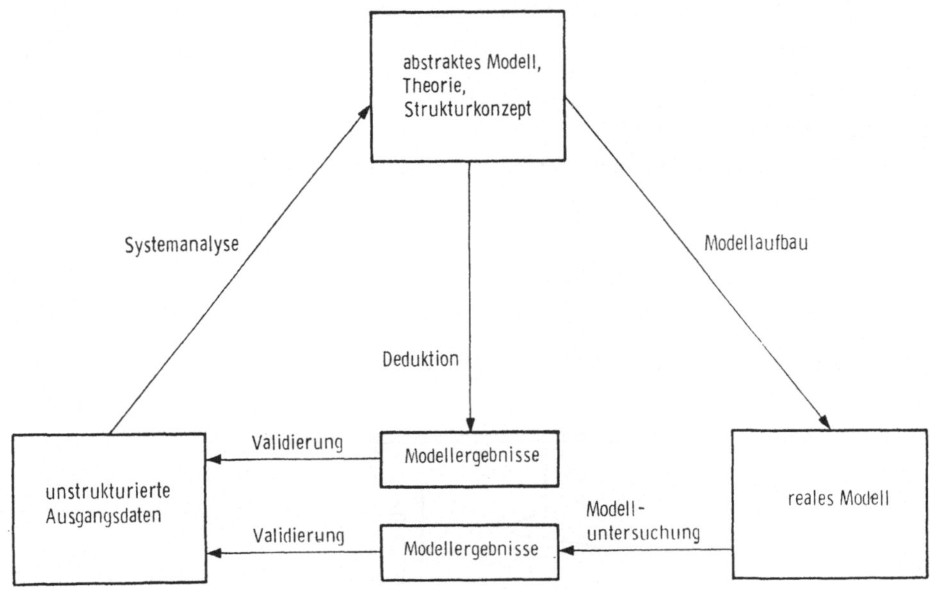


Bild 1: Der wissenschaftliche Erkenntnisprozeß

## 2 Simulation

Voraussetzung für die Möglichkeit der Simulation ist, daß zu dem zu untersuchenden System ein zweites System gefunden wird, für das ein abstraktes Modell vorliegt, das mit dem abstrakten Modell des ursprünglichen Systems übereinstimmt. Das bedeutet, daß beiden realen Systemen das gleiche abstrakte Modell unterlegt werden kann. Ein Beispiel soll diese Vorgehensweise erläutern.

### 2.1. Das mechanische Feder- Stoßdämpfer System

Zunächst soll ein mechanisches System untersucht werden, das aus einer Masse, einer Feder und einem Stoßdämpfer bestehen soll.
Die Masse M sei über die Feder mit der Federkonstanten K und über den Stoßdämpfer mit Dämpfungsfaktor D an einer festen Wand befestigt (Bild 2).
Für das vorliegende mechanische System soll ein abstraktes Modell aufgebaut werden, das über die Bewegung des Schwerpunktes der Masse Auskunft gibt, wenn unterschiedliche Kräfte F(t) angreifen.
Die Systemanalyse löst aus der Menge der Attribute, die das reale System kennzeichnen, diejenigen heraus, die für die Fragestellung relevant sind und verknüpft sie zu einem abstrakten Modell.

Die zunächst wichtigen Attribute sind die folgenden:

x Auslenkung des Masseschwerpunktes aus der Ruhelage

M Masse

K Federkonstante

D Dämpfungsfaktor

Die Abhängigkeit dieser Zustandsvariablen wird durch die folgende Differentialgleichung beschrieben.

$$M*x'' + D*x' + K*x = F(t)$$

Damit liegt ein abstraktes Modell für das reale System vor.

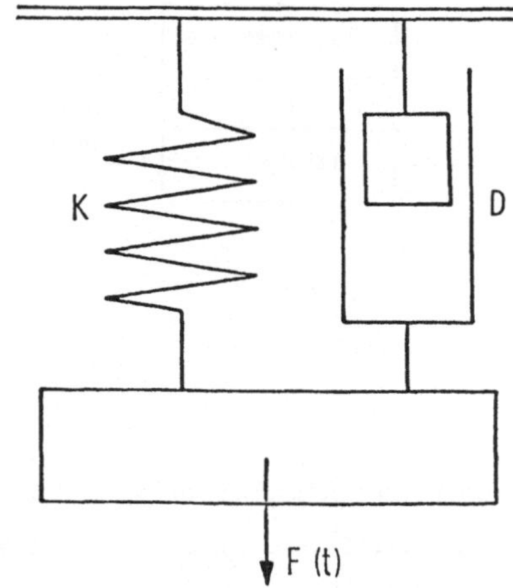



Bild 2: Das Mechanische System

Um das Verhalten des abstrakten Modells zu untersuchen, steht zunächst das analytische Verfahren zur Verfügung. Das würde bedeuten, daß die Differentialgleichung 2. Ordnung gelöst werden muß. Für einfache Funktionen F(t) ist das relativ leicht möglich.

Wie bereits dargestellt, besteht jedoch die weitere Möglichkeit, ein zweites reales System zu suchen, das mit dem zu untersuchenden, realen Feder-Stoßdämpfer-System das abstrakte Modell gemeinsam hat. Ein derartiges System heißt reales Modell zum ursprünglichen System.

Die Untersuchungen werden dann am realen Modell vorgenommen und auf das ursprüngliche System zurückübertragen. Man sagt, daß das reale Modell das ursprüngliche System simuliert.

## 2.2 Das elektrodynamische System

Es soll ein System untersucht werden, das zunächst mit dem Feder-Stoßdämpfer-System vom äußeren Anschein her vollkommen verschieden ist. Es handelt sich um ein elektro-dynamisches System.
In einem Stromkreis werden ein Widerstand R, ein Kondensator mit der Kapazität C, sowie eine Spule mit dem Induktionskoeffizienten L seriell geschaltet (Bild 3).

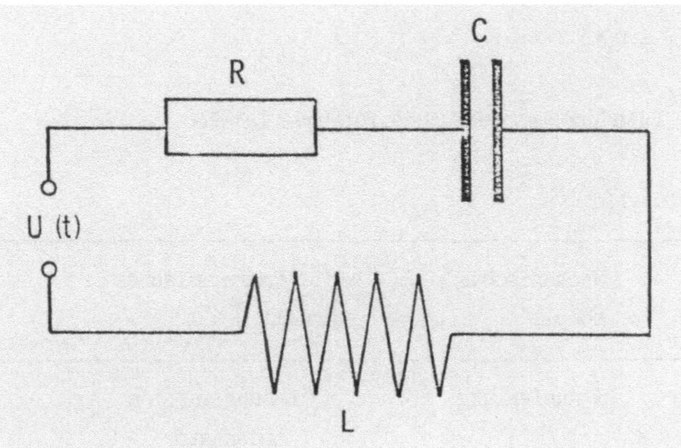


Bild 3: Das elektrodynamische System

Für das vorliegende, reale System soll ein abstraktes Modell entworfen werden, das Antwort auf die Frage geben kann, wie sich die Ladung auf einem Kondensator bei einer Eingangsspannung U(t) verhält.

Ein verhältnismäßig grobes abstraktes Modell benötigt die folgende Zustandsvariable:
x Ladung auf dem Kondensator

Die erforderlichen Koeffizienten sind die folgenden:
L Induktionskoeffizient der Spule
R Widerstand
C Kapazität des Kondensators

Das Verhalten des vorliegenden Systems wird durch die nachfolgende Differential-gleichung beschrieben:

$$L*x'' + R*x' + 1/C*x = U(t)$$

Vergleicht man diese Differentialgleichung mit der Differentialgleichung für das Feder-Stoßdämpfer-Modell, so stellt man fest, daß sie identisch sind. In beiden Fällen handelt es sich um eine Differentialgleichung 2. Ordnung, die eine gedämpfte Schwingung beschreibt. Das bedeutet, daß die beiden realen Systeme das gleiche abstrakte Modell besitzen.

Für das abstrakte Modell läßt sich allgemein schreiben:

$$A*x'' + B*x' + C*x = D(t)$$

Die Zuordnung der Attribute erfolgt durch die folgende Tabelle 1.

Tabelle 1:  Zuordnungstabelle

| Allgemeine Differentialgleichung | Mechanisches Modell | Elektrodynamisches Modell |
|---|---|---|
| x | x Auslenkung | x Ladung auf dem Kondensator |
| A | M Masse | L Induktionskoeffizient |
| B | D Dämpfungs-Faktor | R Widerstand |
| C | K Federkonstante | 1/C Reziproke Kapazität |
| D(t) | F(t) Kraft | U(t) Spannung am Eingang |

Man sieht, daß das mechanische System und das elektrodynamische System trotz aller äußeren Verschiedenheit durch ihr gemeinsames abstraktes Modell miteinander verbunden sind. Das bedeutet, daß ein System in der Lage ist, das Verhalten des anderen Systems zu simulieren.

Welches der beiden Systeme als reales Modell betrachtet wird, hängt von der Behandelbarkeit der Systeme ab. Es ist möglich, daß ein Federstoßdämpfer-System untersucht werden soll und als Modell das elektrodynamische System herangezogen wird , da sich beispielsweise an elektrodynamischen Systemen die Messungen leichter durchführen lassen.

Es wäre jedoch möglich, auch umgekehrt zu verfahren.

Es ist besonders wichtig, daß für die Simulation, die zur Systemuntersuchung ein reales Modell benötigt, auf jeden Fall ein abstraktes Modell erforderlich ist. Dieses abstrakte Modell setzt das zu untersuchende System und das System, das Modell spielt, in Verbindung. Die Zuordnung der Systemkomponenten erfolgt nicht direkt sondern über das abstrakte Modell.

Ein System kann nur Simulationsmodell für ein zu untersuchendes System in Bezug auf die Fragestellung und in Bezug auf die von der Abstraktion als wesentlich erkannten Attribute sein.

## 3  Klassenifikation der Simulationsmodelle

Eine Klassifikation für Simulationsmodelle richtet sich nach praktischen Gesichtspunkten, die ihren Einsatz und ihre Verwendung betreffen. Das bedeutet, daß die Handhabbarkeit, die Kosten beim Modellbau, die Verfügbarkeit usw. im Vordergrund stehen.

Hinweis:
* Simulationsmodelle sind reale Systeme, denen die Aufgabe zuerkannt wurde, Modell zu spielen. Die Klassifikation der realen Modelle ist eine  Einteilung, die berücksichtigt, daß ein abstraktes Modell auf ein  System der realen Welt abgebildet wird.

Eine Klassifikation für Simulationsmodelle könnte eine Form haben, die Bild 4 zeigt.

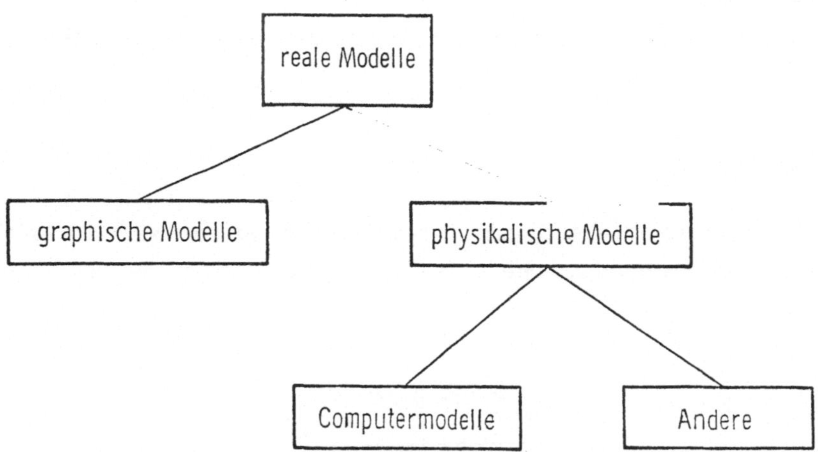


Bild 4: Die Klassifikation für reale Modelle (Simulationsmodelle)

Physikalische Modelle:

Die Systemobjekte sind materielle Körper; die Beziehungen und Wechselwirkungen erfolgen aufgrund der natürlichen, physikalischen Gesetze.

Beispiele:

* Für ein Flugzeug werden im Windkanal an einem verkleinerten Modell ärodynamische Kenngrößen ermittelt.

* Ein Wellensimultor als Modell untersucht den Einfluß der Brandung auf die Stabilität eines Deiches.

* Um den Aufbau eines Moleküls anschaulich zu machen, werden die Atome durch Kugeln und die Verbindungen durch ein Drahtgerüst wiedergegeben.

* Das in Abschnitt 2 beschriebene Feder-Stroßdämpfer-Modell oder das elektrodynamische Modell gehören in die Klasse der physikalischen Modelle.

Die Erstellung eines physikalischen Modells zeichnet sich dadurch aus,daß handwerkliche Tätigkeiten erforderlich sind. Man benötigt eine Werkstatt.

Graphische Modelle:

Die Elemente und Funktionen des abstrakten Modells werden auf graphische Darstellung im 2-dimensionalen Raum abgebildet.

Beispiele:

* Eine mathematische Funktion läßt sich durch eine gezeichnete Kurve in einem Koordinatenkreuz darstellen.

* Der erdachte Bauplan eines Architekten wird als Zeichnung, die den Grundriß darstellt, festgelegt.

* Die Vorstellungen eines Künstlers erscheinen als graphisches Modell in einer Zeichnung oder in einem Gemälde.

Computermodelle:

Computermodelle gehören zu den physikalischen Modellen. Hierbei wird die Rechenanlage als physikalisches System betrachtet. Das Simulationsprogramm auf der Rechenanlage

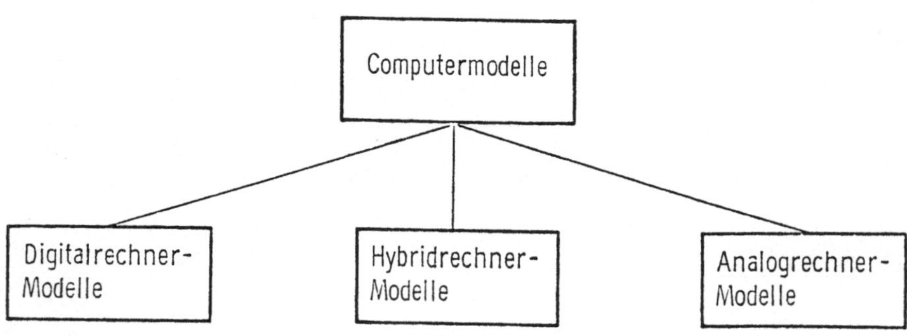


Bild 5: Computermodelle

sorgt dafür, daß die Zustandsübergänge in der korrekten Art und Weise durchgeführt werden.

## 4 Begriffsdefinition

Unter Simultion versteht man ein Verfahren, mit dessen Hilfe, das Verhalten eines realen Systems untersucht werden kann, indem man ein zweites System aufbaut, das mit dem ursprünglichen System in Bezug auf die zu untersuchenden Größen das gleiche abstrakte Modell besitzt. Dieses zweite System heißt reales Modell oder Simulations-modell.
Die Simulation umfaßt zunächst den Aufbau des realen Modells entsprechend den Vorgaben des abstrakten Modells.
Weiterhin gehört zur Simulation das Experimentieren mit diesem realen Modell zum Zweck der Erklärung oder Vorhersage.

Die vorgeschlagene Definition für "Simulation" ist so weit, daß sie auch Begriffe wie z. B. "Flugsimulator" oder "Wellensimulator", die sich im naturwissenschaftlich-technischen Bereich fest eingebürgert haben, einschließt. Die Simulation mit Hilfe, von Simulationssprachen auf einer Rechenanlage erweist sich in natürlicher Weise als Spezialfall.

Literatur
/1/ Schmidt, B.; Systemanalyse und Modellaufbau, Grundlagen der Simulationstechnik, Fachberichte Simulation Bd. 1, Springer Verlag 1985

# Modelle für die medizinische Diagnostik

Berthold Schneider, Hannover

Zusammenfassung. Der Computereinsatz zur Diagnostikunterstützung setzt
entsprechende algorithmisierbare Simulationsmodelle für die Diagnostik
voraus. Es werden folgende Modelle (im Sinne von syntaktischen Modellen) kurz diskutiert: das aussagenlogische Modell (einschließlich der
Erweiterung zum "Fuzzy-Logik"-Modell), das Klassifikationsmodell und
das Entscheidungsmodell. Die aussagenlogischen Modelle wurden in früheren Computerprogrammen häufig verwendet, dürften aber in Zukunft immer
mehr durch Entscheidungsmodelle ersetzt werden.

Summary. The use of computers for help in medical diagnostic needs algorithmic simulation models for the diagnostic process. Three classes
of such models are discussed in the paper: models of propositional logic (including fuzzy-logic), classification models and decision models.
Logic models were frequently used in former computer programs but should
be replaced by decision models in future.

Wenn auch das primäre Ziel ärztlichen Handelns die Heilung und Verhütung
von Krankheiten ist, so hat sich in den letzten Jahrhunderten als eine
wichtige Voraussetzung für die Erreichung dieses Ziels die Diagnostik
immer mehr herausgebildet (vgl. R. Gross [5]). Seit dem Aufkommen der
Computer in den 50er und 60er Jahren ist man bestrebt, zumindest Teile
der Diagnostik durch Computer ausführen oder unterstützen zu lassen
(sog. Diagnoseunterstützung). Dies setzt allerdings voraus, daß für die
Diagnostik entsprechende formale Modelle existieren, die eine Algorith-
misierung gestatten. Es gibt verschiedene Ansätze für solche formalen
Modelle (vgl. Wagner et al. [10]).

## 1. Modelle für die Diagnostik

Modelle werden im folgenden stets als "syntaktische Modelle" verstanden.
Das bedeutet, daß für den zu modellierenden Gegenstand oder Vorgang ein
Sprachsystem aufgestellt wird, in dem die relevanten Elemente durch Zeichen und Wörter (Zeichenfolgen) und die zwischen den Elementen bestehenden Verknüpfungen durch entsprechende sprachliche Verknüpfungs- oder Ableitungsregeln ausgedrückt werden. Mit Hilfe dieser Regeln können aus
den Wörtern Sätze oder allgemeine Ausdrücke gebildet werden, deren Gesamtheit (die "Sprache") das vollständige, sprachliche Modell (die

"Theorie") darstellt. Bevor man ein solches syntaktisches Modell für
die Diagnostik aufstellt, muß man sich erst im klaren sein, welche Elemente und Verknüpfungen bei der Diagnostik eine Rolle spielen.

Unbestreitbar dürften als Elemente der Diagnostik (d.h. des Prozesses
der Diagnosebildung oder Diagnosefindung durch den Arzt) Befunde (Symptome, Meßergebnisse) und Diagnosen (Krankheitsbezeichnungen) angenommen werden (vgl. das Schema der Diagnostik in Abbildung 1 (nach Gross
[5]).

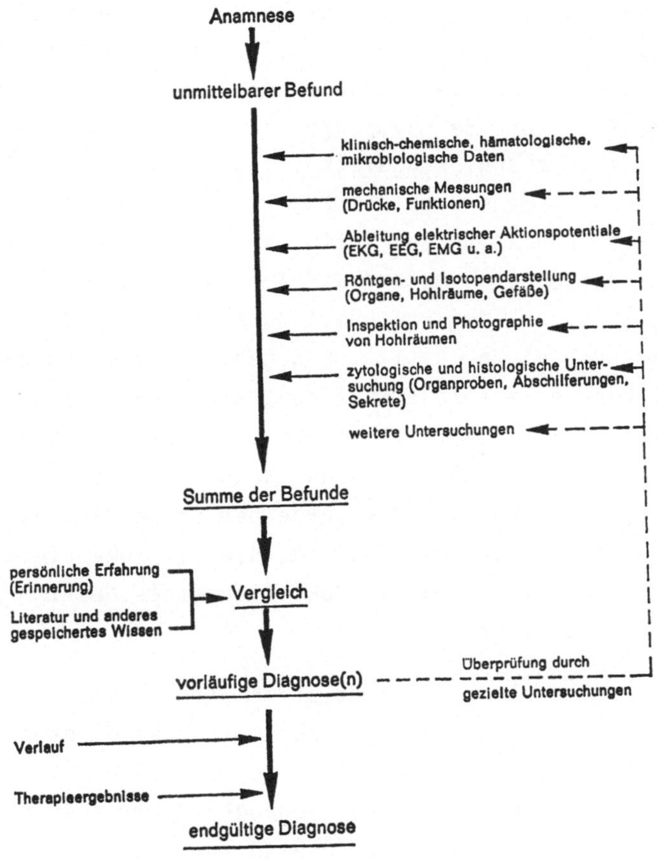


Abbildung 1

Während die syntaktische Formulierung der Befunde keine prinzipiellen
Schwierigkeiten macht, bereitet die genauere Spezifikation der Diagnose
schon größere Probleme. Als wichtigste Fragen, die eine Diagnose beantworten muß, hat R. Gross folgende Punkte zusammengestellt [5]:

| | |
|---|---|
| Was? | Art der Erkrankung |
| Wo? | Lokalisation |
| Seit wann? | Dauer |
| Warum? | Ursache |
| Bei wem? | Kennzeichnung des Patienten |

Formal können diese Elemente einer Diagnose als Sätze oder Ausdrücke aufgefaßt werden und somit syntaktisch ähnlich wie die Daten oder Befunde, aus denen die Diagnose zu erstellen ist, behandelt werden. Inhaltlich ergeben sich aber eine Reihe von Schwierigkeiten. So ist z.B. unklar, was unter "Art der Erkrankung" verstanden werden soll. Primär macht sich diese Art der Erkrankung durch die Symptome und Befunde bemerkbar, aus denen gerade die Diagnose erstellt werden soll. Man könnte daher davon ausgehen, daß die Diagnose nichts weiter als eine zusammenfassende "Klassifikation" der Symptome und Befunde ist. Diese Vorstellung wird vor allem im sog. <u>Klassifikationsmodell</u> nachgebildet. Andererseits zeigt aber die Frage nach dem "Warum", daß offensichtlich mit der Diagnose mehr ausgedrückt werden soll als nur eine klassifikatorische Bezeichnung verschiedener Symptome und Befundkomplexe. Man möchte auch etwas aber die "Ursache" der Krankheit aussagen; d.h. die Symptome und Befunde sollen durch einen bestimmten Gegenstand oder Vorgang "erklärt" werden. Formal kann eine solche Erklärung als eine logische Implikation (wenn-dann-Beziehung) dargestellt werden: z.B. wenn bestimmte Bakterien einen menschlichen Organismus befallen, dann treten die Symptome Fieber, Erbrechen usw. auf. Die Diagnostik würde bei dieser Auffassung in einer Inversion des wenn-dann-Satzes bestehen: die Symptome Fieber, Erbrechen u.ä. wurden beobachtet, also haben Bakterien eines bestimmtes Typs den menschlichen Organismus befallen.

Eine solche Inversion eines hypothetischen Urteils bzw. Schlusses (modus ponens) ist allerdings logisch nicht zulässig (was nicht hindert, daß sie praktisch oft vollzogen wird). Dies zeigt, wie problematisch "Kausalerklärungen" sein können. Die Überlegungen legen aber nahe, die Diagnostik als einen aussagenlogischen Schluß zu formulieren: Wenn ein bestimmtes Symptombild S (formuliert als eine logische (d.h. wahrheitsdefinite) Aussage) vorliegt, dann liegt die Diagnose D (ebenfalls formuliert als logische Aussage) vor. Dies führt zum <u>aussagenlogischen Modell</u> der Diagnostik. Das Problem ist, wie solche Implikationen aus der ärztlichen Erfahrung abgeleitet (begründet) werden können.

Ein weiterer Gesichtspunkt betrifft die Zielsetzung der Diagnostik. Selbst wenn - nach dem Schema von Gross - die Frage nach der Ursache bei der Diagnosestellung eine bedeutsame Rolle spielt, so besteht doch letztlich das pragmatische Ziel einer Diagnose darin, dem Arzt die für den Patienten optimale Therapie anzugeben.

Demnach soll die Diagnose zu einer Entscheidung über die Therapie führen. Diese Entscheidung kann rein aus den Symptomen getroffen werden, sich aus einer nosologischen Diagnose ergeben oder zu einer kausalen Therapie führen, falls in der Diagnose die Ursache der Erkrankung aufgedeckt wurde. Diese Überlegungen führten dazu, den Diagnostikprozeß als Entscheidungsprozeß zu modellieren.

Im folgenden sollen diese drei Ansätze etwas näher beleuchtet werden.

## 2. Die Aussagenlogik als Modell für die Diagnostik

Als Grundelemente der Diagnostik werden folgende 3 Komplexe angesehen:

1. Das ärztliche Wissen (die Erfahrung).
2. Die Symptome und Befunde eines Patienten.
3. Die möglichen Krankheiten (Diagnosen).

Beim aussagenlogischen Modell wird davon ausgegangen, daß diese Grundelemente der Diagnostik jeweils aus einer Menge von elementaren Aussagen (den elementaren Symptomen $s_1,\ldots,s_n$ und Diagnosen $d_1,\ldots,d_m$) bestehen, die über die üblichen logischen Operationen der Negation (dargestellt durch einen - über dem Aussagesymbol), der Konjunktion ("und"-Verknüpfung $\wedge$), der Disjunktion ("oder"-Verknüpfung $\vee$) sowie der Implikation ("wenn-dann"-Verknüpfung $\rightarrow$) zu komplexen Aussagen zusammengesetzt werden können. (Auf die naheliegende Erweiterung zu einer Prädikatenlogik mit Quantoren soll hier nicht näher eingegangen werden.)

Die Symptomatik eines Patienten wird somit syntaktisch modelliert durch einen aussagenlogischen Satz $\varphi_S$ $(s_1,\ldots,s_n)$ (z.B. durch $\bar{s}_1 \wedge s_2$: der Patient hat das elementare Symptom $s_1$ nicht, aber das elementare Symptom $s_2$), die Diagnose durch einen Satz $\varphi_D$ $(d_1,\ldots,d_m)$ (z.B. durch $d_1 \wedge \bar{d}_2$: der Patient hat die Krankheit $d_1$ und nicht die Krankheit $d_2$) und die ärztliche Erfahrung durch einen Satz $\varphi_E$ $(s_1,\ldots,s_n,d_1,\ldots,d_m)$ (z.B. $((\bar{s}_1 \wedge s_2) \rightarrow (d_1 \wedge \bar{d}_2)) \wedge ((\bar{s}_1 \wedge s_2) \rightarrow (\bar{d}_1 \wedge d_2)) \wedge ((s_1 \vee s_2) \rightarrow (d_1 \vee d_2)))$.

Grundlage der Diagnostik ist dann ein Satz der Form

$$\varphi_E \rightarrow (\varphi_S \rightarrow \varphi_D)$$

(Aus der Erfahrung $\varphi_E$ folgt: wenn $\varphi_S$ dann $\varphi_D$).

Nach dem Normalformtheorem der Aussagenlogik können alle diese Sätze (unter Vermeidung der Implikation a→b, die z.B. als Disjunktion ā∨b geschrieben werden kann) als eine Konjunktion aus Disjunktionen, die alle möglichen Paare der elementaren Aussagen $s_i$ bzw. $d_j$ oder ihrer Negationen $\bar{s}_i$ bzw. $\bar{d}_j$ umfassen, geschrieben werden. Es lassen sich also sämtliche Sätze aus den Elementaraussagen durch endliche Anwendung der Konjunktionen, Disjunktionen und Negationen gewinnen. Für die Computersimulation des Modells ist somit lediglich erforderlich, eine geeignete Computerdarstellung der Elementaraussagen und der logischen Operationen der Negation, Konjunktion und Disjunktion zu finden. Eine solche Darstellung ist mit Hilfe der Dualvektoren möglich (vgl. Ledley [7], Schneider [9]). Dabei wird jede der Elementaraussagen $s_i$ und $d_j$ durch einen Dualvektor mit $2^{n+m}$ Komponenten dargestellt (wobei jede Komponente entweder 0 oder 1 ist).

Für 2 Symptome $s_1, s_2$ und Diagnosen $d_1, d_2$ ergibt sich z.B. die Darstellung (bei Schreibweise als Zeilenvektoren):

| Komponenten Nr.: | 0 | 1 | 2 | 3 | 4 | 5 | 6 | 7 | 8 | 9 | 10 | 11 | 12 | 13 | 14 | 15 |
|---|---|---|---|---|---|---|---|---|---|---|---|---|---|---|---|---|
| $s_1 \doteq$ | (0 | 1 | 0 | 1 | 0 | 1 | 0 | 1 | 0 | 1 | 0 | 1 | 0 | 1 | 0 | 1) |
| $s_2 \doteq$ | (0 | 0 | 1 | 1 | 0 | 0 | 1 | 1 | 0 | 0 | 1 | 1 | 0 | 0 | 1 | 1) |
| $d_1 \doteq$ | (0 | 0 | 0 | 0 | 1 | 1 | 1 | 1 | 0 | 0 | 0 | 0 | 1 | 1 | 1 | 1) |
| $d_2 \doteq$ | (0 | 0 | 0 | 0 | 0 | 0 | 0 | 0 | 1 | 1 | 1 | 1 | 1 | 1 | 1 | 1) |

Die Festlegung der 0 oder 1 für die Komponenten kann mit Hilfe des Venn-Diagramms erfolgen. Für Einzelheiten sei auf die Literatur verwiesen ([7], [9]).

Die Negation $\bar{s}$ bedeutet, daß im Vektor von s die 0 in 1 und die 1 in 0 umgewandelt wird. Die Konjunktion bedeutet eine Multiplikation der entsprechenden Komponenten, die Disjunktion eine Addition. Auf diese Weise läßt sich jeder aussagenlogische Satz $\varphi$ der Elementaraussagen $s_i$ und $d_j$ im Computer erzeugen und insbesondere auch die Gesamtheit der Sätze $\varphi_S \to \varphi_D$ bilden, die bei gegebenen Elementaraussagen $s_i$ und $d_j$ sowie der gegebenen "Erfahrung" $\varphi_E$ den logischen Satz $\varphi_E \to (\varphi_S \to \varphi_D)$ "erfüllen". Diese Implikatoren bilden die Gesamtheit der zulässigen diagnostischen Aussagen, die mit der Erfahrung verträglich sind. Man kann sich diese Gesamtheit vom Computer (geordnet nach den möglichen Sätzen $\varphi_S$) auflisten lassen und dem Arzt z.B. in Form von "Entscheidungstabellen" zur Verfügung stellen. Bei einem Patienten mit einer bestimmten Symptomatik muß der Arzt diese Symptomatik zunächst durch einen aussagenlogischen Satz $\varphi_S$ ausdrücken und dann in der Liste nachsehen, welche Diagnoseaussagen

$\varphi_D$ dazu zulässig sind. Im günstigsten Fall gibt es nur eine einzige solche Aussage $\varphi_D$. Dann kann die Diagnose eindeutig gestellt werden. Im allgemeinen werden aber mehrere Diagnoseaussagen zulässig sein und der Arzt steht vor dem Problem, sich für eine dieser zulässigen Diagnosen zu entscheiden bzw. seine Therapiemaßnahmen so einzurichten, daß sie allen zulässigen Diagnosen in etwa entsprechen (falls dies möglich ist). Dabei können ihn aber aussagenlogische Modelle nicht mehr unterstützen, sondern er muß zu anderen Modellen - z.B. zu Entscheidungsmodellen - greifen. Dies zeigt eine der wesentlichen Einschränkungen der aussagenlogischen Modelle. Sie wurden zwar in früheren Anwendungen der Computerdiagnostik (z.B. durch den Wiener Internisten Schmid) benutzt und finden sich auch noch in einigen speziellen Systemen für die nuklearmedizinische Diagnostik oder EKG-Diagnostik. Sie dürften aber in Zukunft - mit zunehmender Verfügbarkeit valider Datenbasen - durch Klassifikations- oder Entscheidungsmodelle ersetzt werden.

## 3. Fuzzy-Logik

In den vergangenen Jahren wurde vereinzelt der Versuch gemacht, die Fuzzy-Logik (fuzzy sets) zur Modellierung der Diagnostik einzusetzen (z.B. bei Esogbue und Elder [4], Adlassnig [1], [2]). Die Fuzzy-set Theorie wurde 1965 von Lotfi A. Zadeh begründet. Der Grundgedanke war, daß der Mensch nicht in präzisen Zahlen und eindeutigen, wahrheitsdefiniten Begriffen denkt, sondern mehr oder minder "unscharf" (fuzzy). Deshalb erschien Zadeh die traditionelle, wahrheitsdefinite Logik zur Beschreibung und Erklärung komplexer Sachverhalte weniger geeignet: "Indeed, the pervasiveness of fuzziness in human thought processes suggests that much of the logic behind human reasoning is not the traditional two-valued or even multivalued logic, but a logic with fuzzy truths, fuzzy connectives and fuzzy rules of inference" [11].

Die Fuzzy-Logik ist gekennzeichnet durch sog. "Zugehörigkeits-Funktionen": Die Gesamtheit der Sachverhalte (universe of discourse) wird als eine Menge U angenommen. Für jede Teilmenge A von U soll eine Funktion $\mu_A(y)$ existieren, die die Elemente y von U auf das Intervall $[0,1]$ der reellen Zahlen abbildet: $\mu_A: U \rightarrow [0,1]$. Die Funktion $\mu_A$ wird interpretiert als ein Maß für die "Zugehörigkeit" (membership) von $y \in U$ zur Teilmenge A. Die Teilmenge A nennt Zadeh eine "Fuzzy-Menge". Dabei steht A für einen Begriff oder Sachverhalt, der durch einen Namen x gekennzeichnet ist. Z.B. kann das Universum aus der Menge der natürlichen Zahlen 1,2,...,10 bestehen. Eine Fuzzy-Menge A, die mit dem Namen "einige" gekennzeichnet ist, kann definiert werden durch die Belegung: $3 \rightarrow 0,5$; $4 \rightarrow$ 0,8; $5 \rightarrow 1$; $6 \rightarrow 1$; $7 \rightarrow 0,8$ und $8 \rightarrow 0,5$. Den Zahlen 1,2,9 und 10 wird der Wert 0 zugeordnet; d.h. sie gehören nicht zum Begriff "einige".

Eine "Fuzzy-Beziehung" (unscharfe Beziehung) zwischen 2 Begriffen, denen zwei Mengen X und Y entsprechen, wird durch eine Fuzzy-Relation R ausgedrückt. Darunter ist eine Funktion $\mu_R(x,y)$ der Elemente x,y aus der Produktmenge X×Y auf das Intervall [0,1] zu verstehen, die den Grad der "Beziehung" zwischen den beiden Begriffen ausdrückt. Wenn beide Mengen endlich viele Elemente enthalten, dann kann $\mu_R(x,y)$ auch als Matrix geschrieben werden.

Zwei Fuzzy-Relationen R und S können zu einer neuen Relation T zusammengesetzt werden (T=R∘S), wobei das Maß $\mu_T$ der zusammengesetzten Beziehung von Zadeh etwas willkürlich definiert wird als:

$$\mu_T(x,z) = \underset{y}{\text{Max}}(\text{Min}(\mu_R(x,y),\mu_S(y,z))$$

Von anderen Autoren wurden auch andere Kompositionsregeln festgesetzt (z.B. die Maximum-Produktregel).

Für die Fuzzy-Mengen können eine Reihe von Operationen (d.h. Funktionen, die angewandt auf eine oder mehrere Fuzzy-Mengen eindeutig zu neuen Fuzzy-Mengen führen) definiert werden, die das ganze methodische System erst zu einer Fuzzy-Logik machen; wie z.B. die Fuzzy-Negation, Fuzzy-Konjunktion, Fuzzy-Disjunktion u.ä. Darauf soll hier nicht näher eingegangen werden (siehe z.B. Zadeh [11]).

Adlassnig hat die Fuzzy-Logik auf die medizinische Diagnostik praktisch angewandt [1], [2]. Sein Modellsystem soll kurz skizziert werden:

Ausgangspunkt bildet wieder eine endliche Menge von Symptomen $(s_1,...,s_n)$ und Diagnosen $(d_1,....,d_m)$, die als Nicht-Fuzzy-Mengen angesehen werden. Jedem Symptom $s_i$ wird eine Fuzzy-Menge durch Angabe eines Maßes $\mu_{s_i}(x)$ zugeordnet (wobei x ein möglicher Wert ist, mit dem das Symptom ausgedrückt werden kann), das angibt, wie stark der Wert x das Symptom ausdrückt. Z.B. kann das Symptom "Fieber" durch folgende Bewertung als Fuzzy-Menge definiert werden: $\mu_{Fieber}(x) = 0$ für $x \leq 36°$; $\mu_{Fieber}(x) = 0,3$ für $36° < x \leq 37°$; $\mu_{Fieber}(x) = 0,8$ für $37° < x \leq 38°$; $\mu_{Fieber}(x) = 1$ für $x > 38°$.

Für jedes Symptom $s_i$ und jede Diagnose $d_j$ werden zwei Fuzzy-Mengen definiert:

$P \doteq \mu_{P_{ij}}(x)$ = Grad des "Vorkommens" (presence) von $s_i$ bei $d_j$

$C \doteq \mu_{C_{ij}}(x)$ = Grad der "Zuverlässigkeit" (conclusiveness) von $s_i$ bei $d_j$

Bei der Fuzzy-Menge "Vorkommen" wird als Referenzmenge U die (absolute) Häufigkeit x angenommen, mit der das Symptom $s_i$ bei 100 Patienten mit der Diagnose $d_j$ vorkommt; bei der "Zuverlässigkeit" wird als Referenzmenge die Häufigkeit x angenommen, mit der die Diagnose $d_j$ bei 100 Patienten richtig ist, die das Symptom $s_i$ haben. Für die Funktionen setzt Adlassnig stückweise quadratische Funktionen an, deren Form mit Hilfe der in einer Datenbank gespeicherten Daten bestimmt werden kann. Eine andere Möglichkeit bietet die Befragung von Ärzten, wobei deren Antworten wieder als Fuzzy-Mengen $P_i$ bzw. $C_i$ charakterisiert werden könnten.

Bezogen auf das Mengenprodukt S×D der Kombinationen von Symptomen und Diagnosen bilden die Fuzzy-Mengen P und C Fuzzy-Relationen $R_P(s_i,d_j)$ und $R_C(s_i,d_j)$. Führt man noch eine Patienten-Symptom Fuzzy-Relation $R_S(s_i,p)$ ein, die den Grad angibt, mit dem bei einem Patienten p das Symptom $s_i$ vorhanden ist, dann kann die Diagnostik durch zusammengesetzte Fuzzy-Relationen modelliert werden:

$R_1 = R_S \circ R_P$ gibt den Grad an, mit dem bei einem Patienten p mit einer Symptomatik S die verschiedenen Diagnosen $d_j$ zu erwarten sind.

$R_2 = R_S \circ R_P$ gibt den Grad der Zuverlässigkeit an, mit dem bei einem Patienten p mit der Symptomatik S die verschiedenen Diagnosen $d_j$ behauptet werden können.

Entsprechend können auch die Fuzzy-Relationen $R_3 = R_S \circ (1-R_P)$ und $R_4 = R_S \circ (1-R_C)$ eingeführt werden, die den Grad angeben, mit dem die verschiedenen $d_j$ nicht erwartet bzw. nicht behauptet werden können.

Für die Computersimulation sind zunächst die Relationen $R_P$ und $R_C$ zu bestimmen. Dies kann - wie bereits erwähnt - aus den in einer großen medizinischen Datenbank gesammelten Informationen geschehen. Adlassnig et al. [2] haben dies z.B. in ihrem System CADIAG-2 für Krankheiten des rheumatischen Formenkreises und für Pankreaserkrankungen getan. Bei einem Patienten p muß der Arzt zunächst dessen Symptomatik erheben und für jedes Symptom $s_i$ den Wert der entsprechenden Zugehörigkeitsfunktion $\mu(p,s_i)$ bestimmen. Hierfür können u.U. Übersetzungsprogramme eingesetzt werden. Dadurch ist dann die Fuzzy-Relation $R_S$ bestimmt und es können mit dem Computer die Werte von $R_1$ bis $R_4$ bestimmt werden. Diagnosen, für die $R_1$ bzw. $R_2$ hohe Werte annimmt, sind wahrscheinlich bzw. können zuverlässig behauptet werden; Diagnosen mit hohen Werten von $R_3$ und $R_4$ sind dagegen unwahrscheinlich. Mittlere Werte von $R_1$ bzw. $R_2$ können als "Hinweise" aufgefaßt werden.

Kritisch an diesem Modell ist zu vermerken, daß die Festlegung der Fuzzy-Mengen und Fuzzy-Relationen ein hohes Maß an Willkür beinhaltet. Will man diese Willkür weitgehend vermeiden, dann ist man auf statistische Methoden angewiesen. Damit reduziert sich aber das ganze Verfahren auf probabilistische Bayes-Klassifikationsverfahren, wie sie im nächsten Abschnitt kurz besprochen werden.

## 4. Klassifikationsmodelle

Unter einer Klassifikation wird eine Zuordnung K von Individuen zu einer (von k möglichen) Klasse $D_i$ aufgrund von beobachteten Merkmalen S verstanden. Da die Individuen durch die Merkmalwerte S vollständig gekennzeichnet sein sollen, kann man auch vereinfachend von einer Zuordnung von Merkmalen S zu einer der möglichen Klassen $D_i$ sprechen. Die Zuordnung soll eindeutig sein; d.h. jeder Merkmalkombination S soll eine und nur eine Klasse $D_i$ zugeordnet werden; $K: S \to D_i$.

In diesem Sinn kann auch das aussagenlogische Diagnostikmodell als ein Klassifikationsmodell verstanden werden, falls die aussagenlogische Formel $\varphi_E \to (\varphi_S \to \varphi_D)$ bei gegebenem $\varphi_S$ eine eindeutige Lösung $\varphi_D$ besitzt, und die Aussage $\varphi_D$ als Definition einer Diagnoseklasse $D_i$ verstanden wird. Die gewählte Zuordnungsregel K wird dabei durch die Erfahrungssätze $\varphi_E$ - also gewissermaßen durch "interne" Eigenschaften des Diagnostikprozesses - bestimmt. Unter Klassifikationsmodellen sollen im folgenden Zuordnungsregeln verstanden werden, die durch "externe" Optimalitätsforderungen bestimmt sind.

Um diese Modelle präziser zu beschreiben nehmen wir an, daß k mögliche und nicht überlappende Diagnoseklassen $D_i$ (i=1,...,k) zur Auswahl anstehen und ein Patient genau einer dieser Klassen zugeordnet werden soll. Man kann sich z.B. diese Klassen als aussagenlogische Kombinationen der Elementardiagnosen $d_1,...,d_m$ denken (z.B. $D_1 \doteq d_1 \wedge \bar{d}_2$; $D_2 \doteq \bar{d}_1 \wedge d_2$; $D_3 \doteq d_1 \wedge d_2$; $D_4 \doteq \bar{d}_1 \wedge \bar{d}_2$). Die Symptomatik S soll nicht als aussagenlogische Formel, sondern als ein n-dimensionaler Vektor mit den reellwertigen Komponenten $s_1,...,s_n$ verstanden werden. Die $s_i$ können entweder den ganzen $R_1$, ein endliches oder unendliches Intervall oder diskrete Werte (z.B. 0 und 1) als Wertebereich annehmen.

Die Diagnostik wird dann aufgefaßt als eine Zuordnung von den (bei Patienten beobachteten) Symptomvektoren $S \in R_n$ zu genau einer Diagnoseklasse $D_i$; $K: S \rightarrow D_i$.

Durch die inverse Abbildung $K^{-1}: D_i \rightarrow S$ wird der $R_n$ in k Bereiche $B_1, .., B_k$ zerlegt, so daß:

Klassifikation zu $D_i$, wenn $S \in B_i$

Das Klassifikationsverfahren K soll bestimmten Optimalitätsforderungen genügen. Wir nehmen an, daß die Klassifikation $S \rightarrow D_i$ fehlerhaft sein kann; d.h. daß ein Patient mit Symptomatik S und richtiger Diagnoseklasse $D_i$ durch K nach $D_j$ eingeteilt werden kann. Wir führen folgende Bezeichnungen ein:

$Q_i$ = Wkt, einen Patienten der Diagnoseklasse $D_i$ einer anderen Diagnoseklasse $(D_j \neq D_i)$ zuzuordnen.

$q_i$ = "Gewicht", das einer solchen Fehlklassifikation zukommt ($0 \leq q_i \leq 1$; $\Sigma q_i = 1$).

Die optimale Klassifikation liegt dann vor, wenn das "Risiko" einer Fehlklassifikation minimal wird:

Risiko $R = q_1 Q_1 + \ldots + q_k Q_k$ = Minimum

Die Lösung dieser Minimierungsaufgabe ist durch folgendes Verfahren gegeben (vgl. Anderson [3]):

Es sei $P(S|D_i)$ die Wahrscheinlichkeit(dichte) für die Symptomatik S bei Vorliegen der Diagnoseklasse $D_i$. Dann ist K optimal, wenn:

$S \rightarrow D_i$ falls $q_i P(S|D_i) = \underset{j}{Max}\, q_j\, P(S|D_j)$

Ein Beispiel für die optimale Einteilung bei stetigem Symptom $S=x$ und 2 Klassen $D_1, D_2$ sowie gleichen Gewichten $q_1=q_2=0,5$ ist in Abbildung 2 gezeigt.

Das Hauptproblem bei diesem Verfahren besteht darin, die Wahrscheinlichkeiten $P(S|D_i)$ zu bestimmen und die Gewichte $q_i$ festzulegen.

a. Bestimmung von $P(S|D_i)$: Es wird eine "Lernstichprobe" von $n_1$ Patienten mit Diagnose $D_1$, $n_2$ Patienten mit Diagnose $D_2, \ldots, n_k$ mit Diagnose $D_k$ ausgewählt (z.B. aus einer medizinischen Datenbank). Für jeden Patienten wird die Symptomatik S bestimmt und daraus werden Schätzwerte $\hat{P}(S|D_i)$ für $P(S|D_i)$ berechnet. Diese Schätzwerte werden statt

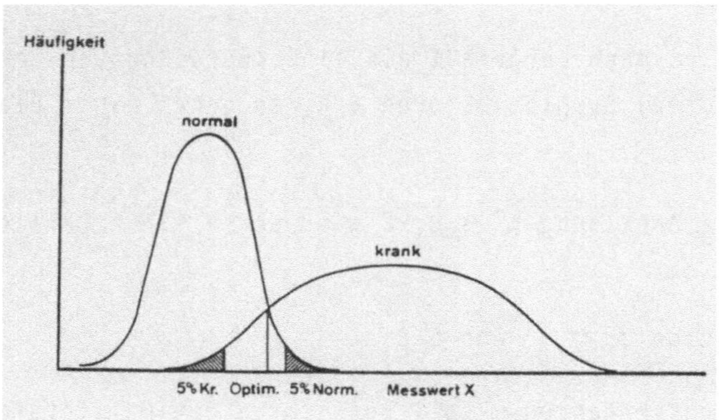


Abbildung 2

der exakten Wahrscheinlichkeiten $P(S|D_i)$ in die obige Klassifikations-
regel eingesetzt (sog. "plug-in-rule"). Die Güte dieser approximativen Klassifikationsregel hängt von der Güte des Schätzverfahrens ab
(vgl. Lachenbruch [6]):

Die Schätzung wird vereinfacht, wenn für $P(S|D_i)$ bestimmte parametri-
sche Verteilungen angenommen werden können, deren Parameter aus den
Daten der Lernstichprobe geschätzt werden. Bei Annahme von multiva-
riaten Normalverteilungen führt dies zur linearen oder quadratischen
Diskriminanzanalyse (vgl. [6]). Eine oft etwas besser angepaßte Ver-
teilungsklasse ist die der logistischen Verteilung oder genereller
die Exponentialklasse. Man kann die Wahrscheinlichkeiten $P(S|D_i)$ auch
"parameterfrei" mit Hilfe von sog. Kernschätzern schätzen (Glätten
der diskreten Häufigkeitsverteilungen durch Integration mit "Kern-
funktionen"). Es existieren mehrere Programmpakete, die verschiedene
Lösungsmöglichkeiten für dieses Problem anbieten (z.B. bei BMDP).

b. Die Gewichte $q_i$ müssen problemgerecht vorgegeben werden. Folgende Be-
merkungen können dabei hilfreich sein:

Die Wahrscheinlichkeiten $P(S|D_i)$ entsprechen den Likelihood-Funktio-
nen. Die Gewichte $q_i$ können als Wahrscheinlichkeiten angesehen werden, daß ein Patient mit der Diagnose $D_i$ zum Arzt zur Diagnostik
kommt (a priori-Wahrscheinlichkeiten von Bayes). Dividiert man das
Produkt $P(S|D_i)q_i$ durch $P(S) = \sum_i P(S|D_i)q_i$, dann erhält man die sog.
a posteriori-Wahrscheinlichkeit von Bayes. Das optimale Klassifikationsverfahren besteht demnach darin, einen Patienten mit der Symptomatik S in diejenige Diagnoseklasse $D_i$ einzuordnen, für die bei gegebenem S die a posteriori-Wahrscheinlichkeit maximal ist. Die a priori-Wahrscheinlichkeiten $q_i$ können z.B. als Häufigkeiten für die frü-

her bei einem Arzt festgestellten Diagnosen $D_i$ geschätzt werden (empirische a priori-Schätzung).

Man nennt dieses Klassifikationsverfahren auch das "Bayes-Klassifikationsverfahren". Es entspricht dem Fuzzy-Modell von Adlassnig, wenn die Symptom-Diagnose Fuzzy-Relation $R_p$ durch die Wahrscheinlichkeiten $P(S|D_i)q_i$ ersetzt und die Symptome S eines Patienten als Nicht-Fuzzy-Variable aufgefaßt werden.

## 5. Entscheidungsmodelle

Die Diagnosen sollen letztlich dem Arzt Entscheidungshilfe für die adäquaten therapeutischen Maßnahmen geben. Dies legt nahe, nicht die Diagnoseklassen $D_i$, sondern die darauf aufbauenden Maßnahmen $A_i$ (die aus einem Komplex von Einzelmaßnahmen $a_j$ bestehen können) als Zielgrößen des diagnostischen Prozesses anzunehmen und diesen als einen sequentiellen Entscheidungsprozeß zu modellieren.

Folgende Elemente umfaßt ein allgemeines Entscheidungsmodell (vgl. [8]):

- Diagnostische Verfahren (Experimente) $E_j$. Diese setzen sich in bestimmter Form (Strategien) aus möglichen Einzelverfahren $e_j$ zusammen. Es wird angenommen, daß bei einer diagnostischen Stufe k nur einer von m Verfahrenskomplexen $E_j^k$ zur Anwendung kommen kann und alle m Komplexe die Gesamtheit der in der k-ten Stufe möglichen Verfahren abdecken.

- Ergebnisse $S(E_j^k)$ des Verfahrens $E_j^k$ in der k-ten diagnostischen Stufe. S wird als ein Vektor im $R_n$ angenommen, wobei die Dimension n vom Verfahren $E_j^k$ abhängt.

- Therapeutische Maßnahmen $A_i$. Diese können aus Einzelmaßnahmen $a_i$ zusammengesetzt sein. Für jede Stufe k kann eine andere Menge $\{A_i;\ i=1,\ldots,n\}$ von Maßnahmen möglich sein. Zur Vereinfachung fassen wir aber die Gesamtheit der auf allen Stufen möglichen Maßnahmen zu einer Gesamtmenge $\{A_i\}$ zusammen und modellieren die Stufenabhängigkeit durch die Entscheidungsfunktion $d^k$.

- Entscheidungsfunktionen $d^k(S)$. Dies sind Zuordnungen der mit dem Verfahren $E_j^{k-1}$ bestimmten Symptomatik S zu den möglichen Maßnahmen $A_i$ oder zu neuen diagnostischen Verfahren $E_j^k$. Im ersten Fall spricht man von terminalen Entscheidungen: $d_t^k(S)$: $S \rightarrow A_i$; im zweiten Fall von experimentellen Entscheidungen: $t_e^k(S)$: $S \rightarrow E_j^{k+1}$. Eine experimentelle Entscheidung bedeutet, daß der diagnostische Prozeß auf der k+1-ten Stufe mit einem Verfahren $E_j^{k+1}$ fortgesetzt wird. Der sequentielle diagnostische Prozeß kann nach folgendem Schema simuliert werden:

Der Arzt wählt nach einem Entscheidungsprinzip aus der möglichen Menge ein Verfahren $E_j^0$ aus (z.B. Anamnese und unmittelbarer Befund; vgl. Abb. 1), wendet es auf den Patienten an und beobachtet die Symptomatik S. Aufgrund dieser Symptomatik trifft

er eine Entscheidung $d^1(S)$, die entweder eine terminale Entscheidung für eine Thera-
piemaßnahme $A_i$ oder eine experimentelle Entscheidung für die Fortsetzung der Diagnostik mit dem Verfahren $E_j^1$ sein kann. Bei experimentellen Entscheidungen wird der Prozeß
auf der nächsten (k+1-ten) Stufe wiederholt bis entweder eine terminale Entscheidung
getroffen wird oder eine vorgegebene Maximalzahl K von diagnostischen Stufen erreicht
ist. Im letzten Fall kommen als Entscheidungen für die K-te Stufe nur terminale Entscheidungen in Frage.

Der diagnostische Prozeß ist demnach durch eine Folge $D \doteq d^0(S), d_1(S), \ldots$ gekennzeichnet. Diese Folge D nennt man die diagnostische Strategie ($d^0$ ist unabhängig von S und
führt nur zu experimentellen Entscheidungen, die letzte Entscheidung $d^K(S)$ führt nur
zu terminalen Entscheidungen). Ist eine obere Grenze K vorgegeben, dann heißt die
Strategie geschlossen, sonst offen. In praxi muß aber die Folge stets endlich sein.
Das Problem besteht darin, "optimale" Strategien anzugeben. Zur Präzisierung des Begriffs "optimal" führen wir folgende Modellannahmen ein:
- Die Symptomatik S bei Anwendung eines diagnostischen Verfahrens $E_j^k$ ist Realisation
  einer Zufallsgröße, deren Verteilung von dem gewählten Verfahren und einem (dem Arzt
  unbekannten) Zustandsparameter $\theta$ des Patienten (z.B. seiner "wahren" Diagnose) ab-
  hängt: $P(S|\theta, E_j^k)$. Die möglichen Zustände $\theta$ werden ebenfalls als Zufallsgrößen mit
  einer a priori-Verteilung $p(\theta)$ aufgefaßt.
- Mit einer terminalen Entscheidung $A_i$ ist ein bestimmter Nutzen (utility) $u(A_i, \theta)$
  verknüpft. Dieser Nutzen kann z.B. monetär ausgedrückt und sowohl positiv (Gewinn)
  als auch negativ (Verlust) sein. Er hängt sowohl von $A_i$ als auch vom Zustand $\theta$ des
  Patienten ab.
- Mit einer experimentellen Entscheidung $E_j^k$ sind Kosten $k(E_j^k, \theta)$ verbunden, die ebenfalls monetär ausgedrückt werden können und sich aus "fixen" Kosten $k_f(E_j^k)$ und zufälligen "Risikokosten" $k_r(E_j^k, \theta)$ zusammensetzen. Die Risikokosten entstehen z.B.
  wenn dem Patienten ein Schaden zugefügt wird. $k_r(E_j^k, \theta)$ sind dann die "erwarteten"
  Schadenskosten.

Bei jedem diagnostischen Schritt k kann nun (unter der Bedingung der vorherigen Verfahren $E_j^{k-1}, \ldots, E_j^0$) der mittlere Gewinn G einer terminalen Entscheidung $A_i = d_t^k(S)$ und
der mittlere Verlust V einer experimentellen Entscheidung $E_j^k = d_e^k(S)$ berechnet werden:

$$G(d_t^k) = \int_\theta \int_S u(d_t^k(S), \theta) dP(S|\theta, E_j^{k-1}) dp(\theta)$$

$$V(d_e^k) = \int_\theta \int_S k(d_e^k(S), \theta) dP(S|\theta, E_j^{k-1}) dp(\theta)$$

(Man beachte, daß die Folge von Verfahren $E_j^k$ eine Markoffkette bildet.)

Es erscheint nun folgende Festlegung plausibel:

Eine Strategie wird an der Stelle K mit der terminalen Entscheidung $A_i = d_t^K(S)$ beendet, falls $G(d_t^K) \leqq V(d_e^K)$ ist.

Eine Strategie D* ist optimal (in einer Klasse von Strategien D), falls der Gesamtgewinn:

$$G = G(d_t^{*K}) - \sum_{k=1}^{K-1} V(d_e^{*k}) = Max(D)$$

Ein endlicher Endpunkt K existiert,falls $G(d_t^k)$ und $V(d_t^k)$ bestimmte Monotoniebedingungen erfüllen. Man kann dann, von diesem Endpunkt aus rückrechnend, die optimale Strategie D* bestimmen (vgl. auch [8]).


## Literatur


[ 1] Adlassnig, K.-P.: A Fuzzy Logical Model of Computer-Assisted Medical Diagnosis. Meth. Inform. Med. 19, 141-148, 1980

[ 2] Adlassnig, K.-P., Kolarz, G., Scheithauer, W.: Present State of the Medical Expert System CADIAG-2. Meth. Inform. Med. 24, 13-20, 1985

[ 3] Anderson, T.W.: An Introduction to·Multivariate Statistical Analysis. John Wiley, New York 1958

[ 4] Esogbue, A.O., Elder, R.C.: Fuzzy Sets and the Modelling of Physician Decision Processes, Part I: The Initial Interview-Information Gathering Session. Fuzzy sets and Systems 2, 279-291, 1979

[ 5] Gross, R.: Zur klinischen Dimension der Medizin. Hippokrates Verlag, Stuttgart 1976

[ 6] Lachenbruch, P.A.: Discriminant Analysis. Hafner Press, New York 1975

[ 7] Ledley, R.S.: Use of Computers in Biology and Medicine. McGraw-Hill, New York 1965

[ 8] Raiffa, H. and Schlaifer, R.: Applied Statistical Decision Theory. The M.I.T. Press, Cambridge, Mass. and London, 1968

[ 9] Schneider, B.: Mathematische Grundlagen der medizinischen Diagnostik. Computer: Werkzeug der Medizin (Herausgeber: C.T. Ehlers, N. Hollberg, A. Proppe), S. 160-182, Springer-Verlag, Berlin, Heidelberg, New York 1970

[10] Wagner, G., Tautu, P., Wolber, U.: Problems of Medical Diagnosis - A Bibliography. Meth. Inform. Med. 17, 55-74, 1978

[11] Zadeh, L.A.: Outline of a New Approach to the Analysis of Complex Systems and Decision Processes. IEEE Transactions on Systems, Man, and Cybernetics, SMC-3, 28-44, 1973

# MODELLBILDUNGS- UND SOFTWAREMETHODIK

MODELLBILDUNGS- UND SOFTWAREMETHODIK

# EIN BEISPIEL FÜR MODELLIERUNG UND SIMULATION MIT PETRINETZ-MODELLEN


Peter Winkler, Berlin



**Zusammenfassung**. Anhand eines kleinen Beispiels wird gezeigt, wie hierarchische Petrinetze zur Modellierung und Simulation diskreter Prozesse verwendet werden. Die zu simulierenden Systeme werden auf der abstraktesten Ebene in physische und steuernde Bereiche gegliedert. Die weitere Konstruktion ist "objektorientiert", d.h. das Modell bekommt die Gestalt von unabhängigen Objekten, die sich gegenseitig durch Botschaften beeinflussen. Diese Objekte entsprechen z.B. Maschinen in der Realität. Die Modellbildung wird unterstützt durch den Netzeditor des TOPAS-N-Systems. Ein Simulationswerkzeug in diesem System interpretiert die Modelle und berechnet Ereignisfolgen.

**Summary**. Modelling and simulation of discrete event processes with Petri nets is shown in a small example. The systems to be simulated are subdivided on the most abstract level of description into physical and control aspects. The further design is "object oriented", i.e. the model has the form of independent objects sending each other messages. The objects correspond to real devices, for instance machines. The TOPAS-N net editor supports model design. A simulation tool contained in this system interprets the models and computes sequences of events.


## 1.0 PETRINETZE ALS MODELLIERSPRACHE

Viele heute gebräuchlichen Simulationssysteme für Prozesse mit diskreten Ereignissen, die nicht für Spezialanwendungen sondern als Werkzeuge konstruiert wurden, weisen zweierlei Mängel auf :

1. Die Phasen der Modellerstellung und des Simulationsexperiments werden unzureichend voneinander unterschieden.

2. Modellerstellung ist zum überwiegenden Teil einfach "Programmieren". Im günstigen Fall existieren Standard-Modellbausteine als vorprogrammierte Unterprogramme. Für komplexere Steuerungsprobleme können aber solche Standards nicht existieren. Die Methoden zur Modellerstellung sind in solchen Fällen die gewöhnlichen Programmiermethoden.

Der Abbildung der Realität in Programmiersprachen setzen wir die Modellierung in Petrinetzen entgegen. Versuche in dieser Richtung sind schon mehrfach unternommen worden (Vgl. Vorträge der vorigen Symposien Simulationstechnik), führten jedoch kaum zu in relevantem Maßstab eingesetzten praktischen Systemen. Unseres Erachtens liegen die Ursachen dafür in der Wahl von Netzklassen mit ungenügender Ausdrucksfähigkeit und in zu wenig praxisbezogenen Modelliermethoden.

Einfache Stellen/Transitions-Netze, die gewöhnlich als Petrinetze bezeichnet werden, sind für große Modelle nicht geeignet. Reale Probleme sind zu umfangreich und komplex für deren praktischen Einsatz.

Die von uns verwendeten Netzmodelle bestehen aus zwei übereinandergeschichteten Netzhierarchien. Die Modellierung beginnt im Groben mit einer informellen Hierarchie von **Kanal/Instanz-Netzen** (K/I-Netze) zur Beschreibung des Informationsflusses zwischen Subsystemen des Modells. Diese Netze bestehen aus Instanzen, die als Rechtecke gezeichnet werden, Kanälen (Kreise) und Pfeilen, die von Instanz zu Kanal oder von Kanal zu Instanz gehen. Man beschreibt mit den Instanzen Teilsysteme, die nur lose miteinander gekoppelt sind. Die Kanäle stellen den Informationsfluß zwischen diesen Systemen dar. Instanzen können in feinere Kanal/Instanz-Netze zerlegt werden. Wir nennen sie dann "Netzmoduln".

Wenn eine detailliertere Beschreibung des Informationsflusses in einer Instanz nicht mehr interessiert und wenn statt dessen der kausale Mechanismus, das Verhalten der Instanz, beschrieben werden soll, ändert sich die Art der Zerlegung. Die Substruktur enthält dann statt eines Kanal/Instanz-Netzes eine Hierarchie von **Prädikat/Transitions-Netzen** (PrT-Netze). Sie stellen ein sehr mächtiges Ausdrucksmittel für dynamische Systeme dar.

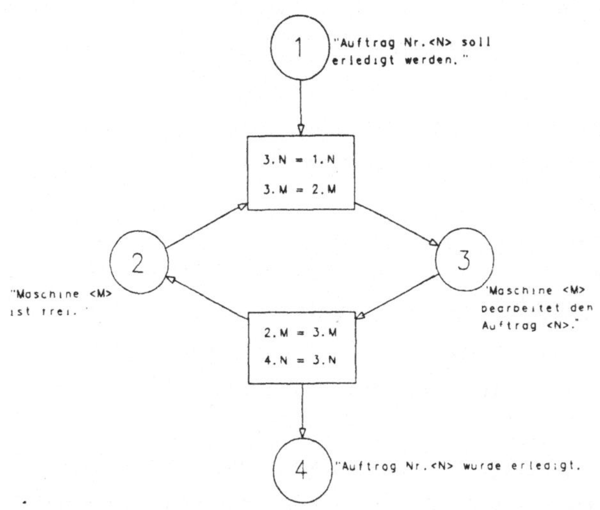


Abb.1    Ein Prädikat/Transitions-Netz

Die Abb.1 zeigt ein einfaches PrT-Netz. Dargestellt ist eine Menge von Maschinen, die Aufträge  bearbeiten können. Die Stellen (1) bis (4) sind mit Prädikaten wie "Auftrag Nr. <N> soll erledigt werden." beschriftet. Diese Prädikate sind informelle Texte bis auf die Variablen, die sie enthalten. <N> ist eine solche Variable. Ein solches Prädikat wird zur wahren Aussage, wenn die Stelle "markiert" wird. Beim Prädikat (1) bedeutet das, daß ein Auftrag vorliegt. Dieser Auftrag hat dann auch eine Nummer, also einen Wert für die Variable <N>. Man kann sich vorstellen, daß die Stelle (1) mit einer Marke belegt ist, die einen Wert für <N> trägt. Es können auch mehrere Marken auf einer Stelle vorhanden sein. Dann liegen bei (1) mehrere Aufträge vor. Beispielsweise gelten dann die Aussagen

> "Auftrag Nr.13 soll erledigt werden."
>
> "Auftrag Nr.4 soll erledigt werden."
>
> "Auftrag Nr.54 soll erledigt werden."
>
> "Auftrag Nr.162 sollerledigt werden."

Damit das Modell funktionieren kann, werden auch Maschinen benötigt. Dazu wird die Stelle (2) mit Marken belegt. Nehmen wir an, wir hätten zwei Maschinen "A" und "B". Durch zwei Marken auf (2) die die Werte A und B für <M> tragen, machen wir die Aussagen

> "Maschine A ist frei."
>
> "Maschine B ist frei."

gültig. Die Markierung von (1) und (2) ist die Voraussetzung für ein Ereignis, das in der oberen Transition (Rechteck) beschrieben ist. Alle Vorbedingungen zu ihrem Schalten sind erfüllt. Wenn das Ereignis stattfindet, wird je eine Marke von den beiden Vorgängerstellen entfernt. Dies können z.B. die Marken mit den Aussagen

> "Maschine B ist frei." und
>
> "Auftrag Nr.54 soll erledigt werden."

sein. Gleichzeitig wird eine neue Marke auf die Nachfolgerstelle (3) gelegt. Beim Ereignis müssen Werte für die Variablen in "Maschine <M> bearbeitet den Auftrag <N>." gefunden werden. Die Regeln dafür stehen in der Transition, die zu dem Ereignis gehört. Da die Variablennamen ·<N> und <M> nicht eindeutig sind sondern in verschiedenen Prädikaten vorkommen, wurden sie durch das Davorschreiben des Labels (1), (2) oder (3) eindeutig gemacht. "3.N=1.N" bedeutet, daß die Nummer des Auftrags, der bearbeitet wird (3.N), identisch ist mit der Nummer des Auftrags, der erledigt werden sollte (1.N). Statt solcher einfachen Gleichungen können hier natürlich in großen Modellen sehr viel umfangreichere Ausdrücke stehen.

Für Simulationen ist es unerläßlich, die Modelle mit Zeiten zu bewerten. Als Zeitmodell enthalten die Netzmodelle eine "Abkürzung" des Modells einer globalen Uhr: In die Transitionen wird eine "Aktivierungszeit" eingetragen, die angibt, wie lange die Vorbedingungen für ein Ereignis gegolten haben müssen, bevor das Ereignis stattfinden kann. Im Beispiel kann die untere Transition mit einer solchen Aktivierungszeit versehen werden. Sie hat die Bedeutung, daß das zugehörige Ereignis (das Ende der Bearbeitung) erst stattfinden darf, wenn diese Aktivierungszeit verstrichen ist. Diese Aktivierungszeit ist also ein Modell der Bearbeitungsdauer. Die Aktivierungszeiten können sowohl Konstanten als auch Werte aus Zufallsverteilungen oder Funktionen von Prädikatsvariablen sein.

## 2.0 METHODIK DER MODELLBILDUNG

Für Simulationsmodelle von Produktionsanlagen wird eine Grundstruktur aus verschiedenen Betrachtungsbereichen verwendet. Es wird mindestens zwischen einem Modell der physischen Anlage und einem Modell der Steuerung dieser Anlage unterschieden. Wenn verschiedene Typen von Produkten oder Werkstücken detailliert betrachtet werden sollen, ist es sinnvoll, Modelle des Bearbeitungsfortschritts bzw. der Bewegung von Produkten und Werkstücken und einen Bereich der Arbeitspläne für die Produkte hinzuzufügen. Die oberste Netzebene enthält diese Betrachtungsbereiche als kommunizierende Netzmoduln. Abb.2 zeigt ein Beispiel der obersten Netzebene. Die Netzmoduln sind die mit 1M und 2M beschrifteten Knoten.

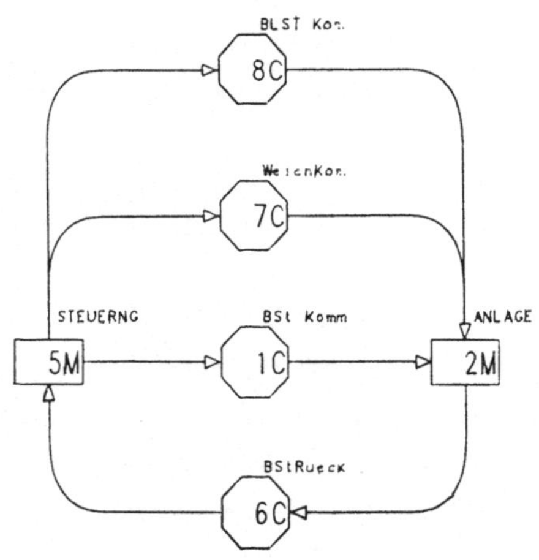



Abb.2    Die abstrakteste Netzebene

Das einzig Spezielle für die in diesem Beispiel zu simulierende Anlage sind die Schnittstellen zwischen den vier Bereichen. Das sind die als Achtecke dargestellten Kanäle.

Grundsätzlich wird objektorientiert modelliert. D.h. Objekte der realen Welt, die ein eigenständiges Verhalten aufweisen, werden als Netzmoduln oder Instanzen in einem der Modellbereiche dargestellt. Die Modellierung beginnt mit dem Bereich der physischen Anlage. Anlagenteile wie Bearbeitungsstationen oder Blockstrecken des Fördersystems werden als Netzmoduln und Instanzen abgebildet. Um die Darstellung anschaulicher zu gestalten, werden eigene grafische Symbole für die Anlagenteile statt der Rechtecke und Kreise eingesetzt.

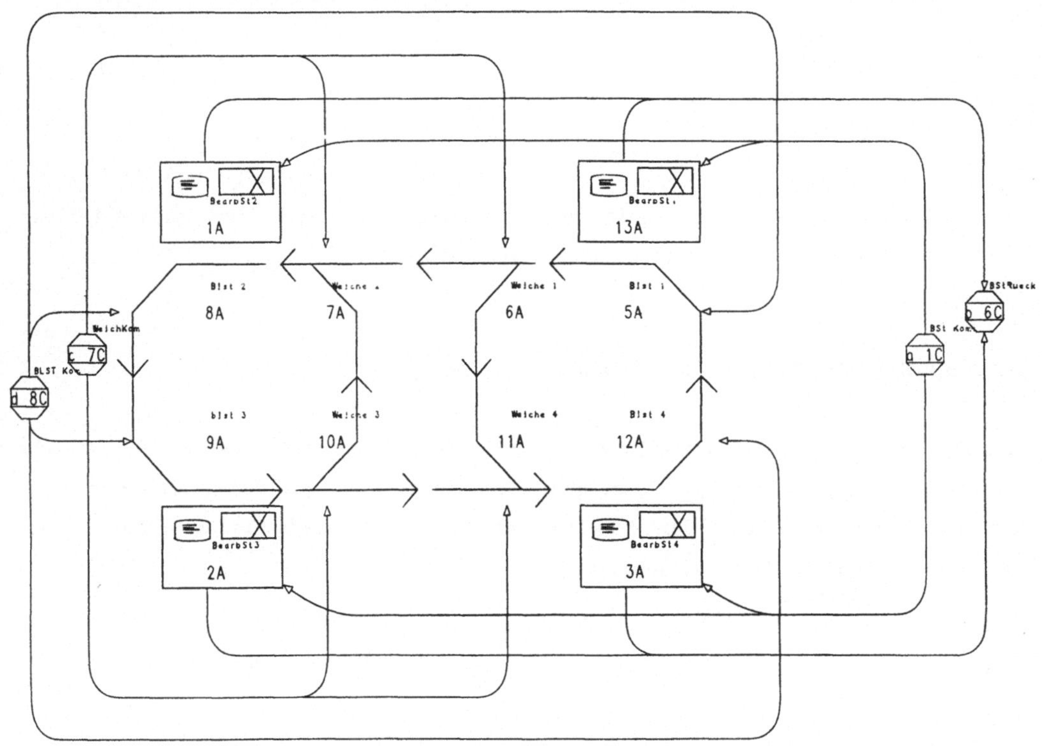


Abb.3  Die Anlage

Abb.3 zeigt eine Anlage mit vier Bearbeitungsstationen und einem Transportsystem, das sie verbindet. Das Transportsystem ist in Blockstrecken und Weichen gegliedert, die einzeln aus dem Bereich der übergeordneten Steuerung kontrolliert werden. Die Achtecke symbolisieren die Schnittstellenkanäle zur Steuerung, die bereits in Abb.2 sichtbar sind.

Die Substruktur einer Instanz beschreibt das Verhalten eines Objekts, wobei wir zwischen Normal- und Ausnahmeverhalten unterscheiden. Es zeigt sich in den Zuständen eines Objekts und den Übergängen dazwischen. Diese werden als Stellen und Transitionen eines Prädikat/Transitions-Netzes abgebildet.

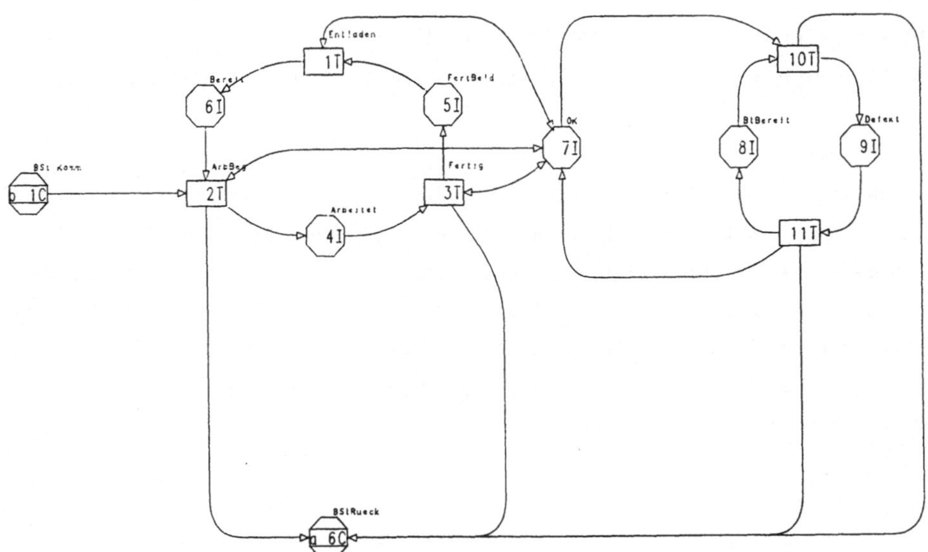

Abb.4   Das Verhalten einer Bearbeitungsstation

Jedes Objekt in der Anlage hat sein Abbild im Steuerungsbereich, das   ausschließlich
mit diesem Anlagenteil und keinem anderen kommuniziert.


## 3.0   TOPAS-N ZUR MODELLERSTELLUNG UND SIMULATION

Die hier besprochenen Netzmodelle werden   mit   dem   Netzeditor   des   TOPAS-N-Systems
erstellt.   Es   handelt   sich   dabei um einen interaktiven grafischen Editor, der die
syntaktische Korrektheit der Modelle   abprüft   und   verschiedene   Arten   von
Dokumentationen von Modellen erzeugen kann.

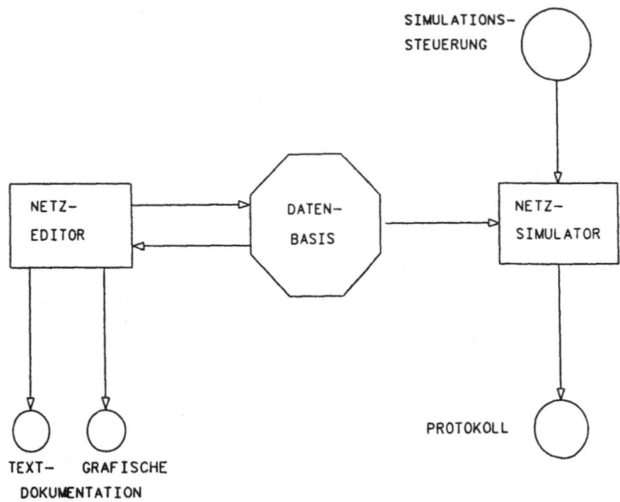


Abb.  Das TOPAS-N-Werkzeugsystem

Die Abbildungen in diesem Aufsatz wurden mit dem TOPAS-Netzeditor erstellt. Das zweite Werkzeug aus TOPAS-N ist der Simulator. Er interpretiert die Netzmodelle und berechnet eine mögliche (zufällige) Folge von Ereignissen. Ereignisse und Stellenmarkierungen werden protokolliert und statistisch ausgewertet. Voraussetzung für die Simulation ist die Angabe von Anfangsbedingungen sowie Protokollierungseinschränkungen und Abbruchbedingungen.


**LITERATUR**

W.Reisig
Systementwurf mit Netzen
Springer 1985

P.Winkler
Anforderungsbeschreibungen und Simulation
mit NET-Modellen
in
Hrsg. G.Hommel, D.Krönig
Requirements Engineering
Springer 1983

#### EIN-MARKEN-PETRINETZE UND SYNCHRONE SCHALTWERKE

Armin Schöne, Bremen

Zusammenfassung: Es wird gezeigt, daß das Zustandsdiagramm einer geeigneten Repräsentation eines Ein-Marken-Petrinetzes durch ein synchrones Schaltwerk auch das Petrinetz beschreibt, wenn man das Zustandsdiagramm in bestimmter Weise interpretiert.

Summary: It is shown that the state diagram of an adequate representation of a marked Petri net with one token by a synchronous sequential system describes the Petri net itself, if the state diagram is interpreted in a certain way.

## 1. Einführung

Einer der Wege zur Bildung eines Modells eines Systems ist die Entwicklung eines Petrinetzes, einer besonderen mathematischen Beschreibung des betrachteten Systems. Man erwartet oder hofft, mit Hilfe eines solchen Modells wichtige Informationen, zum Beispiel über den Aufbau und das dynamische Verhalten des nachgebildeten Systems zu gewinnen.

Zweifellos ist ein besonderes mathematisches Werkzeug nicht in gleicher Weise für die Bildung von Modellen aller überhaupt in Frage kommenden Systeme geeignet. So dienen Petrinetze vor allem dazu, die Organisation von Systemen zu beschreiben, für deren Verhalten unterschiedliche Ereignisse kennzeichnend oder bedeutsam sind. Daher kann man Petrinetze dort anwenden, wo bei einer Systembeschreibung diskrete Werte der Systemvariablen maßgebend sind, mit anderen Worten, bei Systemen, die (auch) als digitale Systeme beschrieben werden können. Als besonderer Vorzug einer Darstellung durch Petrinetze wird u.a. angegeben, daß durch sie kausale Abhängigkeiten innerhalb einer Menge von Ereignissen explizit dargestellt werden können, wohingegen streng sequentielle Modelle das Gefüge von Prozessen kaum widerspiegeln und zum Beispiel nicht erkennen lassen, ob ein Ereignis von einem anderen, zeitlich vorangehenden Ereignis abhängig ist oder nicht /1/.

Man unterscheidet in der Regel zwischen einer abstrakten mathematischen Beschreibung von Petrinetzen und spricht dann auch von einer "Netztheorie" und Interpretationen oder Repräsentationen von Petrinetzen. Letztere können entweder zur Veranschaulichung des Inhalts der Netztheorie dienen oder ergeben sich aufgrund von Anwendungen.

Petrinetze gehören zu den gerichteten Graphen mit zwei unterschiedlichen Arten von Knoten. Für diese wurden unterschiedliche Benennungen eingeführt, zum Beispiel "Ereignis" für die eine Art von Knoten und "Zustand" für die andere Art. Teils einführende, teil eingehendere Definitionen der Petrinetze und Darstellungen ihrer Theorie und Anwendungsmöglichkeiten findet man zum Beispiel in /1/ bis /4/, vgl. auch /5/.

Da Modelle digitaler Systeme als Petrinetze entwickelt werden können, lassen sich gerade auch Schaltwerke (also zum Beispiel digitale Datenverarbeitungsanlagen) mittels Petrinetzen beschreiben. Andererseits werden Schaltwerke oder digitale Datenverarbeitungsanlagen selbst als Modelle anderer digitaler Systeme bzw. als Hilfsmittel zur Erstellung solcher Modelle benutzt.


## 2. Repräsentationen von Ein-Marken-Petrinetzen durch Schaltwerke

Nicht zuletzt die konkurrierende Anwendungsmöglichkeit von Modellen auf der Basis von Petrinetzen und von Schaltwerken wirft die Frage auf, in welchem Verhältnis solche Modelle zueinander stehen. Da ein Petrinetz im Kern abstrakt mathematisch aufzufassen ist, während man bei einem Schaltwerk letztlich an eine technische Realisierung denkt, kann man also nach Repräsentationen von Petrinetzen durch Schaltwerke fragen. Doch hat auch die Realisierung eines Schaltwerkes einen abstrakt mathematisch zu verstehenden und beschreibbaren Inhalt.

Bei Petrinetzen unterscheidet man zwischen der statischen Struktur - gegeben durch die Anordnung der gerichteten Kanten und der Knoten - und der dynamischen Struktur. Letztere ergibt sich durch die Anzahl der zulässigen Belegung jeweils eines "Zustandes" durch "Marken", eine (positiv) ganzzahlige Gewichtung der Kanten und aus Regeln, nach denen ermittelt wird, ob ein "Ereignis" "schalten" kann. Letzteres hängt von der Gewichtung der am "Ereignis" angreifenden Kanten, der jeweiligen Anzahl der zulässigen Markierungen der benachbarten "Zustände" und der Anzahl der bei den benachbarten Zuständen tatsächlich vorhandenen Marken ab. Ob ein "Ereignis" wirklich "schaltet", läßt die Petrinetztheorie offen.

Bei Schaltwerken erwartet man hingegen, daß sie wirklich "schalten", d.h. ihre inneren Zustände ändern. Bei asynchronen Schaltwerken erfolgt dies unter dem Einfluß sämtlicher Schaltvariabler. Bei synchronen Schaltwerken hängt die Art eines Zustandsüberganges zwar auch von sämtlichen Variablen (inneren Zustandsvariablen, Eingangsvaria - blen) ab.Die eigentlichen Zustandsübergänge werden jedoch durch besondere Variable (Taktvariable) ausgelöst. Es ist zweckmäßig, in einem synchronen Schaltwerk nur eine einzige Taktvariable zu verwenden.

An anderer Stelle wurde gezeigt, auf welche Weise die Repräsentation von Synchronisationsnetzen - d.h. von Ein-Marken-Petrinetzen ohne Zustandsverzweigungen - aus dem jeweils zugehörigen Petrinetz abgeleitet werden kann /5/. Das Verfahren ist unmittelbar auch für andere Ein-Marken-Petrinetze anwendbar. Die "Ereignisse" des betrachteten Petrinetzes seien hierfür fortlaufend numeriert. Die "Zustände" (und entsprechend die inneren Zustandsvariablen der Repräsentation durch ein synchrones Schaltwerk) können dann durch $P_{\ldots,\mu,\ldots/\ldots,\nu,\ldots}$ gekennzeichnet werden, wobei die $\mu$ die Nummern der Eingangsereignisse und $\nu$ die Nummern der Ausgangsereignisse des betreffenden "Zustands" sind. In entsprechender Weise, wie in /5/ für Synchronisationsnetze gezeigt wurde, und mit den dort eingeführten Definitionen findet man auch im hier betrachteten allgemeineren Fall die Repräsentation des Petrinetzes durch ein synchrones Schaltwerk, indem man die "Ereignisse" durch bestimmte Schaltnetze und die "Zustände" durch bestimmte Schaltwerke beschreibt. Falls Verzweigungs- oder Wettbewerbskonflikte auftreten, kann man z.B. vorschreiben, daß das Petrinetz nicht schalten darf. In der schaltalgebraischen Beschreibung der Repräsentation des Petrinetzes sind diese Konflikte durch Nebenbedingungen (vgl. /6/) zu berücksichtigen. Am einfachsten ist es jedoch, die aus der zeichnerischen Darstellung des Petrinetzes abgelesenen Zusammenhänge unmittelbar in eine Übergangstabelle zu übertragen. Daraus ergibt sich dann sofort das Zustandsdiagramm.

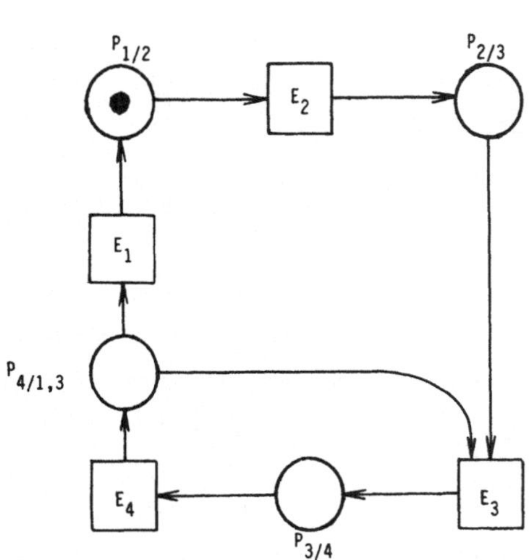

Bild 1. Beispiel eines einfachen Ein-Marken-Petrinetzes, in dem gerade der Zustand $P_{1/2}$ markiert ist.

Ein einfaches Beispiel für ein Ein-Marken-Petrinetz dieser allgemeineren Art zeigt Bild 1. Dieses Petrinetz wird nach dem erwähnten Verfahren durch ein synchrones Schaltwerk "realisiert" (bzw. die abstrakte Beschreibung des Schaltwerks entspricht dem Synchronisationsnetz nach Bild 1), dessen Zustandsdiagramm in Bild 2 dargestellt ist. (Zu dieser Beschreibungsform vgl. man /6/).

In diesem Zustandsdiagramm erkennt man die Markierung eines "Zustandes" im Petrinetz daran, daß die zugehörige "innere Zustandsvariable" des Schaltwerks den Wert L annimmt. Ähnlich wie im Petrinetz die Markierung jeweils auf den oder die nächstfolgenden "Zustände" übergeht, wenn ein Ereignis stattfindet, so wandert im Zustandsdiagramm des synchronen Schaltwerks bei den dem "Schalten" der Ereignisse

139

$E_1, \ldots, E_4$ entsprechenden Zustandsübergängen der Wert L von den die Ein-
gangs-"Zustände" des "Ereignisses"
kennzeichnenden inneren Zustandsvariablen zu den die Ausgangs-"Zustände"
des "Ereignisses" kennzeichnenden.

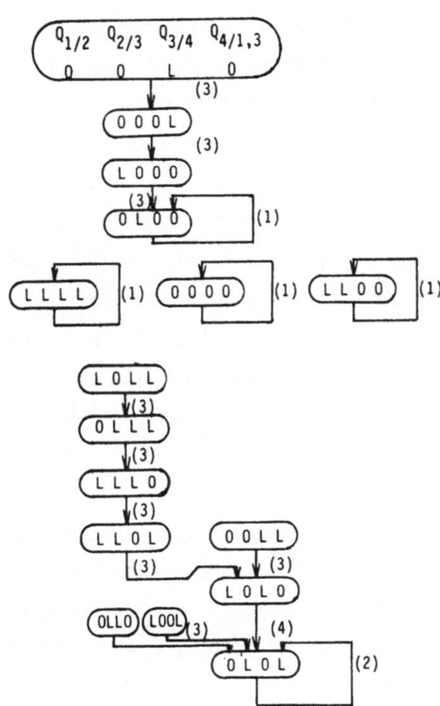


Bild 2. Zustandsdiagramm des Schaltwerks,
durch das das Petrinetz nach Bild 1 repräsentiert
wird.
(1) kein Ereignis schaltet
(2) kein Ereignis schaltet (Verzweigungskonflikt)
(3) ein Ereignis schaltet
(4) zwei Ereignisse schalten

## 3. Interpretation des Zustandsdiagramms eines synchronen Schaltwerks als Beschreibung eines Ein-Marken-Petrinetzes

Vereinbarungsgemäß wird jeder markier-
te "Zustand" des Petrinetzes durch den
Wert "L" der betreffenden inneren Zustandsvariablen und jeder nicht mar-
kierte durch den Wert 0 gekennzeichnet.
Für jeden "Zustand" des Ein-Marken-
Petrinetzes wurde genau eine innere
Zustandsvariable eingeführt. Unter
Beachtung der für Zustandsdiagramme
synchroner Schaltwerke geltenden Zusammenhänge kann man daher die Regel
angeben: Das vollständige Zustandsdiagramm der gewählten Repräsentation
eines Ein-Marken-Petrinetzes durch
ein Schaltwerk gibt alle Möglichkeiten
der Markierung der "Zustände" dieses Petrinetzes und alle Möglichkeiten des "Schaltens"
der "Ereignisse" des Petrinetzes an.

Erwähnt sei, daß bei Anwendungen von Petrinetzen in der Regel keineswegs sämtliche
der aus dem vollständigen Zustandsdiagramm ersichtlichen Markierungen und damit
keinesweg sämtliche möglichen Folgen von Markierungen benötigt werden.

Es ist bekannt, daß Petrinetze auch nebenläufige Vorgänge beschreiben, während ein
(synchrones) Schaltwerk sich immer nur in einem bestimmten (inneren) Zustand, gekennzeichnet jeweils durch eine bestimmte Wertekombination der (inneren Zustands-)varia-
blen, befinden kann. (Die Zeitpunkte von Zustandsübergängen werden beim synchronen
Schaltwerk durch den zeitlichen Verlauf der Taktvariablen in Verbindung mit speziellen
Eigenschaften der Speicherelemente vorgegeben.) Warum beschreibt Bild 2 gleichzeitig
zwei Systeme mit offensichtlich unterschiedlichen Eigenschaften? Der Grund liegt

allein in einer teilweise unterschiedlichen Interpretation von Bild 2. Betrachtet sei als Beispiel der Übergang vom inneren Zustand LOLO. In der Schaltwerkstheorie sagt man, das Schaltwerk geht vom inneren Zustand LOLO in den inneren Zustand OLOL über, sobald die entsprechende Taktbedingung vorliegt. Im übrigen kann sich das (synchrone) Schaltwerk zu irgendeinem Zeitpunkt nur in einem der möglichen inneren Zustände befinden. In der Netztheorie sagt man, irgendwann seien die "Zustände" $P_{1/2}$ und $P_{3/4}$ gleichzeitig markiert (hier entsprechend $Q_{1/2}$=L und $Q_{3/4}$=L). Nach der Schaltregel (d.h. weil $P_{2/3}$ und $P_{4/1,3}$ hier nicht markiert sind) könnten die "Ereignisse" $E_2$ und $E_4$ (gleichzeitig, also nebenläufig) schalten, was zur Folge hätte, daß danach $P_{2/3}$ und $P_{4/1,3}$ markiert und $P_{1/2}$ und $P_{3/4}$ nicht markiert sind. Daß die Ereignisse $E_2$ und $E_4$ hier wirklich schalten, schreibt die Netztheorie nicht vor. Sie überläßt es vielmehr dem Anwender, durch geeignete Interpretationen zu entscheiden, ob $E_2$ und $E_4$ (sogar vielleicht auch nur $E_2$ oder nur $E_4$) schalten.

Die dargestellten Zusammenhänge gelten für sämtliche Ein-Marken-Petrinetze. Erwähnt sei noch, daß zur Beschreibung von Ein-Marken-Petrinetzen Zustandsdiagramme von Schaltwerken in der Form nach Bild 2 zwar ausreichen. Zur Beschreibung von Schaltwerken benötigt man im allgemeinen aber neben "inneren Zustandsvariablen" auch "Eingangsvariable" und "Ausgangsvariable" und dementsprechend erweiterte Formen von Zustandsdiagrammen/6/.


Literatur

/1/ Reisig, W.: Petrinetze. Eine Einführung. Springer-Verlag, Berlin, Heidelberg, New York 1982.

/2/ Starke, P.H.: Petri-Netze. Grundlagen, Anwendungen, Theorie. Deutscher Verlag der Wissenschaften, Berlin 1980.

/3/ Rosenstengel, B. u. U. Winand: Petri-Netze. Eine anwendungsorientierte Einführung. Friedr. Vieweg & Sohn, Braunschweig, Wiesbaden 1982 (2. Auflage 1983).

/4/ Peterson, J.L.: Petri Net Theory and the Modeling of Systems. Prentice-Hall, Englewood Cliffs, N.J. 1981.

/5/ Schöne, A.: Über die Realisierung von Petrinetzen durch Schaltwerke. Angewandte Informatik (1985) H. 4, S. 160-166.

/6/ Schöne, A.: Digitaltechnik und Mikrorechner. Friedr. Vieweg & Sohn, Braunschweig, Wiesbaden 1984.

# Zur Simulation von Zufall und Verläßlichkeit

Hans Fuss, Bonn

*Zusammenfassung:*    *Zufällige Ereignisse in dem betrachteten Real-System (Urbild) und im zugehörigen Modell-System (Abbild).   Erwartungen an den Zufall, globale Randbedingungen; Zufälligkeiten und Regelmäßigkeiten, Fairneß.   Darstellung eines freien und eines (durch den Synchronie-Abstand) gebundenen ("fairen") Zufalls-Generators mittels Petri-Netze.*

*Summary:  Random events in the real system (source) and in its mapping, the model. Expectations on the random of choice and regularities; global restrictions. Constructions of a free and of a 'fair' random number generator (bound through the synchronic distance) with Petri nets.*

## 1.  Einführung, Beispiele

In vielen Simulationsprogrammen spielen **zufällige Ereignisse,** ausgelöst oder gesteuert durch einen Zufallsgenerator *(random number generator)*, eine bedeutende Rolle.

Sie werden vornehmlich benutzt

 ▷ als konfliktentscheidende Instanz, so zum Festlegen einer Reihenfolge unter sonst gleichrangigen oder gleichzeitigen Ereignissen (Aktivitäten);

 ▷ als Input, so z.B. zum Bedienen einer Warteschlange oder zum Erzeugen "stochastischer", also zufällig entstandener Daten.

Dahinter steckt natürlich die Auffassung, daß es in der realen Welt genauso Ereignisse gibt, die man als zufallsgesteuert ansehen muß. Einige Beispiele für solche Situationen:

 ○ An einem Spieltisch, bei dem das Werfen einer Münze den Gewinn bestimmt, trat bei den letzten 20 Würfen nur dreimal "Zahl" ein, davon bei den letzten zwölf hintereinander nur "Adler" – so hat ein neu hinzukommender Mitspieler beobachtet — worauf setzt er sein Geld?

 ○ Das Paradoxon von der unerwarteten Hinrichtung (s. M.Gardener, nach[†] M.Scriven in *Mind* 1951): Dem Verurteilten wird als Bestandteil des Urteils mitgegeben, daß er an einem Tag der nächsten Woche gehenkt werden würde, aber er werde nicht wissen, noch nicht einmal am Vortage, an welchem Tage. Die Argumentation seines Verteidigers: Das Urteil könne gar nicht vollstreckt werden; denn: der Sonntag (7. Tag) fiele aus, denn dann wüßte er es am Samstag. Der Samstag, der es dann ja nur noch spätestens sein könne, kann es nicht sein, denn als nunmehr letzter Tag wüßte man es ja am Freitag, etc. – Doch zufällig und unerwartet klopft der Henker am Mittwochmorgen an die Tür.

 ○ Die Auswahl einer Stichprobe, um von ihr auf die Gesamtheit rückzuschließen, z.B. bei der Hochrechnung von Wahlergebnissen.

 ○ Die Ziehung der Lottozahlen.

 ○ Wie oft betreten Kunden einen Laden, und in welchen Zeitabständen?

---

[†] Möglicherweise schon in Rätselform in der altgriechischen Literatur bekannt; Hinweise sind willkommen

## 2. Terminologie

Zur Terminologie einiger Begriffe aus der Modelliersprache:

Wir wollen hier mit $R$ ein reales System aus der realen Welt bezeichnen, dem unsere Aufmerksamkeit gilt. Dieses reale System $R$ wollen wir in $M$, ein Modellsystem (oder kurz: Modell) in der Modellwelt, abbilden und dort mithilfe von Simulationsmethoden untersuchen.

Daß die Modellwelt wiederum ein Teil der Realität ist, stört nicht – im Gegenteil: deshalb sind Modelle von Modellen möglich; es handelt sich also hier nur um einen abstrakten Unterscheidungsprozeß. Ebensogut mag das betrachtete Original-System auch schon ein Modell sein.

Eine besondere Bedeutung spielt noch *nicht-R*, d.h. der Teil des Universums, der zwar zur Realität (nicht Modell), aber nicht zu $R$ gehört, er heiße die zu $R$ gehörige *Umgebung (environment)*.

Die Abgrenzung zwischen $R$ und *nicht-R* ist dabei zunächst Definitionssache, ist also willkürlich; sie wird sich aber natürlich nach der Situation und der fachlichen Fragestellung richten und ist deshalb oftmals ganz natürlich. Dadurch ergibt sich bei $M$ die Abgrenzung dann zwangsläufig.

Die Abgrenzung zwischen $R$ und *nicht-R* ist andererseits Definitions*pflicht* des Modellbauers, also seine originäre Leistung, die mit über die Güte des Modells und die Qualität der Ergebnisse entscheidet. Denn hier wird festgelegt, welche Zusammenhänge über Modellvariablen modelliert werden sollen, und welche Einflüsse als *"exogene"* Parameter betrachtet werden.

Von *"zufallsabhängigen"* Parametern zu reden ist also eine Umschreibung für solche Einflüsse, die *nicht* kausal im jeweils betrachteten System stattfinden, die also von systemfremden oder *"höhergeordneten"* Parametern gesteuert werden. Solche Parameter haben also ihre Kausalität – zumindest teilweise – in der *System-Umgebung*.

Wir nennen $\vec{M}$, oder kurz: $M$, den Vorgang der *Modellbildung* von $R$ nach $M$, und $\overleftarrow{R}$, oder kurz $R$, den Abblidungs-Vorgang des *Rückschließens* von $M$ nach $R$, es sind Vorgänge, zwischen denen in den verschiedenen Phasen (Modellbildung, Modellverwertung) wohl zu unterscheiden ist.

## 3. Problematik: Zufall gegenüber Verläßlichkeit

Nun ist die Benutzung von Zufallsgeneratoren in Simulationsprogrammen oftmals nicht problemadäquat (definiert sie ja möglicherweise kausale Abhängigkeiten des realen Systems in "unbekannte" Einflüsse im Modellsystem um), aber auch sonst nicht ganz problemfrei in ihrer Anwendung:

 ▷ bei den Zufallszahlengeneratoren handelt es sich wohl eher um *Pseudo*-Zufallszahlen-Generatoren, nämlich um Programme, die, sofern sie mehrfach von derselben Basis aufgerufen werden, auch mehrfach nacheinander dieselben Zahlenkolonnen erzeugen – was beim Programmtest wegen der Wiederholbarkeit zu Irrtümern führen kann;

 ▷ manchmal aber ist der **reine Zufall** gar nicht das, was der Modell-Entwerfer bei der System-Spezifikation angeben möchte. Denkbar ist doch auch, daß er Zufallsverteilung *und* eine gewisse Regelmäßigkeit haben möchte, wenn nämlich bestimmte globale Randbedingungen mit erfüllt werden sollten.

Dem letztgenannten Fall seien die nun folgenden Betrachtungen gewidmet. Er hat seine besondere Bedeutung in der Praxis.

Aus dieser Praxis-Relevanz fragen wir uns: Ist es möglich und sinnvoll, gewisse Anforderungen an den Zufallsmechanismus zu stellen und ihn gar nicht so zufällig wirken zu lassen, wie die mathematische, die wahrscheinlichkeitstheoretische Definition des Zufalls es eigentlich erforderte? Treten irgendwo in der Realität sinnvollerweise solche Anforderungen auf? Benennen wir manchmal in unserer realen Welt etwas als "zufällig", was es in Wirklichkeit gar nicht ist?

Stimmt die Auffassung von "zufällig", die man im praktischen Leben hat, vielleicht gar nicht mit der mathematischen Definition von "zufällig" überein, und liefern damit die mathematischen Zufallsgeneratoren gar nicht das, was der Praktiker haben wollte?

Ergeben sich nicht schon allein daraus (notwendigerweise) Mißverständnisse zwischen denjenigen Fachleuten, die ein System und die Spezifikation des Modells angeben, und den Fachleuten, die das Modell erstellen und die zugehörige Simulation durchführen?

Eine unserer Kernfragen soll sein: Inwieweit kann man sich auf den Zufall derart verlassen, daß er sich a) vernünftig, b) zufällig verhält?

In dem eingangs genannten Spieler-Beispiel kann man
a) von der Annahme ausgehen, unter idealen Spielbedingungen sind die Wahrscheinlichkeiten für *Zahl* und *Wappen* gleich, nämlich 1/2, und man setze deshalb sein Geld mal so, mal so; genauer, bzw. wenn dieses Spiel nur einmal gespielt wird: man baue sich einen Zufallsmechanismus, der ebendiese Wahrscheinlichkeiten (1/2 : 1/2) produziert, und setze sein Geld entsprechend;
b) die Ansicht vertreten "... jetzt muß doch endlich *Zahl* kommen..." und darauf setzen; dabei sind es nicht nur die naiven Auffassungen eines unbedarften Alltagsmenschen, die dazu führen können, sondern ebenso die wahrscheinlichkeitstheoretischen Überlegungen über die Länge von Sequenzen und deren Häufigkeit;
c) schlichtweg vermuten, die Münze bzw. der Wurfmechanismus sei falsch, und zwar in eben dem beobachteten Verhältnis 3:17, und demzufolge auf die öfter fallende *Wappen*-seite setzen.

## 4. Aufgabenstellung: Ein "fairer" Zufallsgenerator

Als Beispiele für genauere Untersuchungen wählen wir die folgende Aufgaben: zwei Stationen A und B sollen zufällig bedient werden; in einem Fall soll A "im Schnitt" doppelt so oft wie B, im anderen (einfacheren) Fall sollen A und B gleichverteilt, also "gleich fair" bedient werden.

Wie "un-zufällig" diese Spezifikation ist, und welche weitreichenden Konsequenzen sie hat, wird auf den ersten Blick gar nicht so deutlich.

Wählen wir einen mathematisch weitgehend korrekten Zufallsgenerator Z, der "a" und "b" gleichverteilt (bzw. im anderen Falle im Verhältnis 2:1) produziert, so erscheint es uns schnell fraglich, ob er tatsächlich das Gewünschte liefert. Denn bei der *endlichen Lebensdauer* des Bedienprozesses, vielleich aber auch schon wegen anderer realer Zwänge viel früher, sollen beide Prozesse A und B auch tatsächlich drangekommen sein, und zwar in dem obengenannten Verhältnis. Doch nichts hindert Z daran, in einem (anfänglichen) Zeitabschnitt *immer nur a* und *niemals* ein *b* zu produzieren — das ist zwar recht unwahrscheinlich, jedoch nicht unmöglich. Insofern erscheint es sinnvoll, die eigentlich mögliche totale Willkür des Zufalls etwas einzuengen.

Ein Zufallsgenerator, der zwecks Gleichverteilung a und b abwechselnd liefert, ist offensichtlich unangebracht, denn dann könnte man ja das nächste Ereignis vorhersagen – und das soll ja bei einem zufälligen Ereignis nun wirklich nicht der Fall sein dürfen.

## 5. Lösungsversuche

Mithilfe von Petri-Netzen wird nun aufgezeigt, wie man den oben spezifizierten Sachverhalt korrekt beschreiben und ein ebenso korrektes Modell hierfür erstellen kann.

Zunächst modellieren wir die einfache Aufgabe, daß ein Zufallsgenerator die Stationen A und B
a) gleich, b) im Verhältnis 1:2   frei bedienen soll, in der Netzsprache.

Vernachlässigen wir hier in der ersten Darstellungs-Phase zunächst einmal die Netz-Ergänzungen, die noch nötig wären, um an den betreffenden Stellen Überlauf zu verhindern, dann zeigt sich die Konstruktionsidee dabei deutlich: während im linken Bild der Zufallsgenerator Z rein zufällig die Stellen (a) oder (b) füllt, von denen dann das Funktionieren der Prozesse [A] bzw. [B] abhängt, ist es im rechten Bild so, daß zwar die Reihenfolge beliebig ist, aber (a) doppelt so stark wie (b) mit Marken versorgt wird (da [b] ja 2 Marken zum Schalten brauchen soll, weshalb [a] doppelt so oft wie [b] schalten kann) — sofern nur die Konfliktregelung zwischen [a] und [b] "fair" ist. Und eben diese Fairneß ist das Problem.

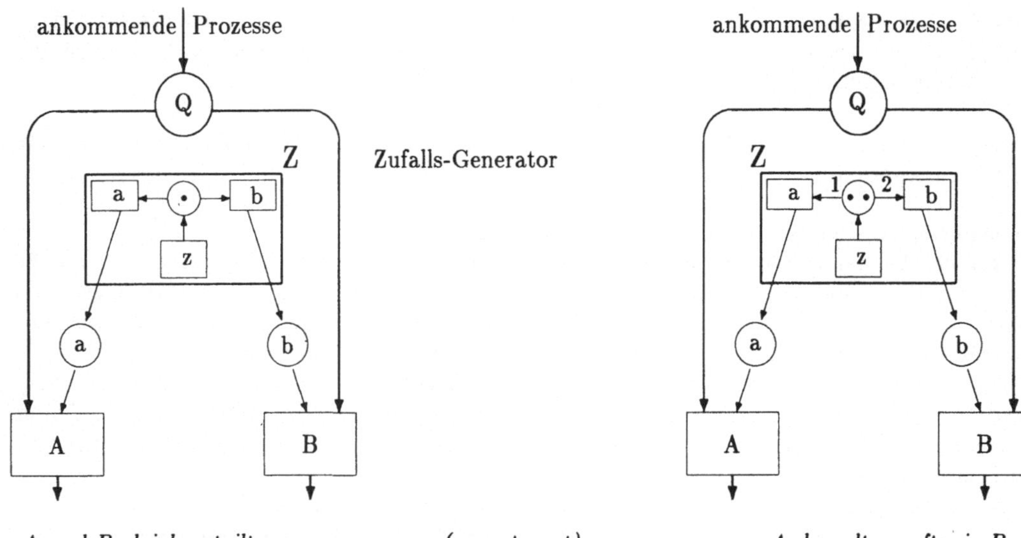


*A und B gleichverteilt*          *(ungesteuert)*          *A doppelt so oft wie B*

Wenden wir uns nun der mangelnden Fairneß zu. Gemeint ist die oben formulierte Möglichkeit, daß der Zufallsgenerator während der Lebensdauer der Prozesse [A] bzw. [B] den einen Ausgang favorisiert hätte bzw. hätte können, und zwar in einem uns (subjektiv!) erscheinenden Ausmaß, das wir nicht mehr als Zufallsabweichung akzeptieren *wollen*.
Dann allerdings müssen wir unser Gefühl objektivieren und *vorher* sagen, *wieviel* Streubreite wir akzeptieren wollen. Dementsprechend muß dann der Spielraum (Schlupf, *slack*) des Zufallsgenerators eingeschränkt werden, indem beide Ausgänge miteinander gekoppelt werden, und zwar in der Spielraum-beschränkenden Art in genau dem akzeptierten Umfang: wenn der Abstand der Ereignishäufigkeiten zu groß wird – und das hieße hier $n$ bzw. $2n$ – dann kann als nächstes nur der andere Ereignisausgang drankommen; eine Abstands-Überschreitung ist nicht möglich.

(Eine etwas subtilere Möglichkeit der Steuerung ist auch denkbar, etwa nach dem folgenden Schema: je mehr man meint, der eine Ausgang sei *zu oft* drangekommen, umso breiter (wahrscheinlicher) mache man den anderen Ausgang. Ein konkretes Beispiel: gelte normalerweise ein Treffer im Intervall $[0, 0.5)$ für den Ausgang *links*, in $[0.5, 1)$ für den Ausgang *rechts*, so verschiebe man, wenn inzwischen beispielsweise *rechts* zu oft eingetreten ist, die Grenzen auf $[0, 0.6)$ für *links*, und $[0.6, 1)$ für *rechts*, und wenn sich *rechts* der Toleranzgrenze nähert, auf $[0, 0.9)$ für *links*, und $[0.9, 1)$ für *rechts*, — und eventuell das ganze dynamisiert. Dieses aufwendigere Verfahren soll hier allerdings nicht dargestellt werden.)

Wir wollen hier den Begriff **Synchronie-Abstand** aus der Netz-Theorie verwenden, um eine Regelung zu konstruieren. Der Synchronie-Abstand (engl. *synchronic distance*) ist – vereinfacht gesagt – der maximale Abstand zwischen zwei Transitionen, gemessen in natürlichen Zahlen, da es sich um eine Zählgröße handelt. Gezählt wird die (max.) Anzahl von Schaltvorgängen, die die eine Transition vornehmen kann, bevor es zu einem Stillstand im System kommt und erst wieder mit dem Schalten der anderen Transition weitergehen kann.

Einschließend die nötigen Netzergänzungen für die Z-Marken-Rückgabe wird nun unten die Möglichkeit dargestellt, wie zwar [A] und [B] zufällig geschehen, aber der Abstand der Ereignishäufigkeiten nicht größer als ein vorgegebenes Limit (hier $n$ bzw. $2n$) sein kann – danach kann es nämlich nicht mehr aktiviert werden (*concession* haben), und das andere Ereignis muß zwangsläufig geschehen.

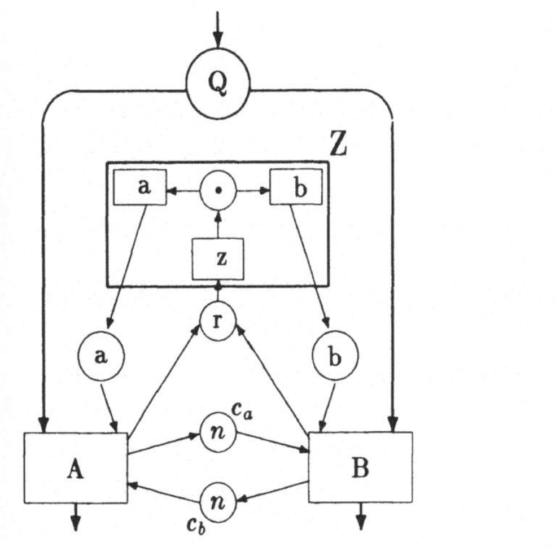

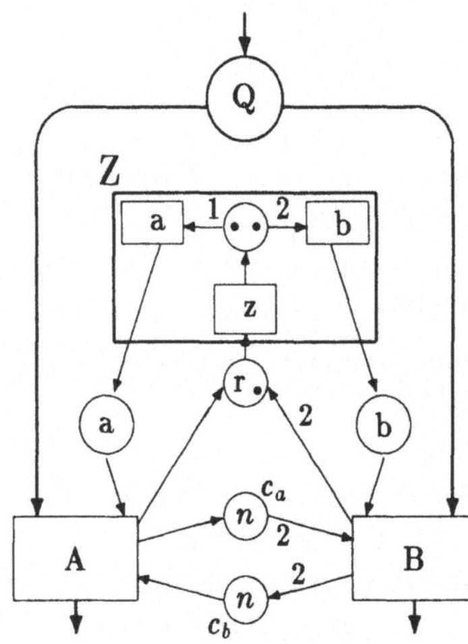

<table>
<tr><td align="center">A und B gleichverteilt</td><td align="center">( Entfernung |A,B| ≤ 2n)</td><td align="center">A doppelt so oft wie B</td></tr>
</table>

## 6. Schlußbetrachtungen

Die Lösungsversuche mögen nicht jedermann voll befriedigen. Man kann sich immer noch fragen, wo ist hierbei der Zufall geblieben?

Die eine Erklärung ist: man hat ihn ja durch die Spezifikation (... soll *im Schnitt* doppelt so oft drankommen wie ...) herausdefiniert. Andererseits ist er ja nicht völlig eliminiert, denn solange der Abstand der Ereignishäufigkeiten nicht *zu groß* ist (was das auch – contextbedingt – heißen mag), kommt das nächste Ereignis ja rein zufällig. Schließlich folgt ja aus der Summen-Anforderung für die Wahrscheinlichkeiten $p_A$ und $p_B$: falls $p_A = \frac{a}{b}$, dann $p_B = 1 - \frac{a}{b}$.

Eine andere Erklärung folgt aus der genauen Betrachtung der zeitlichen Argumentations-Standpunkte. Sie zeigt unterschiedliche *Auffassungen* über das Wesen des Zufalls auf (ähnlich wie die Unterscheidung zwischen *Wahrscheinlichkeit* und *relativer Häufigkeit*).

Wenn eine bestimmte Serie von Ereignissen geschehen ist, kann man *hinterher* abzählen, wie die Verteilung der Ereignisse (Zahl-Adler-Spiel, Stationsbedienung etc.) *war*. Wenn man annimmt, daß man ausreichend genau (zumindest ausreichend lange) beobachtet hat, und wenn man außerdem darauf vertraut, daß sich keine verteilungs-relevanten Parameter ändern, dann kann man annehmen, daß auch zukünftige Ereignisfolgen ähnlich verteilt sein werden. Welche Toleranzen (Fehler ersten, zweiten Grades) auftreten werden, d.h. mit welcher Verläßlichkeit die Ereignisse eintreten werden, kann man allerdings aus prinzipiellen Gründen nicht sagen. Wegen der Endlichkeit unserer Möglichkeiten zu beobachten und abzuwarten (vgl. dazu auch das *Halt*-Problem), kann uns in der Praxis jeder beliebige Ereignis-Abstand überraschen.

Anders ist es, wenn wir einen Mechanismus bauen, der zufällige Ereignisse produziert. Bei ihm kann man die Verteilungsfunktion mit den bestimmenden Parametern (Mittelwert, Streuung) *vorher* angeben.

In der Praxis macht das leider jedoch keinen Unterschied – die Ungewißheit ist zwar auf dem einen (mathematischen) Gebiet behoben, jedoch trotzdem kann uns bei der Anwendung dieses Apparates auch hier widerfahren, daß in der endlichen Anwendungsphase (nämlich höchstens bis zu unserem Tode) auch der – zugegebenermaßen höchst unwahrscheinliche, aber eben nicht unmögliche – Fall eintritt, daß der Zufallsmechanismus *nur a* und *kein b* produziert.

Die Forderung an den Zufall, daß man sich darauf verlassen kann, daß er sich auch *im kleinen* "zufällig genug" verhält, daß er also einigermaßen(?) gleichmäßig(!) in dem erwarteten Bereich streut, ist ein gedanklicher Knoten, der wohl prinzipiell unauflösbar ist.

# 7. References

[Be] E.Best: Non-deterministic Interleaving and The Non-Transitivity of Concurrency. in: News-Letters of the SIG Petri Nets & Related System Models No.15, pp.11-15, (ISSN 0173-7473), GI Bonn (1983)

[Br] W.Brauer (Ed.): Net Theory and Applications. Proc. Advanced Course on General Net Theory of Processes & Systems. LNCS 84, Springer (1979)

[Fu1] H.Fuss: AFMG – Ein asynchroner Fluss-Modell-Generator. Berichte der GMD No.100. GMD (1975)

[Fu2] H.Fuss: Reversal Simulation with Place-Transactor-Nets. in: H.Wedde (Ed.): Adequate Modeling of Systems. Proc. Int. Working Conf. on Model Realism, pp.222-232, Springer (1983)

[Fu3] H.Fuss: Petri Net Languages for Automation of Distributed Systems and Processes. in: IEEE Workshop on Languages for Automation (Nov. 7-9, 1983, Chicago), pp.159-162. IEEE Computer Society Press (506), Silver Spring, Md, USA (1983)

[Fu4] H.Fuss: Improving Simulations with Place-Transactor-Nets. in: A.Javor (Ed.): Simulation in R&D. Proc. IMACS Europ. Simul. Meeting, pp.51-58.; KFKI, Hungary (1984). (augmented version to appear –in selected papers– at N.Holland Publ.Co. 1985)

[Pe] C.A.Petri: State-Transition Structures in Physics & Computation. Int.J.Th.Physics, Vol.21, No.12. pp.979-992 (1982)

[Re] W.Reisig: Petrinetze. Eine Einführung. 158 S. Springer 1982 (*Italienisch:* Le Reti di Petri. A.Mondadori, Milano 1984) (*Englisch:* Petri Nets. EATCS Vol.4, Springer 1985)

[R/W] B.Rosenstengel/U.Winand: Petri-Netze, eine anwendungs-orientierte Einführung. 269 S. Vieweg 1982

[Ss] G.Scheschonk: Vorlesungs-Skriptum Petri-Netze als formale Basis für Informationssysteme. 352 S. (nebst Anh.); FB Informatik, TU Berlin WS 1982/3

[St] P.Starke: Petri Netze. 184 S. VEB Deutscher Verlag d.Wissenschaften Berlin 1980

[Zu] K.Zuse: Petri-Netze aus der Sicht des Ingenieurs. 193 S. Vieweg 1980

# QUANTITATIVE BEWERTUNG FEHLERTOLERANTER HASHTABELLEN-IMPLEMENTIERUNGEN IN DATENBANKSYSTEMEN DURCH SIMULATIONSREIHEN


Klaus Küspert, Heidelberg



Zusammenfassung. Datenbanksysteme sollten Verletzungen der physischen Integrität in den gespeicherten Daten rechtzeitig erkennen. Hierzu sind sog. "online"-Fehlererkennungsmaßnahmen unter Verwendung geeigneter Redundanzen erforderlich. Die Benutzung solcher fehlertoleranter Speicherungsstrukturen führt jedoch stets zu gewissen Mehrkosten bei der DB-Verarbeitung. Für Hashtabellen in Datenbanken wird das Ausmaß dieses Kostenanstiegs exemplarisch untersucht. Dabei zeigt sich, daß im allg. mit einem sehr geringen Kostenzuwachs zu rechnen ist.

Summary. The violation of physical integrity constraints should be detected by the DBMS during normal operation. This kind of online error detection requires suitable redundancies in the database. Fault tolerant database storage structures, however, cannot be maintained without a certain overhead for database processing. We try to quantify these additional costs for hash table processing in database systems. It turns out that in most cases only a very small overhead can be observed.


## 1. Einleitung

Datenbanksysteme müssen mit verschiedenen Arten von <u>Fehlern</u> fertig werden. Insbesondere erwarten die Benutzer solcher Systeme von diesen die Wahrung der Integrität für die gespeicherten Daten. Es ist jedoch festzustellen, daß durch die üblichen Logging- und Recovery-Maßnahmen in Datenbanksystemen /Hä78/ bestimmte Fehlermöglichkeiten nicht oder nur unzureichend berücksichtigt werden. So kann etwa die physische Integrität einer Datenbank (DB) durch Programmfehler im Betriebssystem oder im Datenbank-Verwaltungssystem (DBVS) verletzt werden, ohne daß dies zunächst bemerkt wird. Das DBVS sollte deshalb während der normalen DB-Verarbeitung <u>"online"-Fehlererkennungsmaßnahmen</u> durchführen, die genau jene DB-Strukturen einer Korrektheitsprüfung unterziehen, die aktuell vom DBVS verarbeitet werden. Mit Hilfe von <u>"online"-Fehlerbehandlungsmaßnahmen</u> sollte das DBVS zudem bei einem erkannten Fehler in der Datenbank nach Möglichkeit die Konsistenz selbständig, d.h. ohne Zutun des Benutzers oder Datenbank-Administrators, wiederherstellen.

Fehlererkennungs- und -behandlungsmaßnahmen erfordern geeignete <u>Redundanzen</u> in Datenbanken. Das Mitführen von redundanter Information bedingt jedoch zusätzliche Verarbeitungskosten. Man kann bei den <u>Mehrkosten</u> zwischen einem E/A- und einem CPU-Zeit-Mehraufwand unterscheiden.

Dieser Aufsatz beschäftigt sich mit der simulativen Bestimmung des zusätzlichen <u>E/A-Aufwands</u> bei der Verarbeitung von Hashtabellen in Datenbanken, die in unterschiedlichem Maße redundante Information enthalten. Hashtabellen werden hier als Untersuchungsgegenstand gewählt, da sie eine im DB-Bereich weitverbreitete Speicherungs- und Zugriffspfadstruktur sind.

## 2. Die untersuchten Hashtabellen-Varianten

Fünf verschiedene Implementierungen für Hashtabellen mit "separate chaining" /Kn75/
wurden durch Simulationsreihen hinsichtlich ihrer Auswirkungen auf das Leistungs-
verhalten des DBVS verglichen. Die nachstehende Abbildung zeigt anhand eines Beispiels den prinzipiellen Aufbau einer solchen Hashtabelle. Sie besitzt einen
Primärbereich fester Größe (links im Bild) sowie einen beliebig erweiterbaren
Überlaufbereich (rechts im Bild). Beide Bereiche enthalten Buckets fester Länge,
wobei zwischen Primärbuckets (links) und Überlaufbuckets (rechts) unterschieden
wird. Die Buckets werden mittels NEXT- und PRIOR-Verweisen zu disjunkten
Überlaufketten zusammengefaßt. Das jeweils letzte (am weitesten rechts stehende)
Überlaufbucket einer Kette wird auch Randbucket genannt.

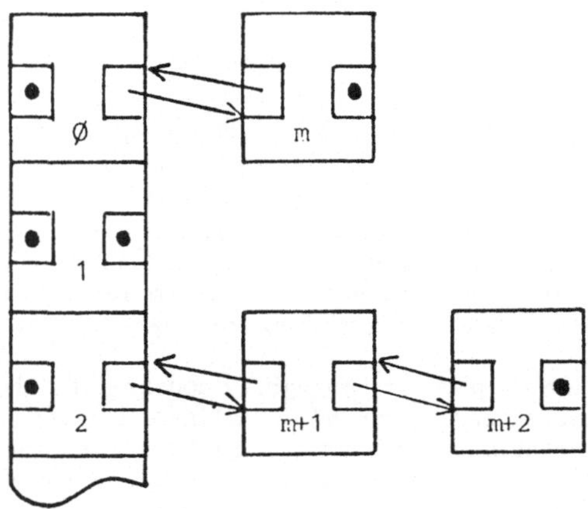


Die fünf von uns betrachteten Hashtabellen-Implementierungen können folgendermaßen
klassifiziert werden:
- Die erste Implementierung entspricht exakt der im Bild gezeigten Struktur.
- Bei der zweiten Implementierung enthält jedes Bucket zusätzlich einen
  Identifikator, der die Zugehörigkeit zu einer bestimmten Hashtabelle ausdrückt.
  Innerhalb einer Hashtabelle besitzen deshalb sämtliche Buckets denselben
  Identifikator. Dieser Wert darf jedoch ansonsten in keiner anderen Hashtabelle
  der Datenbank mehr auftreten.
- Die dritte Implementierung beinhaltet darüber hinaus geschlossene
  Überlaufketten, d.h., auch zwischen einem jeden Randbucket und dem zugehörigen
  Primärbucket existiert eine doppelte Verkettung. Der PRIOR-Verweis im
  Primärbucket zeigt somit zum Randbucket der Kette (das kann u.U. das
  Primärbucket selbst sein), und der NEXT-Verweis im Randbucket führt zum
  Primärbucket zurück.
- Die vierte Implementierung baut wiederum auf der zweiten auf. Hier werden jedoch
  zusätzlich sog. LAST-Verweise von den Primärbuckets zu den Randbuckets
  mitgeführt. Dabei adressiert der LAST-Verweis eines Primärbuckets nicht einfach
  das zugehörige Randbucket, sondern vielmehr ein anderes Randbucket der
  Hashtabelle. Auf jedes Randbucket zeigt genau ein solcher LAST-Verweis. Diese
  Verweisstruktur sorgt dafür, daß jedes Überlaufbucket auf zwei verschiedenen Wegen vom Primärbereich der Hashtabelle aus erreicht werden kann: Zum einen über
  NEXT-Verweise und zum anderen über PRIOR-Verweise, indem nämlich zunächst mit
  Hilfe des LAST-Verweises auf das Randbucket der Überlaufkette zugegriffen wird.
- Die fünfte Implementierung unterscheidet sich von der dritten nur dadurch, daß
  nunmehr die PRIOR-Verweise nicht zum jeweiligen Vorgänger in der Kette führen
  sondern zum Vorvorgänger. Diese Art der Verweisbenutzung basiert auf einem Vorschlag von Taylor /Ta77/.

In /Kü85/ wird erläutert, welche Arten von Inkonsistenzen bei den vorgenannten
Hashtabellen-Implementierungen erkannt bzw. darüber hinaus erfolgreich behandelt

werden können. Wie schon zu vermuten ist, bietet etwa die Implementierung 1 kaum
Möglichkeiten zur Durchführung von Fehlererkennungs- und behandlungsmaßnahmen, da
die hierfür benötigten Redundanzen fehlen. Dagegen können z.B. bei der Implemen-
tierung 5 recht umfangreiche Konsistenzprüfungen unter Verwendung der redundanten
Information durchgeführt werden, und auch eine erfolgreiche Fehlerbehandlung im
Fall einer erkannten Inkonsistenz ist oft möglich.


## 3. Kostenmaße zur Bewertung des E/A-Aufwands

Es soll in diesem Aufsatz untersucht werden, welche E/A-Mehrkosten durch das
Mitführen von redundanter Information verursacht werden. Gleichzeitig geht es aber
auch um die Prüfung der Tauglichkeit verschiedener Kostenmaße zur Leistungsbewertung.

Die folgenden vier Kostenmaße werden benutzt:
- C1: Beim Kostenmaß C1 werden einfach die bei einer Operation (Lesen, Einfügen,
  Löschen) berührten Buckets gezählt. Dies geschieht unabhängig davon, ob ein Bucket
  nur zum Lesen bereitgestellt wird oder ob in ihm auch geändert wird.
- C2: Hier werden bei der Operationsausführung veränderte Buckets kostenmäßig doppelt gewichtet. Dadurch soll das Rückschreiben der geänderten Daten in die Datenbank berücksichtigt werden, das entweder bei Transaktionsende oder aber zu
  einem späteren Zeitpunkt erfolgen muß.
- C3: Bei diesem Kostenmaß wird der Pufferverwaltung des DBVS Rechnung getragen.
  Es werden lediglich die benötigten physischen E/A-Operationen (Lesen eines Blocks
  von der Platte, Schreiben bzw. Rückschreiben eines Blocks auf die Platte) im Fall
  eines LRU-Pufferverwalters gezählt, nicht aber die rein im Systempuffer des DBVS
  ohne E/A-Operation erfolgenden Seitenzugriffe.
- C4: Hier wird auch noch das Schreiben von Log-Daten in die Kostenrechnung einbe-
  zogen. Dabei nehmen wir an, daß vor Änderung eines Buckets dessen "before image"
  und nach Änderung dessen "after image" geschrieben werden muß. Somit kann eine
  einzelne Änderung in der Datenbank u.U. zu vier E/A-Operationen führen:
  - Lesen des zu verändernden Datenbankblocks
  - Schreiben des "before image" (alter Blockinhalt)
  - Schreiben des "after image" (neuer Blockinhalt)
  - Rückschreiben des veränderten Blocks in die Datenbank


## 4. Vorgehensweise bei der Simulation

Die Hashtabellen-Varianten 1 bis 5 wurden in Simulationsprogrammen implementiert,
um die Kosten C1 bis C4 für verschiedene Lastcharakteristika und Datenvolumina zu
bestimmen. Die Programme wurden in der Programmiersprache Pascal erstellt.

Den Simulationen wurden zwei verschieden dimensionierte Hashtabellen zugrunde gelegt. Die erste bestand aus m=1250 Primärbuckets mit maximal 20 Einträgen pro
Bucket. Der Primärbereich bot hier also 25000 Einträgen Platz. Die zweite umfaßte
m=188 Primärbuckets mit maximal b=133 Einträgen pro Bucket, so daß der
Primärbereich 25004 Einträge aufnehmen konnte. Die beiden Varianten sollen unterschiedliche Anwendungen repräsentieren. Im ersten Fall ist dies eine Hashtabelle,
die Datensätze größerer Länge enthält (z.B. Satzlänge 100 Bytes bei einer
Seitenlänge von 2048 Bytes), während man sich im zweiten Fall vorstellen kann, daß
nur relativ kurze Schlüssel-Verweis-Paare in den Hashbuckets gespeichert sind.

Die folgenden Lastprofile fanden Verwendung:
- STORE-Sequenz: 100000 Einträge mit über einen Zufallszahlengenerator erzeugten
  Schlüsselwerten werden in die zuvor leere Hashtabelle eingefügt.
- ERASEC-Sequenz ("erase chain"): Die Hashtabelle wird zunächst wiederum mit 100000
  Einträgen geladen. Im Anschluß daran werden jedoch 100000 Löschungen ausgeführt,
  wobei jeweils ausgehend von einem Primärbucket die Überlaufkette (soweit vorhan-
  den) bis zu dem Bucket, das den zu löschenden Eintrag enthält, durchlaufen wird.
  Durch die Löschungen wird die Hashtabelle wieder vollständig entladen.

- ERASED-Sequenz ("erase direct"): Sie unterscheidet sich nur dadurch von der ERASEC-Sequenz, daß nunmehr auf das den zu löschenden Eintrag enthaltende Bucket direkt zugegriffen wird, also ohne Benutzung der Überlaufkette. Dies kann unter Verwendung irgendeines geeigneten Zugriffspfads geschehen. Ansonsten erfolgen die Löschungen aber wie oben beschrieben.

Bei der Durchführung einer Löschung (ERASEC/ERASED) soll der jeweils davon betroffene Eintrag (dies kann ein Satz oder auch ein Schlüssel-Verweis-Paar sein) zufällig ausgewählt werden. Gleichzeitig muß dafür gesorgt werden, daß die Hashtabelle nach Abschluß der 100000 Löschoperationen auch wirklich wieder völlig leer ist. Diese beiden Forderungen sind nur recht schwer zu erfüllen, wenn eine Hashtabelle Zufallszahlen enthält (vgl. /Kü84/). Zufallszahlen sind aber eine wesentliche Voraussetzung für eine einigermaßen realitätsnahe Untersuchung von Operationsabläufen auf einer Hashtabelle.

Zur Vermeidung der mit der Verwendung von Zufallszahlen verbundenen Probleme wurde ein Verfahren implementiert, das eine zufallsbestimmte Auswahl von Schlüsselwerten erlaubt, ohne daß diese Werte auch vom Simulationsprogramm explizit verwaltet werden müssen. In den Buckets werden also keine Schlüsselwerte gespeichert; statt dessen wird dort nur jeweils ein Zähler mitgeführt, der angibt, wie viele "fiktive" Schlüsselwerte das Bucket enthält.

Im Fall einer Einfügung wird dann ein Primärbucket zufällig ausgewählt und im zugehörigen Randbucket der Zähler um 1 erhöht. Im Fall einer Löschung kann nicht so einfach vorgegangen werden, da die Wahrscheinlichkeit dafür, daß in einem Bucket ein Eintrag gelöscht wird, proportional zur Zahl der in dem Bucket aktuell vorhandenen Einträge (d.h. proportional zum Wert des Zählers) ist. Ein kleines Beispiel möge dies verdeutlichen: Angenommen, in einer Hashtabelle existieren nur drei Buckets, die jeweils maximal b=20 Einträgen Platz bieten und aktuell folgende Belegungen aufweisen:
- Bucket 1: Zähler = 16
- Bucket 2: Zähler = 19
- Bucket 3: Zähler = 15
Eine nachfolgende Löschung bezieht sich hier mit einer Wahrscheinlichkeit von 32% auf Bucket 1. Die entsprechenden Werte für die Buckets 2 und 3 lauten 38% bzw. 30%. In /Kü84/ wird ausführlich erläutert, wie die Verwaltung und Auswahl der Buckets gemäß ihrer - im Zähler wiedergegebenen - Belegung genau erfolgen kann.


## 5. Simulationsergebnisse

Bei den Simulationen hat sich gezeigt, daß für b=20 unter Zugrundelegung des Kostenmaßes C4 die Kostenunterschiede zwischen den fünf betrachteten Hashtabellen-Implementierungen max. 5 bis 6% betragen. Erwartungsgemäß ergaben sich die größten Kostendifferenzen zwischen den Implementierungen 1 und 5. Die untenstehende Tabelle zeigt die Simulationsergebnisse für eine ERASED-Sequenz.

| | ERASED | | | | | | |
|---|---|---|---|---|---|---|---|
| | Verfahren | | | | | DELTA- | |
| | 1 | 2 | 3 | 4 | 5 | 1-2 | 1-5 |
| C1 | 1.059 | | 1.080 | 1.087 | 1.094 | 0% | 3.3% |
| C2 | 2.075 | 2.119 | 2.160 | 2.174 | 2.188 | 2.1% | 5.4% |
| C3 | 2.054 | 2.097 | 2.138 | 2.152 | 2.166 | 2.1% | 5.5% |
| C4 | 4.140 | 4.227 | 4.309 | 4.337 | 4.364 | 2.1% | 5.4% |

Sehr deutlich sind die Unterschiede zwischen den verschiedenen Kostenmaßen zu erkennen. Während C4 als eine weitestgehend realistische Kostenabschätzung anzusehen ist, besitzt etwa C1 stets viel zu kleine Werte. Darüber hinaus ist C1 auch nicht dazu in der Lage, die Kostendifferenzen zwischen den untersuchten Hashtabellen-Implementierungen genügend herauszuarbeiten. So unterscheiden sich z.B. die Implementierungen 1 und 2 bzgl. des Kostenmaßes C1 überhaupt nicht, was aber - wie die anderen Kostenmaße zeigen - offensichtlich an der Realität vorbeigeht. Für $b=133$ liegen die Kostenunterschiede zwischen den Implementierungen stets unter einem Prozent. Die entsprechenden Ergebniszusammenstellungen können /Kü85/ entnommen werden.

## 6. Zusammenfassung

Anhand von fünf verschiedenen Hashtabellen-Implementierungen wurde untersucht, zu welchen Mehrkosten das Mitführen von Redundanzen in einer Datenbank führt. Gleichzeitig wurden mehrere Kostenmaße auf ihre Eignung zur quantitativen Bewertung des Verarbeitungsaufwands hin überprüft. Die Simulationsergebnisse machen deutlich, daß bei Verwendung von redundanter Information im beschriebenen Umfang der Kostenzuwachs (E/A-Operationen) stets weit unter 10% liegt. In /Kü85/ wird übrigens nachgewiesen, daß sich diese Aussage auch auf Redundanzen in B*-Bäumen übertragen läßt.

## Literatur

Hä78 Härder, T.: Implementierung von Datenbanksystemen. Carl Hanser Verlag, München Wien, 1978

Kn75 Knuth, D.E.: The Art of Computer Programming, Vol. 3: Sorting and Searching. Addison-Wesley Publ. Comp., Reading/Mass., 1978

Kü84 Küspert, K.: Überlegungen zur schnellen "online"-Fehlerbehandlung in Speicherungsstrukturen von Datenbanksystemen. Interner Bericht 109/84, Univ. Kaiserslautern, Fachbereich Informatik, 1984

Kü85 Küspert, K.: Fehlererkennung und Fehlerbehandlung in Speicherungsstrukturen von Datenbanksystemen. Springer-Verlag, Informatik-Fachberichte 99, 1985

Ta77 Taylor, D.J.: Robust Data Structure Implementations for Software Reliability. Ph.D. Thesis, Univ. of Waterloo, Dept. of Computer Science, 1977

# ASSOZIATION BEI DER MODELLIERUNG DISKRETER SIMULATIONSSYSTEME: EIN KONZEPT UND ÜBERLEGUNGEN ZU SEINER IMPLEMENTIERUNG


Karl Kohel / Ulrike Maschtera, Linz



Zusammenfassung: Das Ziel einer konzeptionellen Modellierung von diskreten stochastischen Simulationssystemen sollte sein, dem Benutzer ein deskriptives Werkzeug zur Mo-
dellformulierung zur Verfügung zu stellen. Beim Stand der heutigen Simulationssprachen
und -systemen überwiegt aber der prozedurale Aspekt der Beschreibung, was nicht zuletzt
in der mangelnden Abstraktion der verwendeten Datentypen begründet liegt. Mit den Hilfs-
mitteln der Assoziation und der Aggregation kann der Abstraktionsgrad von Datentypen
jedoch derart erhöht werden, daß die zuvor unbedingt notwendige prozedurale Beschreibung von Abläufen nun in einer deskriptiven Form vorgenommen werden kann. Die Anwendung dieser Abstraktionsmethoden auf Mengen und deren Elemente ergibt ein Konzept, das
durch den erreichten Abstraktionsgrad und der damit verbundenen Komplexität der Forderung der deskriptiven Modellbeschreibung gerecht wird.

Summary: The aim of conceptual modelling of discrete event simulation systems should
be to present a descriptive tool for model-formulation to the user. Nowadays, the level
simulation languages have reached represents a more procedural view of formulation.
Last but not least, this is based on the lack of abstraction of the used data types.
By means of association and aggregation the abstraction level of data types can be en-
creased to such an extent that the description of transactions can now be done in a
descriptive manner instead of the usual procedural one. The application of these abstraction methods to sets and their members supplies a concept which fulfills the
demand for a descriptive model representation.


## Einleitung

Die durch den Abstraktionsvorgang ASSOZIATION - die in Beziehungsetzung von Member-Ob-
jekten (Members) zu Objekten höherer Ordnung - gewonnenen Objekttypen, sogenannte Set-
Objekte, erleichtern die Modellierung diskreter stochastischer Simulationssysteme. Über
die Abstraktion mittels AGGREGATION werden für diese Set-Objekte zusätzliche Eigenschaften definiert. Daraus resultieren neuerlich Set-Objekte höherer Ordnung, deren Komplexität vom erreichten Abstraktionsgrad abhängt und die ihre erworbenen Eigenschaften über
Manipulationsprozeduren der in diese Set-Objekte aufzunehmenden Members weitervererben.
Eine entsprechende Aggregation für die Members ist notwendig, um die neuen Eigenschaften der Set-Objekte aufzunehmen und um diese adequat verarbeiten zu können. Durch die
sukzessive Anwendung dieser Abstraktionsformen werden abstrakte Datentypen(ADT) geschaffen, bei denen Mengenmanipulationsoperationen verschiedenster Art (vgl. die Strategien
FIFO, LIFO, PRTY, wahrscheinlichkeitsabhängiges Einfügen, ...) durch Aufruf derselben
Standardmanipulationsprozedur (vgl. Prozedur INTO in SIMULA) automatisch ablaufen, nur
gesteuert durch den gewählten Mengentyp. Dadurch wird der Benutzer von lästigen Mengen-

koordinationsüberlegungen befreit und zu einer deskriptiven Mengen- und Elementdefinition hingeführt, in der alle Charakteristiken angegeben werden.

<u>Warteschlangendefinitionen mittels ASSOZIATION/AGGREGATION</u>: Warteschlangen sind elementare Bausteine eines diskreten Simulationssystems. Bei ihren Implementierungen in Simulationssprachen und -systemen wurden allerdings nur rudimentäre Eigenschaften berücksichtigt. Sehen wir davon ab, daß zumeist die transienten Elemente die Einfügeposition bestimmen, dann werden in GPSS und SIMSCRIPT noch die Verwaltungsstrategien FIFO, LIFO und die Prioritätssteuerung durch das System unterstützt, während in SIMULA der Benutzer ohne Prioritätssteuerung das Auslangen finden muß, es sein denn, daß er selber eine entsprechende Verwaltung aufbaut.

Stützt sich die Darstellung von Warteschlangen in SIMULA auf ein doppelt verkettetes Listenkonzept ab, so treten in GPSS für einfache Anwendungsfälle Warteschlangen nicht explizit auf und statt dessen erfolgt eine systeminterne Verwaltung. Die Notwendigkeit, Warteschlangen als explizite Bausteine eines Simulationsmodells zu betrachten, zeigt sich auch in GPSS deutlich, sobald das einfache Konzept einer FIFO-Verwaltung mit/ohne Prioritätssteuerung aufgegeben werden muß, bzw. sobald eine Warteschlange mehreren Systemelementen zur gleichzeitigen parallelen Abarbeitung zugeordnet werden soll. So muß vom Benutzer bereits eine einfache Erweiterung des Typs Warteschlange um die zusätzliche Bedingung einer begrenzten Aufnahmefähigkeit und einer standardmäßigen Alternative für den Fall der Ablehnung eines Elementes in prozeduraler Form, durch Abfragen der Cardinalität und anschließendem Vergleich mit einem zulässigen Maximalwert, implementiert werden.

Im folgendem sollen durch geeignete Definition von abstrakten Datentypen diese Arbeiten vom Benutzer in die Datentypen verlagert werden. Dadurch erhält der Benutzer ein deskriptives Hilfsmittel für assoziative/aggregative Abstraktion. Ferner wird gezeigt, wie dadurch die Forderung einheitlicher Schnittstellen realisiert werden kann.

## Ein konzeptionelles Mengenmodell

Für die Realisierung von ADTen erweist sich SIMULA mit seinen Möglichkeiten - Definition von hierarchischen Klassen, sowie Definition von VIRTUAL deklarierten Prozeduren zum Zwecke einer späteren Redefinition - als besonders vorteilhaft. Dementsprechend wurde auch das Problem einer Warteschlange mit begrenzter Cardinalität in /1/ mittels SIMULA gelöst. Durch die Definition einer Klasse *NUMERAL* und deren Übergabe als generischer Parameter in der Klasse *ANCHOR* des Set-Objektes wird die (Un-)Beschränktheit der Warteschlange zum Ausdruck gebracht. Mittels der zusätzlich definierten Prozedur *FULL* im Set-Objekt überprüft das Member-Objekt in der Klasse *ELEMENT*, ob das Set noch zusätzliche Members aufnehmen kann oder nicht. Für den Fall einer Ablehnung durch das Set führt das Member die durch die Prozedur *REFUSED* definierte Aktion aus. Diese wird standardmäßig als ein Ignorieren des Einfügeversuchs im Member-Objekt implementiert und kann wegen der VIRTUAL-Deklaration vom Benutzer neu definiert werden. Die Einführung eines generischen Parameters *MAX_CONTENTS* als Referenzvariable auf eine Klasse *NUMERAL* anstelle einer einfachen Integer-Variablen dient dazu, das aus den Datenbanksystemen bekannte Problem der '*nullvalues*' zu lösen, indem für den Fall der Unbeschränktheit des Sets anstelle einer Klasse *NUMERAL* die Nullreferenz *NONE* übergeben wird.

<u>Definition eines allgemeinen Mengenkonzepts</u>: Eine Verallgemeinerung obiger Problemstellung führt zur Definition von zwei Bedingungen, von denen das Einfügen eines Members in ein Set abhängig gemacht wird. Die erste Bedingung stellt das Set-Objekt und lautet: Ein Member darf sich nur dann einfügen, wenn es die *Bedingungen* des *Set-Objektes* erlauben. Im Zuge einer "Gleichberechtigung" und einer Verallgemeinerung stellt die zweite Bedingung das Member-Objekt und diese lautet: Ein Member darf sich nur dann einfügen, wenn es die *Bedingungen* des *Member-Objektes* erlauben.

Da es grundsätzlich verschiedene Arten von Bedingungen gibt, z.B. Bedingungen, die unbedingt eingehalten werden müssen (technische, physikalische Grenzen) und solche, deren Einhaltung nur "wünschenswert" erscheinen (Individualwünsche, Komfortforderungen), kann eine Steuerung der Bedingungen in Form einer Vorrangbeziehung zwischen Set und Member angegeben werden. Die Assoziationsrelation '*is_membership_of*' zwischen Set und Member wird dementsprechend nur dann erfüllt, wenn durch obige Vorrangbeziehung eine gegenseitige Erlaubnis zum Einfügen resultiert. Für eine Vorrangbeziehung *SET-MEMBER* ergibt sich die Erlaubnis aus (1.a), für den umgekehrten Fall der Vorrangbeziehung *MEMBER-SET* folgt (1.b). Bei einer Gleichberechtigung zwischen *SET und MEMBER* wird zwischen Einhaltung und Nichteinhaltung der "Individualwünsche" unterschieden, woraus die strikte Einfügebedingung (1.c) bzw. die auf das notwendige Ausmaß reduzierte Bedingung (1.d) resultieren.

```
SET   akzeptiert  MEMBER      und   MEMBER  erlaubt     EINFÜGEN    Abb.(1.a)
SET   erlaubt     EINFÜGEN    und   MEMBER  akzeptiert  SET              (1.b)
SET   akzeptiert  MEMBER      und   MEMBER  akzeptiert  SET              (1.c)
SET   erlaubt     EINFÜGEN    und   MEMBER  erlaubt     EINFÜGEN         (1.d)
```

Da wir die Forderung nach einheitlichen Schnittstellen erheben, folgt für eine Implementierung der *is_membership_of*-Relation die Forderung (SIMULA-Notation):

```
IF ASSOCIATION.ALLOWED_TO(SET, MEMBER)
    THEN ASSOCIATE                              Abb. 2
    ELSE REFUSE;
```

wobei *ASSOCIATE* die systemspezifische Implementierung des Einfügens eines Members in ein Set exekutiert und *REFUSE* eine system-/benutzerspezifische Aktion darstellt. Wie aus dem Code offensichtlich wird, muß *ASSOCIATION* auf einen ADT verweisen, der durch die Prozedur *ALLOWED_TO* das Einfügen bzw. das Ablehnen des Members steuert und in dem auch die Vorrangbeziehung zwischen Set und Member geregelt sein muß. Da Set und Member als Parameter übergeben werden, sind die Einfügebedingungen - als spezifische Merkmale des Sets bzw. Members - in ihnen selbst enthalten. Darüberhinaus wird der Datentyp *ASSOCIATION* jenem Datentyp (Set/Member) zur Verfügung gestellt, der das Einfügen anstößt (in SIMULA dem Member-Objekt). Wie aus (1.a)-(1.d) weiter hervorgeht, steuern die Vorrangbeziehungen den Erfolg der Assoziationsbemühungen. Diese sind aber für einen speziellen Versuch eindeutig bestimmt, woraus folgt, daß entsprechend viele ADTen der Art *ASSOCIATION* benötigt werden. Jeder dieser ADTen hat über die ADTen Set und Member die Möglichkeit, auf die für Set und Member spezifischen Bedingungen zuzugreifen, die in Form von ADTen der Art *CONDITION* realisiert werden. Jeder ADT *CONDITION* muß zwei Prozeduren *ACCEPT* und *PERMIT* enthalten, um für jede Vorrangbeziehung (1.a)-(1-d) einen entsprechenden Wahrheitswert liefern zu können. Da je nach Art der Bedingung nur eine oder beide Prozeduren definiert werden, empfiehlt sich die Standarddefinition: *PERMIT:=TRUE;* und *ACCEPT:=PERMIT;*. Weiters werden *'NULLOBJECTS'* für jede Art von ADT, d.s. Objekte der Oberklassen der ADTen *'ASSOCIATION'* bzw. *'CONDITION'*, bereitgestellt. Auf diese Art und Weise wird die *'nullvalue'*-Problematik gelöst, falls es gilt, eine Schnittstelle (z.B. *ALLOWED_TO*) aufrechtzuerhalten.

Definition von Einfügestrategien (Ordnungsrelationen auf Mengen): Die Einführung einer Ordnung innerhalb der Members eines Sets führt zur Definition von Ordnungsrelationen, die im Bereich der Simulation und der Warteschlangentheorie zumeist bei den Einfügestrategien FIFO, LIFO oder einer Prioritätssteuerung enden. Zudem steuern in Simulationssprachen/-systemen ausschließlich entweder das Set oder die Members die Einfügestrategie. In einem allgemeinem Konzept sollte es jedoch möglich sein, sowohl für das Member als auch für das Set eine eigene Einfügestrategie definieren zu können. Da jedoch nur eine Strategie zum Tragen kommen kann, erfordert eine entsprechende Auswahl die zusätzliche Definition von Vorrangbeziehungen zwischen einem Set und jedem Member.

Bestehende Mengenmanipulationsprozeduren die anstelle eines Sets ein Member innerhalb eines Sets als Einfügehinweis referenzieren (vgl. FOLLOW, PRECEDE in SIMULA) stellen für sich bereits eine Strategie dar. Um Konflikte zu vermeiden, müssen solche Prozeduren derart umdefiniert werden, daß zusätzlich zum referenzierten Member auch das Set, in dem sich dieses Member befindet, zur Bestimmung der Strategie und der Einfügeposition herangezogen werden.

Diese beiden Anforderungen werden realisiert durch einen ADT *'RULE'*, der gemäß seiner definierten Vorrangbeziehung die entsprechende Strategie des Sets bzw. Members auswählt, und durch einen ADT *'STRATEGY'*, der durch eine Prozedur *'POSITION'* die Einfügeposition des Members im Set bestimmt.

Definition von *SET-OF-SETS* - Auswahl einer Menge: In einer Simulationsaufgabe ist die Wahl einer Warteschlange durch ein transientes Element nicht immer deterministisch bestimmt, sondern von gewissen Systemzuständen abhängig oder zufallsbedingt. In solchen

Fällen mußte bisher die Auswahl einer Warteschlange in prozeduraler Form durch den Benutzer beschrieben werden. Dafür steht z.B. in GPSS, neben dem GATE- und TEST-Block als GPSS-spezifische Testmittel für Systemzustände, der TRANSFER-Block zur Verfügung. (Bezeichnen die im TRANSFER-Block angegebenen Blockadressen Blöcke mit assoziierten Warteschlangen - z.B. SEIZE, ENTER, ... - so lassen sich die durch den TRANSFER-Block beschriebenen Auswahlmöglichkeiten wie in Abb. 3 beschreiben.) Um nun beliebige Auswahlmöglichkeiten zu realisieren, definieren wir ADTen *SET_OF_SETS*, deren Member Mengen des im vorigen Kapitel definierten Typs sind. Die Kriterien für die Auswahl der Membermengen werden als Verfeinerungen des ADTs *CRITERIA* dargestellt und einem Objekt der Art *SET_OF_SETS* als generischer Parameter übergeben. Dieser ADT *SET_OF_SETS* ist mit einer Prozedur *PASS_ON* versehen, die einem *OUT; INTO(nächste Membermenge);* entspricht. Dadurch läßt sich eine hierarchische Modellierung realisieren, da die serielle Kopplung von Teilsystemen dem Einfügen der die Teilsysteme beschreibenden Sets (*SET_OF_SETS*) in das das Gesamtsystem beschreibende *SET_OF_SETS* entspricht und die parallele Kopplung von Teilsystemen durch Vergabe entsprechender *CRITERIA* realisiert werden kann.

```
TRANSFER ,block address  Deterministische Auswahl einer Warteschlange(SIMULA: INTO)
TRANSFER BOTH, ........   Auswahl jener Menge, die als erste die Aufnahme erlaubt;
TRANSFER ALL, .........   letzte Menge erlaubt jederzeit eine Aufnahme
TRANSFER SIM, .........   Bei Eintreffen aller spezifizierten Bedingungen wird die
                         erste Menge gewählt, sonst die zweite
TRANSFER PICK, ........   Die Auswahl einer Menge erfolgt zufällig nach
TRANSFER .zzz, ........   statistischen Gesichtspunkten                    Abb. 3
```

<u>Abschließende Bemerkungen</u>: Dieses Konzept wurde in SIMULA implementiert. Durch die Unterstützung der objekt-orientierten Programmierung seitens SIMULA, ließen sich diese ADTen konzepttreu abbilden, woraus das in Abb. 4 skizzierte Netz der verwendeten ADTen resultiert. Eine der vielen Anwendungsmöglichkeiten dieses Mengenkonzeptes im Bereich der Simulation findet sich bei /2/. Dort spiegelt sich auch die Einhaltung der einheitlichen Schnittstellen der Einfügeoperationen wider.

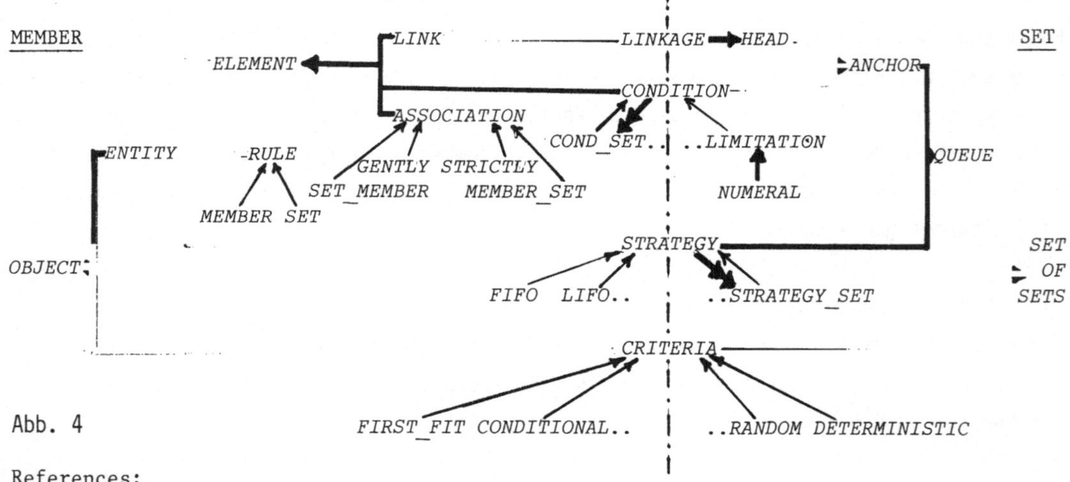


Abb. 4

References:


/1/ Maschtera U.: "Multiple Set Entries and Their Use in Discrete Event Simulation",
    IMACS'85
/2/ Maschtera U.: "Aggregation von Prozessen im Rahmen der konzeptionellen Modellierung
    diskreter Simulationssysteme", ASIM'85

# Aggregation von Prozessen im Rahmen der konzeptionellen Modellierung diskreter Simulationssysteme

Maschtera Ulrike, Linz

Zusammenfassung. Zu den Konzepten zur Unterstützung des Abstraktionsprozesses im Rahmen der konzeptionellen Modellierung zählt neben Klassifikation, Generalisation und Assoziation auch die Aggregation, also die Vereinigung von Komponenten zu einem Objekt höherer Ordnung. Die Anwendung der Aggregation auf Aktivitäten/Prozesse verlangt Synchronisationsmaßnahmen innerhalb der Objekte. Sie ermöglicht es, alternative Modellauslegungen im Rahmen der Experimentierumgebung festzulegen und befreit den Benutzer von - bei komplexer Modellogik notwendiger - Abstraktionsarbeit.

Summary. The tools of conceptual modeling include classification, association and aggregation. Aggregation is the combination of components to form a more complex type. In this paper aggregation is applied to discrete event simulation processes and the resulting synchronisation is treated. Using aggregation in the discrete event simulation modeling environment enables to define models in a descriptive way and to include alternative system configurations within the experimental frame.


## Einleitung

Wesentliches Markmal der konzeptionellen Modellierung ist es, den Modellierungsprozeß der menschlichen Wahrnehmung einer Problemumgebung anzunähern. Im Falle diskreter Ereignissimulation folgt daraus eine deskriptive, hierarchische, prozessorientierte Modellierumgebung, die dem Benutzer die Abstraktionsarbeit insbesondere im Zusammenhang mit der Synchronisation der Prozesse erleichtert bzw. abnimmt. Zu diesem Zweck wird im folgenden das Abstraktionskonzept 'Aggregation' auf Simulationselemente angewendet.


## Aggregation

Aggregation - die Vereinigung von Objekten zu einem Objekt höherer Ordnung - tritt immer dann auf, wenn verschiedene Simulationsobjekte (Teilsysteme) in einem Simulationsobjekt höherer Ordnung (System/Teilsystem) vereint werden. Man kann daher drei Arten der Aggregation unterscheiden, nämlich die durch den Transaktionsfluß bestimmte serielle Kopplung unabhängiger Teilsysteme, die serielle Kopplung von Aktivitäten/Prozessen (Teilsystemen) in einer "Person"(System) und die parallele Kopplung von Teilsystemen. Aus der konzeptionellen Modellierung resultiert ua der zusätzliche Wunsch, die Beschreibung des Systems in *deskriptiver* statt prozeduraler *Form* vornehmen zu können und von Synchronisationsmaßnahmen so weit als möglich befreit zu werden. Als Folge davon soll die *Definition des Modells innerhalb der Experimentierumgebung* vorgenommen werden können.

Die SERIELLE KOPPLUNG UNABHÄNGIGER TEILSYSTEME bestimmt das Aussehen eines Systems für
einen Transaktionstyp. Selbstverständlich kann eine Transaktion nur eine der durch das
System selbst vorgegebenen Kopplungsmöglichkeiten wählen. Diese sind permanenter Natur
und daher getrennt von den transienten Elementen zu definieren, um dann für diese als
generische Parameter zur Verfügung zu stehen. In SIMULA realisiert man dies am besten
durch mehrstufige Mengen verschiedensten Typs (vgl /2/) und einer Transaktionsoberklasse
mit der (zum Zweck der Redefinition *VIRTUAL* deklarierten) Prozedur *PASS_ON*, die den
nächsten Prozess auswählt und gegebenenfalls aktiviert.

Bekanntes Beispiel für die SERIELLE KOPPLUNG ABHÄNGIGER TEILSYSTEME ist die in GPSS
vorhandene 'facility' als Vertreter der (mehrstufigen) prioritätsgesteuerten Aggregation
unterbrechbarer Prozesse. Alle übrigen Aggregationsarten müssen in GPSS in prozeduraler
Form -gesteuert durch Schalter- angegeben werden. Als Beispiel sei der Fall einer Arzt-
helferin erwähnt, die zwei Handlungen abwechselnd durchführt (vgl /3/). Andere System-
kopplungsarten sind verzahnt bzgl der Prozesse (dh der Wechsel von einer Handlung A zur
nächsten erfolgt nur, wenn keine Anforderung für A mehr vorhanden ist) oder Aushilfstätigkeiten (dh der Wechsel zu einer benachrangten Aktivität erfolgt nur, falls keine
Anforderung für die bevorrangte Aktivität da ist, und der Wechsel zu einer bevorrangten
Aktivität ist nach jedem Abschluß einer benachrangten Aktivität möglich).

Der Forderung, dem Benutzer *Aggregationshilfsmittel* in die Hand zu geben, mit Hilfe
derer ein System aus Teilsystemen aufgebaut werden soll, kann nun dadurch entsprochen
werden, daß die *Systemhierarchie ausgedrückt* wird durch GENERISCHE PARAMETER VON PROZESS
PRIMITIVA. Führt man die Aggregation -wie in /3/- auf Aktivitätsbasis durch,[1] so erhält
man mit der in Abb.1 definierten (unterbrechbaren) Aktivität die in Abb.2b-d definierten
Primitiva des *nicht unterbrechbaren Prozesses* und *der unterbrechbaren Prozesse mit/ohne
Wiederaufnahme* der unterbrochenen Handlung, indem die generischen Parameter *KUNDE, ZEIT*
assoziiert werden zu einer *QUEUE* und einer *VERTEILUNG*. Diese Primitiva enthalten zwei
Reaktivierungspunkte, an denen die Kontrolle an andere Prozesse (Teilsysteme) übergeben
werden kann. Die Referenzen auf diese Prozesse werden generische Parameter der Prozess-
primitiva, wobei *BRUDER* denjenigen bezeichnet, dem nach Abschluß einer Handlung die
Kontrolle übergeben wird, und *SOHN* angibt, wer die Kontrolle in Ermangelung von Anforderungen erhält. Eigenreferenz ist selbstverständlich möglich. Da sich ein System im
jeweils dominanten Zustand seiner Teilsysteme befinden soll, muß die in SIMULA für
*PROCESS*-Objekte definierte Prozedur *IDLE* neu definiert werden (Abb 2a).

Mit Hilfe dieser Primitiva kann nun eine Vielzahl von Aggregationen definiert werden:
1) Den *Standardserverprozeß* erhält man dadurch, daß *BRUDER* eine Referenz auf sich selbst
und *SOHN* entweder eine Referenz auf das im *HOLD(SIMDAUER)* befindliche Hauptprogramm
*(MAIN)* oder auf sich selbst ist.

---

[1] Selbstverständlich kann auf diesen Umweg über Aktivitäten verzichtet werden. Er dient
nur zur Veranschaulichung von Synchronisationsmaßnahmen bei Aggregation.

2) Mittels *REACTIVATE server* wird das Objekt *server* auch bei Suspendierung <u>unterbrochen</u>.
Dies ist für die Typen *ACTION/WORK* nicht ˍzulässig und wird außer Kraft gesetzt. Die
*VIRTUAL* deklarierte Prozedur *IGNORE* erlaubt es, in diesem Fall weitere Spezifikationen
durchzuführen. Im Fall eines Prozesses vom Typ *WORK* wird die Unterbrechung durch die
Prozedur *INTERRUPT* ausgeführt, die einen zusätzlichen Reaktivierungspunkt darstellt.
Der Prozeß, dem an diesem Reaktivierungspunkt die Kontrolle übergeben werden soll, ist
Parameter und nicht unbedingt Verwender der Prozedur *INTERRUPT*. Dadurch kann diese
auch von Objekten verwendet werden, die nicht als *PROCESS* deklariert sind, zB. Trans-
aktionen. Eine (mehrstufige),(prioritätsgesteuerte) Aggregation unterbrechbarer
Prozesse (vgl 'facility') erhält man nun entweder

a) durch Definition des Objekts  *ARZT:-NEW WORK(PRIO_QUEUE,ARZT,ARZT,VTLG);*
   und Exekution des Statements  *ARZT.INTERRUPT(ARZT);*

oder

b) durch Definition des Objektes *ARZT:-NEW WORK(ANY_QUEUE,ARZT,ARZT,VTLG);*
   und Exekution von   *ARZT.INTERRUPT(NEW WORK(INTERRUPT_QUEUE,ARZT,ARZT,VTLG1));*

Im Fall a) ist *PRIO_QUEUE* eine priority queue, in die sich der die Unterbrechung Veranlassende einreihte/eingereiht wurde. Dadurch wird die unterbrochene Handlung sofort
wiederaufgenommen, falls der gerade 'behandelte Kunde' höhere Priorität besitzt als
der die Unterbrechung veranlassende Kunde. Im Fall b) ist jeder unterbrechende Prozeß
ein eigenes Objekt vom Typ *WORK* mit eigener *INTERRUPT_QUEUE* und -falls *VTLG1=/=VTLG-*
eigener Verteilung. Zur Realisierung der Wiederaufnahme wird der Parameter *SOHN* immer
auf den unterbrochenen Prozess zeigen. Durch die Definition von *BRUDER* als Referenz auf
den unterbrochenen Prozeß wird die Cardinalität der *INTERRUPT_QUEUE* auf 1 beschränkt,
durch Eigenreferenz beim Parameter *BRUDER* hingegen die gesamte *INTERRUPT_QUEUE* abgearbeitet, bevor der unterbrochene Prozeß wiederaufgenommen wird. Übergibt man als
Parameter *FROM* der Prozedur *INTERRUPT* ein Objekt vom Typ *ACTION*, so beschränkt man die
Unterbrechungstiefe auf 1.

3) Im Fall von <u>*Aushilfstätigkeiten*</u> ergibt sich eine Prozesskette, bei der die Referenz
*BRUDER* immer auf den höchstrangigen Prozeß verweist, die Referenz *SOHN* jeweils auf den
nächstniedrigeren, bzw. im Fall des niedrigstrangigen auf *MAIN*.

    *BLUTABNAHME:-NEW ACTION(Q1,BLUTABNAHME,ANMELDEN,VTLG1);*
    *ANMELDEN   :-NEW ACTION(Q2,BLUTABNAHME,MAIN,VTLG2);*  (benachrangt,*SOHN==MAIN*)

4) <u>*Verzahnte Aggregation bzgl der Prozesse*</u> erfordert die Definition von n+1 Prozeßob-
jekten, je eines für die zu aggregierenden Einzelprozesse und ein weiteres zur Beendigung der durch die Prozeßreferenzen angegebenen Aktivierungsschleife.

    *ULRIKE   :-NEW ACTION(Q2,ULRIKE,VAMPIR,VTLG2);*
    *VAMPIR   :-NEW ACTION(Q1,VAMPIR,U_DOUBLE,VTLG1);*    (benachrangt,*SOHN==exit*)
    *U_DOUBLE:-NEW ACTION(Q2,ULRIKE,MAIN,VTLG2);*         (exit: *SOHN==MAIN*)

5) <u>*Verzahnte Aggregation bzgl einzelner Tätigkeiten*</u> bedingt die Definition von $n^2$ Pro-
zeßobjekten aufgrund der n(n-1) Möglichkeiten der reihungsbedingten Abfrage auf leere
Queues. Für n=2 ergeben sich die folgenden vier Prozeßobjekte, von denen *MARGRET* oder
*CHRISTINE* aktiviert werden und die beiden anderen die Exits aus den Aktivierungs-
schleifen darstellen:

```
MARGRET    :-NEW ACTION(Q2,CHRISTINE,C_DOUBLE,VTLG2);
CHRISTINE  :-NEW ACTION(Q3,MARGRET  ,M_DOUBLE,VTLG3);
M_DOUBLE   :-NEW ACTION(Q2,CHRISTINE,MAIN,VTLG2);      (exit1: SOHN==MAIN)
C_DOUBLE   :-NEW ACTION(Q3,MARGRET  ,MAIN,VTLG3);      (exit2: SOHN==MAIN)
```

Besser ist es, für diese Zwecke einen weiteren Datentyp        (Abb 2e) als Exit
zu definieren. Unabhängig von der Anzahl der derart kombinierten Tätigkeiten benötigt
man einen derartigen Prozeß, der auch der zu aktivierende ist:

```
MARGRET    :-NEW ACTION(Q2,CHRISTINE,CHRISTINE,VTLG2); (scheinbar bevorrangt)
CHRISTINE  :-NEW ACTION(Q3,MARGRET  ,DOUBLE   ,VTLG3);
DOUBLE     :-NEW DISTRIBUTION(M1,MARGRET,MAIN);        (exit: SOHN==MAIN)
mit    M1 :- {MARGRET,CHRISTINE}
```

6) Die *Aggregation bereits aggregierter Prozesse* analog zu 3) bzw. 5) würde die Teilsysteme ändern. Anwendung der bzgl der Prozesse verzahnten Aggregation (Fall 4) ist jedoch leicht möglich, indem ein weiteres Objekt als Exit des resultierenden Systems
definiert wird und die Exits der Teilsysteme die Verkettung herstellen:

```
DOUBLE     :-NEW DISTRIBUTION(M1,MARGRET,ULRIKE);      (scheinbar bevorrangt)
U_DOUBLE   :-NEW ACTION       (Q2,ULRIKE,KOMBI*MM,VTLG2);
KOMBI*MM   :-NEW ACTION       (Q2,CHRISTINE,MAIN,VTLG2); (exit)
```

Wird *ULRIKE* scheinbar bevorrangt, so gilt: *U_DOUBLE.SOHN:-MARGRET;DOUBLE.SOHN:-KOMBI*UU;*
```
KOMBI*UU   :-NEW ACTION       (Q2,ULRIKE,MAIN,VTLG2);
```

Möglich wäre auch *U_DOUBLE.SOHN:-KOMBI*MC;* mit
```
KOMBI*MC   :-NEW DISTRIBUTION(M1,MARGRET,MAIN);
```
als exit.


Die <u>PARALLELE KOPPLUNG VON TEILSYSTEMEN</u> ist in den meisten Fällen eine Assoziation (vgl
in GPSS den Typ 'storage') und daher durch geeignete Mengen darstellbar. In den zuvor
definierten Primitivas müssen die in Zeilen (§,$) stehenden *PASSIVATEs* zu einem
*WAIT(MENGE)* geändert werden, wobei *MENGE* ein weiterer generischer Parameter wird. Die
parallele Kopplung zweier Teilsysteme innerhalb einer entity erfolgt nun durch geeignete Definition von *MENGE* bzw. *QUEUE* (vgl /2/), wobei die Synchronisation in den
Prozeduren *INTO,OUT,REFUSED...* stattfindet.


Ein anderes *Aggregationshilfsmittel* ist die <u>AGGREGATION MIT HILFE VON PAARMENGEN</u>(vgl/4/).
Paarmengen (Typ *PAIR* in /2/) bestehen aus zwei *PARTNER*mengen, zwischen denen einmal
eingefügte Elemente hin und her wechseln. Jedem Prozeßobjekt P werden als generische
Parameter zwei Paarmengen (*PRAE* und *POST*) zugeordnet. Sie realisieren zwei *WAIT_UNTILs*,
bei denen die Bedingung durch den Status eines *PARTNERs* (zB leer) ausgedrückt wird: je
eine der Paarmengen enthält eine Eintragung für jeden Prozeß, der den Beginn (*PRAE*) bzw
das Ende (*POST*) der Exekution von P blockiert, ihr *PARTNER* enthält eine Eintragung für
jeden Prozeß, der P blockieren kann, aber derzeit nicht blockiert. Zur Synchronisation
wird in den Prozeßprimitivas vor (§) eingefügt *WHILE NOT PRAE.EMPTY DO PASSIVATE;* und
vor (*) eingefügt *WHILE NOT POST.EMPTY DO PASSIVATE;*. Ändert ein Prozeß Q seinen Status
(vor (+) und nach (*)), so wechseln alle seine Eintragungen in derartigen Paarmengen in
die zugehörigen *PARTNER*. Gleichzeitig muß die Aktivierung aller *OWNERs* dieser Paarmengen
(hier zB P) überprüft werden, da sie sich in einer der soeben eingefügten Warteschleifen
befinden könnten.

```
Abb 1: (unterbrechbare) Aktivität
PROCESS CLASS ACTIVITY(KUNDE,ZEIT);
          REF(LINK)KUNDE;REAL ZEIT;
       BEGIN KUNDE.OUT;HOLD(ZEIT);END;

Abb 2e: Distributionsprozeß
STATUS CLASS DISTRIBUTION;
BEGIN  REF(STATUS)ANY; BOOLEAN LEER;
       REF(SET_OF_SETS)MENGE;LEER:=TRUE;
       MENGE:-QUEUE QUA SET_OF_SETS.FIRST;
       WHILE MENGE=/=NONE AND NOT LEER DO
       BEGIN ANY:-MENGE.OWNER;
            LEER:=LEER AND ANY.QUEUE.EMPTY;
            MENGE:-MENGE.SUC; END;
       IF NOT LEER THEN ACTIVATE BRUDER
                  ELSE ACTIVATE SOHN;
   END;
```

```
Abb 2a: Aggregierbarer Prozeß
PROCESS CLASS STATUS(QUEUE,BRUDER,SOHN);
        REF(HEAD)QUEUE;
        REF(STATUS)BRUDER,SOHN;
BEGIN   BOOLEAN TRIED;
BOOLEAN PROCEDURE IDLE;
   BEGIN BOOLEAN STATE; STATE:=TRUE;
        IF NOT TRIED
           THEN BEGIN TRIED:=TRUE;
           IF BRUDER=/=MAIN THEN
              STATE:=BRUDER.IDLE;
           IF SOHN=/=MAIN THEN
              STATE:=STATE AND SOHN.IDLE;
           IDLE:=STATE AND THIS PROCESS.
                                   IDLE;
           TRIED:=FALSE;END;
           ELSE IDLE:=TRUE;      END;END;
```

```
Abb 2b: Unterbrechbarer Prozess ohne
        Wiederaufnahme
STATUS CLASS PROZESS(VTLG);

         REF(VERTEILUNG)VTLG;
     BEGIN REF(CUSTOMER)KUNDE; REF(ACTIVITY)HANDLUNG; WHILE TRUE DO BEGIN
           WHILE QUEUE.EMPTY DO BEGIN ACTIVATE SOHN; PASSIVATE; END;
(+)        KUNDE:-QUEUE.FIRST; HANDLUNG:-NEW ACTIVITY(KUNDE,VTLG.NEXT_VALUE);
           ACTIVATE HANDLUNG;
       REACTIVATE CURRENT AFTER HANDLUNG;
       IF NOT HANDLUNG.TERMINATED
          THEN REACTIVATE HANDLUNG;
(*)        KUNDE.PASS_ON; ACTIVATE BRUDER AFTER CURRENT;PASSIVATE; END;END;
```

```
Abb 2c: nicht unterbrechbarer Prozeß (vgl.
        MASIM's DOACTION /1/)
STATUS CLASS ACTION(VTLG);
        VIRTUAL: PROCEDURE IGNORE;


                                                               (§)



       WHILE NOT HANDLUNG.TERMINATED DO BEGIN
           REACTIVATE CURRENT AFTER HANDLUNG;
           IGNORE;END;
                                                               ($)
```

```
Abb 2d: Unterbrechbarer Prozess mit Wiederaufnahme (vgl. MASIM's DOWORK /1/)
STATUS CLASS WORK(VTLG); REF(VERTEILUNG)VTLG; VIRTUAL: PROCEDURE IGNORE;
BEGIN   REF(CUSTOMER)KUNDE; REF(ACTIVITY)HANDLUNG;  REAL ENDZEIT; REF(STATUS)INTERP;
        PROCEDURE INTERRUPT(FROM);REF(STATUS)FROM;
            BEGIN INTERP:-FROM;
                IF ENDZEIT ¬=TIME
                THEN BEGIN KUNDE.RESTZEIT:=ENDZEIT-TIME; KUNDE.PRECEDE(QUEUE.FIRST);
                     REACTIVATE THIS WORK AFTER CURRENT; REACTIVATE FROM AFTER CURRENT;
                     REACTIVATE HANDLUNG AFTER CURRENT; END
                ELSE IF NOT SOHN.IDLE AND SOHN=/=MAIN THEN SOHN.INTERRUPT(FROM)
                                         ELSE REACTIVATE FROM;        END;
        WHILE TRUE DO BEGIN WHILE QUEUE.EMPTY DO BEGIN ACTIVATE SOHN;PASSIVATE;END;
        KUNDE:-QUEUE.FIRST; IF KUNDE.RESTZEIT=0 THEN KUNDE.RESTZEIT:=VTLG.NEXT_VALUE;
        HANDLUNG:-NEW ACTIVITY(KUNDE,KUNDE.RESTZEIT); ENDZEIT:=KUNDE.RESTZEIT+TIME;
        ACTIVATE HANDLUNG; WHILE NOT HANDLUNG.TERMINATED DO BEGIN
                           REACTIVATE CURRENT AFTER HANDLUNG; IGNORE;END;
        IF ENDZEIT=TIME
           THEN BEGIN KUNDE.PASS_ON; ACTIVATE BRUDER AFTER CURRENT;PASSIVATE;END
           ELSE IF INTERP=/=THIS WORK THEN WHILE NOT INTERP.IDLE DO  PASSIVATE;
    END;END;
```

References:
/1/ Auer H.,Maschtera U.:"MASIM - A Process-Oriented Simulation Language and Its
        Implementation Via a Macroprocessor", Simuletter (16)1,1985, p4-19
/2/ Kohel K.,Maschtera U.:"Assoziation bei der Modellierung diskreter Simulations-
        systeme: ein Konzept und Überlegungen zu seiner Implementierung",ASIM'85
/3/ Weber K.,Trzebinger R.,Tempelmeier H.:"Simulation mit GPSS", Haupt 1963,S.180
/4/ Maschtera U: "Multiple Set Entries and Their Use in Discrete Event Simulation",
        11th IMACS World Congress on System Simulation and Scientific Computation 85

# Requirements im Kontext eines Simulationsmodells


K.H. Sturm

Versuchsanstalt für Datenverarbeitung und Prozeßtechnik, Berlin



Zusammenfassung: Ausgehend von einem Simulationsprojekt werden spezifische Requirementsaspekte dargelegt. Hierzu wird im ersten Teil die Requirementsphase als Basis für die geplante Systementwicklung dargestellt. Der Aufgabenbereich ist gekennzeichnet durch einen iterativen Prozeß, der Daten, Erfahrungen und Wissen zu Requirementsdokumenten verarbeitet.
Im zweiten Teil wird im Trend von Methode und Werkzeugen auf die im Projekt benutzte SADT-Technik eingegangen.
Das abschließende Resumee liefert einige Aussagen zur Methoden-Diskussion.


## 0. Einleitung

Die Requirementsphase im Software-Life-Cycle gewinnt – als Basis für ein zukünftiges System – nicht nur wegen der Ausprägung von Leistungsmerkmalen sondern, ebenso auch wegen ihrer bereits im Vorfeld bestimmenden Kostenentwicklung, zunehmend an Bedeutung.

Im Kontext eines Forschungsprojektes* (1) zur simulativen Bilanzierung der Energie- und Massenströme in verfahrenstechnischen (Brau-)Prozessen werden nachfolgende Aspekte des Requirementsansatzes dargelegt und erläutert.

## 1. Requirements

Mit zunehmender Erkenntnis, daß Software-Engineering (2) nicht nur der Entwurf und die Implementierung eines Programms ist, wurden Phasenmodelle (3) entwickelt, die den gesamten Software-Lebenszyklus (Life-Cycle) überdecken.

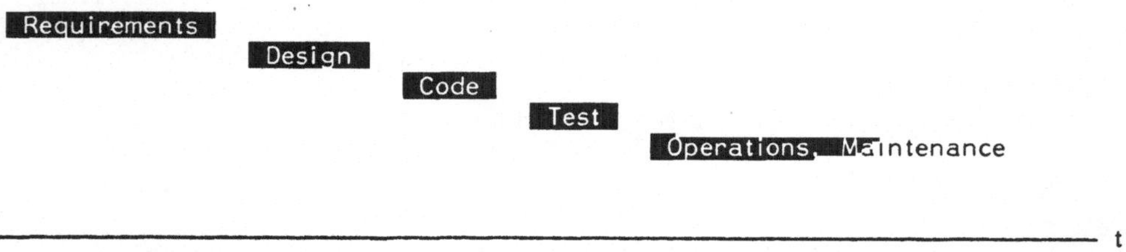

Abb. 1    Life-Cycle-Modell (4)


*"Nutzung solarer Prozeßwärme in Brauereien" gefördert vom BMFT 03E 8035 A.

Bedingt durch die steigenden Softwarekosten wurden im weiteren, zugeordnet diesen Phasen, Untersuchungen und Arbeiten durchgeführt (z. B. (4)), um durch gezielte Maßnahmen die Wirtschaftlichkeit des Produktes "Software" zu verbessern, wobei die Requirementsphase zunehmend an Bedeutung gewinnt. Langfristig wird dies auch zu der gewünschten Umverteilung der Kosten (5) in den einzelnen Phasenbereichen führen.


## 1.1 Requirementsphase

Ähnlich wie bei industriellen Softwareprojekten kann die Requirementsphase eines Forschungsprojektes - zwar unter anderen Randbedingungen - in zwei Abschnitte unterteilt werden.

Abb. 2    Requirementsabschnitte


In dieser Betrachtung ergibt sich, unabhängig differenzierender Randbedingungen, letztlich eine gemeinsame Zielgröße - die Anforderungsspezifikation - als Basis für die zu erstellende Systemlösung.

Basisdokument → ideelles System → Systemlösung

Dabei soll das Basisdokument als Ergebnis der Requirementsphase sowohl – präzise, vollständig, verständlich, realistisch, gewichtet, lösungsneutral – alle wichtigen Anforderungen enthalten als auch formal die nachfolgende Transformation in ein ideelles System unterstützen.

## 1.2 Requirementsprozeß

Allgemein kann davon ausgegangen werden, daß der Requirementsprozeß sukzessiv in Richtung der Zielgröße Dokumente erzeugt und diese neuen Dokumente verknüpft mit Information, Erfahrung und Wissen wieder in seinen iterativen Prozeß einbezieht, bis letztlich die Basis für das zukünftige System erfragt, erfaßt, modelliert, bewertet, ..., entscheidbar und dokumentiert ist.

Ebenso übertragbar auf viele Projekte ist, daß das Ergebnis einer Validation zu einer Rückkopplung in vorangegangene Phasenbereiche führt, so daß diese zu einer Überarbeitung bzw. Neufassung der zugeordneten Dokumente führt.

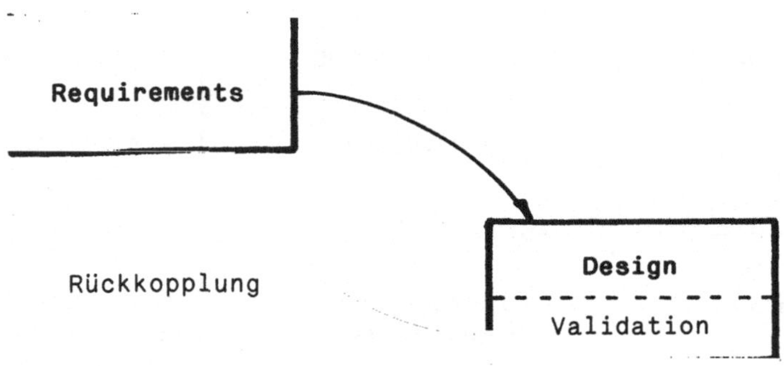


Abb. 3    Rückkopplung auf die Requirementsphase

In dem einleitend angeführten Simulationssystem führten speziell die Ergebnisse der Design-Validation zu einer Vielzahl von Rückkopplungen und im Designbereich abschließend zu drei varianten Strukturspezifikationen (6):

- brauereispezifische Energie- und Massenspezifikation,
- verfahrentechnische Energie- und Massenspezifikation,
- anlagen-/verfahrenstechnisch kausale E/M-Spezifikation.

Neben der Rückkopplung auf die Requirements ist auch zu berücksichtigen, daß sowohl jede Phase ihre eigenen Anforderungen im Rahmen eines Software-Environments hat als auch, daß mit fortschreitender Konkretisierung der Softwarespezifikation neue Anforderungen entstehen.

## 2. Methoden und Werkzeuge

Im Trend einer im klassischen Sinn mehr ingenieurmäßigen Bearbeitung von Software wird speziell im Requirementsbereich gearbeitet (z. B. GI-Fachgruppe 4.3.1 Requirements-Engineering), um durch gezielte Methoden und Werkzeuge effiziente Lösungen zu erreichen.

Informell werden an diese Hilfsmittel folgende Anforderungen gestellt:

- leicht erlernbare und anwendbare Technik,
- verständliche, akzeptable Formalien, die von allen betroffenen Personen akzeptiert werden,
- anhand der Dokumente soll entscheidbar sein, ob das zu entwickelnde System die Anforderungen erfüllt,
- der iterative Requirementsprozeß soll unterstützt werden.

Einen Einblick in die Methodenlandschaft liefert Hesse (7), wobei nach dieser Einordnung Infogramme (8) und SADT (9) geeignete Techniken für die Requirementsphase sind.

### 2.1 SADT

In dem angeführten Anwendungsbeispiel wurde sowohl für die Requirementsphase als auch bei internen Design-Besprechungen die SADT-Methode computer-unterstützt auf einer HP 1000 vielfältig eingesetzt.

Bei einer systemtheoretischen Betrachtung enthält diese Methode:

<u>Funktionale Elemente</u>, um die Transformation der Input-/Output-Daten unter Berücksichtigung zugeordneter Kontrollen (C) und Hilfsmittel (M) zu beschreiben.

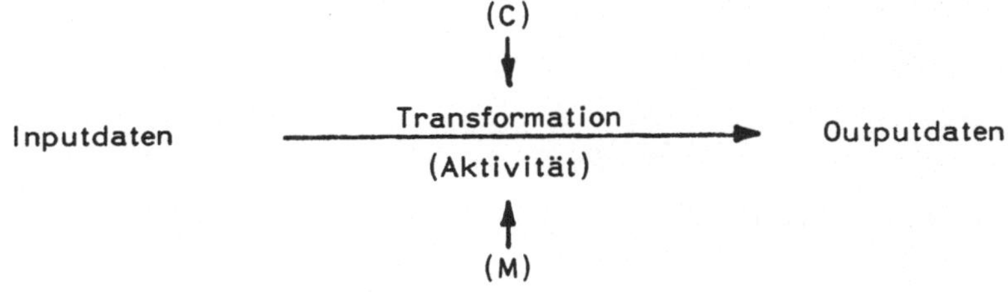

<u>Strukturelle Elemente</u> (▢, →) um sequentielle, iterative und nebenläufige Aktivitäten zu beschreiben.

<u>Hierarchische Elemente</u>, um eine erste grobe Beschreibung sukzessiv nach der TOP-DOWN-Methode aufzulösen.

Begünstigt wird diese Technik durch:

- die grafische Darstellungsform der Diagramme,
- die halbformale Beschreibung (Diagrammformular),
- die verbale Beschreibung der Aktivitäten und Pfeile (Listen).

Am Beispiel des Simulationsmodells ergibt sich auf dem obersten Level folgende Systembetrachtung:

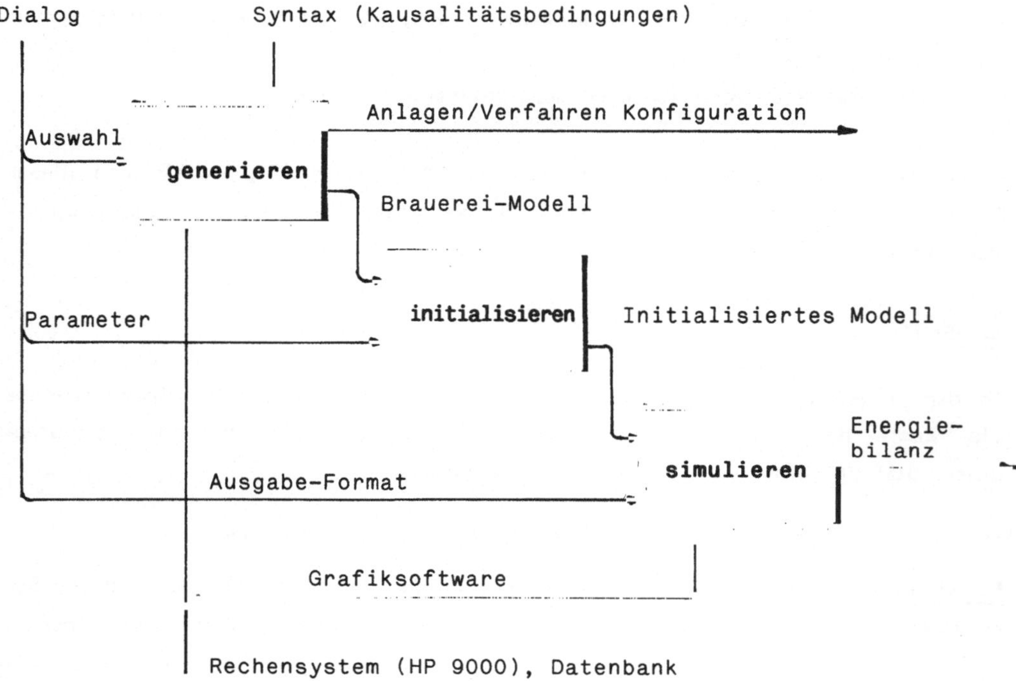


Abb. 4    Simulationssystem

## 3. Resumee

Ausgehend von einigen der auf der Grassauer Tagung (10) geprägten Grundsätzen:

- eine Methode ist besser als keine,
- ein Methodenbündel reicht nicht aus,
- Methoden können nicht die Vernunft ersetzen,

lieferte der hier aufgezeigte Ansatz eine gute Basis für das Energie-Simulationsmodell, selbst wenn die produzierten Requirementsdokumente in den seltensten Fällen formale Objekte bereitstellten für eine perfekte Transformation in ein ideelles System und auch der Einsatz von SADT in einer nicht konsistenten Software-Entwicklungsumgebung erfolgte.

## Literaturliste

( 1)  Perl, J.; Runkel, U.D.; Sturm, K.H., "Nutzung solarer Prozeßwärme in Brauereien", Forum der Brauerei, Nr. 36, S 305-308, Okt. 1983

( 2)  Bauer, F.L.; "Software Engineering", in: "Advanced Course of Software Engineering", Lecture Notes in Computer Science; 30 Springer-Verlag (1975), pp 522-545.

( 3)  Peters, L.J.; Tripp, L.L.; "A Model of Software Engineering", 3rd. International Conference an Software Engineering, May 1978, Atlanta USA, IEEE No. 78 CH 1317-7c, pp 63-69

( 4)  Boehm, B.W.; "Software Engineering", IEEE Transaktions on Computers, Vol. C-25, No. 12, Dec. 1976, pp 1226-1241.

( 5)  End, W.; Gotthardt, H.; Winkelmann, R.; "Softwareentwicklung", Siemens AG, 4. Auflage 1984, (s. S 15).

( 6)  Perl, J.; Sturm, K.H.; "Spezifikation und Modellbildung zur Simulation von Energieflüssen in verfahrenstechnischen (Brau-)Prozessen, in: Breitenecker, F.; Kleinert, W. (ed): Simulationstechnik, 2. Symposium in Wien, Sept. 1984, Informatik Fachberichte 85, Springer Verlag 1984, S 265-273.

( 7)  Hesse, W.; "Methoden und Werkzeuge zur Software-Entwicklung - ein Marsch durch die Technologie-Landschaft", Informatikspektrum 4, S 229-245 (1981).

( 8)  Frölich, C.; "Das Infogramm: Eine Technik zur Analyse, Definition und zum Entwurf von DV-Systemen, SOFTLAB, Interner Bericht 1980.

( 9)  Ross, D.T.; "Structured analysis (SA): A language for communicating ideas", IEEE Trans. on Software Engineering, Vol. SE-3, No. 1 (1977) pp 16-34.

(10)  Floyd, C.; "Ergebnisse des Teilworkshops Entwurfsmethoden" in: Morgenbrod, H.; Remmele, W. (ed): Entwurf großer Software Systeme, Ergebnisse des Teilworkshops, Grassau, Mai 1984.

# SIMULATIONSHARDWARE

Simulation unterschiedlicher Verbindungsnetze im M5PS Multiprozessorsystem
- Modellierung


F. Regen; M. Behrens; W. Ameling  /  Aachen


Zusammenfassung: Das M5PS Multiprozessorsystem verfügt über maximal 56 Prozessoren
in 8 Teilsystemen. Die Leistungsfähigkeit solcher hierarchischer Multiprozessorsysteme hängt nicht nur von der Anzahl der parallelen Rechenelemente sondern in starkem Maße von der Verbindungsstruktur und von den Vergabestrategien auf den einzelnen
Ebenen ab. Hier wird die Simulation eingesetzt, um eine geeignete Struktur für die
Verbindung der Teilsysteme miteinander und um geeignete Vergabetrategien zu finden.
Zur Verringerung der erforderlichen Berechnungszeiten wurde hybride Modellierung und
die sogenannte hierarchische Dekompositionsmethode angewandt, d.h. Teilbereiche des
Systems werden teilweise auch mit Hilfe analytischer Berechnungen getrennt gelöst
und die erzielten Ergebnisse gehen als Parameter in das in der Ebene darüber liegende Gesamtmodell ein. Gegenstand dieses Beitrages sind alle mit der Modellierung zusammenhängenden Aspekte.

Summary: The M5PS Multiprocessor consists of at most 56 processors in 8 subsystems.
The performance of such a hierarchical multiprocessor system is not only affected by
the number of processing elements but also depends to a high degree on the interconnection structure and the allocation strategies at all levels. Here we use simulation to find a well suited structure on the subsystem level and proper allocation
strategies. To reduce simulation time, we apply hybrid modeling and a method termed
hierarchical decomposition. Decomposition involves the off-line solution of subnet-
works. The analysis of the high level model is then carried out using the obtained
parameters. Hybrid modeling means that the off-line solution is at least partially
carried out through analytic computation. In this paper we discuss all modeling aspects.


## Einleitung

Bild 1 zeigt den Aufbau des M5PS Multiprozessorsystems. Es handelt sich um ein hierarchisch aufgebautes Mehrrechnersystem, bei dem bis zu 8 Teilsysteme über Kopplungs-
module verbunden werden können. Maximal 7 Prozessoren an einem asynchronen gemeinsamen Bus bilden ein Teilsystem. Jeder Prozessor besitzt privaten Speicher, auf den er
ohne Behinderung zugreifen kann. Des weiteren verfügt das System über globalen Spei-
cherraum, der auf die Teilsysteme verteilt ist. Zugriffe auf den Speicher des eigenen Teilsystems erfolgen über den Teilsystembus, Zugriffe auf den Speicher anderer
Teilsysteme (externe Aufträge) werden über den Teilsystembus an die Kopplungseinheit
abgegeben, die zur Synchronisation mit dem asynchronen Netzwerk über sogenannte
Teilsystemausgangs- und -eingangspuffer verfügt. Ankommende Aufträge von anderen
Teilsystemen (Fremdaufträge) bzw. zurückkehrende externe Aufträge (Antworten) werden
im Teilsystemeingangspuffer abgelegt, der als Warteschlange ausgelegt ist. Für die
Erledigung von Fremdaufträgen greift die Kopplungseinheit wie ein Prozessor auf den
Teilsystembus zu und legt die Rückmeldung im Teilsystemausgangspuffer ab. Die erhal-
tenen Antworten werden an den entsprechenden wartenden Prozessor weitergegeben. Eine
genaue Beschreibung des Zugriffsablaufs findet man in /BEHR84/.

Nachdem in den letzten Jahren die Leistungsfähigkeit der Teilsysteme mit Messungen
und Simulation /KRIN82, MILD82, REGE83, REGE84/ sowie von zwei gekoppelten Teilsy-

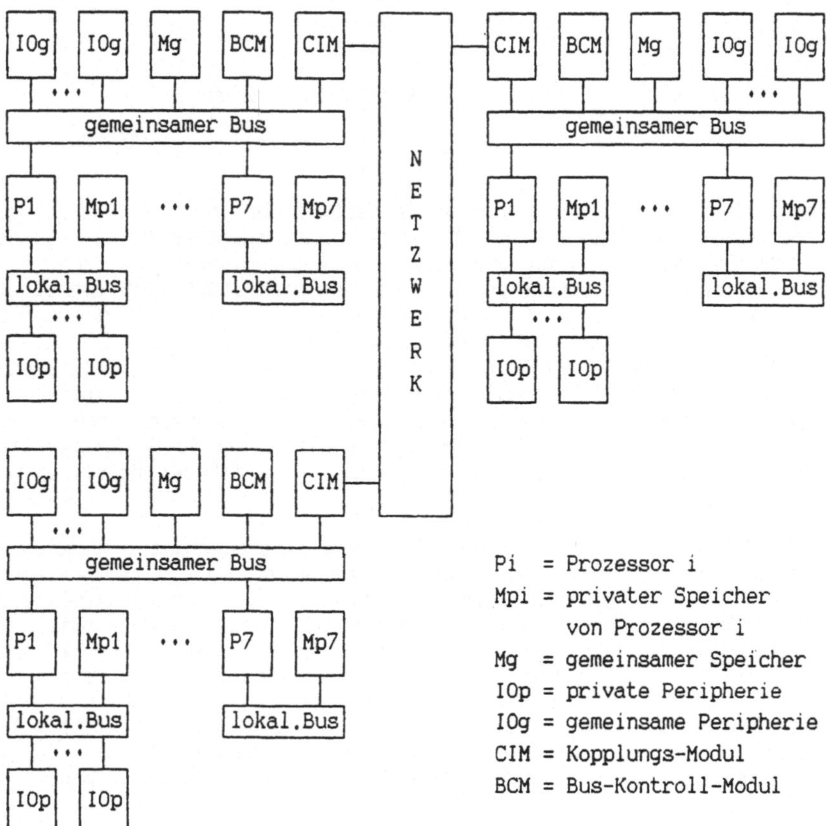



<u>Bild 1</u>: Das M5PS Multiprozessorsystem

stemen mit Hilfe der Simulation /BEHR84/ bestimmt wurde, wird nun die Auslegung des
Verbindungsnetzwerkes zwischen den 8 Teilsystemen untersucht. Als Hilfsmittel wurde
das Simulationssystem FORCASD eingesetzt, ein im Philips Forschungslaboratorium
Hamburg entwickeltes Werkzeug, das sich als sehr geeignet für die Simulation sehr
vieler  Arten von Rechnersystemen erwiesen hat /REGE83, DAHM83/. FORCASD baut auf
den Auswertungsnetzen, einer Art von Petrinetzen auf. Auf die Terminologie der Auswertungsnetze und auf FORCASD soll in diesem Beitrag nicht näher eingegangen werden.


<u>Simulationskonzept</u>

Eine Simulationsuntersuchung ist im allgemeinen sehr aufwendig. Man sollte daher
immer zuerst klären, ob nicht andere Möglichkeiten gefunden werden können. Messungen
scheiden immer dann aus, wenn sich das zu untersuchende System noch in der Kon-
zeptionsphase befindet, und die analytische Berechnung von Warteschlangenmodellen
ist leider nur in eingeschränkten Fällen möglich. In vielen Fällen des Entwurfs von
Rechnern, so auch hier, ergibt sich daher die diskrete Simulation als das einzig
geeignete Untersuchungshilfsmittel. Die gravierenden Nachteile bei Simulationen sind
der Zeitaufwand zur Erstellung des Simulationsprogramms und die hohen Rechenzeiten,
die erforderlich sind, um möglichst genaue Ergebnisse zu erhalten. Die Zeit von den

ersten Überlegungen bis zum fertigen Simulationsprogramm wurde durch das zur Verfügung stehende Simulationssystem FORCASD beträchtlich reduziert (hier ca. 7-8 Mannwochen). Es bleibt das Rechenzeitproblem. Wegen der enormen benötigten Rechenzeiten ließ sich das in /BEHR84/ entwickelte Teilsystemmodell, in dem die Kopplung zweier Teilsysteme auf der Zeitscheibenebene modelliert wurde, im Zusammenhang mit der Kopplung mehrerer Teilsysteme nicht verwenden. Gelöst wurde das Rechenzeitproblem durch eine kombinierte hybride hierarchische Simulation. Die Ergebnisse eines detaillierten Modells auf Zeitscheibenebene eines Teilsystems und eines mit der Mittelwertanalyse berechneten Warteschlangenmodells werden als Parameter für die sich nur innerhalb eines Teilsystems abspielenden Vorgänge benutzt, um in dem auf höherem Level liegenden Gesamtmodell von der Zeitscheibenebene wegzukommen. Die folgenden Abschnitte enthalten eine genaue Modellbeschreibung. An dieser Stelle sollen einige Zahlenangaben einen Einblick vermitteln, welchen Einfluß die Loslösung von der Zeitscheibenebene hat. Beispielsweise werden bei der Simulation des Busses als Verbindung der Teilsysteme in /BEHR85/ je Sekunde CPU-Zeit (Siemens 7536) ca. 6-7 externe Aufträge im Modell erzeugt. Die Anzahl der in dieser Zeit vergangenen Modellzeitscheiben ist abhängig vom Anteil der externen Aufträge an allen Speicherzugriffen. So vergehen bei einem Externanteil von 25% (1%) für ca. 1000 externe Aufträge ungefähr 700-800 (12000-13000) Zeitscheiben. Im Modell aus /BEHR84/ müssten beispielsweise für 1000 externe Aufträge bei einem Anteil von 1% für jedes Teilsystem, d.h. 8 mal 12000-13000 Zeitscheiben simuliert werden. In einer CPU-Sekunde wurden dort ca. 15-17 Zeitscheiben berechnet, d.h. die Rechenzeiten konnten durch das hier verwendete Simulationskonzept um den Faktor 2-50 je nach Externanteil gesenkt werden.

## Modellierung

Da die meisten Leser mit der Terminologie der Auswertungsnetze vermutlich nicht vertraut sind, wird für die Modellierung in diesem Beitrag eine nicht ganz exakte, aber leicht verständliche Beschreibung - eine Kombination aus Warteschlangen und zeitbehafteten Transitionen - verwendet. Zu modellieren war ein komplettes System, d.h. die Topologie, die Verkehrslast und die prozeduralen Eigenschaften der verwendeten Strategien.

Ein wesentlicher Aspekt des Simulationssystems FORCASD ist die Möglichkeit, verschiedene Komponenten getrennt zu modellieren, die dann miteinander verbunden werden. Bild 2 zeigt die Verbindungsebene der "Black Boxes". Der Ausgang jeder Komponente "Teilsystem" ist mit einem Eingang der Komponente "Verbindungsnetzwerk" verbunden und umgekehrt. Die Komponente "Teilsystem" wird nur einmal modelliert, aber

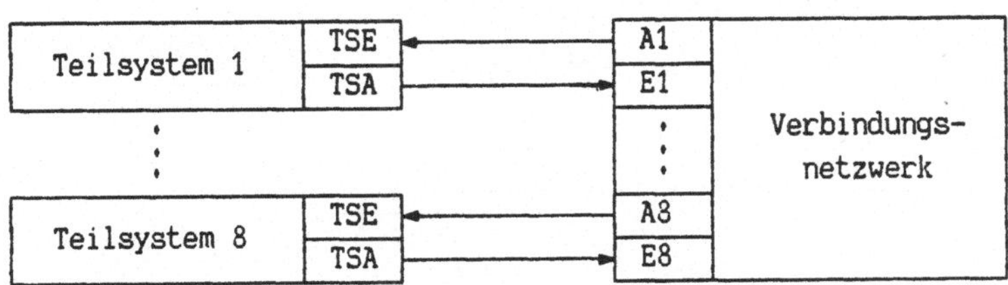


<u>Bild 2</u>: Verbindung der Modellkomponenten

achtmal unter verschiedenen Versionsnummern benutzt. Ein weiterer Vorteil ist, daß man verschiedene Verbindungsstrukturen untersuchen kann, indem man jeweils die entsprechende Modellkomponente in das Modell einbindet. In diesem Beitrag wird auf die Komponente "Verbindungsnetzwerk" nicht weiter eingegangen. In /BEHR85/ werden verschiedene Verbindungsstrukturen und unterschiedliche Strategien auf allen Ebenen bei unterschiedlichen Lastverhältnissen untersucht.

## Modellierung eines Teilsystems

Bild 3 zeigt die Struktur des Teilsystemmodells. Fremdaufträge von anderen Teilsystemen und die Antworten auf die eigenen externen Aufträge werden im Teilsystemeingangspuffer abgelegt. Zur Angleichung des asynchronen Netzwerkes auf den Teilsystemtakt wird für die Übertragung in den Eingangspuffer eine zufällige Zeit zwischen 0 und 1 Zeiteinheit berechnet. Die Warteschlangenstrategie ist FIFO mit der Möglichkeit Antworten eine höhere Priorität zuzuordnen. Die Transition 1 entnimmt jeweils den ersten Token aus dem Eingangspuffer. Haben Antworten eine höhere Priorität, so werden sie sofort in die Prozessor Queue übertragen. Im anderen Fall kann eine Antwort erst dann übertragen werden wenn der letzte vor ihr behandelte Fremdauftrag im Ausgangspuffer angelangt ist. Die eigentliche Übergangzeit ist für Antworten immer 0. Für Fremdaufträge ist sie 0, wenn diese vor internen Speicherzugriffen Vorrang haben. Ansonsten wird sie zufällig in Abhängigikeit von der Anzahl der um einen Speicherzugriff konkurrierenden Prozessoren ermittelt, wobei die entsprechenden Mittelwerte mit Hilfe des weiter hinten beschriebenen Warteschlangenmodells bestimmt wurden. Transition 3 repräsentiert den Speicherzugriff bei Fremdaufträgen bzw. den Zugriff auf das Kopplungsmodul bei externen Aufträgen und überträgt denselben in den Ausgangspuffer. Vorgesehene Strategien sind fair und bevorzugte Zuteilung von Fremdaufträgen. Die Übergangszeit entspricht einer Zeiteinheit plus einer Anpaßzeit an das asynchrone Netzwerk. Transition 2 ist eine reine Verzögerungstransition. Sie repräsentiert die Zeit bis zum nächsten externen Zugriffswunsch eines Prozessors auf ein anderes Teilsystem. Diese Zeit setzt sich zusammen aus einer wie oben zufällig in Abhängigkeit von der Anzahl der im Teilsystem momentan intern zugreifenden Prozessoren nach vorgegeben Mittelwerten und Varianzen ermittelten Zeit plus einer Korrekturzeit. Die Korrekturzeit ergibt sich aus der Anzahl der durch die Transition 3 für interne Zugriffe verlorengegangenen Zeitscheiben multipliziert mit der Wahrscheinlichkeit, daß diese Zugriffe zu Kollisionen auf dem Teilsystembus geführt hätten. Diese Konfliktwahrscheinlichkeit ist ebenso von der Anzahl intern zugreifender Prozessoren abhängig und wird in dem bereits erwähnten Warteschlangenmodell berech-

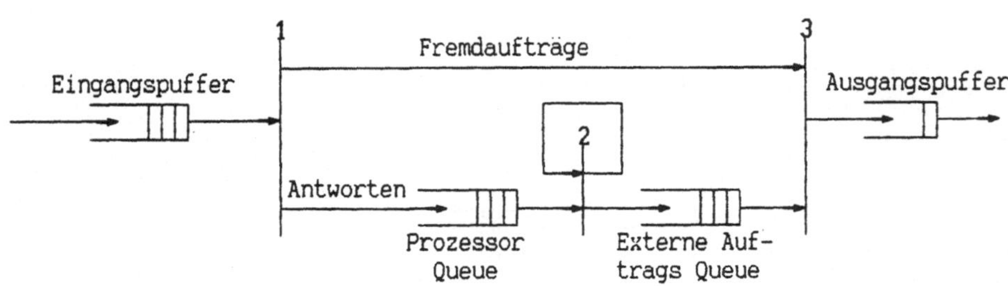


<u>Bild 3</u>: Modellkomponente "Teilsystem"

net. Die für die Übergangszeitberechnung benötigten Mittelwerte und Varianzen werden in dem im nächsten Abschnitt beschriebenen detaillierten Teilsystemmodell auf Zeitscheibenebene bestimmt. Ist eine zufällige Zeit einmal ermittelt, dann kann sie nicht mehr verändert werden. Wenn allerdings eine Antwort ankommt, ändert sich die Anzahl der intern rechnenden Prozessoren. Deshalb wird in diesem Fall die laufende Übergangszeit unterbrochen, eine neue Zufallszeit mit den neuen Werten berechnet und von dieser der Prozentsatz der von der alten Zufallszeit bereits abgelaufenen Zeit abgezogen. In Bild 3 ist dies durch die geschlossene Schleife an Transition 2 gekennzeichnet. Nach Ablauf der Zeit wird ein neuer externer Auftrag in der entsprechenden Warteschlange abgelegt.

<u>Detailliertes Teilsystemmodell</u>: Zur Berechnung der Mittelwerte und Varianzen für die Zeiten zwischen zwei externen Aufträgen wurde das Teilsystemmodell aus /BEHR84/ verwendet, in dem jeder Teilsystembuszugriff auf Zeitscheibenebene detailgetreu nachgebildet ist. Der Ausgangspuffer wird für die Berechnung hier direkt mit dem Eingangspuffer kurzgeschlossen, d.h. jeder externe Auftrag kehrt ohne Verzögerung sofort wieder als Antwort zurück. Dieses Modell wurde dann für alle benötigten Externraten mit allen Prozessoren berechnet, wobei die Zeiten zwischen zwei externen Zugriffen protokolliert und die entsprechenden Mittelwerte und Varianzen berechnet wurden.

<u>Warteschlangenmodell</u>: Bild 4 zeigt das Warteschlangenmodell, mit dessen Hilfe die Verzögerung von Fremdaufträgen bei fairer Strategie und die Busauslastung (= Wahrscheinlichkeit für Konflikte auf dem Bus) eines Teilsystems in Abhängigkeit von der Anzahl der um den Bus konkurrierenden Prozessoren berechnet wurde. Das Modell enthält zwei geschlossene Ketten ohne Klassenwechsel. Kette 1 repräsentiert die Fremdaufträge, Kette 2 die internen Zugriffe der Prozessoren auf den Teilsystembus. Die Wartezeiten der Ketten an den Servern lassen sich leicht berechnen, wenn die Verweildauern in den Servern, die Bedienstrategien und die Kundenanzahlen der Ketten bekannt sind /SAUE81/. Die Tabellen 1 und 2 zeigen die gewählten Werte. Die Verweildauer in Intern hängt vom Anteil der Nutzung des privaten Speichers ab. 3,42 Zeiteinheiten ergibt sich bei Messungen, wenn der private Speicher nicht genutzt wurde /KRIN84/. Die Kundenanzahl 0 in der Kette 1 wurde gewählt um die Busauslastung in

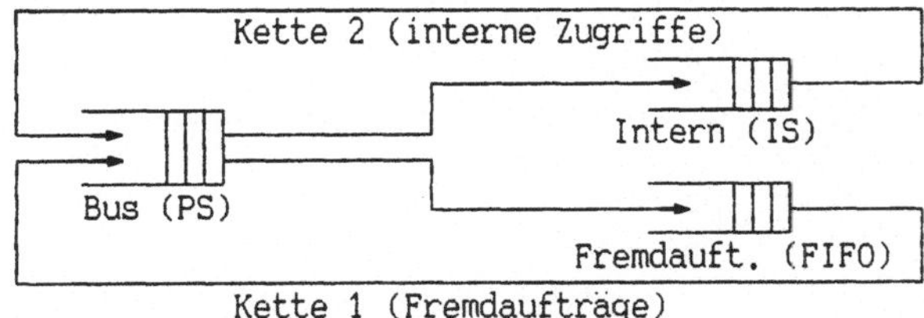


<u>Bild 4</u>: Warteschlangenmodell

<u>Tabelle 1</u>:

| Server | Strategie | Verweildauer |
|---|---|---|
| Bus | PS | 1 ZE |
| Intern | IS | 3,42 ZE |
| Fremdauft. | FIFO | 0 |

<u>Tabelle 2</u>:

| Kette | Kundenanzahl |
|---|---|
| 1 | 0 oder 1 |
| 2 | 0,1,···oder 7 |

Abhängigkeit von der Anzahl der um einen Zugriff konkurrierenden Prozessoren (Kundenanzahl der Kette 2) zu berechnen. Ist die Kundenanzahl gleich 1 in der Kette 1, so entspricht ihre Wartezeit am Server Bus der gesuchten Verzögerung eines Fremdauftrages.


<u>Literatur:</u>

/BEHR84/   Behrens, M.; Regen, F.; Ameling, W.
           *Untersuchung von gekoppelten M5PS Teilsystemen mittels Simulation*
           Informatik Fachbericht 85, pp.79-83, 1984

/BEHR85/   Behrens, M.; Regen, F.; Ameling, W.
           *Simulation unterschiedlicher Verbindungsnetze im M5PS Multiprozessorsystem
           - Lastfälle, Strategien und Simulationsergebnisse*
           Tagungsband zur ASIM85 (Informatik Fachbericht)

/DAHM83/   Dahmen, N.; Killat, U.; Stecher, R.
           *Mixed Traffic Performance Data of CSMA/CD- and DSMA-Access Protocols
           Derived from FORCASD Simulation Runs*
           Informatik Fachbericht 60, pp. 535-553, 1983

/MILD82/   Milde, J.; Krings, L.; Ameling, W.
           *Architektur des Multiprozessor Systems M5PS und Auswertung einiger
           Anwendungen*
           NTG/GI-Fachtagung, Ulm, 1982

/KRIN82/   Krings, L.; Milde, J.; Ameling, W.
           *The Influence of Bus Allocation Algorithms on the System Performance of
           Multiprocessor Systems with a Time-Shared Bus*
           Proceedings 10th IMACS World Congress, Montreal, 1982

/KRIN84/   Krings, L.
           *Minimierung der Ausführungszeit für eine Klasse von Prozeßgraphen in einem
           Multiprozessorsystem mit Zugriffskonflikten am gemeinsamen Bus*
           Dissertation, RWTH Aachen, 1984

/REGE83/   Regen, F.; Krings, L.; Ameling,W.
           *Simulation of Job Execution in the M5PS Multiprocessor*
           Informatik Fachbericht 71, pp. 329-336, 1983

/REGE84/   Regen, F.; Krings, L.; Ameling, W.
           *Berechnung der Ausführungszeiten von Prozeßgraphen in einem
           Multiprozessorsystem mittels Simulation*
           Informatik Fachbericht 85, pp.73-78, 1984

/SAUE81/   Sauer, Ch.H.; Chandy, K.M.
           *Computer Systems Performance Modelling*
           Prentice Hall, Inc., Englewood Cliffs, N.J. 07632, 1981

Simulation unterschiedlicher Verbindungsnetze im M5PS Multiprozessorsystem
- Lastfälle, Strategien und Simulationsergebnisse

Behrens, M.; Regen, F.; Ameling, W. / Aachen

Zusammenfassung: Im Rahmen dieser Veröffentlichung wird die Rechenleistung eines hierarchischen Multiprozessorsystems, des M5PS-Systems, gemessen. Das System besteht aus Teilsystemen, die ihrerseits wieder Multiprozessorsysteme sind. Die Teilsysteme sind über ein Netzwerk miteinander verbunden. Dazu wird ein deterministischer, zentral gesteuerter Zeitscheibenbus mit einem Zeitscheibenring verglichen. Drei deterministische Buszuteilungsstrategien werden untersucht: Vergabe mit festen, zyklischen und komplementären Prioritäten. Dabei ist insbesondere das Problem der Fairneß zwischen den einzelnen Teilsystemen bei überlastetem Bus wichtig. Es wird gezeigt, daß bei niedrig und normal ausgelastetem Bus die Zuteilungsstrategie auf dem Teilsystembus in starkem Maße die Zugriffszeit bei einem Zugriff auf ein anderes Teilsystem bestimmt. Einige Meßwerte der Laufzeit von externen Zugriffen bei unterschiedlichen Lastfällen werden vorgestellt.

Summary: In this paper, we address the performance analysis of a hierarchical multiprocessor system, the M5PS-System. The system consists of microprocessor clusters which are connected by a network. Therefore we compare a deterministic, centrally controlled slotted bus with a slotted ring. Three deterministic bus scheduling algorithms are examined: fixed priorities, cyclic priorities and complementary priorities. Comparison of simulation results will give insight into the question of fairness among clusters in the case of a heavily loaded bus. It will be shown that the selection of a well suited intracluster bus control scheme is decisive for gaining minimal intercluster access delays at low and normal loads. Some characteristic delays of external accesses at different loads will be presented.


Einleitung

Bei dem $M^5$PS-System handelt es sich um ein enggekoppeltes Multiprozessorsystem mit hierarchischer Struktur. Auf der untersten Ebene steht das Prozessormodul, das auf seinen privaten Speicher unbehindert und exklusiv zugreifen kann. Bis zu 7 Prozessormodule sind zu einem Teilsystem zusammengefaßt und greifen konkurrent über einen im TDMA (Time Division Multiplex Access) organisierten gemeinsamen Bus auf gemeinsamen Speicher zu. Dabei wird der Zugriff auf jeweils ein Datenbyte durch ein spezielles Modul mit vorwählbaren Zuteilungsstrategien zu Beginn jeder Zeitscheibe kontrolliert. Der Zugriff auf den Speicher wird innerhalb einer Zeitscheibe abgeschlossen. An den gemeinsamen Bus ist jeweils ein Systemkopplungsmodul /BEHR84/ angeschlossen, das Zugriffswünsche auf Speicher fremder Teilsysteme anhand der Adresse erkennt und abwickelt. Der betroffene Prozessor wird bis zur vollständigen Abarbeitung des Zugriffs angehalten. Die Systemkopplungsmodule kommunizieren miteinander über ein Systemnetzwerk. Durch die Wahl des send and wait...receive and answer-Schemas beim Zugriff auf ein fremdes Teilsystem werden die Laufzeiten eines externen Zugriffs leistungsbestimmend. Ein Teil der Laufzeiten entsteht beim doppelten Durchlaufen des Netzwerkes, ein anderer beim Zugriff des fremden Systemkopplungsmoduls auf den Teilsystemspeicher sowie bei der Übergabe der Antwort an den zugreifenden externen Prozessor. Außerdem kostet das Warten auf ein freies Ausgaberegister Zeit. Die Wahl des

Netzwerkes ist mithin für die Leistung genauso entscheidend wie die Einbindung der Zugriffe des Systemkopplungsmodules in den Zuteilungsalgorithmus des gemeinsamen Busses. In den folgenden Kapiteln werden verschiedene Lösungsansätze untersucht.

## Netzwerktopologien

Das Netzwerk zwischen den Teilsystemen arbeitet nach dem Message-Switching Verfahren, wobei jede Nachricht ein Wort (48 Bit) lang ist. Es werden zwei verschiedene Topologien vorgestellt und miteinander verglichen, der deterministische Zeitscheibenbus (Slotted Bus) mit zentraler Verwaltung, und der Slotted Ring. Beide sollen die Nachricht parallel übertragen. Dies ist möglich, da die räumlichen Entfernungen zwischen den Teilsystemen gering sind. Das zur Bewertung verschiedener Verbindungsstrukturen zwischen Teilsystemen benutzte Simulationskonzept ist in  /REGE85/ beschrieben und wurde entsprechend um zwei Modellkomponenten, Zeitscheibenbus und Slotted Ring, erweitert.

Beim *Slotted Bus* haben alle angeschlossenen Teilsysteme prinzipiell gleichberechtigten Zugriff auf das gemeinsame Kommunikationsmittel, den Bus. Bei der hier vorliegenden engen Kopplung der Teilsysteme ist eine zentrale deterministische Zuteilung nach dem TDMA-Verfahren möglich. Random-Access-Verfahren wie etwa CSMA/CD werden hier aufgrund des Overheads nicht verwendet. Die Wartezeit auf einen Slot hängt von der Zuteilungsstrategie des Busses und der Busauslastung ab, als Nachrichtenlaufzeit wird immer ein Slot benötigt. Es wurden drei verschiedene deterministische Zuteilungsstrategien untersucht.

Bei der Strategie *Feste Prioritäten* erhält jedes der K Teilsysteme eine seiner Nummer entsprechende Priorität. Dagegen erhält bei der Strategie *Zyklische Prioritäten* jedes Teilsystem, das während eines Slots auf dem Systembus die Priorität p (p $\varepsilon$ {1,2,...,K-1}) hat, für den nächsten Slot die nächstniedrigere Priorität p+1. Das Teilsystem mit der Priorität K erhält im nächsten Slot die höchste Priorität, 1. Eine weitere Möglichkeit, mit sich systematisch veränderndern Prioritäten zu arbeiten, sind die *komplementären Prioritäten*. Hierbei erhält das Teilsystem x die Priorität x für einen Slot und die Priorität (K + 1 - x) für den nächsten. Für den darauffolgenden Slot erhält es wieder die Priorität x und so weiter.

Bei der Topologie *Slotted Ring* wird die Zeitachse ebenfalls in Zeitscheiben fester Länge (Slots) eingeteilt /SPAN82/. Die Slots entsprechen dann umlaufenden Nachrichtencontainern, die mit jeweils einer Nachricht, entweder einem Fremdauftrag oder einer Antwort gefüllt werden können. Leere Slots werden durch ein entsprechendes Indikatorbit gekennzeichnet. Erkennt ein sendewilliges Teilsystem einen leeren Slot, so kann es diesen mit der Nachricht füllen; das Indikatorbit wird entsprechend geändert. Eine Nachricht wird aus einem Slot entnommen, wenn die Zieladresse mit der Teilsystemnummer übereinstimmt, der Slot ist danach leer und kann neu gefüllt werden. Es existieren ebensoviele Slots wie Teilsysteme. Alle Slots werden nach Ablauf

der Verweilzeit jeweils dem im Ring folgenden Teilsystem zugesandt. Zu der Wartezeit
auf einen leeren Slot addiert sich hier die Nachrichtenlaufzeit, die ebenso viele
Slots lang ist, wie Teilsysteme passiert werden müssen.

## Untersuchte Lastfälle

Eigene Untersuchungen haben gezeigt, daß die mittlere Last auf höheren Netzebenen
eines hierarchischen Multiprozessorsystems eher niedrig ist. Ähnliche Ergebnisse
sind auch der Literatur zu entnehmen, beispielsweise im Zusammenhang mit dem $CM^*$-
Projekt /JONE80/. Ein gut dimensioniertes Netzwerk muß jedoch zwischenzeitlich auch
ein hohes Nachrichtenaufkommen ohne starke Leistungseinbußen verarbeiten können. Nun
gibt es bei dem hier vorgestellten aufwendigen Multiprozessorsystem eine ganze Reihe
von Parametern, die die Netzwerkbelastung beeinflußen. Die Nachrichtenrate auf der
Ebene der gekoppelten Netzwerke wird durch die Anzahl der angeschlossenen Teilsysteme K bestimmt. Für die hier vorgestellten Untersuchungen wurde $K = 8$ gewählt.
Ebenfalls wichtig ist die Anzahl von Prozessoren PE(k), aus denen jeweils ein Teilsystem besteht, im Rahmen dieser Untersuchung wurde PE(k) für alle Teilsysteme zu 7
gewählt. Des weiteren kann die Zahl der Prozessoren $PE_e(k)$ jedes Teilsystems festgelegt werden, die Fremdaufträge erzeugen (Hier gewählt: 1 oder 7) und die Wahrscheinlichkeit $P_e$, mit der ein Prozessor den Speicheradreßbereich des eigenen Teilsystems
verläßt und damit einen Fremdauftrag generiert. Es besteht die Möglichkeit eine $P_e$
von 1, 5, 10 oder 25% festzulegen. Diese Werte müssen nach einer Analyse des
Prozeßgraphen festgelegt werden. Bei den meisten Simulationsläufen wurde eine sym-
metrische Lastverteilung angenommen, d.h. $P_e$ und  PE waren jeweils für alle Teilsysteme gleich. Aber es wurden auch unsymmetrische Lastverteilungen untersucht. Des
weiteren sind die Verteilungen der Fremdaufträge auf die verschiedenen anderen Teilsysteme mitbestimmend für die Laufzeit, sie können bei dem verwendeten Modell eines
Teilsystems /REGE85/ als Übergangswahrscheinlichkeiten vorgegeben werden. Hier wurden zwei Fälle vorgesehen: Bei der Verteilung <u>gleichverteilt</u> wird jedes andere Teilsystem mit der Übergangswahrscheinlichkeit 1/7 angesprochen, während bei der Verteilung <u>Pipe</u> jeweils 94% der Fremdaufträge vom Teilsystem i (i<K) aus das Teilsystem
i+1 und vom Teilsystem K aus das Teilsystem 1 erreichen. Die restlichen 6% werden
auf die anderen fremden Teilsysteme gleichmäßig verteilt. Alle Lastfälle wurden mit
vier verschiedenen Vergabestrategien am Teilsystembus simuliert:

- *F/A1.* Die Prozessoren werden am Teilsystembus mit fairer Strategie behandelt
(Round Robin). Fremdaufträge werden wie Prozessorzugriffe behandelt. Antworten
haben höchste Priorität, können Fremdaufträge in der Warteschlange jedoch
nicht überholen.

- *F/A2.* Wie F/A1, jedoch erhalten Antworten am Teilsystembus immer die höchste
Priorität .

- *F/F.* Wie F/A1 jedoch sind Fremdaufträge und Antworten gleich priorisiert.

- *F/FA.* Kombination aus den beiden vorangehenden Strategien: Fremdaufträge und Antworten werden bevorzugt, aber Antworten überholen Fremdaufträge.

## Ergebnisse

Es wurde zunächst der Zeitscheibenbus untersucht, wobei die Slotdauer zu 125 ns festgesetzt wurde, das ist ein Viertel der Zeitscheibenlänge auf dem Teilsystembus und entspricht einer maximalen Übertragungsrate von 384 MBaud. Bei gleichverteilter symmetrischer Last ergibt sich eine Busauslastung bis zu 70%. Dabei ist die Beeinflußung der Laufzeit durch die gewählte Systembusstrategie vernachlässigbar. Auch bei festen Prioritäten wird eine eventuell längere Laufzeit des Fremdauftrags auf dem Bus durch eine entsprechend kürzere der Antwort kompensiert. Bei diesen Busauslastungen stellt nicht der Systembus, sondern der Teilsystembus das Haupthindernis dar, wie sich beim Vergleich der Laufzeiten der externen Zugriffe bei den verschiedenen Teilsystembuszuteilungsstrategien zeigt (Bild 1). In Bild 2 ist im unteren Teil die Laufzeit externer Zugriffe als Funktion der Wahrscheinlichkeit externer Zugriffe angegeben. Die resultierende Busauslastung ist im oberen Teil angegeben. Verwendet wurde die Strategie F/FA. In Bild 3 ist die Auswirkung unsymmetrischer Last dargestellt. Es wurde die Verteilung "Pipe" benutzt. Bei $P_e$ von 25% und $PE_e(k)$ = 7 für alle k außer k = 6, $PE_e(6)$ = 1 ergibt sich bei einer verdoppelten Slotdauer (250 ns) eine Busauslastung von knapp 100%, der Bus ist also der Engpaß. In dieser Rahmensituation zeigt nur noch die Strategie "Zyklisch" eine einigermaßen faire Zuteilung. Die anderen Strategien können im Extremfall sogar eine Blockierung eines Teilsystemes hervorrufen.

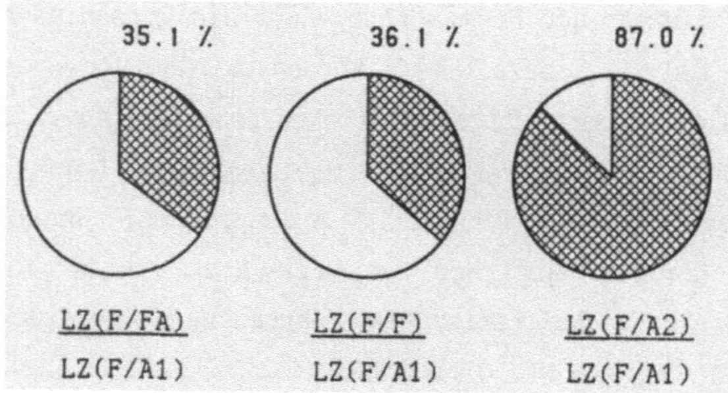


Bild 1: Auswirkung verschiedener Teilsystembuszuteilungsstrategien auf die Laufzeit

Als Alternative wurde der Slotted Ring untersucht. Um das Ergebnis gleich vorwegzunehmen: Die mittleren Laufzeiten externer Zugriffe sind etwas länger als die vergleichbaren des Zeitscheibenbusses. Bei einem Gesamtsystem aus 8 Teilsystemen mit jeweils 7 Prozessoren, symmetrischer Lastverteilung und einer $P_e$ von 25 % beträgt die mittlere Laufzeit externer Zugriffe 5.4 interne Zeitscheiben, also etwa 2.7 ms (gegenüber 2 ms beim Bus). Die Slotdauer des Rings betrug 125 ns und als Strategie

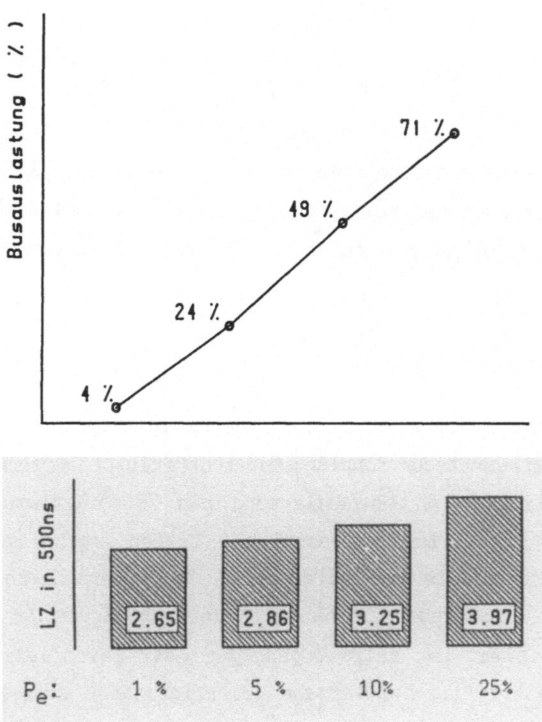

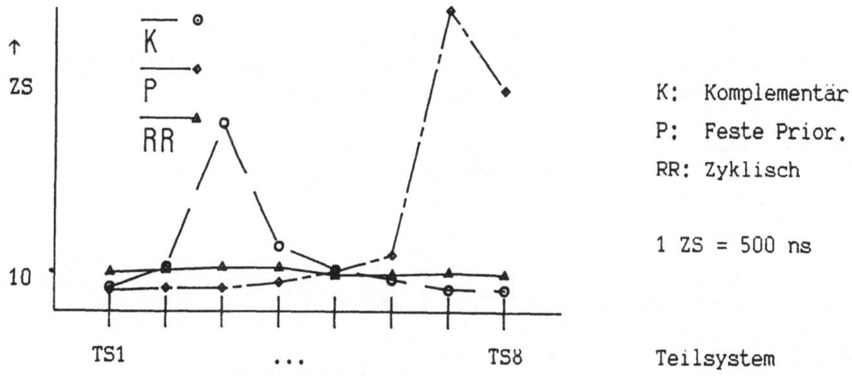

**Bild 2**: Laufzeit externer Aufträge und Busauslastung bei Strategie F/FA in Abhängigkeit von $P_e$



**Bild 3:** Laufzeiten externer Aufträge bei überlastetem Zeitscheibenbus

wurde F/FA verwendet. Die Differenz erklärt sich aus der längeren Verweildauer im Netzwerk: Fremdauftrag und Antwort sind, da der Ring unidirektional betrieben wird, _immer_ für die Dauer von 8 Slots im Netzwerk, während für die Übertragung beim Bus nur 2 Slotdauern notwendig sind. Die konstante Verweildauer hat allerdings auch zur Folge, daß die Laufzeit eines externen Auftrages beim Slotted Ring weitgehend von Unsymmetrien in der Lasterzeugung unbeeinflußt bleibt. Eine Monopolisierung des

Slotted Rings durch eine einzelne Station, wie sie etwa in /KAUF84/ beschrieben ist, muß bei dem hier beschriebenen Multiprozessorsystem nicht befürchtet werden, solange die Slotdauer kleiner als der minimale Abstand zweier Sendewünsche gewählt wird, der hier 500 ns beträgt.

## Wertung

Im Rahmen dieser Untersuchung hat sich der deterministische Zeitscheibenbus als ein leistungsfähiges Instrument zur Kopplung von acht Multiprozessorsystemen gezeigt. Im Nieder- und Mittellastbereich (Busauslastung bis 70 %) dominiert der Einfluß der Zuteilungsstrategie des Teilsystembusses, die besten Ergebnisse werden durch eine Strategie (F/FA) erzielt, die die individuellen Lastunterschiede innerhalb der Teilsysteme umgeht. Bei Hochlastbetrieb hangt es weitgehend von der Zuteilungsstrategie des Busses ab, inwieweit der faire Zugang zum Netz gewährleistet ist, die besten Ergebnisse werden mit zyklischer Vergabe der Prioritäten erzielt. Der Slotted Ring ist bei den hier vorliegenden Rahmenbedingungen eine durchaus gute Lösung, die weitgehende Unabhängigkeit der Laufzeiten von Lastunsymmetrien verkraftet, aber er ist durch seine Topologie bedingt die langsamere Alternative.

## Literatur:

/BEHR84/ Behrens, M.; Regen, F.; Ameling, W.
*Untersuchung von gekoppelten M5PS Teilsystemen mittels Simulation*
Informatik Fachbericht 85, pp.79-83, 1984

/JONE80/ Jones, A.K.; Schwartz, P.
*Experience Using Multiprocessor Systems - A Status Report*
ACM Computing Surveys, 12,2, pp.121-165, 1980

/KAUF84/ Kauffels, F.-J.
*Lokale Netze*
Köln-Braunsfeld: R. Müller, 1984

/REGE85/ Regen, F.; Behrens, M.; Ameling, W.
*Simulation unterschiedlicher Verbindungsnetze im M5PS Multiprozessorsystem - Modellierung*
zur Veröffentlichung vorgesehen beim 3. Symposium Simulationstechnik, ASIM85

/SPAN82/ Spaniol, O.
*Konzepte und Bewertungsmethoden für lokale Rechnernetze*
Informatik Spektrum, Springer, 5, pp. 152-170, 1982

# SIMULATION EINES DATENBANKRECHNERS FÜR DIE PROZESSDATENVERARBEITUNG

Rolf-Peter Liedtke

Forschungszentrum Informatik
an der Universität Karlsruhe
Haid-und-Neu-Straße 10-14
7500 Karlsruhe 1

**Zusammenfassung:** An Datenbanksysteme in der Prozeßdatenverarbeitung
werden neben anderen insbesondere hohe Anforderungen bezüglich ihrer
Effizienz gestellt. Sie müssen kurze Reaktionszeiten aufweisen und in
der Lage sein, hohe Datenraten zu verarbeiten. In diesem Beitrag wird
die Leistungsfähigkeit eines auf einem neuartigen Architekturkonzept
basierenden realzeitfähigen Datenbankrechners durch Simulation untersucht. Es wird gezeigt, daß vor allem das Massenspeichersystem sehr
leicht zum Engpaß werden kann, so daß Beschleunigungsmaßnahmen durch
Parallelisierung in erster Linie hier ansetzen müssen. Parallelisierung der höheren logischen Funktionen des Datenbanksystems hingegen
kann die Leistung nicht unbedingt steigern.

## 1. Architektur des Datenbankrechners

Aus Effizienzgründen werden Datenhaltungssysteme in Anwendungen in der
Prozeßautomatisierung gegenwärtig meist individuell auf der Basis von
Dateisystemen realisiert. Dabei muß man allerdings auf die Nutzung der
spezifischen Eigenschaften von Datenbanksystemen, wie Transaktionsverwaltung, Synchronisation konkurrierender Zugriffe, Konsistenzwahrung
und Datenunabhängigkeit, verzichten. Diese Eigenschaften - vor allem
die Datenunabhängigkeit, d.h. die Möglichkeit Datenstrukturen zu ändern, ohne die Zugriffsprogramme ändern zu müssen - gewinnen jedoch
auch im Bereich der Prozeßautomatisierung an Bedeutung.

In diesem Papier wird mit Hilfe der Simulation untersucht, inwieweit
ein neues Architekturkonzept in der Lage ist, die Voraussetzungen für
die Realisierung eines hinreichend effizienten Datenbankrechners für
die Datenhaltung in der Prozeßdatenverarbeitung zu bieten.

Um sowohl einzelne Datenbankoperationen zu beschleunigen als auch um
den Durchsatz zu erhöhen, wird die Datenbanksoftware in einzelne Funktionseinheiten zerlegt, die auf verschiedene Prozessoren eines speziell entwickelten Multi-Mikrorechnersystems verteilt werden können.
Die Komponenten dieses Systems sind über ein gemeinsames Doppelbus-
System gekoppelt. Folgende Funktionen des Datenbanksystems können dann
einzelnen Rechnern zugeordnet werden: Transaktionsverteilung und -
verwaltung, Suche in Indexstrukturen, Massenspeicherzugriffe, Ausführung relationaler Operationen, Änderung von Primärdaten, Änderung von
Indexstrukturen.

Diese Funktionen können in Form einer (logischen) Pipeline angeordnet
werden und erlauben damit eine weitgehend phasenparallele Verarbeitung
von Transaktionen, da diese die genannten Funktionen oder Teilmengen
davon in jeweils der gleichen Reihenfolge durchlaufen /AF84/ /Fe84/.
Es muß jedoch nicht notwendigerweise jede Datenbankfunktion einer

---

Diese Arbeit wurde aus Mitteln des BMFT unter der
Kennzahl 08IT10428 bzw. 08IT042A9 gefördert.

eigenen Rechnerkomponente zugeordnet werden, sondern es ist beispielsweise sinnvoll, Funktionen mit geringem Leistungsbedarf auf einem gemeinsamen Rechner unterzubringen.

In der Massenspeicherkomponente soll für Lesezugriffe ein sog. Filterprozessor /Ki83/ eingesetzt werden. Dies bedeutet, daß während des Lesens von der Magnetplatte bereits einfache relationale Operationen, wie Selektion, Projektion oder Aggregatfunktionen auf den gelesenen Daten ausgeführt werden können. Dabei werden nicht selektiv eine oder wenige Datenseiten, sondern jeweils eine ganze Relation gelesen, und die qualifizierten Tupel werden "on the fly" herausgefiltert und als Ergebnis zur Weiterverarbeitung (für weitere relationale Operationen oder bereits als Endergebnis) zur Verfügung gestellt. Dies erspart Indexzugriffe und ermöglicht Parallelverarbeitung um den Preis sehr zahlreicher E/A-Operationen. Deren Zeitbedarf wird jedoch nicht von der mittleren Dauer eines Plattenzugriffs bestimmt, sondern lediglich von der reinen Übertragungsdauer der gelesenen Blöcke, wenn es gelingt, alle Seiten einer Relation in aufeinanderfolgenden Blöcken der Platte abzulegen. Damit kann der Aufwand für Positionier-/Suchoperationen des Plattensystems auf ein Minimum reduziert werden.

Schreibzugriffe betreffen unverändert einzelne Seiten. Durch Verwendung eines Datenbank-Cache /El82/ können sie verzögert durchgeführt werden zu Zeitpunkten, zu denen kein Leseauftrag vorliegt. Damit ist eine kurze Antwortzeit für reine Lesetransaktionen gewährleistet.


## 2. Modellbeschreibung

Die eben beschriebene Architektur wurde als Warteschlangennetz modelliert und mit Hilfe des Simulationssystems RESQ2 (Research Queuing Package Version 2) /SMK82/ simuliert. Da Transaktionen in wechselnden Abständen ausgeführt werden und sich im allgemeinen keine konstante Population von Aufträgen im System befindet, wurde eine Modellierung als offenes System gewählt.

Es wurden zwei Varianten des Modells entwickelt. Bei der ersten Variante wurde zugrundegelegt, daß jeder der genannten Datenbankfunktionen ein eigener Prozessor zugeordnet wird (Abb. 1). Daher wird jede Funktion durch eine Bedienstation dargestellt. Die beiden Funktionen, die auf den Indexstrukturen arbeiten, wurden dabei nicht modelliert. Die Bedienstationen sind gemäß der Abfolge der einzelnen Schritte bei der Transaktionsverarbeitung miteinander verbunden. Durch Verzweigungen in den Verbindungen mit entsprechenden Verzweigungswahrscheinlichkeiten für die Aufträge werden verschiedene Transaktionsklassen berücksichtigt, wie z.B. Lesen ganzer Relationen, Lesen von Teilrelationen durch Anwendung relationaler Operationen unterschiedlicher Komplexität, Ändern von Relationen.

In der zweiten Variante wurde angenommen, daß alle logischen Datenbankfunktionen (d.h. solche, die nur auf bereits im Hauptspeicher befindliche Daten zugreifen) demselben Prozessor und das Massenspeichersystem (d.h. die mit einfachen relationalen Operationen kombinierte Plattenein- und -ausgabe) einem zweiten Prozessor zugeordnet werden. Dieses Modell besteht infolgedessen aus nur zwei Bedienstationen für die Datenbankfunktionen (Abb. 2). Die logischen Datenbankfunktionen, die im vorigen Modell durch eigene Bedienstationen modelliert wurden, führen nun zu einer entsprechenden Anzahl von Auftragsklassen für die Station, in der sie jetzt zusammengefaßt sind. Die Verbindung der Auftragsklassen untereinander entspricht genau der Struktur der ersten Variante.

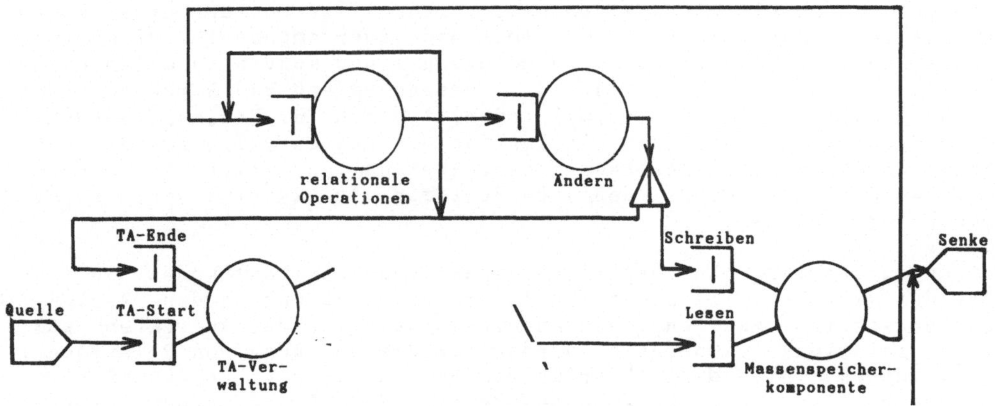


Abb. 1: Modell mit getrennten Prozessoren für logische Funktionen

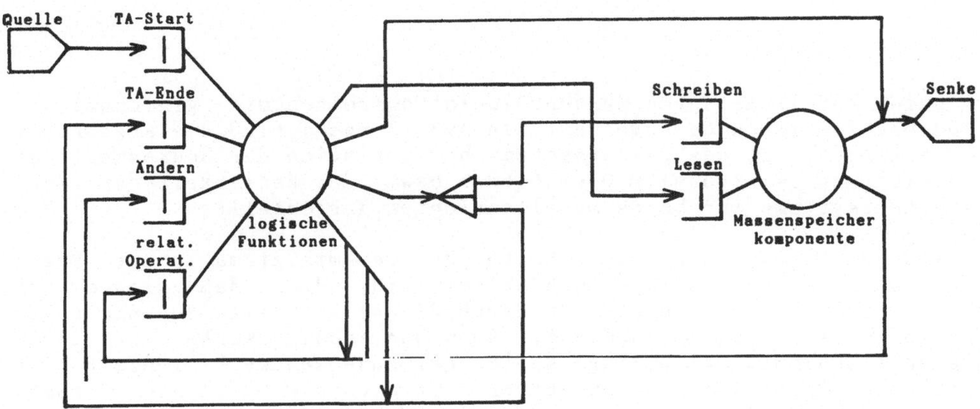


Abb. 2: Modell mit gemeinsamem Prozessor für logische Funktionen

Das Doppelbus-System wurde mit Hilfe des Pool-Konzepts modelliert /SMK82/. Dabei synchronisiert ein Pool die Belegung der beiden Busse, während der Zeitbedarf der Datenübertragungen durch weitere Bedienstationen zwischen je zwei miteinander kommunizierenden Komponenten des Datenbanksystems nachgebildet wird. (Wegen der Übersichtlichkeit sind diese Stationen und die Mechanismen des Pools nicht in den Abb. 1 und 2 dargestellt.) Die Nachrichten, die zwischen den Komponenten übertragen werden, unterscheiden sich z.T. erheblich in ihrer Länge. Daher weisen die verschiedenen Bedienstationen, die die Verzögerung durch den Bustransfer modellieren, unterschiedliche Bedienzeiten auf, je nach der Art der Nachrichten, die an der jeweiligen Stelle über den Bus geschickt werden.

Aufgrund des neuartigen Konzepts (mengenorientierte Verarbeitung bei allen Datenbankfunktionen, keine Einzeltupelverarbeitung) können die Bedienzeiten für die einzelnen Komponenten nur ganz grob abgeschätzt werden. Die verwendeten Parameter für die Bedienzeiten der logischen Datenbankfunktionen orientieren sich an Messungen, die an einem konventionellen CODASYL-Datenbanksystem durchgeführt wurden. Um der Unsicherheit Rechnung zu tragen, wurden Simulationsreihen durchgeführt, bei denen die Bedienzeiten ausgewählter Stationen jeweils stark variiert wurden.

Insbesondere resultiert aus dem skizzierten Filterkonzept eine ungewöhnlich lange Bedienzeit für die Massenspeicherkomponente. Diese wurde abgeschätzt, indem unter Zugrundelegung eines konventionellen Plattensystems und eines Datenbestands, dessen Umfang und Struktur (Relationenanzahl und -größe, Tupelgrößen) typisch für Prozeßsteuerungsanwendungen sind, mittlere Zeiten für das sequentielle Lesen einer ganzen Relation bzw. das Ändern einzelner Seiten ermittelt wurden. Dabei wurde angenommen, daß jede Relation in aufeinanderfolgenden Blöcken abgelegt ist.

Das zugrundegelegte Lastprofil (Transaktionsverhalten) kommt in der Verbindungsstruktur zwischen den Auftragsklassen und in den Verzweigungswahrscheinlichkeiten (Wahrscheinlichkeit für das Auftreten komplexer relationaler Operationen oder für die Änderung von Relationen) zum Ausdruck. Die Werte hierfür wurden aus einer repräsentativen Untersuchung von Datenbankanwendungen in der Prozeßautomatisierung abgeleitet.

Die Strategie des verzögerten Schreibens wird durch Auftragsklassen unterschiedlicher Priorität modelliert.


## 3. Simulationsergebnisse

Für beide Modellvarianten wurden Simulationsreihen mit gleichartigen Parametervariationen durchgeführt. In Abb. 3 und 4 sind die Ergebnisse für die Antwortzeit des Gesamtsystems bei Variation der Bedienzeit für die Ausführung relationaler Operationen bzw. der Bedienzeit des Massenspeichersystems für beide Modellvarianten dargestellt.

Es wird deutlich, daß das Verhalten des Gesamtsystems in der Regel durch das Massenspeichersystem bestimmt wird, d.h. daß dieses zum Engpaß wird. Es wird erst dann durch die relationalen Verknüpfungsoperationen als Engpaß abgelöst, wenn man größere Werte für deren Bedienzeit annimmt. Allerdings steigt bei zunehmender Bedienzeit für relationale Operationen deren Antwortzeit ebenso wie die des Gesamtsystems vor allem in der zweiten Modellvariante extrem steil an.

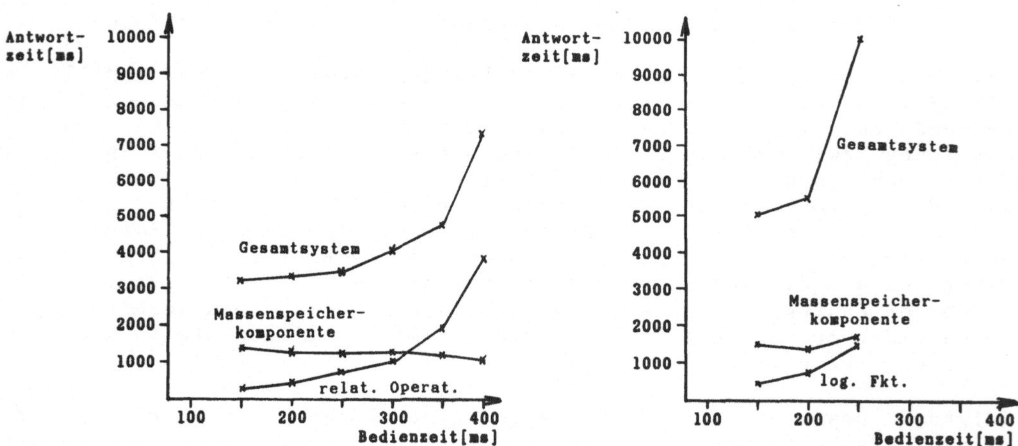


<u>Abb. 3</u>: Antwortzeitverhalten bei Variation der Bedienzeit für die Ausführung relationaler Operationen
a) mehrere logische Stationen      b) eine logische Station

Da die übrigen Funktionen, Transaktionsverwaltung und Änderungsstation, keine nennenswerte Rolle spielen, wird das Systemverhalten bei Variation von deren Bedienzeit hier nicht weiter betrachtet.

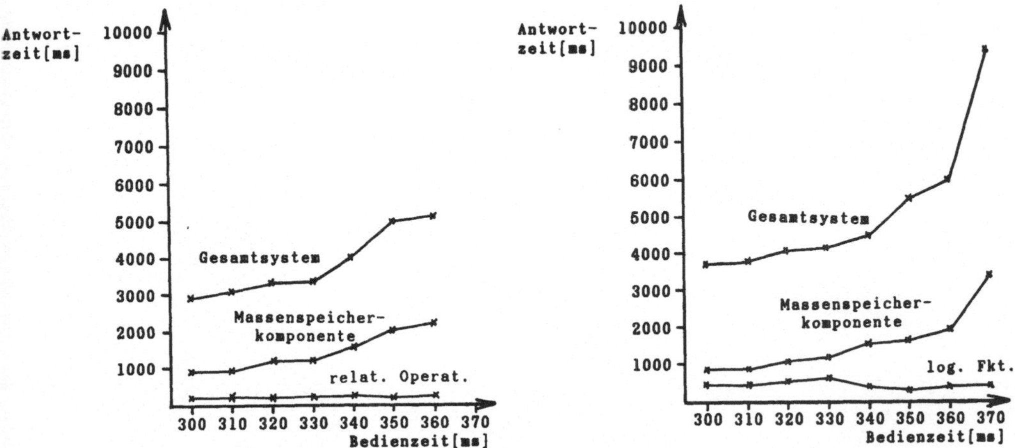

**Abb. 4:** Antwortzeitverhalten bei Variation der Bedienzeit des Massenspeichersystems
a) mehrere logische Stationen    b) eine logische Station

In der ersten Modellvariante ist die Auslastung der einzelnen Stationen sehr ungleichmäßig. Bei der zweiten Variante ist das Verhalten der
beiden Stationen weitgehend ausgeglichen. Allerdings liegt hier die
Gesamtantwortzeit des Systems etwa 30% über der Antwortzeit der ersten
Variante.

Insgesamt kann man aus den Ergebnissen der beiden hier untersuchten
Modelle schließen, daß Parallelverarbeitung im Bereich der logischen
Datenbankfunktionen (Transaktionsverwaltung, relationale Operationen,
Primärdatenänderung) erst dann sinnvoll ist, wenn die Massenspeicherkomponente aufgrund weiterer Maßnahmen hinreichend leistungsfähig
ist. Die Parallelisierung von Datenbankfunktionen sollte daher zunächst an dieser Stelle ansetzen. Jedoch bedarf auch die Realisierung
der relationalen Operationen besonderer Aufmerksamkeit. Es dürfte
sinnvoll sein, dieser Funktion eine eigene Rechnerkomponente zuzuordnen, während die übrigen logischen Funktionen gemeinsam durch eine
weitere Komponente realisiert werden.


## Literatur


/AF84/    M. Adams, B. Ferkinghoff, K. Bender, O. Drobnik, P.C. Locke-
          mann, Konzept für einen Datenbankrechner in der Prozeßauto-
          matisierung. Universität Karlsruhe, Forschungszentrum Infor-
          matik, Interner Bericht Nr. 2/84, Okt. 1984

/El82/    K. Elhardt, Das Datenbank-Cache, Entwurfsprinzipien, Algo-
          rithmen, Eigenschaften. TU München, TUM I8208, 1982

/Fe84/    B. Ferkinghoff: Softwarearchitektur eines Datenbanksystems
          auf der Basis eines Mehr-Mikrorechnersystems für den Einsatz
          in der Prozeßdatenverarbeitung. Universität Karlsruhe,
          Forschungszentrum Informatik, Interner Bericht Nr. 3/84,
          Nov. 1984

/Ki83/    W. Kießling: Datenbanksysteme für Rechenanlagen mit intelli-
          genten Subsystemen: Architektur, Algorithmen, Optimierung.
          TU München, TUM I8307, 1983

/SMK82/   Ch.H. Sauer, E.A. MacNair, J.F. Kurose: The Research
          Queueing Package Version 2: Introduction and Examples.
          Research Report RA 138, IBM Thomas J. Watson Research
          Center, Yorktown Heights, 1982

# SIMULATIONSSPRACHEN

# UND

# SIMULATIOSSOFTWARE

<u>**U P D A T E   O N   A C S L**</u>

WILLIAM A HAVRANEK

RAPID DATA LTD

WORTHING, UK

This paper reviews progress with the Advanced Continuous Simulation Language
(1) since the last ASIM Meeting in Vienna in September 1984 (2).  This is prim-
arily concerned with the area of micro-computer implementation, use with a pre-
processor and control system design suites.

## Improvements in ACSL

The most significant development in ACSL has been the implementation of the
language on the IBM-PC and compatible systems.  The availability of a pre-
processor in conjunction with ACSL has simplified its use, and interfacing with
control system design packages has extended the applications spectrum to the
control system designers, an application for which continuous system simulation
languages have been slanted anyway.  There has been no new version release,
but the features of the next version (which will include Bode, Nichols, Nyquist
and root locus plotting routines) are also geared towards this use by extending
the analytical capability of ACSL.

## Micro-computer Versions

Most engineers or scientists have access to either mainframes or mini-computers,
whilst the utilisation of a dedicated special purpose system is mostly restricted
to project-dedicated, real-time simulation applications, and hence to a specialist
group who need specialist experience to programme and operate the system.

Over the last few years, access and use of powerful scientific computers for
any researcher has become general for CADCAM applications in which simulation
as a design tool plays an increasing role.  ACSL runs on the CRAY super computer;
mainframes from CDC, DEC, IBM and SPERRY UNIVAC; minis from DEC, DATA GENERAL,
GOULD SEL, PERKIN ELMER, PRIME, HARRIS and ELXSI.  We have recently introduced
a system for the APOLLO DOMAIN, Motorola 68.000 based super micro-computer.
This 32 bit micro has super mini performance, and its computing power and very
fast response make the system suitable for interactive simulation applications.
With the introduction of an M 68.000 based system others of this type, eg for

the SUN, will no doubt follow.

Since the conference in Vienna, a micro-computer version was also introduced
on the IBM-PC and compatible systems.  This has made ACSL available to a much
wider circle of potential users, as well as enabling the current users on mainframes to offload some of their development work of simulation models, as this
version is a full implementation of ACSL.  The only limitations of the PC version
versus the other systems are those imposed by the micro-computer in terms of
speed and size.  Nonetheless, performance in terms of speed is quite reasonable,
as illustrated by the following example:-

A model used for stability assessment of high performance aircraft (F16) which
consisted of the simultaneous solution of the 6 degrees of freedom, aerodynamic,
inertial, elastic and servocontrol equations, performed at a ratio of 5 to 1
relative to realtime on a CDC 6600 mainframe, and on an IBM-AT with Math Coprocessor
would be 45 to 1.  Thus a 5 second transient on the CDC takes about 200 seconds on
an AT, and 500 seconds on a PC (3).  For a small model like a pendulum (4), the
time taken is about 7 seconds for an AT with Math Coprocessor.  Link time between
the model and the library on the AT is about 2 minutes.

The minimum configuration is 320 K B main memory, one floppy disk drive and a
monochrome monitor with DOS.  The ideal is an AT with Math Coprocessor, RAM disk,
Hercules Graphics Board and HP Plotter.

The Introduction of ACSL on micro-computers offers the possibility of providing low
cost turn-key simulation systems, the cost efficiency of which are further increased
if other simulation related systems, eg control system development packages or
discrete simulation systems such as SIMSCRIPT II.5 or SIMAN, are installed on the
same computer.

**Computer Aided Modelling Program**

Whilst good graphic post processors have made simulation languages easy to use for
analysis, the modelling process needed improvements for the engineer or scientist
to develop a computer model from the physical system (5).

The Computer Aided Modelling Program (CAMP) is a pre-processor that can reside in
front of ACSL.  It is a bond graph type program which derives non-linear state
equations from bond graphs, or block diagrams or combinations.  The bond graph
method first became popular at several engineering schools in the lates 60's (6)

but has also more recently been in use by industry, in Germany for example by
Bosch and Daimler Benz. The system makes the modelling process still easier
as it permits automated simulation. Despite the fact that almost no real programming
skill is needed to use ACSL, there may still be considerable effort to develop the
input to the program in the required mathematical form. Bond graphs are a concise
pictorial representation of the energy storage, dissipation and exchange of
interacting dynamic systems. They allow immediate identification of physical state
variables, and greatly facilitate derivation of state equations for all types of
energetic, non-linear systems.

The program input to a simulation must be "causal". This means that the internal
variables must not only be restricted by the component constitutive laws, but
also must be arranged in a consistent I/O form throughout the system. This means
that the physical system schematic must first be manually manipulated into equations,
transfer functions or block diagrams before it can be processed by ACSL. This
increases the potential for human error. For simple systems, equations formulation
according to well established rules poses no great difficulties. However, in
many practical cases the analyst is required to use considerable ingenuity to organise
the component models into a system model in the absence of standard procedures.
This often proves to be a major impediment to those who should use simulation for
system design and optimization. A bond graph is often a convenient model for a
physical dynamic system, particularly when several energy domains are involved.
Using a small number of basic elements, bond graph models may be constructed for
systems involving mechanical, electrical, hydraulic, pneumatic, magnetic, fluid,
thermal and other effect. Standard methods for processing one-domain systems such
as electric circuits into differential equations do not work well when many forms
of energy are present in a single system. Bond graph techniques, on the other hand,
work for all energetic systems and even some non-energetic ones.

Bond graph modelling techniques were developed at about the same time as continuous
system simulation languages. Bond graph papers began to appear in some numbers in
the late 60's. Bond graph techniques have since then spread worldwide.
Unfortunately, so far there has been little explicit contact between those involved
in the development of continuous system simulation languages, and those developing
bond graph modelling techniques (7).

CAMP is an advanced equation generator which accepts both bond graph input and
functions as a preprocessor for ACSL. Equations for each component are written in
symbolic and causally compatible form by the computer. The human operator merely
has to supply linear parameters or nonlinear functions. Camp allows one to add
control system block diagrams (or equations) to the physical system model.

There is no need to combine the component equations into an explicit set of differential equations as long as the simulator can sort the equations into a suitable order for execution.  Every system variable can be included in the equations so no extra output equations are needed.  Since each component's constitutive law occurs separately, parameter studies on individual components are readily accomplished.  The proposed form of the equations corresponds closely to those written automatically by CAMP.

There is much to be said in favour of combining the power of bond graph causal studies with ACSL.  Component relations may be entered directly into such a simulation program after the causal information has been applied according to a strict procedure.  No algebraic manipulation of the component equations is required.

Although a large number of equations are generated in this way, each equation is itself as simple as possible, and the constitutive laws of each component of the system appear separately.  Thus, parameter studies, as well as studies of the effect of changing component models entirely, are easily accomplished.

Some internal variables of no particular interest are computed, which does increase processing time and storage requirements.  At the risk of introducing human errors, such variables could be eliminated.  In many cases, the extra costs associated with these variables are trivial compared with the total human and computer costs associated with the modelling project.  Experience with CAMP, which produces the expanded formulation automatically from a coded bond graph, has shown no significant increase in costs for running typical engineering simulations.

## Control System Design

As mentioned in Vienna, more users are starting to use ACSL with a control system design suite.  This now includes CTRL-C for design analysis of multivariable systems, and SUNS, a non-linear, multivariable design suite, originating from the University of Sussex, and which will soon be commercially available (8).

## Conclusions

Through availability of a sophisticated simulation language on inexpensive personal computers, and further advancement in the automation of the model development through a pre-processor, the use of simulation techniques for continuous system studies in research and development will further accelerate.  The period under review has shown the start of this trend in the United States, Europe and the rest of the world in a widely varying range of applications.

**Acknowledgements**

The author wishes to thank Dr E E L Mitchell of Mitchell & Gauthier Associates Inc
for his support in the preparation of this article.

**References**

1.    "ACSL User Guide Reference Manual" Mitchell & Gauther Assoc Inc (1981)

2.    "Advances with the Advanced Continuous Simulation Language" W A Havranek
      2 Symposium Simulationstechnik, Wien 1984, Springen-Verlang Berlin Heidelberg
      Pages 460 - 464

3..   "Aeroservolasticity in the Time Domain" M A Cutchins, J W Purvis & R W Burton
      Journal of Aircraft, Vol 20 No 9 September 1983

4.    "Lets Talk ACSL" Mitchell & Gauthier Assoc Inc

5.    "Direct Programming of Continuous System Simulation Languages Using Bond
      Graph Causality" D Karnopp, Transactions of the SCS 1984, Volume 1, Number 1
      Pages 49 - 60

6.    "Modeling and Simulation in a Computer Aided Design Curriculum" J Granda
      Annual Meeting of the American Society for Engineering Education, University
      of Utah, June 24-28 1984.

7.    "Computer Aided Design of Dynamic Systems" J Granda, Proceedings of the
      Summer Computer Simulation Conference, Boston, Mass, July 23-25 1984.

8.    "An Overview of the Sussex University Nonlinear Control System Software"
      D P Atherton, M D Wadey, O P McNamara and A Goucem. Computer Aided Control
      System Design.  The Institute of Measurement and Control Workshop,
      Brighton, 19-21 September 1984

Kopplung spezieller Simulationsprogramme mit Simulationssprachen
als Modellierungshilfe für kontinuierliche Systeme

Ingrid Bausch-Gall, München

## 1. Einleitung

Die Anwendung blockorientierter Simulationssprachen, wie ACSL /1/, CSSL-IV /2/,
CSMP /3/ hat sich zur Modellierung und Studie kontinuierlicher Systeme weithin
durchgesetzt. Diese Sprachen wurden nach gemeinsamen Standards /4/, als Werkzeug
für Modelle entwickelt, die sich als gewöhnliches Differentialgleichungssystem
oder Blockdiagramm formulieren lassen. Kontinuierliche blockorientierte Simulationssprachen entlasten den Anwender von Programmierarbeit und helfen bei der
Systemstudie.

In vielen praktischen Fällen ist es jedoch schwierig oder gar unmöglich, die Differentialgleichungen ohne grobe Vereinfachungen manuell aufzustellen. Dies ist zum
Beispiel für dreidimensionale Mehrkörpersysteme mit komplizierten Koppelelementen
(Fahrzeug- und Robotersimulation) oder für elektrische Schaltungen mit ausreichend
genauer Bauelementmodellierung der Fall. In manch anderen Fällen ist es zwar möglich, die Differentialgleichungen von Hand aufzustellen, Spezialprogramme erleichtern jedoch die Arbeit (Abb.1).

Zur Lösung von Aufgaben, die sich vollständig durch einen Typ von Ersatzmodell darstellen lassen (z.B. nur elektrisch oder nur mechanisch) wendet man am besten bewährte und dem Anwendungsgebiet angepaßte Simulationsprogramme an. Häufig sind jedoch Systeme zu untersuchen, die sich nur durch eine Kombination verschiedener Er-
satzmodelltypen geeignet modellieren lassen. Hier geht man derzeit wie folgt vor:

- jedes Teilmodell wird für sich mit einem geeigneten Programm simuliert
  und anschließend verknüpft man die Teilergebnisse

- ein vereinfachtes Gesamtsystem wird simuliert

- die Gleichungen werden manuell erstellt und mit einem FORTRAN-Programm
  oder einer Simulationssprache studiert.


Demgegenüber würde eine Kopplung spezieller Simulationsprogramme mit Simulationssprachen den Komfort und die aufwendigen Bauelementmodelle der speziellen Programm-
me erhalten und gleichzeitig die Flexibilität der Simulationssprachen nutzen.
Eine Kopplung ist möglich, da die Modellierung in verschiedenen Anwendungsgebieten
immer auf eine mathematische Formulierung als Differentialgleichungssystem führt.
Um dies zu verdeutlichen, werden hier Kopplungen zu den Programmen SPICE (Schaltungssimulation) und MEDYNA (Mehrkörpersimulation) besprochen.

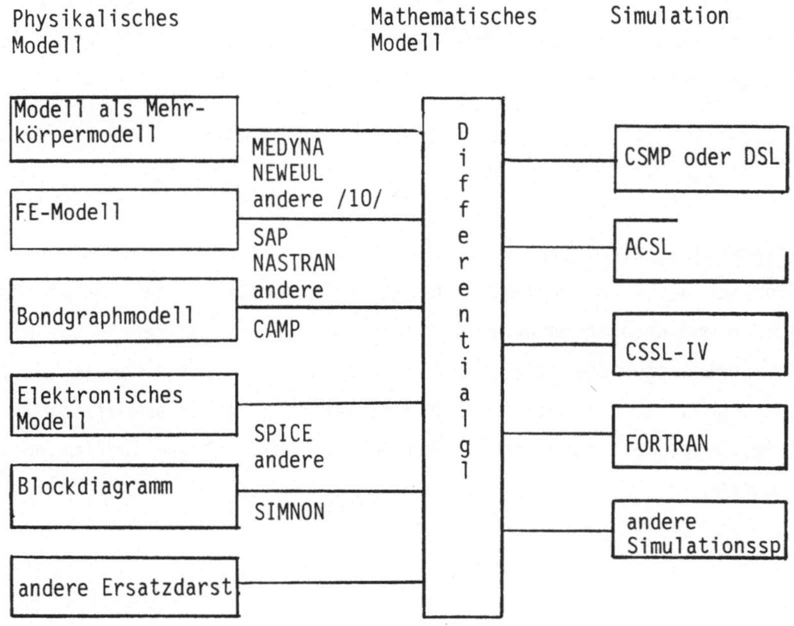



Bestehende Programme:  MEDYNA  -  ACSL
                       NEWEUL  -  Differentialgleichungen
                       CAMP    -  ACSL und DSL

in Entwicklung:        SPICE   -  ACSL

ABBILDUNG 1:

## 2. Realisierungsmöglichkeiten

Die bestehenden Programme zur Zeitsimulation erstellen aus einer anwendernahen Eingabe das Differentialgleichungssystem des physikalischen Modells in geeigneter Form. Gelingt es, auf diese erzeugten Differentialgleichungen zuzugreifen, so können Simulationssprachen zur Erweiterung der Modelle und zur Systemstudie eingesetzt werden. Die speziellen Programme erzeugen explizite oder implizite Differentialgleichungssysteme.

Explizite Differentialgleichungssysteme lassen sich nach der höchsten Ableitung auflösen. Modelle, die auf den Newton'schen Gesetzen beruhen führen z.B. zu:

$$\ddot{y} = f(t, y, \dot{y})$$

Implizite Differentialgleichungssysteme lassen sich nicht nach der höchsten Ableitung auflösen. Bei der elektrischen Schaltungssimulation erhält man z.B. ein System der Art:

$$f(t,y,\dot{y},\ddot{y}) = 0.$$

Explizite Differentialgleichungen können direkt in Simulationssprachen übernommen werden, da sie sich durch fortlaufende numerische Integration lösen lassen. Bei impliziten Systemen muß dagegen entweder $\ddot{y}$ durch ein Iterationsverfahren vor der Integration berechnet werden oder die Iteration wird zusammen mit einem Integrationszeitschritt durchgeführt. Die mögliche Kopplungsart hängt daher sowohl vom Typ der Differentialgleichung, als auch von der Realisierung der Integration im speziellen Simulationsprogramm ab.


## 2.1. Vorlaufprogramme

Diese anwendernahen Programme erstellen entweder die Differentialgleichungen direkt in Form einer lesbaren Datei oder erzeugen sofort die Eingabe für eine Simulationssprache. Sie unterstützen den Benutzer also bei der Gleichungserstellung. Beispiele dafür sind NEWEUL /9/,/10/ und CAMP /7/,/8/.
NEWEUL erstellt aus einem dreidimensionalen Mehrkörpermodell einen vollständigen Satz symbolischer Bewegungsgleichungen. Diese können in ein Simulationssprachenmodell oder in ein FORTRAN-Programm übernommen werden.
CAMP erstellt aus einer Systemformulierung als Bondgraph direkt ein DSL- oder ACSL-Modell, das gut lesbar ist und vom Benutzer ergänzt werden kann.


## 2.2. Spezielle Simulationsprogramme

In den letzten Jahren wurden für mehrere Fachgebiete Programme entwickelt, die sowohl die Modellierung unterstützen, als auch eine Zeitsimulation durchführen. Diese Programme werden hier spezielle Simulationsprogramme genannt. Sie sind anwendernah, komfortabel und enthalten aufwendige Modelle komplizierter Bauelemente, für die viele Jahre Entwicklungsarbeit aufgewandt wurden. Sie sind geeignet für Aufgabenstellungen, die sich vollständig in einem dieser speziellen Programme formulieren lassen. Oft ist es jedoch schwierig oder unmöglich, in diesen Programmen Teile zu modellieren, die nicht von vornherein bei der Programmentwicklung vorgesehen wurden.

## 2.2.1 Explizites Differentialgleichungssystem

Zu Programmen, die explizite Differentialgleichungssysteme erstellen, kann man mit programminternen Kenntnissen die Gleichungen als Kode für eine Simulationssprache auf eine Datei schreiben. Dabei ist zu beachten, daß der Anwender das entstehende Modell ändern kann und die zur Verfügung stehenden Unterprogramme zur Bauelementmodellierung aufgerufen werden (Abb. 2).

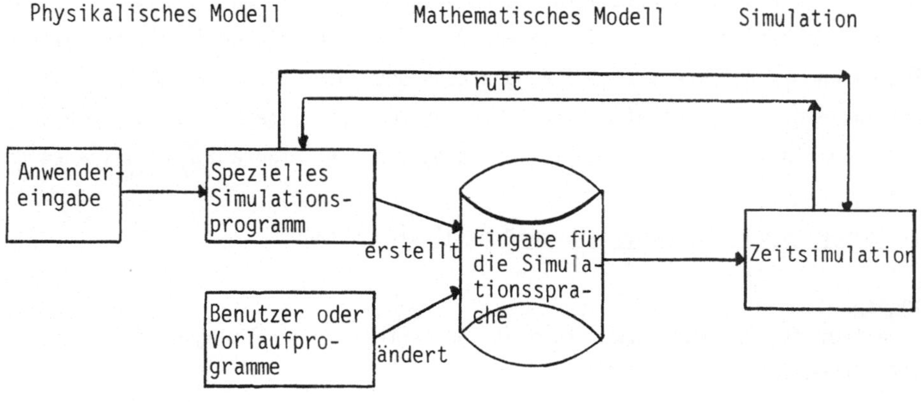


ABBILDUNG 2:

Ein Beispiel ist MEDYNA /10/, das zur Simulation von Rad-/Schiene-Systemen und Magnetbahnen entwickelt wurde und inzwischen allgemein zur Simulation dreidimensionaler Mehrkörpersysteme eingesetzt wird. MEDYNA führt den Benutzer interaktiv bei der Beschreibung seines Mehrkörpersystems, erstellt die Gleichungen und erlaubt vielfache Untersuchungen des Systems, darunter auch die Zeitsimulation. Als Erweiterung von MEDYNA wurde ein Interface zu ACSL entwickelt /6/. Das entstehende ACSL-Modell kann durch nicht in MEDYNA zur Verfügung stehende Teilmodelle ergänzt werden. Dabei können Koppelelemente und externe Anregungen ersetzt, erzeugte Gleichungen ergänzt oder Gleichungen hinzugefügt werden. Bei der Simulation in ACSL werden MEDYNA-Unterprogramme zur Bauelementmodellierung oder für externe Anregungen aufgerufen.

## 2.2.2 Implizites Differentialgleichungssystem

Läßt sich bei diesem Gleichungstyp die Iteration vom Integrationsschritt trennen, so muß in dem erzeugten Modell in der Simulationssprache die höchste Ableitung bei jedem Aufruf der Derivative Section mit einem Iterationsverfahren berechnet werden. Ansonsten kann wie bei expliziten Differentialgleichungen vorgegangen werden. Führt jedoch das spezielle Simulationsprogramm die Iteration zusammen mit einem Zeitschritt durch, so läßt sich das Differentialgleichungssystem nicht direkt zur

Integration in einer Simulationssprache aufstellen. Die benötigten Teile des speziellen Programms können jedoch in abgeänderter Form als Unterprogramme aus dem Simulationssprachenmodell gerufen werden. Die Integration des im speziellen Programm beschriebenen Teilmodells verbleibt dort. Der Datenaustausch zwischen den Teilmodellen findet dabei nur einmal je Zeitschritt statt.

Diese Realisierung bietet sich z.B. für SPICE /5/, das verbreiteste Programm zur Simulation elektrischer Schaltungen, an. Die Schaltung wird zur Eingabe in SPICE auf einer Schaltungsdatei beschrieben. Die Auswertung dieser Schaltungsdatei und das Erstellen der Differentialgleichungen kann aus dem erzeugten Modell in der Pre-Initial-Section aufgerufen werden. In der Derivative Section werden diejenigen SPICE-Programmteile gerufen, die die Iteration und die Integration realisieren.

Gestalt des entstehenden Modells in der Simulationssprache:

```
PROGRAM
      Aufruf des Programms zum Lesen und Auswerten der Schaltungsdatei
INITIAL-SECTION

DERIVATIVE-SECTION
          .          Gleichungen im Kode der Simulationssprache
          .          einmal je Zeitschritt Aufruf der SPICE-Unterprogramme,
          .          die Iteration und Integration durchführen
END
```

Im SPICE-Modell müssen Ausgangs- und Eingabespannungen zum Datenaustausch vorgesehen sein (Abb. 3).

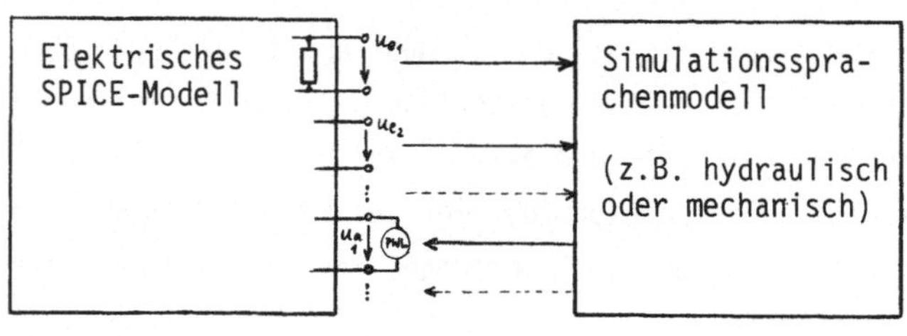


ABBILDUNG 3:

Das entstehende Gesamtmodell ist sehr übersichtlich. Der Datenaustausch findet jedoch nur einmal je Zeitschritt statt, was wie bei Hybridrechnern oder Abtastsystemen zur Instabilität führen kann.

## 3. Zusammenfassung

Spezielle Simulationsprogramme nehmen dem Benutzer die Gleichungserstellung ab und stellen komplizierte Bauelementmodelle zur Verfügung.

Um diese Möglichkeiten auch für Teilmodelle in Simulationssprachen nutzen zu können, bieten sich Kopplungen zwischen Simulationsprogrammen und kontinuierlichen Simulationssprachen an. Bei der Erstellung der Kopplungsprogramme ist darauf zu achten, daß:

- der entstehende Kode vom Benutzer verstanden werden kann
- klar gestaltete und dokumentierte Schnittstellen Ergänzungen durch weitere Teilmodelle erlauben
- das in dem speziellen Programm realisierte Modellierungswissen erhalten bleibt

Durch diese Vorgehensweise kann die Flexibilität von Simulationssprachen und das in speziellen Programmen realisierte Erfahrungswissen kombiniert genutzt werden.

Die Verwendung verbreiteter, gut getesteter Programme als Modellierungshilfe für Simulationssprachen könnte zu einer Standardisierung bei der Entwurfsphase führen.

## 4. Literatur


/1/ ACSL: Advanced Continuous Simulation Language, User Guide/Reference Manual
Mitchell and Gauthier Ass., 1981

/2/ CSSL-IV Simulation Language, User Manual
Nilsen, R.N: Simulation Services, 1981

/3/ CSMP-III: Continuous System Modeling Program III, Program Reference Manual
IBM, 1972

/4/ The SCi Continuous System Simulation Language (CSSL)
Simulation, December 1967, S. 281-303

/5/ Nagel, L.W.: SPICE2, A Computer Program to Simulate Semiconductor Circuits
University of California, Berkley, Memorandum No. ERI-M520, 1975

/6/ Führer, C.; Kortüm, W.; Wallrapp, O.; Bausch-Gall, I.: MEDYNA - A Simulation
Tool for Mechanical Systems and its Interface to Simulation Languages
Proceedings of the 11th IMACS World Congress, OSLO 1985

/7/ Granda, J.: Computer Aided Design of Dynamic Systems
Proceedings of the Summer Computer Simulation Conference, 1984

/8/ Haug, E.J.: Elements and Methods of Computational Dynamics
in: Computer Aided Analysis and Optimization of Mechanical System Dynamics
Springer Verlag, 1984, NATA ASI Series F: Computer and Systems Sciences

/9/ Havranek, W.A.: Update to ACSL
Proceedings 3. Symposium Simulationstechnik, Ebernburg, 1985

/10/ Kortüm, W.: Modeling and Simulation of Actively Contrólled Mechanical Systems
in: Modeling and Simulation in Engineering, Ed. William F. Ames,
North-Holland, 1983

SIDAS II, EIN PROGRAMMPAKET ZUR MODULAREN
BLOCKORIENTIERTEN SIMULATION DYNAMISCHER SYSTEME

Hans Braun, Karlsruhe

Zusammenfassung. SIDAS II ist ein Programmsystem zur digitalen blockorientierten Simulation dynamischer Systeme. Die Eingabe der zu simulierenden Systemstrukturen erfolgt interaktiv graphisch durch das Aufbauen eines Blockschaltbilds. Dabei wird ein modulares Vorgehen im Sinne der strukturierten Programmierung unterstützt. Bei der Implementierung wurde besonderer Wert auf Komfort, Einfachheit und Robustheit der Anwenderschnittstelle gelegt. SIDAS beinhaltet ein Konzept zur kombinierten kontinuierlich/diskreten Simulation, das eine effiziente Behandlung unstetiger Vorgänge gewährleistet. Die Möglichkeit der repetierenden Simulation mit Parametervariation erweitert den zu behandelnden Problemkreis auf Randwert- und Optimierungsaufgaben.

Summary. SIDAS II is a program package for digital block oriented simulation of dynamical systems. The structure of the systems to be simulated is defined by interactive generation of a block diagramme on a graphics display. Structured programming facilities are provided which offer the possibility to divide these systems into modules. Importance was given to implementing a smart, simple and robust user interface. A concept for combined continuous/discrete simulation provides an efficient handling of non-continuous processes. Another feature of SIDAS II, which performs repetitive simulations with parameter variations, makes it possible to tackle boundary value and optimization problems.

## 1. Einführung

In den letzten Jahren ist die digitale Simulation kontinuierlicher Systeme gegenüber analogen Verfahren stark in den Vordergrund getreten. Gründe hierfür sind höhere Flexibilität, höhere Zuverlässigkeit und geringere Kosten. Hinzu kommt der Vorteil der einfacheren Handhabung, wenn dem Anwender geeignete Hilfsmittel zur Verfügung gestellt werden. Einer der wesentlichen Aspekte beim Entwurf eines Programmpaketes zur digitalen Simulation ist daher die Wahl der Schnittstelle zwischen Anwender und Programm. Von dieser Schnittstelle ist zu fordern, sie soll sein:
- einfach und robust
- problemorientiert
- schnell erlernbar
- übersichtlich
- selbstdokumentierend.

Die Darstellung dynamischer Systeme in Form von Blockschaltbildern kann diesen Forderungen genügen. Besonders geeignet ist sie für den Bereich der Systemtechnik, weil das Blockschaltbild hier seit langem ein gebräuchliches Hilfsmittel ist.

Mitte der siebziger Jahre wurde das blockorientierte Simulationssystem SIDAS entwickelt [1], das die beschriebenen Vorteile der interaktiven graphischen Programmierung nutzt. Es hat sich seither in Forschung, Lehre und bei industriellen Anwendungen bewährt [2,3]. Die Systemdarstellung in einem Schaltbild hat jedoch einen schwerwiegenden Nachteil. Die unmittelbare Anschaulichkeit, die ein Signalflußgraph bei einfachen Systemen besitzt, weicht bei komplexen Schaltbildern einer zunehmenden Unübersichtlichkeit. Dies ist nur dadurch vermeidbar, daß Blöcke mit komplexeren Funktionen eingeführt werden.

Aus diesem Grund wurde das Programmpaket SIDAS völlig überarbeitet und neu implementiert. SIDAS II ermöglicht es dem Anwender, eigene Blockfunktionen zu definieren. Hierzu stellt er Teile des Systems in Schaltbildern dar und bezeichnet sie mit einem frei wählbaren Namen. In übergeordneten Schaltbildern können diese Systemteile dann wie Blöcke aus dem Katalog der Grundfunktionen eingesetzt werden. Diese Modularisierung hat über die übersichtliche Darstellung hinaus weitere wesentliche Vorteile. In völliger Analogie zur strukturierten Programmierung kann man von einer Beschreibung des Systems "im Großen" ausgehen und die Teilsysteme bis hin zu den mit Hilfe der Grundfunktionen darzustellenden Details schrittweise verfeinern. Die "Bottom up" Vorgehensweise ist natürlich ebenso möglich. Die Teilsysteme können einzeln auf Korrektheit geprüft werden, was die Zuverlässigkeit der Simulation wesentlich erhöht. Ein wichtiger praktischer Aspekt ist wohl auch die Möglichkeit, für spezielle Anwendungsbereiche in sehr einfacher Weise Bibliotheken häufig benötigter Funktionen aufbauen zu können.

In den folgenden Abschnitten wird in Aufbau und Funktionsweise des Programmpakets SIDAS II eingeführt und die Handhabung des Systems mit Beispielen erläutert.

## 2. Aufbau des Programmpakets

SIDAS II besteht aus den vier Programmen [4]
- Graphischer Editor
- Binder
- Laufzeitsystem
- Auswertesystem.

Sie werden in der angegebenen Reihenfolge benötigt, um eine Simulation durchzuführen. Der graphische Editor dient zur Problemspezifikation. Der Anwender erhält zunächst ein Raster auf dem graphischen Bildschirm ausgegeben (Abb. 1). Durch Auswahl eines Rasterpunktes mit dem graphischen Cursor und Eingabe eines Befehls wird an dieser Stelle ein Block gezeichnet. Die Blöcke werden mit frei wählbaren Namen (3 signifikante Zeichen) bezeichnet. Der Name bestimmt die Funktion das Blocks. Ist er nicht in der Liste der 67 in SIDAS zur Verfügung stehenden Grundfunktionen enthalten, so wird davon ausgegangen, daß es sich um eine vom Anwender in einem Modul zu definierende Funktion handelt. Die Verbindungen zwischen den Blöcken werden durch Anfahren der Ein- und Ausgänge und Eingabe eines Befehls hergestellt. Die Parameter des Systems werden zur Vervollständigung der Problemspezifikation im Dialog abgefragt.

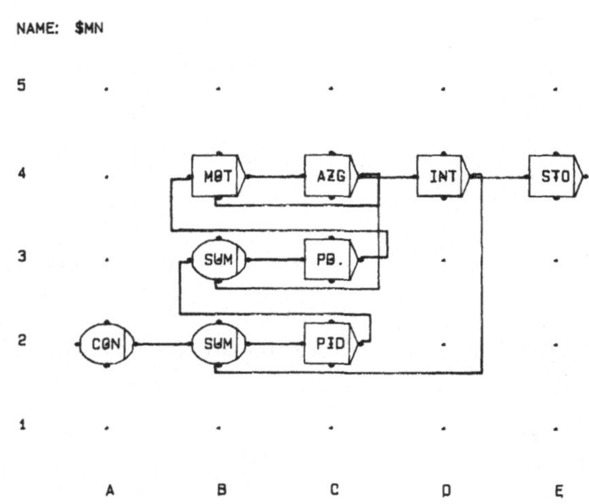



Der Editor ermöglicht es, jederzeit wahlfrei die Systemstruktur graphisch zu editieren, Parameter zu setzen oder zu verändern, das Blockschaltbild auf Plotter auszugeben und Dokumentationslisten zu erstellen.

Die Systeme werden vor der weiteren Bearbeitung auf Files gespeichert. Bei späteren Veränderungen kann mit dem Editor wieder auf diese Files zugegriffen werden.

Abb. 1: Blockschaltbild mit Raster

Zur Erläuterung des weiteren Vorgehens sei als Beispiel die Lageregelung eines Lastenaufzugs betrachtet. Abbildung 2 zeigt das Prinzipschaltbild des Lageregelkreises mit unterlagerter Geschwindigkeitsregelung.

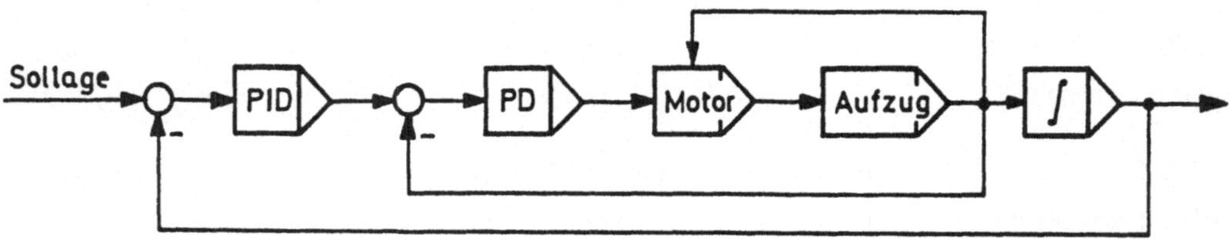


Abb. 2: Lageregelkreis

Obwohl die in diesem Schaltbild vorhandenen Blöcke nicht als Grundfunktionen in SIDAS vorhanden sind, kann das Schaltbild direkt für die Simulation übernommen werden (Abb. 3a). Unterschiede bestehen lediglich in den Namen MOT für Motor und AZG für Aufzug, sowie dem Block CON, der den konstanten Sollwert liefert und dem Speicherblock STO, der für die Speicherung der angeschlossenen Größe sorgt. Die Blöcke AZG, MOT, die Regler PD und PID sowie der im PID-Regler enthaltene Block ING (Integrierer mit Beschränkung) werden nun in einzelnen Editorläufen erstellt. Die Schaltbilder sind in Abbildung 3 zusammengestellt. Auf die realisierten Gleichungen soll hier nicht näher eingegangen werden. Die Funktion der verwendeten Blöcke kann dem Anhang entnommen werden. Zur Erklärung sei nur ergänzt, daß die vom Aufzug zu transportierende Last durch den Block PARO1 (Abb. 3b) als Parameter des Moduls AZG definiert ist und bei der Abarbeitung als aktueller Wert des angeschlossenen Konstantenblocks eingesetzt wird.

Die Vorteile der Modularisierung werden hier unmittelbar deutlich. Es ist möglich, direkt von der technisch-physikalischen Realität auszugehen und sie häufig ohne vollständige mathematische Formulierung in Blockschaltbilder umzusetzen. Durch die Auf-

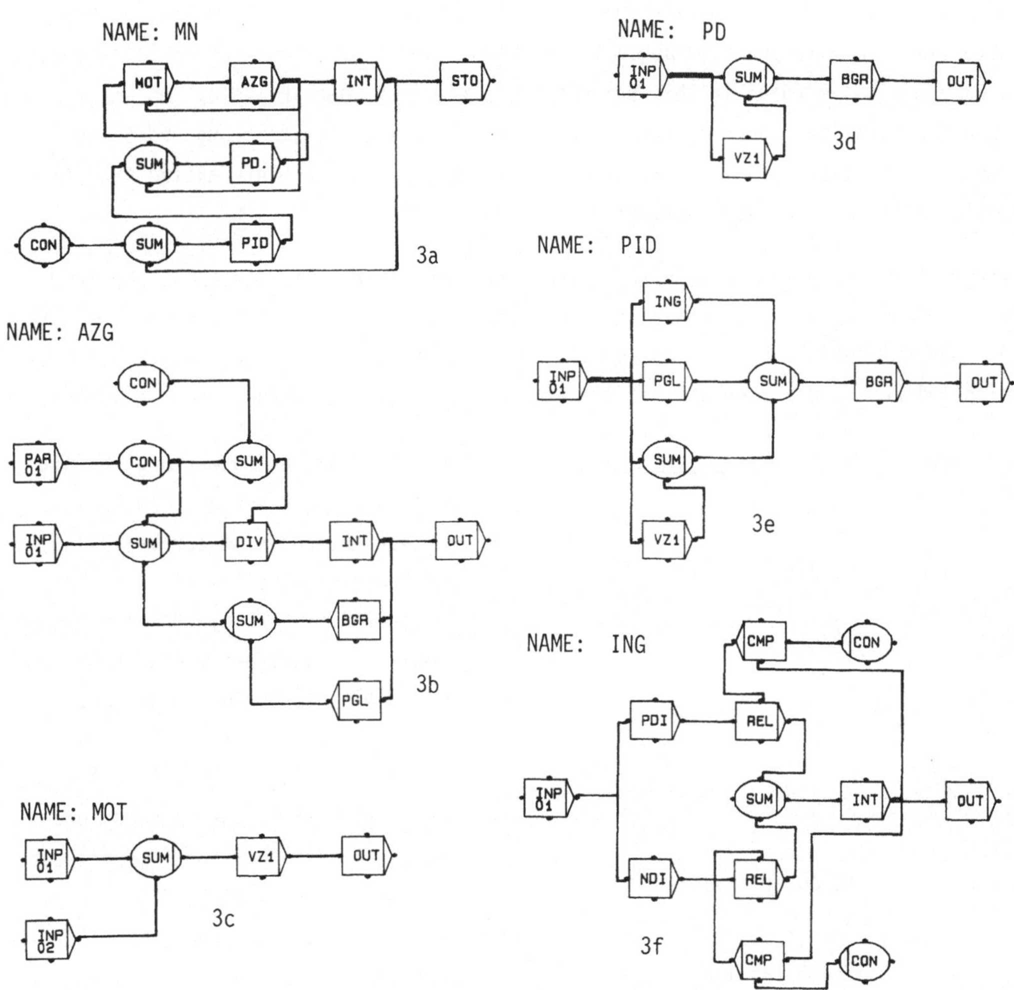



Abb. 3: Module zur Simulation des Lageregelkreises

teilung bleiben die Funktionen der einzelnen Module einfach und die Blockschaltbilder überschaubar. Die Module können einzeln getestet werden, was das Suchen und Beseitigen von Fehlern wesentlich vereinfacht.

Um aus den Moduln ein vollständiges System zu erstellen, wird der Binder benötigt. Er erzeugt aus den vom Editor gespeicherten Daten eine Liste der für die Auswertung des Schaltbilds erforderlichen Funktionen. Die Liste ist in üblicher Weise sortiert [5] und kann als Programm einer virtuellen Maschine mit Neumann-Struktur interpretiert werden, die die SIDAS-Grundfunktionen als Instruktionssatz besitzt. Die Adressrechnung wird relativ ausgeführt und die Module werden in Unterprogrammtechnik aufgerufen. Die Programmschritte für mehrfach verwendete Module sind also nur einmal in der Programmliste enthalten. Dadurch hat SIDAS auch bei größeren Systemen nur einen relativ geringen Speicherbedarf und ist auf Rechnern mit 64 kB Adressraumbeschränkung effizient lauffähig.

Die eigentliche Simulation wird vom Laufzeitsystem ausgeführt, indem die Programmliste vielfach interpretativ abgearbeitet wird. Die Integration (sofern Integrierer
vorhanden sind) erfolgt in üblicher Weise. Es stehen in der aktuellen Implementierung
ein Runga-Kutta-Verfahren zweiter Ordnung ohne Schrittweitensteuerung und eines
vierter Ordnung mit Schrittweitensteuerung zur Verfügung [6]. Interaktive Eingriffsmöglichkeiten während der Simulation bestehen nicht.

Die Simulationsergebnisse werden zur späteren Auswertung auf einer Datei abgelegt.
Dabei werden neben der unabhängigen Variablen (Zeit) alle Größen abgespeichert, die
an einen Speicherblock (STO) angeschlossen sind. Sie werden mit frei wählbaren Namen
gekennzeichnet und können bei der Auswertung mit diesen Namen angesprochen werden.

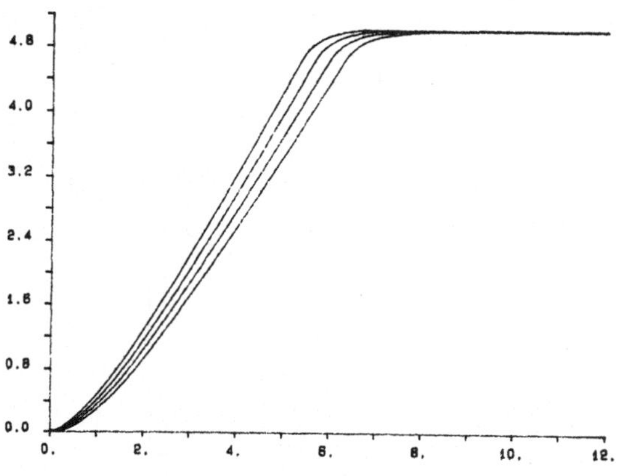

Abb. 4:  Simulationsergebnis

Zur interaktiven Auswertung der Simulationsergebnisse steht dem Anwender
ein Auswerteprogramm zur Verfügung.
Das Programm arbeitet mit einer Ar-
beitsdatei, in der die Daten mehrerer
Simulationsläufe gesammelt werden können. Damit besteht die Möglichkeit,
vergleichende Auswertungen durchzuführen. Die Daten können in beliebiger
Kombination alphanumerisch und graphisch ausgegeben werden. So erzeugt
der Befehl "GRA TIME (1,4), WEG" das
in Abbildung 4 dargestellte Diagramm, das vier Fahrten des oben beschriebenen Aufzugs-
systems bei unterschiedlicher Last zeigt. Zur Zeit steht die Implementierung einer
wesentliche Erweiterung des Auswerteprogramms kurz vor dem Abschluß. Mit ihr wird es
möglich, in einer BASIC-ähnlichen Sprache die Datensätze algebraisch zu verknüpfen,
zu normieren, Zoomfunktionen auszuführen usw., die Daten also in beliebiger Weise
nachzuverarbeiten.


## 3. Ereignisbehandlung

In technischen Systemen treten häufig unstetige Signalformen (Impulse, Sprünge) und
nicht stetig differenzierbare Kennlinien (Diode, Komparator) auf. Bei der Simulation
solcher Systeme mit rein kontinuierlichen Methoden kommt es zu Genauigkeitseinbußen
bzw. zu einer unnötigen Reduktion des Integrationsschrittweite an den Unstetigkeitsstellen [7]. Außerdem ist man häufig gerade daran interessiert, mit spezifizierter
Genauigkeit zu erfahren, wann ein Schaltvorgang stattfindet, wann eine Größe den Wert
Null erreicht oder welchen Wert sie extremal annimmt. Bei rein kontinuierlicher Behandlung sind solche Informationen nur dadurch zu erhalten, daß man sehr kleine
Schrittweiten für die Integration wählt. Dies führt zu hohem numerischen Aufwand und
unnötig großen Mengen von Ergebnisdaten.

Zur Vermeidung dieser Schwierigkeiten führt das SIDAS-Laufzeitsystem eine ereignisgesteuerte Simulation durch [7]. Es wird zwischen Zeit- und Zustandsereignissen unterschieden. Zeitereignisse sind solche, die von Datenquellen herrühren (beispielsweise einem Generator für poissonverteilte Impulsfolgen) und somit a-priori bestimmbar sind. Sie werden über eine Warteschlange abgehandelt. Das zunächst äquidistante zeitliche Grundraster für die Speicherung von Ergebnisdaten wird ebenfalls durch die Einordnung der Zeitpunkte in die Warteschlange erreicht. Das jeweils nächste Zeitereignis in der Warteschlange bestimmt die maximale Länge des aktuellen Integrationsschritts.

Zustandsereignisse entstehen, wenn Unstetigkeitsstellen auf Kennlinien überschritten werden. Tritt innerhalb eines Rechenschritts ein Ereignis ein, so wird der Schritt rückgängig gemacht und der Ereigniszeitpunkt durch ein modifiziertes Sekantenverfahren bis zur vorgegebenen Genauigkeit eingeschachtelt.

Durch einen Schalter kann das Laufzeitsystem dazu veranlaßt werden, nicht nur im äquidistanten Grundraster Ergebnisse abzuspeichern, sondern auch zu allen weiteren Ereigniszeitpunkten. Es werden dann links- und rechtsseitige Grenzwerte abgespeichert, sofern sie sich unterscheiden. Dadurch erscheint beispielsweise ein Schaltvorgang im Ergebnisdiagramm korrekt als Stufe und nicht als Rampe.

Abbildung 5 zeigt als einfaches Beispiel die Simulation eines hüpfenden Balls, wobei der Stoßvorgang beim Auftreffen auf die Unterlage mitsimuliert ist. Die Behandlung der Berührung mit der Unterlage als Zustandsereignis führt hier zu hoher Genauigkeit und unmittelbar zur korrekten graphischen Darstellung des Vorganges.

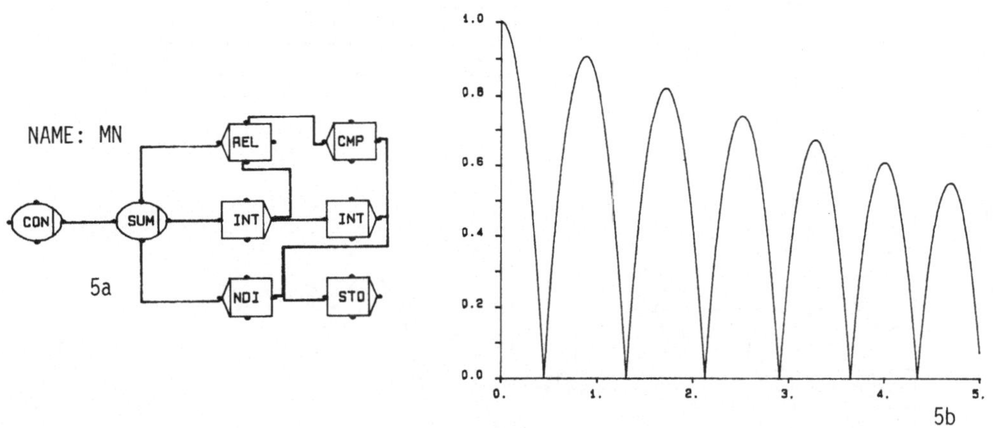


Abb. 5: Hüpfender Ball

## 4. Repetierendes Rechnen

Bei der Untersuchung dynamischer Systeme besteht oft die Notwendigkeit, das Verhalten eines Systems bei variierenden Parametern zu simulieren. Hierzu besitzt SIDAS einen repetierenden Rechenmodus. Während eines Simulationslaufs, im folgenden als Zyklus be-

zeichnet, sind alle Parameter konstant. Durch die "zyklischen" Blöcke PAD (Parameter-
addition) und PVD (Parameterübergabe) können am Ende jedes Zyklus Parameterveränderun-
gen vorgenommen werden, so daß der nachfolgende Simulationslauf mit veränderten Parametern durchgeführt wird. Die Veränderungen können dabei von den Ergebnissen vorange-
gangener Zyklen abhängen, so daß neben der gesteuerten Parametervariation auch die
Lösung von Randwert - und Optimierungsaufgaben möglich ist. Damit wird der mit SIDAS
zu behandelnde Problemkreis wesentlich erweitert.

Abbildung 6 zeigt die Behandlung eines einfachen Optimierungsproblems. Die Dämpfung d
des im Modul SYS dargestellten Verzögerungsglieds 2. Ordnung soll dabei so bestimmt
werden, daß der Güteindex

$$J = \int_0^T (x(t) - x_{stat})^2 \, dt \overset{!}{=} \min_d$$

zum Minimum wird. x(t) bezeichnet hierbei die Systemausgangsgröße und $x_{stat}$ deren
stationären Wert.

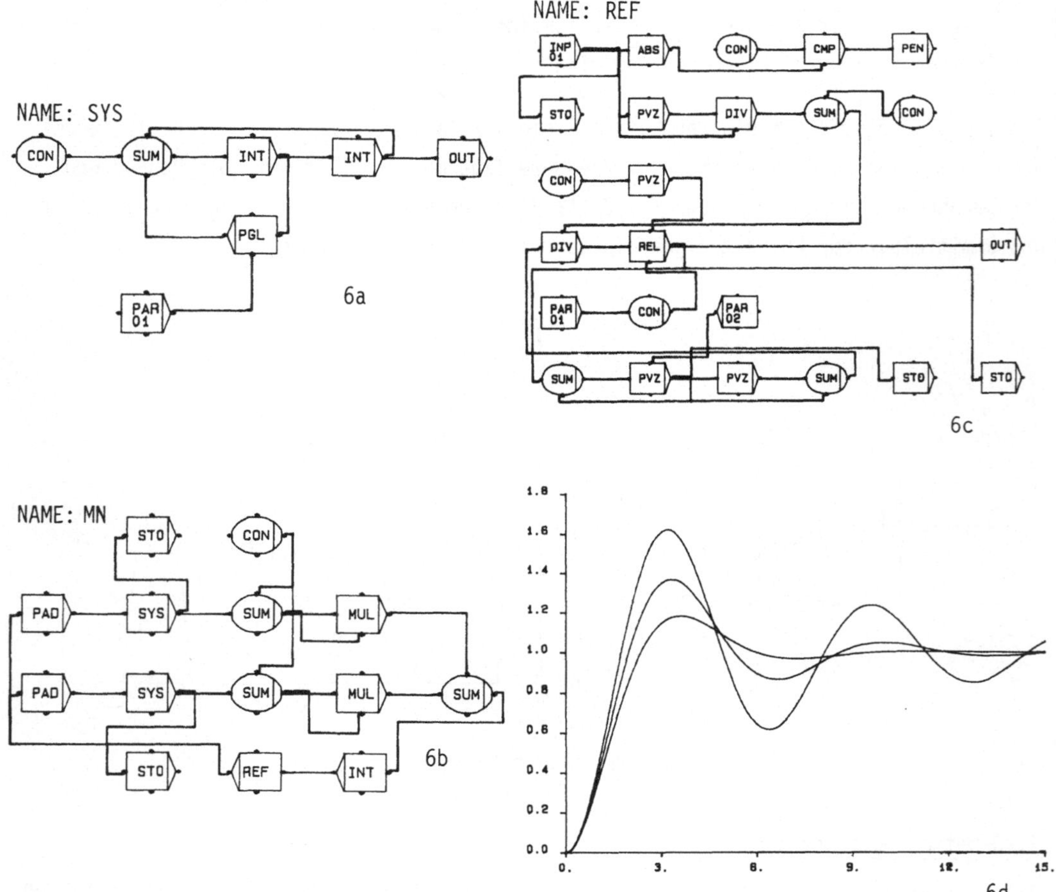



Abb. 6: Optimierungsproblem

Hierzu wird das System SYS in zwei Realisierungen parallel simuliert, wobei sich die Dämpfungsparameter um einen kleinen Betrag unterscheiden. In der Schaltung 6b werden die Abweichungen der Systemausgangsgrößen vom stationären Wert quadriert, und die Differenz dieser Größen wird aufintegriert. Am Ende eines Zyklusses steht somit am Ausgang des Integrierers eine Näherung für den Gradienten des Güteindex bezüglich des Dämpfungsparameters zur Verfügung. Der anschließende Block REF ist ein zyklischer Modul, der nur am Ende des Rechenzyklus ausgewertet wird. Er beinhaltet ein Regula-falsi Nullstellensuchverfahren (Abb. 6b) einschließlich Startsequenz, Speicherung der aktuellen Parameterwerte und bedingtem Iterationsabbruch. Er liefert am Ausgang ein Inkrement für den zu optimierenden Parameter, der über die PAD-Blöcke den Dämpfungswerten beider Systeme zugeschlagen wird. Die Iteration endet, wenn der Betrag des genäherten Güteindexgradienten eine vorgegebene Schranke unterschreitet. In Abbildung 6d ist der Verlauf der Systemausgangsgröße für einige Iterationsschritte gezeigt; die Kurve mit dem geringsten Überschwingen stellt das gesuchte Optimum dar.

## 5. Schlußbemerkungen und Ausblick

Die Erfahrungen der letzten Jahre zeigen, daß SIDAS ein sehr leistungsfähiges Hilfsmittel zur Untersuchung dynamischer Systeme in Forschung, Lehre und bei industriellen Anwendungen darstellt. Der Umgang mit SIDAS ist sehr einfach und schnell erlernbar. Die Robustheit der Anwenderschnittstelle und die umfangreiche Fehlerprüfung schließen Fehlfunktionen aufgrund formal falscher Handhabung weitestgehend aus. Eine online Help-Funktion steht zur Verfügung. Die erweiterten Möglichkeiten von SIDAS II, insbesondere der Vorteil der Modularisierung, werden von den Anwendern sehr begrüßt.

Das Programmpaket wurde in Fortran auf einer PDP 11 unter RSX 11M geschrieben. Abgesehen von wenigen leider systemspezifischen Unterprogrammen, die zur Behandlung von Laufzeitfehlern erforderlich sind, sind die Programme portabel. Die meisten Erfahrungen liegen inzwischen mit Implementierungen auf Rechnern der VAX11-Familie unter VMS vor. Die Maximalgröße der behandelbaren Systeme ist prinzipiell nicht beschränkt. Bei Rechnern mit 64 kB Adressraumbeschränkung liegt die Grenze, je nach Komplexität der Schaltung und verwendetem Integrationsverfahren, bei Systemen mit 200-400 Freiheitsgraden.

SIDAS II wird momentan unter drei Gesichtspunkten weiterentwickelt. Zunächst ist vorgesehen, wie bereits im Kapitel 2 erläutert, das Paket mit universellen Möglichkeiten zur Nachverarbeitung von Simulationsdaten auszustatten. Weiterhin wird an der Implementierung impliziter Integrationsverfahren zur Behandlung steifer Systeme gearbeitet. Längerfristig ist beabsichtigt, die bisher insbesondere aus Gründen der graphischen Darstellung gemachte Einschränkung auf drei Blockeingänge durch die Einführung vektorieller Datenpfade aufzuheben.

ANHANG

In den Beispielen verwendete SIDAS Grundfunktionsblöcke:

| | |
|---|---|
| I N T : Integrierer | C M P : Komparator |
| V Z 1 : VZ1 Glied | R E L : Relais |
| S U M : Summation | C O N : Konstante |
| M U L : Multiplikation | S T O : Abspeichern auf File |
| D I V : Division | O U T : Blockausgang |
| A B S : Absolutbetrag | I N P : Blockeingang |
| B G R : Begrenzer-Kennlinie | P A D : Parameteraddition |
| P D I : Diodenkennlinie positiv | P V Z : Verzögerung um einen Zyklus |
| N D I : Diodenkennlinie negativ | P E N : Bedingter Abbruch der Rechnung |
| P G L : Proportionalglied | |

## Literatur


[1]  M. Wittmann:
Erstellen eines Programmsystems zur Simulation kontinuierlicher, dynamischer Systeme. Diplomarbeit, Institut für Meß- und Regelungstechnik, Universität Karlsruhe, 1974.

[2]  H. Moll; H. Burkhardt:
On an Interactive Digital Simulation System for Hybrid Structured Block-Diagrams. Computer Aided Design of Control Systems, ed. by M.A. Cuenod, Pergamon Press, Oxford/New York 1980.

[3]  H. Moll; H. Burkhardt:
SIDAS, ein interaktives Programmsystem zur blockorientierten digitalen Simulation dynamischer Systeme. Regelungstechnik, Heft 2 und 3, 1978.

[4]  H. Braun:
SIDAS II - Version 1.0 - Benutzer-Anleitung.
Institut für Meß- und Regelungstechnik, Universität Karlsruhe, 1985.

[5]  W. Jentsch:
Digitale Simulation kontinuierlicher Systeme. R. Oldenbourg Verlag, München/Wien, 1969.

[6]  R.D. Grigorieff:
Numerik gewöhnlicher Differentialgleichungen: Band 1 - Einschrittverfahren. B.G. Teubner, Stuttgart 1972.

[7]  F.E. Celliers:
Combined Continuous/Discrete Systems Simulation by Use of Digital Computers: Techniques and Tools. Ph.D. Dissertation, Swiss Federal Institute of Technology, Zürich.

# A COMPILER FOR CONTROL SYSTEMS SIMULATION


D.Matko,M.Šega ,B.Zupančič,R.Karba
Ljubljana, Yugoslavia



Summary. The paper describes a compiler for control systems simulation,
which is included in the interactive program package for analysis and
design of control systems ANA and enables a block oriented universal
computer simulation (UNICUS). By means of general blocks and analog
computer the concept of ANA can be extended to nonlinear and time variable systems. Analog computer and real process included in the simulation require the real time simulation. Due to the concept of UNICUS
the simulation is in spite of its generality as fast as a simulation
in FORTRAN can be. For off line applications the optimization is available. The output of the simulation is in the format of ANA data base
and can be processed by ANA. UNICUS is written in a standard FORTRAN
and can be run on every computer while interpreter (written in FORTRAN
too) is implemented on PDP 11/34  computer with RT 11 operating system.

Zusammenfassung. Diese Veröffentlichung befasst sicht mit einem Compiler, der für die Simulation von Regelsystemen verwendbar ist. Er ist in
ein interaktives Programmpaket  für den rechnergestützten Entwurf von
Regelsystemen ANA eingeschlossen. Durch allgemeine Blöke und durch das
Einschliessen von Analogrechner wird das Konzept von ANA auch auf nichtlineare und zeitvariante Prozesse verbreitet. Analogrechner und reelle
Prozesse verlangen eine Echtzeitsimulation, die durch das Compilerprin-
zip von UNICUS erreicht ist. Die Simulation ist trotz ihrer General-
lität so schnell, wie eine Simulation in FORTRAN schnell sein kann.
Bei dem off-line Betrieb ist auch eine Optimierung möglich. Der Simula-
tionausgang ist mit der Datenbase von ANA kompatibel und kann dementsprechend behandelt werden. UNICUS ist in standard FORTRAN Geschrieben
und kann auf jedem Rechner eingesetzt werden, wobei Interpreter (auch
FORTRAN) am PDP 11/34 - RT11 Betriebesystem installiert ist.


## 1.   Introduction

The paper describes a compiler for control systems simulation, which is
included in the interactive program package for analysis and design of
control systems ANA. The compiler enables an universal computer simulation (UNICUS), which is block oriented and where each block can be either a source of the signal, a signal joining block, a linear transfer
block written by the user in the form of a subroutine, an analog computer block or a general block, written by the user in the form of a subroutine, an analog computer or real process connected to the digital
computer via A/D and D/A converters. All blocks are multivariable. As
signal sources some standard signals (step, pulse, ramp, Gaussian noise), signals generated (computed or recorded) by ANA and signals gene-

rated by an user written subroutine are available. Among signal joining
blocks summing and subtracting are implemented. Linear transfer blocks
are transfer blocks of the ANA (discrete transfer function matrices and
state space description). By means of general blocks and analog computer the concept of ANA can be extended to nonlinear and time variable
systems. Analog computer and real process included in the simulation
require the real time simulation. Due to the concept of UNICUS the simulation is in spite of its generality as fast as a simulation in FOR-
TRAN can be. Also some special blocks for on line implementation are
available: parameter estimator, state estimator and Kalman filter.

## 2.  The language structure

The block in the control structure can be either a source of the signal,
a signal joining block, a linear transfer block, an analog computer or
a general block written by the user in the form of a subroutine. As signal sources some standard signals (step, pulse, ramp, Gaussian noise),
signals generated (computed or recorded) by ANA and signals generated
by an user written subroutine are available. Among signal joining blocks
summing and subtracting are implemented. Linear transfer block are transfer blocks of the ANA (discrete transfer functions matrices and state
space description). The general block written by the user represents
a singificant extension of the simulation possibilities because the
nonlinear and time varying blocks can be included to the simulation
scheme. The general block is written by the user in FORTRAN prior to
entering ANA and describes the desired input output relation. If the
block called "process" is written by the user in the form of a general
block, the simulated delay of the process must be 1 less as the real one.
Also two vectors - "parameters" and "states" of the general block are
available. All other variables (parameters and states of other blocks
are available through their names). An analog computer or a real process
can be included to the UNICUS via A/D and D/A converters. This of course requires the real time simulation and due to the concept of UNICUS
the simulation is in spite of its generality as fast as a simulation in
FORTRAN cna be. The number of "real time" blocks is limited to 1. It
is forseen that a digital simulation language will be included in UNICUS.
As parameter estimation blocks three standard procedures are included
(recursive least squares, recursive extended least squares and recursive maximum likelihood methods), it is  forseen to include also instru-
mental variables and output error methods. The state estimator and Kalman
filter are generated by user in ANA and included into the simulation.

## 3.   Communication with the user

The interpreter of ANA helps the non skilled user to generate the data
base for UNICUS. It is possible to choose the standard control structure, which includes one process, controller in the direct and feedback
path, prefilter, two noise filters on the input and the output of the
process, feed forward controller, process parameter estimation and state observer or Kalman filter. If a more complicated scheme is required,
it is possible to extend the standard structure to the structure required by the user. The interactive definition of concrete scheme is based
on semigraphics capabilities of videoterminal VT 100 which is one of
the input-output units of the package. The screen is divided into three
parts: the last 9 rows are reserved for interactive communication with
the user (SCROLL area). The first 17 rows are devided in two areas: the
left part is the area of the standard structure and the right part is
reserved for additional elements and connections, which enable more
general simulation scheme applications. During the interactive definition of the scheme first the maximal standard structure is shown in the
left upper part of the screen. This maximal structure, shown in Fig.1
is then interactively adjusted to the structure designed by the user.

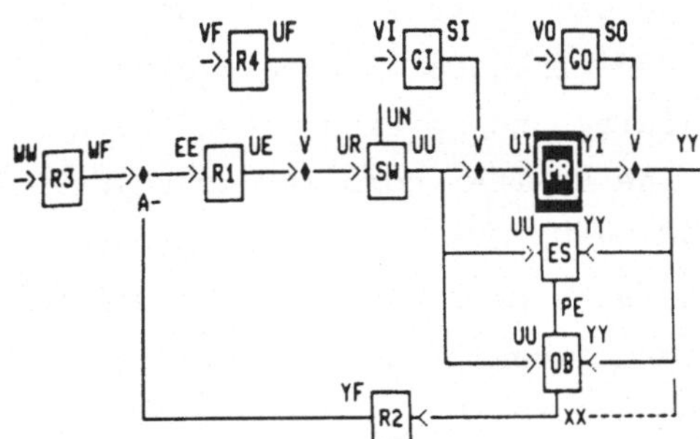


Fig.1. The maximal standard structure of UNICUS

The block being determined is shown in reverse mode and if it exists its
type must be given. The type of each block implies the control structure
and so the determination of the remaining scheme. When every block of
the standard structure is determined, the existing scheme, if necessary
can be extended through additional elements shown on the right upper
part of the screen. The connections of the additional elements with the
subset of the standard scheme are shown by means of markers. The data
base contains also the data of the timing of the simulatin: initial time, final time, maximal number of steps and the data for output, which
is in the format of ANA. Some additional conditions for the terminati-

on of the simulation run can be added in the form of a logical expression. The data for optimization option (discussed later) are also generated interactively and are included into the data base.

For off line applicatons the optimization is available. In this case in each simulation run the criterion function is evaluated and optimization gives the optimal values of the parameters. The criterion function can be chosen from a menu of criterion functions or written by user in form of a subroutine (ex. $\sum (\underline{x}^T \underline{Q} \underline{x} + \underline{u}^T \underline{R} \underline{u})$). $\underline{x}$ and $\underline{u}$ are two vectors of variables of the control scheme and $\underline{Q}$ and $\underline{R}$ corresponding weighting matrices. For the first step, for the last step and for other steps of the simulation three different values of the weighting matrices $\underline{Q}$ and $\underline{R}$ can be specified. As optimization method a method EXTREM /1/ is included. It is forseen to include some other methods. The limitations of the optimization is included in form of logical expressions (maximum 10) or a user written subroutine. By means of this off line optimization the PID controllers, optimal open loop responses of batch processes etc. can be designed.

## 4. The compilation and run procedures

UNICUS compiles the input data base into a program and a subroutine in FORTRAN. The compilation is done in several steps where various tests of the simulation scheme validity and sorting procedure are performed. The interpreter calls first the FORTRAN compiler to compile the program and subroutine generated by UNICUS, then a linker to link the UNICUS program and subroutine with user written subroutines and subroutines of the UNICUS library and finally runs the simulation program. The results of the simulation are in the format of ANA and can be dealt with the interactive package output routines which are accessible directly from the run time interpreter. Also some modification of the simulation scheme can be done without repeated running of the compiler: the parameters of linear blocks and output variable list. So different control possibilities can be tested by UNICUS and evaluated by ANA.

## 5. Conclusion

A compiler for control systems simulation is described. It is included in the interactive program package for analysis and design of control systems ANA. We believe that it might be of great help to the engineers designing all kinds of systems.

References

1/ ANA - interactive CAD package - manual, Faculty of electrical engineering, Ljubljana, 1984 (in slovene).

# INTERAKTIVE GRAPHISCHE SIMULATION

## KONTINUIERLICHER SYSTEME

### Die Benutzerschnittstelle des Systems *IMP*

Robert Schaback, Göttingen

**Zusammenfassung.** Auf den ASIM–Tagungen 1982 und 1983 wurde die Hard– und Software-Architektur eines an der Universität Göttingen entwickelten interaktiven graphischen Simulationssystems (**IMP**) für kontinuierliche Systeme vorgestellt [4,2]. In diesem Beitrag wird die praktische Handhabung des inzwischen weitgehend fertiggestellten Systems einem größeren potentiellen Anwenderkreis an Hand von Beispielen aus den Gebieten Biologie/Medizin und Technik/Physik demonstriert. Ferner wird auf den Benutzerdialog, die graphische Ausgabe und das Zeitverhalten des Systems eingegangen.

**Summary.** This paper presents the user interface of the interactive graphic simulation system **IMP**, whose internals have been described at two earlier ASIM meetings [4,2]. Examples from biology/medicine and engineering/physics illustrate the system's features.

## 1. Benutzerdialog

Das System akzeptiert im Dialog Kommandos in beliebiger Folge aus dem unten auszugsweise aufgelisteten Befehlsvorrat. Dabei steht * für eine beliebige nichtnegative ganze Zahl. Genaueres findet sich in [3].

### 1.1 Modellbildungsphase

Es werden gewöhnliche Differentialgleichungssysteme (oder in analoger Weise auch Systeme von diskreten Differenzengleichungen) definiert durch die Kommandos

DVAR* = beliebige Formel für die Ableitung der Variablen VAR*
VAR* = beliebige Formel für die Variable VAR* als Funktion anderer Variablen

werden Formeln aus Variablen VAR*, Parametern PAR* und reellen oder ganzzahligen Konstanten sowie beliebigen FORTRAN-legalen Funktionen zugelassen. Das Kommando VALID besorgt eine Modellprüfung und bereitet Simulationsläufe vor. Man kann Modellteile laden und ablegen durch spezielle Formen der Kommandos LOAD und SAVE. Dadurch ergeben sich flexible Möglichkeiten zur modularen Modellentwicklung. Diese können aus Platzgründen hier nicht durch Beispiele belegt werden.

### 1.2 Parameterbehandlung

Parameter PAR* unterscheiden sich in **IMP** von Variablen VAR* dadurch, daß sie im Modell nicht zeitabhängig sind. Sie können aber nach Analogrechnerart beim repetierenden Rechnen manuell variiert werden. Deshalb gibt es die folgenden Kommandos:

| | |
|---|---|
| PAR* = Wert | (Festsetzung von Parametern) |
| ASSIGN PAR* POT* | (Zuweisung von Parametern an Potentiometer) |
| SCALE POT* W1,W2 Typ | (Skalierung von POT* von Wert W1 bis Wert W2, wobei Typ = LIN oder LOG) |
| CHECK | (Ablesen der laufenden Poti-Werte) |

Der Anfangswert von VAR* ist PAR100+*.

### 1.3 Zuweisung von Linienformen

Das System kann eine Reihe abhängiger Variablen durch Kommandos der Form ASSIGN VAR* LINE* als farbige Kurven in Abhängigkeit von einer durch ASSIGN VAR* LINE1 als unabhängige Variable ausgewählten Variablen darstellen. Die Zeit ist VAR0; assigniert man LINE1 nicht an VAR0, so erhält man Phasenraumbilder.

## 1.4 Simulationsläufe

Hier gibt es die Kommandos

RUN            (Einzelsimulation)
REPEAT        (Iterative Simulation)
FIT             (Iterative Simulation mit Parameteranpassung, derzeit in der Implementierung)

Dabei haben wir uns aus Platzgründen auf die in den folgenden Beispielen auftretenden Befehle beschränkt. Die obige Langform der Befehle und Operationen kann in naheliegender Weise drastisch abgekürzt werden, was in den Beispielen auch erfolgt ist. Die einzige nichttriviale Abkürzung ist K* für KNOB*, was gleichbedeutend mit POT* und POTENTIOMETER* ist; die Kurzform P* steht für PAR* bzw. PARAMETER*.

## 2. Systemeigenschaften

### 2.1 Entwurfsziel

Im Vergleich zu anderen Simulationssystemen hat **IMP** den Vorteil der Direktinterpretation. Weder Programmiersprachen–noch Betriebssystemkenntnisse werden vorausgesetzt. Erkauft wird dies durch den Nachteil eines begrenzteren Repertoires.

Das System ist für Modellbildungsprozesse in der Forschung und in der Lehre gedacht, bei der das qualitative Studium des Modells und dessen schnelle Weiterentwicklung Vorrang vor Laufzeiteffizienz haben und der Zwang zur Detailprogrammierung sehr störend wirken würde.

Anwendungen, bei denen ein einzelnes, aber hochkompliziertes und dann langfristig unverändertes Modell angestrebt wird, das von qualifizierten Programmierern realisiert werden kann, fallen nicht in den Anwendungsbereich von **IMP**.

### 2.2 Voraussetzungen an Hardware und Software

Das System **IMP** ist im Kern als FORTRAN–Programmsystem ausgelegt. Es ist daher im Prinzip auf jeder FORTRAN–fähigen Maschine einsetzbar, wobei allerdings bei mangelnder Leistungsfähigkeit der Maschine ein unbefriedigendes Geschwindigkeitsverhalten in Kauf genommen werden muß. Von der Hardware her sind ein graphisches Display und eine Analogeingabe sowie ein übliches alphanumerisches Terminal nötig.

## 3. Effizienz

### 3.1 Effizienz des Modellbildungsprozesses

Der Hauptgesichtspunkt bei der Effizienzmessung von **IMP** ist der Zeitbedarf für den Modellbildungsprozeß als Ganzes; es kommt wegen der Entwurfsziele für **IMP** in erster Linie auf die Gesamtarbeitszeit des Modellentwicklers an und nicht auf die Zeit für das Rechnen der Simulationen.

Da der Modellbildungsprozeß in **IMP** keine Compilation, kein Linken und keine intervenierenden Kommandos des Betriebssystems erfordert, kann sich der Benutzer auf sein Modell konzentrieren. Deshalb können **IMP**-Benutzer in Zyklen von ca. 1–3 Minuten eine Modellmodifikation erstellen und testen. Typische **IMP**-Sitzungszeiten für Modelleingabe, mehrere Modifikationen mit Testen und diverse spezielle Produktionsläufe mit verschiedenen Anzeigearten betragen etwa eine Stunde.

### 3.2 Effizienz der Simulation

Die "Zykluszeit" für die Berechnung und Darstellung eines neuen Trajektoriensystems steigt bei **IMP** mit der Komplexität des Modells langsam von ca. 1/20 sec. (bei einfachen diskreten Modellen und fester Skalierung der Ausgabe) bis ca. 3 sec. Realzeit auf der VAX11/780 für Modelle mit 8 Variablen, starker Nichtlinearität, starken Oszillationen, automatischer Skalierung und vielen Ausgabepunkten. Der Benutzer sieht erst "flimmernde", dann "pulsierende" und schließlich "springende" Bilder. Genauere Zahlen finden sich in den Beispielen.

Da bei der Implementierung des **IMP**-Systems bisher keine Effizienzgesichtspunkte im Vordergrund standen, sind eine Reihe von Beschleunigungsmöglichkeiten noch ungenutzt.

Es ist klar, daß speziell programmierte Modelle in der CPU–Laufzeit effektiver sind. Anwendungen, bei denen spezielle Modelle extrem schnell durchzurechnen sind, sollten deshalb individuell nach reinen Effizienzgesichtspunkten programmiert werden. Der Gesamtaufwand inklusive Programmierung ist dann aber sicher wesentlich höher als bei **IMP**.

## 4. Beispiele

Aus Platzgründen können hier nur zwei Beispiele angegeben werden; der Tagungsvortrag wird erheblich mehr Beispiele bringen. Dies gilt insbesondere für die Demonstration der modularen Modellentwicklung.

Leider sind Beispiele in Textform keine vollgültigen Demonstrationen, solange nicht die Funktion der graphischen Anzeige und der Variation der Parameter durch Drehen der Potentiometer durch eigene Versuche beurteilt werden können. Man erhält bewegliche Bilder in Abhängigkeit von den Parametern und kann das qualitative Verhalten des Modells direkt graphisch studieren. Erst dadurch (und durch die einfache Modellbildungsphase) wird die Arbeit mit **IMP** attraktiv.

### 4.1 FitzHugh–Nagumo–Modell

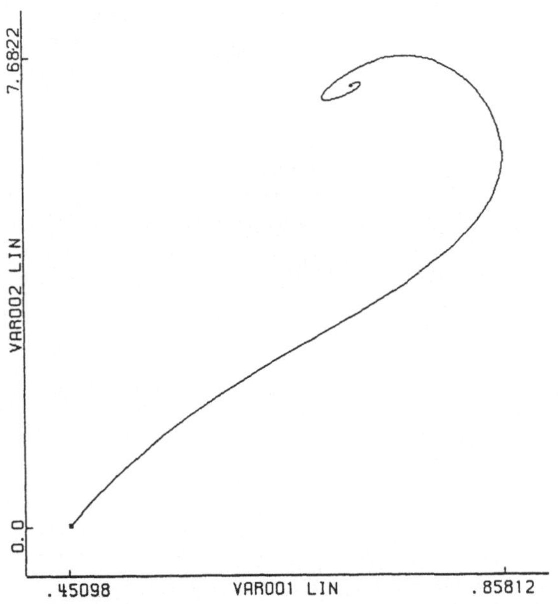


Bild 1 : FitzHugh–Nagumo–Modell : Phasenraum

Dieses beschreibt die Ionenstromstärke und das Membranpotential in einer Nervenzelle. Durch Variation der Parameter kann man deren Einfluß auf den "Schwelleneffekt" studieren.

DVAR1=VAR1*(1–VAR1)*(VAR1–PAR1)–PAR2*VAR2

DVAR2=VAR1–PAR3*VAR2

| | |
|---|---|
| A PAR1 K1 | A ENDTIME K8 |
| A PAR2 K2 | SC K8 0.1,100 |
| SCA K2 0,.01 | A V1 L2 |
| A PAR3 K3 | A V2 L3 |
| SCA K3 0,.1 | VALID |
| A PAR101 K4 | CHECK |

PAR102=0  REPEAT

Die Zykluszeit liegt bei 1/2 sec.

## 4.2 Tragflächenmodell

Es handelt sich um ein mechanisches Modell eines elastisch aufgehängten und von vorn angeblasenen Tragflügels mit zwei Freiheitsgraden (Anstellwinkel und Auslenkung nach oben/unten). Das Modell stammt von Prof. Dr. Dierolf, Trier. Es entsteht ein lineares inhomogenes System mit recht komplizierter Parameterabhängigkeit. Durch Simulation soll festgestellt werden, wann das System instabil wird. Dies tritt bei starker Anblasung irgendwann auf; der Tragflügel wird nach oben weggerissen. Die wichtigsten Parameter werden an Potentiometern justiert (Anblasung: Potentiometer 1, Trimmung: Potentiometer 2) und es kann die Abhängigkeit der Instabilität von anderen Parametern getestet werden.

DV1=V3  DV3=-(P4*P1*V5+V7)*0.02855
DV2=V4  DV4=-(P4*P1*V6+V8)*0.02855
V5=(198+P2*(-10.00+5.654*P2))*V3-V4*(1127+32.20*P2*P2)
V6=(10.00-5.654*P2)*V3+32.20*P2*V4  V7=(P3*15.31*(P2*P2+35.02))*V1+V9
V9=((P2*P2+35.02)*(-P4*P1*P1*5.654)-P2*(P3*463.2-P4*P1*P1*10.00))*V2
V8=-V1*P2*P3*15.31+V2*(P3*463.2+P4*P1*P1*5.654*(P2-5.125))

A P1 K1  SC K3 10,20
A P2 K2  SC K4 1.E-5,1.E-2 LOG
A P3 K3  SC K5 -2,2
A P4 K4  SC K6 -0.7,0.7
P103=0  SC K8 1,20
P104=0  A V1 L2
A P101 K5  A V2 L3
A P102 K6  VALID
A END K8  CHECK
SC K1 0,500  REPEAT

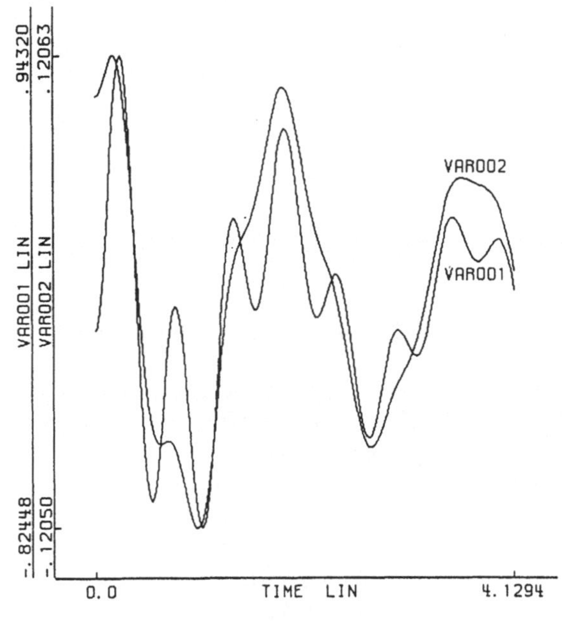


Bild 2 : Tragflügel-Modell

Dieses Modell hat stark oszillierende Trajektorien (bei geringer Anblasung liegt ein gedämpfter Schwinger vor). In der Nähe der kritischen Anblasung ist das Modell numerisch sehr sensibel. Bei wiederholter Überschreitung des a-priori unbekannten, von den anderen Parametern abhängigen kritischen Wertes kann man gut die Stabilität von **IMP** testen; das Programm hat stets einen "korrekten" Abbruch vorgenommen und den Benutzer innerhalb von **IMP** weiterarbeiten lassen (etwa durch leichtes Rückdrehen eines Potentiometers und ein neues REPEAT-Kommando).

Die Zykluszeit liegt bei 3 sec.

## 5. Zusammenfassung

Von den Forderungen, die Frau Dr. I. Bausch-Gall in ihrem Vortrag [1] auf dem Treffen des Arbeitskreises "Simulation technischer Systeme" in Stuttgart am 21.2.1985 an kontinuierliche Simulationssysteme stellte, erfüllt das **IMP**-System die folgenden:

-Anwendernähe
-Reduzierung des Programmieraufwands
-leicht erlernbar für den Anfänger
-Anwender kann Modellteile vorformulieren
-komfortable Ausgabe (graphische Darstellung)
-Hilfe bei der Modellerstellung
-Möglichkeit zur modularen Modellerstellung

Nachteile des Systems sind:

-Nicht geeignet für große und sehr komplexe Modelle
-geringere Mächtigkeit als andere Systeme
-noch nicht bzgl. Effizienz ausgereift

Vorteile :

-niedrige Zykluszeit bei der Modellerstellung
-große Benutzerfreundlichkeit bei der Ein-und Ausgabe
-integriertes Filesystem für Teilmodelle und Daten
-Möglichkeit zur Analog-Eingabe
-Flexible Möglichkeiten zu modularer Modellerstellung
-Möglichkeit zur Parameteridentifikation (zur Zeit noch in der Implementierung)

### Literatur


[1] Bausch-Gall, I. : Kontinuierliche Simulationssprachen und Simulationsprogramme in der Mechanik und Elektronik, Vortrag beim Treffen des ASIM/GI-Arbeitskreises "Simulation technischer Systeme" am 21. Februar 1985 beim IKE in Stuttgart

[2] Krauth,J., Schaback,R. : An Interactive System for Simulation and Graphic Evaluation of Discrete and Continous Systems, in: Informatik-Fachberichte 71, Springer-Verlag 1983

[3] Schaback, R. : **IMP** User's Manual, Institut für numerische und angewandte Mathematik, Göttingen 1985

[4] Schaback, R. : Ein interaktives System zur Simulation, Parameterschätzung und graphischen Auswertung diskreter und kontinuierlicher Modelle, in: Informatik-Fachberichte 56, Springer-Verlag 1982



Ich danke Immo Diener für seine Hilfe bei der Redaktion und der T$_E$Xnischen Aufbereitung des Manuskripts sowie Helge Robitzsch für die Anfertigung der Hardcopy-Plots.

# Entwurf einer Allgemeinen Modellbeschreibungssprache

Peter Eschenbacher, Erlangen

Zusammenfassung: Die Allgemeine Modellbeschreibungssprache SIMPLEX-MDL ist Bestand-
teil des Simulationsystems SIMPLEX II. In einem einheitlichen Konzept werden die
Modellklassen "kontinuierliche Modelle", "ereignisorientierte Modelle" und "transactionsorientierte Modelle mit beschränkten Warteräumen" behandelt.
Die Sprache ist blockorientiert und hierarchisch strukturiert. Eine einmal definierte
Modellkomponente vereinbart eine Klasse, von der beliebig viele Inkarnationen erzeugt
werden können.
Die Modellkomponenten sind bezogen auf Schreibzugriffe autonom, bezogen auf Lesezugriffe transparent. Daher können Modellkomponenten jederzeit ausgetauscht, portiert
oder in einer Modellbank abgelegt werden.

Summary: The General Purpose Model Description Language is part of the simulation
system SIMPLEX II. The model classes "continuous models", "event-oriented models" and
"transaction-oriented models" are handled by a integrated concept.
The language is block-oriented and hierarchically structured. A previously defined
model component defines a class, from which an arbitrary number of incarnations can
be generated.
In respect to write access, model components are autonomous, whereas, in respect to
read access they are transparent. Therefore, model components are easily exchangeable
and portable and can be stored in a model bank.

## 1 Anforderungen und Zielsetzungen

Das Konzept der Allgemeinen Modellbeschreibungssprache SIMPLEX-MDL orientiert sich an
den Anforderungen einer Simulationsumgebung, die im Rahmen des Projekts SIMPLEX II
entsteht und deren Ziel es ist, den Benutzer in allen Phasen einer Simulationsstudie
die größtmögliche Unterstützung zukommen zu lassen und alle Arten von rechnergestützten Simulationsmodellen mit einer gemeinsamen methodischen Vorgehensweise
behandeln zu können /1/.
Modelle, die in SIMPLEX-MDL formuliert wurden, sollen einerseits leicht verständlich
sein und sich an gängige Notationen anlehnen, andererseits haben wir uns zum Ziel
gesetzt, durch eine einheitliche Methodologie Modelle einer wissenschaftlichen Fachrichtung auch einer anderen Fachrichtung zugänglich und verstehbar zu machen.

Es wird daher der Versuch unternommen, die meist getrennt behandelten Modellklassen
- zeitkontinuierliche Modelle
- ereignisorientierte Modelle
- transactionsorientierte Modelle
in einem gemeinsamen Konzept unterzubringen.

Auch wenn sich später eine Trennung der Modellklassen aus Gründen der Effizienz oder Handhabbarkeit als sinnvoll herausstellen sollte, so wird auf diese Weise doch erreicht, daß das Simulationssystem Modelle aller Klassen gleichermaßen handhaben kann und sich der Anwender nicht mit unterschiedlichen Modellierungsphilosophien sowie syntaktischen und anschaulichen Beschreibungsmitteln vertraut machen muß.

Modellkomponenten, die einmal für ein Modell erstellt wurden, sollen auch in beliebigen anderen Modellen zum Einsatz kommen können. Um bequem mit Modellkomponenten hantieren zu können, muß es möglich sein, diese in einer Modellbank abzulegen und beliebig oft zu vervielfachen. Damit die Modellkomponenten auch in einer anderen Umgebung einsetzbar sind, dürfen innerhalb der Komponente keinerlei Verweise auf außenstehende Objekte vorkommen. Die Verbindungen zwischen den Komponenten sind ausschließlich auf der darüberliegenden Ebene zu vereinbaren.

Damit auch der in Programmiersprachen ungeübte Benutzer die Simulation zum Einsatz bringen kann, besteht für ihn die Möglichkeit, mit vorgefertigten Modellkomponenten zu arbeiten, die er nur noch zu initialisieren und miteinander zu verknüpfen hat. Eine solche Initialisierung kann menügeführt auf einfache und übersichtliche Art erfolgen. (menügeführte Modellbeschreibung)

Um die Anschaulichkeit der Modellbeschreibung zu verbessern, soll es möglich sein, Teile der Sprache graphisch statt textuell zu beschreiben. Die gleiche graphische Darstellung kann später zu Verfolgung des Simulationslaufes dienen oder kann so erweitert werden, daß auch Simulationsergebnisse darin eingeblendet werden.

Modelle in SIMPLEX-MDL werden mittels eines Precompilers in ein lauffähiges Programm abgebildet, das eine modifizierte Form von GPSS-FORTRAN Version 3 /2/ als Laufzeitsystem verwendet.
Um auch transactionsorientierte Modelle mit beschränkten Warteräumen ohne großen Aufwand modellieren zu können, wurde GPSS-FORTRAN bereits in geeigneter Weise erweitert /3/.

Dem Konzept von SIMPLEX-MDL liegen weitgehend Überlegungen der Allgemeinen Systemtheorie zugrunde /4/. Einige Sprachelemente und konzeptionelle Gedanken wurden aus der Modellbeschreibungssprache GEST /5/ übernommen.

## 2 Das hierarchische Strukturkonzept

Ein Modell besteht aus Modellkomponenten und den Kommunikationsmechanismen zwischen den Komponenten.

Ein Modell ist ein abgeschlossenes Gebilde. Das bedeutet insbesondere, daß auch Quellen und ggf. Meßeinrichtungen Bestandteile des Modells sind.
Modellkomponenten (in der Systemtheorie als Systeme bezeichnet) hingegen besitzen Vorrichtungen zur Kommunikation mit anderen Komponenten.

Modelle können hierarchisch strukturiert werden.
Jede Modellkomponente kann wiederum aus Modellkomponenten bestehen. Modell-komponenten, die nicht mehr weiter zerlegbar sind, heißen Basiskomponenten.

Die Kommunikation zwischen den Komponenten erfolgt mittels Connections und Transactions.
Über eine Connection wird einer Komponente der Wert einer Zustandsvariablen einer anderen Komponente mitgeteilt.
Transactionen sind Merkmalsträger, die, einer Laufliste folgend, von Komponente zu Komponente weitergegeben werden. Ihre Merkmale können in den Komponenten, die sie durchlaufen, verändert werden.

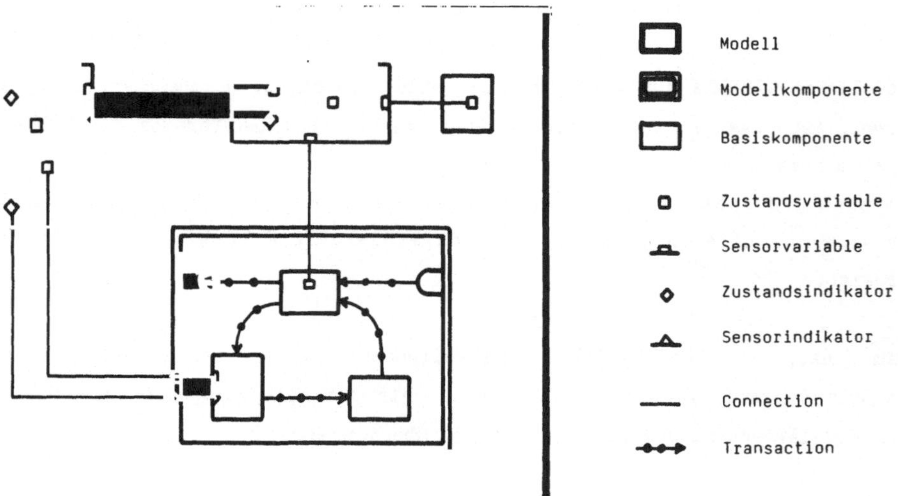


Bild 1:  Hierarchische Struktur und Kommunikation im Modell

## 3 Basiskomponenten

### 3.1 Elemente der Basiskomponente

Eine Basiskomponente kann aus drei Arten von Elementen bestehen:

1) Merkmale (Attribute), repräsentiert durch Variable und Konstanten

2) Indikatoren (Anzeiger für bestimmte Zustandsübergänge)

3) Bedienstation (zur Bearbeitung von Transactionen)


Ein Merkmal ist eine Eigenschaft (Farbe, Länge) einer Komponente mit einer Menge von Ausprägungen (ganze, reelle, boolesche Zahlen; Aufzählungen). Wir unterscheiden zwischen

- Konstanten:               komponenten-eigene, zeitinvariante Merkmale

- Zustandsvariablen:        komponenten-eigene, zeitvariante Merkmale

- Transactionsvariablen: Merkmale derjenigen Transaction, die sich gegenwärtig in der
                          Bedieneinheit befindet

- Sensorvariablen:         Merkmale einer fremden Komponente, die über Connections
                           laufend erfragt werden


Ein Indikator zeigt an, ob eine formulierte Bedingung gerade wahr geworden ist und stößt für diesen Fall vorgesehene Ereignisse an. Wir unterscheiden zwischen

- Zustandsindikatoren:    komponenten-eigene Indikatoren

- Sensorindikatoren:      Indikatoren einer fremden Komponente, die über Connections
                          erfragt werden


Eine Bedienstation besteht aus Eingang, Bedienwarteschlange, Bedieneinheit, Transportwarteschlange und Ausgang.

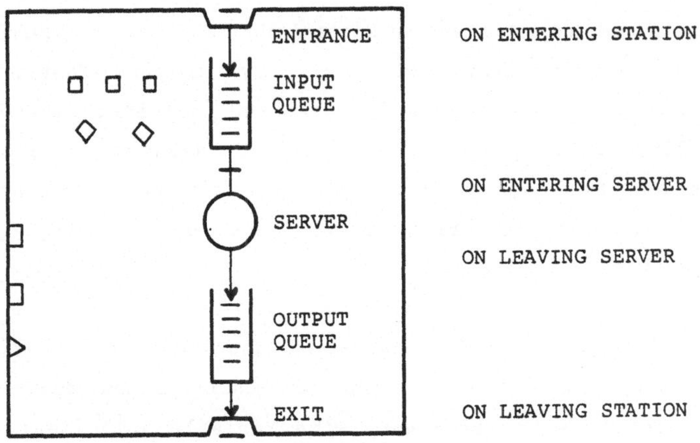


Bild 2:  Basiskomponente mit Bedieneinheit

Die Bedienstation nimmt Transactionen auf, die ihr von der übergeordneten Komponente
zugestellt werden. Diese Transactionen gelangen durch den (verschließbaren) Eingang
in die Eingangs- oder Bedienwarteschlange, in der sie solange verweilen, bis sie zur
Bedieneinheit vorgerückt sind. Die Variablen derjenigen Transaction, die sich in der
Bedieneinheit befindet, können von der Basiskomponente ebenso verändert werden wie
ihre eigenen Zustandsvariablen. Ist die Bearbeitung abgeschlossen, gibt die Basiskomponente die Transaction frei, die jetzt in die Ausgangs- oder Transportwarteschlange vorrücken kann und sich dort solange aufhält, bis sie die Nachfolgestation
betreten kann. Das Weiterrücken der Transactionen wird ganz vom Simulator übernommen,
der auch eventuell auftretende Rückstauungen bei begrenzten Warteschlangenlängen
berücksichtigt. Näheres hierzu findet sich in /3/.

3.2 Die Beschreibung der Dynamik

Um das zugrundeliegende Konzept der dynamischen Beschreibung in seiner Geschlossen-
heit verstehen zu können, gehen wir von der Zustandsraumdarstellung aus.
Zunächst unterscheiden wir abhängige und unabhängige Zustandsvariable. Der Wert einer
abhängigen Zustandsvariablen ist zu jedem Zeitpunkt aus den Werten der unabhängigen
Zustandsvariablen berechenbar.

Die unabhängigen Zustandsvariablen und die Sensorvariablen sowie die Zeit "T" spannen
den Zustandsraum der Komponente auf. Der Zustand der Komponente wird eindeutig durch
die Lage eines Punktes -im folgenden als Zustandspunkt bezeichnet- in diesem Raum
beschrieben.
Die Eigendynamik des Modells zu beschreiben heißt, die Menge aller möglichen Bahnen
dieses Zustandspunktes (Trajektorien) durch den Zustandsraum anzugeben.

Das geschieht durch einen Programmtext, der angibt, welcher Zustandsübergang zum
gerade aktuellen Zeitpunkt und im aktuellen Zustand der Komponente auszuführen ist.
Wir unterscheiden dazu zwischen Zustandsübergängen, die im ganzen Zustandsraum oder
in Bereichen des Zustandsraumes Gültigkeit besitzen (bereichsweise definierte
Zustandsübergänge: Differenzen- und Differentialgleichungen) und solchen, die nur
dann ausgeführt werden, wenn eine Bedingung eintritt, d.h. wenn der Zustandspunkt
eine bestimmte Fläche im Zustandsraum erreicht oder durchdringt (getriggerte
Zustandsübergänge: Ereignisse).

Zur Abgrenzung von Bereichen des Zustandsraumes steht ein IF-THEN-ELSIF-ELSE-
Konstrukt zur Verfügung, das je nach Bedingung nur bestimmte Zustandsübergänge zur
Ausführung bringt. Ist in einer Bedingung eine Variable enthalten, die zeitkontinuierliche Zustandsübergänge ausführt, ist zusätzlich ein Toleranzbereich anzugeben, der besagt, innerhalb welcher Genauigkeitsgrenzen die Bedingung einzuhalten

ist. In einer Bedingung, die die Zeit "T" enthält, darf T nur auf der linken Seite
auftreten und dort nur alleine stehen. Auf der rechten Seite der Bedingung sind keine
Zustandsvariable erlaubt, die kontinuierliche Zustandsübergänge ausführen.

Das Anzeigen des Eintritts einer Bedingung bezeichnen wir als Indikation. Eine
Indikation geht syntaktisch aus einer Bedingung oder boolschen Variablen hervor,
indem der boolsche Ausdruck in Hochkommata eingeschlossen wird. Zur Verknüpfung von
Indikationen ist die OR-Verknüpfung zugelassen. Man beachte den Unterschied zwischen
den Formulierungen 'x>3 OR y>5' und 'x>3' OR 'y>5' !

Zur Formulierung eines Ereignisses dient das Konstrukt
ON indication DO state-transitions END.
Die Indikation gibt dabei an, wann das Ereignis auszuführen ist.

Damit ein Ereignis weitere Ereignisse hervorrufen kann, kann eine Indikation auch
innerhalb der Komponente oder an andere Komponenten weitersignalisiert werden. Hierzu
dient der Indikator und die Anweisung
SIGNAL indicator,
die in einem Ereignis vorkommen darf. Zur näheren Erläuterung sei auf das Beispiel 1
im Anhang verwiesen.

Um die Vorgänge in der Bedienstation, die im wesentlichen vom Simulator übernommen
werden, mit den anderen Vorgängen innerhalb der Komponente abstimmen zu können, gibt
es vier standardmäßig bereitgestellte Indikationen:
ON ENTERING STATION        Betreten der Station
ON ENTERING SERVER         Betreten der Bedieneinheit
ON LEAVING  SERVER         Verlassen der Bedieneinheit
ON LEAVING  STATION        Verlassen der Station

Um umgekehrt auch auf den Transactionsfluß in der Bedieneinheit Einfluß nehmen zu
können, gibt es die Anweisungen:
LOCK / UNLOCK ENTRANCE                       des Eingangs
LOCK / UNLOCK SERVER       schließen/öffnen  der Bedieneinheit
LOCK / UNLOCK EXIT                           des Ausgangs

CLEAR SERVER               Bedienstation freigeben

Soll beispielsweise eine Station modelliert werden, die Fässer füllt, dann wird der
Füllvorgang durch ON ENTERING SERVER in Gang gesetzt und nach beendeter Füllung die
Bedieneinheit mit CLEAR SERVER wieder freigegeben.

## 4 Die Kommunikation im Modell

### 4.1 Connections

Die Merkmale des Modells und ihr dynamisches Zusammenspiel wird in den Basiskomponenten festgelegt. Die darüberliegenden Komponenten dienen dazu, die Beziehungen herzustellen, die zwischen den Basiskomponenten bestehen.

Eine Connection ist eine starre Verbindung zwischen einer Zustandsvariablen einer Komponente und einer Sensorvariablen einer anderen Komponente. Das bedeutet, daß die Sensorvariable stets den gleichen Wert besitzt wie die zugeordnete Zustandsvariable. Das gleiche gilt für Zustandsindikatoren und Sensorindikatoren.
Eine Connection wird ähnlich wie in GEST vereinbart:
component . state-variable  --> component . sensor-variable

Im Gegensatz zu vielen anderen Sprachentwürfen existieren keine explizit erklärten Ausgangsvariablen. Diese schränken die universelle Einsetzbarkeit einer Komponente unnötig ein und räumen dem Experimentator, der alle Variablen beobachten kann, eine Sonderstellung ein.
Nach unserem Entwurf verbindet sich mit der Struktur des Modells die Vorstellung eines Glaskastens, in den man zwar hineinschauen und alle Vorgänge beobachten kann, dessen Zustand von außen jedoch nur beeinflußbar ist, wenn für die Modellkomponente ausdrücklich Reaktionen auf Einflüsse von außen vorgesehen sind.

Alle Modellkomponenten sind gegenüber ihrer Umgebung autonom. Jede Basiskomponente kann nur ihre eigenen Merkmale verändern. Es existiert also kein direkter Schreibzugriff auf die Merkmale fremder Komponenten. Dagegen gilt ein allgemeines Leserecht für alle Komponenten - einschließlich des Experimentators.

### 4.2 Transactions

Neben Connections werden auf Komponentenebene Transactionsklassen und Lauflisten vereinbart.

Die Deklaration einer Transactionsklasse beinhaltet die Vereinbarung der Konstanten und Zustandsvariablen, die Transactionsquelle sowie den Namen der Laufliste. Anstelle einer Quelle kann auch ein Eingang der Komponente angegeben werden. Dadurch ist es möglich, mehrere Ebenen der Modellhierarchie zu durchlaufen.

Modellkomponenten, die Transactionen aufnehmen und bearbeiten können heißen Stationen. Nach der Generierung wird eine Transaction von einer Station zur nächsten weitergereicht und dort bearbeitet. Die Bearbeitungsreihenfolge ist in einer Laufliste festgelegt.

Damit Transactionen verschiedener Klassen von der gleichen Station bearbeitet werden können, fordern wir, daß Variablen mit gleicher semantischer Bedeutung bei der Deklaration mehrerer Transactionsklassen den gleichen Namen tragen. Über eine Äquivalenzliste kann dann eine Namenszuordnung zu den Transactionsvariablen in den Basiskomponenten erfolgen.

Transactionen nehmen in den Stationen Plätze ein. Die Anzahl der Plätze ist häufig begrenzt (begrenzte Warteräume). Dadurch kann der Fall eintreten, daß eine Transaction eine Station nicht verlassen kann, weil die Nachfolgestation keinen freien Platz zur Verfügung stellen kann. Die Transactionensteuerung des Simulators handhabt auch solche Rückstauungen.

Eine nähere Beschreibung dieser Transactionensteuerung, der Laufliste sowie der zusätzlichen Gesichtspunkte, die durch Rückstauungen ins Spiel kommen, ist in /3/ zu finden.


Literatur

/1/  Klaus-Jürgen Langer:  Das Simulationssystem SIMPLEX II
     erschienen im gleichen Band


/2/  Bernd Schmidt:  Der Simulator GPSS-FORTRAN Version 3
     Springer  Berlin 1984


/3/  Sabine Nagel:  Transactionsorientierte Modelle mit
                    beschränkten Warteräumen in GPSS-FORTRAN
     erschienen im gleichen Band


/4/  Franz Pichler:  Mathematische Systemtheorie
     Walter de Gruyter  New York 1975


/5/  Tuncer I. Ören:  GEST - A Modelling and Simulation Language
                      based on System Theoretic Concepts
     in: Simulation and Model Based Methodologies
         An Integrative View, Springer  New York 1984

## ANHANG

Beispielmodell: Es existieren zwei Wirte-Parasiten-Systeme. Übersteigt die Anzahl der Wirte im System 1 einen Grenzwert, wird aus dem System 1 ein Zehntel der Parasiten entnommen und dem System 2 zugeführt.

Zunächst werden die beiden Basiskomponenten Wirpa und Experimentator vereinbart, anschließend wird das Gesamtmodell zusammengestellt. Die Basiskomponente Wirpa ist darin zweimal in den Ausprägungen System1 und System2 vorhanden. Die Überschreitung des Grenzwerts, die der Indikator überschreitung anzeigt, löst im System1 eine Herausnahme, im System2 ein Hinzufügen von Parasiten aus.

```
BASIC COMPONENT  Wirpa

DECLARATION OF ELEMENTS

CONSTANTS  a (REAL) := 0.005 ;
           b (REAL) := 0.05
           C (REAL) := 0.000006

STATE VARIABLES  Wirte (REAL) := 10000.
                 Parasiten (REAL) := 1000.

SENSOR VARIABLE  Anzahl (REAL)

SENSOR INDICATORS  Herausnehmen, Hinzufüllen

DYNAMIC DESCRIPTION

DIFFERENTIAL EQUATION SYSTEM
Wirte     := a * Wirte - ... * Wirte * Pa...
Parasiten := -b * Parasiten + c * Wirte * Pa...
END OF SYSTEM

ON Herausnehmen
DO Parasiten := Parasiten - Anzahl;  END

ON Hinzufüllen
DO Parasiten := Parasiten + Anzahl;  END

END OF Wirpa
```

The catalogue printed on the sheet:

Band 66: Applications and Theory of Petri Nets. Proceedings, 1982. Edited by G. Rozenberg. VI, 315 pages. 1983.

Band 67: Data Networks with Satellites. GI/NTG Working Conference, Cologne, September 1982. Edited by J. Majus and O. Spaniol. VI, 251 pages. 1983.

Band 68: B. Kutzler, F. Lichtenberger, Bibliography on Abstract Data Types. V, 194 Seiten. 1983.

Band 69: Betrieb von DN-Systemen in der Zukunft. GI-Fachgespräch, Tübingen, März 1983. Herausgegeben von M. A. Graef. VIII, 343 Seiten. 1983.

Band 70: W. E. Fischer, Datenbanksystem für CAD-Arbeitsplätze. VII, 222 Seiten. 1983.

Band 71: First European Simulation Congress ESC'83. Proceedings, 1983. Edited by W. Ameling. XII, 653 pages. 1983.

Band 72: Sprachen für Datenbanken. GI-Jahrestagung, Hamburg, Oktober 1983. Herausgegeben von J. W. Schmidt. VII, 237 Seiten. 1983.

Band 73: GI-13. Jahrestagung, Hamburg, Oktober 1983. Proceedings. Herausgegeben von J. Kupka. VIII, 502 Seiten. 1983.

Band 74: Requirements Engineering. Arbeitstagung der GI, 1983. Herausgegeben von G. Hommel und D. Krönig. VIII, 247 Seiten. 1983.

Band 75: K. R. Dittrich, Ein universelles Konzept zum flexiblen Informationsschutz in und mit Rechensystemen. VIII, 246 pages. 1983.

Band 76: GWAI-83. German Workshop on Artifical Intelligence. September 1983. Herausgegeben von B. Neumann. VI, 240 Seiten. 1983.

Band 77: Programmiersprachen und Programmentwicklung. 8. Fachtagung der GI, Zürich, März 1984. Herausgegeben von U. Ammann. VIII, 239 Seiten. 1984.

Band 78: Architektur und Betrieb von Rechensystemen. 8. GI-NTG-Fachtagung, Karlsruhe, März 1984. Herausgegeben von H. Wettstein. IX, 391 Seiten. 1984.

Band 79: Programmierumgebungen: Entwicklungswerkzeuge und Programmiersprachen. Herausgegeben von W. Sammer und W. Remmele. VIII, 236 Seiten. 1984.

Band 80: Neue Informationstechnologien und Verwaltung. Proceedings, 1983. Herausgegeben von R. Traunmüller, H. Fiedler, K. Grimmer und H. Reinermann. XI, 402 Seiten. 1984.

Band 81: Koordinaten von Informationen. Proceedings, 1983. Herausgegeben von R. Kuhlen. VI, 366 Seiten. 1984.

Band 82: A. Bode, Mikroarchitekturen und Mikroprogrammierung: Formale Beschreibung und Optimierung, 6, 1-277 Seiten. 1984.

Band 83: Software-Fehlertoleranz und -Zuverlässigkeit. Herausgegeben von F. Belli, S. Pfleger und M. Seifert. VII, 297 Seiten. 1984.

Band 84: Fehlertolerierende Rechensysteme. 2. GI/NTG/GMR-Fachtagung, Bonn 1984. Herausgegeben von K.-E. Großpietsch und M. Dal Cin. X, 433 Seiten. 1984.

Band 85: Simulationstechnik. Proceedings, 1984. Herausgegeben von F. Breitenecker und W. Kleinert. XII, 676 Seiten. 1984.

Band 86: Prozeßrechner 1984. 4. GI/GMR/KfK-Fachtagung, Karlsruhe, September 1984. Herausgegeben von H. Trauboth und A. Jaeschke. XII, 710 Seiten. 1984.

Band 87: Mustererkennung 1984. Proceedings, 1984. Herausgegeben von W. Kropatsch. IX, 351 Seiten. 1984.

Band 88: GI-14. Jahrestagung. Braunschweig. Oktober 1984. Proceedings. Herausgegeben von H.-D. Ehrich. IX, 451 Seiten. 1984.

Band 89: Fachgespräche auf der 14. GI-Jahrestagung. Braunschweig, Oktober 1984. Herausgegeben von H.-D. Ehrich. V, 26.. Seiten. 1984.

Band 90: Informatik als Herausforderung an Schule und Ausbildung. GI-Fachtagung, Berlin, Oktober 1984. Herausgegeben von W. Arlt und K. Haefner. X, 416 Seiten. 1984.

Band 91: H. Stoyan, Maschinen-unabhängige Code-Erzeugung als semantikerhaltende beweisbare Programmtransformation. IV, 36.. Seiten. 1984.

Band 92: offene Multifunktionale Büroarbeitsplätze. Proceedings, 1984. Herausgegeben von F. Krückeberg, S. Schindler und O. Spaniol. VI, 335 Seiten. 1985.

Band 93: Künstliche Intelligenz. Frühjahrsschule Dassel, März 1984. Herausgegeben von C. Habel. VII, 320 Seiten. 1985.

Band 94: Datenbank-Systeme für Büro, Technik und Wirtschaft. Proceedings, 1985. Herausgegeben von A. Blaser und P. Pistor. X, 3 519 Seiten. 1985.

Band 95: Kommunikation in Verteilten Systemen I. GI-NTG-Fachtagung, Karlsruhe, März 1985. Herausgegeben von D. Heger, G. Krüger, O. Spaniol und W. Zorn. IX, 691 Seiten. 1985.

Band 96: Organisation und Betrieb der Informationsverarbeitung. Proceedings, 1985. Herausgegeben von W. Dirlewanger. XI, 26.. Seiten. 1985.

Band 97: H. Willmer, Systematische Software- Qualitätssicherung anhand von Qualitäts- und Produktmodellen. VII, 162 Seiten. 1985.

Band 98: Öffentliche Verwaltung und Informationstechnik. Neue Möglichkeiten, neue Probleme, neue Perspektiven. Proceedings, 1984. Herausgegeben von H. Reinermann, H. Fiedler, K. Grimmer, K. Lenk und R. Traunmüller. X, 396 Seiten. 1985.

Band 99: K. Küspert, Fehlererkennung und Fehlerbehandlung in Speicherungsstrukturen von Datenbanksystemen. IX, 294 Seiten. 1985.

Band 100: W. Lamersdorf, Semantische Repräsentation komplexer Objektstrukturen. IX, 187 Seiten. 1985.

Band 101: J. Koch, Relationale Anfragen. VIII, 147 Seiten. 1985.

Band 102: H.-J. Appelrath, Von Datenbanken zu Expertensystemen. VI, 159 Seiten. 1985.

Band 103: GWAI-84. 8th German Workshop on Artifical Intelligence. Wingst/Stade, October 1984. Edited by J. Laubsch. VIII, 282 Seiten. 1985.

Band 104: G. Sagerer, Darstellung und Nutzung von Expertenwissen für ein Bildanalysesystem. XIII, 270 Seiten. 1985.

Band 105: G. E. Maier, Exceptionbehandlung und Synchronisation. IV, 359 Seiten. 1985.

Band 106: Österreichische Artifical Intelligence Tagung. Wien, September 1985. Herausgegeben von H. Trost und J. Retti. VIII, 211 Seiten. 1985.

Band 107: Mustererkennung 1985. Proceedings, 1985. Herausgegeben von H. Niemann. XIII, 338 Seiten. 1985.

Band 108: GI/OCG/ÖGJ-Jahrestagung 1985. Wien, September 1985. Herausgegeben von H. R. Hansen. XVII, 1086 Seiten. 1985.

Band 109: Simulationstechnik. Proceedings, 1985. Herausgegeben von D. P. F. Möller. XIV, 539 Seiten. 1985.

```
BASIC COMPONENT Experimentator

DECLARATION OF ELEMENTS
   CONSTANT  Grenzwert (REAL) := 7500.
   STATE VARIABLE    Anzahl (REAL) := 0.
   SENSOR VARIABLES  Wirte1 (REAL),
                     Parasiten1 (REAL)
   STATE INDICATOR   Überschreitung

DYNAMIC DESCRIPTION
   ON 'Wirte1 > Grenzwert (TOLERANCE :=1.)'
   DO
       Anzahl := 0.1 * Parasiten1;
       SIGNAL  Überschreitung;
   END

END OF Experimentator


MODEL  Beispiel1

SUBCOMPONENTS
   System1  OF  CLASS  Wirpa
   System2  OF  CLASS  Wirpa
   Experimentator

COMPONENT CONNECTION
   System1.(Wirte,Parasiten)  -->  Experimentator.(Wirte1,Parasiten1)
   Experimentator.(Überschreitung,Anzahl)  -->  System1.(Herausnahme,Anzahl)
   Experimentator.(Überschreitung,Anzahl)  -->  System2.(Hinzufüllen,Anzahl)

END  OF  Beispiel1
```

Das Simulationssystem SIMPLEX II

Ein Experimentiersystem mit Allgemeiner Modellbeschreibungssprache


Klaus–Jürgen Langer, Erlangen


**Zusammenfassung.** Es wird das Konzept eines Simulationssystems vorgestellt, das auf Grundlagen der Wissenschaftstheorie und Systemtheorie basiert und somit in allen Wissenschaftszweigen Verwendung finden kann. Mit UNIX als Basisbetriebssystem soll eine hohe Portabiltät von Modellen, Modellkomponenten und Simulationsergebnissen sichergestellt werden. Eine komfortable und einheitliche Benutzerführung soll jedermann den Zugang zur Simulation ermöglichen. Der Modellaufbau wird über eine Allgemeine Modellbeschreibungssprache erfolgen.

**Summary.** A concept of a simulation system is presented which is based on scientific method and system theory and is therefore applcable in all branches of science. A high degree of portability for models, model components and simulation results is assured by using UNIX as the basic operating system. A unified and convenient user interface is provided to make simulation accessible to everyone. The model is constructed using a general purpose model description language.


## 1. Zielsetzungen

Das Simulationssystem SIMPLEX II wird an der Universität Erlangen–Nürnberg als komfortable Arbeitsumgebung zum vorhandenen Simulator GPSS–FORTRAN Version 3 (siehe /1/) entwickelt. Das erklärte Ziel ist es, den Benutzer in allen Phasen einer Simulationsstudie so weit als möglich zu unterstützen und ihn von Verwaltungsaufgaben zu entlasten. Zu Beginn des Projekts SIMPLEX II wurde folgender Forderungskatalog erstellt:

(1)  Interaktives Simulationssystem

(2)  Verwendung problembezogener Modellbezeichner

(3)  Benutzerführung durch Menü–Steuerung der Teilfunktionen

(4)  Automatische Datenverwaltung einschließlich Modellbank

(5)  Unterstützung der Dokumentation

(6)  Beschreibung von Experimentierfolgen zur automatischen Ablaufsteuerung

(7)  Statistische Methoden zur Auswertung der Simulationsergebnisse

(8)  Graphische Aufbereitung der Ergebnisse

(9)  Verwaltung mehrerer Experimente eines Modells

(10) Vergleich und Auswertung der Simulationsergebnisse mehrerer Experimente

## 2. Beschreibung der Komponenten von SIMPLEX II

Bild 1 zeigt eine Prinzipskizze des Simulationssystems SIMPLEX II. Die stärker umrandeten Komponenten sind Programme, während die übrigen Daten repräsentieren. Deutlich erkennbar ist die Dreiteilung in Definitions-, Simulations- und Bewertungsphase. In jeder dieser Phasen erhält der Anwender volle Systemunterstützung durch Menüsteuerung sowie formulargestützte Dateneingabe für alle Eingabedateien. Die klare Gliederung fördert die Transparenz des doch recht komplexen Gesamtsystems.

**Definitionsphase:** Zunächst erfolgt die Modellbeschreibung durch den Anwender mit Hilfe einer Allgemeinen Modellbeschreibungssprache, wie sie etwa in /2/ dargestellt wird. Neben der Verwendung problembezogener Modellbezeichner hat der Benutzer hier die Möglichkeit, auf früher definierte Modellkomponenten zurückzugreifen, die bereits in der Modellbank archiviert sind. Der Modellgenerator erzeugt aus dem neuen Modell, den bereits vorhandenen Komponenten sowie den in der Laufzeitbibliothek gespeicherten Routinen des Simulators GPSS-C das ablauffähige Simulationsprogramm und erstellt alle modellrelevanten Datenbereiche einschließlich Vorbelegung. GPSS-C ist die C-Übersetzung von GPSS-Fortran Version 3 mit einigen Erweiterungen; z.B. beschränkte Warteräume (siehe /3/).
Die Vorbelegungen der modellrelevanten Datenbereiche können jetzt noch vom Anwender experimentspezifisch modifiziert werden. Ein Initialisierungsprogramm erzeugt dann den endgültigen Anfangszustand eines Experiments.

**Simulationsphase:** In diesem Abschnitt findet die eigentliche Durchführung eines Simulationsexperiments statt. Das Simulationsprogramm erhält folgende Eingabedaten:

| | |
|---|---|
| Anfangszustand | : Belegung der Datenbereiche des Simulators |
| Steuerdaten | : Benutzerangaben zum Experimentablauf (z.B. Protokollierung) |
| Quelldaten | : Zeitreihen für die verschiedenen Quellen des Modells |
| Funktionstabellen | : Tabellarische Funktionen wie z.B. Verteilungen o.ä. |

Nach der Durchführung des Experiments stehen die eigentlichen Ergebnisse des Simulationslaufes in den Simulationsdaten dem Anwender zur Verfügung. Die Protokolldaten enthalten gesammelte Angaben für eine nachträgliche graphische Prozeßverfolgung sowie detaillierte Informationen über den schrittweisen Ablauf der Simulation. Diese Informationen werden vom Anwender lediglich zur Verifizierung komplexer Modelle benötigt, falls er die interne Arbeitsweise des Simulators nachvollziehen will.
Analog zum Anfangszustand wird auch ein Endzustand des Experiments erzeugt, der wiederum bei einer Fortsetzung des Simulationslaufes als neuer Anfangszustand dienen kann. Dies ist insbesondere dann der Fall, wenn der Anwender eine Simulationsstudie im Einzelschrittverfahren ablaufen lassen will, um etwa die korrekte Funktionsweise seines Modells zu überprüfen.

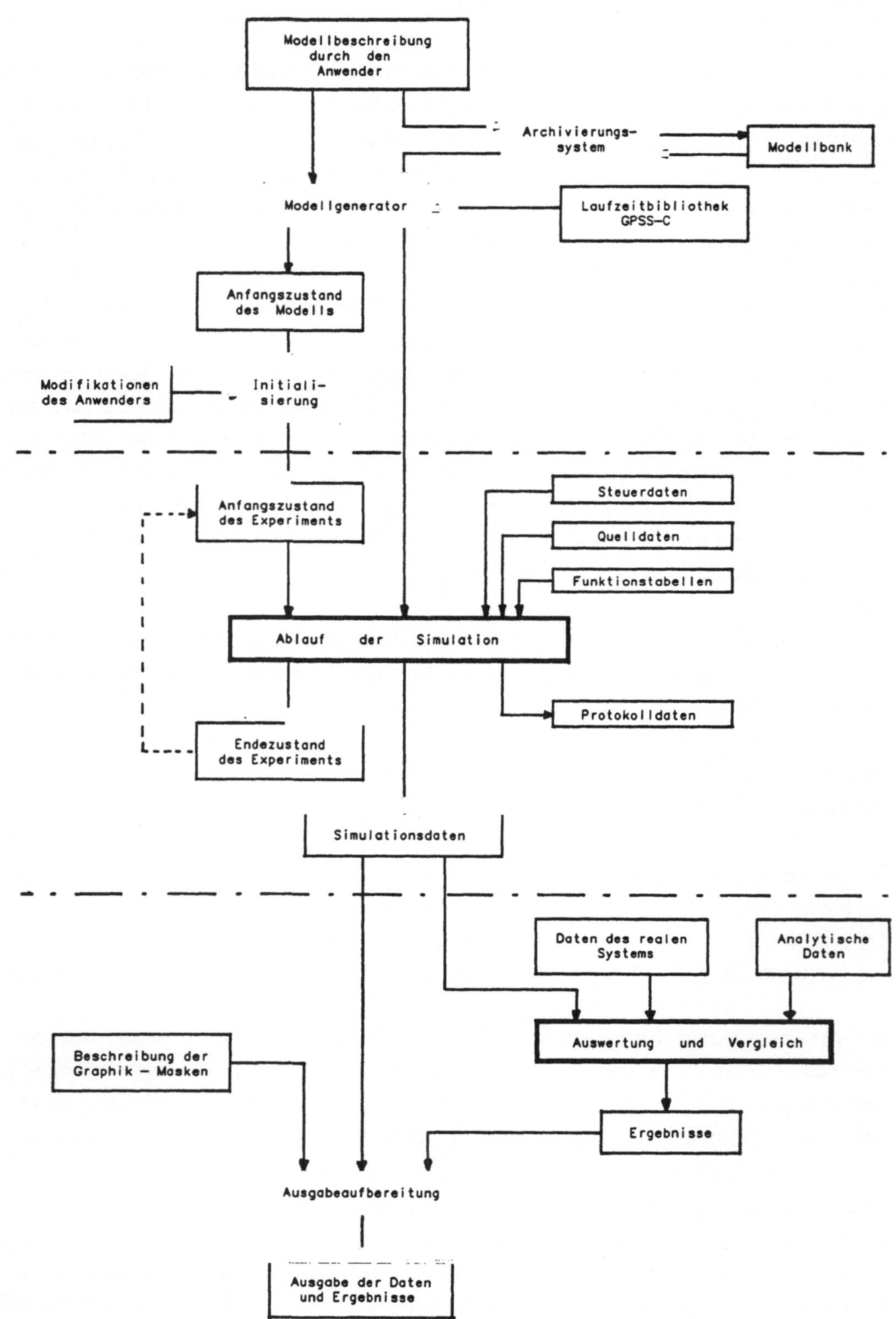


Bild 1   Prinzipskizze des Simulationssystems SIMPLEX II

**Bewertungsphase:** Hier erfolgt die Auswertung und Aufbereitung der Simulationsdaten in
für den Anwender übersichtlichen Darstellungen. Die simulativ gewonnenen Informatio-
nen können mit Daten verglichen werden, die entweder vom Anwender durch analytische
Auswertung des abstrakten Modells ermittelt wurden oder aber durch Beobachtung des
realen Systems zur Verfügung stehen. Diese Vergleichsmöglchkeiten erleichtern die
Validierung des Simulationsmodells beträchtlich. Durch eine Beschreibung der Graphik-
Masken kann der Benutzer weitestgehend selbst entscheiden, in welcher Form er die
Ergebnisse des Experiments präsentieren will: ob etwa als Plots, Balkendiagramme oder
aber auch in numerischer Form. Die Beschreibung dieser Masken erfolgt mit Hilfe eines
interaktiven Graphikeditors über vordefinierte Graphiksymbole. Für sämtliche Dar-
stellungen existieren Standardmasken, so daß der Anwender im Idealfall nur aus einer
Reihe von vorgegebenen Komponenten die gewünschten auswählen muß.


## 3. Experimentbeschreibung in SIMPLEX II

Es wird unterschieden zwischen der Modellbeschreibung mittels der Allgemeinen Modellbeschreibungssprache **SIMPLEX-MDL** (**SIMPLEX**-**M**odel Description **L**anguage; siehe /2/) zur
Definition des Simulationsmodells mit seinen Komponenten sowie seiner Struktur, und
der Experimentbeschreibung über die Experimentbeschreibungssprache **SIMPLEX-EDL**
(**SIMPLEX**-**E**xperiment Description **L**anguage), die es gestattet, den Ablauf eines Experiments zu einem vorhandenen Modell festzulegen.

SIMPLEX-EDL enthält Sprachkonstrukte sowohl zur Durchführung eines Einzelexperiments
als auch zur Abwicklung von Experimentreihen. Letzteres wird durch die Bereitstellung
von Verfahren und Kommandoprozeduren zur
 —— Parametervariation,
 —— Parameterschätzung sowie zur
 —— Parameteroptimierung bezüglich einer Zielfunktion
erreicht.

Ein Einzelexperiment überführt den Anfangszustand eines Modells in einem Simulations-
lauf in einen Endzustand. Dem Anwender stehen hierfür folgende Hilfsmittel zur Ver-
fügung:
 —— Problembezogene Modellbezeichner aus SIMPLEX-MDL
 —— Wahl eines beliebigen Anfangszustands
 —— Sichern eines Modellzustands auf Datei
 —— Verwendung externer Quellen und Funktionstabellen
 —— Selektive Protokollsteuerung
 —— Mehrere Integrationsverfahren und Zufallszahlengeneratoren
 —— Diverse Abbruchkriterien (Endezeit, maximale Transaktonszahl usw.)
 —— Unterbrechung des Simulationslaufes durch Hardwareinterrupt

## 4. Einsetzbarkeit von SIMPLEX II

Das hier vorgestellte Konzept eines interaktiven Simulatonssystems soll den Benutzer
in allen Phasen einer Simulationsstudie unterstützen:
— bei der System- und Problembeschreibung
— beim Modellaufbau
— beim Modelltest
— bei der Modellvalidierung
— bei der Experimentabwicklung
— bei der Auswertung der Ergebnisse
— bei der Darstellung der Ergebnisse
— bei der Dokumentation der Simulationsstudie

Es wird das Ziel angestrebt, daß nicht nur ganze Modelle, sondern bereits Modellkomponenten portabel sind. Durch den Zwang zu einer genauen Schnittstellendefinition in
der Modellbeschreibungsphase können erprobte Komponenten jederzeit in einem anderen
Gesamtmodell wiederverwendet werden. Ein wohlgeordnetes Datei- und Dokumentations-
system erlaubt die Zusammenarbeit mehrerer Wissenschaftler unterschiedlicher Fach-
richtungen am gleichen Projekt.

## Literatur

/1/ Bernd Schmidt: Der Simulator GPSS-FORTRAN Version 3
    Springer Berlin 1984

/2/ Peter Eschenbacher: Entwurf einer Allgemeinen Modellbeschreibungssprache
    erschienen im gleichen Band

/3/ Sabine Nagel: Transactionsorientierte Modelle mit beschränkten Warteräumen
                in GPSS-FORTRAN
    erschienen im gleichen Band

# Transactionsorientierte Modelle mit beschränkten Warteräumen in GPSS-FORTRAN


Sabine Nagel, Erlangen



Zusammenfassung: Viele reale Systeme, z.B. aus dem fertigungstechnischen Bereich,
verfügen nur über endliche Stau- und Warteräume, deren optimale Dimensionierung oft
mit Hilfe der Simulation ermittelt werden soll. Deshalb wurde die Klasse der transactionsorientierten Modelle, die mit GPSS-Fortran Version 3 bearbeitet werden kann,
so erweitert, daß auch Modelle mit beschränkten Warteräumen unterstützt werden.
Derartige Modelle benötigen eine besondere Steuerung, die die Transactionen gemäß den
Angaben aus einer Laufliste von Station zu Station befördert.



Summary: Many real systems, for example, those in the area of production engineering,
are only provided with limited back-up spaces and queue sizes, whose optimal dimen-
sioning should often be determined with the assistance of simulation. For this rea-
son, the class of transaction-oriented models, which can be handeld with GPSS-Fortran
Version 3, has been expanded to support models with limited queue sizes.
Such a model requires a special flow control, which transfers the transactions from
station to station according to a station sequence list.


## 1 Einleitung

Viele Fragestellungen aus dem betrieblich-technischen Bereich befassen sich mit
Varianten des Kapazitätsproblems, also mit der optimalen Ausnutzung endlicher Betriebsmittel. Gerade bei Anwendungen in der Fertigungstechnik, etwa bei der Planung
einer pufferarmen Produktionsanlage, ist die Simulation als Prognose- und Analyse-
hilfsmittel von großer Bedeutung. Mit der Hilfe von Digitalrechnern ist sie heute ein
leistungsfähiges Instrument zur Lösung der verschiedensten Managementaufgaben.

Zur Simulation auf Digitalrechnern stehen einige Sprachen und Programmsysteme zur
Verfügung, die bereits eine Reihe vorgefertigter Elemente und und Funktionen enthalten, die de Erstellung derartiger Modelle sehr erleichtern. Eine solche Sprache ist
GPSS-FORTRAN Version 3 (siehe /1/). Es handelt sich dabei um ein Programmpaket, das
sich für diskrete, kontinuierliche und kombinierte Modelle eignet. Besonders unterstützt wird die Behandlung von Warteschlangensystemen; bei der Behandlung beschränkter Warteräume erfährt der Benutzer allerdings bisher keine besondere Unterstützung.

Deshalb wurde die Klasse der transactionsorientierten Modelle, die mit GPSS-FORTRAN
behandelt werden kann, dahingehend erweitert, daß auch Modelle mit beschränkten

Warteräumen bearbeitet werden können. Die Grundzüge dieser erweiterten Modellklasse werden im folgenden dargestellt.


## 2 Transactionsorientierte Modelle mit beschränkten Warteräumen

Grundbausteine transactionsorienterter Modelle sind Stationen und Transactionen.

**Transactionen** sind mobile Merkmalsträger, die in einer besonderen Komponente (Quelle) erzeugt und von dort zur nächsten Station weitergegeben werden. Dabei können die Merkmale der Transaction in den Komponenten verändert werden. Die Reihenfolge der zu durchlaufenden Stationen wird durch die **Laufliste** festgelegt.

**Stationen** können Transactionen aufnehmen und diese bearbeiten, also deren Merkmale verändern. Vor den Stationen können sich Warteschlangen aus Transactionen aufbauen, deren Bedienwunsch bisher noch nicht erfüllt werden konnte. Die maximale Länge dieser Warteschlangen kann der Benutzer festlegen.
Je nach Art der Modifikation der Transactionsparameter unterscheidet man verschiedene Stationstypen (z.B. Facility, Pool, Storage usw.).

Die Übergabe der Transaction von einer Station zur nächsten erfolgt durch die **Transactionensteuerung.** Eine derartige Steuerung wird bei Modellen mit beschränkten Warteräumen notwendig, da nicht mehr sichergestellt ist, daß eine Transaction in der Nachfolgestation noch Platz findet. Vor Verlassen der gerade belegten Station muß eine übergeordnete Instanz prüfen, ob die Transaction ihre Station verlassen und die nächste Station belegen darf, oder ob sie an ihrem gegenwärtigen Aufenthaltsort warten muß.
Die Transactionensteuerung sieht von den Stationen nur die Ein- und Ausgänge. Den Weg der Transaction von Station zu Station entnimmt sie der Laufliste.


## 2.1 Die Bedienstation

Eine Station hält mindestens einen Platz reserviert, auf dem sich Transactionen aufhalten können. In der Mehrzahl der Fälle wird es eine Obergrenze für die Anzahl der Plätze geben. Es wird unterschieden zwischen reinen Warteplätzen und Bearbeitungsplätzen (= Bedieneinheiten).
Zudem verfügt jede Station über mindestens einen Eingang und mindestens einen Ausgang, über deren Öffnen und Schließen sie selbst entscheidet. Eine Transaction betritt eine Station durch einen Eingang und reiht sich in die Eingangs- oder Bedienwarteschlange ein, bis sie in der Bedieneinheit der Station bearbeitet werden kann. Sie gibt die Bedieneinheit nach Beendigung der Bearbeitung wieder frei und reiht sich

in die Ausgangs- oder Transportwarteschlange ein. Sobald die Nachfolgestation beleg-
bar ist, schleust sich die Transaction aus der Transportwarteschlange aus und verläßt
die Station durch einen Ausgang. Beide Warteschlangen können auch entfallen; sie sind
kein notwendiger Bestandteil einer Station (vgl. /2/).

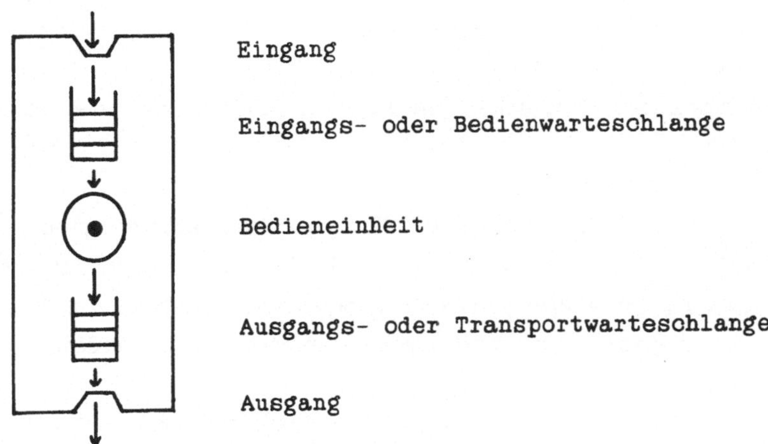


Abb. 1: Allgemeiner Stationstyp

Der Eingang einer Station wird verschlossen, wenn
- die Aufnahmekapazität der Station erschöpft ist,
- die Station defekt ist,
- die Station stillgelegt werden soll.
Wird ein bisher verschlossener Eingang wieder geöffnet, so wird dies der Steuerung
gemeldet, die dann eine neue Transaction zu dieser Station schickt.

Ein Ausgang wird geöffnet, wenn
- eine Transaction fertig bearbeitet wurde,
- die Station geräumt werden muß.
Der Ausgang bleibt verschlossen, wenn die fertig bearbeitete Transaction die gewünschte Nachfolgestation nicht betreten darf. Diese Transaction blockiert dann die
gerade belegte Bedieneinheit der Station solange, bis sie weiterlaufen darf.


## 2.2 Festlegung des Weges von Station zu Station : Die Laufliste

Die Laufliste enthält eine Sequenz von Stationen und Steueranweisungen. Sie ist
blockorientiert aufgebaut und wird interpretativ von der Transactionensteuerung abgearbeitet.
Für die Beschreibung der Laufliste stehen mehrere Sprachkonstrukte zur Verfügung:
1) Strenge Sequenz
    Die Reihenfolge der Stationen ist fest vorgegeben.

2) Kommutative Sequenz

Die Steuerung wählt nach einem angebbaren Kriterium die Bearbeitungsreihenfolge
von n Stationen.

3) Alternative Sequenz

Die Transactionensteuerung wählt anhand einer vom Benutzer angebbaren Strategie
eine von n alternativen Stationen aus.

4) Verzweigung

Entsprechend dem Wert einer vom Benutzer beliebig definierten Bedingung wird
verzweigt.

5) Verzweigungsnetzwerk

Zwischen einem Start- und einem Endknoten können weitere Knoten definiert werden,
an denen nach einer angebbaren Bedingung zum nächsten Knoten verzweigt werden
kann. Die Kanten dieses Netzwerkes repräsentieren beliebige Stationsfolgen, die
beim Übergang von einem Knoten zum anderen abgearbeitet werden.

6) Schleifen

In der Laufliste können beleibige Schleifenformen (Endlosschleife, Zählschleife,
repeat-until-Schleife und Kombinationen dieser Typen) vereinbart werden.

7) Subsequenz

Es kann eine Stationenfolge als Untersequenz vereinbart werden. Nach Durchlaufen
dieser Untersequenz wird die Bearbeitung mit dem nachfolgenden Element der ursprünglichen Laufliste fortgesetzt.

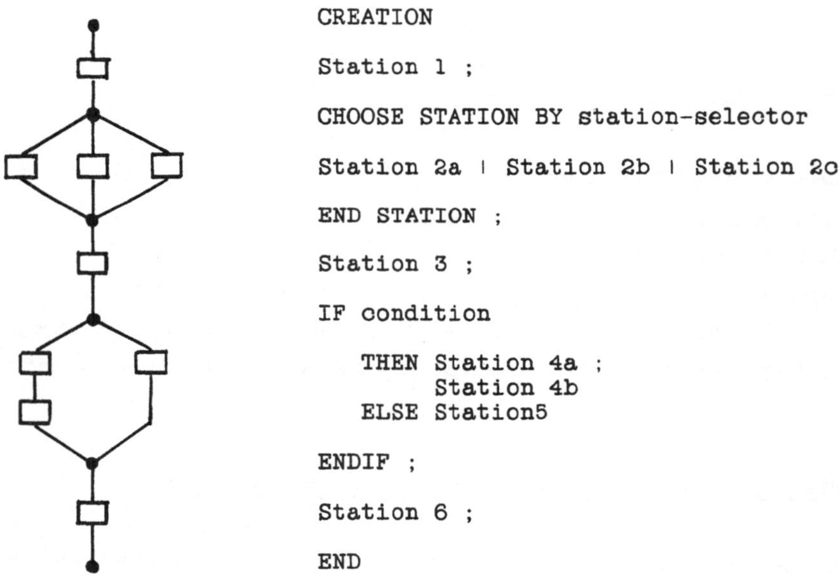


Abb. 2: Beispiel eines Transactionsflußgraphen

Die oben aufgeführten Sprachkonstrukte, die die Laufliste beschreiben, können auch
zur Definition eines gerichteten Graphen, der der Laufliste äquivalent ist, dienen.
Einen derartigen Graphen bezeichnen wir als **Transactionsflußgraphen.**

An einem solchen Graphen läßt sich leicht erkennen, daß das blockorientierte Sprach-
konzept in allen Einzelkonstrukten eingehalten wurde. Sämtliche (Teil-) Graphen
müssen nämlich genau einen Anfangs- und genau einen Endknoten besitzen. Nur bei
Einhaltung dieser Bedingung läßt sich jeder Teilgraph durch eine Kante in einem
übergeordneten Graphen ersetzen, und die Blockstruktur der Laufliste bleibt erhalten.


## 2.3 Die Transactionensteuerung


Die Transactionensteuerung hat die Aufgabe, die Transactionen gemäß den Angaben aus
der Laufliste von einer Station zur nächsten zu befördern. Sie sieht nur die Eingänge
und Ausgänge der Stationen und erkennt, ob diese offen oder geschlossen sind.

Die Transactionensteuerung wird aufgerufen,
- sobald eine Transaction in einer Station fertig bearbeitet wurde,
- wenn ein bisher verschlossener Eingang wieder geöffnet wird.


Im ersten Fall ermittelt die Steuerung aus der aktuellen Laufliste, anhand derer die
Transaction gerade bearbeitet wird, die nächste zu besuchende Station.
Ist diese Station noch aufnahmebereit, d.h. ist ihr Eingang offen, so kann die
Transaction die bisher belegte Station verlassen. Die Transactionensteuerung veran-
laßt diese Station, ihren Ausgang zu öffnen und übergibt dann die Transaction an die
Nachfolgestation.
Wollen mehrere Transactionen gleichzeitig dieselbe Station belegen, so wählt die
Transactionensteuerung nach einer angebbaren Strategie (z.B. nach Priorität) eine von
ihnen aus.


Ist jedoch die Aufnahmekapazität der nächsten zu belegenden Station erschöpft bzw.
ihr Eingang aus sonstigen Gründen verschlossen, so wird die Transaction von der
Transactionensteuerung in der Station, in der sie sich gerade befindet, solange
zurückgehalten, bis die Nachfolgestation wieder aufnahmefähig ist und ihren Eingang
öffnet.
Durch dieses Zurückhalten kann ein Rückstau entstehen, der sich noch weiter fort-
pflanzen kann.


Wurde der Eingang einer Station wieder geöffnet, überprüft die Steuerung, ob in den
Vorgängerstationen dieser Komponente Transactionen warten, die die Komponente betreten wollen und durch den verschlossenen Eingang bisher daran gehindert wurden. Ist
dies der Fall, wird unter den wartenden Transactionen diejenige ausgewählt, die die
freigewordene Station als erste belegen darf. Diese Auswahl wird nach lokalen oder
globalen Gesichtspunkten vorgenommen, denkbar sind Rotationsverfahren oder Priori-
tätsregelungen (z.B. nach längster Wartezeit, Dringlichkeit des Auftrages).

## 3 Realisierung der neuen Modellvorstellungen

Gemäß den geschilderten Modellvorstellungen wurde auf GPSS-Fortran - Basis ein Laufzeitsystem entwickelt, das auch dem unerfahrenen Benutzer die Simulation von Systemen mit beschränkten Warteräumen leicht macht. Die Erstellung eines solchen Modells besteht dann nur noch aus der geeigneten Besetzung der Datenbereiche für die im Modell verwendeten Stationen, sowie der Festlegung der Laufliste(n) für die Transactionen. Alle zur Behandlung beschränkter Warteräume notwendigen Maßnahmen, wie Weiterleiten der Transactionen von Komponente zu Komponente, Zurückhalten in einer Komponente, werden vom Laufzeitsystem übernommen.
Derzeit sind alle wichtigen Mechanismen bereits implementiert, auch die meisten Stationstypen aus GPSS-Fortran Version 3 können mit beschränkten Warteräumen versehen werden.

Dieses Laufzeitsystem wird den Unterbau der **Allgemeinen Modellbeschreibungssprache SIMPLEX-MDL**, die im Rahmen des Projektes SIMPLEX II entsteht, bilden. Mit Hilfe dieser Modellbeschreibungssprache wird der Anwender in der Lage sein, seine Modelle auf höherer Ebene mit problemangemessenen Sprachelementen zu beschreiben. Näheres hierzu siehe /2/ und /3/.

## Literatur

/1/ Bernd Schmidt:   Der Simulator GPSS-FORTRAN Version 3
         Springer Berlin 1984

/2/ Peter Eschenbacher: Entwurf einer Allgemeinen Modellbeschreibungssprache
         erschienen im gleichen Band

/3/ Klaus-Jürgen Langer: Das Simulationssystem Simplex II
         erschienen im gleichen Band

# Die Bedienstation in SPIRO

Robert K. Bell, Uttenreuth

Zusammenfassung. Es wird die Implementation von Bedienstationen in SPIRO beschrieben und mit einfachen Beispielen erläutert. Der Text enthält: Berechnung der Bedienzeit, Schließen und Öffnen, Einschalten und Ausschalten, MTBF, MTTR, Vorgänger und Nachfolger, Priorität, Verdrängung, Einzel-, Skalar-, Vektor- und lineare Bedienstationen.

Summary. The implementation of servers in SPIRO is described and explained with simple examples. It contains: calculation of the service time, closing and opening, switching on and switching off, MTBF, MTTR, predecessors and successors, priority, displacement, single, scalar, vector , and linear servers.

Bei SPIRO (Simulation Programs Including Realtime Operations) handelt es sich um eine Reihe von Programmen, die für verschiedene Arten programmierter Simulation entwickelt wurden. In der vorliegenden Arbeit wird das Konzept der Bedienstation in SPIRO erklärt.

In einem warteschlangenorientierten Modell bewegen sich Marken (englisch: tokens in SPIRO, transactions in GPSS und GPSS-F) durch einen gerichteten Graph von Knoten zu Knoten. Diese Knoten können Warteschlangen, Verzweigungen, Verzögerungen, Sperren usw. sein. Eine der wichtigsten Arten solcher Knoten ist die Bedienstation (englisch: server). Als Beispiel für ein solches Modell betrachten wir einen Supermarkt. Die Kunden werden durch Marken, die Kassen und die verschiedenen Schalter für Käse, Fleisch usw. werden durch Bedienstationen dargestellt. Eine oder mehrere Marken belegen eine Bedienstation für eine bestimmte Zeit, zum Beispiel wenn ein Kunde an einer Kasse bedient wird. Wichtig ist, daß die Verweilzeit beim Betreten der Bedienstation bekannt oder berechenbar ist.

Diese Bedienzeit ist entweder:
1) eine Konstante
2) eine Zufallszahl mit einer gegebenen Verteilung, z.B. einer Gleichverteilung.
3) eine vom Benutzer gelieferte Funktion
4) eine Eigenschaft der Marken

```
z.B.  name = Kasse;
      type = single server;
      service time = random (distribution = uniform;
                                    minimum = 5;
                                    maximum = 10):
```

Eine Kasse ist eine Einzelbedienstation, weil sie nur von einem Kunden
jeweils besetzt ist. Ein Parkhaus wäre ein Beispiel für eine Skalarbedienstation (englisch: scalar server), falls alle Parkplätze als
gleichwertig betrachtet werden, und falls die Verweilzeit beim Einstel-
len eines Autos bekannt oder berechenbar ist.

```
z.B.  name = Parkhaus;
      type = scalar server;
      capacity = 30;
      service time = 1.5:
```

Ein Hotel mit einer feststehenden Anzahl von Zimmern, die unterschiedliche Preise, Geräuschpegel, Ausblicke und Ausstattung haben, ist ein
Beispiel für eine Vektorbedienstation (englisch: vector server). Hier
können im Gegensatz zur Skalarbedienstation die Komponenten individuell
angesprochen werden. Eine lineare Bedienstation unterscheidet sich von
einer Vektorbedienstation darin, daß Speicherplätze für die einzelnen
Komponenten nicht reserviert werden. Ein Beispiel für eine lineare
Bedienstation wäre der Hauptspeicher eines Rechners, der eine bestimmte Anzahl von Aufträgen gleichzeitig enthalten kann. Jeder Auftrag
belegt einen zusammenhängenden Speicherbereich.

Eine Bedienstation ist entweder geschlossen oder geöffnet (englisch:
locked oder unlocked). Solange sie geschlossen ist, kann keine neue
Marke die Bedienstation betreten. Will eine Kassiererin unterbrechen
oder aufhören, so gibt sie bekannt, daß sie keine weiteren Kunden
bedienen wird, z.B.  lock (Kasse)

Eine Bedienstation ist entweder ein- oder ausgeschaltet (englisch:
on oder off). Ist sie ausgeschaltet, wird keine neue Marke hereinge-
lassen und eine sich eventuell in der Station befindende Marke wird
nicht bedient, d.h. die Zeit, die eine Marke in einer ausgeschalteten
Station verbringt, zählt nicht zur Bedienzeit.
Zu den geplanten Abschaltungen kommen zusätzliche Ausfälle, die durch
Ausfälle des Gerätes verursacht werden oder andere Ursachen haben.
Gründe, die zum Ausfallen einer Kasse führen können, wären in England
ein Streik, in den USA ein Raubüberfall, in Rumänien ein Stromausfall,
in der Bundesrepublik eine Personalversammlung oder ein selbst zum

Einkauf gegangener Kassierer in der UDSSR.

Die Zeit zwischen aufeinanderfolgenden Ausfällen (englisch: meantime between failures, MTBF) ist entweder konstant, eine Zufallszahl mit einer vorgegebenen Verteilung oder eine vom Benutzer geschriebene Funktion. Zur Zwischenzeit zwischen Ausfällen zählt nur die Zeit, die die Station auch eingeschaltet ist,

```
z.B. name = Roboter 1;
     type = single server;
     service time = 5;
     mtbf = random (distribution = exponential;
                    maximum = 7);
     mttr = random (distribution = normal;
                    mean = 5;
                    maximum = 15;
                    standard deviation = 2):
```

Die Zeit zwischen den Ausfällen und der Wiederaufnahme der Bedienung (englisch: meantime to repair, MTTR) ist auch konstant, eine Zufallszahl nach vorgegebener Verteilung oder eine vom Benutzer geschriebene Funktion.

Eine Bedienstation besitzt einen oder mehrere Vorgänger (englisch: predecessor). Ist eine Bedienstation teilweise oder ganz frei, so müssen deren Vorgänger überprüft werden, ob eine Marke von den Vorgängern in die Bedienstation eintreten kann. Die Vorgänger sind selber Knoten verschiedener Art. Wir unterscheiden zwischen direkten Vorgängern, die unmittelbar mit der Bedienstation gekoppelt sind, und indirekten Vorgängern. Der komplexe aber sehr nützliche Begriff des indirekten Vorgängers wird an einem Beispiel erläutert:

| Roboter 1 | ---> | Tür 1 | ---> | Roboter 2 |

```
name = Roboter 1;
type = single server;
service time = 5;
successor = Tür 1:

name = Tür 1;
type = barrier;
successor = Roboter 2:

name = Roboter 2;
type = single server;
service time = 10:
```

Roboter 1 und Roboter 2 sind Bedienstationen. Tür 1 ist eine Sperre (englisch: barrier), die entweder geöffnet oder gesperrt ist. Es verläßt eine Marke den Roboter 2. Der direkte Vorgänger ist Tür 1. Falls Tür 1 geschlossen ist, so tritt keine neue Marke in Roboter 2 ein.

Ansonsten muß Roboter 1 untersucht werden. Hat Roboter 1 eine Marke, deren Bedienzeit abgelaufen ist, so kann diese Marke Roboter 1 verlassen und nach dem Passieren der Tür 1 in Roboter 2 eintreten. Man bezeichnet Roboter 1 als indirekten und die Tür 1 als direkten Vorgänger des Roboters 2.

Ein Knoten kann mehrere Vorgänger haben:
z.B.

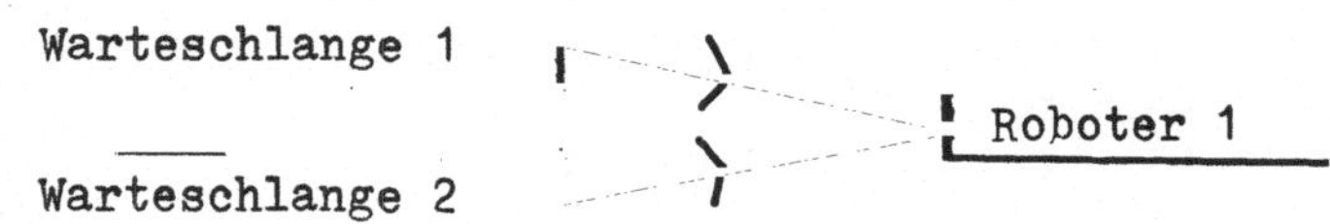


```
name = Warteschlange 1, Warteschlange 2;
type = queue:

name = Roboter 1;
type = single server;
service time = 10:
predecessor = Warteschlange 1, Warteschlange 2:
```

Die Gesamtheit aller Vorgänger bildet einen zyklusfreien, gerichteten Graph. Der Graph muß durchsucht werden bis entweder eine Marke gefunden wird, die eine höhere Priorität als alle anderen in Frage kommenden Marken besitzt, oder bis der ganze Graph durchsucht worden ist.

In den folgenden Fällen ist es nicht notwendig, die Vorgänger eines Knoten, der selbst ein Vorgänger ist, zu untersuchen:
1) Der Knoten ist eine Warteschlange
2) Der Knoten ist eine Bedienstation, die keine Marke enthält, deren Bedienzeit abgelaufen ist.
3) Der Knoten ist eine geschlossene Sperre

Der Graph der Vorgänger, die untersucht werden müssen, ist durch solche Knoten abgegrenzt oder durch Knoten, die selber keine Vorgänger haben.
Es ist möglich, daß mehrere Marken im Vorgängergraph der Bedienstation sind, die in der Lage sind, die Bedienstation zu betreten. Für solche Fälle muß ein Auswahlkriterium (englisch: policy) definiert werden, das entscheidet, welche Marken die Bedienstation betreten: Es gibt zwei einfache Möglichkeiten

1) Die Priorität wird durch die Lage der Knoten innerhalb des Graphen festgelegt. Bei Warteschlangen wird immer die Marke gewählt, die am längsten in der Warteschlange stand.

2) Jede Marke besitzt eine Priorität. Die Marke mit der höchsten Priorität wird gewählt. Falls mehrere Marken die höchste Priorität

besitzen, so wird die Auswahl unter diesen wie bei 1) getroffen.

Ähnlich dem Vorgängergraph gibt es auch einen Nachfolgergraph. Sobald
die Bearbeitung einer Marke in einer Bedienstation abgeschlossen ist,
so darf sie die Bedienstation verlassen. Durch Untersuchung des Nachfolgergraphes wird der nächste Knoten ausgewählt, wo die Marke eintreten wird, oder es wird festgestellt, daß in keinem der Nachfolger
ein Platz zur Verfügung steht.
Ähnlich dem Vorgängergraph sind die Grenzen des Nachfolgergraphes
und der Auswahlkriterien bei mehreren möglichen Nachfolgerplätzen
definiert.
Wie schon erwähnt, können verschiedene Marken verschiedene Prioritäten haben, die bei der Wahl einer Marke in dem Vorgängergraph berücksichtigt werden. Es ist auch möglich, daß eine Marke mit höherer
Priorität eine Marke mit niedrigerer Priorität aus einer Bedienstation
verdrängt  (englisch: displaces in SPIRO and preempts in GPSS-F).
Verdrängung findet nur statt, falls die Priorität der wartenden Marke
die Priorität der Marke, die in der Bedienstation bearbeitet wird,
um einen bestimmten Wert übertrifft. Man nennt diesen Wert Auslösungswert (englisch: threshold). Der Auslösungswert muß vom Benutzer als
Konstante oder als Funktion definiert werden. Ebenso muß der Benutzer
die Zeit angeben, die benötigt wird, eine Marke zu verdrängen und die
neue Marke einzuladen.

```
z.B. name = queue 1;
     type = queue:
     •
     •
     •
     name = server 1;
     type = single server;
     displacement;
     service time = 5;
     set up time = 1;
     close down time = 1;
     threshold = 2;
     node for displaced tokens = queue 1:
```

Eine etwas komplizierte Bedienstation ist die Mehrfachbedienstation
(englisch: multiple server).Diese enthält verschiedene Abteilungen
(englisch: compartments). Eine Abteilung enthält eine Marke oder ist
leer. Zum Beispiel enthält ein Friseurladen mehrere Frisierplätze.
Ein solcher Platz ist eine Mehrfachbedienstation mit zwei Plätzen,
einem für den Friseur und einem für den Kunden. Die Verhaltensweise
der Bedienstation stellt die Zusammenarbeit der verschiedenen Abteilungen dar. Die Mehrfachbedienstation befindet sich in einer von meh-

reren Phasen, in unserem Beispiel Waschen, Schneiden, Trocknen
usw. Während der Phase Trocknen kann die Abteilung Friseur unbesetzt
bleiben. Jede Abteilung hat eigene Vorgängergraphen, Nachfolger-
graphen, Bedienzeiten usw.

```
z.B. name = Frisierplatz;
     type = multiple server;
     compartments = Kunde, Friseur;
     phases = Waschen (service time = 10),
              Schneiden (service time = 20),
              Trocknen (service time = 15, not needed = Friseur):
```

Diese Implementierung der Bedienstation wird umfangreicher und
komplexer sein als die frühere Implementierung in SPIRO und anderer
Simulationssoftware wie GPSS-F, SLAM und SIMAN. Für den Benutzer
hat das den Vorteil, daß er im allgemeinen weniger zu programmieren
hat, um ein Modell mit Bedienstationen darzustellen. SPIRO kann
auch als Modellbeschreibungssprache benutzt werden, ohne daß
Simulationssoftware vorhanden ist.


## Weitere Veröffentlichungen über SPIRO

1) SPIRO - A New Simulation Package, Robert K. Bell
         and Pervez-Walter Ernest, Proceedings of
         the Summer Computer Simulation Conference
         1982, Denver, USA.
         Society for Computer Simulation, P.O.Box 2228,
         La Jolla, California 92038, USA.

2) SPIRO - ein neues Simulationspaket, Robert K. Bell
         und Pervez-Walter Ernest, ASIM 1982 Erlangen.
         In: Informatik Fachberichte 56, Simulations-
         technik, Springer Verlag, Berlin, Heidelberg,
         New York 1982.

3) Station Types in GPSS, GPSS-F, SLAM and SPIRO,
         Robert K. Bell and Pervez-Walter Ernest,
         First European Simulation Conference, Aachen 1983.
         In: Informatik Fachberichte 71, Springer Verlag
         Berlin, Heidelberg, New York, Tokyo 1983.

4) The Four Levels of Flow Control in SPIRO,
           Robert K. Bell und Pervez-Walter Ernest,
           First European Simulation Conference,
           Aachen 1983. In: Informatik Fachberichte 71,
           Springer Verlag Berlin, Heidelberg, New York,
           Tokyo 1983.

5) The User-Interface in SPIRO, Robert K. Bell,
           Pervez-Walter Ernest, Ejob Tecle-ab,
           UKSC Conference on Computer Simulation 1984,
           Bath, England.
           Butterworths, London.

6) Simulation, Steuerung und Zuteilung der Betriebsmittel
   mit SPIRO: Robert K. Bell, Pervez-Walter Ernest,
           Ejob-Tecle-ab, 2. Symposium Simulationstechnik,
           Wien 1984. In: Informatik Fachberichte 85,
           Springer Verlag, Berlin, Heidelberg, New York,
           Tokyo 1984.

7) The Use of Directed Graphs in the Implementation of SPIRO.
           Robert K. Bell, Rainer Rimane, Peter Wilkinson.
           11th IMACS World Congress 1985,
           Oslo, Norwegen, August 1985

MAPLIS - Matrixorientierte Simulation als Fortsetzung der
Statistik in den Sozialwissenschaften


Wilfried Tettweiler
Brahmsstr. 12
8033 Krailling


Die Anwendung der Simulationstechnik ist in den Sozialwissenschaften noch nicht sehr weit verbreitet, vornehmlich deshalb,
weil Struktur und Objekte der gebräuchlichen Simulationssprachen
nicht hinreichend komplementär zu Struktur und Objekten der in
den Sozialwissenschaften verbreiteten Statistiksprachen sind.

Dieser Vortrag beschreibt zunächst allgemein die Entsprechungen
zwischen den Objekten von Simulationssprachen zu den durch statistische Methoden gewonnenen Inhalten dieser Objekte. Dadurch
wird die Stellung von MAPLIS als eine weitere Methode festgelegt, die ebenfalls lediglich aufgrund modellhafter Algorithmen
Inhalte von Objekten verändert oder erzeugt.

Sodann werden beispielhaft Verwandtschaften zwischen MAPLIS und
SPSS sowie MAPLIS und P-STAT aufgezeigt, um zu zeigen, daß die
Gewöhnung an die Sprachelemente dieser Statistiksprachen beim
Verständnis der MAPLIS-Sprache behilflich sein können.

# ECHTZEITSIMULATION

# Software Konzept für Echtzeit-Simulation


Reinhard Kodweiß, Friedrichshafen



Zusammenfassung. Am Simulationslabor bei Dornier werden zwei Cockpits jeweils mit einer Reihe von Untersystemen und eine Steuerkonsole eingesetzt. Für die Simulation werden mehrere Modelle ständig betriebsbereit gehalten, während Software und Hardware laufend an neue Aufgaben angepaßt oder erweitert werden müssen. Das Software Konzept für Entwicklung und Betrieb der Simulatoren wird beschrieben.

Summary. At the simulation laboratory of Dornier we operate two cockpits each with several sub systems and a console. For simulation several models are maintained with software and hardware to be fitted or extended with new problems all the time. The software concept for development and use of the simulators is des ribed.


## 1.Einführung

Die Firma Dornier betreibt in ihremSimulationslabor zwei Flugzeug-Cockpits mit den dazu gehörenden Untersystemen und verschiedenen mathematischen Modellen für Flugzeuge. Da sowohl die Modelle als auch die Hardware ständig an neue Aufgaben angepaßt und erweitert werden, ergeben sich für die Programmierung der Simulation besondere Anforderungen:

- Die Modell-Software muß weitgehend unabhängig  von der Ansteuerung der Hardware sein.
- Die Wartung der Software muß möglichst so geschehen, daß alle Programme immer ohne besonderen Aufwand auf demselben Stand sind.
- Es müssen umfangreiche Testhilfen für Hardware und Software vorhanden sein.

## Aufbau der Simulation

Die Ausrüstung der Simulation mit Hardware wird in Bild 1 schematisch dargestellt.
Die vorhandenen Rechner sind jeweils mit einem geeigneten,oft der speziellen Aufgabe angepaßten echtzeitfähigen Betriebssystem ausgerüstet. Darüberhinaus sind auf dem Simulationsrechner eine Reihe echtzeitgeeigneter Programmierwerkzeuge schon vom Hersteller bereitgestellt.
Die bei Dornier entwickelte und eingesetzte Software umfaßt
- Entwicklungsprogramme  (Crossassembler für Microprozessoren)
- Testhilfen
- Betriebsprogramme  (Datentransfer, Simulatorsteuerung) sowie die spezielle Modellsoftware für Flugzeuge und alle Untersysteme.

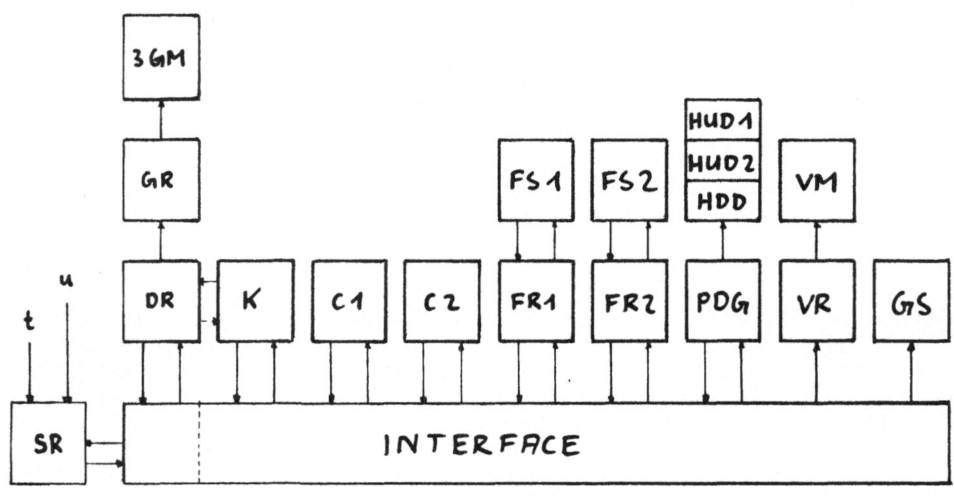


Bild 1          Simulations-Hardware

SR       Simulationsrechner

DR       Datenrechner

GR, 3GM Graphikrechner mit 3 Monitoren

K        Steuerkonsole

C1, C2  Cockpit 1 und 2

FR1, FS1, FR2, FS2  Steuerkraftrechner 1 und 2 mit Steuerkraftsimulation

PDG, HUD1, HUD2, HDD  Programmierbarer Display-Generator mit Head Up / Head
                      Down Display

VR, VM  Sichtrechner mit Monitoren und opt. System

GS       Geräuschsimulation

t        Zeitsteuerung

u        Steuerung durch den Operator

Die Programmstruktur der Untersysteme soll hier nicht beschrieben werden. Sie sind
über fest definierte Datenfelder an das Interface zwischen Simulator und Rechner an-
gebunden. Ihre Prozessoren werden vom Datenrechner oder vom Simulationsrechner aus
geladen. Die Programmentwicklung für die Untersysteme erfolgt auf dem Simulationsrechner.
Die Unabhängigkeit der Simulationsmodelle von der Hardware wird durch den Datenrechner
gewährleistet, der die physikalischen Werte aus  dem Simulationsprogramm für die Hardware aufbereitet. So muß nur das Programm im Datenrechner an die Hardware angepaßt

werden. Der Datenrechner enthält auch alle Testhilfen zur Fehlersuche an der Hardware.

<u>Struktur der Software.</u>

Grundlegend an der Software im Simulationsrechner ist, daß ein Simulationsprogramm aus mehreren vollständigen Programmen (Tasks) besteht, die von außen vom Betreiber der Simulation oder intern vom Betriebssystem gesteuert werden. Es gibt Programme für die Steuerung, für den Datentransfer, zur Initialisierung und für das mathematische Modell selbst. So kann auch hier der Aufwand für Wartung gering gehalten werden.

Die Schnittstelle zwischen allen Programmen ist ein gemeinsamer für alle voll zugänglicher Speicherbereich. Dieser enthält die Blocks:
- Steuerung und Eingabe/Ausgabefelder
- allgemeine Modell- und Untersystemparameter
- spezielle Modellparameter, die vom Benutzer selbst definiert werden können.

Die Organisation dieses gemeinsamen Speichers läßt beliebig viele Programme zu, die darauf zugreifen. So ist eine Testhilfe möglich, die über Variablennamen arbeitet. Der Stand des Testsystems erlaubt zur Zeit folgende Zugriffsmöglichkeiten in Echtzeit:
- Ausgabe von Speicherinhalten in beliebigen Datenformaten.
- Änderung von Speicherinhalten (formatfreie Eingabe)
- Steuerung der Eingabe und Ausgabe (Dateinamen, Belegung des Kanalschreibers usw.)
- Steuerung des Simulators.

In Entwicklung befindet sich ein Generator für Steuereingaben, wie sie im Flugversuch und zur Beurteilung der Steuercharakteristik eines Flugzeuges verwendet werden.

Mit dem Simulationssystem können umfangreiche Modelle auch auf mehrere Zeitebenen verteilt werden, ohne daß der Benutzer sich um die Verwaltung und Steuerung der verschiedenen Ebenen kümmern muß. So werden Teile des Modells, die sich über der Zeit nur langsam ändern, mit einem Vielfachen des Grundtakts gerechnet.


<u>Anwendung</u>

Mit dem beschriebenen System werden zur Zeit eine Reihe von Aufgaben praktisch parallel durchgeführt.
- Simulation zur Weiterentwicklung des Alpha Jet
- Aufbau von Hilfsmittel für rechnerunterstützte Schulung,
- Studie zur Beurteilung von Bedienelementen (z.B. Side-Stick) mit dem Modell eines geregelten Kampfflugzeugs.
- Entwicklungssimulation für ein vollgeregeltes Flugzeug.

Der Simulationsrechner und die Steuerkonsole kann immer nur ein Cockpit betreiben. Die Struktur des Betriebssystems ermöglicht es jedoch, daß die freie Rechenkapazität für andere Aufgaben zur Verfügung steht. So können auch während einer Echtzeit-Simulation Programme entwickelt und getestet oder Auswertungen gerechnet werden.

COMPUTER ASSISTED PROCEDURE TRAINER (CAPT),
EIN NEUES AUSBILDUNGSMITTEL ZUR PILOTEN-
SCHULUNG

Dipl.-Ing. H.J. Munser
Dornier GmbH
Abt. BA6o - Simulation -
Postfach 142o

Innerhalb des DOCATS (Dornier Computer Assisted Training System)
ist der CAPT ein Ausbildungsmittel das den computerunterstützten
Unterricht praxisnäher fortführt und ergänzt sowie das Simulator-
training bzw. Flugtraining optimal vorbereitet.

Im einzelnen werden vorgestellt:

- Hardware Struktur

    - Computer
    - Darstellungsmedien
    - Ein/Ausgabe Systeme
    - Dialogsystem
    - Arbeitsplatz
    - Lehrerstation

- Software Struktur

    - Drehbuch / Schülersoftware / Lehrersoftware
    - Grafik / Bilderstellung / Bilddynamik
    - Funktionsmodelle, Untersysteme
    - CAPT-Management

Am Beispiel einer Musterlektion wird das computerunterstützte
Procedure Training in den Lern-, Übungs- und Testphasen erläutert
und evtl. in einem kurzen Videofilm demonstriert.

ANFORDERUNGEN AN DAS DATENPAKET ZUM DESIGN UND BETRIEB VON FLUGSIMULATOREN FÜR
AUSBILDUNG UND TRAINING VON COCKPITBESATZUNGEN


Georg Schütz, Frankfurt


Zusammenfassung. Zunehmende Verlagerung der Ausbildung von Verkehrsflugzeugführern
vom Flugzeug in den Simulator führt zu steigenden Anforderungen an den Realismus
der Simulation und damit an Umfang und Qualität des verwendeten Datenpaketes.
Die Bestandteile eines typischen Datenpaketes werden aufgeführt und behördliche
Forderungen angegeben. Es folgen Hinweise zur laufenden Aktualisierung der Daten
in der Betriebsphase.

Summary. The increasing transfer of airline pilot flight training from aircraft to
simulator leads to growing requirements with regard to simulation realism and sub-
sequently to extent and quality of the data package used.
The elements of a typical data package are listed, and requirements of goverment
authorities are stated. It is outlined how the data are kept up to date during the
operation.


Einführung - Warum ist die Qualität des Datenpaketes so wichtig?

Die Vorteile des Simulatortrainings gegenüber dem Flugtraining dürfen in Fachkreisen
wohl als bekannt vorausgesetzt werden und sollen an dieser Stelle nicht näher erläutert werden. In wenigen Stichworten seien die Vorteile nur nochmals kurz in Er-
innerung gerufen:

- Sicherheit
- Effektivität
- Trainingsqualität
- keine Umweltbelastung
- Wirtschaftlichkeit

Die logische Konsequenz dieser Situation ist das kontinuierliche Bemühen der Fluggesellschaften, Flugtraining abzubauen und zunehmend Ausbildung in den Simulator zu
verlagern. Bild 1 zeigt die Entwicklung des Anteils Flugtraining am Gesamttraining
bei der Deutschen Lufthansa für die Flugzeugmuster Boeing 737 und 747. Das Kurz-
streckenflugzeug B 737 dient als sog. "Eingangsmuster" für Nachwuchsflugzeugführer,
die noch relativ wenig Flugerfahrung, speziell auf Strahlflugzeugen, haben und daher
einen höheren Bedarf an praktischer Ausbildung im Flugzeug haben, als dies bei Piloten für das Langstreckenflugzeug B 747 der Fall ist. Mit der Flugzeuggröße steigt
auch der ökonomische Druck für eine Verlagerung, da die Flugstundenkosten sowohl in
Relation zu den Simulatorstundenkosten als auch absolut drastisch steigen.

Seit 1982 gibt es bei United Airlines überhaupt kein Flugtraining für die B 727 Besatzungen mehr; mit FAA Genehmigung werden Initial-Training (Grundausbildung), Transitionstraining (Erwerb der Musterberechtigung) und Recurrent-Training (Auffrischung von Kenntnissen und praktischen Fähigkeiten) zu 100% im Simulator durchgeführt.

Bei dieser Entwicklung übernehmen die Fluggesellschaften und die staatlichen Aufsichtsbehörden, die die erforderliche Genehmigung dazu erteilen, eine hohe Verantwortung. Sie müssen dafür einstehen, daß den Cockpitbesatzungen während ihrer Ausbildung keine wesentlichen Eindrücke und Erfahrungen vorenthalten werden, die beim Flugbetrieb in der Wirklichkeit gesammelt werden.

Dieser Verantwortung versucht man dadurch gerecht zu werden, daß man die Übertragbarkeit von Wirklichkeit und Simulation auf immer größere Höhen treibt. Man analysiert die Wirklichkeit zunehmend feiner und läßt immer mehr Details in die Simulation einfließen (z. B. Sprechfunkverkehr, Wetterradar, Niederschlagseffekte etc.), um die noch vorhandenen Unterschiede zur Wirklichkeit so weit wie möglich zu verwischen.

Der letzte und nicht eliminierbare Unterschied ist das Wissen, in einem Simulator zu sitzen und damit keiner realen Gefahr ausgesetzt zu sein.

Durch den ständig gesteigerten Aufwand zur Erzeugung eines höheren Realismus wird erreicht, daß die im Simulator erflogene Erfahrung derjenigen im Flugzeug immer gleichwertiger wird.

Das Ergebnis der Analyse der Wirklichkeit ist das Datenpaket. Die Quantität und Qualität des Datenpaketes in Verbindung mit einem optimalen Simulationsmodell bestimmen ganz direkt die Qualität der Simulation und speziell die Übertragbarkeit zur Wirklichkeit.

Üblicherweise gilt beim Thema Simulation das Augenmerk überwiegend der Modellierung und der technischen Realisierung; dem notwendigen Datenpaket wird wenig Beachtung geschenkt. Das Datenpaket ist aber Teil der Simulationskette, und die ist bekanntlich stets so stark wie ihr schwächstes Glied.

## 2. Herkunft und Elemente eines Datenpaketes

Es reicht heute nicht mehr aus, Daten und Informationen aus den verschiedensten
Quellen zu besorgen und diese Sammlung der Simulation zur Verfügung zu stellen. Vielmehr muß darüberhinaus erheblicher Aufwand getrieben werden, erforderliche Daten
überhaupt erst zu erzeugen. Als Beispiel sei die Durchführung von mehrstündigen Testflügen des Flugzeugs genannt, die ausschließlich der Aufzeichnung einer Vielzahl von
Parametern bei definierten Flugmanövern dienen, um den Simulatorherstellern praktikable Sollvorgaben an die Hand zu geben (im Fall A 310: 40 Flugstunden).

Hinzu kommt, daß im Simulator nicht nur das Normalverhalten des Flugzeugs und aller
seiner Systeme dargestellt werden soll, sondern zusätzlich einige hundert Fehler von
einer kleinen Systemstörung bis zu katastrophalen Schäden - und dies in jeder beliebigen Kombination. Modellierung und Datenpaket müssen so detailliert sein, daß
Schäden mit allen Folgewirkungen möglichst naturgetreu nachgebildet werden.

Lieferanten des Datenpaketes sind im wesentlichen der Flugzeughersteller und zum
kleineren Teil die Ausrüstungsindustrie. Es haben sich jedoch auch Firmen mit dem
ausschließlichen Tätigkeitsfeld "Erstellen von Datenpaketen" gebildet, z. B. Kohlmann Systems Research in USA.

Bestandteile eines Datenpaketes sind - ohne Anspruch auf Vollständigkeit:

- Ausrüstungslisten
  komplette Aufstellung aller festen und losen Teile im Cockpit des darzustellenden
  Flugzeugs (Teilnummern und Bezeichnung);

- Mechanische Zeichnungen
  kompletter Zeichnungssatz, der auch für die Konstruktion des Simulatorcockpits verwendet wird;

- Elektrische Prinzip-Diagramme
  Ein Satz von elektrischen Zeichnungen, die je ein System bzw. einen in sich geschlossenen Schaltkreis vollständig zeigen. Die Vorteile der Prinzip-Diagramme
  sind die große Übersichtlichkeit (kein umständliches Hin- und Herblättern wie im
  Schaltplanhandbuch) und die hohe Aktualität. Die Prinzip-Diagramme sind nämlich
  die Arbeitsunterlagen der Entwicklungsingenieure beim Flugzeughersteller und werden bis zur Flugzeugauslieferung auf dem neusten Stand gehalten. Erst mehrere Monate später und evtl. noch mit Fehlern behaftet, wird das Schaltplanhandbuch revidiert;

- Modifikationslisten
  Produktionsdokumente, die ein Flugzeug im Auslieferungszustand exakt definieren.
  Über die Flugzeugbasisdefinition hinaus bietet der Hersteller durchnumerierte Modifikationen an (für bereits ausgelieferte Flugzeuge als Service Bulletin), die
  abgegrenzte mechanische und/oder elektrische Änderungen eines Systems beinhalten.
  Eine Großzahl der Modifikationen werden standardmäßig inkorporiert, einige jedoch
  nur auf Wunsch einzelner Fluggesellschaften;

- Aerodynamik / Flugmechanik / Triebwerk-Datenbank
  Es handelt sich um die vollständige Aufstellung aller Koeffizienten und Derivativa,
  abhängig von Anstellwinkel, Machzahl, Staudruck, Klappenstellung, Flughöhe, Schub-
  hebelposition etc., um die Berechnung aller Kräfte und -momente durch Anströmung
  und Triebwerk zu ermöglichen und damit die resultierende Bewegung des simulierten
  Flugzeuges.

  Bei einem neuen Flugzeugtyp ist es schwierig, rechtzeitig diese erforderliche Datenbank zu erhalten. Daher müssen zur Konzeption des Simulators in solchen Fällen zunächst die errechneten Daten des Flugzeugherstellers über Flugleistung und Flugeigenschaften zugrundegelegt werden. Dieses mathematische Modell wird dann durch
  Resultate aus dem Windkanal verfeinert.
  Die maximale Realitätsnähe wird jedoch erst erreicht, wenn die bei der Flugerpro-
  bung ermittelten Werte in diese Datenbank integriert sind.

  Die großen Flugzeughersteller liefern die Datenbank seit einigen Jahren als Magnetband. Die Form des Computermediums erleichtert allen Nutzern (Performance Abteilung der Fluggesellschaften, Simulatorhersteller etc.) die rationelle Verarbeitung
  mit Digitalrechnern. Zur Größenvorstellung: Die Länge des "Datenfiles" für den
  A 310 ist größer als 230 KW bei 32 bit Wortlänge;

- Flugleistungs- und Flugeigenschaften - Zusatzinformationen
  Alle Zusatzinformationen, zusätzliche Berichte und Datensammlungen wie auch Antworten des Flugzeugherstellers auf Fragen zu diesem Thema werden als Technical Notes
  bezeichnet, die eine fortlaufende Numerierung erhalten und Bestandteil der offi-
  ziellen Dokumentation werden;

- Abnahmedokument für Flugsimulatoren
  Seitdem staatliche Behörden, speziell die FAA in den Vereinigten Staaten, konkret
  und detailliert vorschreiben, welche Flugmanöver für eine Simulator-Anerkennung zu
  absolvieren sind, liefern die Flugzeughersteller ein Dokument ausschließlich für
  Simulationserfordernisse, den "Acceptance Test Guide", ATG.

Alle geforderten Flugmanöver werden von einem speziell instrumentierten Flugzeug
durchgeführt, und alle relevanten Parameter werden in einem genormten Koordi-
natensystem aufgezeichnet (Bild 2). Ausgenommen sind Manöver mit unvertretbarem
Risiko, wie z. B. die Ermittlung der VMCG. Zusätzlich rechnet der Flugzeughersteller unter Verwendung der erwähnten Aerodatenbank das gleiche Manöver durch
und läßt den Computer die relevanten Parameter im gleichen Maßstab über der Zeitachse zeichnen. Damit hat er gleichzeitig eine Plausibilitätsprüfung seiner Aerodatenbank geleistet.

Mit Hilfe des ATG's können nun Fluggesellschaften und Behörden fundiert die Güte
der Flug- und Triebwerkssimulation gegenüber dem Simulatorhersteller überprüfen.
Die einzelnen Tests können bei gleichen Eingangsbedingungen im Simulator entweder
manuell oder automatisch nachgeflogen und - wieder im gleichen Maßstab - aufgezeichnet werden. Im automatischen Betrieb werden alle Eingangsbedingungen samt
Pilotenaktivität mit größtmöglicher Übereinstimmung zum Flugversuch vom Simulationsrechner vorgegeben ("ATG-Treiber"-Software). Hat man die Flugzeug-ATG Aufzeichnungen auf Klarsichtfolie kopiert, kann man sie direkt auf die Simulatorergebnisse
auflegen und damit die Größe der Abweichungen optimal beurteilen;

- Systembeschreibungen
Geordnet nach ATA-Kapiteln liegen für alle Flugzeugsysteme und Komponenten ausführliche Dokumente vor, die Aufbau, elektrische Verschaltung und Funktion beschreiben.
Oftmals reicht jedoch die Funktionsbeschreibung nicht vollständig für die Simula-
tionsbedürfnisse aus. In diesen Fällen müssen vertiefende Informationen vom jeweiligen Gerätehersteller zusätzlich beschafft werden;

- Flugsteuerungscharakteristik
Spezielle Unterlagen befassen sich mit der Kinematik aller Flugsteuerungselemente
und den Betätigungskräften, die sowohl statisch (Funktion des Steuerflächenaus-
schlags) als auch dynamisch (Zeitfunktion) angegeben werden.

- Flugzeugwartungs- und Betriebsdokumentation
Hierbei handelt es sich um die Standarddokumente, die bei Fluggesellschaften für
einen Flugzeugtyp geführt werden, von denen genannt seien:

Mikrofilme:
AMM (Wartungshandbuch), AWM (Schaltplanhandbuch), IPC (Teilekatalog),
ASM (Schematische Zeichnungen) etc.

Bücher:
FM (Flughandbuch), AOM (Betriebshandbuch), FCOM (Trainingshandbuch),
PEM (Flugleistungsdokument, auch als Magnetband) etc.

- Diverse Zusatzinformationen

  Alle über die genannten Daten hinausgehende Informationen.
  Hauptsächlich gehören hier Antworten der Flugzeug- und Gerätehersteller auf Anfragen des Simulatorentwicklers dazu sowie Beobachtungen und Aufzeichnungen von Cockpitbesatzungen, speziell des für den Simulator verantwortlichen Kapitäns.


## 3. Anforderungen der Zulassungsbehörden

Die amerikanische Federal Aviation Administration hat weltweit Maßstäbe gesetzt für die Methodik von Simulator-Anerkennungsverfahren. Anfang 1983 veröffentlichte die FAA das Advisory Circular AC 120-40 mit dem Titel "Airplane Simulator and Visual System Evaluation". Es enthält eine komplette Beschreibung des Prüfverfahrens und eine Aufstellung aller Tests. Dabei wird unterschieden in 4 Abstufungen von Realismus, wobei Phase III die größte Annäherung an die Wirklichkeit bedeutet und damit die intensivste Prüfung erfordert. Andererseits können in Simulatoren mit FAA Phase III-Zulassung wesentlich mehr Flugübungen durchgeführt werden als z. B. bei Phase I-Simulatoren, wo die Piloten noch auf mehr Flugtraining angewiesen sind.

Grundlage des gesamten Prozesses ist wieder das Datenpaket. Alle Prüfungen erfolgen nur gegen offizielle (Flugzeug-) Herstellerdaten, belegt durch Dokumentnummer und Seite. Keinesfalls werden Sollwerte anerkannt, die während des Flugbetriebes durch Personal der Fluggesellschaft notiert wurden.

Das in Kap. 2 erwähnte ATG spielt hierbei eine entscheidende Rolle und ist direkt auf die FAA-Anforderungen zugeschnitten. Toleranzen werden für jeden Check von der FAA im AC 120-40 angegeben und sind "hart", d.h., jede  noch so kleine Überschreitung bedeutet die Nichtanerkennung.
Dies unterstreicht die essentielle Notwendigkeit, vom Flugzeughersteller ein optimales Datenpaket zu erhalten.


## 4. Betriebserfordernisse und neue Erkenntnisse; wie hält man einen Simulator "up to date"

Auch wenn ein Flugsimulator - endlich - fertiggestellt, von dem Abnahmeteam der Fluggesellschaft für trainingsbereit befunden, von den Behörden geprüft und anerkannt worden ist und seinen "Normalbetrieb" aufgenommen hat, ist der Prozess der Datenbeschaffung nicht zu Ende.

Die Hauptursache sind die ständigen Produktverbesserungen, die Flugzeug-, Triebwerk- und Gerätehersteller an Komponenten und Systemen vornehmen, vgl. Absatz "Modifikationslisten" in Kap. 2. Sie werden als Service Bulletins den Fluggesellschaften angeboten, die sie dann - evtl. etwas verändert - als Ingenieuranweisung zur Einarbeitung in die Flugzeuge und den Simulator veranlassen.

Alle betroffenen Zeichnungen, Schaltpläne etc. des Simulators müssen für jede dieser
Änderungen sorgfältig auf den letzten Stand gebracht werden, um als Arbeitsunterlage
jederzeit aktuell zu sein.

Werden neue Systeme eingebaut und im Simulator nicht die Original Flugzeugcomputer
verwendet, benötigt man vom Hersteller alle Informationen (Flußdiagramm, Regelge-
setze, Schaltpläne), um die Funktion mit dem Simulationsrechner realistisch nachbilden zu können.

Von den Flugzeugherstellern werden manchmal neue Datenpakete bezüglich Aerodynamik
und Flugmechanik zum Kauf angeboten. Sie werden erstellt, wenn Fehler oder Ungenau-
igkeiten in der Originalversion entdeckt werden, zusätzliche Flugversuchsergebnisse
vorliegen, z. T. auch für neue Konfigurationen, und dergleichen mehr.

Entscheidet sich eine Fluggesellschaft für die Inkorporation der neuen Aerodaten,
müssen größere Programmierarbeiten geleistet werden, eine neue fliegerische Abnahme erfolgen und das Gesamt-Datenpaket revidiert werden.

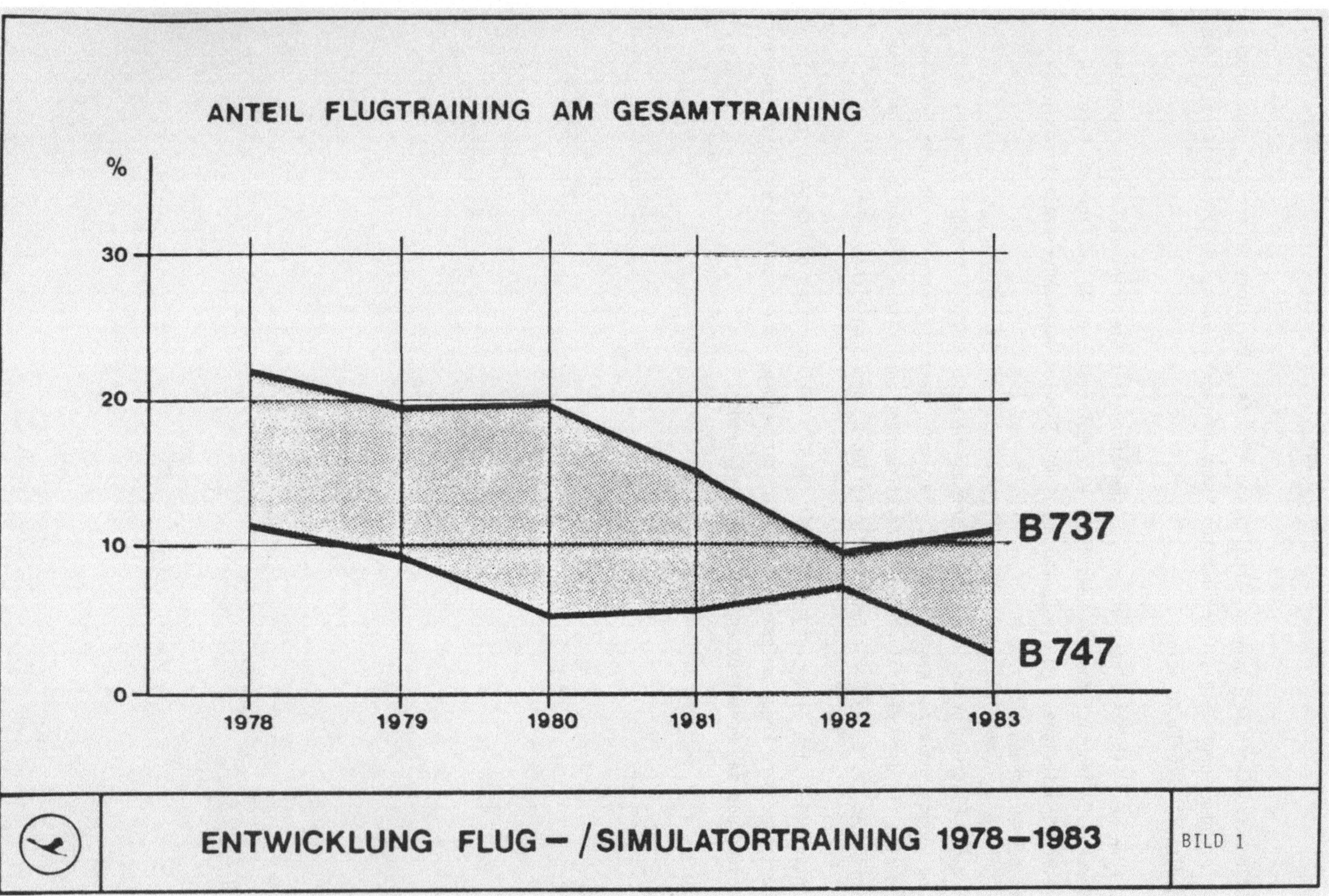

ANTEIL FLUGTRAINING AM GESAMTTRAINING
%
30
20
10
0
1978
1979
1980
1981
1982
1983
B 737
B 747
ENTWICKLUNG FLUG-/SIMULATORTRAINING 1978-1983
BILD 1

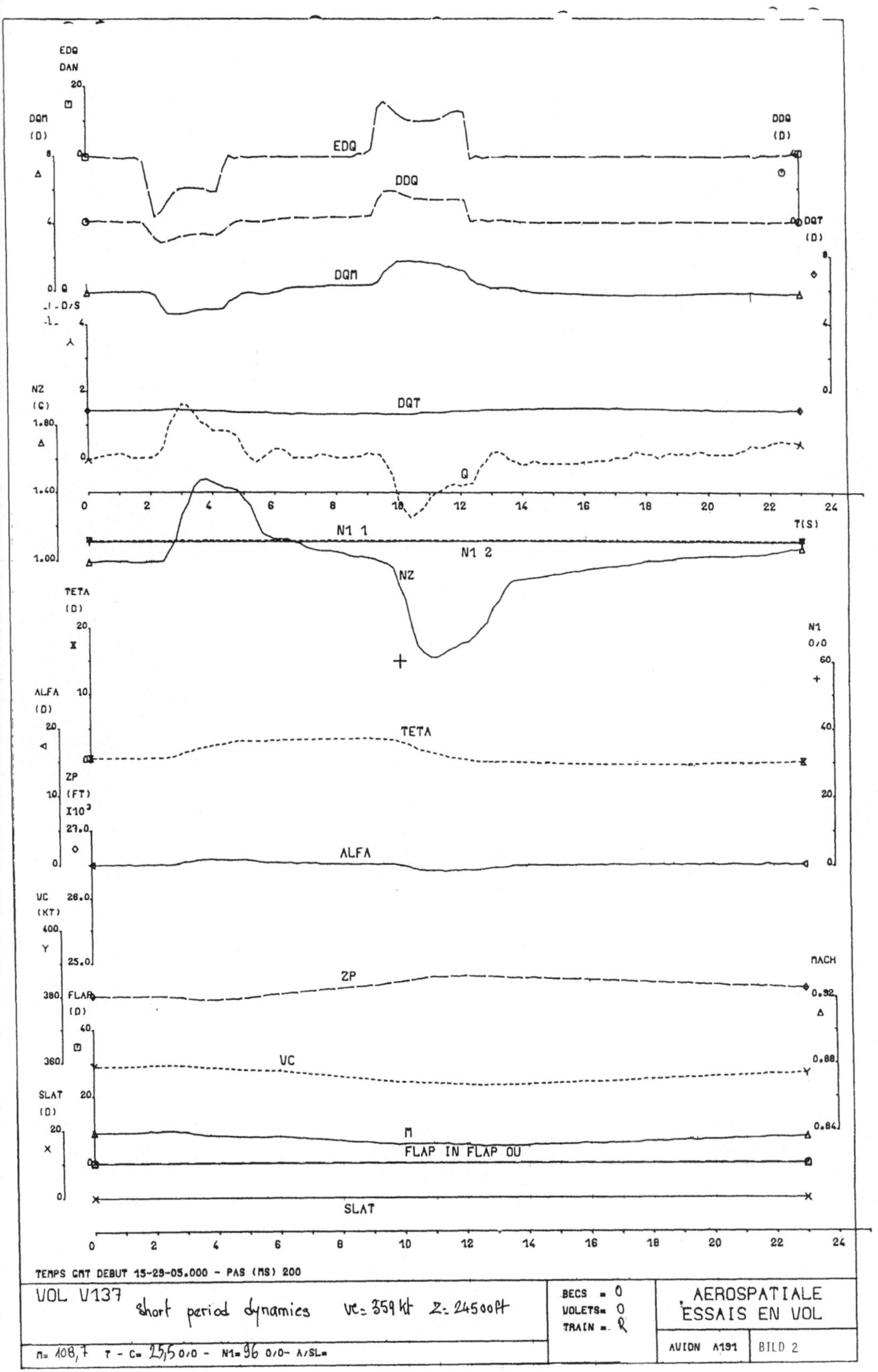
EDQ
DAN
DQM
(D)
EDQ
DDQ
DQM
DQT
N2
(C)
Q
N1 1
N1 2
NZ
DDQ
(D)
DQT
(D)
TETA
(D)
ALFA
(D)
ZP
(FT)
X10³
VC
(KT)
FLAP
(D)
SLAT
(D)
N1
0/0
TETA
ALFA
ZP
VC
M
FLAP IN FLAP OU
SLAT
MACH
T(S)
TEMPS CNT DEBUT 15-29-05.000 - PAS (MS) 200
VOL V137   short period dynamics   Vc= 359 kt   Z= 24500ft
n= 108,7   T - C= 25,5 0/0 - N1= 96 0/0- A/SL=
BECS = 0
VOLETS= 0
TRAIN = R
AEROSPATIALE
ESSAIS EN VOL
AVION A191   BILD 2

# COMPUTER GENERATED IMAGES FOR AIRCRAFT SIMULATORS

D. Shorrock, Rediffusion Sim. Inc. USA

( Vortrag wird während ASIM´85 verteilt )

# Multiview™ Display

J.L. Bentz
Manager, Advanced Engineering, Product Development
McDonnell Douglas Electronics Company

McDonnell Douglas Electronics Company offers several types of display
hardware for providing out-the-window scenes to flight crews training in
aircraft simulators.  Marketing personnel defined a need for a visual display
offering everyone on the flight deck a uniform field of view of at least 40°
vertical by 150° horizontal.  Requirements included minimum feature resolution
comparable to that provided by existing modular displays, and scene brightness
meeting the highest values specified by the Federal Aviation Administration.

As major system components we chose a large inclined curved mirror, a
rear-projection screen assembly, and an array of three-color projectors.  We
examined seven candidate techniques for fabricating the required 200-sq-ft
mirror surface and used three of them to build reduced-scale models.  The
approach we selected has a metallized polyester film for the mirror surface.
The film is edge-attached to a curved closed chamber, and a vacuum behind the
film creates and maintains the desired mirror shape.

Projectors had to be developed to meet our brightness and resolution
goals.  We chose a configuration having high-intensity red, green, and blue
projection cathode ray tubes with separate projection lenses.

We believe that the Multiview Visual Display System can be effective in
training aircraft, naval, and ground crews in many applications.

KONZEPTE NEUER ALGORITHMEN ZUR
INTEGRATION STEIFER UND HOCHFREQUENTER PROBLEME


(CONCEPTS OF NEW ALGORITHMS FOR THE
INTEGRATION OF STIFF AND/OR HIGHLY OSCILLATORY PROBLEMS)


by


H.J. Halin and K. Tichy

Department of Energy
ETH (Swiss Federal Institute of Technology)
Clausiusstr. 33
CH-8092 Zurich, Switzerland

Concepts of new algorithms suitable for the integration of stiff and/or highly oscillatory problems are outlined in the first part of the paper. A common characteristics of the presented methods is, that they employ higher derivatives of the state variables which are calculated analytically by means of automated symbolic differentiation techniques. Moreover, for the solution of the system of algebraic equations, which is solved after each integration step, algebraic manipulation techniques are applied in order to derive the Jacobian of the system of ODEs. All methods have been implemented in the semianalytical simulation package PSCSP (Powers Series Continuous-System Simulation Program) [1] which provides a number of attractive features for engineering and scientific applications that are not available in other present-day simulation languages.

The first discussed algorithm can be looked at as a modification of the well-known Gear-type methods based upon backward-difference techniques in form of the Nordsieck-vector notation. However, instead of using the elements of the Nordsieck-vector, which are approximations of the higher derivatives of the state variables, these higher derivatives will be evaluated accurately from analytical formulae. These higher derivatives are calculated from the values of the independent variables and from values of state variables at the beginning of each integration step. Consequently, when comparing a conventional Gear-type method with the modified version of this method, it becomes clear that the latter one achieves a higher accuracy per integration step. Moreover, the modified method has an additional advantage of being self-starting, since it is a single-step method.

The second algorithm consists in a variable-order-variable-stepsize Hermite-type method which uses higher derivatives at either end of the integration step.

The third method is based on the idea of representing the solution as a sum of two parts. The first part entails an analytical expression that takes the stiffness into account and is a linear combination of two exponentials and/or sinusoidal functions, where the eigenvalues are taken from guesses of the locally largest eigenvalues of the system. Very good approximations to these eigenvalues can be easily obtained from the ratios of the derivatives of successive orders. The second part of the solution is found by the application of the Hermite-type integration formula mentioned above. This second part contains both the non-stiff contributions and the corrections to the analytical approximation of the first part as well.

The second section of the paper summarizes numerical results and preliminary experience with the new algorithms compared with the codes EPISODE and LSODE and applied to a number of benchmark-problems.

Ref.: H.J. Halin
       "The Applicability of Taylor Series Methods in Simulation"
       Proceedings of the 1983 Summer Computer Simulation Conference,
       July 11-13, 1983, Vancouver, B.C., Canada,
       Vol. II (State-of-the-Art Topics), pp. 1032-1078.

Ueber die Vorteile semianalytischer Methoden zur Loesung von
"Optimal Control Problems" dargestellt an einem Beispiel aus der Robotik


(The Usefulness of Semianalytical Integration Techniques for Solving
Optimal Control Problems Demonstrated by Means of an Example from
the Area of Robotics)


by


H.J. Halin, S.A.R. Hepner, and H.P. Geering
ETH (Swiss Federal Institute of Technology)
CH-8092 Zuerich
SWITZERLAND


ABSTRACT

The solution of optimal control problems has been of growing practical importance for more than two decades. Therefore a number of numerical methods got developed which lend themselves to the solution of various classes of control problems. Software implementation of these methods entails algorithms for solving ordinary differential equations within a framework that serves to iteratively improve the control vector for instance by solving a two-point boundary-value problem.

It is well known that the application of all these methods often goes along with severe numerical difficulties causing unreliable results and excessive computing times. These computational problems are often due to the fully numerical integration methods applied and to various numerical approximations (e.g. inaccurate integration across discontinuities, replacement of differential quotients by difference quotients etc. during the process of computation.

In the first part of this paper itwill be outlined that these numerical difficulties can be completely avoided when using so called semianalytcal techniques. It is known from the literature that such methods, the implementation of which can be fully automated, lead to piecewise analytical approximations of the states and other variables. It is also shown how semianalytical techniques can be readily implemented in order to provide software which is especially suited for handling complicated engineering simulation problems efficiently and accurately.

The second part of the paper deals with such a language referred to as PSCSP (Power Series Continuous-System Simulation Program) which was recently completed at ETH. It is shown, how some of the features of PSCSP, which are not available in other simulation programs currently in use, can readily be exploited for handling optimal control problems. Among these features are:

a) PSCSP allows a highly accurate integration by using a method of variable order and variable stepsize. Typical orders range from 10 to 30 permitting integration steps which are often by two orders of magnitude larger than those used by a fourth-orderRunge-Kutta method. Of course these advantages include adequate savings in computing time.

b) Due to the piecewise analytical character of the method it is readily possible to localize discontinuities, extrema etc. The analytical character also permits the accurate storage of trajectories of states and other variables for later usage.

c) PSCSP supports a variety of options for symbolic formula manipulation. For
   instance it is possible to code the Lagrange- formulation of the equations
   of motion of a mechanical system while using generalized coordinates and to
   let the program derive the corresponding time dependent state-space description.

d) An additional feature of PSCSP is the availability of partial derivatives
   of any complexity which are automatically derived in an analytical form.
   Hence it is possible to calculate gradients, Jacobians, Hessians etc. without any approximation.

In a third part, a sample problem taken from the area of robotics is solved.
In this the semianalytical methods of PSCSP as well as conventional fully numerical techniques are applied to the corresponding optimal control problem.
It will be shown that the semianalytical approach leads to substantial savings
in computing time, more accurate results and a significantly shorter and more
readable code.

SIMULATION DES LINEAR- QUADRATISCHEN REGELUNGSPROBLEMES

F.Breitenecker, Technische Universität Wien
Wiedner Hauptstrasse 6-10, A-1040 Wien

Zusammenfassung. Dieser Beitrag beschäftigt sich mit dem linear- quadratischen Rege-
lungsproblem. Es wird zunächst ein Verfahren, "Erweitertes Invariantes Einbetten"
vorgestellt, das das Problem unabhängig von den Randbedingungen löst. In der Folge
wird gezeigt, daß dieses Verfahren sich auch sehr  gut zur Simulation des Problemes
eignet. Implementationsmöglichkeiten und Beispiele in den  Simulationssprachen ACSL
und HYBSYS werden angegeben.

Summary. This contribution deals with the simulation of the linear- quadratic regulator problem. First the method of "extended invariant imbedding" is shown which
allows to solve the problem independently from the initial values. In the following
it is  shown that this method can be used as well for the simulation of the problem.
Examples of implementations within the simulation languages ACSL and HYBSYS are
given.

## Mathematische Grundlagen.

Viele technische Prozesse können in erster Näherung durch ein zeitinvariantes lineares

System $\dot{x}=A.x+B.u$ (Zustandsgleichung), $y=C.x$ (Ausgangsgleichung) um einen Arbeitspunkt

herum beschrieben werden. Dabei bedeuten $x(t)$ einen n- dimensionalen Zustandsvektor

("inneres Prozessverhalten"), $u(t)$ einen m- dimensionalen Steuerungsvektor ("äußere

Eingriffsmöglichkeiten") und $y(t)$ einen r- dimensionalen Ausgangsvektor ("messbares

(beobachtbares) Prozessverhalten"). Eine häufig auftretende Regelungsaufgabe ist nun

die sogenannte linear- quadratische (LQ- Problem), bei der eine Steuerung (Regelung)

$u(t)$ zu finden ist, die das System von einem Zustand $(x_o=x(t_o))$ in einen anderen

$(x_T=x(T))$ überführt  ("fester Rand") oder das System von einer "Auslenkung"

$(x_o=x(t_o))$ wieder zur Ruhelage regelt ("freier Rand"), wobei möglichst wenig Energie

verbraucht und die Bewegungen möglichst "glatt" (smooth) erfolgen sollen. Diese For-

derung wird mathematisch beschrieben durch die quadratische Gütefunktion

$$J_1(u)=\int_{t_o}^{T} (x'.Q.X+u'.R.u)dt, \qquad J_2(u) = x_T'.L.x_T + J_1(u)$$

($J_1$- fester Rand, $J_2$- freier Rand), die zu minimieren ist. Anwendung des Minimumprin-

zipes von Pontryagin (z.B./2/) führt das Minimierungsproblem auf die Randwertaufgabe

$$\dot{x} = A.x - BR^{-1}B'.p, \quad \dot{p} = -Q.x - A'.p, \quad x(t_o)=x_o, \; x(T)=x_T \; (p(T)=L.x(T)) \qquad (1)$$

mit dem n- dimensionalen Kozustandsvektor $p(t)$ zurück, wobei für die optimale Steue-

rung  $u(t) = -R^{-1}B'.p(t)$  gilt.

Eine direkte numerische Lösung der Randwertaufgabe (1) ist wegen ihrer Instabilität

nicht möglich (/3/), außerdem ist man aus technischen Gründen an der Berechnung einer

Steuerung $u(t)$ bzw. Regelung $u(x(t))$ interessiert und nicht am Kozustand  $p(t)$.

Die klassische Lösungsmethode besteht im Lösen einer Matrix- Riccatidifferential-

gleichung für $K(t)$, mit der dann $u=-R^{-1}B'K(t).x$ gilt. Ein Nachteil ist nun, daß diese

Methode einerseits nur bei Problemen mit freiem Rand anwendbar ist (beim festen Rand

kommen weitere Differentialgleichungen hinzu) und andererseits die Methode (die
Riccatigleichung) von den Randwerten abhängt, d.h. für neue Randwerte $(x_O, x_T, L)$
müssen die (nichtlinearen) Differentialgleichungen nochmals gelöst werden.

In /3/ wird nun ein "Erweiterter Einbettungsalgorithmus" vorgestellt, der diese Nachteile nicht besitzt. Er beruht auf den Matrixdifferentialgleichungen (MDGL)

$$\dot{W} = A.W + W.A' + W.Q.W - B.R^{-1}.B' \quad \text{bzw.} \quad \dot{\overline{W}} = -A'.\overline{W} - \overline{W}.A + \overline{W}.B.R^{-1}.B'.\overline{W} - Q \tag{2}$$

$$\dot{G} = (A + W.Q).G, \quad \dot{F} = -G'.Q.G \quad \text{bzw.} \quad \dot{\overline{G}} = (-A' + \overline{W}.B.R^{-1}.B').\overline{G}, \quad \dot{\overline{F}} = -\overline{G}.B.R^{-1}.B'.\overline{G}$$

mit den Anfangswerten $W(t_O)=\overline{W}(t_O)=F(t_O)=0_n$, $G(t_O)=\overline{G}(t_O)=E_n$, die unabhängig von den

Randbedingungen des Problems sind und (üblicherweise) konträres Stabilitätsverhalten
aufweisen (abhängig von den Eigenwerten von $A+A'$ bzw $-A'-A$). Die (punktweisen)
Lösungen der MDGL (2) sind die Koeffizienten für die linearen Gleichungssysteme (LGS)

$$x(t) = W(t).p(t) + G(t).x_O \quad \text{bzw.} \quad p(t) = \overline{W}(t)x(t) + \overline{G}(t)p_O$$

$$p_O = G'(t)p(t) - F(t).x_O \qquad x_O = \overline{G}'(t)x(t) - \overline{F}(t)p_O \tag{3}$$

zunächst im Zeitpunkt $t=T$, woraus sich dann die fehlenden Randbedingungen $p_O$, $p_T$
(und $x_T$) berechnen lassen und dann für jeden Zeitpunkt $t_k \in (t_O, T)$, woraus dann die
Werte für $x(t_k)$ und $u(t_k)$ berechenbar sind.

<u>Anwendung und Implementation in Simulationssprachen</u>

Das vorgestellte Verfahren eignet sich nun auch gut für die Simulation des Problems.
Algorithmisch dafür aufbereitet, besteht es aus folgenden Schritten:

1. Auswahl der stabilen MDGL in (2) durch Eigenwertanalyse

2. Integration und Abspeichern der Lösungen der MDGL (2) (als "Regelungsdatenbasis"
   organisiert) über einem maximal interessierenden Simulations- (=Regelungs-)
   Horizont $[t_O, T_{max}]$

3. Lösen des LGS $x_T=W_T.p_T+G_T.x_O$, $p_O=G'_T.p_T-F_Tx_O$ bzw. $p_T=\overline{W}_T.x_T+\overline{G}_T.p_O$,

   $x_O=\overline{G}'_T.x_T-\overline{F}_T.p_O$ $(p_T=L.x_T)$ für die aktuelle Störauslenkung $x_O$ und/ oder den

   aktuellen neuen Arbeitspunkt $x_T$ für $T \leqslant T_{max}$ zur Ermittlung der unbekannten
   Randbedingungen $p_O$, $p_T$ $(x_T)$.

4. Lösen der LGS $x_k=W_k.p_k+G_k.x_O$, $x_O=G'_k.p_k-F_k.x_O$, $u_k=R_k^{-1}.B'_k.p_k$ bzw.

   $p_k=\overline{W}_k.x_k+\overline{G}_k.p_O$, $x_O=\overline{G}'.x_k-\overline{F}_kp_O$, $u_k=...(x_k=x(t_k), W_k=W(t_k),...)$ zur Ermittlung

   von Steuerung $u$ und Zustand $x$ zum (diskreten) Zeitpunkt $t_k$.

Zu bemerken ist, daß die ersten zwei Schritte, die umfangreichsten des Verfahrens,
nur ein einziges Mal durchgeführt werden müssen, um die "Regelungsdatenbank" anzu-
legen. Von dieser Datenbank, die unabhängig von Form und Werten der Randbedingungen
ist, wird dann im 3. und 4. Schritt die optimale Steuerung berechnet (was auch
"online" geschehen kann).

Das Verfahren kann nun sicher als eigenes Programmpaket zur Simulation implementiert
werden. Aus verschiedenen Gründen ist es jedoch (meiner Meinung nach ) vorteilhafter,
auf bestehende Simulationssoftware (-Sprachen) aufzubauen. Generell bieten sich hier

die Makro- Features von Simulationssprachen (SP) an, um mehr als nur- wie üblich- im
Zeitbereich zu simulieren; für Dokumentationszwecke wird sinnvollerweise auf die
Standard- Features der SP zurückgegriffen.

In /5/ wird zur Implementation von "höheren Ebenen" in SP, die z.B. auch Modellbildung
erledigen und Entscheidungen treffen können, ein Supermakro- Konzept vorgeschlagen.
Ausgehend von der Trennung Modell (MO)- Methode (ME)- Experiment (E; Anwendung einer
Methode (Z.B. Simulationsablauf) auf ein Modelll) ist ein Supermakro ein Makro auf
Experimentebene mit rekursiven Fähigkeiten. Gemäß Abb.1 ist er ein variabel steuerbarer
Ablauf von Teilexperimenten, die das Modell erzeugen ($E_{MODEL}$), die Methoden zur Analyse
des Modells generieren  bzw. verbinden ($E_{METHODS}$) und die dann wahlweise die generier-
ten Methoden auf die  definierten Modelle anwenden ($E_1,..,E_N$).
Im Falle des LQ- Problemes muß ein das Problem mit dem vorgeschlagenen Verfahren lösen-
den Supermakro "LQREG" folgende Teilexperimente beinhalten:

* $E_{MODEL}$: Auswählen und Erzeugen (=Methode $ME_{MODEL}$) einer Zustandsraumbeschreibung
  (eines Modelles MO) in der Syntax der SP für die MDGL (2) mit interaktiver Eingabe
  der Systemmatrizen und Eigenwertanalyse  (1.Schritt des Verfahrens).
* $E_{METHOD}$: Bereitstellung der Methoden  (=Methode $ME_{METHOD}$) "Integration der erzeugten MDGL und Abspeichern auf Regelungsdatenbasis" ($ME_1$),  "Lösen von LGS mit
  Koeffizienten aus der Datenbasis" ($ME_2$) und "Schnittstelle zu Dokumentationsfea-
  tures der SP" ($ME_3$)  mit geeigneten Schnittstellen.
* $E_I$ = $ME_1$(MO): 2. Schritt des Verfahrens- Integration und Abspeicherung der MDGL (2)
* $E_{II}$ = $ME_2$(MO): 3. Schritt des Verfahrens- Lösen eines LGS zur Ermittlung der unbe-
            kannten Randwerte

* $E_i$ = $ME_2$(MO), i= 1(1)n : 4. Schritt des Verfahrens- Lösen von LGS für jeden Zeit-
            punkt $t_k$ zur Ermittlung von $x_k$ und $u_k$
* $E_{III}$ =$ME_3$(MO): "Übergabe" der Ergebnisse an die SP zur weiteren Dokumentation

Sinnvollerweise ist zu fordern, die Abfolge der Teilexperimente mit $E_{MODEL}$ (Neubeginn),
$E_I$ (Vergrößerung von $T_{max}$) und $E_{II}$ (neue Störauslenkungen) beginnen zu können.

## Implementation in ACSL und HYBSYS

Die vorgestellte Supermakro- Technik kann in den derzeitig verfügbaren SP nur teilweise
implementiert werden (derzeit fehlen vor allem die Möglichkeiten zum Verbinden von
Modellen und zum Definieren von Methoden). Im folgenden wird dargestellt, wie der
Supermakro "LQREG" in ACSL und HYBSYS als Vertreter für eine compiler- und eine
interpreterorientierte SP implementiert werden kann.
In ACSL (/1/), einer sehr weit verbreiteten SP, wird ein Modell in einer spezifischen
ACSL- Syntax im Modellteil definiert, der dann von einem Precompiler und "folgendem"
FORTRAN- Compiler übersetzt wird. Ein interaktiver  "Runtime - Interpreter"  (RTI)
erlaubt es, dieses Objekt- Programm (=das Modell) zu starten (=Simulationslauf), Konstante zu ändern,Ergebnisse zu dokumentieren und verschiedenartige andere Modellanalysen
durchzuführen. Der Modellteil besteht aus einer INITIAL SECTION, in der Anfangswertbe-
rechnungen zum Zeitpunkt $t_o$ festgelegt werden, aus einer DYNAMIC SECTION, die in einer

Schleife über Teilintervallen $[t_{i-1}, t_i]$ abgearbeitet wird und jeweils die Integration über einem Teilintervall aufruft, die errechneten Werte ausgibt, mit ihnen zusätzliche Berechnungen durchführt und die Endbedingung abprüft, und aus einer TERMINAL SECTION, in der Endwertberechnungen definiert werden. Die eigentliche Systemdynamik wird in der DERIVATIVE SECTION, die innerhalb der DYNAMIC SECTION angegeben wird, in Form von Differentialgleichungen festgelegt. Auf Modellbeschreibungsebene verfügt ACSL über Makro- Fähigkeiten, d.h. Modellteile können als Makro vordefiniert werden (am Anfang des Modellteiles); in einer beliebigen Section "aufgerufen", werden sie vom Precompiler durch den gesamten definierten Code mit aktuellen Parametern (Werten) ersetzt.

Diese Makro-Möglichkeit kann nun zur automatischen Definition der MDGL (2) verwendet werden, indem ähnlich wie beim ACSL- Standardmakro TRAN auch die Dimension für Zustand, Ausgang und Eingang variabel definiert wird; die DERIVATIVE SECTION besteht dann nur aus dem "Aufruf" dieses Makros, womit $E_{MODEL}$ teilweise implementiert ist und gleich beim Starten von ACSL, wo der Modellteil übersetzt wird, durchgeführt wird.

Die Standardmethode der Integration über $[t_o, T_{max}]$ (=Simulationslauf) braucht nicht eigens definiert zu werden, das Lösen eines LGS wird beim Starten von ACSL mitgeladen, womit $E_{METHOD}$ durchgeführt ist. Der 2.Schritt des Verfahrens, die Integration der MDGL (2) ist ein "normaler" Simulationslauf, der vom RTI aus gestartet wird; beim Durchlaufen der INITIAL SECTION können die Werte für die Systemmatrizen interaktiv eingegeben und nach einer Eigenwertanalyse die Koeffizienten für stabile MDGL berechnet werden (Teil von $E_{MODEL}$), zusätzlich werden die Werte in der DYNAMIC SECTION (zu jedem Kommunikationszeitpunkt $t_k$) auf ein File ausgegeben, womit die Regelungsdatenbasis erzeugt ist ($E_I$). Der 3. und 4.Schritt des Verfahrens, das Lösen eines LGS zur Bestimmung der fehlenden Randwerte ($E_{II}$) und das Lösen eines LGS zu jedem Zeitpunkt $t_k$ ($E_i$, i=1(1)n) werden in einem modifizierten Simulationslauf durchgeführt: in der INITIAL SECTION wird nun das LGS für $p_o$, $p_T$ (und $x_T$) gelöst, wobei die Werte $W_T$, $G_T$,.. aus der Datenbasis (File) verwendet werden; in der DYNAMIC SECTION wird zu jedem Zeitpunkt $t_k$ ein LGS für $x_k$ und $u_k$ mit Koeffizienten aus der Datenbasis gelöst - die automatisch aufgerufene Integration über $[t_k, t_{k+1}]$ wird nicht beachtet (sie läßt sich leider nicht unterbinden, sondern nur mit Algorithmus IALG=0, also "data sampling" durchführen). Die Kommunikation zwischen dem  Supermakro  und dem RTI ($E_{III}$) ist durch die Synchronisation von Kommunikationsintervall CINT und dem Beschreiben/Lesen der Regelungsdatenbasis in der DYNAMIC SECTION gegeben. Zwischen einem "normalen" Simulationslauf ($E_I$) und dem modifizierten ($E_{II}$; $E_i$, i=1(1)n) wird im RTI mit einer logischen Flag umgeschaltet. Abbildung 2 faßt diese Implementierungsmöglichkeit, die derzeit im Teststadium ist, zusammen.

HYBSYS (/8/), eine am Hybridrechenzentrum der TU Wien entwickelte interpreterorientierete SP, kann sowohl analoge als auch digitale Integration durchführen. Im Falle analoger Integration (Simulation) stehen ein AUTOPATCH- System und automatische Skalierung zur Verfügung, die eine Schaltung von einer digitalen Modelldatenbasis weg generieren. Diese Modelldatenbasis kann interaktiv durch Befehle erzeugt, erweitert und geändert werden. Ein sehr leistungsfähiges Feature von HYBSYS sind die Makros auf Experimentebene, die in FORTRAN programmiert und in Overlay- Technik exekutiert werden. In einem derartigen Makro kann nun all das programmiert werden, was in HYBSYS direkt getan werden kann, denn jeder HYBSYS- Befehl hat einen äquivalenten FORTRAN- Unterprogrammaufruf - möglich sind z.B. Parameteränderung, Starten eines Simulationslaufes, aber auch Änderung der Modelldatenbasis. Mit dieser Makro- Möglichkeit können z.B. sehr effizient Optimierungen implementiert werden (/6/).

Der Supermakro "LQREG" kann nun mit Hilfe eines einzigen derartigen Makros implementiert werden. Abhängig von Flags, die interaktiv in HYBSYS gesetzt werden, wird der Makro ganz oder nur teilweise durchlaufen, wobei folgende Teile verfügbar sind (Abb.3):

* Interaktive Eingabe der Dimensionen und Systemmatrizen des LQ-Problems, Eigenwertanalyse und Laden eines maximal dimensionierten Modelles für die MDGL (2), das entsprechend den Dimensionen reduziert wird ($E_{MODEL}$ - 1.Schritt des Verfahrens)

* Durchführung eines Simulationslaufes und Abspeichern der Werte auf eine Regelungsdatenbasis ($E_I$ - 2.Schritt des Verfahrens, "INTMDE" in Abb.3)

* Lösung von LGS zur Berechnung der fehlenden Randwerte und der Zustände $x_k$ und Steuerungen $u_k$ mit Koeffizienten aus der Regelungsdatenbasis nach interaktiver Eingabe von Störauslenkung $x_0$ und/oder neuem Arbeitspunkt $x_T$ ($E_{II}$; $E_i$, i=1(1)n - 3. und 4.Schritt des Verfahrens, "CALCXU" in Abb.3)

* "Übergabe der berechneten Werte an HYBSYS für Dokumentation ($E_{III}$, "DISPXU" in Abb.3)

Eine zusätzliche Implementation von Methoden ($E_{METHOD}$) geschieht durch Laden der entsprechenden Programme im Makro. Eine in /4/ beschriebene Teilimplementation dieses Verfahrens in HYBSYS wird derzeit erweitert und adaptiert.

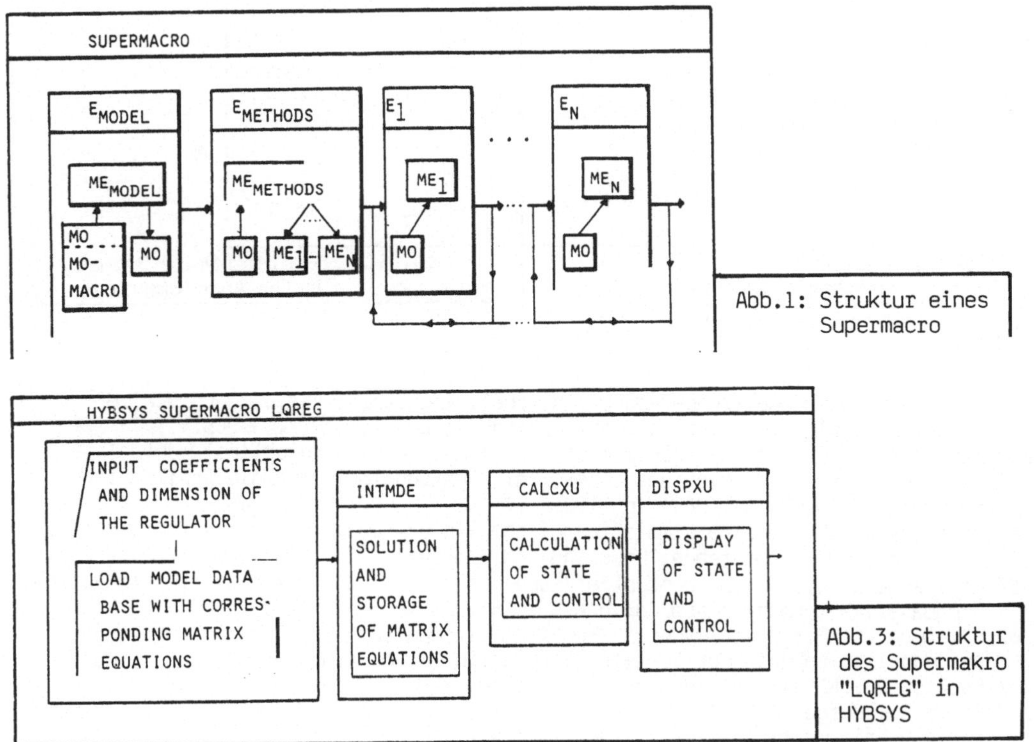



Abb.1: Struktur eines Supermacro

Abb.3: Struktur des Supermakro "LQREG" in HYBSYS

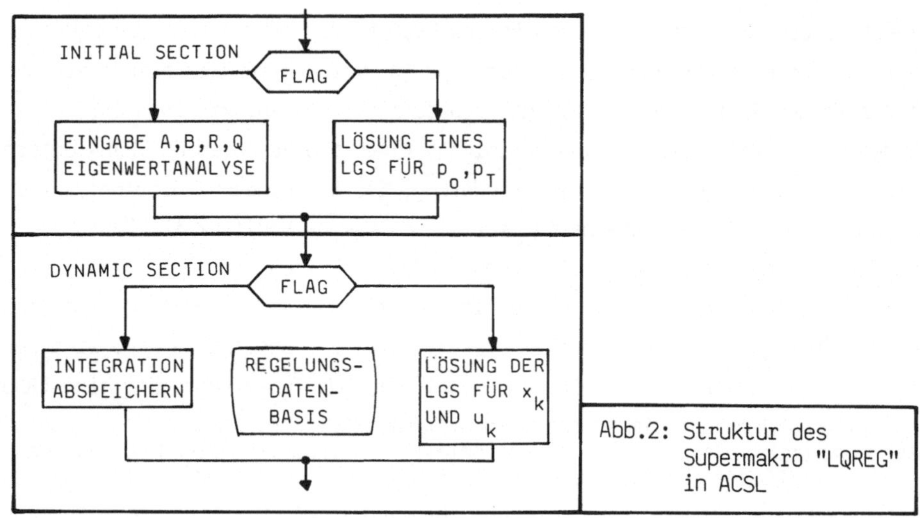



Abb.2: Struktur des Supermakro "LQREG" in ACSL

## Beispiel: Andockmanöver

Mit den bestehenden Grundversionen des Supermakro "LQREG" in ACSL und HYBSYS wurde das energieminimale Andockmanöver zweier Satelliten simuliert. Die Dynamik kann nach /7/ in erster Näherung durch ein System 4.Ordnung mit zweidimensionaler Steuerung (Tangential- und Radialschub) beschrieben werden. Die Abbildung 4 zeigt Teile der Lösungen der MDGL (Regelungsdatenbasis), Abbildungen 5 und 6 veranschaulichen zwei Andockmanöver (Ergebnis der Berechnung von $x_k$).

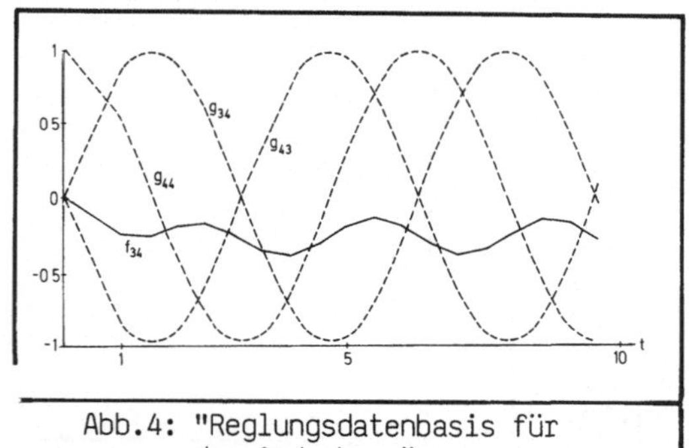



Abb.4: "Reglungsdatenbasis für das Andockmanöver

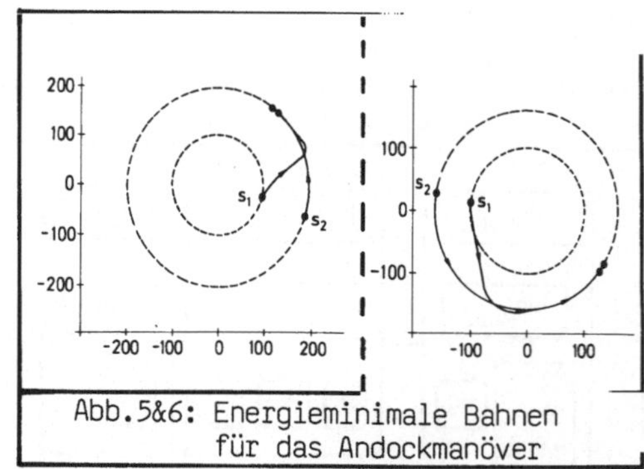



Abb.5&6: Energieminimale Bahnen für das Andockmanöver

## Literatur


/1/ ACSL User Guide/ Reference Manual. Mitchell & Gauthier Ass., Concordia, MA.

/2/ Athans M., Falb P.L.: Optimal Control. Mac Graw- Hill, N.Y., 1966.

/3/ Breitenecker F.: On the solution of the linear- quadratic optimal control problem by extended invariant imbedding. OACM (Optimal Control- Applications and Methods), vol. 4 (1983), pp 129.

/4/ Breitenecker F.: Online simulation of the linear- quadratic regulator problem. Proc. Int. AMSE Conference "Modeling and Simulation", Paris, July 1982, vol.3,pp37.

/5/ Breitenecker F.: On the concept of supermacros in today's and future simulation languages. Mathematics and Computers in Simulation XXV (1983), pp. 279.

/6/ Breitenecker F.: Optimierung in kontinuierlichen Simulationssprachen: Aspekte bei Modellen technischer Systeme. Informatik-Fachbericht 85(1984), pp 656.

/7/ Sagirow P.: Satellitendynamik. BI - Verlag, Manheim, 1970.

/8/ Solar D., Berger F., Blauensteiner A.: HYBSYS - interactive simulation software for a hybrid multiple user system. Informatik-Fachbericht 56 (1982), pp 257.

Simulation des Nachbeulverhaltens
Achsensymmetrischer Kugelschalen

Martin Gräff, Wien

Zusammenfassung. Es wird das Nachbeulverhalten einer elastischen Kugel-schale für große achsensymmetrische Deformation untersucht. Der gesamte Nachbeulpfad wird für die experimentell bestätigte "single dimple" Lösung, die eine starke lokale Eindellung darstellt, anhand eines Druck-Deformations-Diagramms angegeben.

Summary. The post-buckling behaviour of an elastic spherical shell is studied for large axisymmetric deformations. The complete post-buckling path is given for the experimentally confirmed single-dimple solution in a load-deformation diagram.


## 1. Modell und Schalengleichungen

Betrachten wir eine dünne Kugelschale, die durch den äußeren Druck p quasistatisch belastet wird, d.h. untersuchen wir das Stabilitätsver-halten des momentanen Gleichgewichtszustandes bei festem Wert der Belastung p; dynamische Einflüsse sind im Modell nicht berücksichtigt. Nehmen wir an, daß das Material der Schale isotop, homogen und linear elastisch ist.

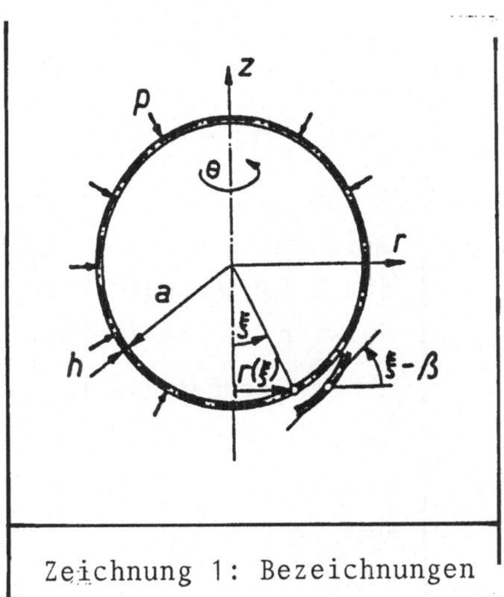


Zeichnung 1: Bezeichnungen

Reissner [1] gibt Gleichungen für diesen Fall an, die in dimensionsloser Form wie folgt lauten bei gleichmäßiger Dicke (h(ξ) = const.):

$$d\left[\beta^{m} + \beta'\,ctg\,\xi + ctg^{2}\xi\,\frac{cos(\xi-\beta)}{cos\,\xi}\,\frac{sin(\xi-\beta)-sin\,\xi}{cos\,\xi} - \nu\,\frac{cos(\xi-\beta)-cos\,\xi}{sin\,\xi}\right] =$$

$$= -\,\psi^{+}\,\frac{sin(\,-\beta)}{sin} - \mu\lambda\frac{cos(\,-\beta)}{sin}\int\limits_{0}^{\xi} cos\,\phi(n)sin\eta\;d\eta\;,$$

$$\delta\left[\psi^{+''} + \psi^{+'}ctg\,\xi - \psi^{+}(ctg^{2}\xi\,\frac{cos^{2}(\xi-\beta)}{cos^{2}\xi} - \nu(1-\beta')\frac{sin(\xi-\beta)}{sin\,\xi})\right] =$$

$$= \frac{cos(\xi-\beta)-cos\,\xi}{sin\,\xi} + \left[-4\lambda ctg\,\xi\int\limits_{0}^{\xi}cos(\phi(n))sin\eta\;d\eta\left[\frac{sin2(\xi-\beta)}{sin2\xi} + \right.\right.$$

$$\left.\left. + \nu(1-\beta')\frac{cos(\xi-\beta)}{cos\xi}\right] + 4\lambda\nu sin(\overline{\phi}-\xi+\beta) + 4\lambda\,\frac{(sin^{2}\xi sin\,\overline{\phi})'}{sin\xi}\right]$$

$$\beta(0) = A(\pi) = \psi^{+}(0) = \psi^{+}(\pi) = 0$$

Die Größen $\lambda$ und $\delta$ bezeichnen dabei dimensionslose Belastungs- beziehungsweise Formparameter. $\psi^{+}(\xi)$ ist die dimensionslose Spannungsfunktion,
$\xi$ ist eine Materialkonstante, $\xi$ ist die unabhängige Variable und $\beta(\xi)$
beschreibt die Deformation, es ist die Winkeldifferenz der Tangenten
an die gebeulte und an die perfekte Schale.

Mit Hilfe der Funktion $\overset{\sim}{\phi}(\xi)$ können wir zwei Modelle für die Belastung
realisieren:

$$\overset{\sim}{\phi}(\xi) = \xi \quad\ldots\ldots\ldots\ldots\ldots\text{ dead-load}$$
$$\overset{\sim}{\phi}(\xi) = \xi - \beta(\xi) \quad\ldots\ldots\ldots\ldots\text{Folgebelastung}$$

## 2. Lösungsverfahren

Ein Blick auf die Form des Nachbeulpfades zeigt das Hauptproblem der
Berechnungen. Die kanonische Parametrisierung
der Lösungen durch den Belastungsparameter
$\lambda$ ist nicht eindeutig.

Wir kennen die Lösung der Randwertaufgabe
für Werte $\lambda \approx$ u,d $\|\beta\| \approx 0$. Die Berechnung
des Nachbeulpfades durch Differenzenverfahren
bei festem $\lambda$ und Fortsetzungsmethode bezüglich $\lambda$ liefert Ergebnisse nur für den
linken, absteigenden Ast des Pfades. An der
Umkehrstelle versagt diese Methode. Abhilfe
bietet ein Verfahren zur Kurvenverfolgung von
Schwetlick [2], das eine lokale Umparameteri-
sierung des Problems durchführt.

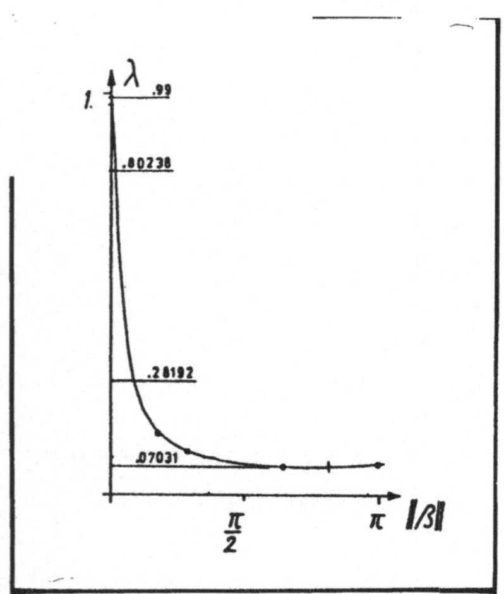



Zeichnung 2: Nachbeulpfad

Es wurde schließlich ein Programmsystem zur Berechnung des Nachbeulpfades entwickelt, das folgende Möglichkeiten bietet:

(1) Berechnung von Startlösungen ($\lambda \approx 1$, $\|\beta\| \approx 0$)

(2) Vor- oder Rückschritt am Nachbeulpfad mit Fortsetzungs- oder
Schwertholzmethode (d.h. Lösen eines RWP)

(3) Datenmanipulationen: Speichern und Zeinen von Lösungen.


## 3. Ergebnisse

Zeichnung 2 zeigt die typische Form des Nachbeulpfades, der durchge-
zogene Weg stammt aus numerischen Rechnungen. Die Stellen, die mit
"o" markiert sind, wurden in Gräff, Scheidl, Troger und Weinmüller [3]
mit Hilfe der singulären Strömungstheorie berechnet. Dort wird auch
eine ausführliche Interpretation der Ergebnisse geliefert. Zeichnung 3
zeigt das Ansehen der Kugel bei wachsender Belastung (kleinerwerdendem
$\lambda$).

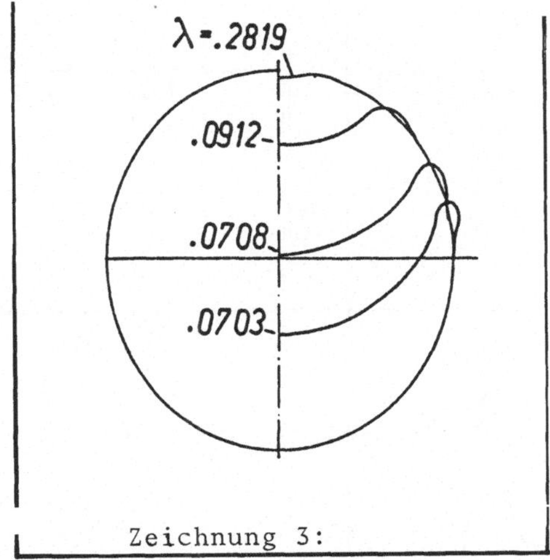


Zeichnung 3:

Die restlichen Diagramme zeigen die Lösungen des Randwertproblems
zu den in Zeichnung 2 markierten Stellen.

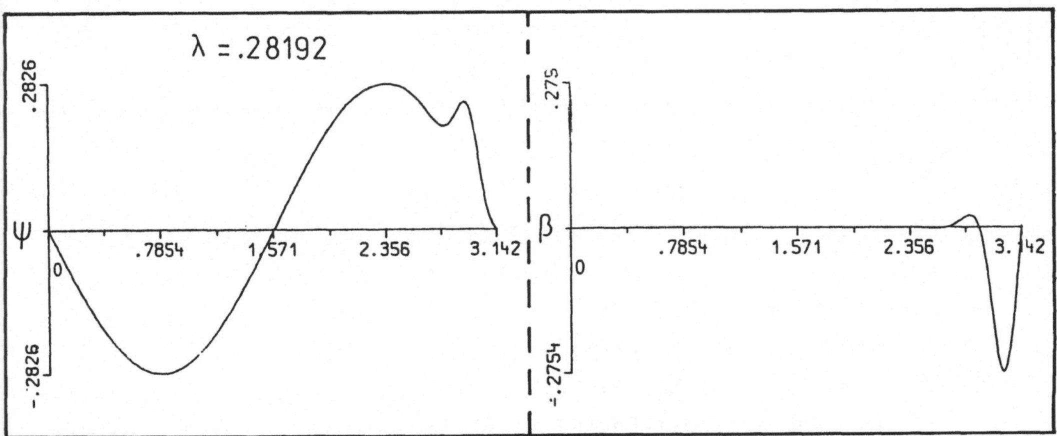

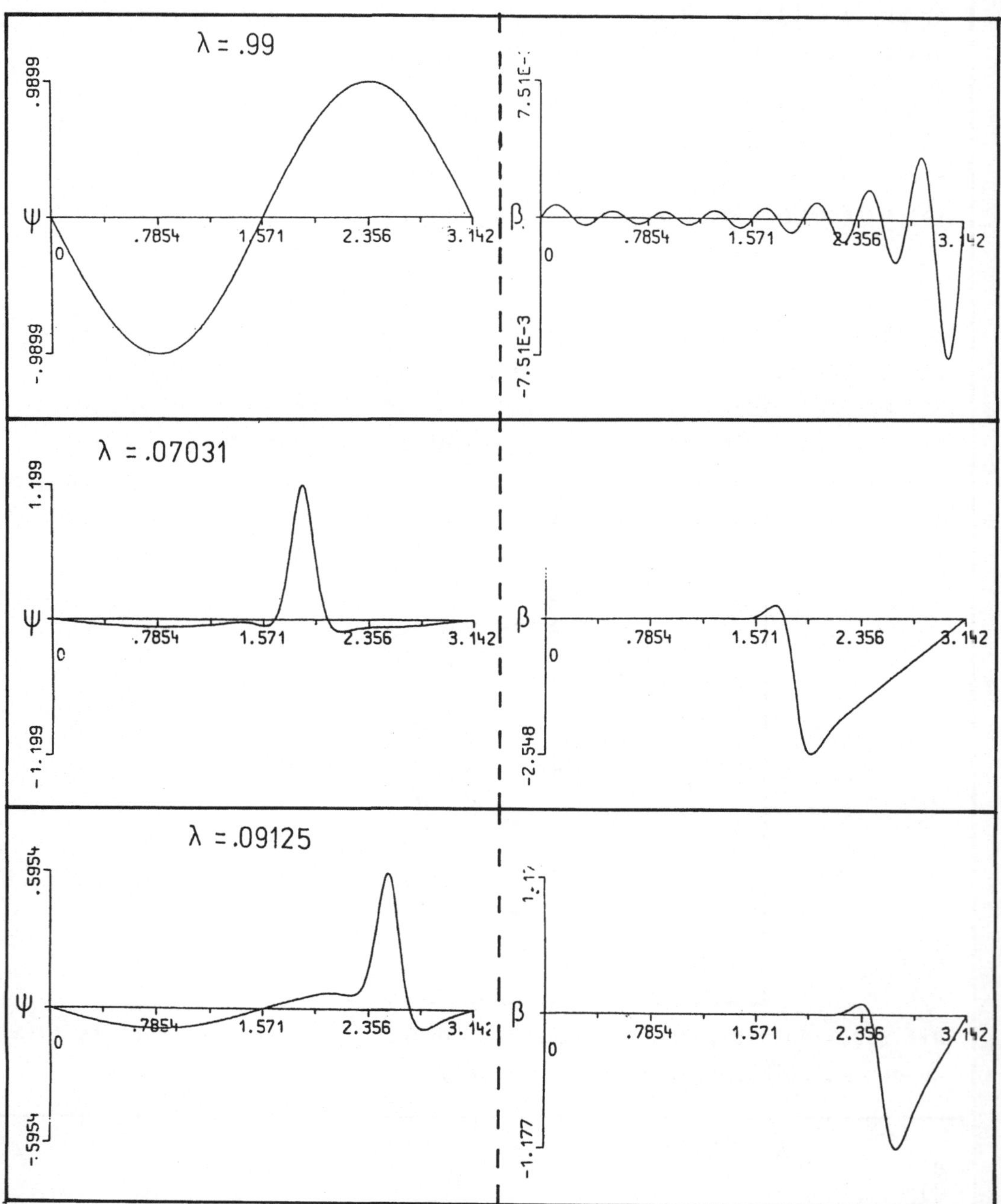

## Literatur

/1/ Reissner E., On axisymmetrical deformations of thin shells of
revolution, Proc. Symp. in Appl. Math., vol.3 (1950)27 - 52.

/2/ Schwetlick H., Numerische Lösung nichtlinearer Gleichungen,
Oldenburg Verlag, München, Wien, 1979.

/3/ Gräff M., Scheidl R., Troger H., Weinmüller E., An investigation
of the complete post-buckling behviour of axisymmetric spherical
shells, to appear.

PARAMETERIDENTIFIKATION

# SELBSTTÄTIGE FEHLERERKENNUNG UND MODELLANPASSUNG
## BEI DER SIMULATION

Klaus Diekmann, Bochum

Zusammenfassung. Parallel zum Prozeßbetrieb arbeitende on-line Simulationen erfordern eine ständige Aktualisierung des Simulationsmodells. Nach einer Prozeßveränderung muß unabhängig von überlagerten Prozeßstörungen eine sichere und schnelle Modellanpassung erfolgen. In dieser Arbeit wird eine selbsttätige Erkennung von Parametervariationen vorgestellt, mit der eine gezielte Anpassung des Simulationsmodells erfolgen kann.

Summary. On-line simulations working parallel to the real process require a permanent adaption of the simulation model. After a variation of the process the adaption of model parameters must be certain and fast, independent of the superposed process noise. In this paper an automatically recognation of parameter variations is suggested, which allows an optimal adaption of the simulation model.

## 1.Einleitung

Das Aufgabengebiet der Simulationstechnik kann nach der Art der Simulationsdurchführung aufgeteilt werden. Off-line Simulationen mit meist theoretisch erstellten Modellen werden für Fallstudien und kritische Untersuchungen vor Inbetriebnahme des realen Prozesses verwendet. On-line Simulationen, d.h. Simulation des Prozeßverhaltens parallel zum Prozeßbetrieb, dienen dem Bedienungspersonal zur Prozeßüberwachung oder zur Entscheidungshilfe. Bereits mit geringen Kosten für Hard- und Software kann bei letzterer Simulationsart dem Bedienungspersonal ein effizientes Arbeitsmittel zur sicheren und optimierten Prozeßführung zu Verfügung gestellt werden.

Da viele reale Prozesse die Eigenschaft besitzen, daß sich die Beschreibungsparameter mit der Zeit durch Verschleiß, Umwelteinflüsse oder externe Manipulation verändern, verlangt die on-line Simulation ein stets aktuelles Prozeßmodell, um die o.a. Anforderungen erfüllen zu können. Die Simulation solcher zeitvarianter Prozesse bereitet dann Schwierigkeiten, wenn der Zeitpunkt und die Art der Variation unbekannt ist. Als notwendige Forderung ist daher eine selbsttätige Fehlererkennung und anschließende Modellanpassung zu stellen.

In dieser Arbeit wird die Problematik einer selbsttätigen Fehlererkennung diskutiert, um anschließend einen Lösungsweg aufzuzeigen, der eine sichere und schnelle Entscheidung ermöglicht, um gezielt eine Parameteranpassung vornehmen zu können.


## 2. Die Simulationsanordnung

Zur Überprüfung, ob das Prozeß- und das Modellverhalten übereinstimmen, werden Prozeß und Modell parallel zueinander angeordnet. Bild 1 zeigt die sich daraus ergebende Simulationsanordnung.

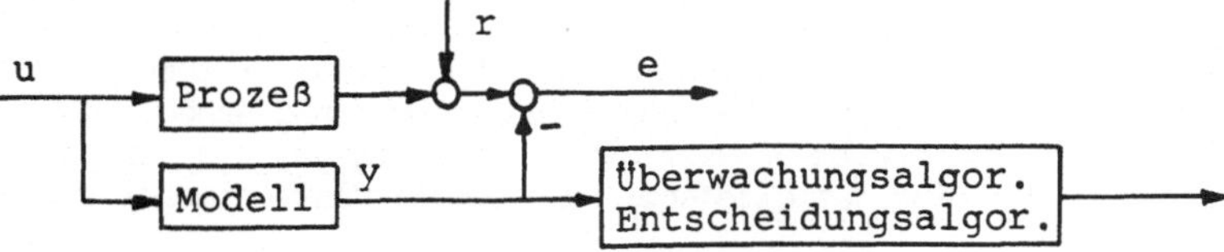


Bild 1. Simulationsanordnung

Der Fehler e als Differenz zwischen gemessenem Prozeßausgangssignal und simuliertem Modellausgangssignal kann als Steuergröße zur Modellanpassung verwandt werden. Jedoch muß dabei berücksichtigt werden, daß im Fehlersignal e auch die Störsignale r enthalten sind. Während der Fehleranteil aus einer Prozeßänderung zu einer Modellanpassung führen soll, darf das Störsignal keine Parameterveränderung bewirken. Da eine Fehleraufteilung bislang nicht möglich war, führte man eine sehr vorsichtige Modellanpassung durch. Zwar wurden dadurch nach einer Prozeßänderung die Simulationsparameter nur sehr langsam adaptiert, aber so konnten die Störungen keine großen Modellveränderungen bewirken. Ein Kompromiß, der viele Probleme beinhaltet.


## 3. Die Simulationsgleichungen

Für die Simulation werden diskrete Differenzengleichungen verwendet. Das ungestörte Ausgangssignal kann danach berechnet werden mit

$$y(k) = - \sum_{i=1}^{n} a_i \, y(k-i) + \sum_{i=1}^{n} b_i \, u(k-i) \tag{1}$$

Die Parameter der Simulationsgleichung werden zusammengefaßt im Parametervektor

$$\underline{p}^T = \begin{bmatrix} a_1 & \cdots & a_n & b_1 & \cdots & b_n \end{bmatrix} \tag{2}$$

Werden in der Gl.(1) auf der rechten Gleichungsseite anstelle der simulierten Ausgangssignale die vorherigen gemessenen Ausgangssignale eingesetzt, so können in der on-line Simulation die Prozeßstörungen berücksichtigt werden. Es ist dann nur noch eine Einschritt-Vorhersage (one-step-ahead prediction) möglich, welche jedoch den aktuellen Prozeßzustand besser wiederspiegelt.

Die Parameter der Simulationsgleichung werden vorab theoretisch oder experimentell ermittelt. Verändert sich das Prozeßverhalten durch interne oder externe Ereignisse, so müssen diese Parameter der Variation angepaßt werden. Dies erfolgt mit der Anpassungsgleichung

$$\hat{\underline{p}}(k+1) \quad = \quad \hat{\underline{p}}(k) \quad + \quad \underline{q}(k+1) \cdot e(k+1) \tag{3}$$
neue Param.　　alte Param.　Korrekturv.　Fehler

wobei der Fehler e die Steuergröße und der Korrekturvektor $\underline{q}$ die Anpassungsgeschwindigkeit und - richtung bestimmt. Wie bereits oben ausgeführt, sollte der Fehler jedoch nur den Simulationsfehler aufgrund der Parametervariation enthalten und nicht die Prozeßstörungen. Dies ist jedoch nur dann möglich, wenn ein zusätzlicher Störsignalschätzer eingeführt wird, welcher ebenfalls parallel zum Simulationsmodell arbeitet, s. <u>Bild 2.</u>.

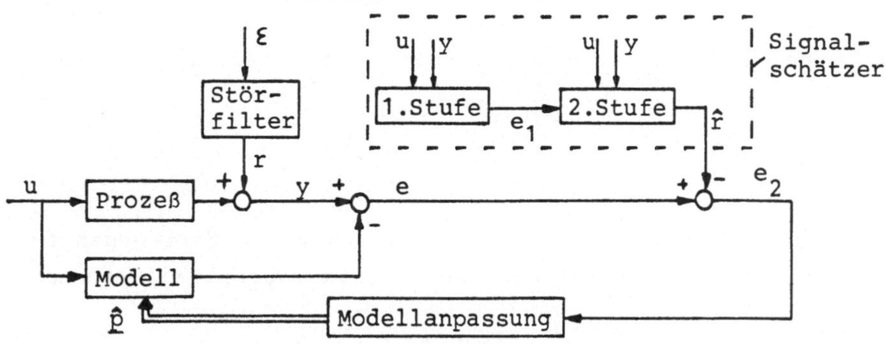


<u>Bild 2.</u> Parallel arbeitender Störsignalschätzer


## 4. Die Erkennung einer Prozeßveränderung

Ein effizientes und doch relativ einfaches Verfahren zur Schätzung von Prozeßstörungen wurde von Astroem und Mayne 1982 im Rahmen eines Parameterschätzverfahrens vorgestellt. Es geht von der Annahme aus, das dem Prozeß ein farbiges Rauschen überlagert ist, welches durch Filterung aus einem weißen Rauschsignal entstanden ist. Es wird daher versucht, zunächst das weiße Rauschsignal zu schätzen, um anschließend die Parameter des Störsignalfilters und damit auch das farbige Rauschen zu bestimmen.

<u>1.Schritt</u>: Geht die Ordnung n in der Differenzengleichung Gl.(1) gegen Unendlich, so müßten alle systematischen System- und Rauscheigenschaften durch diese Gleichung beschrieben werden können. In der Praxis genügt aufgrund der begrenzten A/D-Wandlergenauigkeit eine Ordnung von

n=8. Mit Hilfe eines einfachen Least-Squares Verfahrens werden die Parameter $\underline{a}$ und $\underline{b}$ in der Differenzengleichung

$$\hat{y}_1(k) = - \sum_{i=1}^{8} a_i\, y(k-i) + \sum_{i=1}^{8} b_i\, u(k-i) \tag{4}$$

geschätzt. Der Fehler $e_1$ zwischen gemessenem und geschätztem Ausgangssignal

$$e_1(k) = y(k) - \hat{y}_1(k) \tag{5}$$

müßte der nicht systematische Signalanteil sein und kann daher als das weiße Rauschen angenommen werden.

<u>Schritt 2</u>: Mit den gemessenen Ein- und Ausgangssignalen u und y und dem geschätzten Störsignal $e_1$ werden dann mit Hilfe des erweiterten Least-Squares Verfahrens die Parameter $\underline{a}$, $\underline{b}$ und $\underline{c}$ in der Differenzengleichung

$$y_2(k) = - \sum_{i=1}^{n} a_i\, y(k-i) + \sum_{i=1}^{n} b_i\, u(k-i) + \sum_{i=1}^{n} c_i\, e_1(k-i) + e_1(k) \tag{6}$$

geschätzt, wobei $\underline{c}$ die Parameter des Störfilters sind. Bildet man nun den Fehler

$$e_2(k) = y(k) - \hat{y}_2(k)$$

so müßte dieser bei einer on-line Schätzung mit der Zeit gegen Null gehen, da neben dem Prozeßverhalten auch das Störverhalten nachgebildet wird.

Dies bildet nun die Grundlage für die Erkennung einer Prozeßveränderung: Wird der Fehler $e_2$ größer, so kann dies nur durch eine Parametervariation und nicht durch eine Prozeßstörung entstanden sein. Liegt also ein Simulationsfehler vor, so müßte man dies aus dem Verlauf von $e_2$ ersehen können.

Zu Beginn dieser Arbeit waren jedoch an die Simulationsfehlererkennung die Forderungen gestellt worden, daß sie selbsttätig, schnell und sicher sein sollte. Dies wird durch die einfache Betrachtung von $e_2$ nicht erreicht. Ein verbessertes Beurteilungsmaß wäre der quadratische Fehler, da große Fehler stärker bewertet werden. Die Untersuchungen haben aber gezeigt, daß dadurch nur die Forderung nach Schnelligkeit, nicht aber nach Sicherheit und Selbsttätigkeit erfüllt werden.

Größere Sicherheit erhält man, wenn man einen gemittelten, quadrierten Fehler über einen begrenzten, vergangenen Meßzeitraum betrachtet. Dies soll anhand eines Beispiels gezeigt werden:

<u>Beispiel</u>: In einem Verzögerungssystem 2.Ordnung wird der Verstärkungs-
faktor zu beliebigen Zeitpunkten verändert. Dem Ausgangssignal wurde
ein farbiges Rauschen überlagert. <u>Bild 3</u> zeigt den Verlauf des gemittelten, quadrierten Fehlers über einen Zeitraum der jeweils letzten
40 Meßwerte.

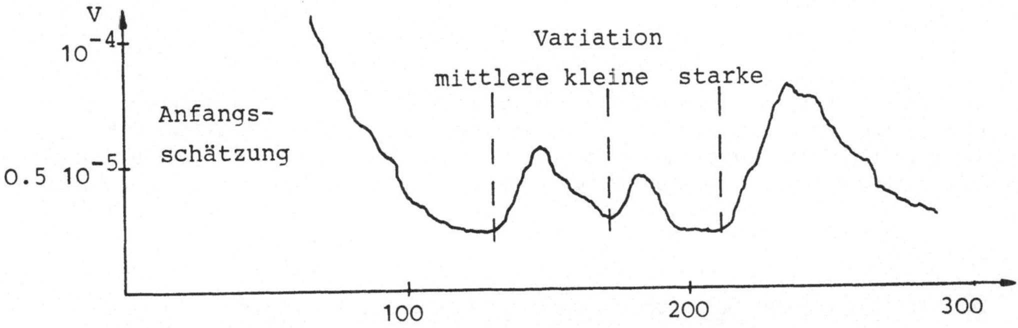


<u>Bild 3.</u> Verlauf des gemittelten, quadrierten Fehlers $e_2$

Anhand des Signalverlaufs sind eindeutig die Zeitpunkte der
Prozeßveränderungen ersichtlich. Die Forderung nach Selbsttätigkeit
der Fehlererkennung kann durch einen numerischen Vergleich des kleinsten Fehlers mit dem aktuellen Fehlerquadrat erzielt werden

$$V = \frac{V_{aktuell}}{V_{minimal}}$$

Überschreitet V ein vorgegebenes Maß, so liegt eine Parametervariation
vor.


## 5. Simulationsmodellanpassung

Wurde der Simulationsfehler anhand der Berechnung von V erkannt, so
kann der Korrekturvektor in Gl.(3) auf ein bestimmtes Maß hochgesetzt
werden, der eine geeignete Modellanpassung erlaubt. Dabei kann eine
Empfindlichkeitssteuerung des Korrekturvektors in Abhängigkeit von der
Größe V erfolgen. Die Richtung der Korrekturänderung wird mit Hilfe
des Least-Squares Verfahrens bestimmt. Sobald die Simulation wieder
mit dem Prozeßverhalten übereinstimmt, kann der Korrekturvektor zu
Null gesetzt werden. In der Praxis bedeutet dies, daß Simulationsfehler je nach Störungsart schon nach 10 Abtastungen erkannt und nach
weiteren 10 Werten behoben sein können.


<u>Literatur</u>


Astroem, K., Mayne, D.Q., A new algorithm for recursive estimation of
controlled ARMA processes, 6th IFAC-Symposium on "Identification and
System Parameter Estimation", Washington, 1982

# Ein universelles Optimierungsmodul zur Loesung von Entscheidungsproblemen in der Simulation


Karl-Josef Krechel-Mohr, Polch
Istvàn Molnàr, Budapest



**Zusammenfassung.** Der vorliegende Beitrag beschreibt die effiziente Verbindung von Simulationssystem und Optimierungssoftware zur Unterstützung automatisierter Entscheidungsvorbereitung. Im Vordergrund steht dabei die Auswahl eines universell einsetzbaren Algorithmus der nichtlinearen Optimierung und die Gestaltung des Optimierungsmoduls.


## 1. Die Integration eines Optimierungsmoduls in ein Simulationssystem

Eine große Anzahl von Entscheidungssituationen aus allen wirtschaftlichen und gesellschaftlichen Bereichen kann aufgrund ihrer Komplexität nur als Simulationsmodell beschrieben werden. Das Entscheidungsproblem besteht darin, die optimalen Entscheidungswerte eines Simulationsmodells, im Hinblick auf eine operational definierte Zielfunktion, zu finden, ohne die durch Restriktionen beschriebenen Grenzen zu verletzen.

Bei der Lösung von Entscheidungsproblemen mit Hilfe der digitalen Simulation ist man bestrebt, die optimalen Parameter des Modells automatisch, d.h. durch die Verknüpfung von Simulationsmodell und Optimierungsalgorithmus, zu bestimmen. Durch die Einbettung des Simulationssystems in eine übergeordnete Regelkreisstruktur (Optimierungsmodul) kann die Suche nach den optimalen Werten der Entscheidungsvariablen durch automatische Parametervariation erreicht werden.

Ausgehend von einer Anfangskonstellation der Entscheidungsvariablen $(z_1)$, die vom Benutzer vorzugeben ist, wird das Simulationsmodell berechnet und die Zielfunktion ausgewertet. Dabei kann der Wert der Zielfunktion insbesondere auch vom Output $(E_i)$ der Simulation abhängig sein. Der Zielfunktionswert $(F_i)$ wird an das Optimierungsmodul übergeben und dort analysiert. Solange das Abbruch- oder Zielkriterium der Optimierung nicht erreicht ist, wird eine neue Parametervariante $(z_i)$ mit Hilfe eines geeigneten Optimierungsalgorithmus generiert und an das Simulationssystem für das folgende Simulationsexperiment weitergegeben. Das Optimierungsmodul steuert in einem Iterationszyklus die Suche nach den optimalen Werten der Entscheidungsvariablen automatisch und benötigt dazu von "außen" lediglich die Vorgabe des Abbruchkriteriums und einer zulässigen Anfangskonstellation $(z_1)$.

Die Integration eines Optimierungsmoduls in ein Simulationssystem, mit dem Ziel der automatischen Parameteroptimierung, stellt, aufgrund der breiten Anwendungsmöglichkeiten der Simulation, hohe Anforderungen an die Optimierungssoftware.

Der Suchvorgang bei der Optimierung kann dabei im Allgemeinen nur durch Verfahren der nichtlinearen Optimierung gesteuert werden. Diese Algorithmen stellen somit eine unerläßliche Hilfe für einen Auswahl- oder Entscheidungsprozeß dar. Ihr Nachteil besteht darin, daß sie meist nur für eine spezielle Struktur des mathematischen Modells konstruiert sind.

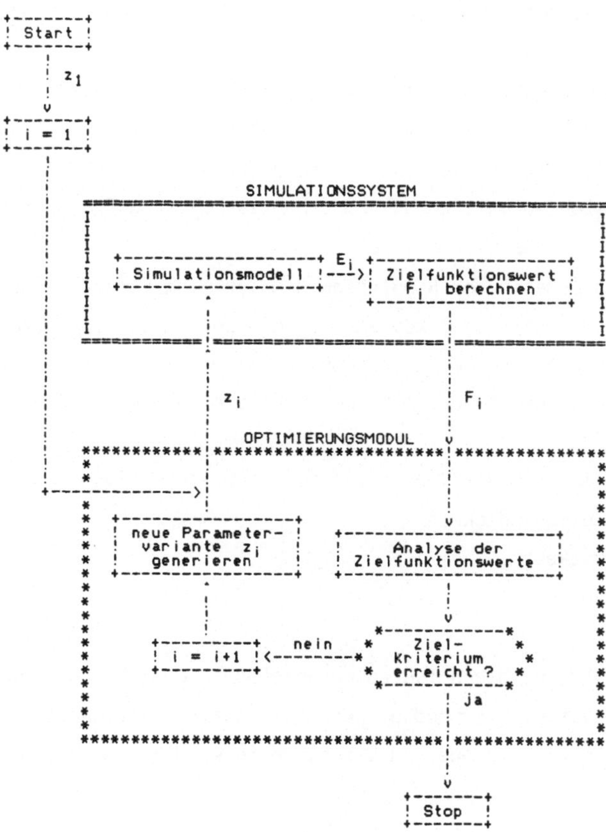


Bild 1: Kopplung von Simulationssystem und Optimierungsmodul

## 2. Auswahl der Komponenten des Optimierungsmoduls

Ein für die Simulation geeignetes universelles Optimierungsmodul sollte folgende Algorithmen beinhalten:

1. Ein <u>universelles Optimierungsverfahren</u>, das in der Lage ist, alle in der Simulation auftretenden Optimierungsprobleme mit vertretbarem Aufwand zu lösen.

2. Eine äquidistante Rasterstrategie (Faktorentwurf), mit der auf einem definierbaren, gleichmäßigen Gitternetz der Entscheidungsvariablen die Zielfunktion an den Knotenpunkten ausgewertet wird. Mit diesem Algorithmus soll auch eine Sensitivitätsanalyse in der Umgebung eines gefundenen Optimums möglich sein.

3. Spezielle Optimierungsverfahren, welche die Struktureigenschaften spezifischer,
   häufig in der Simulation auftretender Optimierungsprobleme berücksichtigen und
   deshalb besonders effizient (d.h. mit einer sehr geringen Anzahl von Simulationsläufen) arbeiten.

In der nichtlinearen Optimierung existiert eine riesige Anzahl von Optimierungsalgorithmen, die jeweils bei einem speziellen Typ der Zielfunktion anwendbar sind. Bei
der Optimierung in der Simulation ist der Typ bzw. die Struktur der Zielfunktion oft
nicht erkennbar, weil die Simulationsergebnisse (die in die Zielfunktion eingehen)
meist stochastische Variablen sind. Deshalb kann eine a priori Entscheidung für den
einen oder anderen Optimierungsalgorithmus, unter den Aspekten der Anwendbarkeit und
Effizienz, nur selten gefällt werden /5/. Man ist somit auf ein universell einsetzbares Optimierungsverfahren angewiesen.

Da Optimierungsprobleme in der Simulation hinsichtlich Struktur und Informationsge-
halt sehr verschiedenartig sein können, muß ein universell einsetzbarer Lösungsalgorithmus eine Vielzahl von Anforderungen erfüllen:

- Allgemeiner Anwendungsbereich, d.h. keine Einschränkung der Zielfunktion und der
  Restriktionen
- Hohe Wahrscheinlichkeit der Konvergenz zum globalen Optimum
- Hohe Konvergenzgeschwindigkeit
- Einfache Anwendbarkeit
- Wenig Steuerparameter

Optimierungsalgorithmen, die auf Gradientenmethoden oder Newton-Methoden basieren,
können niemals universell verwendbar sein. Sie setzen Stetigkeit und Differenzier-
barkeit der Zielfunktion voraus und benötigen meist die expliziten partiellen Ableitungen der Zielfunktion. Damit erfüllen sie nicht die Forderung nach allgemeiner
Anwendbarkeit und scheiden von vornherein aus.

Ein universell einsetzbares Optimierungsverfahren ist somit nur als direkte Such-
methode möglich. Unter den Suchmethoden bieten Zufallssuchverfahren die höchste
Wahrscheinlichkeit für globale Konvergenz, weil sie, im Gegensatz zu deterministischen Verfahren, nicht nur in der unmittelbaren Umgebung des Startpunktes Tastschrit-
te durchführen. Zufallsverfahren haben aber den schwerwiegenden Nachteil, daß sehr
viele Funktionswertberechnungen notwendig sind.

Deterministische Suchverfahren approximieren relativ schnell das nächstgelegene lokale Optimum zum Startpunkt. Die Forderung nach schneller lokaler Konvergenz führt aber
selten zum globalen Optimum.

Eine Mischung zwischen Zufallsstrategie und deterministischer Strategie kommt dem Bemühen, das globale Optimum zu finden und dem Wunsch nach schneller Konvergenz, entgegen.

Auf der Grundlage dieser Überlegungen bietet das Complex-Verfahren von Box /2/ folgende Vorteile:

- Partielle Ableitungen werden nicht benötigt
- Die Zielfunktion muß nicht explizit vorliegen
- Die Wahrscheinlichkeit für globale Konvergenz ist relativ hoch
- Beliebige konvexe Restriktionen werden berücksichtigt
- Robust gegen Funktionswertschwankungen und Rundungsfehler
- Relativ hohe Konvergenz in der Anfangsphase
- Mehrpunktverfahren
- Bietet viele Möglichkeiten der Modifikation

Einen Teil der Anforderungen, die an ein universelles Optimierungsverfahren gestellt werden, kann Complex-Box nicht erfüllen. Deshalb wurde der Algorithmus von Box durch geeignete Strategieerweiterungen modifiziert. Das hierzu entwickelte Programm (BOX-MOD) /4/ ermöglicht die Lösung beliebiger kontinuierlicher Optimierungsprobleme mit und ohne Restriktionen und kompensiert die in der Literatur oft angeführten Nachteile des Complex-Verfahrens. Die Variablen der Zielfunktion können bei BOX-MOD auch mittelbare Funktionen anderer Parameter sein oder von stochastischen Störungen überlagert werden, d.h. der Wert der Zielfunktion kann insbesondere auch vom Output der Simulation abhängig sein. Die Restriktionen dürfen bei BOX-MOD, im Gegensatz zu fast allen anderen Optimierungsalgorithmen, sogar konkav sein. Außerdem ist die heuristische Lösung diskreter bzw. gemischt-diskreter Optimierungsprobleme möglich.

Wie die empirischen Tests von BOX-MOD zeigen, ist das modifizierte Box-Verfahren ein leistungsfähiger Algorithmus, der durchaus als universell bezeichnet werden kann.


## 3. Beschreibung des Optimierungsmoduls

Das Optimierungsmodul (OPTMOD) wurde mit dem kombinierten Simulationssystem GASP IV /6/ gekoppelt und besteht aus vier Submodulen:
-Steuerroutine SIMRUN zur Bestimmung der Anzahl der Simulationsruns
-Routinen zur Parameteroptimierung (OPTALG, OPTAL1, ..., OPTALn)
-Eingaberoutinen (OPTINP, INPUT1, ..., INPUTn)
-Ausgaberoutinen (OPTOUT, OUTPU1, ..., OUTPUn)

OPTMOD steuert den Ablauf von Dateneingabe, Optimierungsalgorithmus und Ergebnisausgabe des Optimierungsmoduls.
SIMRUN bestimmt für jede Konstellation der Entscheidungsvariablen die Anzahl der Simulationsläufe und schätzt den Erwartungswert der Zielfunktion.
OPTALG ruft den Optimierungsalgorithmus Nummer i (OPTALi) auf.
OPTINP liest die allgemeinen Daten des Optimierungsmoduls ein und ruft die algorithmusspezifische Inputroutine Nummer i (INPUTi) auf.
OPTOUT ruft die algorithmusspezifische Ausgaberoutine Nummer i (OUTPUi) auf.

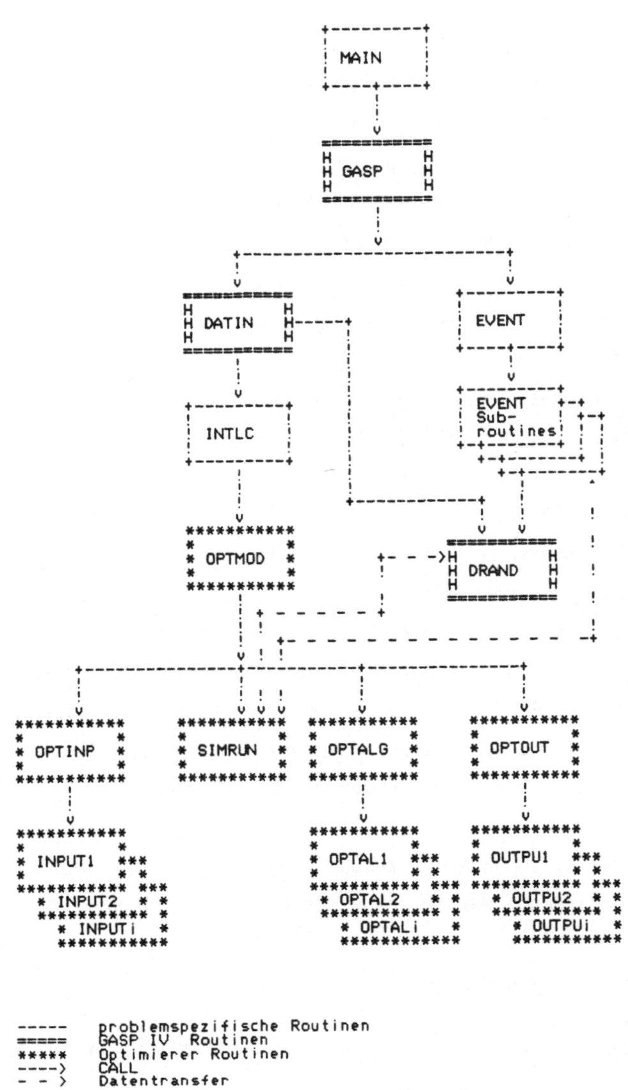

Bild 2: Beschreibung des Optimierungsmoduls und seine Kopplung an GASP IV

OPTINP wird nur einmal, nach dem ersten Aufruf von SUBROUTINE OPTMOD, ausgeführt.
OPTINP liest insbesondere die Nummer i des vom Benutzer gewünschten Algorithmus zur
Parameteroptimierung ein. Der Algorithmusnummer i sind die Eingaberoutine INPUTi, die
Optimierungsroutine OPTALi und die Ausgaberoutine OUTPUi zugeordnet. Dabei wird
OUTPUi nur einmal, vor dem letzten Simulationslauf, mit den optimalen Entscheidungs-
werten aufgerufen. Um die Computerkosten (Anzahl der Simulationsläufe) gering zu
halten, wird (bei Heteroskedastizität der Zielfunktionsergebnisse) die Anzahl der
Simulationsläufe von SIMRUN, für jede Parameterkonstellation, dynamisch bestimmt.

Zur Zeit sind im Optimierungsmodul zwei Algorithmen zur Parameteroptimierung imple-
mentiert:
- OPTAL1: Ein universelles Optimierungsverfahren = BOX-MOD
- OPTAL2: Eine äquidistante Rasterstrategie

Die algorithmusspezifischen Eingabe- bzw. Ausgaberoutinen dazu sind INPUT1, OUTPU1
bzw. INPUT2, OUTPU2.
Aufgrund der flexiblen Schnittstellendefinition ist die Integration weiterer Optimierungsalgorithmen, deren inneres Modell auf die spezifischen Struktureigenschaften
der Zielfunktion eingeht, unproblematisch durchzuführen. Dazu sind für den Algorithmus $i$ ( $i > 2$) die Routinen INPUTi, OPTALi und OUTPUi zu schreiben und OPTINP, OPTALG
und OPTOUT entsprechend zu ergänzen.

## 4. Ergebnisse

An zwei von Pritsker /6/ definierten Simulationsmodellen (Lagerhaltungsmodell, Modell der Tankerflotte) ist die entwickelte Optimierungssoftware getestet worden.
Hierzu sind die Ausgangsmodelle entsprechend den Modifikationen von Gately /3/ verändert worden. Die Testergebnisse übertreffen die Resultate vergleichbarer Veröffent-
lichungen und zeigen, daß durch die effiziente Verbindung von Simulationssoftware
und Optimierungssoftware die Anwendung automatisierter Entscheidungsvorbereitung in
der Simulation auf einem hohen Niveau möglich ist.


## Literatur

/1/ Azadivar F.; Optimization of Stochastic Systems Through Simulation Using
Stochastic Approximation Method; Dissertation, Purdue University, 1979

/2/ Box M.J.; A new method of constrained optimization and a comparsion with other
methods; Computer Journal, Vol. 8, 1965

/3/ Gately M.P.; Decision Optimization Module for the GASP IV Simulation Language;
PATRIOT Project Office Redstone Arsenal, AL35809, 1978

/4/ Krechel-Mohr K.-J.; Ein universelles Verfahren zur Lösung von Optimierungspro-
blemen; Studienarbeit, Technische Hochschule Darmstadt, 1984

/5/ Mandl C.E.; Simulationstechnik und Simulationsmodelle in den Sozial- und Wirt-
schaftswissenschaften; Lecture Notes in Economics and Mathematical Systems;
Springer Verlag, 1977

/6/ Pritsker A.A.B.; The GASP IV Simulations Language; John Wiley and Sons, New York, 1974

/7/ Schwefel H.-P.; Numerische Optimierung von Computer-Modellen mittels der Evolutionsstrategie, Basel und Stuttgart, 1977

/8/ Smith D.E.; Automatic optimum-seeking program for digital simulation; Simulation, July 1976, S. 27-31

DER EINFLUSS DES STATISTISCHEN MODELLS FÜR DEN MESSPROZESS

AUF DIE AUSWAHL DES VERFAHRENS DER PARAMETERSCHÄTZUNG


W. Renn, H.M. Frauer, R. Maulbetsch, M. Eggstein, Tübingen


Zusammenfassung. Mit Hilfe eines realistischen und allgemeinen Modells, für die bei Messungen an biologischen Systemen unausweichlich auftretenden Fehler, wird gezeigt, wie man Testdaten für die Validierung von Parameterschätzverfahren erzeugt. Parallel dazu werden mit Hilfe der Maximum Likelihood Methode die dem Fehlermodell entsprechenden Schätzer abgeleitet. Dazu werden zwei einfache Beispiele - ein lineares Modell, das den Methodenvergleich im klinisch-chemischen Laboratorium beschreibt, und ein nicht-lineares Modell für die Ligand Rezeptor Bindung - durchgerechnet. Einschränkungen des allgemeinen statistischen Modells, die zu den Methoden der kleinsten Quadrate und der gewichteten Regression führen, werden diskutiert, um die enge Beziehung zwischen dem statistischen Modell und dem verwendeten Schätzer aufzuzeigen.


Summary. Using a realistic and general model for the errors ocurring inevitably with measurements on biological systems, the generation of test-data for parameter estimation is demonstrated. In addition the estimator corresponding to the statistical model is derived by means of the maximum likelihood method. Two examples are presented: A linear model describing the comparison of methods in the clinical laboratory and a non-linear model for radioligand receptor binding. Simplifications of the general model leading to least squares and weighted regression estimation are discussed, to emphasize the tight connection between the statistical model and the estimator.


## 1. Einführung

Bei der systemtheoretischen Analyse experimentell gewonnener Daten werden oft sehr komplexe Modelle verwendet, um das zu analysierende System zu beschreiben. Für die bei der Gewinnung der Daten auftretenden Fehler begnügt man sich jedoch mit sehr einfachen statistischen Modellen. So nimmt man z.B. bei dem Regressionsmodell an, daß die unabhängige Variable ohne Fehler gemessen werden kann. Bei den Modellen der Korrelation und der Strukturrelation /1/, bei denen diese Annahme wegfällt, wird meist nur ein linearer Zusammenhang zwischen den Variablen untersucht. Außerdem wird bei all diesen Modellen eine Normalverteilung der Fehler und eine Proportionalität zwischen der Varianz der Meßfehler und der Varianz der Meßpunkte angenommen. Bei realistischen Meßreihen, besonders im Bereich der Biologie und Medizin, sind diese Voraussetzungen nur selten erfüllt. Um zu zeigen, daß man ein realistisches System auch ohne diese Einschränkungen analysieren kann, werden zwei einfache Modelle vorgestellt, bei denen das statistische Modell für den Meßprozeß und die dabei auftretenden Fehler im Vordergrund stehen. Dazu werden, ausgehend von einem allgemeinen Ansatz für die Fehlerquellen beim Versuchsablauf, die entsprechenden Testdaten als Zufallszahlen mit der zugehörigen Wahrscheinlichkeitsdichte generiert. Außerdem werden die den verschiedenen statistischen Modellen entsprechenden Maximum Likelihood Schätzer abgeleitet.


## 2. Ein lineares Modell

Im klinisch-chemischen Laboratorium wird der Vergleich von zwei Methoden, die den gleichen Laborparameter mit verschiedener Präzision und Richtigkeit messen, folgendermaßen durchgeführt: Man entnimmt den im Labor routinemäßig gemessenen Patientenproben eine zufällige Auswahl von Stichproben. Die einzelne Probe wird geteilt und auf den beiden zu vergleichenden Analysegeräten gemessen.

Um diesen Sachverhalt in einer Monte Carlo Simulation zur Erzeugung von Testdaten darzustellen, definieren wir die Zufallsvariablen (ZV) b1,b2 und b3 für die Fehler der Meßmethode X, die Fehler der Meßmethode Y und die "wahren" Werte des Laborparameters Z. Die dazugehörenden Wahrscheinlichkeitsdichten (WD) sind $f_{b1}$, $f_{b2}$ und $f_{b3}$. Als erstes werden Zufallszahlen erzeugt, die mit der WD $f_{b3}$ verteilt sind und der Verteilung eines Laborparameters im Patientenkollektiv der Klinik entsprechen. Aus der Praxis ist bekannt, daß diese Verteilung entweder normal ( bei den Elektrolyten und den meisten Substraten ) oder logarithmisch ( bei den Enzymen ) ist.

$$f_{b3} = \exp(-1/2(Z - \mu_z)^2 / \sigma_z^2) \ / \ \sqrt{2\pi} \ _z \qquad (2.1)$$

oder

$$f_{b3} = \exp(-1/2(\ln Z - \mu_z)^2 / \sigma_z^2) \ / \ \sqrt{2\pi} \, \sigma_z \cdot Z \qquad (2.2)$$

Die Generierung von normalverteilten Zufallszahlen geschieht bekanntlich durch die Summation von gleichverteilten Zufallszahlen. Logarithmisch verteilte Zahlen bekommt man am einfachsten, indem man normalverteilte Zahlen exponenziert.

Zu den so generierten Zufallszahlen werden nun weitere Zufallszahlen addiert, die mit $f_{b1}$ bzw. $f_{b2}$ verteilt sind. Dadurch erhält man die "Meßwerte" der Methode X bzw. Y, die sich aus der Überlagerung der statistisch verteilten "wahren Patientenwerte" Z und den Meßfehlern der beiden Methoden ergeben. Bei den Meßfehlern nehmen wir an, daß sie normalverteilt sind - analog wie (2.1) - mit

Mittelwerten und Standardabweichungen, die quadratische Funktionen des "wahren" Wertes Z sind.

$$\mu_x = m_x^0 + m_x^1 Z + m_x^2 Z^2 \tag{2.3}$$

$$\sigma_x^2 = s_x^0 + s_x^1 Z + s_x^2 Z^2 \tag{2.4}$$

Die obigen Gleichungen beinhalten das statistische Modell. Das funktionale Modell, das den Zusammenhang zwischen den nicht beobachtbaren Werten Z und den unverfälschten Meßwerten X bzw. Y beschreibt, soll linear sein :

$$X = \alpha_1 + \beta_1 Z \quad \text{und} \quad Y = \alpha_2 + \beta_2 Z \tag{2.5}$$

Mit dieser Vorgehensweise kann man Verteilungskurven von Laborparametern erzeugen, die von den tatsächlich gemessenen nicht zu unterscheiden sind. Den diesem Versuchsaufbau und Fehlermodell entsprechenden Maximum Likelihood Schätzer bekommt man folgendermaßen: Da die drei betrachteten ZV unabhängig sind, ergibt sich die gemeinsame WD aus dem Produkt der einzelnen WD.

$$f_{b1,b2,b3}(U,V,Z) = f_{b1}(U) * f_{b2}(V) * f_{b3}(Z) \tag{2.6}$$

Geht man nun über zu den meßbaren ZV, die sich aus der Summe von tatsächlichem Wert und Meßfehler ergeben,

$$a1 = X + b1 \quad \text{und} \quad a2 = Y + b2 \tag{2.7}$$

und eliminiert die nicht meßbare ZV b3 durch Übergang zur Marginalverteilung - d.h. Integration über Z - , so erhält man die bivariate Verteilung für die Meßpunkte $X_i$ und $Y_i$ :

$$f_{a1,a2}(U,V) = \int f_{b1}(U-X) * f_{b2}(V-Y) * f_{b3}(Z) \, dZ \tag{2.8}$$

Daraus berechnet man die Likelihood Funktion ( LF ) /2/ - d.h. die Wahrscheinlichkeit dafür, daß die Meßwerte durch (2.8) beschrieben werden - , indem man die Variablen U,V in (2.8) durch $X_i, Y_i$ ersetzt und das Produkt über alle Meßwertpaare N bildet. Diese Wahrscheinlichkeit soll maximal sein. Um die Analogie mit der Methode der kleinsten Quadrate zu erhalten, geht man noch zum negativen Logarithmus der LF über und erhält den Schätzer S :

$$S = - \sum_{i=1}^{N} \ln f_{a1,a2}(X_i, Y_i) \quad \text{mit} \quad S(\alpha, \beta, m, s) = \text{Min} \tag{2.9}$$

Aus dieser Minimimalbedingung erhält man Schätzungen für die unbekannten Parameter des statistischen und des funktionalen Modells - (2.3,4) und (2.5). Die numerische Anwendung der dargelegten Methode und insbesondere das Problem der Identifizierbarkeit der verwendeten Modellparameter wird in einer weiteren Arbeit untersucht /3/. Hier soll nur die Ableitung des Schätzers S aus dem statistischen Modell dargestellt werden.

### 3. Ein nicht-lineares Modell

Bei den üblichen Anwendungen nicht-linearer Modelle in Biologie und Medizin sind der Versuchsaufbau und die Fehlermöglichkeiten vom bisher untersuchten Modell folgendermaßen verschieden :

1. Man hat im einfachsten Fall nur zwei ZV, die unabhängige a1 und die abhängige a2. Um die Ableitung des Schätzers (2.9) übernehmen zu können, setzt man deshalb rein formal :

$$X = Z \quad \text{und} \quad f_{b3} = \delta (Z - X_i) \tag{3.1}$$

mit den fest vorgegebenen Sollmeßpunkten $X_i$. Beispiele dafür sind die Zeit bei pharmakokinetischen Experimenten oder Konzentrationen bei der Erstellung von Kalibrierungskurven.

2. Bei biologischen Experimenten weist die unabhängige Variable ebenfalls Fehler auf, die unter Umständen die Meßfehler der abhängigen ZV a2 sogar übersteigen können. Diese fehlerhaften Werte sind jedoch nicht meßbar. Man kennt im allgemeinen nur die Sollmeßpunkte, aber nicht die durch die Schwierigkeit des Experimentes bedingten Abweichungen davon. Man ist deshalb gezwungen, anstelle der bivariaten WD (2.8), eine univariate Marginalverteilung zu verwenden, die aus (2.8) durch Integration über U entsteht.

3. Die fehlerfreie, abhängige Variable Y ist eine nicht-lineare Funktion G der ZV a1, sodaß man zwischen a2 und a1 folgenden Zusammenhang bekommt :

$$a2 = G(a1) + b2 \tag{3.2}$$

Berücksichtigt man die Punkte 1. - 3., so erhält man nach (2.1 - 9) :

$$S = - \sum_{i=1}^{N} \ln \int f_{b1}(U-X_i) * f_{b2}(Y_i - G(U)) \, dU \tag{3.3}$$

Dies ist der Ausdruck des Maximum Likelihood Schätzers für den allgemeinsten Fall mit beliebigen Verteilungen der Fehler.

Dazu betrachten wir folgendes Beispiel: Bei der Bestimmung von Insulinrezeptoren an Erythrozyten wird das Insulin radioaktiv markiert und mit den Konzentrationen $X_i$ den verschiedenen Proben zugegeben. Anschließend wird die Aktivität des gebundenen Insulins $Y_i$ gemessen. Verwendet man das einfache Clark Modell /4/, so ergibt sich :

$$Y = G(U) \quad \text{mit} \quad G(U) = R * U / ( K + U ) \tag{3.4}$$

Hierbei ist R die Kapazität und 1/K die Affinität des Rezeptors. Wir nehmen nun an, daß die Fehler bei der Präparation der Erythrozytenproben und deren radioaktiver Markierung normal verteilt sind mit einer Streuung, die proportional zu den Konzentrationen ist, d.h. $\sigma_x = S_x * X_i$. Die Messwerte der Radioaktivität des gebundenen Insulins besitzen eine Poissonsche Verteilung :

$$f_{b2}(Y_i,Y) = (Y/Y_i)^{Y_i} * \exp(-(Y-Y_i)) / \sqrt{2\pi Y_i} \tag{3.5}$$

wobei die Fakultät durch die Stirlingsche Formel ausgedrückt wurde.

Die Generierung von Testdaten, die dem statistischen Modell entsprechen, ist damit festgelegt. Zunächst werden die normalverteilten Werte von a1 generiert und damit die "exakten" Y - Werte mit der Modellgleichung (3.4) berechnet. Diese definieren die Poisson Verteilung (3.5), mit der dann Zufallszahlen erzeugt werden, die den gemessenen Werten $Y_i$ entsprechen. Dazu wurde die Methode von Marsaglia, wie sie in /5/ dargestellt ist, verwendet.

Die Auswertung von (3.3) benötigt sehr viel Rechenzeit, da bei der Parameterschätzung für jeden Parametersatz und jeden Term in der Summe ein Integral ausgewertet werden muß. Durch die folgende Näherung vereinfacht sich der Rechenaufwand : Zunächst geht man in (3.3) von der Integrationsvariablen U zu Y über. Wenn nun die Fehler der X - Werte groß gegenüber den Fehlern der Y - Werte sind, so kann man sämtliche Terme mit Ausnahme von $f_{b2}$ aus dem Integral an der Stelle $Y = Y_i$ herausziehen.

$$\tag{3.6}$$
$$S = \sum ((KY_i/(R-Y_i) - X_i)^2/2S_x^2 X_i^2 - \ln(KR/(R-Y_i)^2)) + N\ln S_x$$

Hierbei wurde der konstante Term $\sum \ln\sqrt{2\pi}\, X_i$ weggelassen, da er bei der Schätzung der unbekannten Parameter R, K, $S_x$ durch die Minimalisierung von S (3.6) wegfällt. Bei der Ableitung von (3.6) wurde die Normierung der WD verwendet. Durch Verlängern der Zählrate kann man im Prinzip immer erreichen, daß die obige Annahme erfüllt ist.

## 4. Vergleich mit anderen Schätzverfahren

Wie in der Einleitung dargelegt, werden bei den üblichen Schätzverfahren die Fehler der unabhängigen Variablen vernachlässigt. Angewandt auf den oben abgeleiteten allgemeinen Schätzer (3.3), bedeutet dies, daß man die WD $f_{b2}$ an der Stelle $U=X_i$ aus dem Integral ziehen kann. Da $f_{b1}$ normiert ist, bekommt man dann für den Maximum Likelihood Schätzer einer ZV, die Poisson verteilt ist, folgenden Ausdruck:

$$S = - \sum ( \ln(G(X_i)/Y_i) - (G((X_i)-Y_i) ) \qquad (3.7)$$

Hier wurde analog zu (3.6) der konstante Term $\sum \sqrt{2\pi Y_i}$ unterdrückt.

Entwickelt man nun das Argument des Logarithmus in (3.7) nach dem relativen Fehler $(G(X_i)-Y_i)/Y_i$ bis zum quadratischen Glied und vernachlässigt die Terme höherer Ordnung, was bei genügend hohen Zählraten eine sehr gute Näherung ergibt, so geht die Poisson Verteilung in eine Gauß Verteilung über und man erhält den entsprechenden Markov Schätzer :

$$\qquad (3.8)$$
$$S = \sum (Y_i - G(X_i))^2/\sigma_y^2 \quad \text{mit} \quad \sigma_y^2 = S_y^2 \cdot Y_i$$

Die Schätzung der Parameter durch Minimalisierung von (3.8) entspricht der nicht-linearen, gewichteten Regression. Der Parameter $S_y$ kann durch

$$S_y^2 = \sum (Y_i - G(X_i)^2/Y_i \, df \qquad (3.9)$$

biasfrei geschätzt werden, wobei df die Anzahl der Freiheitsgrade ( Anzahl der Meßpunkte - Anzahl der Parameter ) ist. Ergibt sich dabei $S_y=1$, so weiß man, daß das statistische Modell exakt gilt. In der Praxis bekommt man jedoch $S_y \neq 1$. Dies muß jedoch nicht bedeuten, daß keine Poisson Verteilung vorliegt, sondern die Ursache dafür sind, nach unserer Erfahrung, die vernachlässigten Fehler der X - Werte. Falls $S_y$ wesentlich größer als 1 ist, erhält man mit dem neu abgeleiteten Schätzer (3.6) bessere Schätzungen für R und K, wie man mit Hilfe der Testdaten zeigen kann.

Vernachlässigt man noch die Abhängigkeit $\sigma_y$ von $Y_i$ und behandelt $\sigma_y$ als Konstante, so erhält man aus (3.8) den least squares Schätzer, der bei den meisten Arbeiten über Rezeptor Ligand Bindungen benützt wird.

$$S = \sum (Y_i - G(X_i))^2 \tag{3.10}$$

Auch bei der Behandlung anderer Probleme im Bereich der Biologie und Medizin wird dieser Schätzer verwendet, ohne eine eingehende Prüfung der entsprechenden Voraussetzungen. In der obigen Ableitung ist aufgezeigt, welche Näherungen angenommen oder welche Voraussetzungen erfüllt sein müssen, damit man die Methode der kleinsten Quadrate anwenden darf.

Das Ziel der vorliegenden Arbeit ist darzulegen, wie man spezielle Schätzer ableiten kann, die der Fehlerstatistik des untersuchten Experiments genau entsprechen. Solche Methoden sind vor allem dann anzuwenden, wenn es um höchste Genauigkeit geht und wenn die tatsächliche Fehlerverteilung wesentlich ist. Ein Beispiel dafür ist die Erstellung von nicht-linearen Kalibrierungskurven im medizinischen Laboratorium, wie sie bei der Durchführung von Radio- oder Enzymimmunoassays notwendig sind /6/. Jeder Fehler bei der Parameterschätzung überträgt sich auf die mit der Kalibrierung berechneten Patientenwerte. Außerdem wird gezeigt, wie man Testdaten erzeugt, die dem statistischen Modell entsprechen. Damit kann man dann das verwendete Parameterschätzverfahren und Optimierungsprogramm testen. Daneben kann man durch Generieren geeigneter Zufallszahlen den Einfluß der Sollmeßpunkte $X_i$ auf die Schätzung der Parameter untersuchen, was zu einer Verbesserung der Versuchsplanung führt.

## 5. Literatur


/1/ Haekel,R.B.,Schneider,B.,(1980): Statistische Modelle und Verfahren beim Vergleich von Analysenmethoden, GIT Labor-Medizin 3,97 - 104 .

/2/ Van der Waerden,B.L.,(1965): Mathematische Statistik, Springer Verlag.

/3/ Renn,W., et al.,(1985): Ein allgemeines statistisches Modell für den Vergleich von Analysenmethoden, ( In Vorbereitung ).

/4/ Boeynaems,J.M.,Dumont,J.E.,(1980): Outlines of Receptor Theory, Elsevier / North-Holland Biomedical Press.

/5/ Abramowitz,M.,et al.(1965): Handbook of Mathematical Functions, Dover Publication, Inc. New York.

/6/ Renn, W., et al.,(1985): Die umfassende EDV-Unterstützung für das Radio-Immunologische-Laboratorium, in Medizin-Technik'85, Biomedizinische Technik ( Ergänzungsband ).

# Neuere Verfahren zur Parameteridentifizierung dargestellt am Beispiel der Modellierung von Rübenwachstum

Johannes Schlöder, Annette Conrads und Tobias Frank, Bonn

Zusammenfassung: Effiziente numerische Verfahren zur Identifizierung von Parametern in Systemen nichtlinearer gewöhnlicher Differentialgleichungen werden vorgestellt. Die adäquate Formulierung dieser inversen Probleme führt auf komplexe überbestimmte Mehrpunktrandwertprobleme. Ihre Diskretisierung mit einem Mehrzielverfahren ergibt hochdimensionale beschränkte Ausgleichsprobleme, die mit einem verallgemeinerten Gauss-Newton-Verfahren gelöst werden. Eigenschaften dieser Vorgehensweise und ihrer Realisierung im Programmpaket PARFIT werden besprochen. Als Anwendungsproblem wird die Identifizierung eines Modells für das Wachstum von Rüben behandelt.

Summary: Efficient numerical methods for parameter identification in non-linear o. d. e. are presented. The adequate formulation of these inverse problems leads to complex overdetermined multipoint boundary value problems. Their discretisation with a multiple shooting method yields large scale constrained non-linear least-squares-problems, which are solved by a generalised Gauss-Newton method. Some properties of this procedure and its realisation in the PARFIT algorithm are discussed. As practical application the identification of a model for the growth of sugar-beets is treated.

## 1.0  Parameteridentifizierungsprobleme

Bei PI-Problemen sind Parameter p in einem i.a. nichtlinearen System gewöhnlicher Differentialgleichungen zu bestimmen.

$$\dot{y}(t) = f(t,y(t,p),p) \tag{1}$$

Dieses System dient als Modell für einen Prozess, von dem Beobachungen in Form von Funktionen der Prozessvariablen y und der Parameter zu Zeitpunkten $t_j$ vorliegen.

$$n_{ij} = g_{ij}(t_j,y(t_j),p) + \varepsilon_{ij} \tag{2}$$

Unter der Annahme, daß die Messfehler $\varepsilon_{ij}$ statistisch unabhängig sind und einer Normalverteilung $N(0,\sigma_{ij}^2)$ genügen, liefert die Minimierung des Zielfunktionals

$$J(p,y) = \|r_1(y(t_1),\ldots,y(t_k),p)\|_2^2 := \sum_{i,j} \sigma_{ij}^{-2}(n_{ij} - g_{ij}(t_j,y(t_j),p))^2 \tag{3}$$

eine Maximum-Likelihood-Schätzung

Weitere fehlerfrei vorgegebene Modelleigenschaften können als Gleichungsbeschränkungen

$$r_2(y(t_1),\ldots,y(t_k),p) = 0 \tag{4}$$

oder auch Ungleichungsbeschränkungen berücksichtigt werden.

Als Beispiel betrachten wir

## 1.1  Ein Modell für das Wachstum von Rüben [3]

Zur Beschreibung der Dynamik der Masse von Rübenkörper R und Rübenblatt B werden
modifizierte Verhulstgleichungen zugrunde gelegt.

$$\dot{R}(t) = r_R \cdot B(t) \cdot (1 - R(t)/K_R) \tag{5}$$

$$\dot{B}(t) = r(\alpha,\beta,T) \cdot \varphi(B_{MAX},BF) \cdot B(t) \cdot (1-B(t)/K_B) - r_A \cdot B(t)$$

Werte für den Temperaturverlauf T und die Bodenfeuchte BF liegen tabelliert vor. Die
sieben Parameter $r_R$, $K_R$, $\alpha$, $\beta$, $B_{MAX}$, $K_B$ und $r_A$ sowie zwei Anfangswerte $R_{START}$ und
$B_{START}$ sollen so bestimmt werden, daß 32 im Jahr 1979 gemessene Daten der Rübenkörper-
und Rübenblattmasse möglichst gut approximiert werden.


## 2.0  Mehrzielverfahren

Zur Lösung der obigen Klasse von PI-Problemen haben sich die von Bock [1] entwickelten
*Randwertproblemmethoden*, insbesondere ein im Programmpaket PARFIT realisiertes Mehr-
zielverfahren als sehr effizient erwiesen.
Die Idee des Mehrzielverfahrens besteht darin, über einem geeignet gewählten Gitter

$$\tau_1 < \tau_2 < \ldots < \tau_m \tag{6}$$

- z.B. einer Teilmenge der Beobachtungspunkte - Lösungen $(t;s_j,p)$ von m-1 unabhängigen
Anfangswertproblemen zu berechnen.

$$\dot{y}(t) = f(t,y(t,p),p) \quad y(\tau_j) = s_j \quad t \in [\tau_j,\tau_{j+1}] \tag{7}$$

Man erhält eine unstetige, von den zusätzlich eingeführten Variablen $s_j$ abhängige
Lösungstrajektorie.


Abb. 1  Starttrajektorie für das Rübenproblem

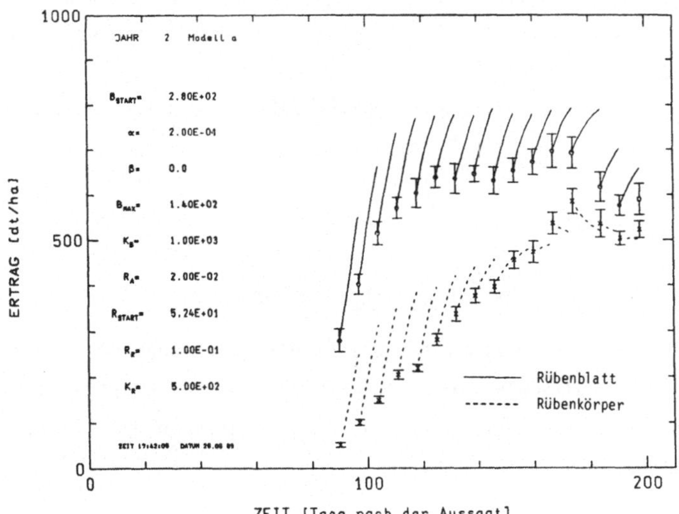

Durch diese Parametrisierung hat man eine Umformulierung des PI-Problems in ein *großes beschränktes nichtlineares Ausgleichsproblem* in den Variablen $(s_1,\ldots,s_m,p)$ erreicht.

BAP:
$$\| R_1(s_1,\ldots,s_m,p)\|_2^2 = \min \tag{8}$$

unter den Bedingungen

$$R_2(s_1,\ldots,s_m,p) = 0 \tag{9}$$

und den Anschlußbedingungen zur Gewährleistung der Stetigkeit der Lösung

$$h_j(s_{j+1},s_j,p):=y(\tau_{j+1};s_j,p)-s_{j+1} =0 \quad j =1,\ldots,m-1 \tag{10}$$

Der entscheidende Vorteil dieser Formulierung liegt darin, daß die in den Beobachtungsdaten enthaltene Information über die Lösung durch die Startschätzung für die Variablen
$s_j$ in das Verfahren eingebracht werden kann.

*Dies macht das Verfahren weitestgehend unabhängig von schlechten Startschätzungen
für die Parameter.*

Außerdem können mit diesem Ansatz PI-Probleme gelöst werden, die als Anfangswertproblem instabil sind.
Zur Lösung des Problems BAP eignen sich


## 2.1  Verallgemeinerte Gauss Newton (VGN) Verfahren

In jedem Schritt dieses Iterationsverfahrens wird das Problem BAP linearisiert und eine
gegebene Näherung $x_k$ der Lösung durch die Lösung $x_k$ des linearisierten Problems
verbessert.

$$x_{k+1} = x_k + \lambda_k \Delta x_k$$

Der Dämpfungsfaktor $0 < \varepsilon \le \lambda_k \le 1$ sorgt für globale Konvergenz. Lokal ist die *Konvergenz* linear mit einem Konvergenzfaktor, der von der Kompatibilität des Modells mit
den Daten abhängt. Bei guter Kompatibilität konvergiert das Verfahren *im wesentlichen
wie ein Verfahren zweiter Ordnung.*
Praktisch wichtig ist, daß das Vollschritt-VGN-Verfahren *nur gegen statistisch signifikante Minima* konvergiert.


## 3.0  Eigenschaften von PARFIT

## 3.1  Auswertung der Verfahrensfunktion und ihrer Ableitungen

Im Verlauf des VGN-Verfahrens müssen immer wieder die Funktionen $R_1$ (8), $R_2$ (9) und
die Anschlußbedingungen (10) sowie die Jacobimatrizen  dieser Funktionen ausgewertet
werden. Der wesentliche Aufwand dabei ist, die Anfangswertprobleme (7) zu lösen und
die Lösung $y(t;s_j,p)$ nach $(s_j,p)$ abzuleiten.

Zur Behandlung der *Anfangswertaufgaben* stehen mehrere leistungsfähige *numerische Integratoren* zur Verfügung, von denen entsprechend den Eigenschaften des aktuellen Problems (z.B. steif oder nichtsteif, Anzahl der Unstetigkeiten, Anzahl der Beobachtungspunkte) der geeignete ausgewählt werden kann.

Fehlerhafte Jacobimatrizen führen in einem VGN-Verfahren nicht nur zur Verschlechterung der Konvergenz sondern auch zu falschen Ergebnissen. Daher werden in PARFIT die erforderlichen *Jacobimatrizen automatisch* durch sog. *interne numerische Differentiation* schnell und zuverlässig erzeugt. Dies entlastet den Benutzer von mühsamer analytischer Vorarbeit und vermeidet die bei komplexen realistischen Problemen leicht auftretenden Programmierfehler.

## 3.2 Singuläre Probleme

Bei der Behandlung von PI- Problemen - vor allem in der Anfangsphase der Modellierung eines Prozesses - kann es vorkommen, daß Parameter nicht oder nur schlecht durch die Beobachtungsdaten bestimmt sind. Dies führt dazu, daß die Jacobimatrix des VGN-Verfahrens singulär bzw. fast singulär wird. Die Lösung des linearen Problems ist nicht eindeutig. In diesem Fall wird im PARFIT automatisch eine *Regularisierung* vorgenommen. Das VGN-Verfahren konvergiert gegen ein reduziertes Modell. Die Analyse der Jacobimatrix im Lösungspunkt gibt Hinweise darauf, wie das Modell zu ändern ist bzw. welche zusätzlichen Daten erforderlich sind.

## 3.3 Statistische Analyse

Mit der Lösung des Approximationsproblems BAP ist die Lösung des PI-Problems noch unvollständig. Man benötigt auch statistische Kriterien zur Beurteilung der Güte der Parameterschätzung und - vor allem, wenn das Modell für *Prognosen* eingesetzt werden soll - der Güte der Lösungstrajektorie. Im Fall des VGN-Verfahrens erweist sich diese statistische Analyse als besonders einfach. Aus der im letzten Schritt des Verfahrens erzeugten Jacobimatrix läßt sich leicht eine Approximation der *Kovarianz–Matrix* für die Parameter und Werte der Lösungstrajektorie berechnen.

## 4. Numerische Ergebnisse

Mit PARFIT wird die Lösung des Rübenwachstumsmodells nach 12 Iterationen mit einer Genauigkeit von $10^{-3}$ erreicht.

Während die Beobachtungsdaten offensichtlich gut approximiert sind, zeigen die Schätzungen der Standardfehler allerdings, daß einige Parameter durch die Daten nur schlecht bestimmt sind. Daher sind weitere Modellierungsarbeiten erforderlich. Hierzu sollen auch Daten aus anderen Jahren für ein Mehrfachexperimentproblem [2] herangezogen werden. Darüber wird an anderer Stelle zu berichten sein.

Abb. 2  Lösung

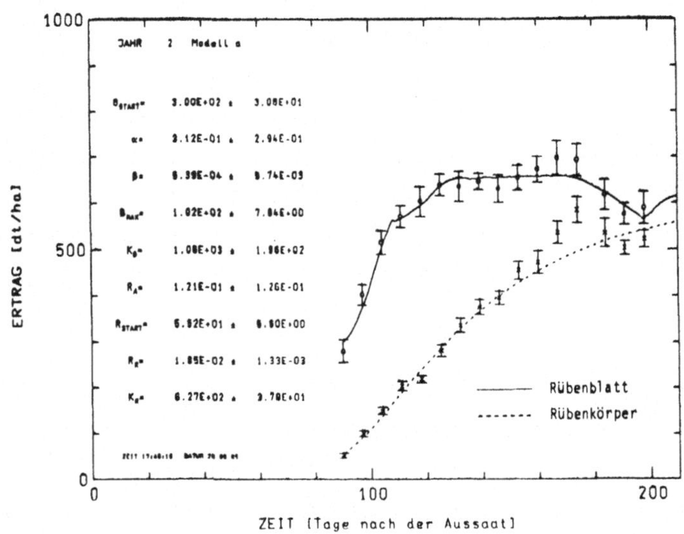


Die Autoren danken Herrn Dipl.-Ing. agr. Thoer für die Überlassung des Rübenwachstumsmodells einschließlich aller erforderlichen Daten. Herrn Prof. Dr. Richter und Herrn
Prof. Dr. Steffen sei für Diskussionen gedankt.
Diese Arbeit ist mit Unterstützung des von der Deutschen Forschungsgemeinschaft
getragenen Sonderforschungsbereiches 72 entstanden.

## Literatur

1  Bock, H.G.:  Recent Advances in Parameteridentification Techniques for O.D.E.
               in: Numerical Treatment of Inverse Problems in Differential and Integral
               Equations; Deuflhard, Hairer (eds) Boston 1983

2  Schlöder,J.; Bock H.G.: Identification of Rate Constants in Bistable Chemical Reac-
               tions  in: Numerical Treatment of Inverse Problems in Differential and
               Equations; Deuflhard, Hairer (eds) Boston 1983

3  Thoer, K.:  Betriebswirtschaftliche Untersuchungen zur Verbesserung des Schadschwel-
               lenkonzeptes zur Beurteilung der Unkrautbekämpfung im  Zuckerrübenan-
               bau mit Hilfe eines Simulationsmodells, Dissertation, Bonn 1985

# SIMULATION IN

# BIOLOGIE UND MEDIZIN

Simulation von Ökosystemen
O. Richter, Institut für Landwirtschaftliche Betriebslehre
der Universität Bonn, Abt. für Angewandte Statistik und Mathematik

## 1. Allgemeine Formulierung der Massenbilanzgleichungen

In einem Ökosystem fließt Biomasse und damit Energie in Form von ener-
giereichen organischen Verbindungen von den Primärproduzenten über die
Herbivoren zu den Karnivoren und von dort letztlich zu den Destruenten,
wobei der Wirkungsgrad der Energieumwandlung von Ebene zu Ebene abnimmt.
Eine trophische Ebene in einem Ökosystem ist durch ihre Position innerhalb dieser Hierarchie gekennzeichnet. Abb. 1 zeigt das Blockbild eines
minimalen Ökosystems mit den Komponenten Primärproduzent (PP), Herbivor
(H), Karnivor (K), Destruenten (D) und Nährstoffen (N).

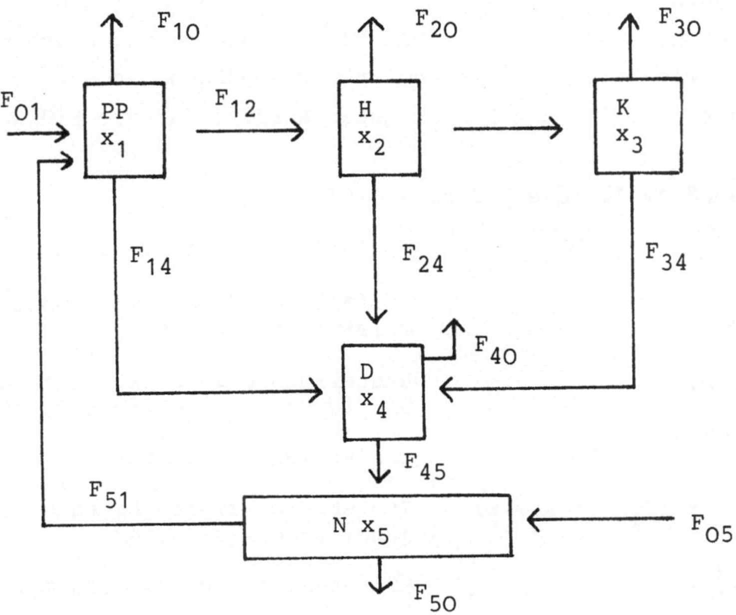


Ökosystemmodelle können als Massenbilanzgleichungen für die Biomassen
in Form von Differentialgleichungen dargestellt werden. Es gelten die
folgenden Bezeichnungen:

$x_i$ :   Biomasse der i-ten trophischen Ebene
$F_{ij}$:   Biomassefluß von der i-ten zur j-ten Ebene
$F_{io}$:   Biomassefluß in die Umgebung, z. B. Verlust von $CO_2$ durch
          Respiration

$F_{0i}$:    Zufluß von der Umgebung in das System (z. B. Mobilisierung von Nährstoffen)

$\mu$  :   Zerfallskonstante (Sterberate)

$\rho$  :   Respirationsrate

Für das in Abb. 1 dargestellte System erhält man formal die Massenbilanzgleichungen:

$$\dot{x}_1 = F_{01} - F_{12} - F_{10} - F_{14} + F_{51} \tag{1}$$

$$\dot{x}_2 = F_{12} - F_{20} - F_{23} - F_{24} \tag{2}$$

$$\dot{x}_3 = F_{23} - F_{30} - F_{34} \tag{3}$$

$$\dot{x}_4 = F_{14} + F_{24} + F_{34} - F_{40} - F_{45} \tag{4}$$

$$\dot{x}_5 = F_{05} - F_{50} - F_{51} \tag{5}$$

Bis auf einfache Zerfallsreaktionen sind die Flüsse $F_{ij}$ nichtlineare Funktionen der Systemkomponenten und können außerdem noch von äußeren Einflußgrößen wie Strahlung und Temperatur abhängen. In der folgenden Tabelle sind einige der gebräuchlichsten Ansätze für die Flüsse dargestellt.

Tabelle 1: Ansätze für die Flüsse

| Fluß | Biologische Interpretation |
|---|---|
| $k_{ij} \, x_i$ | Zerfall von Organismen, monomolekulare Reaktion |
| $k_{ij} \, x_i \, x_j$ | Räuber-Beute Interaktion ohne Sättigung, bimolekulare Reaktion |
| $r \, x_i \, (1 - x_i / K)$ | logistisches Wachstum |
| $r \, x_i \, (1 - (x_i + \alpha \, x_j)/K)$ | Kompetition zweier Arten um eine gemeinsame Ressource |
| $\beta \, x_i \, x_j^a / (x_j^a + L)$ | Räuber-Beute Interaktion mit Sättigung |
| $\dfrac{p_{max} \, (T)}{k} \ln\left[\dfrac{K + I\,(t)}{K + I\,(t)\, e^{-k\,A}}\right] - \rho\, A$ | Primärproduktion von Biomasse als Funktion der Temperatur T, der Einstrahlung I und des Blattflächenindex A (n. Richter 1985). K: Halbsättigungskonstante der Lichtabhängigkeitsfunktion k: Absorptionskonstante des Blätterdaches $p_{max}$ (T): maximale Biomasseproduktionsrate |

## 2. Dynamisches Verhalten nichtlinearer Systeme

Im Gegensatz zu technischen Systemen, die in Hinblick darauf konstruiert sind, in der Nähe des Arbeitspunktes linear zu reagieren, sind
die Nichtlinearitäten in Ökosystemen wesentlich. Die Nichtlinearitäten
bewirken ein komplexes dynamisches Verhalten selbst bei Systemen mit
nur wenigen Komponenten. Obwohl es bei der verfügbaren Computerkapa-
zität keine besonderen Schwierigkeiten bereitet, auch sehr große Systeme zu simulieren, d. h. durch numerische Lösungen für bestimmte Para-
metersätze das dynamische Verhalten zu explorieren, kann auf die mathematische Analyse kleiner Systeme nicht verzichtet werden: sie liefern
Einsichten in allgemeine Eigenschaften nichtlinearer dynamischer Systeme, die durch die Simulation allein prinzipiell nicht zu erhalten sind.
Als Beispiel wird die einfache Situation der Beweidung eines Graslan-
des durch einen festgehaltenen Huftierbestand betrachtet, die sich durch
eine nichtlineare Differentialgleichung beschreiben läßt:

$$\dot{x} = rx \, (1 - x/K) - \text{ß}Hx^a \, / \, (x^a + L) \qquad\qquad (6)$$

Bezeichnungen:

K: maximale Biomasse (Kapazität)

r: Wachstumsrate

ß: maximaler Konsum pro Herbivor

L: Halbsättigungskonstante

H: Huftierbestand

Der 1. Term beschreibt das logistische Wachstum der Vegetation, der 2.
Term die Verlustrate durch die Herbivoren der Dichte H, wobei Sätti-
gungsverhalten angenommen wird: die Aufnahmerate pro Herbivor als Funktion der Nahrung x ist beschränkt.
Für $a = 2$ besitzt das System in einem Intervall $I = (H_1, H_2)$ drei von
Null verschiedene Lösungen. Die Stabilitätsanalyse zeigt: die obere
Lösung und die untere Lösung sind stabil, die mittlere Lösung ist instabil (s. Abb. 2). Die instabile Lösung trennt die Attraktionsbereiche
der stabilen Lösungen. Das bedeutet: das System kann im Intervall I in
zwei stabilen Zuständen hoher und niedriger Primärproduzentendichte
existieren. Wenn das System sich im Zustand hoher Dichte befindet, kann
es diesen Zustand nur verlassen, wenn eine Störung den Trennpunkt der
Attraktionsbereiche überschreitet. Mit wachsender Herbivorendichte,
d. h. mit wachsender Belastung, wird der Attraktionsbereich der oberen
Lösung immer kleiner, das System wird immer verwundbarer gegenüber
Störungen. Ab $H_2$ existiert nur noch der Zustand geringer Dichte.

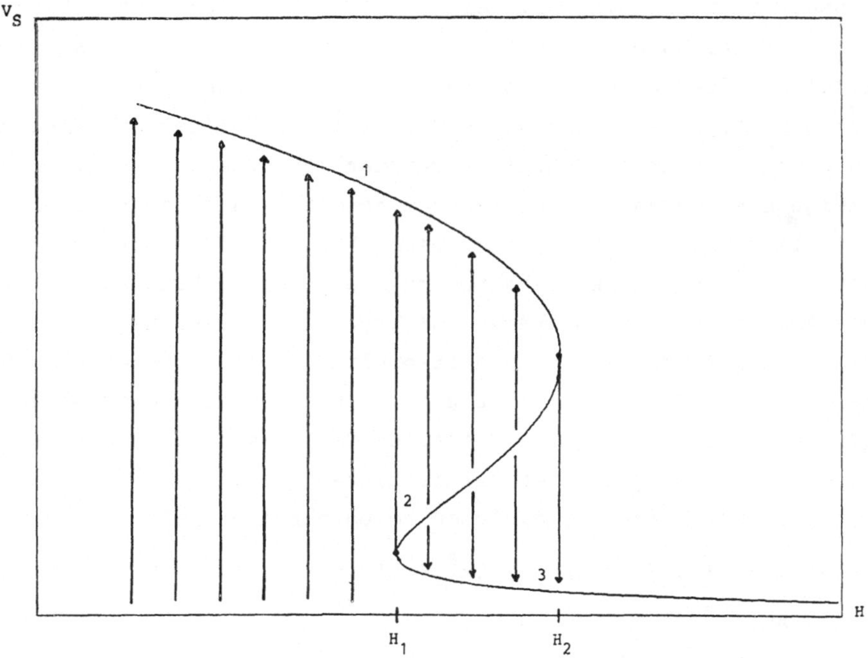



Abb. 2: Stationäre Vegetationsgröße als Funktion des Bestandes.
Zwischen den beiden kritischen Bestandesdichten $H_1$ und $H_2$
existieren drei von Null verschiedene stationäre Zustände.
Die Pfeile verdeutlichen die Attraktionsbereiche der stabilen
Lösungen.

Überläßt man das System sich selbst, dann benötigt man eine weitere
Differentialgleichung für die Herbivoren, die nun mit $x_2$ bezeichnet
werden:

$$\dot{x}_1 = rx_1 \left(1 - \frac{x_1}{K}\right) - \frac{\beta x_1 x_2}{x_1 + L} \tag{7}$$

$$\dot{x}_2 = x_2 \left(\frac{\gamma x_1 x_2}{x_1 + L} - \mu\right) \tag{8}$$

Die Stabilitätsanalyse für den Fall a = 1 zeigt, daß der stationäre Zu-
stand $x_{1s} > 0$, $x_{2s} > 0$ stabil ist, wenn die Bedingung $K < L \frac{\gamma + \mu}{\gamma - \mu}$
erfüllt ist. Die Anwendung des Satzes von Kolmogoroff (May 1974) zeigt,
daß das System im Falle der Instabilität einen Grenzzyklus besitzt.
Abb. 3 zeigt die Bewegung des Systems im Phasenraum: unabhängig vom
Startwert münden alle Trajektorien asymptotisch in den Grenzzyklus ein:
das System vollführt stabile nichtlineare Oszillationen.

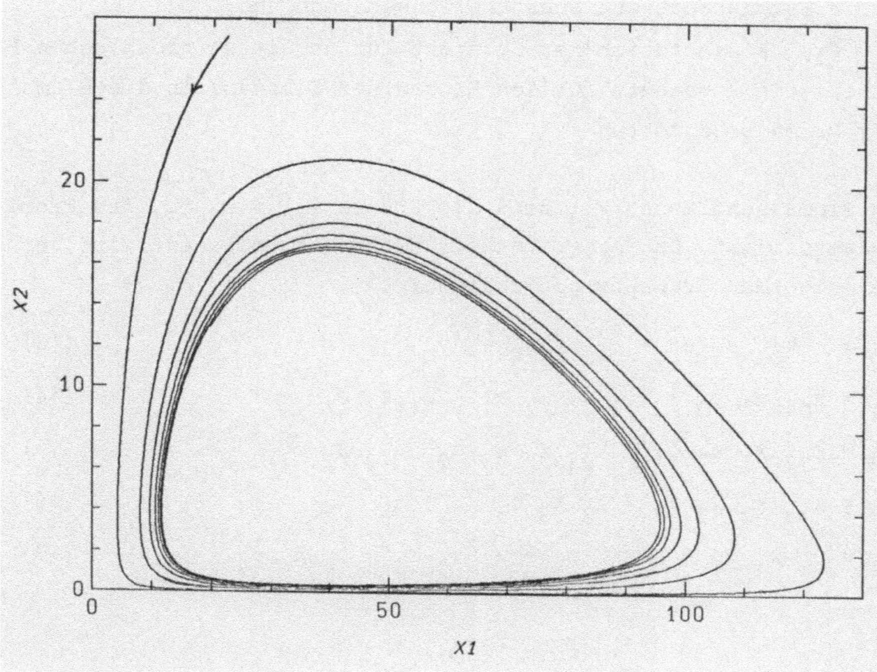


Abb. 3: Grenzzyklus in einem Räuber-Beute-System

## 3. Ein Simulationsmodell für den Transport von Fremdstoffen durch die Nahrungsketten

Das folgende Modell ist in Spain (1984) beschrieben. Zugrunde gelegt wird das minimale Ökosystem der Abb. 1. Der Massenfluß zwischen zwei trophischen Ebenen durch Räuber-Beute Interaktion wird durch $F_{ij} = k_{ij}\, x_i\, x_j$ dargestellt, der Massenverlust durch Atmung und Zerfall durch eine Reaktion 1. Ordnung. Die Bildung von Biomasse des Primärproduzenten erfolgt mit der als konstant angenommenen Rate $F_{01}$. Die Massenbilanzgleichungen (ohne die Komponente Nährstoff) lauten:

$$\dot{x}_1 = F_{01} - k_{12}\, x_1\, x_2 - (\mu_1 + \rho_1)\, x_1 \tag{9}$$

$$\dot{x}_2 = k_{12}\, x_1\, x_2 - k_{23}\, x_2\, x_3 - (\mu_2 + \rho_2)\, x_2 \tag{10}$$

$$\dot{x}_3 = k_{23} x_2\, x_3 - (\mu_3 + \rho_3)\, x_3 \tag{11}$$

$$\dot{x}_4 = \mu_1\, x_1 + \mu_2\, x_2 + \mu_3\, x_3 - \mu_4\, x_4 \tag{12}$$

Es gelten die zusätzlichen Bezeichnungen:

$y_0$: Menge der Substanz in der Umgebung

$y_i$: Menge der Substanz auf der i-ten trophischen Ebene

$\delta$ : Zerfallskonstante der Substanz in der Umgebung

$c_i$ : $= y_i/x_i$ Konzentation der Substanz auf der i-ten trophischen Ebene

$k_O$: Kinetische Konstante für den Einbau der Substanz in die Biomasse der Primärproduzenten

Mit den Biomassenflüssen $F_{ij}$ sind die Flüsse $\phi_{ij} = F_{ij}\, c_i$ des Fremdstoffes assoziiert. Da der Fremdstoff nicht metabolisiert wird, erhält man die folgenden Transportgleichungen:

$$\dot{y}_O = - k_{O1}\, x_1\, y_O + \mu_4\, x_4\, c_4 - \delta y_O \tag{13}$$

$$\dot{y}_1 = k_{O1}\, x_1\, y_O - k_{12}\, x_1\, x_2\, c_1 - \mu_1\, x_1\, c_1 \tag{14}$$

$$\dot{y}_2 = k_{12}\, x_1\, x_2\, c_1 - k_{23}\, x_2\, x_3\, c_2 - \mu_2\, x_2\, c_2 \tag{15}$$

$$\dot{y}_3 = k_{23}\, x_2\, x_3\, c_2 - \mu_3\, x_3\, c_3 \tag{16}$$

$$\dot{y}_4 = \mu_1\, x_1\, c_1 + \mu_2\, x_2\, c_2 + \mu_3\, x_3\, c_3 - \mu_4\, x_4\, c_4 \tag{17}$$

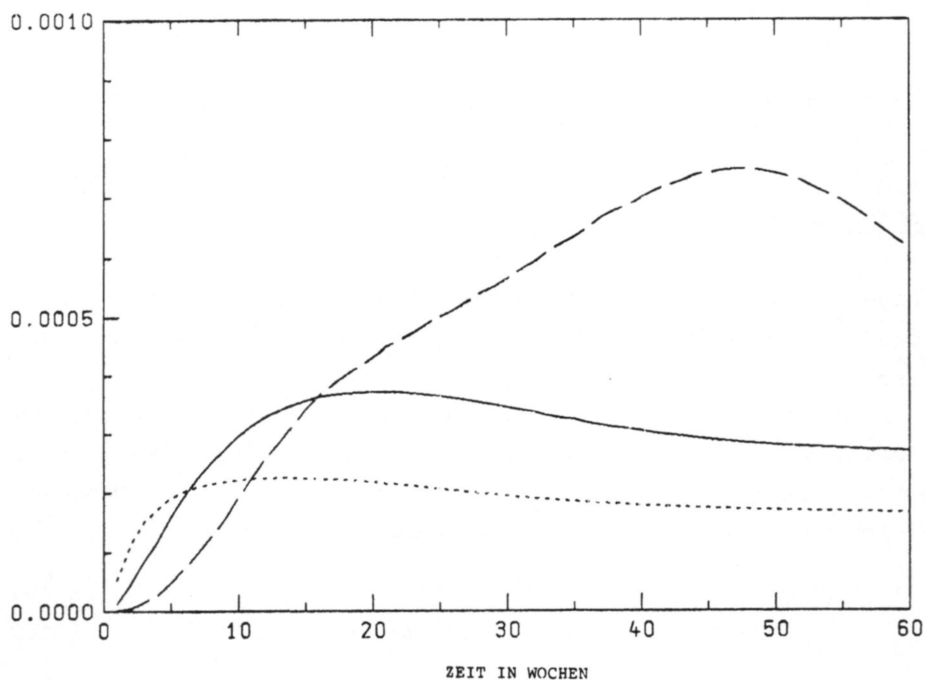


Abb. 4: Konzentrationsverläufe einer Fremdsubstanz in den Kompartimenten eines Ökosystems.
.....: im Primärproduzenten; ————: in den Herbivoren; - - -: in den Karnivoren.
Die Kurven stellen numerische Lösungen des Differentialgleichungssystems (Gleichungen (9 - 12) und Gleichungen (13 - 17)) dar.

Abb. 4 zeigt den Verlauf der Konzentrationen des Fremdstoffes auf den trophischen Ebenen nach einmaliger Belastung des Systems für den in Richter (1985) angegebenen Parametersatz. Die Konzentration der Substanz wächst von Ebene zu Ebene: auf der höchsten trophischen Ebene ist die Substanz am stärksten angereichert.


## 4. Neuere Entwicklungen

Auf mathematischem Gebiet wird das Problem der Verletzbarkeit (Vulnerability Analysis, Goh 1976) von Ökosystemen mit den Methoden der Kontrolltheorie angegangen. Dabei betrachtet man Störungen als Kontrollfunktionen und untersucht die Menge der unter einer bestimmten Klasse von Störfunktionen erreichbaren Systemzustände. Es sei S ein Gebiet im $R^n$, das die erlaubten Systemzustände enthält, U die Menge der zulässigen Störungen, Z die Menge der unerwünschten Systemzustände. Ferner sei ein Ökosystemmodell $\dot{y}_i = f_i (y_1, \ldots, y_n, u_1, u_2, \ldots, u_n)$ $i = 1, \ldots, n$ gegeben. Es wird das Systemverhalten im Intervall $(0, t_1)$ betrachtet. Das System heißt <u>unverletzlich</u> bezüglich $(U, S, Z, t_1)$, wenn <u>keine</u> Trajektorie y (t) mit y (0) $\epsilon$ S im Intervall $(0, t_1)$ das Gebiet Z erreicht.
Beispiele findet man im Band 40 der Lecture Notes in Biomathematics.


## Literatur

Goh, B.S.: Nunvulnerability of Ecosystems in Unpredictable Environments. Theor. Pop. Biol. 10 (1976), 83-97

Lecture Notes in Biomathematics, Bd 40, Springer Verlag Heidelberg 1981

May, R. M.: Stability and Complexity in Model Ecosystems, Princeton University Press, Princeton 1974

Richter, O.: Simulation des Verhaltens ökologischer Systeme, VCH-Verlag, Weinheim 1985

Spain, J. D.: BASIC Microcomputer Models in Biology, Addison-Wesley, London (1982)

# SIMULATION KOMPLEXER POPULATIONSDYNAMIK


Wilfried Gabriel, Plön



**Zusammenfassung.** Simulation ist ein wichtiges Instrument bei der Suche nach Gesetzmäßigkeiten und Funktionszusammenhängen in Ökosystemen. Realistische Populationsmodelle müssen die individuellen physiologischen Randbedingungen berücksichtigen. Anhand solcher Modellkonzeption zum Studium des Einflusses von Kannibalismus auf räuberisches Zooplankton werden einige speziell in der Ökologie auftauchende Probleme der Modellbildung erläutert. Mit einer Kompartmentierung in fein unterteilte Entwicklungsstadien gelingt es, eine unter dem Einfluß von Kannibalismus sehr instabile Altersstruktur zu erfassen. Das Modell ermöglicht generelle, populationsdynamische Aussagen darüber, wann Kannibalismus zur Selbstzerstörung einer Population führt, und wie er andererseits stabilisierend auf eine Räuber-Beute-Beziehung wirken kann.

**Summary.** Simulation is an essential tool for the investigation of laws and functioning in ecosystems. Models of populations are only realistic if the physiological constraints of the individuals are considered. Some specific problems of ecological modelling are demonstrated on such a model concept asking for the consequences of cannibalism on predacious zooplankton. With finely structured compartments of detailed developmental stages it is possible to follow an age structure, which is highly instable under cannibalism. General statements are given on the conditions, when cannibalism destroys its own population and when cannibalism is a stabilizing factor in predator-prey-systems.


## 1. Einleitung und Fragestellung

Technik und Biologie unterscheiden sich wesentlich in der Durchschaubarkeit funktioneller Zusammenhänge: Bei der vom Menschen konzipierten Technik sind die zugrundeliegenden Prinzipien, die Funktionen der Einzelkomponenten und ihre logischen Verknüpfungen von vornherein bekannt bzw. (zumindest prinzipiell) durch gültige physikalisch-chemische Gesetze beschreibbar; bei Organismen, biologischen Teilsystemen oder gar Ökosystemen können jedoch - abgesehen von der höheren Komplexität - Bauplan und Funktionalität meist nur als Arbeitshypothesen postuliert werden. Simulation in Biologie und speziell Ökologie dient häufig dem Auffinden von Gesetzmäßigkeiten und bleibt dann in hohem Maße spekulativ. Nur selten werden Prozesse nachgebildet, die bis ins Detail mit schon bekannten Naturgesetzen quantitativ beschreibbar sind. Innerhalb der Biologie ist die Populationsökologie die älteste Disziplin, in der mathematische Beschreibungsversuche unternommen wurden. Eine historische Darstellung findet sich bei *Hutchinson (1978)*. Viele der heutigen Fragestellungen in der Populationsdynamik können nur mit Computer-Simulation bearbeitet werden, da sich analytische Lösungen meist nur für sehr eingeschränkte, oft unrealistische oder uninteressante Bedingungen finden lassen. Einige für den Bereich der Ökologie spezielle Probleme der Modellbildung und Simulation sollen anhand eines Modells verdeutlicht werden, dessen Zielsetzung es ist, mögliche populationsdynamische Konsequenzen von Kannibalismus (= die eigene Art wird gefressen) zu untersuchen und dabei auch allgemeingültige qualitative Aussagen zu erlauben.

In welchem Ausmaß kann eine Population ihren Nahrungsbedarf durch Kannibalismus decken, ohne in die Gefahr der Selbstauslöschung zu geraten? Diese Fragestellung wird besonders interessant für Populationen, die zumindest prinzipiell ihren Bedarf an tierischer Nahrung ausschließlich durch Kannibalismus befriedigen könnten. Dies ist nur möglich, wenn innerhalb der Population gleichzeitig pflanzliche und tierische Ernährungsweise vorkommt und genügend pflanzliche Nahrung in tierische Körpersubstanz umgewandelt wird, wenn also z.B. die Neugeborenen Pflanzenfresser sind, und die Tiere erst mit zunehmendem Alter tierische Nahrung zu sich nehmen. Solches Fraßverhalten findet man - wie auch bei vielen Fischarten - innerhalb des Zooplanktons z.B. bei den "cyclopoiden Copepoden". Die Populationsdynamik solcher sogenannten Räuber kann sehr stark die Zooplankton-Lebensgemeinschaft und damit das gesamte Ökosystem eines Sees beeinflussen *(Kerfoot 1980)*. Deshalb wird versucht, die Fragestellung anhand eines aus Literaturdaten konstruierten Modellorganismus wirklichkeitsnah zu beantworten.

## 2. Modellierung des Einzeltieres

Viele populationsdynamische Modelle sind ausschließlich in Variablen formuliert, die nur die Gesamtpopulation charakterisieren. Die Einzeltiere werden dabei als gleichartige Objekte betrachtet und nur in ihrer Quantität erfaßt. Wie stark simplifizierend solche Modellansätze sind, zeigt sich im Versagen bei ihrer Anwendung auf konkrete Populationen in Labor oder Freiland. Eine der oft unzulässigen Vereinfachungen kann darin liegen, daß die immer vorhandenen und u.U. entscheidenden Variabilitäten von Merkmalen der Einzeltiere nicht explizit mitmodelliert werden bzw. als stochastische Prozesse sozusagen nachträglich und ohne Kausalstruktur hinzugefügt sind. Sollen - als verdeutlichendes Beispiel - beobachtbare Genfrequenzverschiebungen oder Phänotypveränderungen, die z.B. durch Selektionsmechanismen oder jahreszeitliche Sukzessionen erklärbar sind, zu den möglichen Modellaussagen gehören, dann ist es offensichtlich, daß die populationsdynamische Beschreibung auch Eigenschaften der Einzeltiere beinhalten muß. Bei der Modellerstellung für konkrete Populationen liegt ein entscheidendes Problem darin, alle für die Fragestellung wesentlichen Merkmale und Randbedingungen (z.B. physiologischer Art) kennen und adäquat berücksichtigen zu müssen.

Wichtige Einzelheiten für die Modellierung des Kannibalismus sind z.B.: größenabhängige (maximale) Freßraten, Effizienz der Futterumwandlung in somatisches Wachstum bzw. Eiproduktion, minimale Futteraufnahme zur Abdeckung der metabolischen Verluste, ertragbare Hungerzeit, Gewichtsverlust bei Hunger, Mortalitätserhöhung durch Hunger,. natürliche Mortalität, altersbedingte Änderung des Anteils tierischer Nahrung an der Gesamtnahrung. Mit Kenntnis bzw. Abschätzung dieser Größen *(Gabriel & Lampert 1985)* kann für ein "mittleres" Einzeltier der zeitliche Ablauf des Körperwachstums (W = Körpergewicht) in Abhängigkeit vom Nahrungsangebot modelliert werden, z.B. durch einen differentiellen Ansatz (analog zu *v.Bertalanffy 1941 und 1964, Gabriel 1982)*:

$$\frac{dW}{dt} = a\,W^b - c\,W^d$$

Dabei ist die Nettoproduktionsrate dW/dt als Differenz von Assimilations- und Respirationsrate dargestellt, wobei die Koeffizienten a, b, c und d gewichtsabhängig sind und auch mit der aktuellen Futterkonzentration variieren. Schon ein solch relativ einfacher Modellierungsversuch wie das Nachbilden von individuellen Wachstumskurven kann Hinweise liefern, welche Größen für ein ausreichendes Verständnis bislang zu wenig beachtet oder zu ungenau gemessen wurden. Der dabei zutage tretende Mangel an verfügbaren Daten ist ein generelles Problem bei der Modellierung im Bereich der Ökologie. Die meisten Messungen sind nämlich nur für spezielle örtliche und zeitliche Bedingungen gültig, selbst wenn man von mannigfaltigen innerartlichen und zwischenartlichen Unterschieden schon innerhalb eines Biotops absieht. Eventuell allgemeingültige Prinzipien und Funktionszusammenhänge sind meist noch nicht präzise genug formulierbar, um Grundlage für eine kausalanalytische Modellierung zu bilden.


3.  Einige methodische Probleme von Populationsmodellen

Die naheliegendste Methode für den Übergang vom Einzeltier zur Population bietet eine "discret event simulation", d.h. der Versuch, die Gesamtpopulation durch die Wechselwirkung genau beschreibbarer Einzeltiere zu simulieren. Um zum Beispiel die stochastischen Einflüsse bei geringer Populationsdichte zu studieren, ist dies sicher ein geeignetes Instrument; allgemeingültige Aussagen sind jedoch nur schwer zu erzielen. Die Beschreibung dichteabhängiger Prozesse kann sehr schnell zu hochkomplexen Programmstrukturen führen, da z.B. nicht nur die Wechselwirkung zwischen allen Einzeltieren wichtig ist, sondern auch deren aktuelle räumliche Positionen explizit berücksichtigt werden müßten. Bei mittleren Zooplanktonpopulationsdichten von $10^5$ bis $10^6$ Tieren pro m$^2$ Seeoberfläche erreicht man mühelos die Grenzen der Kapazität und verfügbaren Rechenzeit von Großrechnern. Sinnvollerweise wird man dann ähnliche Tiere zu Klassen zusammenfassen und letztlich die Veränderung dieser Klassen studieren. Spätestens hierbei wird es dann problematisch, welche Detailinformation a priori als relevant betrachtet wird und wie dann solche "repräsentativen" Klassen definiert werden. Solange z.B. nicht alle entscheidenden Faktoren bekannt und richtig modelliert sind, kann ein zusätzlich berücksichtigtes Detail ein Modell sogar verschlechtern, wenn bestimmte Zusammenhänge zwar genauer wiedergegeben sind aber in den Gesamtzusammhang inadäquat oder gar falsch eingebunden werden.

Geht man beim Modellansatz nicht vom Einzeltier aus, sondern versucht von vornherein
in einer Kompartmentstruktur die wesentlichen Eigenschaften der Individuen zu berücksichtigen, dann sind zwar die grundsätzlichen Probleme ähnlich wie bei der
"discret-event"-Simulation, jedoch bietet sich eher die Möglichkeit für allgemeingültige
Aussagen und analytische Untersuchungen. Die Übergänge zwischen den einzelnen
Kompartments resultieren aus biologischen Vorgängen, die sich aus einer Mischung
von zeitlich kontinuierlichen und diskontinuierlichen Prozessen zusammensetzen. Bei
der üblichen auf Differentialgleichungen basierenden Beschreibung muß deshalb vermieden werden, zwar mathematisch korrekt aber in biologisch sinnlosen Bereichen zu
rechnen. Eine Formulierung mit Differenzengleichungen mag oftmals realitätsnäher sein.

Ein typisches populationsdynamisches Problem, das bei einem Kompartmentmodell besonders deutlich hervortritt, ist die Behandlung der Altersstruktur. Die Altersverteilung innerhalb eines Kompartments wird in Modellansätzen meist als homogen oder
zumindest als zeitlich konstant betrachtet, da sich nur eine stabile Altersstruktur
beim Übergang von Kompartment zu Kompartment analytisch berücksichtigen läßt.
Nutzlos sind Beschreibungen oder gar vollständige Lösungen, die eine (in der Natur
selten andauernde) stabile Altersverteilung voraussetzen, wenn das Interesse der
Untersuchung sich gerade auf die dynamischen Prozesse vor Erreichen einer stabilen
Altersstruktur richtet. Als Ausweg bietet sich an, so viele Kompartments zu wählen,
daß in jedem einzelnen die Altersverteilung als nahezu homogen betrachtet werden
kann, selbst wenn die Altersstruktur der Gesamtpopulation starker Dynamik ausgesetzt
ist. Im Falle des hier vorgestellten Kannibalismusmodells sind dafür mehr als 35 Kompartments nötig. Eine korrekte Kompartmentbeschreibung ist jedoch u.U. an mehr
analytische Vorarbeit gebunden als eine "discret event simulation"; im Kannibalismus-
modell z.B. muß eine Formel für die durch Kannibalismus bedingte Mortalität in jedem
Kompartment gefunden werden.

## 4. Details des Kannibalismusmodells

Anhand dieses Problems soll nun gezeigt werden, zu welch stark rückgekoppeltem
System der Kannibalismus führt. Die Population wird in n Kompartments eingeteilt,
die in etwa als Alters- oder Gewichtsklassen aufgefaßt werden können. Um ein Modell-
tier zu beschreiben, das über verschiedene Arten und Umweltbedingungen gemittelt
ist, sind alle Zeitabläufe auf die Entwicklungszeit bis zum adulten Tier und alle Längen
auf die Größe eines ausgewachsenen Tieres normiert. Die einzelnen Kompartments
beschreiben somit Entwicklungsstadien (die morphologisch unterscheidbaren Stadien
der Copepoden werden dabei im Modell noch feiner unterteilt), die von Einzeltieren
je nach Futterbedingungen mehr oder weniger schnell durchlaufen werden. Im n-ten
Kompartment sind die Eier der Adulten gereift. Unter Berücksichtigung der adulten-

spezifischen Mortalität werden die Tiere danach in die erste Adultenklasse (Entwicklungsbeginn der Eier) zurückgestuft. Wenn $N_i$ die relative Populationsdichte im i-ten Kompartment bezeichnet, so läßt sich ihre zeitliche Änderung differentiell ausdrücken als

$$\frac{dN_i}{dt} = f_1 N_{i-1} - f_2 N_i + \delta_{ii_a} f_3 N_n - f_4 N_i$$

wobei mit f (teilweise komplizierte) zeit- und dichteabhängige Funktionen gemeint sind:

$f_1$     Eintrag aus nächstniedrigerem Kompartment. Im einfachsten Fall (homogene Altersverteilung) gilt $f_1 = 1/T_{i-1}$ mit $T_{i-1}$ als Dauer des entsprechenden Entwicklungsstadiums (abhängig vom aktuellen Futterangebot). Für i=1 beschreibt $f_1$ die Geburtsrate, und für $N_{i-1}$ ist entsprechend $N_n$ zu setzen.

$f_2$     analog zu $f_1$, jedoch Übergang in nächsthöheres Kompartment.

$f_3$     trägt nur zur ersten Adultenklasse ($i=i_a$) bei und beschreibt, wieviel Tiere aus der höchsten in die niedrigste Adultenklasse (nach dem Schlüpfen der Eier) zurückgestuft werden.

$f_4$     ist die Mortalitätsrate. Diese setzt sich (additiv) aus vier Komponenten zusammen: natürliche Mortalität (z.B. durch Krankheit), durch Hunger ausgelöste, durch externe Räuber verursachte und durch Kannibalismus bedingte Mortalität.

Eine starke Vernetzung der einzelnen Kompartments erfolgt durch die kannibalismusspezifische Mortalitätsrate in $f_4$, die im Folgenden genauer beschrieben wird. Um das größenselektive Verhalten bei der Beutesuche zu berücksichtigen, wird eine Präferenzmatrix berechnet, deren Elemente $P_{ij}$ angeben, mit welcher relativen Präferenz ein Tier der Klasse j ein Tier der Klasse i frißt. Für die Beuteselektion ist die Grössendifferenz zwischen Räuber und Beute entscheidend. Das beobachtete Verhalten kann durch eine Normalverteilung um eine optimale Beutegröße $L_{j,opt}$ mit Varianz V beschrieben werden:

$$P_{ij} = c \exp( -(L_i - L_{j,opt})^2 / 2 V_j )$$

wobei c sich aus der Normierungsbedingung

$$\sum_{i=1}^{j-1} P_{ij} = 1 \quad ( P_{ij} = 0 \text{ für } i \geqq j )$$

ergibt und die Präferenzmatrix neu normiert werden muß,
sobald ein Kompartment leer wird oder sich wieder füllt.

Mit dieser Präferenzmatrix läßt sich die durch Kannibalismus verursachte Mortalitätsrate $m_i$ für jedes Kompartment berechnen:

$$m_i = \sum_{j=i+1}^{n} \left( N_j P_{ij} a_j b_j \Big/ \sum_{k=1}^{j-1} (w_k N_k P_{kj}) \right)$$

mit

i,j,k    Kompartmentindizes,

N       relative Populationsdichte in einem Kompartment,

P       relative Präferenz,

a       karnivorer Futterbedarf in Einheiten des Gewichtes
         eines adulten Tieres,

b       durch Kannibalismus befriedigter Anteil am karnivoren
         Futterbedarf,

w       mittleres relatives Gewicht eines Tieres in einem
         Kompartment (bezogen auf adulte Tiere).

Diese Formel enthält die relativen Populationsdichten in den Kompartments mehrfach explizit für die Berechnung der Mortalitäten. Damit wird auch formelmäßig die starke Vernetzung und Rückkopplung der einzelnen Kompartments sichtbar.

Grundlage für diese Kompartment-Beschreibung ist die Modellierung der individuellen Wachstumskurve des Einzeltieres aufgrund von Futterangebot und Futterverwertung. Hier liegt auch ein Verknüfpungspunkt zu anderen Populationen, die entweder als Beutetiere gefressen werden oder um gemeinsame Futterquellen konkurrieren. Dienen die cyclopoiden Copepoden selbst als Nahrung für andere Räuber, erfolgt eine Wechselwirkung über die externen Mortalitätsraten.


5. <u>Modellaussagen</u>


Bei der Vorstellung des Modellkonzepts konnten nicht alle Details geschildert werden, z.B. ist das Modell nicht als Differentialgleichungssystem realisiert, sondern es werden Differenzengleichungen benutzt, allerdings mit einer variablen zeitlichen Schrittweite, die vom momentanen Populationszustand geregelt wird. Der Modellentwurf ist von der Zielsetzung geprägt, in einer theoretischen Vorstudie experimentell testbare Hypothesen aufzustellen. Dafür muß größtmögliche Realitätsnähe durch die Beschreibung einer konkreten Population mit ihren physiologischen Randbedingungen gewährleistet sein; um jedoch relevante generelle Aussagen zu ermöglichen, muß das Modell in ökologisch

interpretierbaren und meßbaren Variablen (wie Wachstums- und Mortalitätsraten) formuliert werden.

Mit dem beschriebenen Modell können für Populationen, bei denen ein Wechsel von
herbivorer zu carnivorer Ernährung mit zunehmendem Alter beobachtet wird, und
deren räuberisches Verhalten sich nicht nur auf andere Arten (= Alternativbeute)
sondern auch auf die eigene Art erstreckt (= Kannibalismus), folgenden Hypothesen
aufgestellt werden:

a) Ohne Alternativbeute kann eine Population nur überleben, wenn die ersten Alters-
   klassen vom Kannibalismus verschont werden.

b) Bei Anwesenheit von Alternativbeute ist Kannibalismus ein stabilisierender Faktor
   für die Räuber-Beute-Beziehung, denn er garantiert Koexistenz selbst bei Beute-
   dichten noch weit unterhalb der kritischen Dichte, die ohne Kannibalismus zur
   Vernichtung der Beute- und damit auch der Räuberpopulation führen würde
   *(Gabriel 1985)*.

Ein wesentlicher Wert solcher Modellaussagen liegt darin, daß sie Anstoß zu gezielten
experimentellen Untersuchungen geben können. Dann bilden sie wichtige Bausteine
zum Verständnis unaufgeklärter Funktionszusammenhänge in Ökosystemen.


## Literatur:


*Bertalanffy, L. von (1941)*: Stoffwechseltypen und Wachstumstypen. - Biol.Zbl. <u>61</u>:
510-532.

    --    *(1964)*: Basic concepts in quantitative biology of metabolism. - Helgoländer
wiss. Meeresunters. <u>9</u>: 5-37.

*Gabriel, W. (1982)*: Modelling reproductive strategies of *Daphnia*. - Arch. Hydrobiol.
<u>95</u>: 69-80.

    --    *(1985)*: Overcoming food limitation by cannibalism: A model study on
cyclopoids. - In: *W. Lampert* (Ed.): Food limitation and the structure of
zooplankton communities. - Arch. Hydrobiol. Beih. Ergebn. Limnol. <u>21</u>
(in press).

*Gabriel, W. & W. Lampert (1985)*: Can cannibalism be advantageous in cyclopoids?
A mathematical model. - Verh. Internat. Verein. Limnol. <u>22</u> (in press).

*Hutchinson, G.E. (1978)*: An introduction to population ecology. - Yale Univ. Press.
New Haven and London.

*Kerfoot, W.C., (Ed.), (1980)*: Evolution and ecology of zooplankton communities. -
Univ. Press of New England, Hanover NH.

# COMPUTERSIMULATION IN DER VERHALTENSBIOLOGIE

Lioba Galke, Remscheid

ZUSAMMENFASSUNG. Die Verhaltensforschung kennt verschiedene Modelle tierischen Verhaltens. Die funktionelle Komplexität von Verhaltensmodellen ist in der Regel zu hoch, um das behauptete Modellverhalten aus der Modellbeschreibung alleine herleiten zu können. Mithilfe der Computersimulation ist es jedoch möglich, Modell-"Verhalten" zu studieren. Die Implementierung eines Triebmodells nach LORENZ u. HASSENSTEIN wird skizziert.

SUMMARY. In Behavioural Science different models of animal behaviour are under discussion. Their functional complexity is too high to deduce the proposed model's reactions from the description of the model alone. Computer-simulation makes it possible to study model-"behaviour" directly. An Inplementation of a "Triebmodell" after LORENZ u. HASSENSTEIN is briefly shown.

## I. Einleitung

Computersimulationen sind meines Erachtens für den Verhaltensbiologen ein geeignetes Werkzeug, sich rasch Konsequenzen seiner Modellvorstellungen vor Augen zu führen.

Eine Theorie kann nicht verifiziert werden, sie kann als wahr vermutet werden. Eine nicht falsifizierbare Theorie nennt POPPER eine metaphysische Theorie.[1] Die Theorie nach LORENZ fällt unter diese Kategorie: weder von LORENZ noch von anderen Autoren konnten bisher falsifizierbare Aussagen aufgestellt werden.

Mit meinen Simulationen möchte ich erreichen, dass verschiedene Modelle untereinander sowie die Simulationsergebnisse mit in der Natur beobachteten Werten verglichen werden können. Damit wäre eine empirische Überprüfbarkeit gegeben, die ohne Simulationsexperimente nicht erreicht werden könnte.

## II. Modelldenken in der Verhaltensbiologie

Der Verhaltensforscher sieht sich einem System gegenüber, dessen innerer Aufbau sowie der Ablauf seiner internen Vorgänge unbekannt sind. Er befindet sich also in einer Situation, in der er das ihn interessierende Objekt zunächst als Black-box beschreibt. Feststellbar ist nur das Verhalten, Reaktionen (output) auf vermutete Eingangssignale (input).[2] Da Tiere in ihrer natürlichen Umwelt mit unüberschaubar vielen Reizen konfrontiert werden, sind die Eingangssignale nicht alle bekannt oder feststellbar. In Experimenten muss man sich daher mit

Annahmen behelfen.

Um Verhaltensmodelle programmieren zu können, müssen sie in eine mathematische Form gebracht werden. Mehrdeutig formulierte Modelle müssen durch Annahmen so ergänzt werden, dass die mathematische Form eindeutig ist. Während der Transformation in mathematische Modelle und Programme können somit aufgrund der notwendigen Exaktheit Erkenntnisse gewonnen werden, die allein aus der umgangssprachlichen Beschreibung der Modelle nicht erkennbar wären. Die Phase der Implementation ist mit Erkenntnisgewinn verbunden.

Verhaltensweisen von Tieren erklären verschiedene Forscher mit verschiedenartigen Modellen, teilweise mit Triebmodellen. Triebmodelle zeichnen sich dadurch aus, dass ihre Reaktionen, die ausgeführten Aktionen, abhängen von äusseren Grössen, den Reizen, und von inneren Grössen, die das innere Millieu widerspiegeln. Die inneren Grössen steigen mit der Zeit oder anderen Faktoren an und werden nach verschiedenen Auffassungen wieder herabgesetzt. Konrad Lorenz ordnet jeder angeborenen Verhaltensweise (Erbkoordination) eine innere Grösse zu, die er mit aktionsspezifischer Erregung oder aktionsspezifischer Energie bezeichnet (ASE). Die aktionsspezifische Erregung steigt mit der Zeit an und wird nach dem Ausführen einer Handlung zurückgesetzt.

Im folgenden kürze ich Erbkoordinationen nach LORENZ mit EK ab.

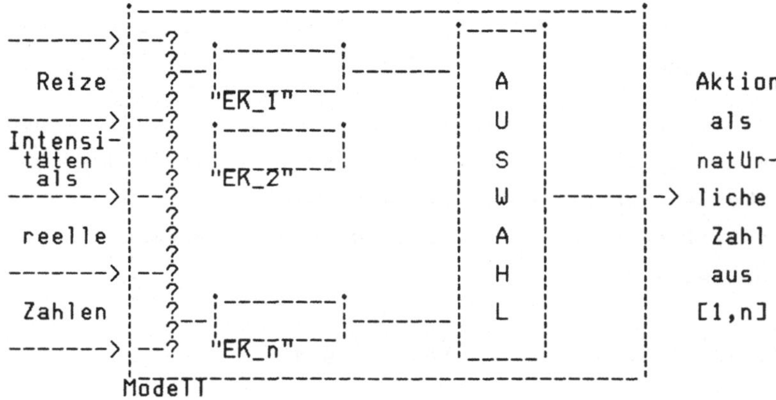


Eine Relation zwischen einzelnen Reizen und Aktionen ist allerdings bei den verschiedenen Autoren nicht näher spezifiziert. Denn welche Reize zu welchen Aktionen führen, ob Reize selektiert werden und nur zu bestimmten Aktionen gelangen oder ob alle Reize für alle Aktionen verantwortlich sind, konnte von mir nicht in Erfahrung gebracht werden.

In der mit "Auswahl" bezeichneten Grösse wird entschieden, welche EK ausgeführt werden soll. Diejenige EK setzt sich durch, die die anderen stark genug hemmt. Für die mathematische Form des LORENZschen Modell bedeutet dies, dass diejenige EK ausgeführt wird, die in der Berechnung, die die gegenseitige Hemmung realisiert, den höchsten Wert erhalten hat. HASSENSTEIN bezeichnet dies mit Maximalwertdurchlass.[3]

Eine Erbkoordination ist demnach wie folgt aufgebaut:

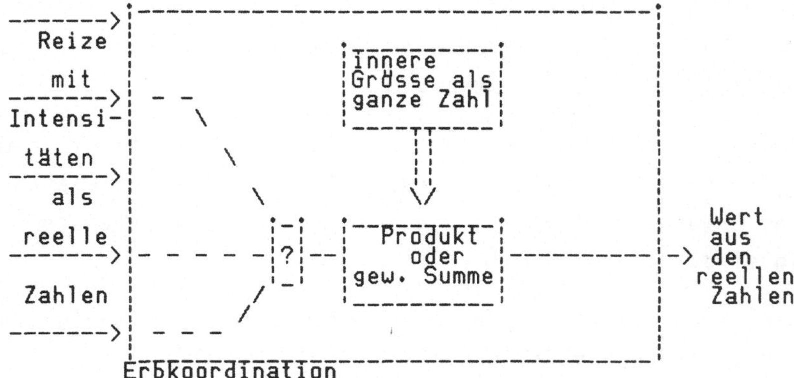


Nach LORENZ und SEITZ werden alle spezifischen Reize eines Triebes summiert (Reiz-Summen-Theorem [4]), jedoch gibt es auch andere Möglichkeiten, die Einflüsse der äusseren Grössen zu beschreiben.

Zur Verrechnung der inneren und äusseren Grössen schlägt HASSENSTEIN die Multiplikation dieser beiden Grössen vor.

III.   Simulationsmethoden

Die Simulation der Verhaltensmodelle habe ich wie folgt strukturiert:

1. die Simulation der verschiedenen Modelle mit der Möglichkeit, einige Parameter zu verändern

2. die Simulation der Umwelt

3. die Auswertung der Simulationsergebnisse

Ich habe mich für Simulationen mit stochastischen Modellen entschieden, da ich von den Wahrscheinlichkeitsaussagen der Simulationsergebnisse eine empirische Überprüfbarkeit der Modelle erhoffe. Ein Umwelt-"modell" lässt sich meiner Ansicht nach nur in dieser stochastischen Form verwirklichen, wenn allgemeingültige Aussagen der Simulationsexperimente erwartet werden.

In einem Simulationsdurchlauf wird ein Verhaltensmodell mit den im Umwelt-"modell" erzeugten Reizungen konfrontiert. Modellspezifisch wird eine von n verschiedenen Aktionen ausgewählt. Ein inkrementierender Stunden-Zähler protokolliert die Stunden und die ausgeführten Aktionen pro Stunde. Bei Simulationsläufen über mehrere Tage, werden die Ergebnisse stundenweise summiert.

In meinen Experimenten habe ich die Simulationsdauer auf 30 Tage festgelegt und ausserdem die Anzahl der möglichen Aktionen pro Stunde auf 5 gesetzt. Ich nehme an, dass die Summe dieser Daten ausreichend ist, um statistische Aussagen zu erlauben. POHLEY hat in seiner Arbeit mit einem Protokoll über 30 Tage und nur einer Aktion (von zwei möglichen) pro Stunde seine Aussagen belegt.[2]

Um das Modell nach LORENZ zu präzisieren, muss ich diejenigen Modellparameter mit ihren Einflüssen auf das Modellverhalten untersuchen, über die keine Angaben vorliegen, die aber zu einem lauffähigen Programm notwendig sind.

Zum einen kann die Anzahl der Erbkoordinationen beliebig festgelegt werden, muss jedoch grösser als 1 sein.
Zum anderen können die Zuwachsraten der Erbkoordinationen im LORENZschen Modell in ihrer Höhe wie folgt variieren:

- Alle Zuwachsraten haben den gleichen Wert

- Die Zuwachsraten nehmen linear steigende Werte an. Den Erbkoordinationen 1 ... n sind die Zuwachsraten 1 ... n zugeordnet.

Mithilfe der Variabilität dieser Modellparameter möchte ich untersuchen, welchen Einfluss die Zuwachsraten auf das Modellverhalten haben.

Der Ursprung der Theorie der Zuwachsraten liegt bei LORENZ darin, dass die Zuwachsraten in der Natur den Häufigkeiten entsprechen, mit der diese Aktionen in der Regel benötigt werden. Sie haben sich im Laufe der Evolution eingestellt. Wird eine Aktion oft ausgeführt, so muss, wenn eine doppelte Quantifizierung angenommen wird, auch die entsprechende Zuwachsrate (im Modell) hoch sein, damit diese Aktion (fast) direkt wieder mit den anderen Aktionen konkurrieren kann.

Eine vorgegebene Anzahl von Erbkoordinationen mit den variabel hohen Zuwachsraten (Zuw-R) und ihrer aktionsspezifischen Erregung (ASE) werden in einer Liste geführt. Die Erbkoordinationen werden in dieser Liste durch ihre Position identifiziert. Eine Erbkoordination ist also ein Paar ( ASE . Zuw-R ).

Eine spezifische Reizung der Erbkoordinationen wird mit dem Umwelt-"modell" erzeugt, das für jede Erbkoordination eine Reizsummenintensität (RSI) liefert.

Nach der Konfrontation der Liste der Erbkoordinationen mit den Reizsummen wird nach HASSENSTEIN das Produkt    ASE * RSI    gebildet. Nach der Berechnung des Produktes wird die aktuelle ASE um ihre Zuwachsrate erhöht. Diejenige Erbkoordination wird ausgewählt, deren Produkt den höchsten Wert besitzt. Die ASE der ausgewählten Erbkoordination wird zurückgesetzt.

## Die Problematik eines Umweltmodells

Ein sogenanntes Umwelt- "Verhalten", das den Verlauf und das Auftreten von Reizen in der Umwelt darstellen soll, ist an keiner Stelle beschrieben. Um den angestrebten Vergleich der Verhaltensmodelle durchführen zu können, müssen die Reaktionen der Modelle unter gleichen Bedingungen untersucht werden. Das heisst insbesondere, die Umwelt, die das Verhalten eines Tieres beeinflusst, muss für alle Modelle gleich sein.

Den Zusammenhang zwischen dem Umweltmodell und den Verhaltensmodellen soll die folgende Skizze ein wenig verdeutlichen:

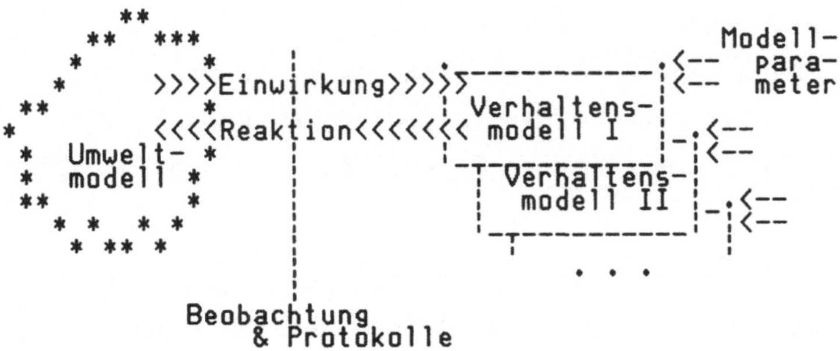


Die Verhalten der verschiedenen Modelle könnten indirekt über die Protokolle der Simulationsergebnisse verglichen werden. Rückwirkungen des Modellverhaltens in die Umwelt werden nicht mit berücksichtigt.

In Anlehnung an die Arbeit von H. und H.J. POHLEY in [2] betrachte ich im folgenden nur, ob eine Erbkoordination Reize erhalten hat. Ich nehme an dieser Stelle an, alle Reize, mit denen ein Trieb oder eine Erbkoordination konfrontiert wird, unterlägen derselben Wahrscheinlichkeitsverteilung.

## IV. Ergebnisse

### Modelle

2 Triebmodelle nach LORENZ & HASSENSTEIN, 11 Triebe
a) alle Erbkoordinationen haben die gleiche Zuwachsrate 1
b) jede Erbkoordination hat ihre eigene Zuwachsrate. Die Zuwachsraten liegen zwischen 1 und 11.

<u>Simulationsläufe</u>
Simulierte Beobachtungsdauer:  30 Tage à 24 Stunden; 5 Aktionen/Stunde.
Eingabe für beide Läufe: Standardnormalverteilte Reizwerte.

<u>Resultate</u>
a) Erwartet:  Gleiche Häufigkeiten aller Triebhandlungen.  Häufigkeiten
gleichverteilt über den Tag mit Erwartungswert:

$$\frac{5 * 30}{11} = 13.64 \quad \frac{\text{Aktionen Tage}}{\text{Trieb Stunde}}$$

Beobachtet:  Die gemessenen Mittelwerte stimmen sehr gut mit dem Erwartungswert  überein.  Die angenommene Gleichverteilung der Aktionen über
den  Tag ist aber keineswegs zu beobachten;  statt dessen ist ein  zyk-
lisches  Aktionsmuster erkennbar (Test:  Sukzessive  Differenzstreuung.
Ergebnisse hochsignifikant [5]).

b)  Erwartet:  Unterschiedliche Häufigkeiten der Triebausführungen  die
proportional  zu  den  Zuwachsraten der  Aktionsspezifischen  Energieen.
Aktionen werden gleichverteilt erwartet.
Beobachtet:  Auch hier bestätigt sich die erste Erwartung.  Die Annahme
einer  Gleichverteilung  der ausgeführten Erbkoordinationen  muss  auch
hier zugunsten eines zyklischen Verhaltensmusters aufgegeben werden.

<u>Interpretation</u>
Die  gemessenen Häufigkeiten der Triebausführungen verhalten  sich  so,
wie  es die Zuwachsraten der zugehörigen aktionsspezifischen  Energieen
erwarten lassen.  Die rhytmischen Verläufe der Handlungsmuster sind als
Epiphänomene  erst  durch die Simulation sichtbar geworden.  Sie  haben
keine  direkte  Ursache  im Modell sondern sind  als  seine  Konsequenz
anzusehen.


V. Literatur

[1] K. Popper / J. Eccles: "Das Ich und sein Gehirn". München 1982

[2] G. Schaefer / G. Trommer / K. Wenk (Hrsg.): "Denken in Modellen".
    Braunschweig 1977

[3] B. Hassenstein: "Instinkt – Lernen – Spielen – Einsicht". München
    1980

[4] K. Lorenz: "Vergleichende Verhaltensforschung". München 1982

[5] J.R.Geigy A.G. Basel (Hrsg.): "Dokumenta Geigy, wissenschaftliche
    Tabellen", 6. Auflage

$$\text{SIMULATION BIOCHEMISCHER PROZESSE IN DER PFLANZENPHYSIOLOGIE:}$$

$$\text{DYNAMIK UND REGULATION DER PHOTOSYNTHETISCHEN } CO_2\text{-FIXIERUNG IM CALVIN-ZYKLUS}$$


Christoph Giersch, Düsseldorf



<u>Zusammenfassung</u>.  Die Regulation der photosynthetischen $CO_2$-Fixierung durch höhere
Pflanzen ist biochemisch ausreichend charakterisiert, systemanalytisch aber nur z.T.
verstanden. Wesentliche Beiträge hierzu können dynamische Simulationsmodelle liefern.
An charakteristischen Beispielen werden Ansätze, Vorgehensweise und bisherige Ergebnisse von Simulationsmodellen dargestellt, und es werden Probleme der Regulation angesprochen, zu deren Klärung künftige Simulationsmodelle beitragen können.

<u>Summary</u>.  Regulation of photosynthetic $CO_2$-fixation is adequately characterized in
experimental terms. However, theoretical understanding of the dynamics of photosynthesis is poor and should be aided by dynamic mathematical models. The biochemical basis,
the mathematical formulation and the results of characteristic models of biochemical
aspects of photosynthesis are reviewed , and problems to be attacked by future models
are suggested.


## 1. Einführung

In den vergangenen Jahren hat sich unser Bild von Bau und Funktion einer typischen
grünen Pflanzenzelle ganz bedeutend erweitert und präzisiert; für Teilaspekte (etwa
des Elektronentransportes oder enzymatischer Reaktionen) sind molekulare Mechanismen
bekannt. Dennoch spielten Simulationstechniken in der Pflanzenphysiologie bisher eine
eher bescheidene Rolle. Das liegt vor allem an dem äußerst komplexen Reaktionsgesche-
hen, das es hier zu beschreiben gilt: Chloroplasten absorbieren als primäre photosyn-
thetische Organellen Lichtenergie und liefern relativ stabile Verbindungen, die Trio-
sephosphate, an das Cytosol, wobei sie anorganisches Phosphat und $CO_2$ aus der Umgebung
aufnehmen. Das System biochemischer Reaktionen, in dem $CO_2$ fixiert und Triosephosphat
gebildet wird, ist der Calvin-Zyklus. Im Cytosol findet u.a. die Produktion von Saccharose, dem wichtigsten pflanzlichen Zucker, statt; dabei (wie auch bei anderen Prozessen)
kann die große Zentralvakuole der ausdifferenzierten Pflanzenzelle die Rolle eines
Zwischenspeichers übernehmen. Mitochondrien spielen nicht nur bei der Veratmung orga-
nischer Moleküle, also während Perioden der Dunkelheit, sondern auch bei der Photores-
piration und beim Crassulaceen-Säure-Metabolismus (CAM) eine wesentliche Rolle. Dieser
komplexe Reaktionsablauf hat sich bislang einer konsistenten Beschreibung durch ein
globales Modell entzogen. Im folgenden sollen an ausgewählten Beispielen exemplarisch
Vorgehensweise, Probleme und Ergebnisse von Simulationsrechnungen in der Pflanzenphysiologie unter besonderer Berücksichtigung des Kohlenstoff-Umsatzes im Calvin-
Zyklus dargestellt werden.

## 2. Photosynthetische Reaktionen

Bei der photosynthetischen $CO_2$-Assimilation im Calvin-Zyklus wird das Kohlendioxid an ein Akzeptormolekül, Ribulose-1,5-bisphosphat (RuBP), gebunden; die entstehende Phosphoglycerinsäure (PGA) wird mit Hilfe von ATP und NADPH zur Stufe des Zuckerphosphates reduziert. ATP entsteht bei der Photophosphorylierung, die an den Transport von Reduktionsäquivalenten vom Wasser zum NADP gekoppelt ist. Die Regeneration des Akzeptors RuBP erfolgt durch eine komplexe Reaktionsfolge (regenerative Phase des Calvin-Zyklus), wobei letztlich aus 5 $C_3$-Molekülen 3 $C_5$-Moleküle entstehen. Da die $CO_2$-Fixierung das Vorhandensein von RuBP erfordert, dessen Konzentration mit Hilfe des fixierten $CO_2$ erhöht werden kann, handelt es sich beim Calvin-Zyklus um einen autokatalytischen Prozess. Die biochemischen Grundlagen des Calvin-Zyklus sind seit etwa 30 Jahren bekannt. In jüngerer Vergangenheit rückten mit dem allgemeinen Interesse an neuen und zusätzlichen Energieressourcen auch Fragen nach Dynamik und Regulation dieses für die heterotrophe Lebensweise grundlegenden Prozesses in den Vordergrund. Während experimentell auch auf diesem Gebiet mittlerweile viele Einzeltatsachen zusammengetragen wurden (siehe z.B. (1)),ist für die theoretische Analyse ein deutlicher Nachholbedarf zu verzeichnen.

## 3. Mathematische Modelle zur $CO_2$-Fixierung im Calvin-Zyklus

### Elektronentransport und Photophosphorylierung

Die bei der photosynthetischen Wasserspaltung entstehenden Reduktionsäquivalente werden mit Hilfe zweier in Serie geschalteter Photosysteme auf einen geeigneten Akzeptor, etwa $NADP^+$, übertragen. Einer der unklaren Punkte ist dabei der Transport der Reduktionsäquivalente im Bereich von Cytochrom f. Eine Computersimulation (2) der Kinetik der Redoxreaktionen von Cytochrom f (Cyt f) sowie der vorausgehenden und der nachfolgenden Reaktion (Plastochinon $\rightarrow$ Cyt f $\rightarrow$ $P_{700}$) sollte klären, ob Cyt f ein obligatorischer Bestandteil der Elektronentransportkette ist oder auf einem Seitenweg liegt. Die errechneten Kinetiken der Redoxreaktionen hingen, wie die Simulationsläufe zeigten, nur schwach von der angenommenen Reihenfolge der Redoxcarrier ab (2). Da zudem die kinetischen Konstanten nur ungenau bekannt waren, erlaubte diese Untersuchung letztlich keine Klärung des angesprochenen Problems. - Zur Beschreibung der oxidativen Phosphorylierung in Mitochondrien entwickelte Bohnensack (3) ein mathematisches Modell der ATP-Bildung in Mitochondrien. Dieses Modell beschreibt die ATP-Produktion unter stationären Bedingungen in guter Übereinstimmung mit experimentellen Tatsachen (4). Interessanterweise lassen sich aus diesem Ansatz die den Prozess der oxidativen Energiekonservierung limitierenden Schritte identifizieren, wozu neben der Cytochromoxidase die Nachlieferung von Substrat und der Transport von Adenylaten über die Mitochondrienmembran zählen. Eine Beschreibung der Dynamik der Phosphorylierung erlaubt dieses Modell allerdings nicht.

<u>Calvin-Zyklus</u>

In der gegenwärtig existierenden Literatur lassen sich hierzu im wesentlichen zwei
Typen von Modellbildung finden: zum einen wird die Reaktionsfolge des Calvin-Zyklus
möglichst komplett in Differentialgleichungen umgesetzt, wobei man ca. 18 DGln erhält,
die numerisch gelöst werden, zum anderen werden heuristische Teilmodelle, die oft nur
zwei und drei Variable enthalten, untersucht, diese z.T. auch analytisch. Ein Beispiel
zur ersten Vorgehensweise ist das Modell von Hahn (5) mit 17 gekoppelten nichtlinearen
Differentialgleichungen. Zusätzlich zum Calvin-Zyklus betrachtet Hahn auch die Stärke-
synthese im Chloroplasten sowie die Synthese von Saccharose im Cytosol und den Transport dieses Zuckers ins Phloem und in die Vakuole. Dieses Modell liefert Fließgleich-
gewichtskonzentrationen für die betrachteten Metabolite, vorausgesetzt die 20 Konstanten des Modells sind bekannt. Interessant für die Dynamik des Systems ist, daß auch
nach drastischen Störungen des Fließgleichgewichtes das System stabil reagiert. Haupt-
ziel ist die dynamische Simulation der biochemischen Reaktionen über einen 24-Stunden
Zyklus mit Tag/Nach-Wechsel und entsprechendem Umschalten von Stärke-Synthese auf
Stärke-Abbau. Das vorgeschlagene Modell ist auch tatsächlich in der Lage, dies zu lei-
sten; allerdings ist fraglich, ob eine der Voraussagen des Modells, das biochemische
System käme jeweils nach Umschalten auf Tag- bzw. Nachtbedingungen nicht ins Fließgleichgewicht, regulatorisch sinnvoll ist und so aufrecht erhalten werden kann.

Zu dem anderen Typ der Modellbildung des Calvin-Zyklus zählt z.B. eine Arbeit von
Kaitala u.a. (6). Hier werden in einem System mit nur zwei Variablen sowohl die Licht-
als auch die Dunkelreaktionen des Calvin-Zyklus beschrieben, die ausschließlich über
die Produktion von Reduktionsäquivalenten (NADPH) miteinander gekoppelt sind. Dieses
Modell ist in der Lage, die Abhängigkeit der Photosyntheserate von der Lichtintensität
und der $CO_2$-Konzentration richtig wiederzugeben. Während dieses Modell wie auch z.B.
das von Peisker (7) hauptsächlich die Regulation der Fixierung von $CO_2$ auf dem Hintergrund der vorhandenen Energie (Licht) und der regulatorischen Eigenschaften der Ribulo-
sebisphosphatcarboxylase/oxygenase (Rubisco) betrachtet, bringt eine Arbeit von Dvorák
und Sel'kov (8) einen weiteren Aspekt in die Diskussion: nicht die Rubisco, sondern die
Phosphoribulokinase sei das für Regulation und Dynamik des Calvin-Zyklus entscheidende
Enzym; das Produkt dieser letzten Reaktion, RuBP, wurde experimentell als Produktakti-
vator der Phosphoribulokinase erkannt. Dvorák und Sel'kov beschreiben diesen Aspekt
mit Hilfe eines Systems von 3 gekoppelten nichtlinearen Differentialgleichungen. Sie
erhalten Hinweise dafür, daß die Durchsatzrate durch den Calvin-Zyklus nicht durch die
Carboxylierungs-Reaktion der Rubisco, sondern durch den regenerativen Zweig des Systems limitiert sei. Gleichzeitig kommen sie zu dem Schluß, daß die Phosphoribulokinase
für die *in-vivo*-Regulation der Photosynthese wohl eher von untergeordneter Bedeutung
sei.

## 4. Zur Parameterschätzung und -optimierung

Viele der Enzyme des Calvin-Zyklus sind mittlerweile isoliert und enzymkinetisch charakterisiert worden, für die meisten dieser Enzyme liegen also Daten für die $K_m$- und $V_{max}$-Werte vor. Allerdings erlauben die ermittelten kinetischen Konstanten oft keine komplette enzymkinetische Beschreibung der Reaktionsraten, da - besonders bei Bisubstratreaktionen - selten sämtliche kinetischen Konstanten bestimmt wurden. In aller Regel (und bei allen o.a. Modellen) werden daher die kompletten enzymkinetischen Ansätze durch Reaktionen erster oder zweiter Ordnung ersetzt. Da für derartige kinetische Ansätze die gemessenen kinetischen Daten nur noch bedingt brauchbar sind, werden diese jetzt zu bestimmenden Parameter häufig über bekannte Daten wie stationäre Raten der $CO_2$-Fixierung oder Poolgrößen einzelner Metaboliten abgeschätzt. Neben der üblichen "trial and error"-Methode werden die Parameter auch mit Hilfe von Optimierungsalgorithmen ermittelt. Als mathematisch aufwendige Arbeit ist in diesem Zusammenhang der Versuch von Milstein und Bremermann (9) zu nennen, zu einer Modellierung des Calvin-Zyklus durch 17 Differentialgleichungen mit 22 Parametern eine Parameteroptimierung vorzunehmen. Das Differentialgleichungssystem stellt eine exakte Modellierung des Calvin-Zyklus dar (noch stärker an den biochemischen Gegebenheiten orientiert als das Modell von Hahn (5)), sowie eine etwas vereinfachte Beschreibung der Stärke-Synthese in den Chloroplasten. Den Autoren gelingt es, mit Hilfe von sechs vorgegebenen experimentellen Datensätzen die 22 Parameter mit erstaunlicher Genauigkeit zu schätzen. Trotz der mathematischen Konsistenz bleibt allerdings fraglich, ob dieses Modell viel zur Klärung der Dynamik des Calvin-Zyklus beiträgt; das vorgegebene Differentialgleichungssystem gilt z.B. nur in unmittelbarer Umgebung der experimentell bestimmten Punkte, so daß eine dynamische Simulation mit Hilfe der errechneten Parameter durchaus fragliche Aussagen liefert.

## 5. Kriterien für die Plausibilität dynamischer Modelle des Calvin-Zyklus

Als Kriterien für die Plausibilität eines Modelles ist zunächst zu prüfen, ob die errechneten Raten (etwa der $O_2$-Entwicklung, der $CO_2$-Aufnahme) und die Poolgrößen der Intermediate innerhalb der physiologischen Bandbreite liegen. Wurden allerdings Parameter aus bekannten Poolgrößen oder Raten abgeleitet, so ist dieses Kriterium hinfällig. Ferner ist im Hinblick auf die bekannten Stabilitätseigenschaften des Calvin-Zyklus auch von dem Modell dynamische Stabilität zu fordern. Ein weiteres Kriterium ergibt sich aus kürzlich wieder aufgegriffenen Untersuchungen (10) der Photosyntheseoszillationen: danach können - je nach experimentellen Bedingungen - die Stabilitätspunkte des Calvin-Zyklus nicht nur Knoten, sondern auch Foci sein. Das dynamische Modell sollte also zu Schwingungen befähigt sein, wie das z.B. für die einfachen Modelle von Laisk (11) und Giersch (12) der Fall ist. Nach diesem letzten Kriterium geben die Modelle von Kaitala u.a. (6) und von Dvorák und Sel'kov (8) die Dynamik des untersuchten Systems nicht korrekt wieder, da diese Modelle keine oszillatorischen Lösungen haben.

## 6. Ausblick

Abschließend sollen einige Punkte genannt werden, zu deren Klärung noch zu erstellende Simulationsmodelle beitragen können. In vielen Fällen wird schon zur Formulierung des Modelles noch experimentelle Vorarbeit geleistet werden müssen. Die im folgenden angesprochenen Fragen können daher auch zur Anregungen für experimentelles Vorgehen führen:

- Wie erfolgt die Umschaltung von der anfänglichen "Brutphase" des Calvin-Zyklus zur Fließgleichgewichtssituation mit dem bekannten hohen Anteil von Export an neu fixiertem Kohlenstoff in das Cytosol? Welche Größe(n) regulieren die Flux-Verteilung?
- Welche Prozesse regulieren im Fließgleichgewicht den Durchsatz durch den Calvin-Zyklus? Wie groß sind die aus einem Simulationsmodell abgeleiteten Kontrollkoeffizienten (13) einzelner Reaktionen?
- Welchen Erkenntniswert besitzen dynamische Modelle des Calvin-Zyklus, die für den Stoffdurchsatz das Massenwirkungsgesetz, nicht aber den Einfluß von Effektoren berücksichtigen?
- Besitzt das biochemische System "Calvin-Zyklus" nur einen oder mehrere stationäre Zustände? (Für die letzte Möglichkeit sprechen Untersuchungen von Hahn (5)). Besitzt das System Bifurkationen?
- Die photosynthetischen Oszillationen enthalten Information über die Größe der partiellen Ableitungen der Reaktionsraten einzelner Enzyme. Wie lassen sich hieraus Aussagen über die Reaktionsraten gewinnen?

## Literatur


1. R.C. Leegood, D.A. Walker and C.H. Foyer (1985) Regulation of the Benson-Calvin Cycle *in* Photosynthetic mechanisms and the environment, Vol. 6 (J. Barber and N.R. Baker, eds.), Elsevier, Amsterdam
2. J. Whitmarsh and W.A. Cramer (1980) Meth. Enzymol. 69, 202-223
3. R. Bohnensack (1981) Biochim. Biophys. Acta 634, 203-218
4. R. Bohnensack, U. Küster and G. Letko (1982) Biochim. Biophys. Acta 680, 271-280
5. B.D. Hahn (1984) Ann. Bot. 54, 325-339
6. V. Kaitala, P. Hari, E. Vapaavuori and R. Salminen (1982) Ann. Bot. 50, 385-396
7. M. Peisker (1974) Photosynthetica 8, 47-50
8. I. Dvorâk and E.E. Sel'kov (1980) Photosynthetica 14, 564-574
9. J. Milstein and H.J. Bremermann (1979) J. Math. Biol. 7, 99-116
10. D.A. Walker, M.N. Sivak, R.T. Prinsley and J.K. Cheesbrough (1983) Plant Physiol. 73, 542-549
11. A.K. Laisk (1983) Fiziologia Rastenii 30, 837-851
12. C. Giersch, eingereicht Arch. Biochem. Biophys.
13. R. Heinrich, S.M. Rapoport and T.A. Rapoport (1977) Progr. Biophys. Molec. Biol. 32, 1-82

# Simulation zentraler Regulationsstörungen bei intrakranieller Drucksteigerung

Oskar Hoffmann, Gießen

Zusammenfassung: Es wird die Ergänzung des Modelles des isolierten intrakraniellen Systems um kardiovaskuläre Komponenten beschrieben. Dabei wird eine Regelung des arteriellen Mitteldruckes über Verstellungen von Herzfrequenz und peripherem Widerstand einbezogen. Störungen dieses Regelkreises werden in Abhängigkeit von einer Minderdurchblutung des Hirnstammes angenommen. Der Modellaufbau wird beschrieben, und Simulationsbeispiele werden demonstriert.

Summary: An extension of the model of the isolated intracranial system by cardiovascular components is reported. Mean arterial blood pressure is regulated in the model via adaequate changes of heart rate and peripheral resistance. Disturbances of this control circuit are assumed to be related to the degree of reduction of regional blood flow in the brain stem. The features of the model are described and simulations are demonstrated.

Intrakranielle Drucksteigerungen stellen eine erhebliche Gefährdung für neurochirurgische Patienten dar. Durch Massenverschiebungen, Behinderung des venösen Abflusses und Verminderung der cerebralen Durchblutung kann sie zu Schädigungen des Hirnstammes führen, und damit zu Störungen der zentralen Regulation /5/.

Die bisher entwickelten Modelle bildeten den isolierten intrakraniellen Raum nach /1,2/. Die Einbeziehung der cerebralen Hämodynamik erlaubte die Simulation der Autoregulation der cerbralen Durchblutung. Der Einfluß hämodynamischer Variabler auf den intrakraniellen Druck und daraus abgeleitete Größen konnte mit diesem Modell untersucht werden /3/.

Die Umkehrung, nämlich die Auswirkung einer Steigerung des intrakraniellen Druckes (ICP) auf die Hämodynamik, kann dagegen nur mit einem um kardiovaskuläre Komponenten erweiterten Modell simuliert und untersucht werden. Dazu wird das Modell des intrakraniellen Raumes /2/ unter Einbeziehung von linkem Herzventrikel, Aorta und extracerebralem peripheren Widerstand von einer stark vereinfachten Nachbildung des kardiovaskulären Systems umgeben (Abb. 1). In Anlehnung an das Kreislaufmodell

von MÖLLER /4/ wird eine Regelung des arteriellen Mitteldruckes (MABP)
über Verstellungen von Herzfrequenz (HR) und peripherem Widerstand (PR)
angenommen. Die Modellvorstellung geht von einer Erfassung des Blut-
druckes durch die Barorezeptoren aus. Die dadurch erzeugten Entladungs-
muster werden über afferente Nervenbahnen an die auch mit höheren Strukturen verbundenen Kreislaufzentren in der Medulla oblongata übermittelt,
von wo aus über efferente Bahnen diese Verstellungen bewirkt werden. Die
hierbei wirksamen Reglerkennlinien sind bei MÖLLER /4/ beschrieben.

Als Maß für die Störung der zentralen Regulation wird die aktuelle regionale Durchblutung des Hirnstammes in Relation zum Normalwert gewählt.
Durch Rückgriff auf Ergebnisse tierexperimenteller Untersuchungen /6/
kann die Hirnstammdurchblutung als Funktion der totalen cerebralen
Durchblutung abgeleitet und in das Modell einbezogen werden (Abb. 3).
Die Störung selbst soll darin bestehen, daß die über afferente Nerven an
die Kreislaufzentren übermittelten Impulsfolgen nicht mehr richtig erkannt oder verarbeitet werden. Im Modell leitet der Regler daher die
Stellgrößen aus dem reduzierten Signal $DRF^{NHR} \cdot ABP$ (für Herzfrequenz),
bzw. $DRF^{NPR} \cdot ABP$ (für peripheren Widerstand) ab. Der Dysregulationsfaktor
DRF resultiert dabei aus der Minderdurchblutung des Hirnstammes. Einen
Überblick über das gesamte Modell gibt die blockorientierte Darstellung
in Abb. 2.

Mit diesem Modell lassen sich pathologische Entwicklungen, wie z.B. eine
Raumforderung mit konstanter Wachstumsrate mit ihren Auswirkungen auf die
Blutdruckregulation simulieren (Abb. 4). Dabei wird angenommen, daß der
Liquorabsorptionswiderstand (RO) mit zunehmender Raumforderung ansteigt,

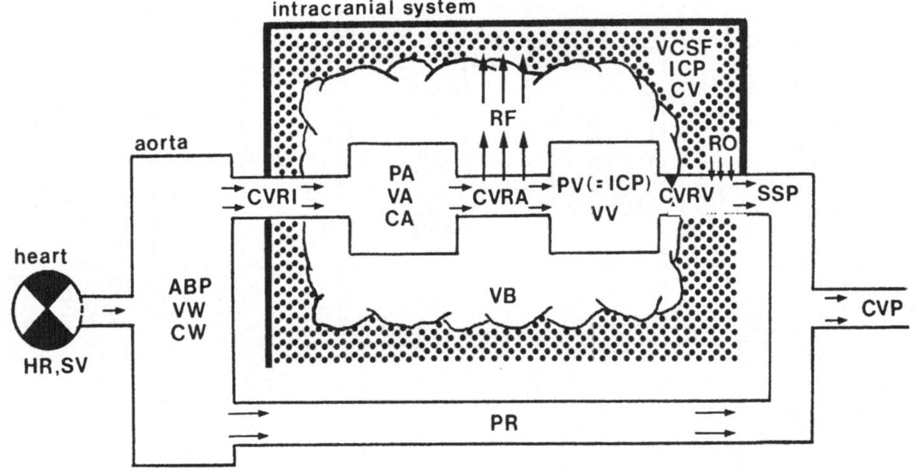


Abb. 1: Kombiniertes Modell des intrakraniellen und kardiovaskulären
Systems.

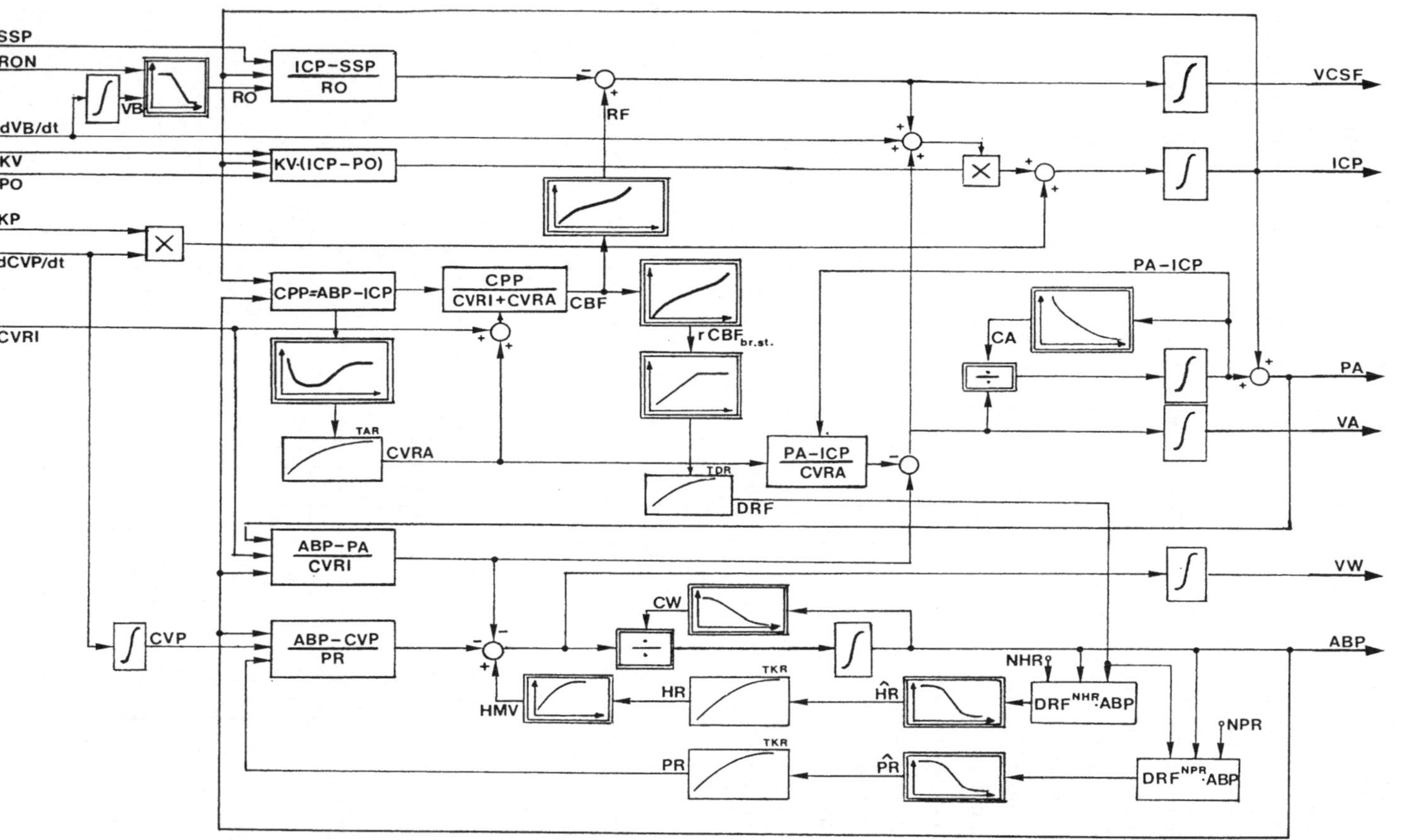


Abb. 2: Blockorientierte Darstellung des kombinierten Modells des intrakraniellen und kardiovaskulären Systems. (ICP-intrakranieller Druck, SSP-Sinus sagittalis-Druck, ABP-arterieller Blutdruck, RF-Liquorformationsrate, CPP-cerebraler Perfusionsdruck, RO-Liquorabsorptionswiderstand, CVP-zentral venöser Druck, PA-Druck im arteriellen Kompartment des cerebralen Gefäßbettes, HR-Herzfrequenz, PR-peripherer Widerstand, CVR-cerebro-vaskuläre Resistenz)

Abb. 3: Regionale Durchblutung des Hirnstammes als Funktion der totalen cerebralen Durchblutung bei intrakranieller Drucksteigerung

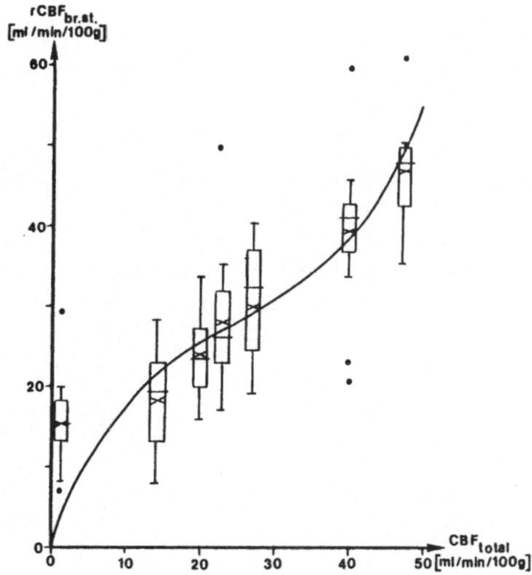


Neben der absoluten Höhe des intrakraniellen Druckes wird als weiterer Irritationsfaktor für die Hirnstammfunktion die Anstiegsgeschwindigkeit des ICP gesehen. Es wird daher zusätzlich eine Stressgröße (STG) eingeführt, die bei steigendem ICP der zeitlichen Ableitung dieser Variablen entspricht, ansonsten aber verschwindet. Die Stressnachwirkung wird über ein Verzögerungsglied erster Ordnung berücksichtigt. Aus dieser Stressgröße wird ein Stressfaktor (STF) nach

$$STF = 1 - \frac{1 - STFB}{1 + \frac{STG}{2}} \qquad mit\ 0 < STFB < 1$$

hergeleitet. Dieser bewegt sich zwischen dem Basiswert STFB und 1. Der Dysregulationsfaktor DRF wird nun ersetzt durch den Dysregulationsfaktor unter Stress (DRFS) nach

$$DRFS = 1 - STF \cdot (1 - DRF) \qquad .$$

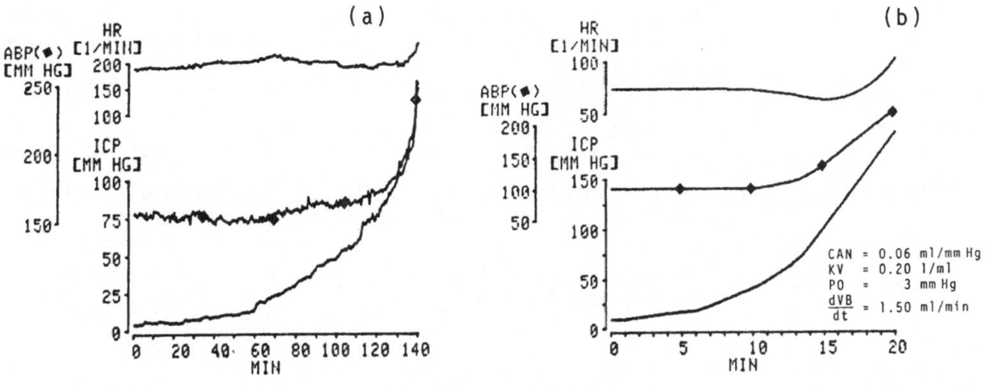


Abb. 4: Raumforderung mit konstanter Wachstumsrate im Tierexperiment (a) und im Modell (b).

Abb. 5: Synchrone Rhythmen
unterschiedlicher Aus-
prägung und Frequenz
bei zentraler Dysregu-
lation im Modell

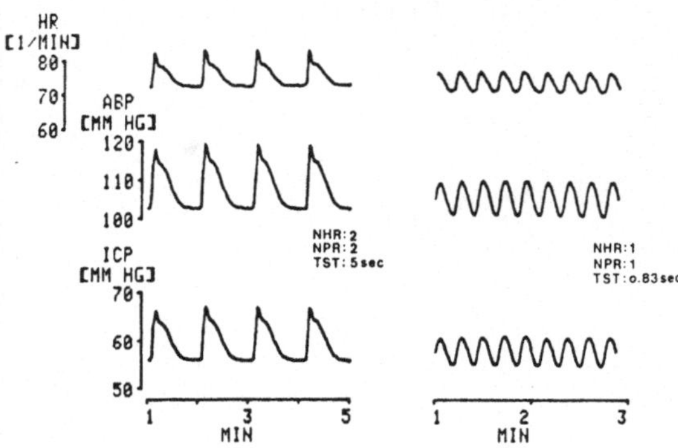


Diese Modellmodifikation führt in der Simulation zu typischen Reizaus-
brüchen von ICP, ABP und HR, wie sie als Folge zentraler Dysregulation
auch bei der Intensivüberwachung neurochirurgischer Patienten zu beobachten sind (Abb. 5).


## Literatur

/1/ Hoffmann, O.: Ein mathematisches Modell zur Simulation der Liquor-
dynamik. In: Informatik Fachber. Bd. 56: Simulationstechnik (M. Goller, ed.), 343-350, Berlin-Heidelberg-
New York, Springer 1982

/2/ Hoffmann, O.: Simulation der intrakraniellen Liquor- und Hämodynamik
unter Einbeziehung der cerebralen Autoregulation.
In: Informatik Fachber. Bd. 85: Simulationstechnik
(F. Breitenecker, W. Kleinert, eds.), 383-387,
Berlin-Heidelberg-New York-Tokyo, Springer 1984

/3/ Hoffmann, O., Zierski, J.: Analysis of the ICP pulse-pressure-
relationship as a function of arterial blood pressure.
Acta Neurochir. 66, 1-21 (1982)

/4/ Möller, D.: Ein geschlossenes nichtlineares Modell zur Simulation
des Kurzzeitverhaltens des Kreislaufsystems und seine
Anwendung zur Identifikation.
Berlin-Heidelberg-New York, Springer 1981

/5/ Pia, H.W.: Central dysregulation in brain stem lesions.
Excerpta Medica Int. Congr. Series ICS 320, 290-299 (1973)

/6/ Zierski, J., Kurzaj, E., Hoffmann, O., Winkler, B.: Cerebral blood
flow in the brain stem during increased ICP.
In: Intracranial Pressure V (S. Ishii, H. Nagai,
M. Brock, eds.), 452-457, Berlin-Heidelberg-New York-
Tokyo, Springer 1983

EIN PROGRAMMSYSTEM ZUR SIMULATION DES KREISLAUFSYSTEMS UND
ZUR IDENTIFIKATION VON KREISLAUFPARAMETERN


Heribert Pösinger, Graz


Zusammenfassung. Es wird ein Programmsystem vorgestellt, mit dessen Hilfe eine neue
Art der Bestimmung der Funktionsfähigkeit ('Kontraktilität') des linken Ventrikels
möglich ist. Es enthält ein Kreislaufsimulations- und ein Identifikationsprogramm.
Die Beschreibung der Kontraktilität besteht aus drei Parametern, was eine bessere
Beschreibung als einzelne bisher übliche Kontraktilitätsindices erlaubt.

Summary. A program-system allowing a new kind of description of the left ventricle's
function ('contractility') is presented. It contains a program for the simulation
of a circulation model and an identification program. The contractility in this
system is described by three parameters allowing a better characterization than
single contractility-indices commonly used up to now.


1. Einführung

Die Bestimmung der Kontraktilität des linken Ventrikels des Herzens ist eines der

schwierigsten meßtechischen Probleme bei der Untersuchung des Kreislaufs. Zu den

meßtechnischen Problemen kommt noch das Fehlen einer einheitlichen Definition des

Begriffes 'Kontraktilität' /1/.


Zur Überwindung dieser Probleme wurde am Institut für Elektro- und Biomedizinische

Technik der TU Graz in Zusammenarbeit mit dem Ludwig-Boltzmann-Institut für experi-

mentelle Traumatologie in Wien ein Programmsystem zur Simulation des Kreislauf-

systems und zur Identifikation von Parametern des Kreislaufsystems entwickelt /2/.


2. Identifikation

Zur Ermittlung der Kenngrößen des untersuchten Kreislaufes wird zunächst eine

Modellstruktur gewählt. Allen Parametern des Modelles werden Anfangswerte zu-

gewiesen. Die darauf folgende Simulationsberechnung ergibt Verläufe von Druck und

Flow (Blutstrom), die sich aus der Struktur des Modelles und den gewählten Start-

werten ergeben.


Diese Druck- und Strömungsverläufe werden mit entsprechenden, am untersuchten Kreis-

lauf gemessenen, verglichen. Die Ähnlichkeit der Simulationsergebnisse und der ge-

messenen Kurven ist ein Maß für die Übereinstimmung zwischen Modell und unter-

suchtem Kreislauf.

In einem automatisierten Verfahren werden die zur Identifikation freigegebenen Parameter des Modells entsprechend den Vorschriften des gewählten Identifikationsverfahrens geändert, die Simulationsberechnung wiederholt und das Ergebnis mit den Referenzdaten verglichen, bis die Übereinstimmung zwischen dem Simulationsergebnis und den Meßdaten optimal ist.

Die Parameterwerte des Modells, auf das der untersuchte Kreislauf solcherart abgebildet wurde, entsprechen den Werten der entsprechenden Parameter des Kreislaufes.

## 3. Kreislaufmodell

Da die Aufgabe des Programmsystems die Bestimmung der Kontraktilität des linken Ventrikels ist, wurde auf die Nachbildung des physiologisch geschlossenen Kreislaufsystems verzichtet.

Das Modell besteht aus Teilmodellen für den Einstrombereich, die Atrio-Ventrikular-Klappe, den linken Ventrikel, die Aortenklappe und den Ausstrombereich (Abb.1). Da mit dem Modell das Kurzzeitverhalten des linken Ventrikels nachgebildet werden soll, wurde auf die Simulation von Regelmechanismen verzichtet.

Das hydraulische Verhalten des Kreislaufsystems wird auf ein elektrisches Modell abgebildet. Der elektrische Strom dient als Abbild des Volumenstromes (Blutstromes), die elektrische Spannung als Modell des Druckes.

## 3.1. Modell für den Ein- und Ausströmbereich

Die Teilmodelle für Ein- und Ausströmbereich, in Abb. 1 mit 'VENE' und 'ARTE', für venösen und arteriellen Teil des Kreislaufmodells, bezeichnet, können aus konzentrierten linearen Elementen aufgebaut werden (Abb. 2). Die möglichen Bauteile sind ein Widerstand, RL, oder ein Leitwert, GQ, zur Nachbildung der Reibung, eine Kapazität, CQ, zur Nachbildung der Volumselastizität des Blutgefäße, eine Induktivität, LL, als Modell der Massenträgheit des Blutes und eine Spannungsquelle, UQ, zur Nachbildung eines Gegendruckes als Abschluß eines Teilmodells. Das Element 'V2' ermöglicht die Nachbildung von Verzweigungen der Blutgefäße. Das Element 'EN' gibt das Ende der Definition eines Teilmodells an.

## 3.2. Modell für Herzklappen

Die möglichen Strukturen für das Modell einer Herzklappe reichen von einem einfachen Rückschlagventil (Abb. 3a) bis zu einem Modell, das sowohl das zum Klappenschluß nötige Rückstromvolumen, als auch Reibung und Trägheit des Blutes im Bereich der Klappe berücksichtigt (Abb. 3b) /2/.

## 3.3. Modell für den linken Ventrikel

Das Modell für den linken Ventrikel besteht aus einer zeitvarianten Kapazität und einem Widerstand (Abb. 4). Der zeitliche Verlauf des Kapazitätswertes ist die treibende Funktion des Kreislaufmodells. Er bildet die Funktion der Herzmuskulatur nach.

Aus rechentechnischen Gründen wird der Kehrwert der Kapazität

$$E_V(t) = \frac{P_V(t)}{(V_V(t) - V_{VO})} \,, \tag{1}$$

mit dem Ventrikeldruck $P_V$, dem Blutvolumen im Ventrikel $V_V$ und einem Referenzvolumen $V_{VO}$, zur Definition der Ventrikelkapazität verwendet.

Die Kurvenform für $E_V(t)$ für die Zeit vom Beginn eines Pulses (t=0) bis zur Zeit $2 \cdot t_{max}$, wurde der Literatur entnommen /3/. Zur Bestimmung des aktuellen Form von $E_V(t)$ reichen nach dieser Definition die vier Parameter $E_{min}$, $E_{max}$, $t_{max}$ und $t_p$ aus.

Bei der Identifikation ergibt sich die Pulsdauer $t_p$ aus den am untersuchten Kreislauf ermittelten Daten. Zur Beschreibung der Kontraktilität bleiben $E_{min}$, $E_{max}$ und die Zeit vom Beginn des Pulses bis zum Erreichen von $E_{max}$, $t_{max}$.

Der Widerstand $R_V$ bildet die Reibung im Myokard und im Blut im linken Ventrikel nach.

## 4. Implementierung der Programme

Die Programme zur Kreislaufsimuation und -identifikation wurden unter dem Betriebssystem RT11 in FORTRAN 4 auf einer PDP 11/34a implementiert.

Für die beiden Teilmodelle für Ein- und Ausstromteil ist Speicherplatz für etwa 150 Elemente vorgesehen. Die genaue Zahl hängt von der gewählten Struktur ab, da in diesem Bereich intern zusätzliche Elemente zur Steuerung der Berechnung eingebaut werden.

Bis zu 8 Ströme oder Spannungen können ausgegeben und zur Definition des Qualitätskriteriums verwendet werden.

Programme zur Digitalisierung und Vorverarbeitung der Meßdaten stehen zur Verfügung.

Zur Identifikation kann man zwischen drei Verfahren wählen /2/. Als Qualitätskriterium dient die gewichtete Summe der Quadrate der relativen Abweichungen der Ergebnisse der Simulation von den entsprechenden Meßwerten. Die Gewichtung ist vom Benützer zu wählen.

## 5. Schluß

Mit diesem Programmsytem ist es möglich, vier Parameter zu ermitteln, die gemeinsam den Zustand des linken Ventrikels beschreiben. Diese Parameter erlauben eine bessere Beschreibung der 'Kontraktilität' des linken Ventrikels als bisher übliche Kontraktilitätsindices.

## 6. Literatur

/1/ KRÖSL, P.: Die Kontraktilität des linken Ventrikels. Graz: Technische Universität, Dissertation 1980.

/2/ PÖSINGER H., P. WACH, P. KRÖSL: Ein Programmsystem zur Identifikation von Parametern des Kreislaufsystems, in Gell, G. und Eichtinger, Ch. (Hrsg.): Medizinische Informatik '84, R. Oldenbourg, Wien München 1984

/3/ SUGA, H., K. SAGAWA, A. A. SHOUKAS: Load independence of the instantaneous pressure-volume-ratio of the canine left ventricle. Circulation research, Vol. 32 (1973), 314 - 322

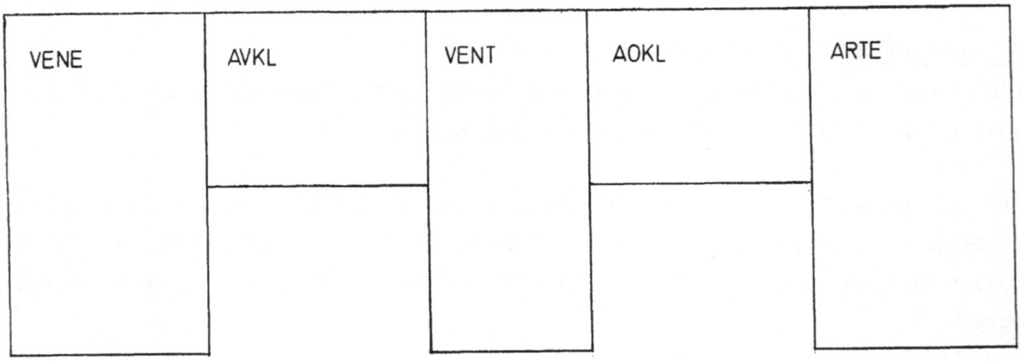

Abb. 1: Struktur des Kreislaufmodells:
VENE ... Modell des Einstromteiles    AVKL ... Modell der A-V-Klappe
VENT ... Modell des linken Ventrikels    AOKL ... Modell der Aortenklappe
ARTE ... Modell für Aorta und Arterien

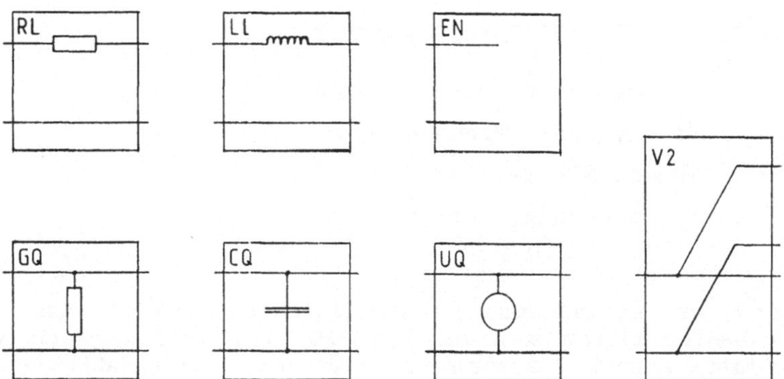

Abb. 2: Elemente der Ersatzschaltung für Ein- und Ausstromteil des Kreislaufmodells

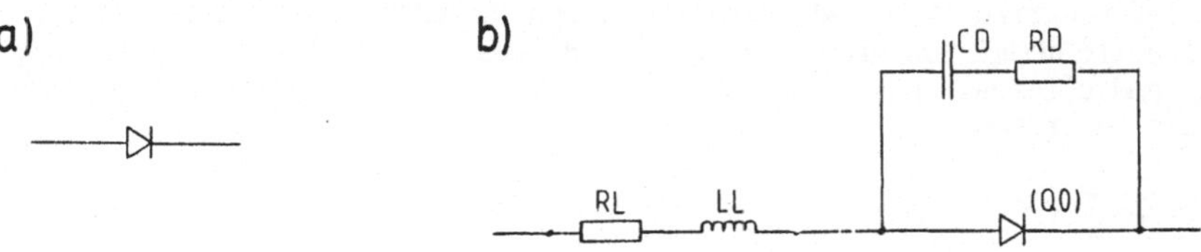

Abb. 3: Modell für Herzklappen:
   a) einfachste Version (Rückschlagventil)
   b) Version mit Rückströmvolumen, Parallelkapazität und Berücksichtigung des
      Blutvolumens im Klappenbereich

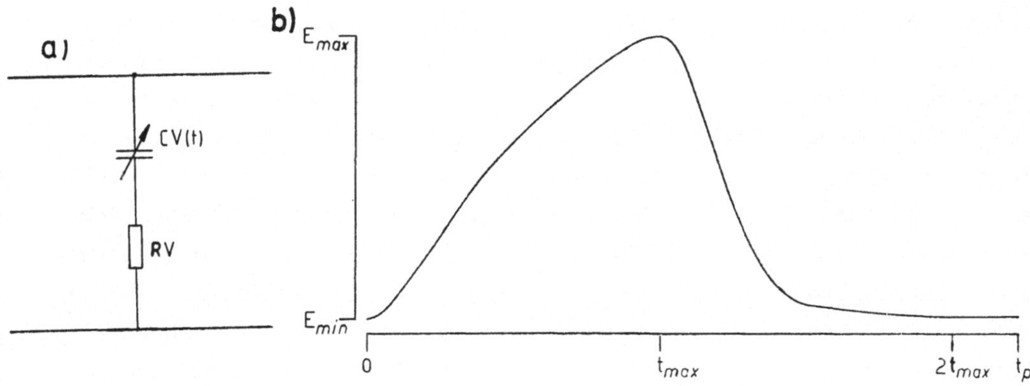

Abb. 4: Modell des linken Ventrikels:
   a) elektrische Ersatzschaltung
   b) Verlauf von $E_V(t)$

SIMULATION  EINES UNGEREGELTEN  PULSATILEN

MODELLES  DES  HERZKREISLAUFSYSTEMS


Dietmar P. F. Möller, Mainz

Vaclav Pohl, Bremen

Thomas Sikora, Berlin

Ewald Hennig, Berlin



Zusammenfassung: Es wird ein mathematisches Modell des Herzkreislaufsystems vorgestellt, welches die Pulsatilität berücksichtigt. Das Modell wird ausgehend, von einem
nichtpulsatilen Mittelwertmodell entwickelt. Der Entwurf eines pulsatilen Kreislauf-
modelles ist für die Untersuchung hämodynamischer Einflüsse beim Totalherzersatz und
bei den verschiedenen Unterstützungsmethoden (Linksherz-, Rechtsherz- und Biventriku-
läre Herzunterstützung ) von besonderem Interesse. Darüber hinaus ist ein pulsatiles
Herzkreislaufmodell auch für physiologische, sportphysiologische und klinische Fragestellungen von Bedeutung. Es werden erste Ergebnisse des Modelles vorgestellt.
Summary: A mathematical model of the circulatory system is outlined, including the
pulsatation of the real biological system. The model is based on a nonpulsatile model,
a so called average model. A pulsatile model is of importance studying the haemodyna-
mic influence which occur with a total artificial heart or at different heart support
systems ( leftventrikular-, rightventricular and biventricular bypass-systems ). Moreover a pulsatile model ist proper to use in the research fields of physiology,  sports-
physiology and clinical applications. First result obtained by simulation with the
model should be presented.


## 1. Einleitung

Für die Auslegung von Regelstrecken bei biologischen Systemen ist die

mathematische Modellbildung und Simulation von großer Bedeutung. Gerade

das komplexe Regelungssystem Herzkreislauf ist prädestiniert für die An-

wendung systemtheoretischer Methoden. Die rechnerunterstützte Simulation

kann z.B. tierexperimentelle Forschungen ergänzen, indem sie z.B. die

Möglichkeiten und Probleme einer adaptiven Anpassung des Perfusionsvo-

lumens von Blutpumpensystemen an die Erfordernisse des Versuchstieres

erfaßt, beziehungsweise den Ersatz einer im regelfall nicht vorhandenen

geschlossenen mathematischen Lösung darstellt, da die mathematische Be-

handlung nichtlinearer Beziehungen im Regelfall die Lösung komplizierter

und teilweise verkoppelter Differentialgleichungssysteme erfordert.

In einer früheren Arbeit /1/ wurde, ausgehend von bekannten physiolo-

gischen Zusammenhängen des Herzkreislaufsystems, durch mathematische

Abstraktion in Form von Differentialgleichungen, welche die relevanten

biologischen Prozesse beschreiben, ein mathematisches Kreislaufmodell

entwickelt. Dabei wurden nur diejenigen Systemelemente mit ihren Attri-

buten berücksichtigt, die den Prämissen des Anwendungszusammenhanges

- hier das Herzersatz- beziehungsweise Herzunterstützungssystem -, ge-

nügen. Es sind dies die folgenden Systemelemente:

- arterielle elastische Kompartimente CAS und CAP

- resistive Kompartimente RA und PR
- venös kapazitive Kompartimente CVS und CVP
- kardiale Kompartimente ( Herzmodell ).

Um ein pulsatiles Verhalten zu realisieren, sind die kontraktilen Elemente des Herzens zeitvariant anzusetzen, was beim früheren Modellansatz /1/ nicht der Fall war. Linker und rechter Ventrikel erfordern zum Druckaufbau - dieser ist die treibende Kraft für die Perfusion - eine zeitvariante Kontraktilität KKL(t) und KKR(t), die z.B. in Form einer Funktion vorliegen kann. Dir Pulsatiliät erfordert darüber hinaus die Berücksichtigung der vier Herzklappen. Herzklappen befinden sich an den Ein- und Auslaßöffnungen beider Ventrikel. Die Atrio-Ventricularklappen zwischen Vorhöfen und Kammern ( Mitralklappe links, Tricuspidalklappe rechts ) dienen zur Abdichtung der Ventrikel gegen die Atrien während der Systole; die Aorten- und die Pulmonalklappe an der Wurzel der großen Arterien verhindern den Rückstrom des Blutes in die Ventrikel während der Diastole. Das Spiel der Herzklappen wird im wesentlichen vom Verhalten des Druckes in den angrenzenden cardialen cavaes bzw. Gefäßen bestimmt. Die Funktion der Herzklappen kann z.B. durch entsprechend bewertete Begrenzerfunktionen realisiert werden.


## 2. Simulationsmodell

Ausgehend von dem in /1/ beschriebenen mathematischen Modell des kardiovaskulären Systems, wird dessen Basisregelkreis Orbis Cardiovascularis für einen pulsatilen Modellansatz zugrunde gelegt, dessen hydromechanisches Analogen in Bild 1 dargestellt ist.

Das Modell wurde sowohl in SLCS-4 als auch in ASS ( Allgemeines Simulationssystem ) implementiert und simuliert. SLCS-4 ist ein gleichungsorientierter Simulator, vergleichbar CSMP. ASS ist ein Wirkungsdiagramm orientierter Simulator bei dem nicht auf Gleichungen übergegangen werden muß, sondern es kann im Dialog mit dem Rechner die Wirkungsstruktur direkt eingegeben werden.

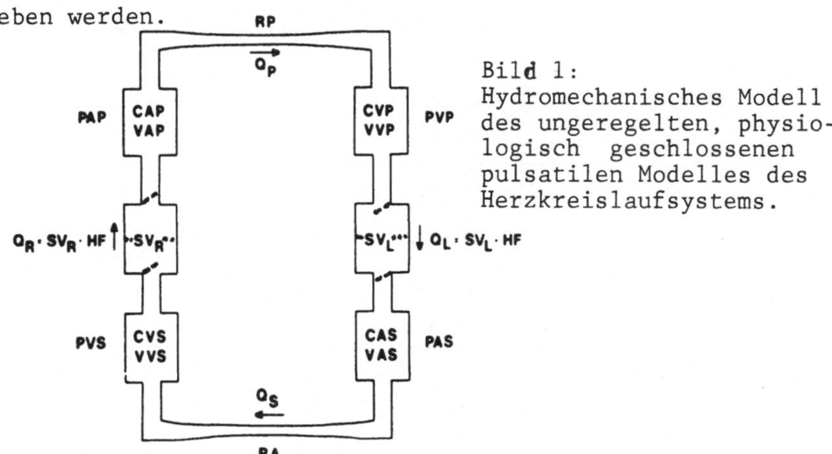


Bild 1:
Hydromechanisches Modell des ungeregelten, physiologisch geschlossenen pulsatilen Modelles des Herzkreislaufsystems.

## 3. Ergebnisse

Für das Mittelwertmodell ( nichtpulsatil ) wurde im stationären Fall
die folgenden Werte erreicht:

- PAS (arterieller Mitteldruck):        117,5 mmHg
- PAP (arteriopulmonaler Mitteldruck):  17,2 mmHg
- PVS (zentralvenöser Druck):           7,2 mmHg
- PVP (venöspulmonaler Mitteldruck)     10,9 mmHg.

Mit den in /1/ ausgeführten vereinfachten Ansätzen für den diastolischen
Blutdruck

$$Pd = 0,8 \cdot PAS \quad (mmHg)$$

und den systolischen Blutdruck

$$Ps = 1,2 \cdot PAS \quad (mmHg)$$

erhält man unter Berücksichtigung des oben angegebenen Mitteldruckes
PAS = 117,5 mmHg:

$$Pd = 94 \ mmHg$$

beziehungsweise

$$Ps = 141,5 \ mmHg.$$

Vergleicht man die zugehörigen vorläufigen Simulationsergebnisse des
pulsatilen Modelles, wie sie in Bild 2 gezeigt sind, so ergibt sich
bereits eine qualitativ gute Übereinstimmung mit obiger Abschätzung:
PAS = 127 mmHg ( Pd = 84 mmHg; Ps = 170 mmHg ).

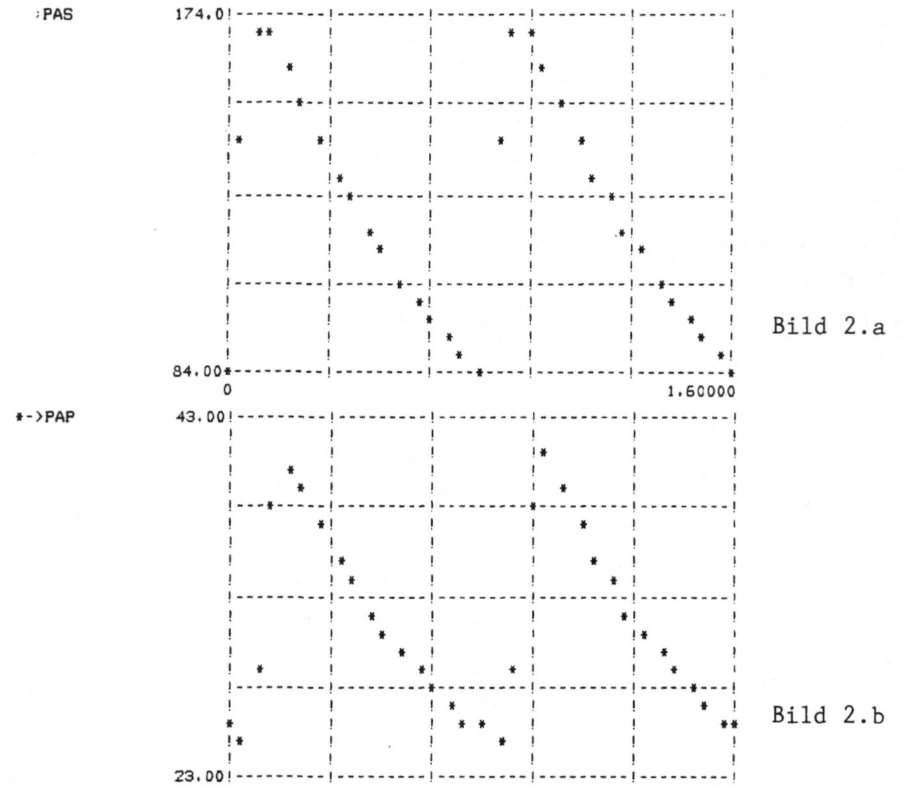

Bild 2.a

Bild 2.b

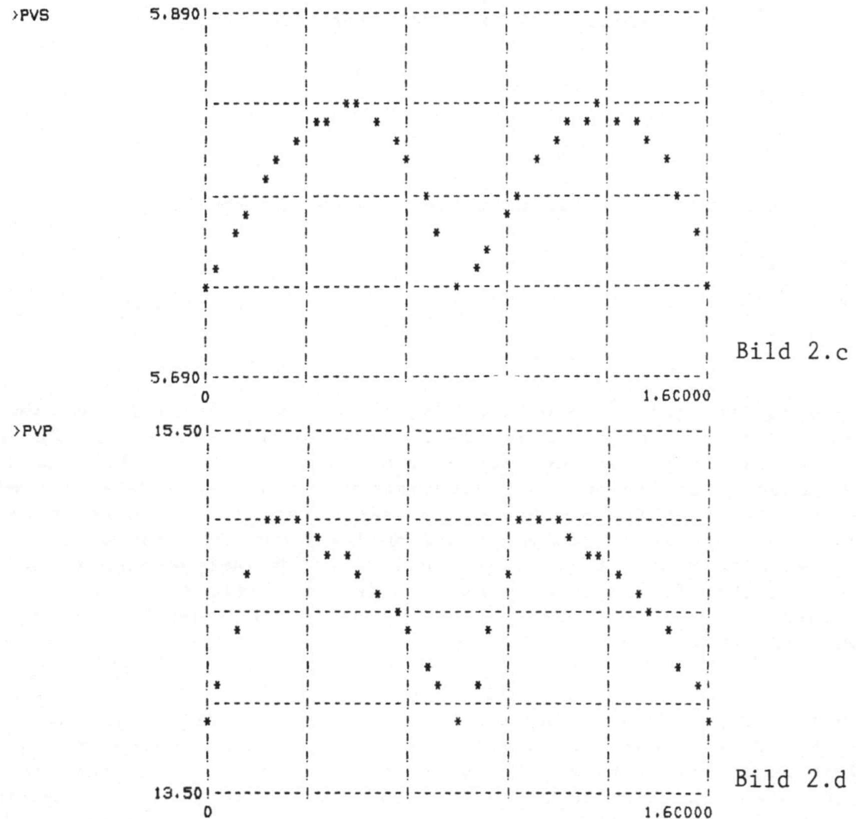



Bild 2. Ordinate: Druck in mmHg ; Abszisse: Zeit t in s - $t_s + t_d = 0,8s$ -

Die relativ zu hohen Ergebnisse für Pd und Ps, und damit auch für PAS,
haben ihre Ursache in den noch nicht optimierten Werten der druckbe-
stimmenden Parameter, die den Simulationen zugrunde gelegt wurden. Die
Optimierung dieser Parameter ist Gegenstand weiterer Arbeiten; ebenso
die differenziertere Modellbeschreibung im Sinne eines physiologisch
vollständig geschlossenen und geregelten pulsatilen Modelles des Herzkreislaufsystems. Mit Hilfe dieses Modelles sollen dann verschiedene
Regelstrategien für Herzunterstützungs- und -ersatzsysteme untersucht
und optimiert werden.

## Literatur


/1/ Möller, D.: Ein geschlossenes nichtlineares Modell zur Simulation des Kurzzeit-
verhaltens des Kreislaufsystems und seine Anwendung zur Identifikation
Springer-Verlag, Berlin-Heidelberg-New Yorg, 1981
Reihe: Medizinische Informatik und Statistik, Bd. 30



Die Arbeit wurde von der Deutschen Forschungsgemeinschaft im Rahmen des Vorhabens
He 1265/2-1 finanziell gefördert.

# ZUR MODELLIERUNG ZEITVERZÖGERTER BIOLOGISCHER PROZESSE


Björn A. Gottwald

Fakultät für Biologie der Universität Freiburg



**Zusammenfassung.** In biologischen Modellen treten häufig zeitlich verzögerte
Vorgänge auf, die in block-orientierten Simulations-Systemen die Einführung
von Totzeit-Blöcken erforderlich machen. Dabei stellt sich das Problem der
Kopplung solcher Totzeit-Blöcke mit numerischen Integrations-Verfahren mit
automatischer Schrittweiten-Steuerung. In diesem Beitrag werden verschiedene Interpolations-Verfahren (Polynome und Splines) mit numerischen Integratoren für gewöhnliche und steife Differential-Gleichungen gekoppelt und im
Hinblick auf ihre Effizienz untersucht. Als Testbeispiele dienen dabei ausgewählte einfache Modelle mit Zeit-Verzögerungen aus dem Bereich der Popu-
lations-Dynamik und der Enzym-Kinetik.

**Summary.** Retarded processes often occur in biological models which ne-
cessitates in block-oriented simulation systems the introduction of lag
blocks. This poses the problem of coupling such lag blocks with numerical
integration methods with automatic step size control. In this contribution
different interpolation methods (polynomes and splines) are coupled with
numerical integrators for ordinary and stiff differential equations and
tested with respect to their efficiency. The test examples (simple models
with time delays) are chosen from population dynamics and enzyme kinetics.


## 1. Einleitung

Bei der Modellierung biologischer Prozesse sind häufig zeitliche Verzögerungen in den Wirkungs-Mechanismen zu berücksichtigen. Dies macht in blockorientierten Simulations-Systemen (vergl. hierzu /GOTT85/) die Einführung
von Totzeit-Blöcken ("lag") und somit bei der numerischen Lösung der betreffenden Differential-Gleichungen die Kopplung von Integratoren mit Interpolations-Verfahren (vergl. /ARND84/) erforderlich. Zur Beurteilung der Effizienz verschiedener unterschiedlich aufwendiger Interpolations-Algorithmen
werden diese daher hier in Verbindung mit robusten Integratoren auf einfache, jedoch für biologische Prozesse typische, verzögerte Anfangswert-Pro-
bleme angewandt.

## 2. Integrations-Verfahren

Für diese Untersuchungen werden drei verschiedene numerische Integrations-
Verfahren mit automatischer Schrittweiten-Steuerung bei Vorgabe einer Tole-
ranz für den jeweiligen Schrittfehler benutzt :

**RK4** Dabei handelt es sich um das übliche Runge-Kutta-Verfahren 4. Ordnung.
Die Abschätzung des Fehlers geschieht dabei nach der Richardson-Extrapola-
tion, indem jeder einzelne Integrationsschritt zusätzlich in zwei Teil-
schritten ausgeführt wird.

**DOP** Dabei handelt es sich um das als RK5(4)7M in /DORM80/ angegebene Verfahren, bei dem die Abschätzung des Fehlers durch die Kopplung von Runge-
Kutta-Verfahren 4. und 5. Ordnung geschieht.

**ROW** Dabei handelt es es sich um das für steife Differential-Gleichungen als
ROW4A in /GOTT81/ angegebene Verfahren, bei dem die Abschätzung des Fehlers
durch die Kopplung von impliziten Runge-Kutta-Verfahren 3. und 4. Ordnung
geschieht.


## 3. Interpolations-Verfahren

Bei der numerischen Integration sind für verzögerte Variable $y(i)$ jeweils
die Werte zu einem um die Verzögerungszeit tlag zurückliegenden Zeitpunkt
als $ylag(i,tlag)$ erforderlich. Diese werden durch Interpolation zwischen
den bereits vorliegenden Werten der betreffenden Variablen gewonnen. Dabei
werden vier verschiedene Interpolations-Verfahren benutzt :

**LIN** Lineare Interpolation zwischen zwei vorliegenden Werten

**QUA** Quadratische Interpolation zwischen zwei vorliegenden Werten unter Verwendung des nächsten zeitlich zurückliegenden Wertes

**KUB** Kubische Interpolation zwischen zwei vorliegenden Werten unter Verwendung der gleichfalls berechneten und gespeicherten 1. Ableitungen der betreffenden Variablen

**DOU** Skalierte Runge-Kutta-Verfahren (vergl. /HORN83/) gestatten es, die bei
der numerischen Integration innerhalb eines Schrittes berechneten Zwischenwerte auch für eine sehr genaue Interpolation ("dense output") zu benutzen.
Dies wird hier auf die DOP-Integration angewandt, indem zusätzlich die erforderlichen Zwischenwerte gespeichert werden.


## 4. Test-Beispiele

Als Test-Beispiele werden die auch analytisch lösbare Differential-Gleichung $y''=-y$ (SIN), eine gemäß /HALB72/ modifizierte logistische Gleichung
(BRA) sowie ein in /OKAM84/ diskutierter enzymatischer Rückkopplungs-Me-

chanismus (OKA) benutzt :

<u>SIN</u> ydot(1) = ylag(2,tlag)          ydot(2) = -ylag(1,tlag)
    mit  tlag = 2 * pi  und den Anfangswerten  y(1) = 0  und  y(2) = 1
    für  t = 0  sowie  ylag(1,tlag) = sin(t)  und  ylag(2,tlag) = cos(t)
    im Bereich t = 0..tlag
Testgröße : absoluter Fehler von y(1) bei t = 4 * pi


<u>BRA</u> ydot(1) = r * y(1) * ( 1 - ylag(1,tlag)/k )
    mit  tlag = 1.9     r = 0.82     k = 59.0  und den Anfangswerten
    y(1) = 10  für  t = 0  sowie  ylag(1,tlag) = 10   für den Bereich
    t = 0..tlag
Bei dieser Wahl der Parameter oszilliert y(1) mit abnehmender Amplitude.
Testgröße : absoluter Fehler von y(1) bei t = 18.0 bezogen auf den Bestwert
49.812935


<u>OKA</u> ydot(1) = inflow   -  z * y(1)      ydot(3) = k2 * y(2) - k3 * y(3)
    ydot(2) = z * y(1) - k2 * y(2)      ydot(4) = k3 * y(3) - k4 * y(4)
    mit  z = k1/(1.0+alfa*ylag(4,tlag)**n)    tlag = 4.0     k1 = 1.0
    k2 = 1.0      k3 = 1.0      k4 = 0.5      alfa = 0.0005     inflow = 10.5
    n = 3  und den Anfangswerten  y(1) = 1.0 , y(2) = 1.0 , y(3) = 1.0 und
    y(4) = 2.0  für  t = 0  sowie  ylag(4,tlag) = 0   im Bereich t = 0..tlag
Bei dieser Wahl der Parameter oszilliert y(4) nach einem Einschwingvorgang
mit konstanter Amplitude.
Testgröße : absoluter Fehler von y(4)
bei t = 100 bezogen auf den Bestwert
33.601395


## 5. Ergebnisse

Bei der Anwendung der Integrations-
Verfahren RK4, DOP und ROW auf das
SIN-Problem wurden die in den Abb. 1,
2 und 3 dargestellten Werte erhalten.
In gleicher Weise sind die Ergebnisse
der Anwendung von DOP auf das BRA-
und das OKA-Problem in den Abb. 4 und
5 dargestellt. Dabei werden für die
Interpolations-Verfahren die folgenden Symbole verwendet :


        X LIN

        O QUA

        O KUB

        + DOU

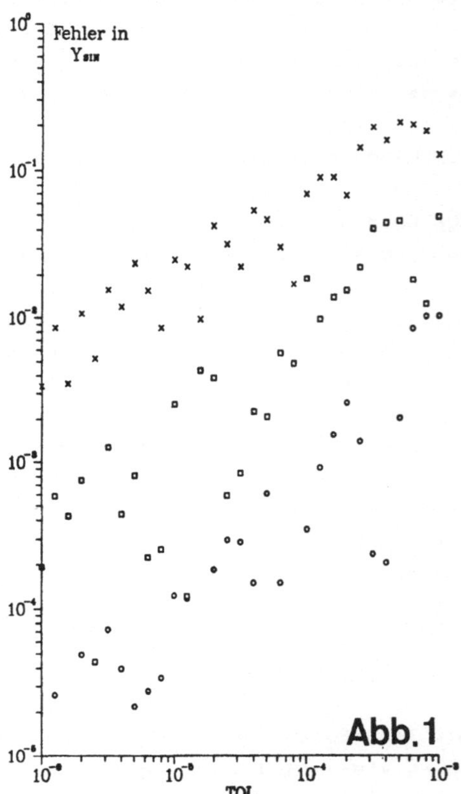

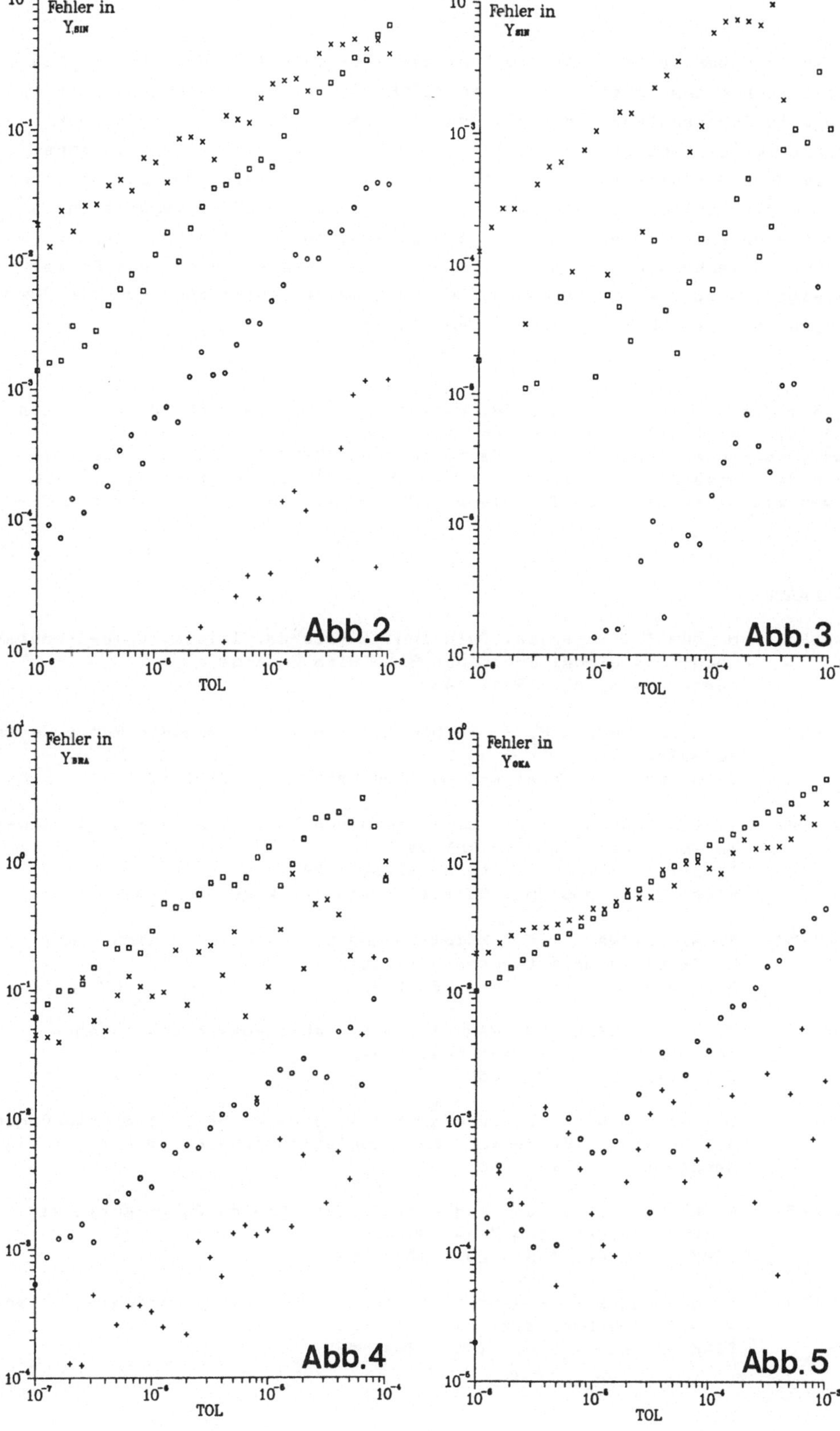
Fehler in
Y,SIN
TOL
Abb.2
Fehler in
Y,SIN
TOL
Abb.3
Fehler in
Y,BRA
TOL
Abb.4
Fehler in
Y,OKA
TOL
Abb.5

Die Abbildungen zeigen, daß die kubische Interpolation der linearen bzw.
quadratischen abweichend von den in /ESCH84/ mitgeteilten Ergebnissen um
etwa eine Zehnerpotenz und somit deutlich überlegen ist. Es ist daher
zweckmäßig, für Totzeit-Blöcke in einem block-orientierten Simulations-
System auch die ohnehin berechneten Werte der 1. Ableitungen zu speichern
und für die kubische Interpolation zu benutzen. Die DOU-Interpolation
bringt eine weitere Verbesserung, die allerdings auch die Speicherung
weiterer Zwischenwerte erforderlich macht. Inwieweit dadurch die Effizienz
gesteigert wird, kann erst dann untersucht werden, wenn auch für die ROW-
Integration die DOU-Koeffizienten vorliegen.


Für die Koeffizienten der DOU-Interpolation danke ich Gerhard Wanner aus
Genf. Die den Abbildungen zugrundeliegenden Berechnungen wurden in der Programmiersprache SIMULA auf der Rechenanlage SPERRY 1100/82 des Rechenzentrums der Universität Freiburg durchgeführt. Für die Erstellung der Abbildungen mit Hilfe des Plot-Systems DISSPLA danke ich Frank Totzke aus Freiburg.


## Literatur

/ARND83/    H. ARNDT : Numerical Solution of Retarded Initial Value Problems
            Local and Global Error and Step Size Control
            Numer. Math. 43 (1984) 343

/DORM80/    J. R. DORMAND & P. J. PRINCE : A family of embedded Runge-Kutta
            formulae
            J. of Computational and Applied Maths. 6 (1980) 19

/ESCH84/    P. ESCHENBACHER : Die Behandlung von Totzeitvariablen im Simu-
            lationspaket GPSS-FORTRAN Version 3
            Informatik-Fachberichte 85 (1984) 354
            Proc. 2. Symposium Simulationstechnik, Wien (Springer-Verlag)

/GOTT85/    B. A. GOTTWALD : Zur Modellierung biologischer Prozesse mit
            Hilfe block-orientierter Simulations-Systeme
            Ber. Deutsch. Bot. Ges. 98 (1985) 13

/GOTT81/    B. A. GOTTWALD & G. WANNER : A Reliable Rosenbrock Integrator
            for Stiff Differential Equations
            Computing 26 (1981) 355

/HALB72/    U. Halbach & H. J. Burckhardt : Sind einfache Zeitverzögerungen
            die Ursachen für periodische Populationsschwankungen ?
            Oecologia 9 (1972) 215

/HORN83/    M. K. HORN : Fourth- and Fifth-Order, Scaled Runge-Kutta Algo-
            rithms for Treating Dense Output
            SIAM J. Numer. Anal. 20 (1983) 558

/OKAM84/    M. Okamoto & K. Hayashi : Frequency conversion mechanism in en-
            zymatic feedback systems
            SIAM J. Theor. Biol. 108 (1984) 529

# SIMULATIONEN AN EINEM ZEITABHÄNGIGEN MODELL DES GEGENSTROMSYSTEMS DER NIERE


Albert  Gilg, München



**Zusammenfassung**. Die mathematische Modellierung des Gegenstromsystems der Niere durch Stephenson war grundlegend für die weitere Erforschung dieses physiologischen Mechanismus. Die Simulation interessanter zeitabhängiger Prozesse, wie der Wasserdiurese oder der Blockade der aktiven Transportraten, stellt hohe Anforderungen an die Leistungsfähigkeit der numerischen Lösungsmethoden. Eine adaptive Kollokations-Linienmethode erweist sich als zuverlässig, genau und schnell bei der Lösung dieser Probleme. Die Resultate der Simulationen liefern aufschlußreiche Einblicke in den Konzentrierungsmechanismus. Das numerische Verfahren kann auch auf aktuelle Modellerweiterungen angewandt werden, da es nicht modellspezifisch ist.

**Summary**. The mathematical model of the kidney countercurrent system by Stephenson promoted research for this physiological mechanism. Simulation of transient processes, e.g. water diuresis or partial blockade of active transport rates, requires highest performance on numerical methods. An adaptive collocation-based method of lines shows to work reliable, exact and fast for these problems. Simulation results lead to interesting aspects on the concentrating mechanism. The numerical method is independent of specific models and therefore simply applicable to further extensions.



## 1. Einführung

Zu den wichtigsten Organen der Säugetiere gehören die Nieren, die Volumen, Osmolarität und Konzentration gelöster Substanzen in der extrazellulären Flüssigkeit regulieren. Um diese Aufgabe zu erfüllen sind die Nieren befähigt einen Urin zu bilden, dessen Osmolarität von der des Blutplasmas deutlich verschieden ist.

Eine Niere besteht aus einem Röhrensystem, das aus einer großen Zahl funktioneller Einheiten, den Nephronen (siehe Bild 1), aufgebaut ist. Die haarnadelförmig angeordneten Henleschen Schleifen bilden ein Gegenstromsystem, dessen qualitative Bedeutung für den Konzentrierungsmechanismus von Kuhn und Ryffel (1942) entdeckt wurde: Die gegensinnige parallele Anordnung bewirkt mit geringem Aufwand (aktivem Salztransport aus TALH und DT) einen großen Konzentrationsgradienten im Nierenmark, der die Konzentrierung in den ebenfalls parallel verlaufenden Sammelrohren ("Gegenstromaustauscher") verursacht.

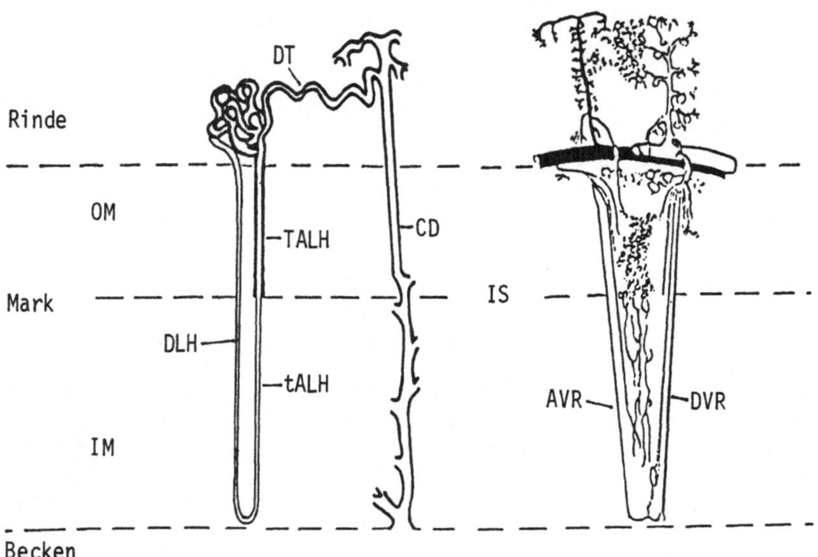


**Bild 1:** Schematische Darstellung eines Nephrons (absteigende (DLH), dünne aufsteigende (tALH) und dicke aufsteigende (TALH) Henlesche Schleife, distales Konvolut (DT) und Sammelrohr (CD)) und eines Blutgefäßes (absteigendes (DVR) und aufsteigendes Vas rectum (AVR)) im interstitiellen Raum (IS) des äußeren (OM) und inneren Nierenmarks (IM).

## 2. Mathematische Modellierung

Zur quantitativen Analyse des Gegenstromsystems wurden mathematische Modelle entwickelt (z.B. von Jacquez et al. (2), Knepper et al. (3), Moore und Marsh (4), Barret und Packer (5), Lory et al. (6), Lory (7) ), die auf der grundlegenden Modellierung durch Stephenson (1) basieren: Die Nephrone und Vasa recta werden durch Röhrenschleifen modelliert. Die aufsteigenden Vasa recta kann man aufgrund ihrer hohen Röhrenmembranpermeabilitäten mit dem Interstitium zu einer funktionellen Einheit, dem sog. Central Core, zusammenfassen, die mit den übrigen Röhren kommuniziert (siehe Bild 2).

Es werden die Konzentrationen $C_{ik}$ zweier gelöster Substanzen (k=1 Salz, k=2 Harnstoff) in den jeweiligen Röhrensegmenten (i=1,...,5) und im Central Core (i=6) berücksichtigt. Die Transportgleichungen in den Röhren haben die Form (x bezeichne die Orts-, t die Zeitkoordinate):

$$\frac{d}{dt} C_{ik}(x,t) = D_k \cdot \frac{d^2}{dx^2} C_{ik}(x,t) - \frac{d}{dx}( C_{ik}(x,t) \cdot V_i(x,t) ) - J_{ik}(x,t)$$

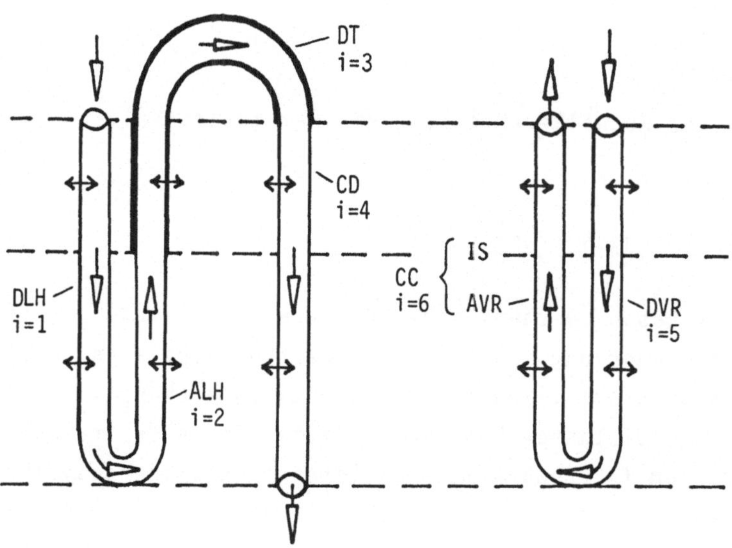

**Bild 2:** Röhrenmodell eines Nephrons und eines Vas rectums
(─▷ Volumenstromrichtung,  ↔  transmurale Flüsse zwischen den Röhren und Central Core)

$D_k$ bezeichnet den Diffusionskoeffizienten der k-ten Substanz. Die Geschwindigkeit $V_i$ des Lösungsmittels in der i-ten Röhre genügt der Differentialgleichung

$$\frac{d}{dx} V_i(x,t) = p_i \cdot [\ C_{i1}(x,t) - C_{a1}(x,t) - (C_{i2}(x,t) - C_{a2}(x,t))\ ]$$

$p_i$ hydraulische Lösungsmittelleitfähigkeit der i-ten Röhrenmembran,
$C_{ak}$ Konzentration der k-ten Substanz außerhalb der Röhre.
Die transmurale Flußrate $J_{ik}$ wird bestimmt durch

$$J_{ik}(x,t) = h_{ik}\ (C_{ik}(x,t) - C_{ak}(x,t)) - Akt_{ik}\ ,$$

$h_{ik}$ Permeabilität der i-ten Röhrenmembran für die k-te Substanz.
$Akt_{ik}$ beschreibt die Rate des aktiven Transports, der nur für Salz im dicken aufsteigenden Teil der Henleschen Schleife und im distalen Tubulus auftritt.
Die Gleichungen für das Central Core resultieren aus der Erhaltung der Massenbilanz im Nierenmark.
Das Modell für alle Nierensegmente wird beschrieben durch ein partielles Differentialgleichungssystem von zwölf parabolischen Differentialgleichungen mit Integraltermen. Die Randbedingungen für dieses System setzen sich zusammen aus gemessenen Einstromwerten für die absteigende Henlesche Schleife und Vas rectum und den Übergangsbedingungen der einzelnen

Röhrensegmente.

Eine ausführliche Modellbeschreibung mit Parametertabellen ist in (9)
enthalten.

## 3. Numerisches Lösungsverfahren

Zur numerischen Lösung parabolischer Differentialgleichungen bietet sich
eine getrennte Behandlung von Orts- und Zeitkoordinate an. Die gängigen
Linienmethoden diskretisieren die Differentialgleichungen in der Ortskoordinate an äquidistanten Punkten und integrieren das resultierende
Anfangswertproblem für gewöhnliche Differentialgleichungssysteme mit numerischen Verfahren. Da bei dieser Semidiskretisierung große Differenti-
algleichungssysteme entstehen wurden die Verfahren an ein spezielles Modell angepaßt und ohne Schrittweitenkontrolle numerisch integriert.
Hier wurde ein neues Verfahren angewandt, eine adaptive Kollokations-
Linienmethode, die folgende Vorteile aufweist:
* Durch den Kollokationsansatz mit Polynomsplinefunktionen erhält man in
der Ortskoordinate eine hohe Konvergenzordnung.
* Man kann eine Abschätzung der Diskretisierungsfehler berechnen.
* Mit Hilfe dieser Fehlerabschätzung lassen sich die Kollokations-"Linien"
adaptiv dem Lösungsverlauf anpassen, so daß mit geringer Linienzahl eine
hohe Genauigkeit erzielt wird und die häufig zu beobachtenden Oszillati-
onen der numerischen Näherung vermieden werden.
* In der Zeitkoordinate wird das i.a. steife Anfangswertproblem mit den
Verfahren von Gear mit variabler Ordnung und Schrittweite gelöst und dadurch effizient eine hohe Genauigkeit gesichert.
Eine detaillierte Beschreibung der Kollokations-Linienmethode mit adap-
tiver Linienverteilung befindet sich in (9). Dieses Verfahren ist nicht
modellspezifisch und hat sich auch bei großer Linienzahl bewährt, die auf
Systeme von mehr als 400 Differentialgleichungen führte.
In den bisherigen mathematischen Modellen wurde die Diffusion in den Röhren vernachlässigt, was zwar die Berechnungen vereinfacht, aber bei zeitabhängigen Modellen Probleme bzgl. der Existenz einer Modellösung verursachen kann.

## 4. Simulationen und Ergebnisse

### 4.1 Das stationäre Modell

Die numerische Lösung des Stephenson-Modells wurde von Lory (8) mit hoher
Genauigkeit berechnet. Sie diente als Anfangsdaten für dieses modifizierte Modell. Die Gleichungen wurden bis zum Erreichen des stationären Zustandes ( $d/dt\ C_{ik}$ = 0 ) integriert. Dabei zeigte sich, daß für stationäre Modelle die Vernachlässigung der Diffusionseffekte in den Röhren be-
rechtigt ist, da die Resultate nur geringfügig von den Daten von Lory (8)
abweichen. Eine Genauigkeitskontrolle ist die Überprüfung der Massener-
haltung im Nierenmark, die hier kleiner als 0.005% ist.
Eine Zusammenfassung der Resultate ist in Bild 3 bzw. Bild 4 (— —) enthalten: Die Salzkonzentration steigt im äußeren Mark steil an bis auf
758 mOsm und bleibt dann im inneren Mark nahezu konstant. Aufgrund des
aktiven Salztransports fällt die Konzentration im TALH und im distalen
Tubulus rasch ab und steigt im Sammelrohr nur bis auf 0.35 mOsm. Die
Harnstoffkonzentration steigt im DLH um nahezu dieselben Faktoren wie
die Salzkonzentration und wird im distalen Tubulus und außermedullären
Sammelrohr durch Wasserentzug rasch erhöht bis auf 834 mMol/l beim Einstrom ins Nierenbecken.
Die vorzugsweise Konzentrierung von Harnstoff ist nicht realistisch und
war ein Grund für Weiterentwicklungen des Stephenson-Modells. Aber der
Gesamtkonzentrierungsfaktor aller gelösten Substanzen ist mit 2.65 im Ein-
klang mit Meßwerten. Der Volumenstrom nimmt in der außermedullären DLH
und im distalen Konvolut rasch ab und die Geschwindigkeit beträgt beim
Ausstrom ins Nierenbecken nur noch $1.3_{10}$-2 cm/min gegenüber 1 cm/min beim
Einstrom in die DLH. Das Central Core nimmt hauptsächlich im äußeren Mark
Wasser auf. Die Symmetrie der Konzentrationen von DVR und AVR bzw.
Central Core zeigt, daß aufgrund der hohen Permeabilitäten nahezu ein
osmotisches Gleichgewicht herrscht. Auch die Konzentrationen im DLH sind
fast gleich denen im Central Core.

### 4.2 Wasserdiurese

Entsprechend dem Hydrierungszustand des Körpers kann die Niere nicht nur
konzentrieren, sondern auch einen Harn produzieren, dessen Osmolarität
geringer ist als die des Blutplasmas. Die Steuerung vom Normalzustand
(Antidiurese) zur Wasserdiurese erfolgt durch das antidiuretische Hormon
(ADH), dessen Fehlen eine Senkung der Wasserleitfähigkeiten der Röhren-
membrane des distalen Konvoluts und des Sammelrohrs bewirkt.
Es wurde ein Zeitintervall von 150 Minuten simuliert. Das Programm benötigte dazu bei 34 Linien fünf Minuten Rechenzeit auf der CDC Cyber 175

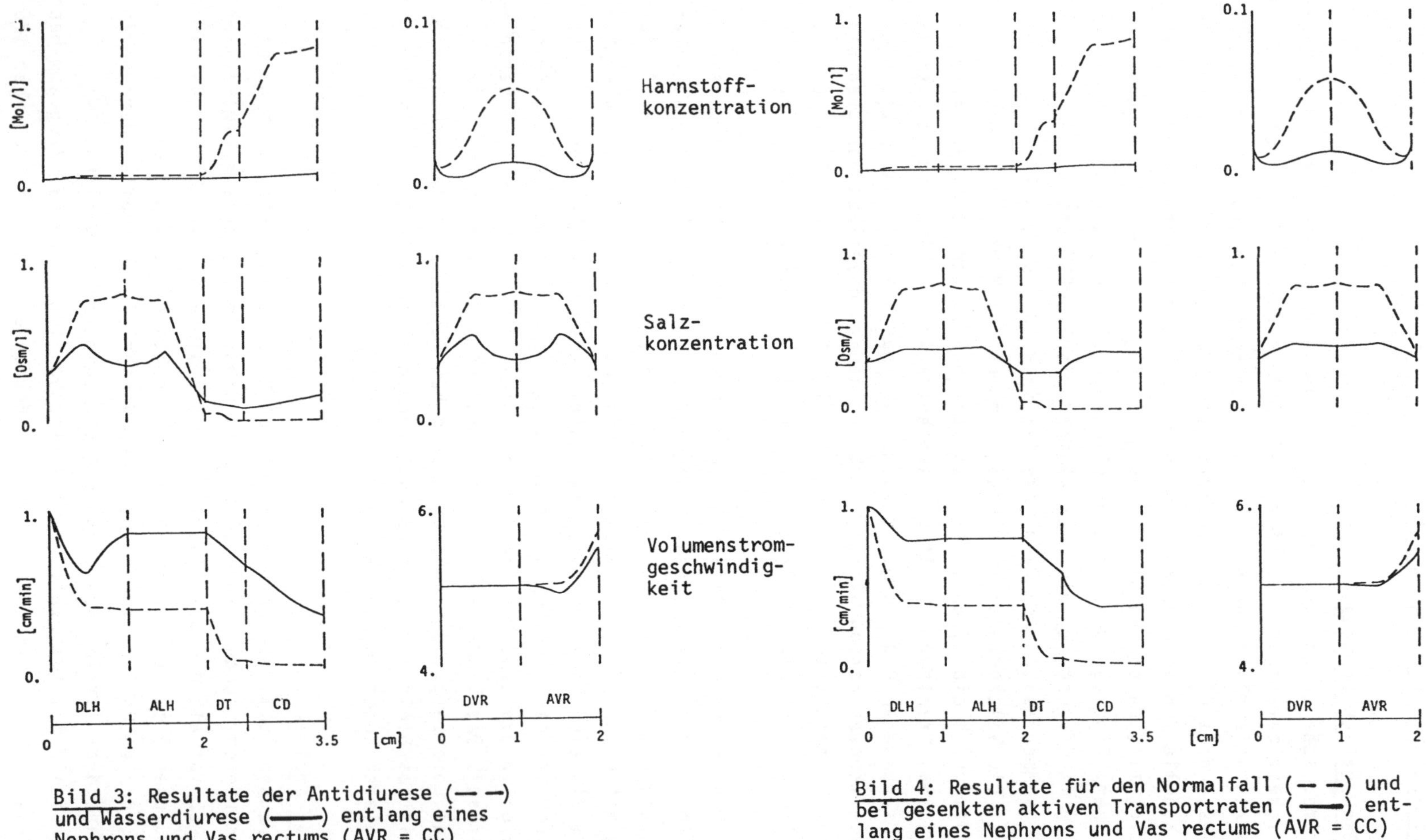


Bild 3: Resultate der Antidiurese (— —) und Wasserdiurese (———) entlang eines Nephrons und Vas rectums (AVR = CC)

Bild 4: Resultate für den Normalfall (— —) und bei gesenkten aktiven Transportraten (———) entlang eines Nephrons und Vas rectums (AVR = CC)

360

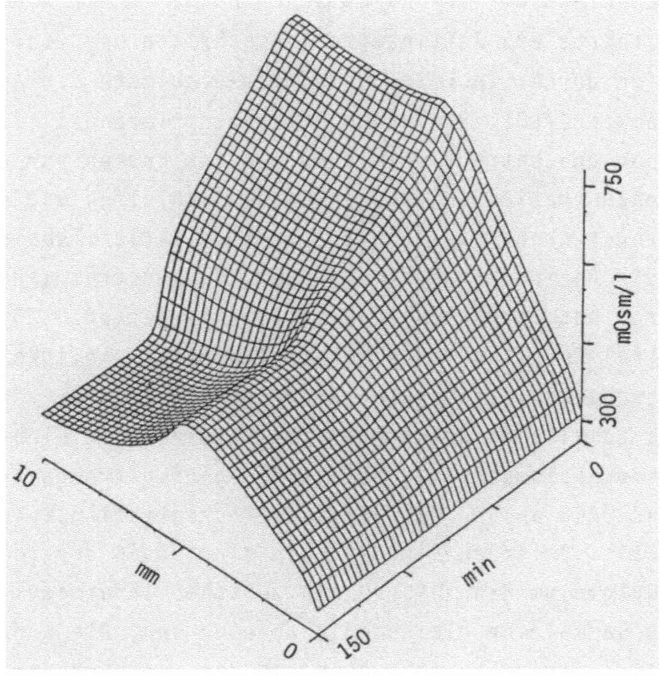

**Bild 5:** Salzkonzentration im Central Core ($C_{61}$) beim Übergang zur Wasserdiurese

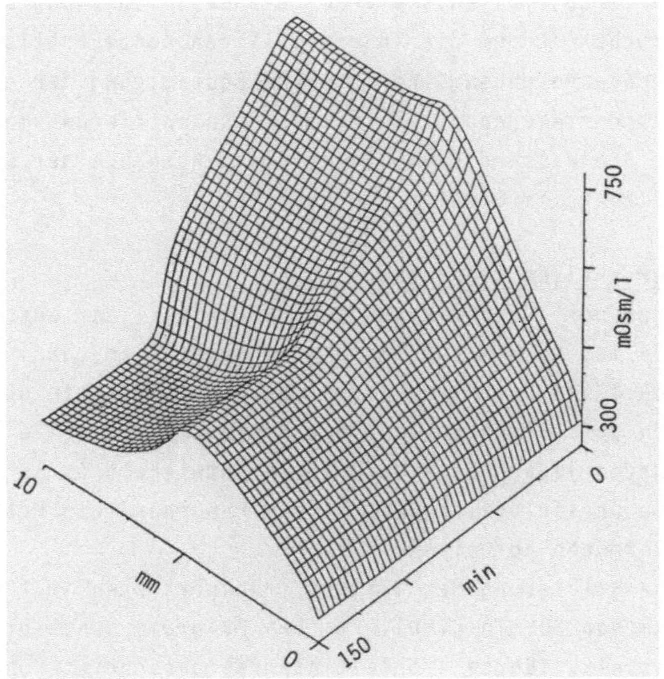

**Bild 6:** Harnstoffkonzentration im Sammelrohr ($C_{42}$) beim Übergang zur Wasserdiurese

des Leibniz Rechenzentrums der Bayerischen Akademie der Wissenschaften in München und führte 845 Zeitintegrationsschritte und fünf Neuvertei- lungen der Linien durch. In Bild 3 sind die Resultate der Anti- und Was- serdiurese zusammengefaßt: Die Harnstoffkonzentrierung ist fast völlig zusammengebrochen und beträgt beim Ausstrom ins Becken nur noch 23 mMol/l. Auch die Salzkonzentration in den Henleschen Schleifen und im Central Core ist weit abgesunken, sie steigt aber im distalen Tubulus und Sammel- rohr bis über die Antidiuresewerte an. Der Volumenstrom wird deutlich größer im Nephron und beträgt beim Ausstrom ins Becken 0.33 statt 0.013 cm/min. Im Central Core sinkt die Volumenstromgeschwindigkeit, da die ab- steigende Henlesche Schleife Wasser resorbiert.

Die Analyse des zeitlichen Übergangs gibt interessante Einblicke in den Konzentrierungsmechanismus (Bild 5,6): Die Volumenstromgeschwindigkeit steigt im DT und OMCD an und die Harnstoffkonzentration in diesen Tubu- lussegmenten fällt. Zwischen 9 und 15 min sinkt dann der Volumenstrom wieder geringfügig ab um dann bis 90 min zwischen innermedullärer DLH und außermedullärem Sammelrohr gleichmäßig anzuwachsen. Die Konzentrationen sinken in diesem Zeitraum ab (mit Ausnahme der Salzkonzentration im Sam- melrohr) bis sie im inneren Mark geringer sind als im Außenmark. Dann steigt der Volumenstrom in der innermedullären DLH rasch (auf nahezu den doppelten Wert!) und die Konzentrationen (wiederum mit Ausnahme der Salz- konzentration im CD) fallen steil ab. Die Beschleunigung des Konzentrati- onszusammenbruchs nachdem die innermedullären Konzentrationen unter die außermedullären abgesunken sind ist eine Bestätigung der großen Bedeutung des Innenmarks der Nierenpapille für den Konzentrierungsmechanismus. Die Resultate für die Wasserdiurese liegen (mit Ausnahme der Salzkonzentra- tion im Sammelrohr) im Bereich von Meßdaten.

## 4.3 Senken der aktiven Transportraten

Der aktive Transport von Salz aus dem dicken Teil der aufsteigenden Henle- schen Schleife ist der "Motor" des Konzentrierungsmechanismus. In dem "aktiven" Modell von Moore und Marsh (4) wird sogar ein aktiver Transport aus dem dünnen aufsteigenden Teil der Henleschen Schleife untersucht. Inzwischen wurden jedoch passive Modelle entwickelt (z.B. Lory et al. (6)) die ohne diese physiologisch umstrittene Hypothese ein realistisches Kon- zentrierungsvermögen aufweisen.

Hier wird eine Halbierung der aktiven Transportraten im TALH und DT über einen Zeitraum von 30 min simuliert. Das Programm benötigte bei 34 Linien 225 sec Rechenzeit, führte 476 Zeitintegrationsschritte und sechs Linien- neuverteilungen aus.

Die Resultate sind in Bild 4 zusammengefaßt.

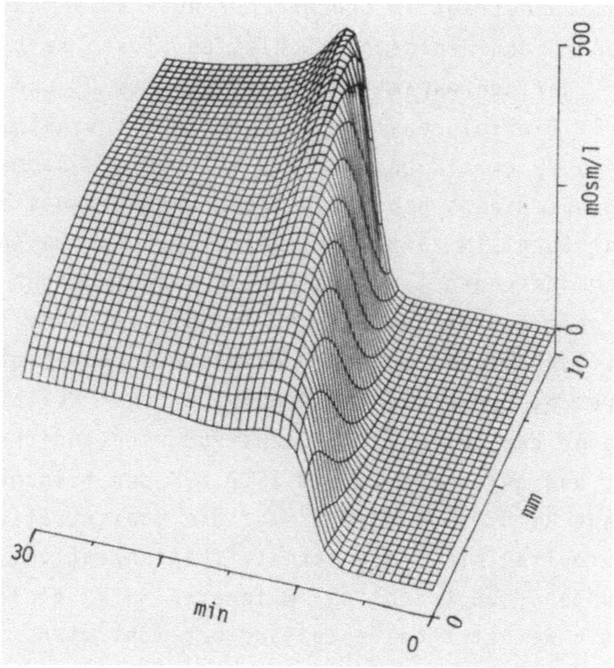

**Bild 7:** Salzkonzentration im Sammelrohr ($C_{41}$) bei Senkung der aktiven Transportraten

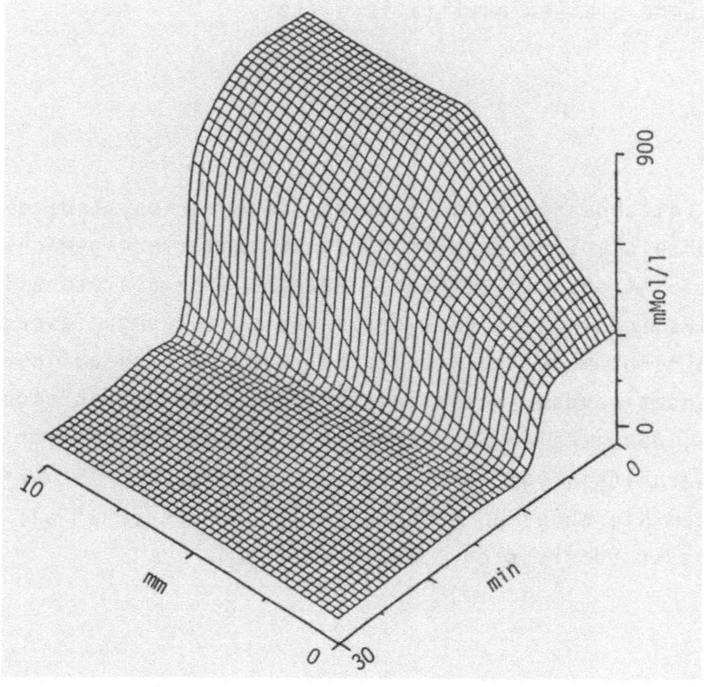

**Bild 8:** Harnstoffkonzentration im Sammelrohr ($C_{42}$) bei Senkung der aktiven Transportraten

Die Harnstoffkonzentration beträgt im Endharn nur noch 43.4 mMol/l. Auch
die Salzkonzentrationen in den Henleschen Schleifen sinken weit ab, steigen jedoch aufgrund des geringeren aktiven Transports im DT und Sammelrohr bis auf 352 mOsm/l. Die Volumenstromgeschwindigkeit sinkt im außermedullären DLH nur auf 0.79 cm/min und beträgt am Ende des Sammelrohrs
noch 0.38 cm/min. Aufgrund dieses hohen Ausstroms ins Becken sinkt der
Volumenstrom im Central Core. Im zeitlichen Ablauf setzen die Konzentra-
tions- und Volumenstromänderungen langsam ein und beschleunigen dann, bis
die Salzkonzentration nach 6.6 min am Eingang ins distale Konvolut ihr
Maximum überschreitet. Dann wächst entlang des distalen Konvoluts die
Salzkonzentration so rasch, daß sich eine Konzentrations-"Welle" im OMCD
ausbildet, die sich wegen der geringen Volumenstromgeschwindigkeit ab
9 min weiter aufsteilt und zwischen 9.6 und 16.2 min den Ausgang des Sammelrohrs erreicht (siehe Bild 7,8). Dort steigt die Konzentration von
0.32 auf 457 mOsm/l. Simultan sinkt die Harnstoffkonzentration. Ab 16 min
setzen sich die Änderungen (hauptsächlich im inneren Mark) gleichmäßig
fort, bis bei ca. 30 min der stationäre Zustand erreicht wird.
Die Änderungen der aktiven Transportraten wirken sich also sehr schnell
auf die Endharnkonzentrationen aus. Im Gegensatz zur Wasserdiurese tritt
kein Einbruch der Konzentrationen im inneren Mark ein sondern die Konzen-
trationsverteilungen in den Henleschen Schleifen und in den Vasa recta
bzw. im Central Core bleiben qualitativ gleich.


## 5. Diskussion


Simulationen an zeitabhängigen Modellen des Gegenstromsystems der Niere
liefern aufschlußreiche Einblicke in diesen Konzentrierungsmechanismus.
Die adaptive Kollokations-Linienmethode erweist sich als schnelles, ge-
naues und zuverlässiges numerisches Verfahren zur Lösung dieser Probleme.
Da das Verfahren nicht modellspezifisch ist kann es auch auf neue Modellvarianten angewendet werden, deren zeitabhängiges Verhalten noch nicht
untersucht wurde. Dazu zählen insbesondere Modelle, die geometrische Aspekte, wie das Verhältnis von kurzen zu langen Henleschen Schleifen, und
Rückflüsse aus dem Nierenbecken berücksichtigen (Horster et al. (10) )
oder neue Hypothesen untersuchen (z.B. Lory (7) ).

Literatur

(1) Stephenson, J.L.:
Concentration of urine in a central core model of the renal counterflow system.
Kidney Int. 2, 1972, 85-94.
(2) Jacquez, J.A., Foster, D., Daniels, E.:
Solute concentration in the kidney - I. A model of the renal medulla and its
limit cases.
Math. Biosci. 32, 1976, 307-336.
(3) Knepper, M.A., Saidel, G.M., Palatt, P.J.:
Mathematical model of renal regulation of urea excretion.
Med. & Biol. Eng. 16, 1976, 408-426.
(4) Moore, L.C., Marsh, D.J.:
How descending limb of Henle's loop permeability affects hypertonic urine
formation.
Am. J. Physiol. 239, 1980, F57-F71.
(5) Barret, G.L., Packer, J.S.:
Dynamic simulation of the renal medulla.
Med. & Biol. Eng. 21, 1983, 324-332.
(6) Lory, P., Gilg, A., Horster, M.:
Renal countercurrent system: role of collecting duct convergence and pelvic
urea predicted from a mathematical model.
J. Math. Biol. 16, 1983, 281-304.
(7) Lory, P.:
Ein Semi-Kollokationsverfahren zur numerischen Lösung von Nierenmodellen.
Habilitationsschrift, Mathematisches Institut der Technischen Universität
München, TUM-M8501, März 1985.
(8) Lory, P.:
Numerical solution of a kidney model by multiple shooting.
Math. Biosci. 50, 1980, 117-128.
(9) Gilg, A.:
Eine adaptive Kollokations-Linienmethode zur numerischen Lösung parabolischer
Differentialgleichungen mit Anwendung auf Röhrenmodelle aus der Biologie.
Mathematisches Institut der Technischen Universität München, TUM-M8407, 1984.
(10)Horster, M., Gilg, A., Lory, P.:
Determinants of axial osmotic gradients in the differentiating countercurrent
system.
Am. J. Physiol. 246, 1984, F124-F134.

# COMPUTERSIMULATION DER RENALEN HÄMODYNAMIK

Dietmar P. F. Möller, Mainz

Zusammenfassung: Es wird ein mathematisches Modell des renalen Systems vorgestellt, welches den sogenannten Guytonschen Basisregelkreis der lang-
zeitregulativen Blutdruckstabilisierung als Sonderfall enthält. Das Modell ist von parametrischer Struktur; es enthält die funktionell und
biologisch relevanten Parameter des biologischen Systems explizit und
eindeutig. Anhand der durch Simulation gewonnenen Ergebnisse kann im
Vergleich zum Guytonschen Basisregelkreis gezeigt werden, daß das entwickelte Modell physiologisch eindeutige Ergebnisse liefert. Dies betrifft insbesondere das stationäre Verhalten des Herzzeitvolumens im
fixierten Stadium der renopriven Hypertonie. Darüber hinaus ist das Modell beliebig erweiterbar, um Einflüsse anderen Ursprunges zu untersuchen wie zum Beispiel das Renin-Angiotensin-Aldosteron System oder
das Antidiuretische Hormon.
Summaray: A mathematical model of the renal system is outlined, including Guyton´s so called basic feedback circuit for longterm circulatory regulation as exceptional case. The developed model is a parametric
model. Its structure contains explicitely the biological parameters.
The model is studied by simulation. In comparison with results obtained
from Guyton´s basic feedback circuit, it can be shown that the developed model matches the real system well, especially in the case of the
stationary behaviour of cardiac output in the fixed state of renopri-
val hypertension. Moreover the renin-angiotensin-aldosteron or the
anti-diuretic hormonal mechanism can be implemented into the model,
outlined.

## 1. Einleitung

Durch den Einsatz der Simulation beim Studium biologischer Abläufe ist

die  Möglichkeit gegeben, Funktionen des Organismus sowohl als Teil-

system, und bei Kombination der teilsysteme als Gesamtsystem, abstra-

hiert durch eine hinreichend genaue Nachbildung des realen biologischen

Prozesses, im rechner nachzubilden. Anhand dieses Modelles können Ak-

tionen und Interaktionen untersucht werden. Ist das Modell erfolgreich

validiert, dann sind Modellvorhersagen möglich, oder es können auf

Grund von Modellberechnungen gezielte experimentelle Untersuchungen an-

geregt werden.

Bei der mathematischen Abstraktion realer biologischer Prozesse müssen

zwei Randbedingungen erfüllt werden: Erstens darf die Vereinfachung zum

Zwecke der Modellbildung nicht soweit getrieben werden, daß das reale

System verzerrt abgebildet wird, denn dann sind die Modellaussagen bio-

logisch nicht mehr von Bedeutung. Zweitens ist der formale Aufwand bei

der Modellbildung so zu begrenzen, daß das Modell noch handhabbar

bleibt. Hierin ist implizit die Ordnung des mathematischen Modelles

enthalten. Bei der Modellbildung wird man stets einen Kompromiß zwischen
der Modellgüte, d.h. der Genauigkeit der Modellaussagen und dem Modell-
aufwand, d.h. den Kosten für den Modellentwurf und die Modellnachbildung
suchen, was nachfolgende Abbildung zeigt /6/.

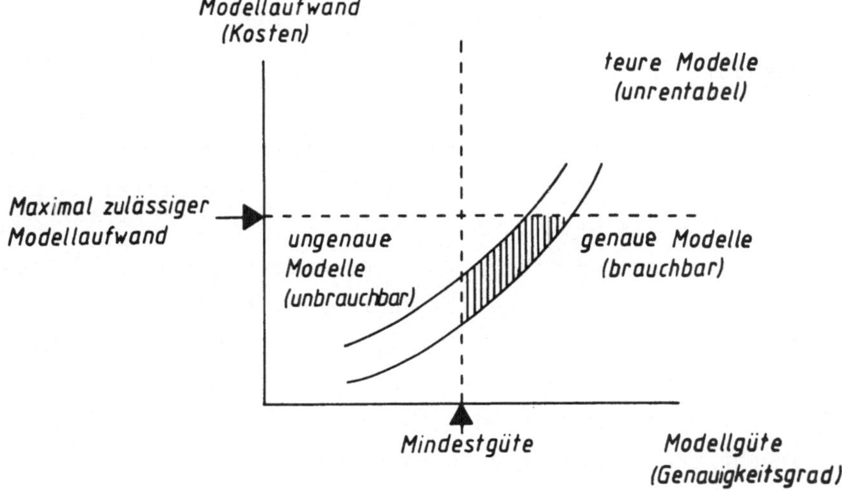


In einer früheren Arbeit /1/ wurde ein mathematisches Modell des renovaskulären Systems vorgestellt, welches auf dem sogenannten Basisregelkreis
des Guytonschen Modelles aufbaut. Der Guytonsche Basisregelkreis beinhaltet den Nieren-Blutvolumen-Druck-Rückkopplungsmechanismus zur langfristigen Blutdruckstabilisierung /2/. Für den Guytonschen Basisregelkreis der renalen Volumenregulation zeigten die in /1/ dargestellten
Modellergebnisse bei Nachbildung einer Hypertonie, daß sie mit tierexperimentellen Beobachtungen, wie sie zum Beispiel in /3/ publiziert wurden, unvereinbar sind. Danach kommt es im Rahmen der Regulationsstörung
innerhalb der fixierten Phase der Hypertonie nicht zu einer Erhöhung des
Herzzeitvolumens, und zwar bei Kontrolltieren und hypertonen Ratten. Demgegenüber bedarf das Guytonsche Modell der Erhöhung des Herzzeitvolumens
im Rahmen der Regulationsstörung /2/.
Ein persistierend erhöhtes Herzzeitvolumen wird in einer Reihe von Simulationsmodellen des renalen Systems gefordert, die auf dem Guytonschen
Basisregelkreis aufbauen. Diese Modelles sind bereits sehr komplex und
von höherer Ordnung. Für den Fall des Basisregelkreises stehen deren Ergebnisse jedoch im Widerspruch zu tierexperimentellen Befunden. Daher
wurde in /4/, durch geeignete Erweiterung des Basisregelkreises von Guyton, ein mathematisches Modell des renalen Systems entwickelt, mit dem
die klinisch relevanten Hochdruckformen richtig nachgebildet werden
können. Darüber hinaus genügt dieses Modell den eingangs aufgestellten
Randbedingungen: Es ist biologisch direkt interpretierbar parametrisiert

und von niedriger Ordnung. Mit dem in /4/ erfolgreich validierten Modell
kann deshalb im Rahmen einer Modellerweiterung der Einfluß von Natrium
- dies ist das am häufigsten vorkommende Kation der extrazellulären
Flüssigkeit - und Proteinen - sie sind neben Phosphaten die wichtigsten
Anionen - auf die Flüssigkeitsräume des Körpers sowohl im orthologischen
wie auch im pathologischen Zustand untersucht werden.

## 2. Simulationsmodell

Ausgehend von dem in /4/ dargestellten mathematischen Modell des renalen
Systems, wird ein erweitertes nichtlineares mathematisches Modell der
Niere vorgestellt, welches den Einfluß von Natrium und Proteinen auf
die Flüssigkeitsräume des Organismus enthält.

Symbolisch wird das renale System durch eine Anzahl von Blöcken (Kästen)
dargestellt, welche die Hüllfläche als Abgrenzung zur Umgebung charakterisieren. Die Verbindungen des Systems (Blöcke) mit seiner Umwelt
sind die Ein- und Ausgangsgrößen, deren Wirkungsfluß durch die Richtung
eines Pfeiles festgelegt wird. Sind keine Verbindungen mit der Umgebung
vorhanden, spricht man von einem geschlossenen System. Demgegenüber weist
weist das offene System immer Verbindungen zur Umgebung auf.

Betrachtet man die in Bild 1 angegebene blockorientierte Darstellung
des renalen Systems, fällt auf, daß das Gesamtsystem Orbis Renalis aus
einer Vielzahl von Subsystemen mit mehreren Ein- und Ausgangsgrößen besteht. Die Eingangsgrößen (Ui) generieren die Ausgangsgrößen (Yi), die
im Regelfall von Störgrößen (Zi) überlagert sind ( i=1,2,...,n ). Darüber hinaus bilden Teile des Gesamtsystems Orbis Renalis eine Steuerkette, da mehrere Subsysteme in Hintereinanderschaltung am Steuervor-
gang beteiligt sind. Das dynamische Verhalten der Steuerkette wird von
den Abbildungsoperatoren der Teilsysteme bestimmt. Andere Teile des Gesamtsystems bilden einen Regelkreis, das heißt einen nicht rückwirkungs-
freien Signalfluß, da die Ausgangsgröße (Y) die Eingangsgröße (U) beeinflußt. Die Regelkreisglieder als teilsysteme des Regelkreises legen mit
ihren Abbildungsoperatoren das dynamische Verhalten der Regelung fest.

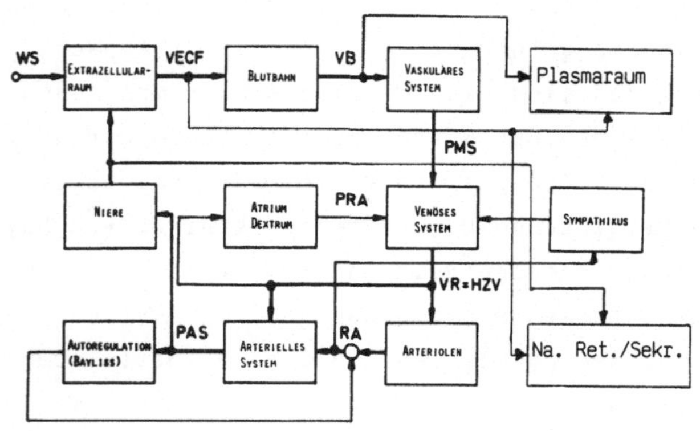


Bild 1: Blockorientierte
Darstellung des renalen
Modelles mit Erweiterung
der Natrium-und Protein-
Abhängigkeit.

## 3. Ergebnisse

### 3.1 Goldblatt Hochdruck

Der Goldblatt Hochdruck ist eine experimentell ausgelöste Hochdruckform infolge einseitiger renaler arterieller Unterbrechung der arteriellen Versorgung.

Das klinische Bild zeichnet sich bei juvenilen Formen primär durch fibromuskuläre Veränderungen im Bereich der großen und mittleren Nierenarterien aus. Bei älteren Patienten dagegen führen hauptsächlich aterosklerotische Alterationen der Nierenarterien zur Stenosierung und als Folge dessen zur Hypertonie  mit ihrer funktionell bedeutsamen Beeinflussung der renalen Hämodynamik.

Der Goldblatt Hochdruck wurde unter Berücksichtigung der zugehörigen Randbedingungen (Exkretionsfunktion der Niere) im Modell nachgebildet. In Bild 2 ist die Exkretionsfunktion der Niere in vergleichender Gegenüberstellung für den Normotoniker und für den Goldblatt induzierten Hochdruck dargestellt.  Bild 3 zeigt die Simulationsergebnisse des Modelles nach Bild 1.

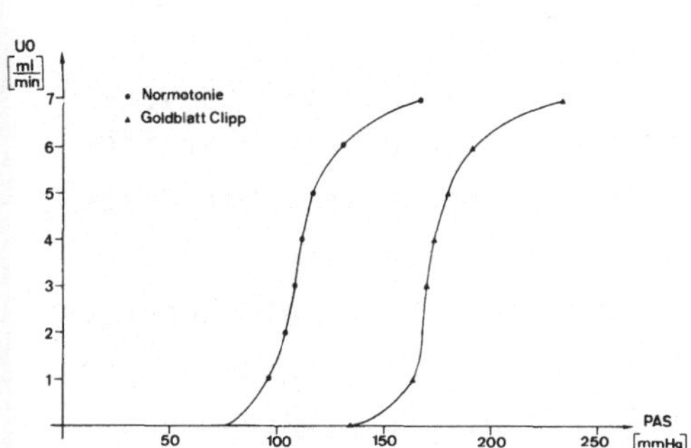

Bild 2: Abhängigkeit der $Na^+$ und $H_2O$-Exkretion (UO) vom mittleren arteriellen Druck (PAS)

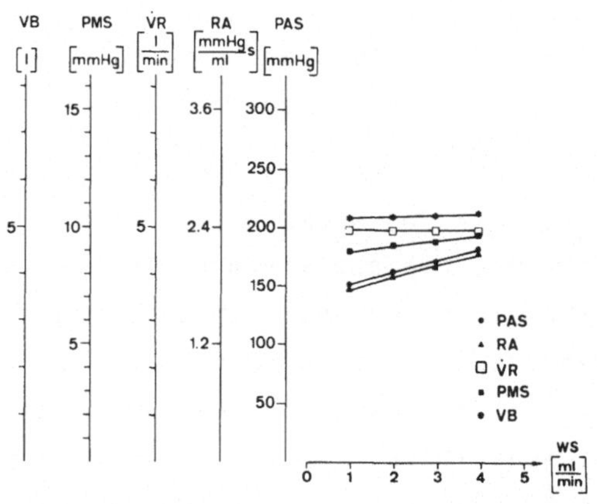

Bild 3: Stationäre Werte des mittleren Druckes (PAS), des peripheren Widerstandes (RA), des venösen Rückstromes (VR), des mittleren Fülungsdruckes (PMS) sowie des Blutvolumens (VB) in Abhängigkeit der isotonischen Belastung (WS)

Wie aus Bild 2 ersichtlich, nimmt bei einer erhöhten Zufuhr von isotoner Flüssigkeit (WS) das Blutvolumen (VB) und damit das Plasmavolumen im Vergleich zum Normotoniker verstärkt zu. Simulatan dazu ist der mittlere Füllungsdruck (PMS) gegenüber dem Normotoniker erhöht, wodurch ein größerer Druckgradient zwischen Peripherie und rechtem Atrium auftritt. ( PMS=7,5 mmHg beim Normotoniker; PMS=9,52 mmHg beim Goldblatt Hochdruck)

Der erhöhte Druckgradient stabilisiert - bezogen auf den veränderten Füllungszustand des vaskulären Systems - den venösen Rückstrom (VR), was aus tierexperimentellen und humanbiologischen Untersuchungen zum renovaskulären Hochdruck bekannt ist /5/. Die Modellergebnisse, wie sie Bild 3 zeigt, befinden sich somit in guter Übereinstimmung mit klinischen Beobachtungen, was der Bedeutung des Modelles bei der Vorhersage nichtmeßbarer Systemzustände zugute kommt.

3.2 Natrium- und Proteineinflüsse

Für den Fall des Goldblatt Hochdruckes wurden die Auswirkungen einer isotonischen Flüssigkeitsbelastung auf die Renale Natrium Exkretion RNE=f(UO, VECF) und die Plasma Protein Konzentration PPK=f(VB, VECF) untersucht. Im Vergleich zum Normotoniker sind die Simulationsergebnisse nachfolgend tabelliert dargestellt.

WS=1 ml/min

|  | Normotoniker | Goldblatt Hochdruck | Goldblatt Hochdruck |
|---|---|---|---|
| RNE | 0,0928 | 0,0789 | ——— |
| PPK | 70,098 | ——— | 70,098 |

Aus Tabelle 1 ist ersichtlich, daß beim Goldblatt Hochdruck, im Vergleich mit dem Normotoniker, eine verminderte renale Natriumexkretion vorliegt, was aus tierexperimentellen Befunden bekannt ist. Die Ursache dafür liegt begründet in der eingeschränkten Nierenfunktion, die als adäquate Antwort der Nieren auf einen erhöhten mittleren Füllungsdruck (PMS) eine Zunahme des Blutvolumens (VB) und damit des extrazellulären Volumens (VECF) die Na- und Wasserretention stimuliert. DEmgegenüber hat der Goldblatt Hochdruck keinen Einfluß auf die Plasma Protein Konzentration, da, im Vergleich zum Normotoniker, das Interstitialvolumen unverändert ist, und die Schwankungen des Plasmavolumens adäquat mit der extrazellulären Proteinkonzentration korrelieren.

Aus dem dargelegten ist ersichtlich, daß das Modell das reale System hinreichend genau wiederspiegelt.

Literatur
/1/ Möller, D.P.F.: Ein mathematisches Modell zur Simulation der Hypertonie. Inform. Fachberichte Band 85, S. 379-382. Hrsg. F.Breitenecker, W.Kleinert Springer Verlag, Berlin-Heidelberg-New York-Tokyo, 1984
/2/ Guyton, A.C.: Arteriel pressure and hypertension. Saunders Publ. Philadelph.1980
/3/ Flohr, H. et al.: Herzzeitvolumen bei renaler, genetischer und DOCA-Hypertonie der Ratte. Pflügers Arch. Suppl. 335(1972) R21
/4/ Möller, D.P.F.: Mathematische Modellierung der renopriven Hypertonie. Funkt. Biologie und Med.: 3(1984),253-259
/5/ Dissmann, Th. et al.: Arch. Kreislaufforschg. 63(1970),226ff
/6/ Mansour, M.: VDI-Bericht Nr.276(1977),S. 5-12

SPECIFIC CASES OF DRUGS MULTIPLE DOSING USING ANALOG - HYBRID
SIMULATION


R.Karba, A.Mrhar, F.Kozjek,M.Atanasijević,D. Matko
Ljubljana, Yugoslavia


Summary. For successful treatment of deseases multiple dosing is required in most cases. The work deals with the multiple dosing simulation
using analog-hybrid computer EAI-580. Through such simulation the influence of the possible practical situations in multiple dosing on drugs
plasma levels can be studied such as influence of dose and dosage interval, influence of different initial dose versus loading dose in order
to attain steady state in shorter time, influence of the case when the
dose (doses) is omited according to the problems of patients compliance,
influence of the case when the dosing for acute treatment (higher dose
in shorter dosing intervals) is changed to the chronic treatment (lower dose in longer dosing intervals) during the time of observation.
All the mentioned cases were studied for the concrete drugs with different pharmacokinetic and pharmacologic properties.

Zusammenfassung. Erfolgreiche Behandlung fordert häufig eine mehrfache
Heilmittelanwendung. Diese Arbeit befasst sich mit der Simulation der
Mehrfachdosierung auf dem Analog - hybridrechner EAI-580, wobei die
Einwirkung der Situationen, die bei der mehrfachen Heilmittelanwendung
in der Praxis vorkommen könnten, auf das Heilmittelnivo in Plasma, untersucht wurde und zwar: Einfluss der Dose und des Dosenintervals,
Einfluss der Verschiedenen Anfangsdosen in der Beziehung auf die nächsten Dosen mit der Absicht der schnellsten Stationierung, Einfluss auf
den Fall wo eine (mehrere) Dose (n) ausgelassen wird (werden), Einfluss
auf den Fall wo die akute Behandlung (grössere Dosen in kürzeren Inter-
vallen) durch die chronische Behandlung (kleinere Dosen in längeren In-
tervallen) erstezt wird. Alle erwähnten Fälle wurden auf konkreten
Heilmitteln mit verschiedenen pharmakokinetischen und pharmakologischen
Eigenschaften untersucht.


## 1. Introduction

For successful treatment of deseases multiple dosing is required in

most cases /1/. The choice of optimal dosage regimen (dose and dosage

interval) is faster and more rational when corresponding mathematical

model together with efficient simulation tool is available /2/. Analog-

hybrid computer proved to be very useful in such cases because of its

speed and flexibility /3,4/. It namely enables simple dosage regimen

adjustments taking into account all practical limitations (possibly

equal doses which must consider the properties of the dosage form,

possily equal dosage intervals, patient compliance and other specific

conditions). So the range of prescribed therapeutic limits can be at-

tained only with some changes of model parameters or logic conditions
what can be very easily and most illustrative realized using analog-
hybrid simulation /5/.

## 2. Simulation of specific dosage regimen

Dosage regimen must be correspondingly designed in order to maintain
drug concentration within therapeutic range through the whole course
of therapy. Here the drug pharmacokinetics as well as patient and dese-
ase characteristics must be taken into account. Generally used schedu-
le "three times a day" may namelly cause either drug cumulation in
human body and consequently undesired side effect or inefficacity of
drug resulting in the prolonged therapy. So for the drugs with very
short or very long halflives the special dosage regimen must be designed.
Figure 1. shows the modifications of conventional multiple dosing which
were studied in the present work.

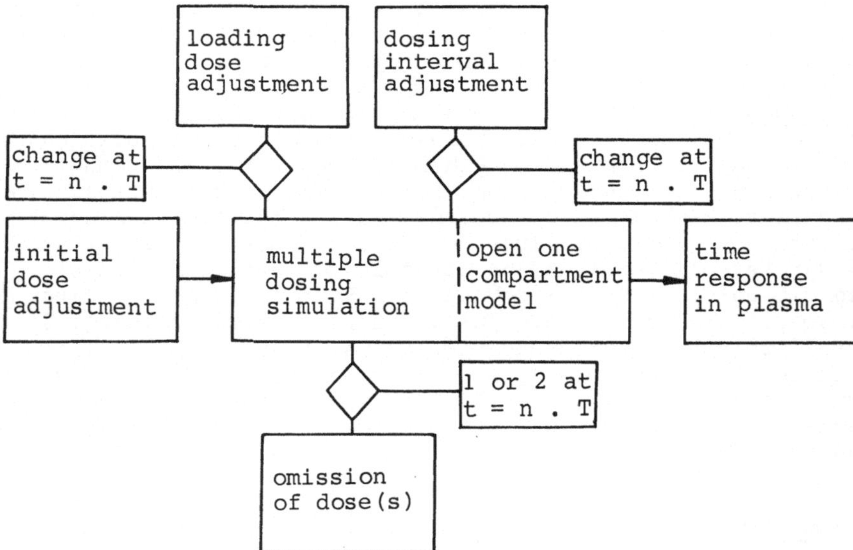


Figure 1. Block  scheme of the possible options in multiple dosing
          simulation

In Figure 1 the following cases of multiple dosing are summarized regarding the attained drug plasma concentrations:
- influence of various dose and dosing interval (unchanged on the observation interval),
- influence of various initial doses (shorter time needed for the minimal effective concentration attainement),
- influence of the case when the dose (doses) is (are)  omited acording
  to the problems of patient compliance (for the simulation the number

of omited doses must be given as well as the time (t) where t=n.T
(T - dosing interval, n - number of dose at which the change starts)),
- influence of the case when the dosing for acute treatment (higher
  dose in shorter dosing intervals) is changed to the chronic treatment
  (lower dose in longer dosing intervals) during the time of observation. The moment of the dosage regimen change (t) can be designed or
  previously prescribed time can be verified.

The corresponding simulations were realized on EAI-580 analog-hybrid
computer. Analog diagrams are shown in Figure 2.

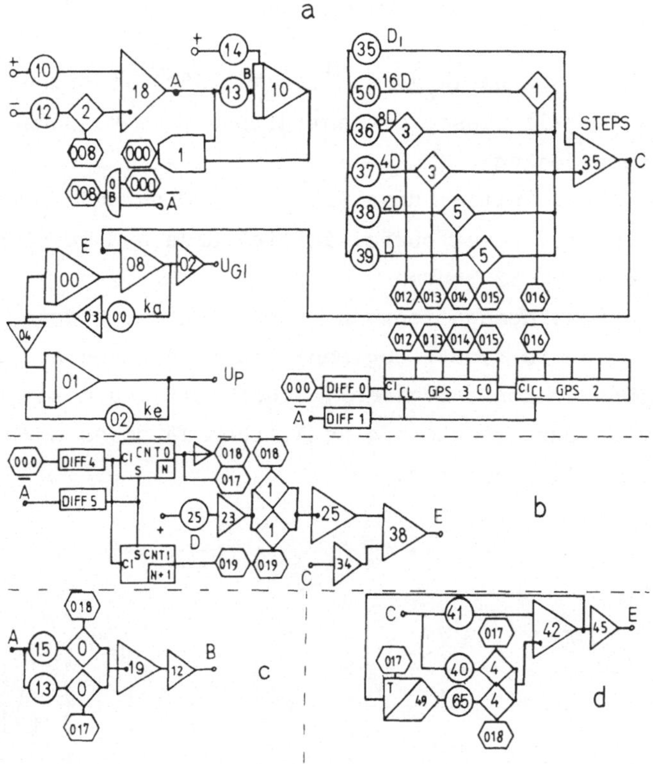

Figure 2.   Analog diagrams for the discussed problems simulation
   a.   Open one compartment model with generator of steps function
        simulating multiple doses ($D_i$-initial dose, D-loading dose,
        $U_{GI}$-compartment of gastrointestinal tract, $U_p$-compartment
        of plasma, $k_a$-absorption rate constant, $k_e$-elimination rate
        constant)
   b.   Scheme for one or two doses omission (inserted between po-
        ints C and E in Figure 2a)
   c.   Scheme for changing the duration of dosage interval (inserted
        between points A and B in Figure 2a)
   d.   Scheme for changing the loading dose (inserted between points
        C and E in Figure 2a)

The proposed approach was used for the treatment of some concrete drugs
having different pharmacokinetic and pharmacologic properties. The results are shown in Figures 3, 4 and 5.

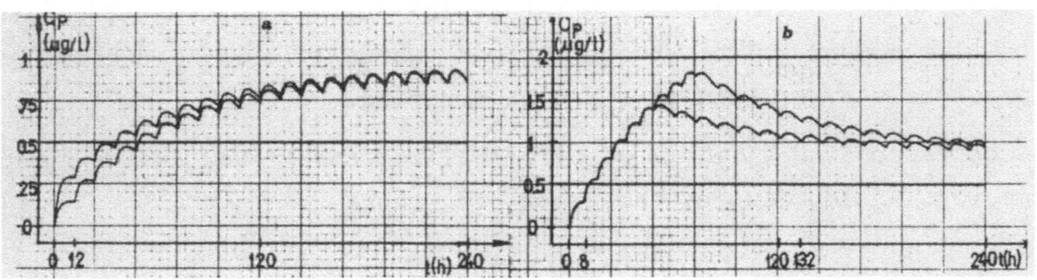

Figure 3.   $\beta$-methyldigoxine ($k_a$=0.4h$^{-1}$, $k_e$=0.016h$^{-1}$, therapeutic range
0.5-2.0 ug/l) plasma concentrations time responses after
multiple dosing
a.   Upper curve: initial dose 0.2 mg, looding doses 0.1 mg every 12 hours, lower curve: initial dose and loading doses
0.1 mg every 12 hours
b.   Two various dosage regimen.  Upper curve: 9 doses a 0.2 mg
every 8 hours (acute regimen), then 14 doses a 0.1 mg every
12 hours (chronic regimen), lower curve: 6 doses a 0.2 mg
every 8 hours (acute regimen), then 16 doses a 0.1 mg every
12 hours (chronic regimen)

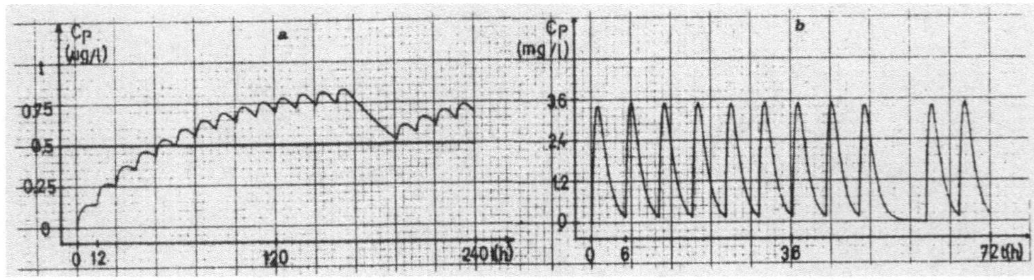

Figure 4a.   $\beta$-methyldigoxine plasma concentrations time response after
multiple dosing for the dosage regimen: 0.1 mg every 12
hours, 15$^{th}$ and 16$^{th}$ dose omited, then 0.1 mg every 12 hours
b.   Ampicillin ($k_a$=1.18h$^{-1}$, $k_e$=0.84h$^{-1}$, F=0.4) plasma concentrations time response after multiple dosing for the dosage re-
gimen: 500 mg every 6 hours, 10$^{th}$ dose omited, then 500 mg
every 6 hours

## 3.  Conclusion

The results of the work clearly explain the influence of discussed dosage

regimen of drugs plasma levels. In the simulation scheme any pharmaco-
kinetical model can be included without problems. The proposed approach
in our opinion enables more profound studies of possible cases in multiple dosing and their influence on drugs efficacy. So it represents an
effective tool for the decisions in the routine clinical practice.

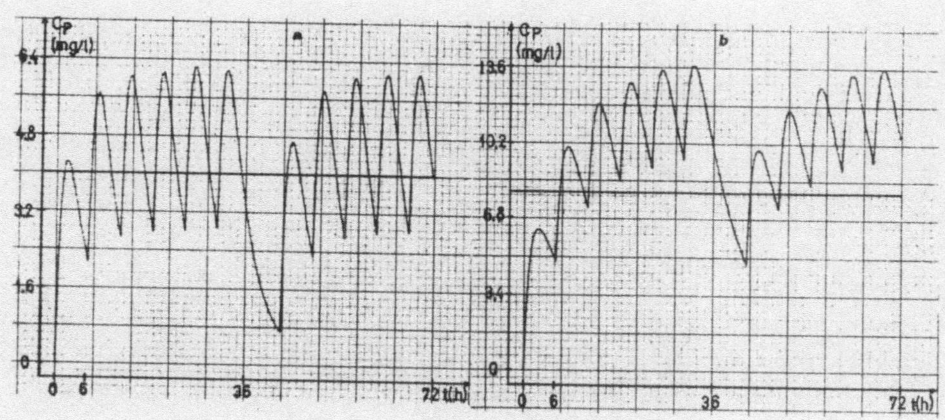

Figure 5a. Procainamide ($k_a$=1h$^{-1}$, $k_e$=0.231h$^{-1}$, F=0.85, therapeutic
range 4-8 mg/l) plasma concentration time response after
multiple dosing for the dosage regimen: 1000 mg every
6 hours, 7th dose omited, then 1000 mg every 6 hours
b. Theophylline ($k_a$=0.9h$^{-1}$, $k_e$=0.116h$^{-1}$, therapeutic range
8-20 mg/l) plasma concentrations time response after multiple dosing for the dosage regimen: 300 mg every 6 hours,
7th dose omited, then 300 mg every 6 hours

## References


/1/ Knoben, J.E., Anderson, F.O., Handbook of clinical drug data. Drug
Intelligence Publication Inc.,Hamilton, 1983.

/2/ Peck, C.C., Computer assisted clinical pharmacokinetics. In. Benet,
L.Z., Massoud, N., Gambertoglio, J.G., eds., Pharmacokinetic basis
for drug treatment, Raven Press, New York, 1984, 367-415.

/3/ Kozjek, F., Karba, R., Mrhar, A., Computer aided individual theophylline dosage regimen design, Proceedings of the 1984 summer computer simulation conference, Boston, Vol.2, 1984, 769-774.

/4/ Karba, R., Kozjek, F., Mrhar, A., Bremšak, F., Matko, D., Evaluation
of incomplete absorption using analog-hybrid simulation, Proceedigs
of 2. Symposium Simulationstechnik, Wien, 1984, 427-431.

/5/ Mrhar, A., Kozjek, F., Karba, R., Bremšak, F., Drinovec, J., Ampicillin, pharmacokinetics and dosage regimen design in patients on hae-
modialysis, Acta Pharm. Jugosl., Vol. 33, 1983, 121-128.

# SCHALTKREISSIMULATION

SMILE

Multi-Level-Simulator für den Entwurf

logischer Schaltungen


Franz Egger, Siemens AG, München


Zusammenfassung:

Die rapid wachsende Komplexität von Bausteinen und Funktionseinheiten erfordern für den Designprozeß neue Werkzeuge, die bereits auf höheren abstrakten Entwurfsebenen Unterstützung bieten und durchgängig bis auf Realisierungsebene anwendbar sind.
Das Multi-Level-Simulationssystem SMILE wurde mit dieser Zielsetzung konzipiert und soll sowohl den Logikentwurf und die Verifikation über unterschiedliche Darstellungsebenen (von der Register-Transfer- bis zur Gatterebene) unterstützen wie auch für die Prüfdatenermittlung einsetzbar sein.


## 1. Einführung

Aufgrund fortschreitender Technologien und höherer Leistungsanforderungen nimmt die Integrationsdichte und damit die Komplexität beim Entwurf von Rechnersystemen und integrierten Schaltungen stetig zu.
Um dennoch mit möglichst geringem Entwicklungsrisiko große Entwurfssicherheit zu erreichen, ist es erforderlich, rechnergestützte Entwurfsverfahren einzusetzen.
Mit SMILE /1/ wird ein leistungsfähiges Simulations-System für die Verifikation eines Entwurfs über mehrere Darstellungsebenen (Top-Down-Entwurf), sowie für die Prüfdatenermittlung angeboten.
Das Einsatzgebiet von SMILE erstreckt sich vom Entwurf von Rechnersystemen über Flachbaugruppen und LSI-Bausteinen hin bis zum Entwurf von VLSI-Chips.


## 2. Allgemeine Systemeigenschaften

Der Ausbau und die Funktionsauslegung des Simulationssystems SMILE wurde im wesentlichen durch folgende allgemeine Systemeigenschaften geprägt:

### Breite Einsetzbarkeit
Simulationsobjekte beliebiger Technik, Komplexität und Aufbaustruktur können mit hoher Genauigkeit zur Entwurfsunterstützung und Prüfdatenermittlung simuliert werden.

### Geschlossenes System
Das Simulationssystem enthält alle Funktionen, die zur autonomen Abwicklung der Simulation erforderlich sind (z.B. Datenaufbereitung, Ergebnisauswertung, Externschnittstellenanschlüsse, Dienstfunktionen, Datenverwaltung).

## Anpaßbarkeit an verschiedene Einsatzgebiete

Durch geeignete Konfiguration können nichtbenötigte Funktionsblöcke
aus dem System ausgegliedert werden und erscheinen dann nicht mehr
im Benutzerinterface (Baukasten-Prinzip).

## Einheitliche Benutzeroberfläche

Alle Komponenten des Simulationssystems sollen unter einer Benutzer-
oberfläche ablaufen. Die Dialogführung zwischen Anwender und System
kann über Kommandos oder Masken erfolgen. Wichtig ist dabei die Ge-
schlossenheit der Kommandosprache bzw. des Maskenaufbaus über alle
Funktionen des Systems, wobei funktionell gleiche Vorgänge u. Sach-
merkmale syntaktisch und semantisch gleich ausgedrückt werden.

## Einbeziehung von Workstations

Da heute verfügbare Workstations leistungsfähige interakiv, grafische
Funktionen anbieten, sollen diese vorallem für die Dialogführung,
die Stromlaufbearbeitung und Ergebnisauswertung von SMILE genutzt
werden.
Abhängig von der Leistungsfähigkeit der Workstation und der Komplexität der Simulationsobjekte können auch alle Funktionen von SMILE
auf einer Workstation abgewickelt werden, so daß die Performance
des Gesamtsystems gesteigert und die Verfügbarkeit von Rechnerleistung
erhöht wird.

## Portabilität

Die Implementierung von SMILE erfolgt unter Einhaltung von Portabili-
tätsgesichtspunkten (Verwendung der Programmiersprache Siemens-PASCAL,
Betriebssystem- und Hardware- abhängige Teile in zentralen Prozeduren
usw.), so daß eine Anpassung an unterschiedliche Hardware-Komponenten
und Betriebssysteme mit relativ geringem Aufwand möglich ist.


## 3. Systemarchitektur

Die Systemarchitektur ist nach hierarchischen Gesichtspunkten angelegt,
d.h. das Gesamtsystem gliedert sich in unterschiedliche Ebenen. Damit
ergibt sich eine eindeutige Aufrufhierarchie der Komponenten, was
wesentlich zur Realisierungssicherheit des Gesamtsystems beiträgt.
Die Verbindung zwischen den einzelnen Hierarchieebenen wird durch
einheitliche Schnittstellen hergestellt. Im wesentlichen sind folgende
drei Hierarchieebenen realisert:

## Benutzerebene

Alle Benutzereingaben in Form von Grafik, Sprache, Masken oder Menüs
werden von einem einheitlichen Monitor verarbeitet. Dieser Monitor
prüft die Eingabedaten auf ihre syntaktische und semantische Richtigkeit und steuert dann die entsprechenden Teilfunktionen an.

## Funktionsblockebene

Das Simulationssystem SMILE ist in mehrere Funktionsblöcke unterteilt.
Diese Funktionsblöcke bilden eine eigene Hierarchieebene und weisen
definierte Schnittstellen zum Ablaufmonitor und der Datenbasis auf.

## Datenbasisebene

Alle Daten (Produkt- oder Bibliotheksdaten) werden in einer zentralen
Datenbasis verwaltet. Der Zugriff zu dieser Datenbasis erfolgt über
eine einheitliche Schnittstelle. Jede Teilfunktion kann die für sie
erforderlichen Daten aus der Datenbasis entnehmen, gegebenenfalls neu
erstellte oder angereicherte Daten für eine spätere Verwendung wieder
in der Datenbasis ablegen.

Die hierarchische Systemarchitektur und die einheitlichen Schnittstellen zwischen den einzelnen Hierarchieebenen ermöglichen eine
Konfigurierung von SMILE im Sinne eines Baukastensystems. Der Lei-
stungsumfang kann dabei den spezifischen Anwendungsfällen so angepaßt werden, daß nicht benötigte Funtkionsblöcke aus dem System ausgegliedert werden. Das Baukastensystem ermöglicht ebenso einfach
neue Leistungen einzubringen. Neue Funktionsblöcke sind entsprechend
den Schnittstellenkonventionen zu implementieren und können dann
in das Spektrum der verfügbaren Funktionen aufgenommen werden.

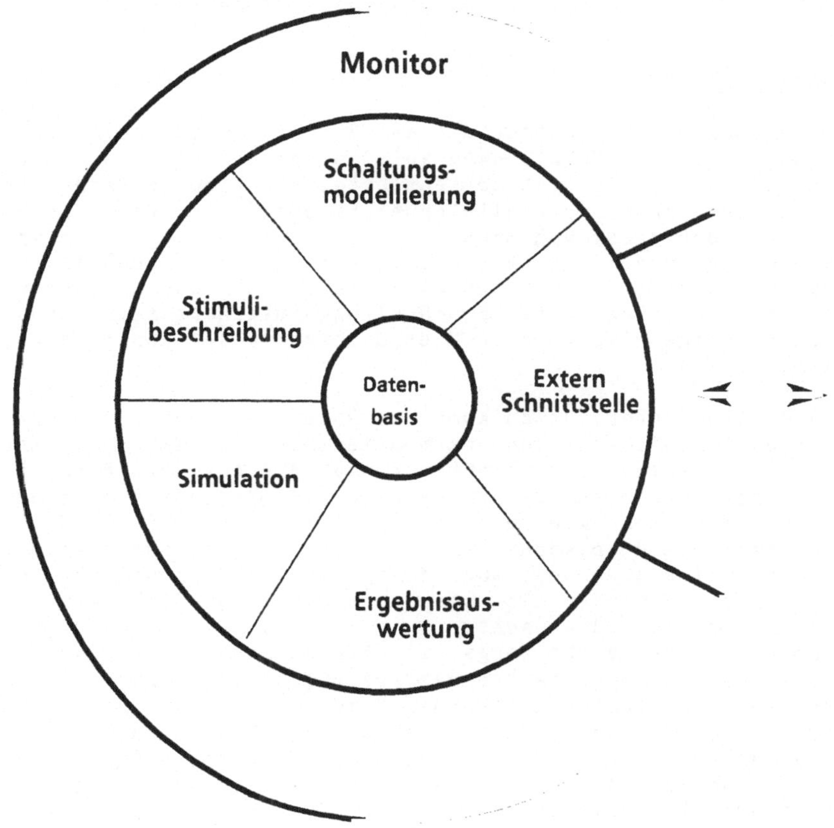


Bild 1: prinzipielle Systemstruktur


## 4. Systemfunktionen

### Monitor

Über den Monitor wird die Bedienung aller Funktionen von SMILE ab-
gewickelt. Dabei kann die Systembedienung dialogorientiert oder in
Form von Batch-Aufträgen erfolgen.
Über Auskunftsfunktionen kann der Anwender jederzeit den Bearbeitungs-
zustand seines Modells abfragen, sich über aufgetretene Fehler in-
formieren oder bei der Bedienung des Systems durch eine hierarchische
HELP-Funktion unterstützt werden.
Der Monitor bietet Unterstützung beginnend von der Ersterfassung der
Daten bis hin zur Auswertung der Simulationsergebnisse. Spezielle
DV-Kenntnisse sind dadurch praktisch nicht erforderlich.

Alle Funktionen des Simulationssystems können über den Monitor explizit aktiviert werden. Wird eine Funktion aufgerufen, die den erforderlichen Abschluß anderer Funktionen voraussetzt, dann werden diese
implizit angestoßen (z.B. fehlende Modellaufbereitung vor einer Simulation).
Das System kann sowohl über formatierte Bildschirmmasken als auch
über eine Kommandosprache bedient werden. Ein Wechsel zwischen beiden
Modi und die Verwendung von Kommandos innerhalb des Maskenmodus ist
möglich. Eine Makroverarbeitung auch auf Kommandosprachebene in Verbindung mit der Sicherung im Dialog eingegebener Kommandofolgen für
wiederholbare Funktionsläufe reduziert den Bedienungsaufwand auf
ein Minimum.

<u>Schaltungsmodellierung</u>

Die Beschreibungsmöglichkeiten, die das System bietet, erlauben die
Modellierung digitaler Schaltungen auf den verschiedensten Ebenen.
Am oberen Ende steht die systemorientierte, funktionale Betrachtungsweise, am unteren Ende die realisierungsbezogene, strukturelle Beschreibung auf der Basis von Bausteinen, Zellen und logischen Grundelemente wie z.B. einem Transfergatter. Das Simulationsmodell für
eine Schaltung kann nicht nur aus einer rein funktionalen oder einer
rein realisierungsorientierten Beschreibung aufgebaut sein, sondern
auch eine beliebige Mischform in diesem Spektrum der Abstraktionsebenen
darstellen.

Auf Transferebene unterstützen komplexe Datenstrukturen, überlagert
mit verschiedenen Sichten, den dokumentierenden Charakter der Modellbeschreibung und erleichtern darüber hinaus die Auswertung der Simulationsergebnisse. Nebenläufige und parallele Prozesse lassen sich
hier ebenso beschreiben wie sequentielle Vorgänge.
Unterbrechungsstrukturen können unmittelbar durch entsprechende Sprachkonstrukte formuliert werden. Unzulässige Ansteuerung oder Verletzungen
von Zeitbedingungen werden als sogenannte Betriebsbedingungen definiert
und bei der Simulation überwacht.
Die Logikelemente der verbindungsorientierten Beschreibung auf Schalt-
werkebene können komplex wie Prozessorbausteine oder einfach wie
UND-Gatter sein. Logikelemente können Simulator-Grundelemente (Gatter,
FF, Register, Zähler, usw), funktional beschriebene Elemente oder
Subschaltungen sein. Spezielle Grundelemente wie das bidirektionale
Transfergate oder die speichernde Busverbindung unterstützen zusätzlich
die Beschreibung technologiespezifischer Eigenschaften.

Die Modellierung großer Schaltungen wird durch einen hierarchischen
Aufbau der Beschreibung erleichtert. So können Module gebildet werden,
die getrennt bearbeitet und über Makrobildung (auch geschachtelt)
oder über die Binder-Funktion zu einem Gesamtmodell zusammengeschaltet
werden.

Die Modellgenauigkeit wird entscheidend bestimmt durch die Genauigkeit,
mit der das Laufzeitverhalten nachgebildet werden kann.

Auf Transferebene kann jedem Transfer und jeder Zuweisung eine Zeit
zugeordnet werden, wobei auch eine Unterscheidung von Anstiegs- und
Abfallzeiten möglich ist.

Auf Schaltwerksebene können Leitungslaufzeiten und Schaltelement-
laufzeiten definiert werden. Die Schaltelementzeit kann differenziert
werden in eine Elementlaufzeit und in eine Schaltzeit, diese getrennt
in Anstiegs- und Abfallzeit.

## Stimulibeschreibung

Die Testdaten, wie z.B. Eingangsmuster oder Speicherinhalte, werden
mit der Stimulibeschreibungssprache formuliert. Neben leicht erlern-
baren Anweisungen für die inkrementale Beschreibung von Bitmustern
oder Signalverläufen bietet sie den erfahrenen Anwendern auch algo-
rithmetische und logische Funktionen. Eine kompakte und übersichtliche Beschreibung wird ermöglicht durch Vektor- und Makrobearbeitung.
Die Stimulibeschreibungssprache ermöglicht auch die für Prüfzwecke
erforderliche Gliederung in Zyklen, die Definition von Abtastkriterien
und Ansteuerungsbedingungen für Prüfautomaten.

## Simulation

Der Mehrebenensimulator in SMILE ermöglicht die Bewertung und Verifikation eines Logikentwurfs in den verschiedenen Entwurfsphasen, von
den ersten Konzeptüberlegungen auf Transfer-Ebene bis hin zur endgültigen Realisierung auf Gatter- oder Zellenebene.
Die 16 logischen Zustände, die aus der Überlagerung der drei Grund-
zustände (0,1. undefiniert) mit vier verschiedenen Signalstärken
und dem Tristate-Zustand entstehen, ermöglichen eine genaue Nachbildung des logischen Verhaltens.
Das Zeitverhalten wird über die getrennte Behandlung von Leitungslaufzeiten, Elementdurchlaufzeiten und Elementschaltzeiten präzise
nachgebildet. Die Trennung in Zeiten für steigende und fallende
Flanken wird dabei automatisch durchgeführt. Bei einer Auflösung
von 1ps kann eine Zeitspanne von bis zu 999 sec. simuliert werden.

Der Simulator führt automatisch eine Reihe von Überwachungsfunktionen
durch. So werden auftretende Spikes gefiltert, Konflikte auf Bussen
gemeldet (z.B. gleichzeitige Aktivität mehrerer Treiber), Oszillationen
erkannt und benutzerdefinierte Betriebsbedingungen (z.B. Setupzeiten)
werden auf Einhaltung überwacht.

Die Möglichkeit, Fixpunkte zu setzen und zu definierten Simulations-
zeitpunkten wieder aufzusetzen, unterstützt zum einen den interaktiven
Betrieb der Simulation, zum anderen trägt dies wesentlich zur effizienten, kostengünstigen Nutzung der Simulation bei.
Für eine spätere Auswertung werden über den gesamten Simulationszeit-
raum die logischen Zustände aller Signale gesichert. Zur Reduzierung
der dabei entstehenden Datenmengen, vor allem bei der Simulation
großer Schaltungen, kann die Anzahl der zu betrachtenden Signale
vor der Simulation eingeschränkt werden.

Neben der Entwurfsverifikation ist auch die Prüfdatenermittlung Bestandteile von SMILE. Der dafür vorgesehene Prüfsimulator enthält
Steuerfunktionen, mit denen die wichtigsten Charakteristika von Prüfautomaten wie z.B. Taktgeneratoren, Eingangsverzögerungen von Test-
vektoren und Abtastzeitpunkte nachgebildet werden können. Die dafür
erforderlichen zyklenorientierten Prüfbitmuster können für beliebige
Teilschaltungen aus einer vorangegangenen Entwurfsverifikation der
Gesamtschaltung automatisch abgeleitet werden. Dabei besteht die
Möglichkeit Toleranzbereiche, Takt- und Triggersignale vorzugeben.
Die Qualität der Prüfbitmuster kann mit einem Fehlersimulator verifiziert werden. Der dabei verwendete Concurrent-Algorithmus bietet
den Vorteil, daß auch funktional beschriebene Bibliothekselemente
für die Fehlersimulation verwendet werden können und somit für die
Prüfdatenermittlung die selbe Bibliothek wie für die Entwurfsverifikation einsetzbar ist.

Ergebnisauswertung
=====

Die Ergebnisse der Simulation können wahlweise über Bildschirm oder
Drucker und soweit sinnvoll auch über Plotter und Grafikbildschirm
ausgegeben werden. Neben der Aufbereitung in Signaldiagrammdarstellung
können die Simulationsergebnisse auch nach speziellen Kriterien ausgewertet werden, so die Ausgaben von Instabilitäten aufgrund von Rückkopplung oder die Ausgabe von Buskurzschlüssen.

Zur Auswahl der auszugebenden Signal- und Zeitbereiche gibt es sehr
komfortable Auswahlkriterien. Die Dialogausgaben werden durch Blätter-
funktionen sowohl in der Zeitachse als auch in der Signalachse und
durch eine ZOOM-Funktion unterstützt.

Logisch zusammengehörige Signale können zu Gruppen zusammengefaßt
werden.
Der Signalverlauf kann mit einem variablen Zeitraster oder komprimiert
ereignisbezogen dargestellt werden.
Zur Unterstützung des Tests funktionaler Modelle (auch funktional
beschriebener Bibliothekselemente) kann für jeden Signalwechsel die
dieses Ereignis auslösende Zeile in der Beschreibung protokolliert
werden, wodurch die Zusammenhänge zwischen Simulationsereignissen
und Modellbeschreibungen leicht zu verfolgen sind.


5.  Ausblick
=====

Der Multi-Level-Simulator SMILE wird z.Z. im Rahmen eines CAD-Systems
für VLSI-Bausteine (VENUS) /2/ eingesetzt. Das Simulationssystem
ist auf Siemens-Rechnern unter dem Betriebssystem BS 2000 und auf
einer UNIX-based Workstation ablauffähig.
Neben stand-alone-Anwendungen ist der Einsatz im Rahmen eines CAD-
System für die Großrechnerentwicklung und für ein Standard-Techno-
logie-System geplant.
Funktionserweiterungen erfolgen in nächster Zeit vorallem in Verbindung mit Spezialhardware. So wird in Kürze ein REALCHIP-Zusatz an-
schließbar sein, mit dessen Hilfe die Modellierung von bereits verfügbaren, komplexen Bausteinen wesentlich vereinfacht wird.
Eine bedeutende Steigerung der Simulationsgeschwindigkeit in Verbindung mit großen Schaltungskomplexen auf Realisierungsebene (bis zu
1 Mill. Gatterfunktionen) soll durch den Einsatz eines speziellen
Simulationsrechners erreicht werden.


6.  Literaturhinweis
=====

/1/ M. Gonauser, F. Egger, D. Frantz:
    SMILE - a multilevel simulationssystem
    S 188-193, IEEE Computer Society Reprint, 1984

/2/ Dr. E. Hörbst, P. Birzele:
    Das CAD-Entwurfssystem VENUS für komplexe Semicustom-Bausteine
    mit Standardzellen, allgemeinen Zellen oder Gate Arrays
    Kongreßprogramm VDI Okt. 85

# MuSiC: Ein Höchstleistungsrechner für die Simulation Digitaler Systeme

Kristian Fischer und Winfried Hahn, Passau

**Zusammenfassung.** Mit dem Munich-Simulation-Computer wird ein hochgradig paralleler Spezialrechner für die schnelle Simulation digitaler, durch Programme einer Mehrebenen-Rechnerentwurfssprache dargestellter Systeme vorgestellt. Grundlage für die hohe Simulationsleistung ist die Kombination von für Datenflußrechner entwickelten Konzepten mit der Ereignissimulation durch das Ereignisfluß-Modell. Dieses Modell, das die Arbeitsweise des Rechners beschreibt sowie seine Implementierung als MuSiC-Organisation, werden vorgestellt und die Simulationsleistung, die einige Milliarden Ereignisauswertungen pro Sekunde erreicht, wird in Abhängigkeit von verschiedenen Parametern diskutiert.

**Summary.** The Munich-Simulation-Computer, a special-purpose, highly-parallel programmable machine, is an approach to transfer concepts (developed for data flow computers) to fast, mixed-design-level simulation of digital systems. To gain high performance, however, the operation principle is modified from data flow computation to event flow computation. This paper presents the event flow computation scheme and its implementation by the MuSiC organisation. It is shown that MuSiC can simulate more than 8 million gates and flipflops at a speed of up to some billion events per second.

## Einleitung

Logik-Simulatoren sind heute hauptsächlich als Programme für Universalrechner implementiert. Beim Entwurf größerer Systeme wie z.B. von VLSI-Chips wird jedoch die Anwendung dieser Programme durch die zu geringe Rechenleistung sequentieller Wirtsrechner stark behindert, weil nur einige $10^5$ Ereignisse pro Sekunde (E/s) ausgewertet werden können. Als Antwort auf diese Herausforderung sind Spezialrechner[1] wie z.B. ZYCAD's Logic Engine (LE)[2] und IBM's Yorktown Simulation Engine (YSE)[3] entstanden. Dabei erreicht die LE durch apparative Realisierung von Algorithmen der Ereignissimulation eine Leistung von bis zu $1.6 * 10^7$ E/s und die YSE durch Ausnutzung von Parallelität eine Leistung von bis zu $3.2 * 10^9$ Gatterauswertungen pro Sekunde. Bezeichnet man mit $p_e$ den mittleren Anteil der Gatter im zu simulierenden System, bei denen sich der Zustand mindestens einer Eingangsleitung ändert, so kann man die YSE-Leistung zum Vergleich angeben durch $3.2 * p_e * 10^9$ E/s. Der Wert für $p_e$ hängt von dem Detaillierungsgrad der Beschreibung des Entwurfs und von der Zeitauflösung der Simulation ab und wird in der Literatur[1,4] mit $0.4 \ldots 0.1$ bzw. auch mit $0.038$ angegeben. Mit diesen Werten ist die YSE der derzeit leistungsfähigste in der Literatur erwähnte Simulationsrechner und dient daher als Vergleichsmaschine zu MuSiC.

Zur weiteren Steigerung der Simulationsleistung wird für MuSiC ein neuartiges Operationsprinzip, das Ereignisfluß-Modell[5], verwendet, das im ersten Abschnitt angegeben wird. In der MuSiC-Organisation, die im zweiten Abschnitt dargestellt wird, spiegeln sich Eigenschaften der zur "Programmierung" verwendeten Rechnerentwurfssprache[6,7] wieder. Dies sind zum einen die vierwertige Logik mit den

Werten 0, 1, "hochohmig"(Z) und "unbekannt"(?) und zum anderen das Mehrebenenkonzept, das es erlaubt ein System modular zu strukturieren und jeden Modul entweder auf algorithmischer Ebene, auf Befehlssatzebene oder auf Gatterebene zu beschreiben. Im dritten Abschnitt wird auf Grundlage eines Leistungsbewertungsmodells die Simulationsleistung von MuSiC geschätzt. Zugunsten der YSE werden dabei nur die Gatterebenensimulation sowie der "Zero-Delay"- und "Unit-Delay"-Simulationsmodus betrachtet. Dies ist die einzige Sprachebene und sind die einzigen Simulationsmodi, die von der YSE unterstützt werden. MuSiC kann zusätzlich Mehrebenenbeschreibungen simulieren und unterstützt den "Precise-Delay"-Simulationsmodus.


## 1. Operationsprinzip

Ein zu simulierendes System kann als Graph dargestellt werden, in dem die Knoten die speichernden Elemente sowie logischen Gatter repräsentieren und die Kanten die sie verbindenden Leitungen. Faßt man einen solchen Graphen als Datenflußprogrammgraphen[8] auf, so entspricht der Fluß von Signalen durch das digitale System genau den Fluß von Daten durch das Programm: Durch die Ausführung des Datenflußprogramms wird also das Verhalten des Systems simuliert.

Mit diesem Ansatz ist es möglich, bei einer datengetriebenen Programmauswertung eine hochgradig parallele Simulation zu erreichen. Andererseits ist die Ereignissimulation eine bewährte Methode durch die Einsparungen von Komponentenauswertungen die Effizienz programmierter Simulatoren zu steigern. Um beide Konzepte für eine schnelle Simulation auszunutzen, erfolgt die Steuerung der Auswertung des Programmgraphen im Ereignisfluß-Modell nicht durch den Fluß von Daten, die Leitungszustände repräsentieren, sondern durch den Fluß von Ereignissen, die Leitungszustandsänderungen repräsentieren. Dazu wird

(1) der Graph durch Befehlsworte (engl.: template) repräsentiert, die jeweils aus einem Operationskode, einer beschränkten Anzahl von Verweisen auf Folgebefehle sowie Feldern zur Annahme und Speicherung der Operanden bestehen,

(2) ein Befehl bereits durch die Ankunft eines neuen Operandenwertes ausführbar, wobei die Verfügbarkeit eines Wertes für jede Operandenposition durch die Pufferung der jeweils zuletzt verarbeiteten Werte sichergestellt wird, und

(3) das Ergebnis einer Befehlsausführung nur dann an die Nachfolgebefehle übermittelt, wenn es von dem zuletzt übermittelten Ergebnis abweicht.

Durch den Übergang vom Datenfluß-Ausführungsmodell (Ankunft eines Wertes für jede Operandenposition macht einen Befehl ausführbar) zum Ereignisfluß-Ausführungsmodell (Ankunft eines Wertes für mindestens eine Operandenposition macht einen Befehl ausführbar) entsteht das Problem, daß Befehle u.U. zunächst mit vorläufigen Operandenwerten ausgeführt werden. Bei MuSiC wird dieses Problem durch die Schrittsteuerung der Simulation umgangen. Dazu wird zunächst ein Programmgraph, der aus Befehlen für speichernde Elemente und logische Gatter besteht, in Stufen (engl.: ranks) eingeteilt: Für einen Knoten s ist

- rank(s) = 0, wenn s ein speicherndes Element darstellt und
- rank(s) = n+1, wenn für alle unmittelbaren Vorgänger t von s rank(t) < n+1 gilt, es mindestens einen unmittelbaren Vorgänger u von s gibt mit rank(u) = n und s kein speicherndes Element darstellt.

Die Schrittsteuerung bewirkt die sequentielle, zyklisch wiederholte Auswertung der Stufen, wobei jeweils nur die ausführbaren Befehle einer Stufe (ggf. parallel zueinander) ausgeführt werden. Die Ausführung von Befehlen mit vorläufigen Operanden ist ausgeschlossen, weil

- alle Befehle einer Stufe datenunabhängig sind und
- in jedem Schritt der Simulation alle zur Ausführung der jeweiligen Stufe notwendigen Operanden berechnet sind.

Der Nachteil der Schrittsteuerung ist jedoch, daß bei in Fließbandtechnik organisierter Befehlsausführung das Fließband nach jedem Schritt neu anlaufen muß. Dies reduziert die Leistung dann erheblich, wenn die Anzahl der in einem Schritt auszuführenden Befehle gering ist.


## 2. Organisation

MuSiC besteht aus 16*16 "processing units"(PUs), die jeweils Speicher für 64k Befehlsworte haben sowie Operationswerke zur Ausführung von Programmen einer höheren Programmiersprache (PLI) für die Simulation algorithmisch beschriebener Teile des Entwurfs, zur Ausführung komplexer Funktionen - z.B. Multiplikation - für die Simulation von Beschreibungen auf Befehlssatzebene und zur parallelen Ausführung der booleschen Grundfunktionen auf bis zu 8 Bit breiten Operandenvektoren für die Gatterebenensimulation.

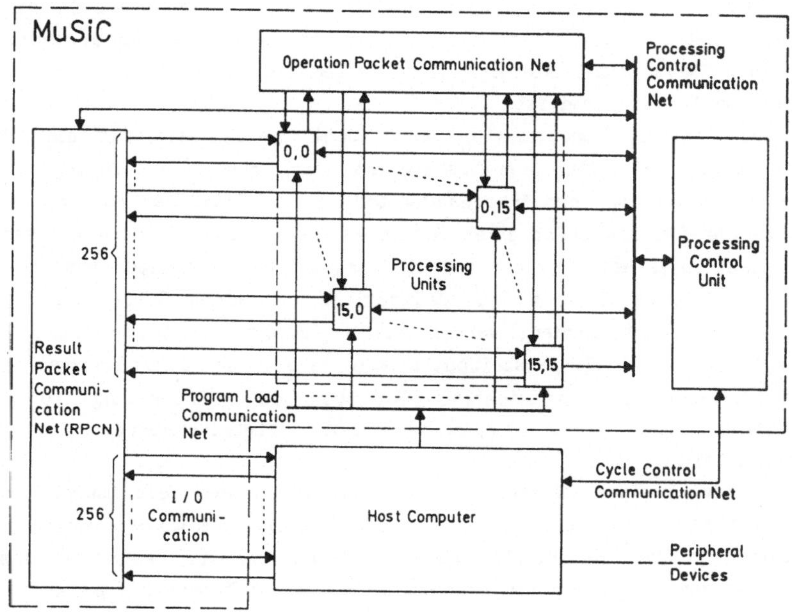


Figur 1: Die Struktur von MuSiC

Wie in Figur 1 gezeigt, sind die PUs untereinander sowie mit einem "Host-Computer" durch die folgenden fünf Kommunikationsnetze verbunden:

(1) Program Load Communication Net: Der "Host-Computer" übersetzt Programme aus Rechnerentwurfssprachen in MuSiC-Befehlsworte und lädt sie über das Netz in die PUs.

(2) Result Packet Communication Net: Ergebnisse, die von einer PU berechnet und von einer anderen PU benötigt werden, werden als "result-packets" durch ein synchrones Delta-Netz[9] übermittelt, über das auch der Ein-/Ausgabe-Datenverkehr

vom/zum "Host-Computer" fließt. Da somit 256 E/A-Kanäle zur Verfügung stehen, sind die erforderlichen E/A-Datenraten ein alleiniges Problem des "Host-Computers".

(3) Operation Packet Communication Net: Durch das Ereignisfluß-Modell bedingt, muß für die einzelnen Schritte der Simulation zwischen der statischen und dynamischen Auftragslast der PUs unterschieden werden:
   - Die statische Auftragslast ist die Anzahl der Befehlsworte der entsprechenden Stufe des Graphen geteilt durch die Anzahl der PUs.
   - Die dynamische Auftragslast in einem Schritt der Simulation ist der Teil der Befehlsworte einer statischen Auftragslast, die wegen der Verfügbarkeit neuer Operandenwerte auszuführen sind.

   Während die statische Auftragslast für alle PUs (annähernd) gleich ist, differriert die dynamische Auftragslast von PU zu PU und zwischen den aufeinander folgenden Auswertungen der gleichen Stufe. Wie in einem Leistungsbewertungsmodell[11] gezeigt werden konnte, ist diese Ungleichheit bei hohen statischen Auftragslasten vernachlässigbar. Bei der Simulation höherer Sprachebenen, bei der die Stufen relativ wenige Befehle enthalten, die Befehle jedoch jeweils beträchtliche Ausführungszeiten haben können, müssen die verschiedenen dynamischen Auftragslasten der PUs jedoch dynamisch ausgeglichen werden. Dazu werden "operation packets" (auszuführende Befehle), die von dem geeigneten Operationswerk der eigenen PU nicht sofort bearbeitet werden können, durch das Netz von solchen PUs "angesogen", bei denen das geeignete Operationswerk z.Zt. frei ist.

(4) Processing Control Communication Net: Durch dieses Netz und die "Processing Control Unit" ist die Schrittsteuerung der Simulation implementiert. Die Kommunikation zwischen der "Processing Control Unit" und den PUs besteht aus dem Signal an die PUs zum Start eines Schrittes der Simulation sowie aus den Signalen "last operation packet fetched" und "last result packet mailed" von den PUs.

(5) Cycle Control Communication Net: Jedesmal wenn in einem Schritt die Befehle der Stufe 0 ausgeführt werden, werden die im Programm verarbeiteten Daten dem jeweils folgenden Simulationszeitpunkt zugeordnet. Die Simulationszeit wird, über das Cycle Control Communication Net von der "Processing Control Unit" kontrolliert, im "Host-Computer", dem "Betriebssystem von MuSiC", fortgeschaltet.

Die Hauptbestandteile einer PU sind der "cell block", in dem Befehlsworte gespeichert werden und Listen für die jeweils ausführbaren Befehle verwaltet werden, sowie die "function unit", in der die Befehle ausgeführt werden. Die restlichen Bestandteile dienen vor allem dem Austausch von "result packets" und "operation packets" innerhalb der PU sowie mit der Umgebung der PU.

Ein "cell block" enthält acht unabhängige "memory units", die jeweils 8K Befehlsworte aufnehmen können. Ankommende "result-pakets" werden in zwei Stationen eines Fließbandes verarbeitet, die eine Ausführungszeit von jeweils 4 Taktperioden haben. Der Ablageplatz des Ergebnisses im adressiertem Befehlswort wird in der ersten Station bestimmt, um in der zweiten Station in die entsprechende memory-unit schreiben zu können. Außerdem muß in der ersten Station bestimmt werden, ob es sich um den ersten für das Befehlswort ankommenden Operanden handelt, um ggf. in der zweiten Station den Befehl in die Liste der auszuführenden Befehle einzuhängen. Diese Liste ist so abgespeichert, daß beim Befehlsabruf jeweils gleichzeitig ein auszuführender Befehl und die Adresse des nächsten auszuführenden Befehls gelesen werden können. Damit kann die durch die Zugriffszeit des Speichers bestimmte

Datenrate voll für das Absenden von "operation packets" genutzt werden, weil ein Programm so abgespeichert werden kann[11], daß in einem Schritt bei einer "memory-unit" entweder Ergebnisse eingetragen werden, oder "operation packets" ausgelesen werden.

Die drei Operationswerke für die von MuSiC unterstützten Sprachebenen, die in der "function unit" zusammengefaßt sind, führen parallel zueinander die vom "cell-block" bzw. von überlasteten PUs angebotenen Befehle aus.

Im Werk für die Operationen der Gaternetzebene werden bitweise definierte Grundfunktionen (z.B. $\neg$, $\wedge$, $\vee$, $\overline{\wedge}$, $\overline{\vee}$) auf Operandenvektoren der Länge acht durch Tabellenzugriff in vier Taktperioden ausgeführt. Das Werk für die Operationen der Befehlssatzebene führt wortweise definierte Funktionen (z.B. +, $\neg$, *, /, shift) auf acht Bit breiten Operanden in einigen zehn Taktperioden aus und das Werk für die algorithmische Sprachebene, das einen handelsüblichen Mikroprozessor enthält, führt die in einen Entwurf eingebundenen Programme einer höheren Programmiersprache aus, deren Ausführungszeit mindestens einige hundert Taktperioden beträgt.

## 3. Abschätzung der Leistung

Wie eingangs erwähnt, beträgt die theoretische Leistung der YSE

$$R_{YSE} = p_e * 3.2 * 10^9 \text{ E/s},$$

wenn man n = 256 Prozessoren, eine Fließbandtaktperiode von t = 80ns und die ausschließliche Verarbeitung von 1-Bit-Operanden (Vektorisierungsgrad v = 1) zugrunde legt. Für $p_e$ = 0.4 ergibt sich

$$R_{YSE} = 1.28 * 10^9 \text{ E/s}.$$

Für die theoretische Leistung von MuSiC werden ebenfalls n = 256 Prozessoren, jedoch eine Fließbandtektperiode von 120ns (synchroner Entwurf mit einer Taktperiode von $\tau$ = 30ns, der mit handelsüblichen "Gatearrays" oder Semi-Custom-VLSI-Chips implementiert werden kann) und ein maximaler Vektorisierungsgrad der Operanden von v = 8 zugrunde gelegt. Bei der Verarbeitung von Vektoren der Länge v als Operanden muß jedoch berücksichtigt werden, daß im Mittel nur

$$ee = v * p_e/(1-(1-p_e)^v)$$

Ereignisse ausgewertet werden. Im Gegensatz zur YSE fällt außerdem in jedem Schritt der Simulation die Anlaufzeit des Fließbandes von

$$t_0 = ( 37 + 2 * (1 + \lceil \text{ld } n \rceil) ) * \tau$$

an. Bei der Auswertung einer Stufe rk mit statischer Auftragslast $e_{rk}$ ist die theoretische MuSiC-Leistung dann

$$R_{rk} = (t_0/(p_e * e_{rk}) + t/(n * ee))^{-1}.$$

Für eine Entwurfsgröße von $10^5$ Gattern und $p_e$ = 0.4 ist

$$R_{MuSiC} = 6.73 * 10^9 \text{ E/s}.$$

Bei beiden Maschinen kann die theoretische Leistung im realen Betrieb aus verschiedenen Gründen nicht erreicht werden. Die Leistung der YSE setzt eine die Datenabhängigkeiten berücksichtigende, optimale Verteilung der Befehle auf die Prozessoren voraus. Der Einfluß von nicht-optimalen Verteilungen, mit denen man sich angesichts der Komplexität des Problems zufrieden geben muß, auf die Leistung konnte mit den über die YSE verfügbaren Informationen nicht ermittelt werden. Im folgenden wird daher die theoretische YSE-Leistung als Bezug verwendet. Für MuSiC konnten dagegen die Hauptfaktoren, die ein Abweichen von der theoretischen Leistung bewirken, in einem Leistungsmodell[11] berücksichtigt werden:

- Der maximale Vektorisierungsgrad kann nicht in allen Teilen
  der Entwurfsbeschreibung
  ausgenutzt werden.
- Wegen der begrenzten Zahl von
  Verweisen auf Nachfolgebefehle
  im Befehlsformat müssen teilweise kopierbefehle eingefügt
  werden.
- Die Verteilung der dynamischen
  Auftragslast über die Prozessoren kann ungleichmäßig sein.
- Die gegenseitige Blockierung
  von Datenpaketen kann die
  Übermittlungszeit in den
  Kommunikationsnetzen erhöhen.
- Die Eintragung von Ergebnissen
  in die "memory-units" kann
  aufgrund von Schreib-/Schreib-
  Konflikten verzögert werden.

Eine Auswertung des Leistungs-
modells, bei der ein existierender
Rechner[12] als zu simulierendes
System zugrunde gelegt ist, ergibt
die in Figur 2 und 3 gezeigten
Leistungsdaten.

Der Vergleich der theoretischen und
praktischen MuSiC-Leistung für den
Zero- und Unit-Delay-Simulations-
modus mit der theoretischen YSE-
Leistung ist in Figur 2 dargestellt. Im Bereich großer Werte für
$p_e$ resultiert die Überlegenheit von
MuSiC hauptsächlich aus der Verarbeitung von Vektoren als Operanden, die im Gegensatz zur YSE wegen
der Paket-Kommunikation mit vertretbarem Aufwand möglich ist. Im
Bereich kleiner Werte für $p_e$, die,
wie eingangs erwähnt, typisch sein
dürfen, führt die Verwirklichung
des Konzeptes der Ereignissimulation zu einer weiteren Vergrößerung der Leistungsdifferenz.

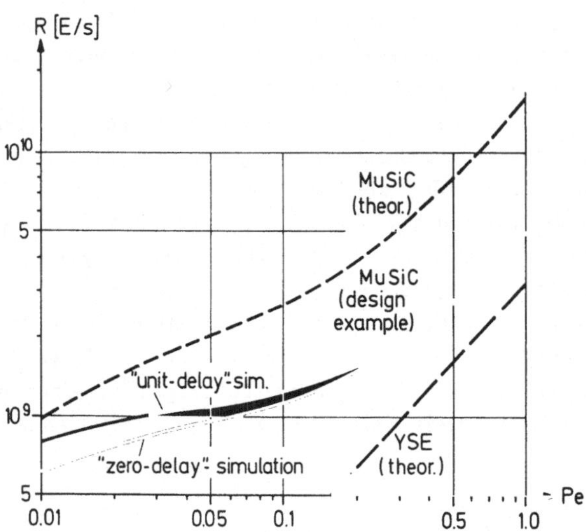


Figur 2: Leistung in Ereignisauswertungen pro
Sekunde als Funktion der Ereignis-
wahrscheinlichkeit

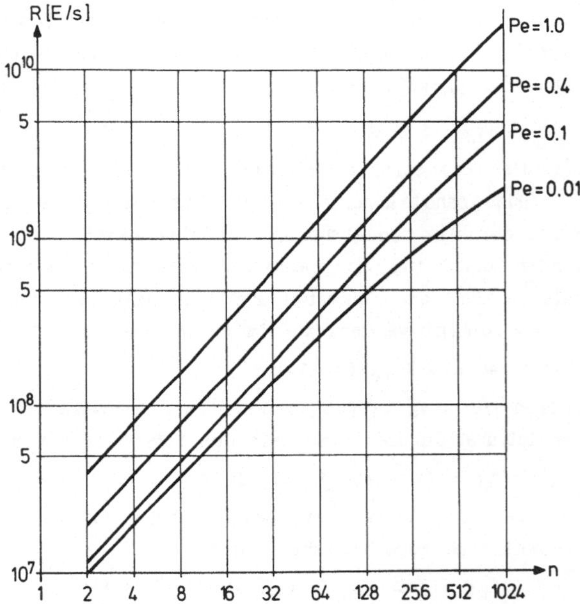


Figur 3: Leistung in Ereignisauswertungen pro
Sekunde als Funktion der Anzahl der
"processing units" für verschiedene
Ereigniswahrscheinlichkeiten

Da der Aufwand für das Kommunikationssystem nur mit $O(n * ld\ n)$ mit der Anzahl
der Prozessoren zunimmt, können Systeme mit mehr als 256 Prozessoren gemäß der
MuSiC-Struktur aufgebaut werden. Wie in Figur 3 gezeigt, bringt bei solchen Systemen
jede Verdoppelung der Anzahl der Prozessoren auch annähernd eine Verdoppelung der

Leistung, solange die Größe von simulierendem und simuliertem System in einem vernünftigen Verhältnis stehen. Dies resultiert aus der Ausnutzung von Parallelität durch das Operationsprinzip von MuSiC und rechtfertigt - im Gegensatz zu den Resultaten für konventionelle Mehrprozessorsysteme[13] - den Bau von Systemen mit sehr vielen Prozessoren.


Schlußbemerkung:

Es wurde eine neuartige Rechnerarchitektur für die Simulation digitaler Systeme vorgestellt. Das zugrunde liegende Operationsprinzip, das dem der simulierten Grundbausteine gleicht, ermöglicht bei der Gatterebenensimulation eine Leistung im Bereich von einigen $10^9$ Ereignisauswertungen pro Sekunde, die durch Hinzufügen von Prozessoren bis über $10^{10}$ Ereignisauswertungen pro Sekunde gesteigert werden kann. Die effiziente Ausführung von Programmen einer Mehrebenen-Rechnerentwurfssprache wird durch sprachebenenspezifische, in jedem Prozessor konkurrent zueinander arbeitende Operationswerke erreicht.


Literatur


1    Blank, T.: A Survey of Hardware Accelerators Used in Computer-Aided Design, Design & Test of Computers, Aug. 1984, S. 21-89
2    ZYCAD Corp.: Settling for less than ZYCAD .., Design & Test of Computers, Mai 1984, S. 17-21
3    Denneau, M.M.: The Yorktown Simulation Engine, ACM IEEE 19th Design Automation Conference, Juni 1982, S. 55-59
4    Barto, R. and Szygenda, S.A.: A Computer Architecture for Digital Logic Simulation, Electronic Engineering, Sept. 1980, S. 35-66
5    Fischer, K.: Ereignisfluß-Modelle für die effiziente Simulation digitaler Systeme, Universität Passau, Fakultät für Mathematik und Informatik (Dissertation in Vorbereitung)
6    Hahn, W.: Computer Design Language / Version Munich - Eine moderne Rechnerentwurfssprache, HSBw München, FB Informatik, Bericht 8002/2, Juli 1983
7    Hahn, W.: Computer Design Language Version Munich (CDLM): A Modern Multi-Level Language, ACM IEEE 20th Design Automation Conference, Juni 1983, S. 4-11
8    Dennis, J.B.: First Version of a Dataflow Precedure Language, Lecture Notes in Computer Science, Vol. 19, Springer 1974, S. 362-376
9    Patel, J.H.: Processor-Memory Interconnections for Multiprocessors, 6th Ann. Symp. on Computer Architecture, April 1979, S. 168-177
10   Dias, D.M. and Jump, J.R.: Analysis and Simulation of Buffered Delta Networks, IEEE Trans. on Computers, April 1984, S. 273-282
11   Hahn, W. and Fischer, K.: MuSiC: an Event-Flow Computer for Fast Simulation of Digital Systems, 22nd Design Automation Conference, Juni 1985, Tagungsband (im Erscheinen)
12   Regenspurg, G., et al.: Einheitsbausteinrechner, GMD-Studien Nr. 67, Gesellschaft für Mathematik und Datenverarbeitung, Bonn, F.R. Germany, Febr. 1982
13   Jones, A.K. et al.: Experience Using Multiprocessor Systems - A Status Report, Computing Surveys, Vol. 12, No. 2.

# Algorithmische Spezifikation von MOSFETs für Mixed-Design-Level Simulation


F. Mündemann, Neubiberg                    W. Hahn, Passau



**Zusammenfassung**

Effiziente Rechner-Unterstützung für VLSI-Entwurf erfordert Entwurfshilfsmittel zur Beschreibung und Simulation von digitalen Systemen auf allen Entwurfsebenen, aber normalerweise ist diese Unterstützung erst für eine Teilmenge der Entwurfsebenen verfügbar. Es wird gezeigt, daß in Hardware-Entwurfssprachen mit Modul- und Verzögerungskonzept unter Benutzung einer algorithmischen Sprachebene eine Erweiterung auf Beschreibungen von Entwürfen unterhalb der Gatterebene durch die Einführung von Verhaltensmodellen für Schaltkreiselemente innerhalb eines bestehenden diskreten Simulationssystems möglich ist.


**Summary**

Efficient support of VLSI design requires designing aids for description and simulation at all design levels, but usually support is given for a subset of them only. It is shown, that it is possible to extend computer hardware description languages with module and delay concepts for design descriptions at circuit level using an algorithmic language level and introducing behavioral models for circuit components within existing discrete simulation systems.



**Einführung**

Computer Design Language (Version München) /Hahn 83/, als homogenes Werkzeug für den Top-Down Entwurf digitaler Systeme entworfen, ist gleichermaßen gut geeignet zur Benutzung auf

- der Systemebene, indem sie algorithmische Modul-Spezifikationen durch den Einsatz der Sprache PL/I unterstützt,
- der Befehlssatzebene, indem es prozedurale Modul-Beschreibungen zuläßt, und auf
- der Register-Transfer-Ebene, indem es nichtprozedurale Anweisungen hierfür bereitstellt.

CDLM mit seiner vierwertigen diskreten Logik (H = logisch HIGH, L = logisch LOW, Z = hochohmig, U = wegen der Zeitbedingungen während der Simulation nicht entscheidbar, ob H/L/Z, aber eines von diesen) enthält ein Modul-Konzept mit speziellen Anweisungen zur Verbindung und Instantiierung von Moduln. Unter den bereitgestellten Datentypen sind unter anderen sowohl REGISTER zur Aufnahme von Werten speichernder Entwurfselemente als auch TERMINALE für die Modellierung nicht-speichernder Elemente.

Der Simulationsteil von CDLM erlaubt es, Moduln auf unterschiedlichen Ebenen der Abstraktion miteinander in ein und demselben Simulationslauf zusammen zu simulieren (Mixed-Design-Level Simulation).

## Problemstellung

Diese Eigenschaften mögen für den klassischen Hardware-Entwurf ausreichend sein, aber für Systembeschreibungen unterhalb der Gatterebene ist heutzutage zusätzliche Unterstützung notwendig, zum Beispiel für die Beschreibung von Transistor-Netzwerken und das Schaltungs-Lay Out, um die Anforderungen des VLSI Entwurfs ebenfalls abdecken zu können.

Das Modellieren von Transistoren ist mit Hilfe analoger Simulationssysteme möglich /Nage 75/, aber dies ist für realistische Entwürfe zu zeitaufwendig und erfordert zusätzliche Diskretisierungsschritte, um die errechneten Werte innerhalb von Mixed-Level Simulationssystemen verwenden zu können. Weiterhin wurde in der Literatur /Flak 83/ gezeigt, daß vierwertige Logik für die diskrete Simulation von Transistor-Netzwerken nicht ausreicht.

Weil kontinuierliche Simulation durch in höheren Programmiersprachen geschriebene Simulationsprogramme erreicht werden kann, sollte sich dieses Problem durch den Einsatz der algorithmischen Sprachebene von CDLM ebenfalls lösen lassen, aber spezifische Abbildungen sind zu definieren, um die Vorteile diskreter Simulation zu erhalten, die Beschränkungen der vierwertigen Logik jedoch zu umgehen.

## Lösungsansatz

Die Modulstruktur von CDLM macht es möglich, daß man pro Schaltkreis-Element einen eigenen Modul definieren, sein Verhalten mit Hilfe von PL/I modellieren und an allen Auftretensstellen innerhalb eines Entwurfes instantiieren kann.

Verbindungen innerhalb eines Schaltkreises werden als idealisierte Verbindungen betrachtet und durch Modul-Verbindungs-Deklarationen in einer Entwurfsbeschreibung repräsentiert. Ihr korrektes Zeitverhalten wird mittels spezieller WIRE-Moduln beschrieben unter Benutzung des Verzögerungskonzeptes (delay) von CDLM /Hahn 83/.

Jede Modul-Verbindung, die einen einzelnen Draht oder eine einzelne Leiterbahn im Entwurf darstellt, wird durch eine Gruppendeklaration von n Terminalen beschrieben, anstatt durch eine Einzeldeklaration. Dadurch wird der Wertebereich von $4^1$ eines einzelnen Terminals auf $4^n$ ausgeweitet, wobei die $4^n$ Werte als Unterwerte der einzelnen Hauptwerte interpretiert werden können. An der Schnittstelle zu Moduln, die nicht Schaltkreise beschreiben, wird eine geeignete Abbildung $4^1$ nach $4^n$, bzw. $4^n$ nach $4^1$ ausgeführt.

Dieser Lösungsansatz, der auf der Mächtigkeit der algorithmischen Sprachebene von CDLM basiert, hat den Vorteil, daß er sofort implementierbar ist und er erlaubt die Benutzung des Simulationsteils von CDLM ohne Änderungen.

**Implementierung**

Angeregt durch einen Ansatz in /Brya 84/, wurden spezifische Modelle für MOS Pull Up-/Down Transistoren, Pass-/Schalttransistoren, Resistoren und Leiterbahnen/Drähte entwickelt /Münd 84/.

Dabei zeigte sich, daß die Schaltkreis-Simulation vereinfacht wird, wenn man Transistoren generell als schaltbare Ladungstransfer-Elemente betrachtet, wobei ihre Ausgabewerte als Funktion ihrer Eingabewerte angesehen werden. Um ihr Verhalten, das in Form von Tabellen innerhalb von PL/I Moduln spezifiziert wird, als Folge von Komponentenzuständen während der Simulation korrekt berechnen zu können, benötigt man Informationen über den Transistortyp, die logischen Pegel, Ladungswerte und Ladungsflußrichtung für jeden Ein-/Ausgabe-Pin. Daher werden pro physikalischer Leitung drei Attribute definiert, von denen jedes jeweils einen von drei möglichen Attributwerten annehmen kann.

| Attribut | Werte | Erläuterung |
|---|---|---|
| Logikpegel | H logisch HIGH<br>L logisch LOW<br>U unentscheidbar | U bedeutet, daß auf Grund der Zeitbedingungen während der Simulation unentscheidbar ist, welcher der beiden anderen Logikpegel sich auf dem Anschluß eingestellt hat. |
| Ladungsversorgung | A aktiv getrieben<br>P passiv geladen<br>X unbekannt | Anzeige, ob andere Schaltkreiskomponenten Ladung auf diesen / von diesem Anschluß transferieren: A: ja, P: nein, X: wegen der Zeitbedingungen unbekannt |
| Verbindung | O offen<br>G geschlossen<br>Y unentscheidbar | leitungsbezogene Verbindung zu anderen Schaltkreiskomponenten: die Komponente, die Ladung auf diesen Anschluß transferiert, ist im Zustand O oder G bzw. wegen der Zeitbedingungen ist dies unentscheidbar. |

Weil jede physikalische Leitung in einer CDLM-Beschreibung normalerweise durch ein Terminal repräsentiert wird, auf dem genau einer der vier diskreten logischen Werte von CDLM weitergereicht werden kann, bedeutet dies einen Übergang von der Ein-Terminal-Notation pro Leitung zu einer Drei-Terminal-Notation pro Leitung und der Wertebereich von CDLM wird dadurch aufgespreizt auf $4^3$ verschiedene Werte, - ausreichend zur korrekten Simulation von Transistoren.

Bei diesem Ansatz sieht der CDLM Simulator nur die Terminale als Modul-Verbindungen, die die Syntax eines Entwurfes darstellen, während die Semantik der ausgetauschten Werte innerhalb der algorithmischen Moduln von CDLM mit Hilfe von PL/I interpretiert wird. Auf diese Weise kann jede Werte-Interpretation innerhalb dieser Moduln ausgedrückt werden. Diese mögliche Werteaufspreizung ist eine Konsequenz der Benutzung der algorithmischen Sprachebene von CDLM.

Die Einführung dieser Attribute vereinfacht besonders die Simulation von Passtransistoren und erlaubt es, diese mit den Modellen für Schalttransistoren zusammenzulegen. Netzwerke, die Passtransistoren enthalten, können ohne Iteration berechnet werden, weil es möglich ist, die Ladungsquellen und -senken eines jeden Schaltkreiselementes im Augenblick seiner Aktivierung während des Simulationslaufes zu bestimmen und die Zustände von Leitungen in Datenfluß-Manier /Pase 85/ zu berechnen.

Ein spezielles Modell WIRE wurde eingeführt, um in der Lage zu sein, für logische Chip-Simulation die Signal-Ausbreitungsgeschwindigkeiten auf Leitungen als Verzögerungen modellieren zu können. Wie in Figur 1 gezeigt, können Geometriedaten aus einem Lay Out extrahiert und von einem Modul WIRE verwendet werden, um die Matrix der Übergangszeiten $t_{ij}$ proportional zu den geometrischen Abständen der Kontakte $C_i$ und $C_j$ zu definieren. Zusätzlich können die Geometriedaten durch elektrische Parameter attributiert werden. Wegen der Mächtigkeit von PL/I können auch recht subtile elektromagnetische Ausbreitungs-, Ausgleichs- und Auslöschungsprozesse berücksichtigt werden, die stattfinden, wenn die Leitungspotentiale durch steigende oder fallende Impulsflanken verändert werden /Gust 83/, aber für rein logische Simulation können alle $t_{ij}$ auf Null gesetzt werden.

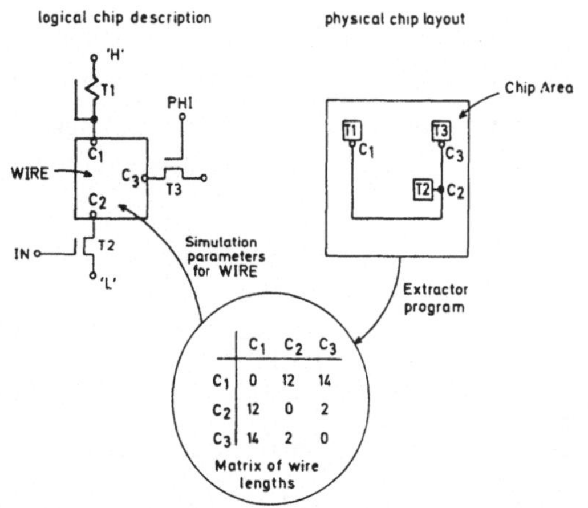


Figur 1:

Herausziehen geometrischer Leitungsdaten durch einen Lay-Out Extraktor.

Das Problem der Zusammenführung von physikalischen Leiterbahnen wird mit Hilfe eines speziellen Moduls TRANSIENT gelöst. Er akzeptiert drei oder vier Terminalgruppen als Eingänge in Übereinstimmung mit den in zweidimensionaler VLSI-Technik auftretenden T-förmigen oder gekreuzten Verbindungen und berechnet die resultierenden Attribute für alle beteiligten Leitungen /Münd 84/. Zur gemischten Verwendung von Moduln, die Schaltkreise beschreiben, und anderen CDLM Moduln werden die notwendigen eins-zu-drei bzw. drei-zu-eins Abbildungen definiert /Münd 84/, so daß nur die Logikpegel-Attribute an andere Moduln weitergereicht bzw. von diesen entgegengenommen werden.

Weiterhin wird das Verzögerungskonzept von CDLM (Angabe von Toleranzbereichen) verwendet, um eine genügend genaue Modellierung kontinuierlicher Signale zu ermöglichen /Hahn 83/.

## Zusammenfassung

Die Erweiterung von Hardware-Entwurfssprachen mit Modul- und Verzögerungskonzept ist für die Beschreibung von Entwürfen unterhalb der Gatterebene durch den Einsatz einer algorithmischen Sprachebene möglich.

Dieses Konzept wird in CDLM verwendet und damit das Verhalten von MOS-Transistoren sowie physikalischen Leitungen mittels PL/I-Moduln modelliert. Auf diese Weise wird zu nahezu denselben Kosten wie auf den übrigen Beschreibungsebenen eine VLSI-gerechte Schaltkreisbeschreibung und diskrete Simulation erreicht. Die durch die Verdreifachung der Leitungen als während der Simulation zu berechnende Objekte eintretende Leistungseinbuße kann gegenüber der durch eine generelle Erweiterung der CDLM-Logikwerte dann in allen Entwurfssimulationen eintretende Leistungseinbuße vernachlässigt werden.

Auf der ELEKTRONIKA '84 wurde eine PASCAL-Implementierung /Münd 84/ dieses Teils von CDLM gezeigt und Entwurfsbeispiele aus dem Buch von Mead/Conway /Mead 80/ simuliert.

Die aufgezeigte Lösung kann auch für die kontinuierliche Simulation von digitalen Systemen verwendet werden, indem zum Beispiel Aufrufe des SPICE Systems /Nage 75/ innerhalb der Modulrümpfe notiert werden und die Semantik der Modulverbindungen auf den Wertebereich der reellen Zahlen durch Benutzung vektorisierter Verbindungsdeklarationen ausgedehnt wird.

## Literatur

/Brya 84/  Bryant, R.E.: A Switch-Level Model and Simulator for MOS Digital Systems, IEEE Trans. on Computers, Vol. C-33, Febr. 1984, pp. 160-177
/Flak 83/  Flake, P.L. et al.: An Algebra for Logic Strength Simulation, Proc. 20th Design Automation Conf., June 1983, pp. 615-618
/Gust 83/  Gustavson, D.B.; Theus, J.: Wire-OR Logic on Transmission Lines, IEEE MICRO, June 1983, pp. 51-55
/Hahn 83/  Hahn, W.: Computer Design Language - Version Munich (CDLM): A Modern Multi-Level Language, Proc. 20th Design Automation Conf., June 1983, pp. 207-212
/Mead 80/  Mead, D.; Conway, L.: Introduction to VLSI Systems, Addision-Wesley Publishing Company, Reading, Mass. 1980
/Münd 84/  Mündemann, F.: ISD-MOS. Interactive Simulation Packet (Discrete Logic) for MOS-Transistor Networks, preliminary System Handbook, München 1984
/Nage 75/  Nagel, L.W.: SPICE2: A Computer Program to Simulate Semiconductor Circuits, Electronics Research Laboratory, Univ. of Calif., Berkeley, Calif., Memorandum No. ERL-M 510, May 1975
/Pase 85/  Pasemann, W.G.: Data Flow Concepts speed Simulation in CAE Systems, Computer Design (Jan. 1985), pp. 131-140

# Simulation digitaler integrierter Schaltungen

Djamshid Tavangarian, Frankfurt am Main

Zusammenfassung:  Der Beitrag beschreibt die wichtigsten Abstraktionsebenen für die Simulation digitaler Schaltungen und Systeme.  Schwerpunktmäßig werden die Simulatoren der Gatterebene betrachtet.  Es werden die unterschiedlichen Modellierungsverfahren der Elemente und Signale erläutert und die gängigsten Berechnungsverfahren diskutiert.

Summary:  This paper describes the usual abstraction levels for the simulation of digital circuits and systems.  The main subject of the paper is the describtion of simulation methods of gate level circuits.  The different modeling methods of the elements and signals will be illustrated and some calculation methods will be discused.

## 1. EINFÜHRUNG:

Die Realisierung komplexer integrierter Schaltungen ist heute ohne den Einsatz von wirkungsvollen Simulations- und Entwurfshilfen nicht denkbar.  Diese Hilfsmittel werden zur Spezifizierung, Berechnung, logischer und zeitlicher Analyse sowie Dokumentation der zu realisierenden elektronischen Schaltungen eingesetzt.  Je nach Aufgabenstellung werden heute vielfältige Simulationssysteme benutzt, die sich im Aufbau unterscheiden und verschiedene Berechnungsverfahren verwenden.

Bei der Beschreibung und Simulation komplexer Schaltungen können hierarchisch gegliederte Abstraktionen der Schaltungskomponenten vorgenommen werden, die unterschiedliche Sichten einer Schaltung konstituieren.  Die unterschiedlichen Sichten einer Schaltung führen zur Bearbeitung der Schaltungen in unterschiedlichen Ebenen, den sogenannten Abstraktionsebenen.  Diese unterscheiden sich in ihren beobachtbaren Objekten (Modelle, Signale) und den auf der Ebene verwendeten Berechnungsmethoden. Dadurch werden die benötigten Simulationszeiten, die Komplexität der Eingaben sowie die Exaktheit der Ergebnisse stark beeinflußt, so daß die Schaltungen in Abhängigkeit der Entwurfsphasen mit den entsprechenden Sichten zu bearbeiten sind.

Die wichtigsten und heute verfügbaren Simulationssysteme lassen sich sinnvoll in folgende Abstraktionsebenen aufteilen:

## - Schaltungsebene

Eine Schaltung auf dieser Ebene wird als eine Einheit simuliert, die Transistoren, Widerstände, Kondensatoren u.ä. als Grundelemente beinhaltet.  Im Simulator werden die Elemente durch algebraische Modelle und geeignete Ersatzbilder definiert.  Zur Berechnung einer Schaltung werden algebraische bzw. Differentialgleichungen zugrunde gelegt, die linear oder nichtlinear sein können.  Unterschiedliche Verfahren werden bei der Aufstellung der Gleichungen sowie bei ihrer Lösung verwendet.  Eine Schaltung auf dieser Ebene kann sowohl im Zeit- als auch im Frequenzbereich analysiert werden.

- Gatterebene

Eine zu simulierende Schaltung auf dieser Ebene beinhaltet als Grundkomponenten boolesche Gatter unterschiedlicher Komplexität. Die Elemente werden durch Delay-Modelle beschrieben. Die Ein- und Ausgangssignale der Elemente werden je nach Konstellation einer Schaltung und gestellten Anforderungen an die Genauigkeit der Ergebnisse mit mehrwertigen logischen Signalen bearbeitet. Eine Schaltung wird durch boolesche Gleichungen formuliert und im Zeitbereich simuliert /2-5/.

- Register-Transfer-Ebene

Eine Schaltung auf dieser Ebene enthält als Elementarkomponenten Register, Busse, Schalter, Speicher, Operationswerke u.ä. Die Schaltung wird im allgemeinen in eine Steuereinheit zur Bewältigung der Steuerungsaufgaben und in eine Operationseinheit zur Manipulation der Daten aufgeteilt. Die beobachtbaren Werte sind geordnete "Bitgruppen": Bytes und Worte. Zur Simulation einer Schaltung im Zeitbereich wird das Daten-Transfer-Modell in Verbindung mit einem (synchronen) Taktschema verwendet.

- Systemebene

Eine Schaltung auf dieser Abstraktionsebene beinhaltet kooperierende semiautonome Module, wie z.B. Prozessoren, I/O-Einheiten u.ä. Im allgemeinen wird hier eine Kausalitätsüberprüfung einer Schaltung bzw. der zugrunde gelegten Algorithmen vorgenommen, bevor die Elemente in allen ihren Einzelheiten bekannt sind. Dabei können sowohl allgemein verwendbare Simulations- und Programmiersprachen als auch spezielle für die Beschreibung elektronischer Schaltungen entwickelte Sprachen verwendet werden.

Darüberhinaus können elektronische Schaltungen Teile beinhalten, die in zwei oder mehreren Ebenen simultan bearbeitet werden sollen. Hierfür existieren Simulatoren, die eine solche Anforderung erfüllen. Sie werden allgemein als Mixed-Mode-Simulatoren bezeichnet. Die wichtigsten Vertreter der Mixed-Mode-Simulatoren sind die Hybridsimulatoren, die zur Bearbeitung von Schaltungen eingesetzt werden, die sowohl analog arbeitende Schaltungselemente (Schaltungsebene) als auch digital arbeitende Komponenten (Gatterebene) beinhalten /1,3/.
Im Rahmen dieses Beitrages werden die Eigenschaften der Simulatoren der Gatterebene schwerpunktmäßig diskutiert, da zur Zeit die für diese Ebene realisierten Simulatoren neben den Schaltungssimulatoren am häufigsten beim Entwurf integrierter Schaltungen verwendet werden. Dabei werden die unterschiedlichen Modellierungsverfahren der Grundkomponenten einer digitalen Schaltung auf dieser Ebene angegeben und beschrieben. Die Gestaltung und die Behandlung der Signale in einer digitalen Schaltung in einem Simulator der Gatterebene stellen weitere Themen des Beitrages dar. Die gängigsten Berechnungsverfahren (laufzeitorientierte, laufzeitbereichorientierte und ereignisorientierte Verfahren), die zur dynamischen und logischen Analyse einer digitalen Schaltung bei den Simulatoren ihre Verwendung finden, werden geschildert.

## 2. SIMULATIONSVORGANG

Zur Spezifikation und Eingabe einer Schaltung für die Simulation werden Schaltungstopologie, Verknüpfungsoperationen und Zeitverhalten der Elemente sowie die Anfangswerte der Einangssignale und inneren Zustände zugrunde gelegt. Eine Simulation kann interpretierend oder kompilierend arbeiten. Interpretierende Simulatoren ermöglichen einen interaktiven Einsatz zur direkten Manipulation der Schaltung. Sie erfordern jedoch höhere Simulationszeiten und größrere Speicherräume.

Der Vorteil eines kompilierenden Simulators liegt in den kürzeren Simulationszeiten bei der Bearbeitung einer Schaltung. Sie sind teilweise inflexibel, da die Übersetzung auf ein bestimmtes Simulationsziel erfolgt und die ermittelten Datenstrukturen anschließend schwer manipulierbar sind. Eine Kombination beider Verfahren wurde in /3/ implementiert, wodurch die Vorteile beider Verfahren zur Geltung kommen.

Zur Umsetzung der Daten für die Simulation werden Modelle für die logischen Elemente (Gatter, Flipflops u.ä.) und Signale zugrunde gelegt. Die Modelle haben einen entscheidenden Einfluß auf die Arbeit und Berechnungsgenauigkeit eines Simulators.

Bei der Simulation digitaler Schaltungen werden im allgemeinen aktivitätsorientierte Verfahren und laufzeitorientierte Verfahren eingesetzt.

Bei einem aktivitätsorientierten Logiksimulator werden die auftretenden Aktivitäten (Ereignisse) erfasst und deren Fortpflanzung in den von der Fortpflanzung der Signale betroffenen Pfaden der Schaltung berücksichtigt. Das Verfahren ist besonders günstig für die zeitsynchron arbeitenden Schaltungen. Hier erfolgen die Signalzustandsänderungen nur während der aktiven Zeitphase von Synchrontaktsignalen der Schaltung.

Das Laufzeitsimulationsverfahren stellt zur Bestimmung der Variablenwerte die Laufzeiten der Gatterelemente in Vordergrund. Die Gatter können unterschiedliche Laufzeiten als konstante Laufzeiten oder Laufzeitbereiche aufweisen. Bei der Simulation wird ein Zeitraster für die Simulationszeitschritte gewählt. Ein Simulationszeitschritt kann maximal die Länge der kleinsten Gatterlaufzeit in der Schaltung aufweisen. Für jeden Zeitschritt wird die Schaltung mit den vorliegenden Logikfunktionen, Signalzuständen und Gatterlaufzeiten bzw. Laufzeitbereichen sowie Laufzeitkombinationen simuliert. Dieses Verfahren erfordert einen höheren Zeitaufwand gegenüber dem ersten Verfahren.

Eine Kombination beider Verfahren ist ebenfalls möglich/2/. In diesem Fall werden sowohl die auftretenden Ereignisse als auch die entsprechenden Gatterlaufzeiten bzw. Laufzeitbereiche bei der Simulation herangezogen. Eine Simulation erfolgt zu den Zeitpunkten, bei denen jeweils ein Ereignis auftritt. Ab diesem Zeitpunkt erfolgt eine laufzeitsimulation der Schaltung, bis ein stationärer Zustand der Schaltung vorliegt. Das Verfahren bietet die Vorteile beider Simulationsarten und ist geeignet zur Erfassung logischer und dynamischer Fehler einer Schaltung und zur Ermittlung von Signalvezögerungszeiten bei minimalen und maximalen Laufzeitgrößen der einzelnen Gatter.

## 3. MODELLIERUNG DER ELEMENTE

Zur Verhaltensbeschreibung eines Grundelementes wird ein zweistufiges Modell verwendet (Abb. 1). In einer Stufe wird die Funktion des Gatters (f) erfasst (Gl. 1). In der anderen Stufe wird das Zeitverhalten (V) des Gatters modelliert (Gl. 2).

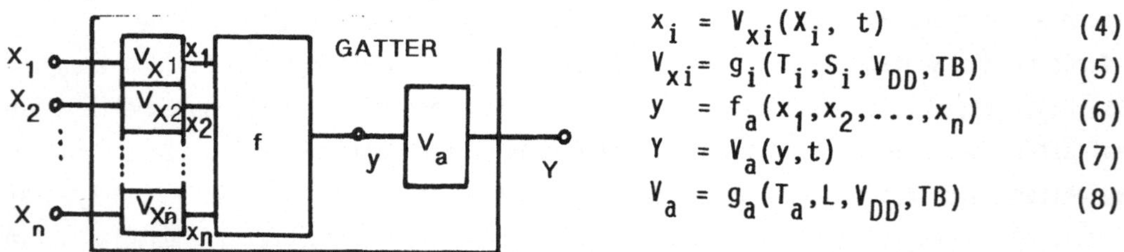


$$y = f(X_1, X_2, \ldots, X_n) \qquad (1)$$

$$Y = V(y, t) \qquad (2)$$

$$\text{mit } V = T :$$

$$Y(t) = y(t-T) \qquad (3)$$

Abbildung 1: Einfache Modellierung eines Gatters mit den zugehörigen Funktionen

Die Funktion f des Gatters wird durch eine Boole'sche Gleichung mit den Variablen xi (i=1,2,...n) charakterisiert. Bei der Modellierung des Zeitverhaltens können außer der Verzögerungszeit T des Gatters, die durch innere Beschaltung des Gatters zustande kommt, je nach Anforderungen an das Modell weitere Einflüße berücksichtigt werden. Für die MOS-Technologie, die heute eine weitverbreitete Technologie zur Realisierung großintegrierter Schaltungen (VLSI) darstellt, werden die Ausgangslast (L) bestehend aus der Summe der Kapazitäten der angeschlossenen Leitungen und Gattereingänge der Folgegatter, die Flankensteiheit (S1,S2,...Sn) der Eingangssignale (X1,X2,...Xn), die Höhe der Vesorgungsspannung des Gatters (VDD-VSS) und die Betriebstemperatur (TB) als wichtigste Faktoren berücksichtigt (Abb. 2).



$$x_i = V_{xi}(X_i, t) \qquad (4)$$

$$V_{xi} = g_i(T_i, S_i, V_{DD}, TB) \qquad (5)$$

$$y = f_a(x_1, x_2, \ldots, x_n) \qquad (6)$$

$$Y = V_a(y, t) \qquad (7)$$

$$V_a = g_a(T_a, L, V_{DD}, TB) \qquad (8)$$

Abbildung 2 : Erweitertes Modell eines Gatters mit den zugehörigen Funktionen

In diesem Modell sind Va bzw. Vxi (i=1,2,...,n) die eingangs- und die ausgangsseitige Verzögerungen des Gatters, die durch die Funktionen ga bzw. gi bestimmt werden, da die Ein-/Ausgangspfade unterschiedlich lang sein können. Der Einfluß der Parameter werden als diskrete oder parametrisierte Größen tabellenorientiert verarbeitet, um die Rechenzeiten der Funktionen minimal zu halten.

Als Beispiel wird die Last eines MOS-Gatters infolge nachgeschalteter Eingangskapazitäten betrachtet (Abb. 3), die durch eine parametrisierte Größe berücksichtigt werden kann. Ordnet man jedem Gatter (G1,G2,...) eine konstante Kapazität C (oder vielfache von C) zu, so erhält man in Verbindung mit dem Innenwiderstand Ri der Ausgangsstufe des Gatters GO eine Zeitkonstante, die mit der wachsenden Zahl der Eingangskapazitäten linear wächst und die Flankensteilheit des Ausgangssignals vermindert (Abb. 3b).

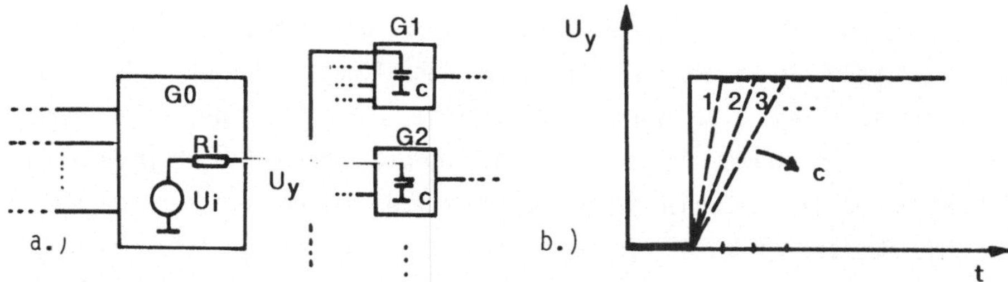


Abbildung 3 : Modellierung der Ausgangslast eines MOS-Gatters
a. Modell, b. Lastabhängige Flankensteilheit am Gatterausgang

Auf ähnliche Weise können die Einflüße weiterer Parameter bestimmt und bei der Simulation der Schaltung eingesetzt werden.  Zur Bestimmung der Parametereinflüße können Simulatoren der Schaltungsebene verwendet werden.

Bei der Fortschaltung kurzer Impulse am Eingang eines Verzögerungsgliedes werden zwei Verfahren zugrunde gelegt. Das Transport-Delay-Verfahren nimmt an, daß jeder Impuls am Eingang eines Verzögerungsgliedes, unabhängig von seiner Impulsdauer, mit entsprechender Verzögerung zum Ausgang übertragen wird.  Im Gegensatz dazu werden beim trägheitsbehafteten Verzögerungsverfahren (Interial-Delay-Verfahren) nur solche Impulse übertragen, die eine längere Impulsdauer als die Verzögerungszeit des Gliedes aufweisen.  Ohne Kenntnis der inneren Struktur eines Gatters kann nicht vorhergesagt werden, welche der beiden Verfahren tatsächlich eingesetzt werden müssen.  Ein Ausweg stellt die Erhöhung der Zahl der logischen Signalzustände "0" und "1" durch einen weiteren als unbestimmt interpretierbaren Zustand "X" dar.  Damit wird angezeigt, daß eine genaue Analyse des o.g.  Falles weitere Informationen erfordert.


## 4.  SIGNALZUSTÄNDE BEI DER SIMULATION


Die funktionale Beschreibung einer digitalen Schaltung erfordert nur die Boole'schen Signalzustände "0" und "1".  Die dynamische Simulation und Überprüfung einer Schaltung erfordert jedoch die Erfassung und die Berücksichtigung von Gatterlaufzeiten in Verbindung mit erweiterten Signalzuständen, damit außer logischer Fehler auch die dynamischen Fehler einer Schaltung (z.B.  Hazards, Races u.ä.) weitgehend ermittelt werden können.  Die Signale in einer Schaltung werden durch Strom- und Spannungsgrößen repräsentiert.  In Abhängigkeit des Pegels eines Signals erhält man Bereiche, die eindeutig den logischen Zuständen "0" und "1" zu zuordnen sind.  Beim Zustandswechsel werden die Übergangsbereiche, die beim Signalanstieg innerhalb 0- und 1-Pegel und beim Signalabfall innerhalb 1- und 0-Pegel liegen, als unbestimmt "X" betrachtet.

Die Signalzustände 0, 1, und X führen zu Simulatoren, die dreiwertige Signale verarbeiten können.  Mit einem solchen Simulator können das Logik- sowie das Zeitverhalten einer Schaltung simuliert und die signifikanten Hazards entdekt werden.  Die Grenzen eines solchen Simulators werden erreicht, wenn die zu simulierende Schaltung "Transmissiongates" oder "Tri-State-Gates" enthält.  Diese Elemente beinhalten einen weiteren hochohmigen (vierten) Zustand am Ausgang.  In diesen Fällen können mehrere Gatter-Ausgänge miteinander verbunden werden, die z.B. zur Realisierung von Busstrukturen in der Schaltung führen. Eine derartige Schaltungsstruktur liegt z.B. vor, wenn mehrere Gatterausgänge, die jeweils ein Transmissiongate in ihrem Ausgangskreis haben, und mehrere Gattereingänge über eine Busleitung miteinander verbunden sind. Beim Durchschalten eines Transmissiongates besitzt die Busleitung nach der entsprechenden Einschwingzeit einen statischen Zustand. Wird das Transmissiongate in hochohmigen Zustand gebracht, so bleibt durch parasitäre Kapazität der Busleitung der statische Zustand für eine gewisse Zeit erhalten. Die Dauer des statischen Zustandes hängt von der angeschlossenen Last der Leitung ab. Dieser Effekt wird z.B. bei Speicherschaltungen ausgenutzt.

Zur Erfassung der korrekten Zustände solcher Leitungen bei der Simulation werden die früheren Leitungszustände ebenfalls mit einbezogen. Die früheren Zustände können selbst wiederum drei Bereiche umfassen (Oh, 1h und Xh), wobei die Indizes h für hochohmig (high impedance) stehen. Damit erhält man insgesamt 6 statische Zustände der Signale in einer Schaltung. Wenn jedoch gleichzeitig mehrere Transmissiongates durchgeschaltet sind, die unterschiedliche Übergangswiderstände aufweisen, stellt sich ein Potential auf der Busleitung ein, das ohne Kenntnis der Widerstandswerte nicht eindeutig bestimmbar ist. Unter Annahme von konstanten Widerstandswerten (Ron, Roff) für die Transmissiongates kann dieser Fall in einer ersten Näherung durch weitere Zustände Os, 1s und Xs (index s ist für soft) erfasst werden. Damit erhält man 9 Signalzustände, die bei der Simulation eingesetzt werden können. Weiterhin können Signalanstiegszeit (Rising=R) und Signalabfallzeit (Falling=F) als jeweils unterschiedliche Signalzustände betrachtet werden. Bei der Überlagerung beider neuen Zustände in Verbindung mit bestimmten logischen Funktionen kann wiederum ein unbestimmter Bereich entstehen, der zu einem weiteren Signalzustand U (als unbestimmt) führt. Mit diesen Zuständen können jedoch nicht alle Typen von digitalen Schaltungen vollständig und korrekt erfasst und simuliert werden. Z.B. können durch Transmissiongates, die bidirektional eingesetzt werden, oder durch Transmissiongates in Abhängigkeit ihrer Geometrie auf einem Chip bzw. durch die Variation der parasitären Kapazitäten entlang ihrer Signaltransferstrecken neue Effekte entstehen, die zu weiteren Signalzuständen in der Schaltung führen. Durch eine höhere Auflösung der Signalzustände, d.h. mehr Zustände, können zwar diese Effekte erfasst werden, jedoch steigt der Simulationsaufwand (Simulationszeit und Speicherbedarf) überproportional. Für solche Fälle ist es sinnvoll, wenn Timing- oder Hybridsimulatoren eingesetzt werden.

## 5. FEHLERSIMULATION

Die Fehlersimulatoren stellen ein Bestandteil vieler Simulatoren auf der Gatterebene. Hier werden Prüfdaten (Testpattern) und Vorschriften erzeugt, die dem Schaltungsdesigner beim Test seiner Schaltung behilflich sind, wenn die Schaltung irgend welche Defekte aufzeigt. Mit Hilfe der Prüfdaten können die fehlerhaften und von außen nicht zugänglichen Bauelemente auf einem Chip für einen späteren Redesign weitgehend lokalisiert werden.

Um eine Schaltung testfreundlich zu gestalten, kommt der Prüfbarkeit der Schaltung während des Entwurfs große Bedeutung zu. Es sind Verfahren bekannt, die die Prüfbarkeit einer Schaltung fördern, z.B. Einsatz eines Prüfbusses, Scan-Path-Methode u.ä. Die Erstellung von Prüfdaten erfolgt durch Fehlersimulatoren mit entsprechenden Fehler-Modellen. Ein weitverbreitetes Modell stellt das sogenannte "Stuck at model" dar. Dabei werden einzelnen oder mehreren Signalen in der Schaltung statische Werte (0 oder 1) infolge eines angenommenen Fehlers zugeordnet und die Ausgangszustände ermittelt. Durch wiederholte Anwendung dieses Verfahrens werden Fehlerlisten erstellt, die zur Überprüfung der fehlerhaften Schaltung eingesetzt werden.

## 6. SCHLUSSBEMERKUNGEN

Der Eisatzbereich der Logiksimulatoren als Entwicklungs- und Entwurfswerkzeuge erstreckt sich auf Architektur- sowie Logikentwicklung einer Schaltung (CAE), Layoutsentwurf (CAD) und Schaltungstest (CAT). Mit zunehmender Entwicklung der Technologie und Verbreitung großintegrierter Schaltungen wird von Designern und Anwendern integrierter Schaltungen wirklichkeitsgetreue und zuverläßige Simulatoren zur Analyse der Schaltungen verlangt, da die Prototypherstellung einer Schaltung mit hohen Kosten verbunden ist.

Korrekte Analyse einer Schaltung mit adequaten Simulatinszeiten stellt hohe Anforderungen an einem Simulator. Durch die Vielfältigkeit der Eigenschaften der Elemente bzw. Technologie- und Prozessparameter wird von einem Simulator genaue und variable Definitionsmöglichkeit für Zeitparameter und Modelle gefordert. Um möglichst genaue Simulationsergebnisse zu erzielen, muß der Simulator über ausgereifte Berechnungsmethoden und Verfahren in Verbindung mit einer neuen Algebra verfügen, die die erhöhte Anzahl logischer Signalzustände berücksichtigt. Viele vorhandene Simulatoren erfüllen diese Anforderungen.

## 7. LITERATUR:


1. Tavangarian, D., Waldschmidt, K. :
   Interaktive graphische Simulation elektrischer Netzwerke mit dem SANDRA - Programmsystem, Informatik-Fachberichte, Simulationstechnik, 1982
2. Jentsch, W. :
   Simulation binärer Schaltwerke, Nachrichtentechnische Fachberichte 49, 1974
3. Bechtold, M., Möheken, G., Tavangarian, D., Waldschmidt, K. :
   HADIS A Hybrid Analogue-Digital Simulator, IMACS 85, North-Holland Publ. Co. 1985
4. Falke, P. L., Musgrave, G., White, I. J. :
   A Digital System Simulator - HILO, Digital Processes 1, 1975
5. Siemens AG :
   Semicustom, Zellenorientierter Baustein-Entwurf, VERDIPUS-Simulationsprogramm, Siemsns AG, 1983

# Analyse nichtlineaer frequenzabhängiger
# Übertragungssysteme mit Volterra-Reihen und
# dem Simulationsprogramm SPICE

Peter Jedele, Haybatolah Khakzar, Stuttgart



Zusammenfassung. Die formale Analyse der nichtlinearen frequenzabhängigen Übertragungssysteme mit Volterra-Reihen ergibt ein System mit drei linearen Gleichungen. Diese stellen die drei Subsysteme erster, zweiter und dritter Ordnung. Es wird gezeigt, daß das lineare Subsystem durch den linearen Teil des Netzwerkes mit dem Eingangssignal gegeben ist, während die Subsysteme zweiter und dritter Ordnung durch das lineare Netzwerk und Oberwellenquellen beschrieben sind. Es zeigt, daß der Postulat von Feldtkeller und Wolman, formuliert für quasilineare Zweipole ohne Speicher, auf Vierpole mit Speichern verallgemeinert werden kann. Ein einstufiger Verstärker in Emitterschaltung wird mit Netzwerkanalyseprogramm SPICE simuliert und der Einfluß der nichtlinearen Quellen auf die nichtlineare Verzerrung des Verstärkers wird aufgezeigt.

Summary. The formal analysis of a nonlinear network using Volterra series representation of the signals yields a system of three linear equations which represent the first-, second- and third-order subsystems. It is shown that the linear subsystem is given by the linear part of the network and the input current source, whereas the second and the third order subsystems are discribed by the linear network and distortion current sources. Thus the thesis of Feldtkeller and Wolman, originally proposed for a restive network, is also valid for quasiliear networks with memory. A single stage amplifier in commom emitter configuration is simulated with networkanalysisprogram SPICE and the influence of the different nonlinear sources on the nonlinear distortion of the amplifier is shown.


## 1. Einführung

1931:       Postulat formuliert durch Feldtkeller und Wolman

"Jeder quasilineare Zweipol ohne Speicher kann durch einen linearen Zweipol und Oberwellenquellen ersetzt werden."


Ziel dieses Vortrags:

Verallgemeinerung des obigen Postulats für Vierpole mit Speichern.

## Die Volterra-Reihen und die multidimensional Laplace-Transform

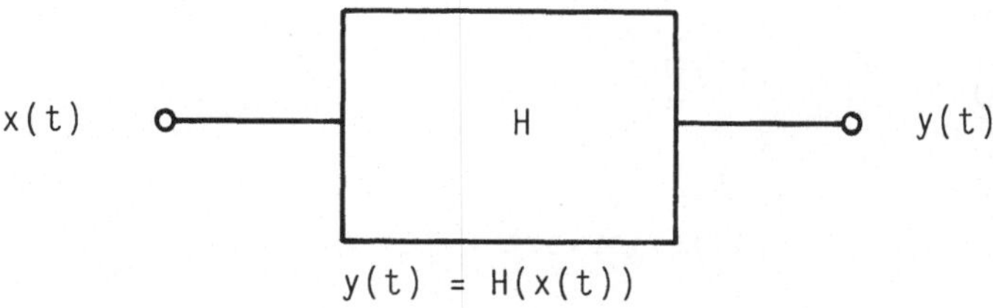



Fig. 1    Schematische Darstellung eines Übertragungssystems

## Nichtlineare Systeme ohne Speicher

Die Funktion

$$y = f(x)$$

kann durch eine Taylor-Reihe ersetzt werden

$$y = \sum_{n=1}^{\infty} c_n x^n$$

Für kleine Nichtlinearitäten und kleine Werte von $x(t)$

$$y(t) = \sum_{n=1}^{3} c_n x^n(t) = \sum_{n=1}^{3} y_n(t)$$



Fig. 2    Schematischwe Darstellung eines nichtlinearen Systems ohne
          Speicher

## Nichtlineare Systeme mit Speicher

Eindimensionales Faltungsintegral bekannt durch die lineare Systemtheorie

$$y_1(t) = \int_0^{\infty} h_1(\tau) x(t-\tau) d$$

wird auf Systeme höherer Ordnung durch die Volterra-Integrale <u>n-ter</u> Ordnung verallgemeinert

$$y_n(t) = \int_0^\infty \ldots \int_0^\infty h_n(\tau_1 \ldots \tau_n) \prod_{i=1}^n x(t-\tau_i)\,d\tau_i = H_n(x(t))$$

$h_n(\tau_1 \ldots \tau_n)$ ....  Volterra-Kerne n-ter Ordnung

Impulsantwort n-ter Ordnung

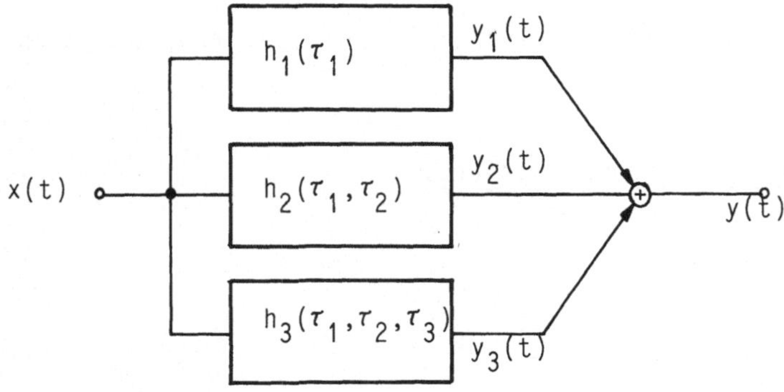


Fig. 3    Schematische Darstellung eines nichtlinearen Systems mit Speicher

## Die n-dimensionale Laplace-Transformation

$$y_n(t) = \int_0^\infty \ldots \int_0^\infty h_n(\tau_1 \ldots \tau_n) \prod_{i=1}^n x(t-\tau_i)\,d\tau_i$$

$$Y_n(p_1 \ldots p_n) = H_n(p_1 \ldots p_n) \prod_{i=1}^n X(p_i)$$

$H_n(p_1 \ldots p_n)$ ....  Laplace-Transformation der Kerne n-ter Ordnung

Übertragungsfunktion n-ter Ordnung

## Analyse eines nichtlinearen Netzwerks am Beispiel eines Transistorverstärkers in Emitterschaltung

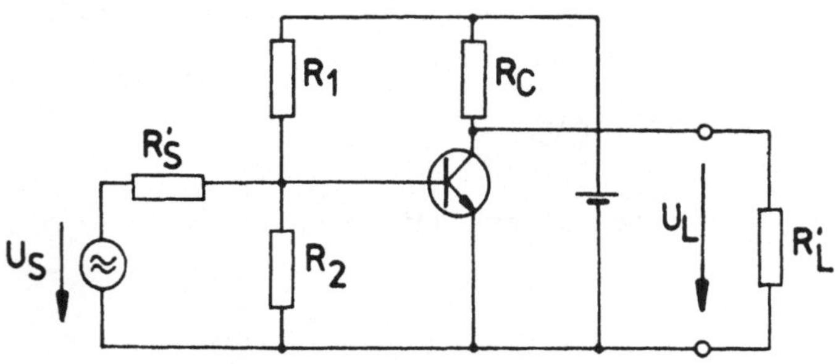


Fig. 4    Einstufiger Verstärker in Emitterschaltung

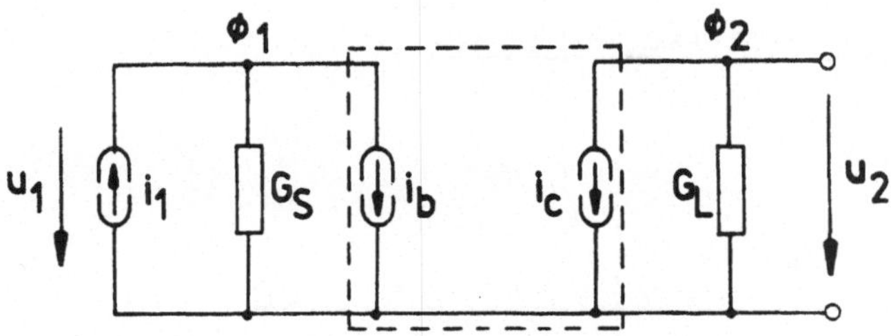

Fig. 5    Kleinsignal-Ersatzschaltung

## Ersatzschaltung des Transistors

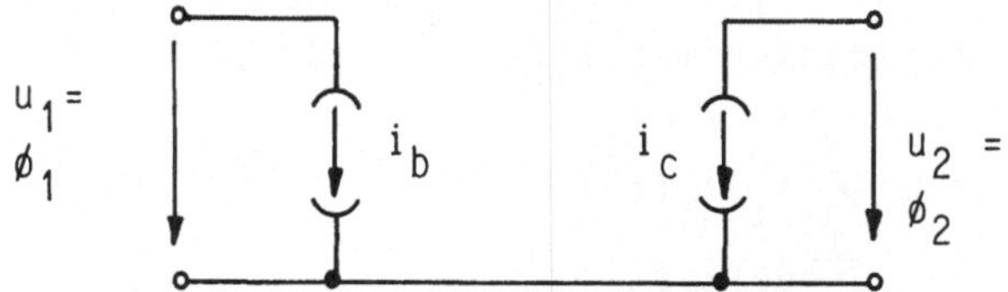

Fig. 6    Kleinsignal-Ersatzschaltung eine bipolaren Transistors in
          Emitterschaltung

Ohm'scher und kapazitiver Anteil für jeden Strom wird berücksichtigt

$$i_b = g_b(u_1,u_2) + \frac{d}{dt}c_b(u_1,u_2)$$

$$i_c = g_c(u_1,u_2) + \frac{d}{dt}c_c(u_1,u_2)$$

$g_b$, $g_c$, $c_b$, $c_c$ sind nichtlineare Funktionen von $u_1$ und $u_2$

Taylor-Reihenentwicklung

$$i_b = \sum_{n=1}^{3} \sum_{k=0}^{n} \left(g_{bik}u_1^{i}u_2^{k} + \frac{d}{dt}c_{bik}u_1^{i}u_2^{k}\right)$$

$$j_c = \sum_{n=1}^{3} \sum_{k=0}^{n} \left(g_{cik}u_1^{i}u_2^{k} + \frac{d}{dt}c_{cik}u_1^{i}u_2^{k}\right) \qquad i=n-k$$

$g_{bik}$, $g_{cik}$, $c_{bik}$, $c_{cik}$ .... Taylor-Koeffizienten

## Knotenanalyse des Verstärkernetzwerks

a) Zeitbereich

| $\phi_1(t)$ | $\phi_2(t)$ | $=$ |
|:---:|:---:|:---:|
| $G_S$ | $0$ | $i_1(t) - i_b(t)$ |
| $0$ | $G_S$ | $- i_c(t)$ |

Die unbekannten Funktionen $\phi_1(t)$, $\phi_2(t)$, $i_b(t)$, $i_c(t)$ werden durch Volterra-Reihen des Eingangsstromes $i_1(t)$ ausgedrückt:

$$\phi_1(t) = A(i_1(t)) = \sum_{i=1}^{3} A_i(i_1(t))$$

$$\phi_2(t) = B(i_1(t)) = \sum_{i=1}^{3} B_i(i_1(t))$$

$$i_b(t) = D(i_1(t)) = \sum_{i=1}^{3} D_i(i_1(t))$$

$$i_c(t) = E(i_1(t)) = \sum_{i=1}^{3} E_i(I_1(t))$$

b) Frequenzbereich

$$G(p) \begin{bmatrix} A_1(p) \\ B_1(p) \end{bmatrix} = \begin{bmatrix} 1 \\ 0 \end{bmatrix} \longrightarrow \begin{matrix} A_1(p) \\ B_1(p) \end{matrix}$$

$$G(p_1,p_2) \begin{bmatrix} A_2(p_1,p_2) \\ B_2(p_1,p_2) \end{bmatrix} = \begin{bmatrix} -D_2^*(p_1,p_2) \\ -E_2^*(p_1,p_2) \end{bmatrix} \longrightarrow \begin{matrix} A_2(p_1,p_2) \\ B_2(p_1,p_2) \end{matrix}$$

$$G(p_1,p_2,p_3) \begin{bmatrix} A_3(p_1,p_2,p_3) \\ B_3(p_1,p_2,p_3) \end{bmatrix} = \begin{bmatrix} -D_3^*(p_1,p_2,p_3) \\ - E_3^*(p_1,p_2,p_3) \end{bmatrix} \longrightarrow \begin{matrix} A_3(p_1,p_2,p_3) \\ B_3(p_1,p_2,p_3) \end{matrix}$$

wobei die Matrix

$$G(p) = \begin{bmatrix} G_S + Y_{b10}(p) & Y_{b01}(p) \\ Y_{c10}(p) & G_L + Y_{c01}(p) \end{bmatrix}$$

die komplexen Admittanzen sind

$$Y_{bik} = g_{bik} + p \cdot c_{bik}$$

$$Y_{cik} = g_{cik} + p \cdot c_{cik}$$

## Oberwellenquellen und lineare Netzwerke

Verallgemeinerung des Postulats formuliert durch Feldtkeller und Wolman)

Darstellung der drei Subsysteme:

- System erster Ordnung

- System zweiter Ordnung

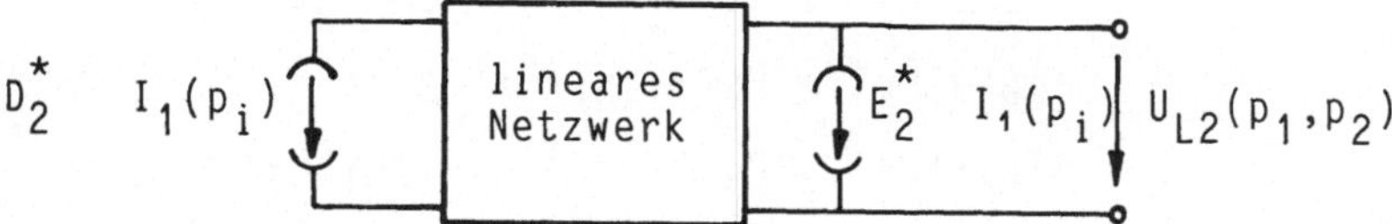


- System dritter Ordnung

Fig. 7   Die drei Systeme

## Berechnung der drei Oberwellenquellen

$$D_2^*(p_2,p_2) = Y_{b20}(p_1+p_2)A_1(p_1)A_1(p_2)$$
$$+Y_{b02}(p_1+p_2)B_1(p_1)B_1(p_2)$$
$$+Y_{b11}(p_1+p_2)A_1(p_1)B_1(p_2)$$

$$D_3^*(p_1,p_2,p_3) = 2Y_{b20}(p_1+p_2+p_3)A_1(p_1)A_2(p_2,p_3)$$
$$+2Y_{b02}(p_1+p_2+p_3)B_1(p_1)B_2(p_2,p_3)$$
$$+Y_{b11}(p_1+p_2+p_3)A_1(p_1)B_2(p_2,p_3)$$
$$+Y_{b11}(p_1+p_2+p_3)B_1(p_1)A_2(p_2,p_3)$$
$$+Y_{b30}(p_1+p_2+p_3)A_1(p_1)A_1(p_2)A_1(p_3)$$
$$+Y_{b03}(p_1+p_2+p_3)B_1(p_1)B_1(p_2)B_1(p_3)$$
$$+Y_{b21}(p_1+p_2+p_3)A_1(p_1)A_1(p_2)B_1(p_3)$$
$$+Y_{b12}(p_1+p_2+p_3)A_1(p_1)B_1(p_2)B_1(p_3)$$

$$E_2^*(p_1,p_2) = Y_{c20}(p_1+p_2)A_1(p_1)A_1(p_2)$$
$$+Y_{c02}(p_1+p_2)B_1(p_1)B_1(p_2)$$
$$+Y_{c11}(p_1+p_2)A_1(p_1)B_1(p_2)$$

$$E_3^*(p_1,p_2,p_3) = 2Y_{c20}(p_1+p_2+p_3)A_1(p_1)A_2(p_2,p_3)$$
$$+2Y_{c02}(p_1+p_2+p_3)B_1(p_1)B_2(p_2,p_3)$$
$$+Y_{c11}(p_1+p_2+p_3)A_1(p_1)B_2(p_2,p_3)$$
$$+Y_{c11}(p_1+p_2+p_3)B_1(p_1)A_2(p_2,p_3)$$
$$+Y_{c30}(p_1+p_2+p_3)A_1(p_1)A_1(p_2)A_1(p_3)$$
$$+Y_{c03}(p_1+p_2+p_3)B_1(p_1)B_1(p_2)B_1(p_3)$$
$$+Y_{c21}(p_1+p_2+p_3)A_1(p_1)A_1(p_2)B_1(p_3)$$
$$+Y_{c12}(p_1+p_2+p_3)A_1(p_1)B_1(p_2)B_1(p_3)$$

## Nichtlineare Verzerrung eines Verstärkers

Gütefaktor

$$M_{2E}(f_1,f_2) = 20\lg\frac{B_2(f_1,f_2)\; 2R_L\,1mW}{2B_1(f_1)B_1(f_2)}$$

$$M_{3E}(f_1,f_2,f_3) = 20\lg\frac{B_3(f_1,f_2,f_3)\; R_L\,1mW}{2B_1(f_1)B_1(f_2)B_1(f_3)}$$

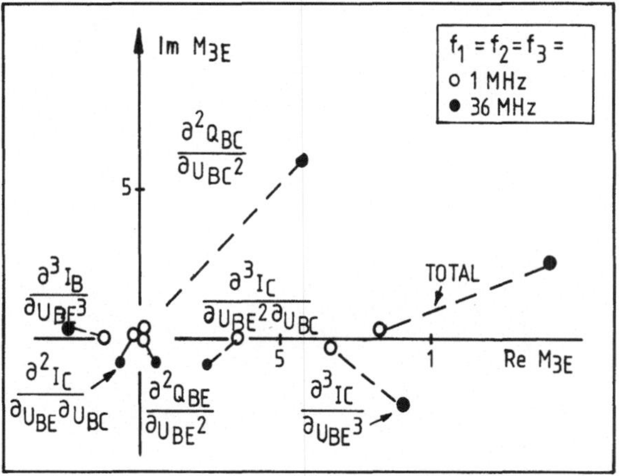



Fig. 8    Beitrag der verschiedenen nichtlinearen Parameter zur $M_{3E}$

## Schrifttum


/1/   Feldkeller, R. / Wolman, W.: Fastlineare Netzwerke, Telegra-
      phen- und Fernsprechtechni, 1931, p. 167-171 and 242-248

/2/   Schetzen, M.: Nonlinear Syst. Modeling Based on the Wiener
      Theory, IEEE Proc., 1981, No. 12, p. 1557-1573

/3/   Volterra, V.: Sopra le funzioni che dipendone de altre funzioni,
      Rend. R. Academi dei Lincei 2 sem.., 1887

4//   Narayana, S. / Poon, H.C.: An Analysis of Distortion in Bipolar
      Transistor Using Integral Charge Control Model and Volterra
      Series IEEE Transactions on Circuit

/5/   Wölk, J.: Ersatzschaltbilder des bipolaren Transistors für den
      fast-linearen Betriebsfall
      Diplomarbeit, Institut für elektrische Nachrichtentechnik
      Stuttgart

/6/   Jedele, P.: Analyse der nichtlinearen Verzerrungen einer gegen-
      gekoppelten Verstärkerstufe durch Volterra-Reihe.
      Zweite Semesterarbeit, Institut für elektrische Nachrichten-
      technik Stuttgart

/7/   Jedele, P., Khakzar, H.: Generalization of Distortion Sources
      Sugested by Feldtkeller and Wolman using Volterra Series Repre-
      sentation, European Conference Circuit Theory and Design,
      Stuttgart 1983

# SIMULATION IN

# TECHNISCHEN ANWENDUNGEN

VEHICLE CRASHWORTHINESS SIMULATION
THE ROLE OF SUPERCOMPUTER (*)


Moshe R. Heller
Simulation Technology
CONTROL DATA GMBH
8000 München 80, Germany


ABSTRACT
Optimization of the structural crashworthiness is an essential problem and also a
marketing tool in vehicle development. To identify promising design measures and to
reduce the experimental effort, numerical simulation techniques are being used.
Current finite element codes for simulation crash behaviour are ineffective because
they do not possess special features for appropriate modelling the highly non-linear
kinematics involved (in the crash process). One of the most serious limitations under
inelastic material response is the lack of a method to handle 'folding mechanisms'.

KEYWORDS
VEHICLE ENGINEERING, FOLDING MECHANISMS, FINITE-ELEMENT-METHODS, CRASHWORTHINESS,
SUPERCOMPUTER.

INTRODUCTION

This CRASHWORTHINESS Project is based on:

1.    Survey of existing codes

2.    Published Literature

3.    The 'field' experience

and will be developed for finite element models which are:

4.    Large (thousands of DOF's)

5.    With large displacement

6.    Nonlinear

7.    Elastic-Plastic

8.    Dynamic

when all of the above brings us to conclude that present codes on regular computers
are:

A.    Much too slow

B.    Not well suited to evaluate design changes rapidly

C.    Not extremely accurate in predicting crash response

Therefore, this paper will introduce:

THE NEED FOR A NEW CODE WHICH RUNS ON A SUPERCOMPUTER.


(*) first published at the SCS-85, Chicago, July 22 - 25/85

## AN IMPROVED CAR CRASH CODE

As mentioned before, the existing codes are in the stage of scientific methods, and they are not really user oriented for designers in all stages of car body development. This is calling for the following four (4) main objectives:

1.  CRASH RELATED MODELS which include:

    1.1     Geometrical non-linear formulation for:

            1.1.1     Large displacement
            1.1.2     Large rotation
            1.1.3     Large strains

    1.2     Additional State-of-the-Art features:

            1.2.1     Buckling and/or folding
            1.2.2     Contact Control and Friction
            1.2.3     Transition elements

2.  A NEW CODE structured as follows:

    2.1     PREPROCESSOR which has:

            2.1.1     Mesh generation and control graphics
            2.1.2     Interactive processing

    2.2     ANALYSIS which will have:

            2.2.1     An effective data management
            2.2.2     Optimized performance for a specific computer
                      (i.e. solvers for supercomputer)
            2.2.3     Interactive processing
            2.2.4     A mesh adaption/redefinition-technics

    2.3     POSTPROCESSOR will include:

            2.3.1     Interactive graphics
            2.3.2     Visualization of the results (i.e. image post processor)

3.    A SUPERCOMPUTER for:

      3.1          Code written for large production to compute in core

      3.2          Special data flow/structure or new solvers

      3.3          Avoiding data reshuffling

      3.4          Interactive use as postprocessing in parallel


4.    USER ORIENTED with:

      4.1          Following a fimiliar format

      4.2          Fast easy input of design changes

      4.3          Fast graphic output-results easily understood


## THE CRASH MODEL

The crash naturally will handle:

1.    Material Behaviour

2.    Methodology of Analysis

3.    Software Requirements


and the material description for it includes:

A.    Large Strain Elasto-Plastic

B.    Rigid-Plastic

C.    Elasto-Viscoplastic

D.    Rigit-Viscopolastic

E.    Thermomechanical Coupling Phenomena


The structural modelling contains two major parts as follows:

1.    Structural Modelling-I with:

      1.1          Mechanical Models

            1.1.1  Collapse Mechanisms

            1.1.2  Hinges

            1.1.3  Folds


which are inadequate for general situations.

      1.2          Finite elements of

            1.2.1  Beams

            1.2.2  Plates

            1.2.3  Shells

which are currently inadequate for modelling of confined deformations.

2. Structural Modelling-II, the Folding-Mechanisms

    2.1         Adaptive mesh refinement technics - local refinement

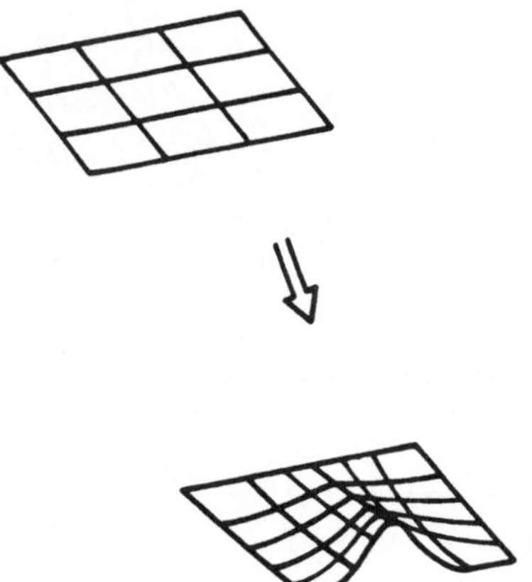

Figure 1. Problem size increases progressively with confined deformation

    2.2         Combined models

            incorporation of adequate mechanical models into finite elements

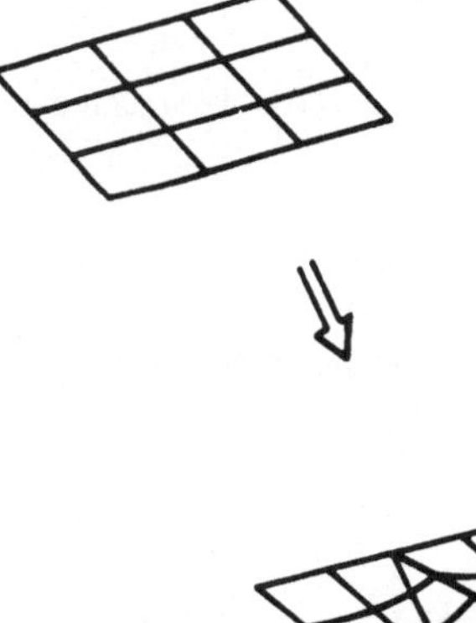

Figure 2. Model should keep problem size independent of confinement of
        deformation

## METHODOLOGY OF ANALYSIS

The methodology will be with the aid of:

1.    Current capabilities
2.    Advanced model
3.    Solution technics

and the advanced dynamics model is:

A.    Semidiscrete equation of motion
B.    Discretisation in time
C.    Vector interaction
D.    Matrix solution with solver technics

using all the above for a simple lumped model will get the deformation as described
in figure 3.

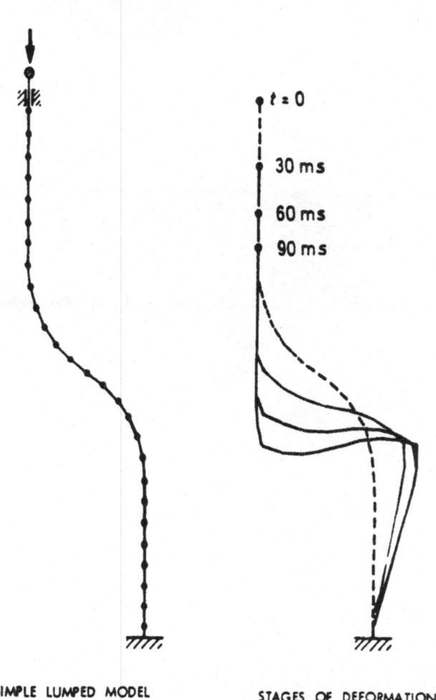


Fig. 3    SIMPLE LUMPED MODEL
STAGES OF DEFORMATION DURING IMPACT

<u>CRAHSWORTHINESS PROGRAM MILESTONES</u>

1. <u>PHASE I</u>

   The first six months
   will handle the
   buckling/folding
   problem of
   'a simple' structure

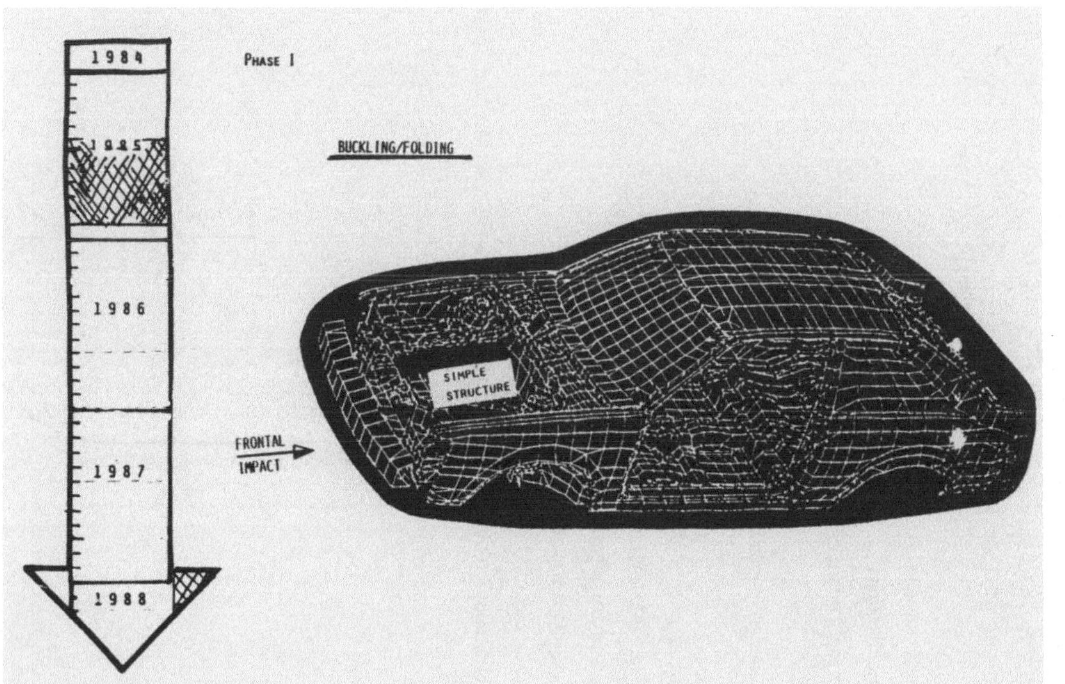



Figure 4. Phase I of Part I of the Crashworthiness

## 2.  A SIMPLE STRUCTURE

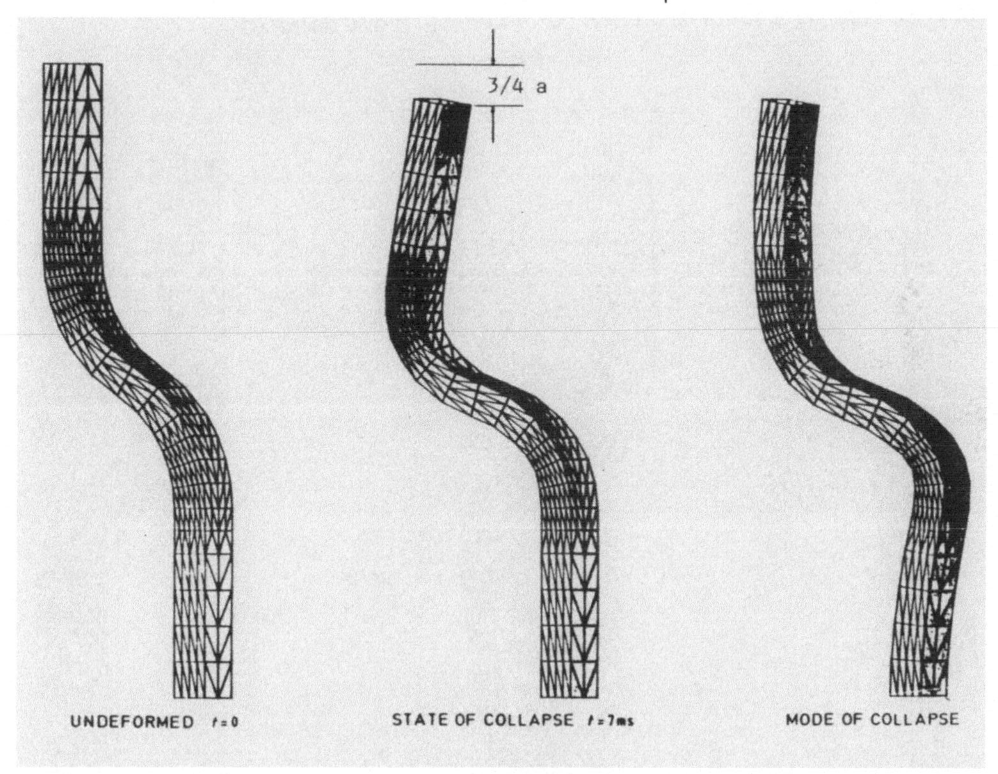


Figure 5. A 'Simple-Structure' Elasto-Perfect Plastic Analysis of Impact

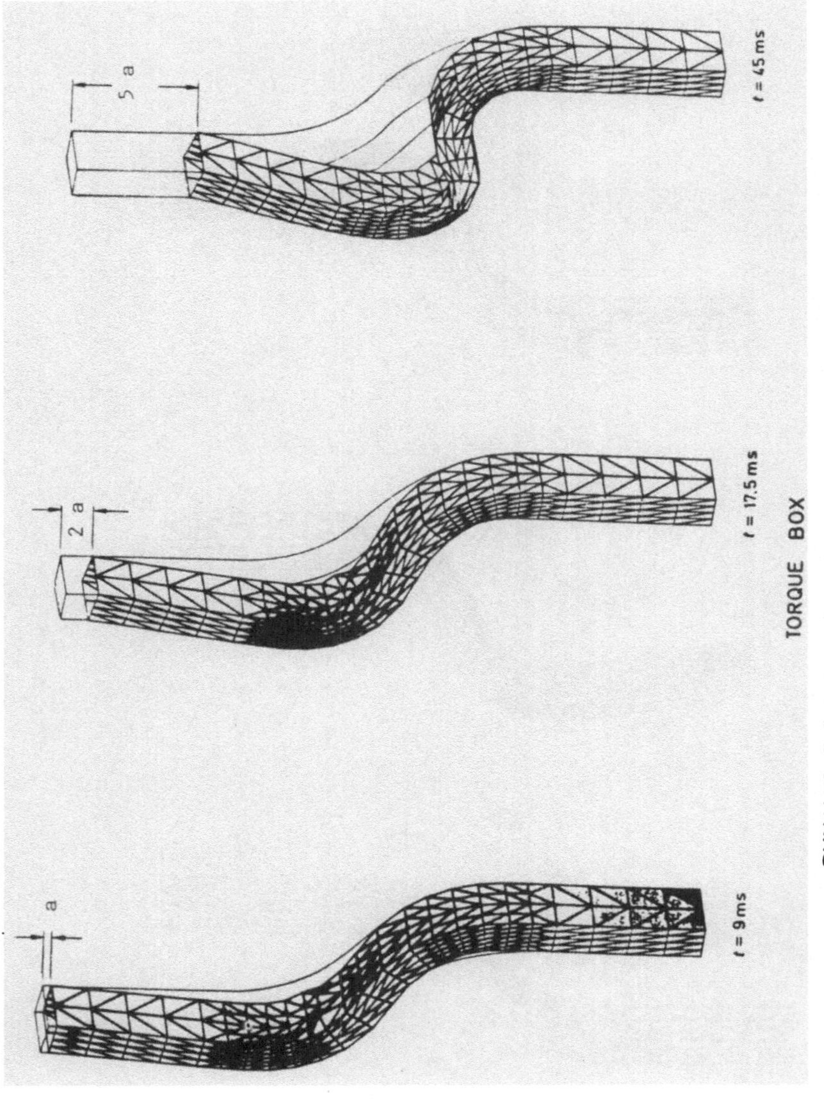



Figure 6. A 'Simple-Structure' Dynamic, Rigit-Viscoelastic Analysis - Deformation Stages

3.    <u>A FRONT END I OF CRASH</u>

PHASE II
part one will
take care of
the front end
impact

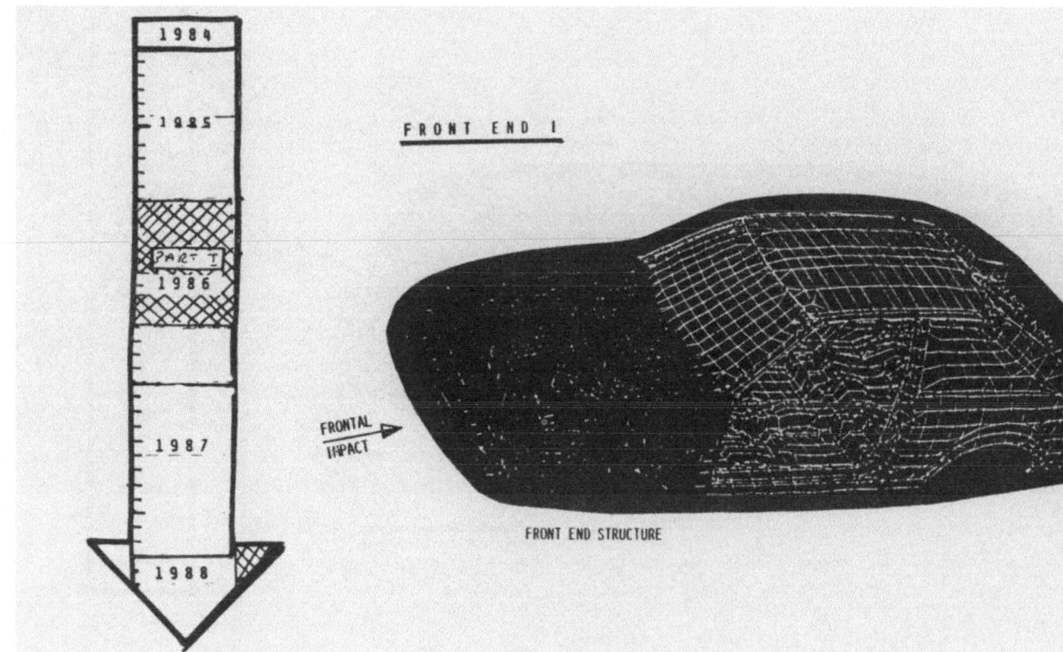



Figure 7. Phase II, Part I of Crashworthiness

4.     A FRONT END II OF CRASH

PHASE II
part two will
handle the
front end
impact and
also oblique
and off-set
one

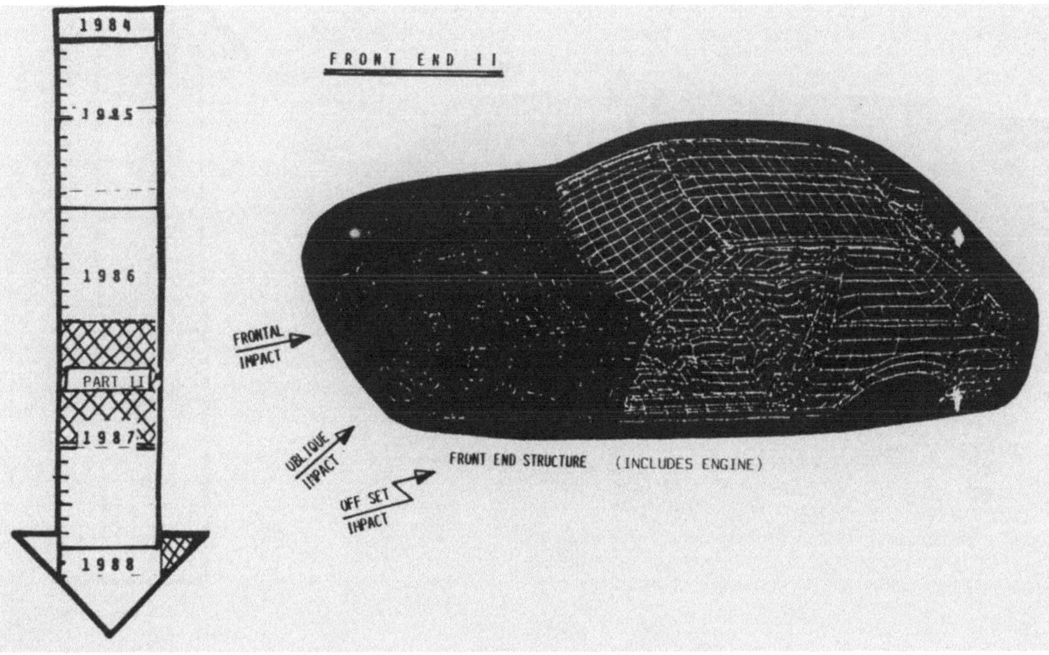



Figure 8.   Phase II, Part II of Crashworthiness

## 5. A FULL CAR CRASH

The final part
will also add
to part two
the side and
the rear
impact

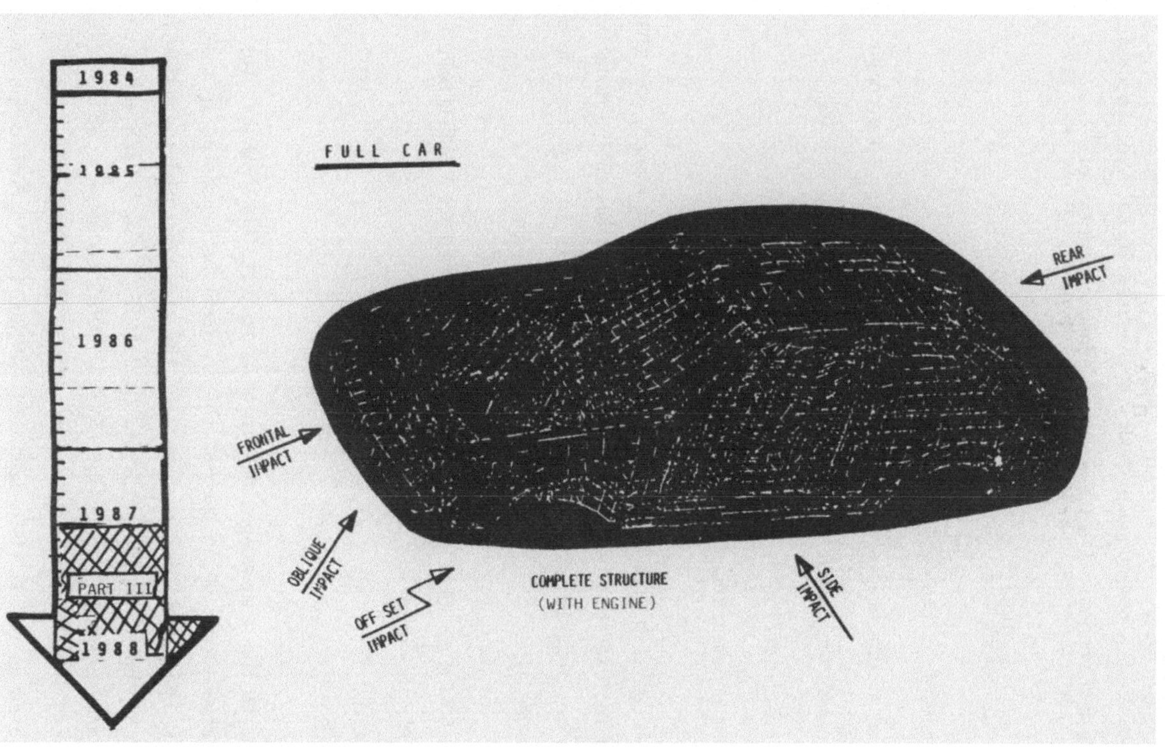


Figure 9.    Phase II - Final Part of Crashworthiness

SUMMARY

The goal of the total project is to conduct a research program which has as objective
the development of a new computer model to be used in the vehicle design phase for
the accurate and economical simulation of crash performance.

The project will include:

1.    development of theory

2.    writing of computer software, desinged specially for supercomputers

3.    development or use of pre- and postprocessors

4.    model verification by experimental testing

5.    program documentation

The global model is planned to consider first front-end impact, and then is to be
expanded to include oblique, off-set, side and rear impact. The model will be
designed to be flexible and user optimized so that it is easy for the desinger/
engineer to use it.

THESE CRASH SPECIFIC SOLUTIONS MUST BE NEW, PERFORMED ON A SUPERCOMPUTER, AND BETTER
THAN THE STATE-OF-THE-ART.

ACKNOWLEDGEMENTS

I would like to thank my co-partner in this project, GERT RUETER, for the many fruit-
ful conversations from which much of the information presented in this paper has been
cleaned.  The design and the structure of the crashworthiness program is the work of
many talented people, including J. St. DOLTSINIS, K.-J. MELZER and a whole group of
scientists and engineers from BATTELLE-INSTITUTES to whom  I would like to extend my
thanks.
My  thanks also go to all the members of CONTROL DATA's Supercomputer Operation and
Marketing who have been involved beyond everyday's work in the promotion of this
program.

# EINSATZ VON MKS-FORMALISMEN ZUR
# KFZ-SIMULATION

Karl-Heinz Senger, Oberpfaffenhofen



**Zusammenfassung.** Diese Untersuchung beschreibt den Einfluß linearer bzw. nichtlinearer Bewegungsgleichungen auf die Ergebnisse einer Zeitsimulation an einem
einfachen Modell einer Fahrzeughinterachse unter Verwendung allgemeiner Mehrkör-
perprogramme. Mit Hilfe dieses Testbeispiels mit Zwangsbedingungen und linearen
Koppelelementen wurden die Programme ADAMS, MEDYNA, MESA VERDE, MULTIBODY und NE-
WEUL getestet. Es zeigt sich, daß das nichtlineare Verhalten der Hinterachse schon
mit einer nichtlinearen Beschreibung der Feder-Dämpfer-Kinematik allein erfaßt
werden kann. Die Integration benötigt in diesem Fall jedoch nur die Hälfte der
Rechenzeit, die für eine voll nichtlineare Simulation erforderlich ist.



**Summery.** This paper discusses the influence of linear and nonlinear equations of
motion on the results of a time simulation for a simple model of a vehicle rear
axle using general purpose multibody programs. Applying this test example with
bearings and linear suspension force laws, the programs ADAMS, MEDYNA, MESA VERDE,
MULTIBODY and NEWEUL are tested. It can be shown, that the nonlinear behaviour of
the rear axle can be described using only nonlinear representation of the
spring-damper-kinematics. In this case the intgration needs only half of the time
required for a completely nonlinear simulation.


## 1. EINLEITUNG

Um in der Fahrzeugentwicklung schon frühzeitig Aussagen über das Fahrverhalten und
während des Betriebs auftretende Kräfte ohne den Bau von Prototypen machen zu können, wird die rechnergestützte Simulation unter Verwendung von Mehrkörper-Formalismen bzw. -Programmen eingesetzt [1]. Bei der Untersuchung der Fahrzeugbewegung
wird man in der Regel mit der Linearisierung der Bewegung der einzelnen Fahrzeug-
komponenten um die Gesamtschwerpunktsbewegung hinreichend gute Resultate
erzielen. Es sind jedoch auch extreme Fahrmanöver (z.B. schnelle Slalomfahrt,
Fahrspurwechsel) zu untersuchen, bei denen die lineare Beschreibung der Bewegung
möglicherweise nicht mehr ausreichend ist. Insbesondere mit dieser Fragestellung
befaßt sich die vorliegende Arbeit. Ziel dieser Untersuchung ist es, Aussagen über
die Notwendigkeit nichtlinearer Formalismen zu machen und den Einsatz verschiedener MKS-Programme anhand eines Beispiels zu testen.

## 2. MODELLBESCHREIBUNG UND MODELLBILDUNG

Als Testbeispiel wurde zunächst ein einfaches Modell einer Fahrzeughinterachse
ausgewählt (s. Bild 1). Es besteht aus drei Körpern (Aufbau, Rad links, Rad
rechts), die mit Gelenken, Federn und Dämpfern untereinander verbunden sind. Aufgrund der Zwangsbedingungen in den Lenkerlagern verbleiben unter der Voraussetzung

der ebenen Bewegung insgesamt 5 Freiheitsgrade mit den Lagezustandsvariablen $Y_I$ und den Geschwindigkeitszustandsvariablen $Y_{II}$. Die Reifen werden durch parallel geschaltete Feder/Dämpfer in horizontaler und vertikaler Richtung modelliert. Alle Federn und Dämpfer werden mit Hilfe linearer Kraftgesetze beschrieben. Für den Kraftangriffspunkt der horizontalen Reifenkraft wurden zwei verschiedene Ansätze verwendet (s. Bild 2):

1. Die Kräfte greifen am Punkt A am Reifen an. Zur Berechnung der Federkraft in vertikaler Richtung wird die z-Verschiebung von Punkt A bzgl. Punkt C verwendet, zur Berechnung der Seitenkraft die y-Verschiebung.

2. Der Kraftangriffspunkt (Punkt B) der Seitenkraft liegt immer in der Fahrbahnebene, senkrecht unter Punkt A. Die Kräfte werden wie unter 1) berechnet, aber das Moment der Seitenkräfte auf das Rad ändert sich infolge des zustandsabhängigen Hebelarms.

Der 1. Ansatz ergibt sich aus der teilweisen Linearisierung des zweiten Modells.

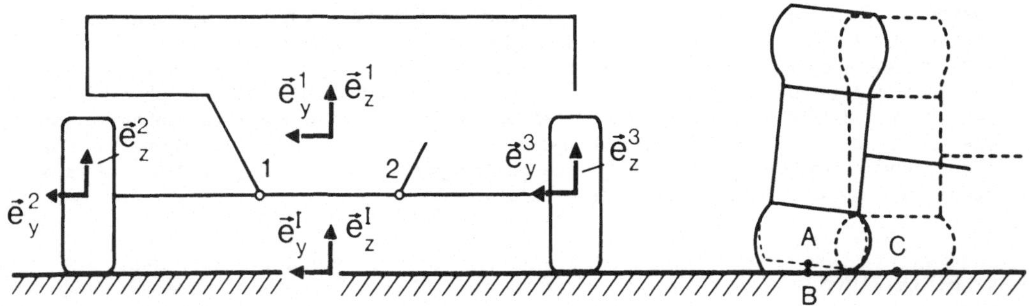

Bild 1.   Verwendetes Simulationsmodell;
1,2 Lenkerlager

Bild 2.   Modellierung der Kraftangriffspunkte am Rad

Zum rechnergestützten Aufstellen der Bewegungsgleichungen werden die Programme ADAMS [2], MEDYNA [3], MESA VERDE [4], MULTIBODY [5] und NEWEUL [6] verwendet. Von diesen Programmen erstellt MEDYNA die linearen Bewegungsgleichung, bei MESA VERDE und NEWEUL stehen diese Optionen zusätzlich zur Verfügung. Um außer der Bearbeitung der oben beschriebenen Fragestellung auch unterschiedliche MKS-Formalismen und Programmrealisierungen zu vergleichen, wurden die nichtlinearen Bewegungsgleichung mit vier verschiedenen Programmen, die auf unterschiedlichen Formalismen basieren, aufgestellt. ADAMS verwendet die LAGRANGE'schen Gleichungen gemischten Typs, MESA VERDE und MULTIBODY den ROBERSON/WITTENBURG Formalismus und NEWEUL die NEWTON/EULER'schen Gleichungen. Nur MESA VERDE und NEWEUL erstellen die Bewegungsgleichung in symbolischer Form.

Von den fünf getesteten Programmen bieten nur ADAMS und MEDYNA eine Koppelelement-Bibliothek. Bei den Programmen MESA VERDE, MULTIBODY und NEWEUL hat der Benutzer die Feder-Dämpfer-Kräfte in Abhängigkeit der Zustandsvariablen zu definieren [1]). MEDYNA arbeitet als einziges Programm dialog-orientiert. Das bietet den Vorteil,

---

[1]) Vom Programm MESA VERDE stand nur eine ältere Version zur Verfügung. Mittlerweile wurde die Eingabe geändert [7].

Fehler schon bei der Eingabe zu erkennen und dem Benutzer Hilfstexte zur Verfügung stellen zu können.

## 3. INTEGRATION DER BEWEGUNGSGLEICHUNGEN

Die Bewegungsgleichung wurden bei Verwendung von ADAMS, MEDYNA und MULTIBODY mit den in diesen Programmen implementierten Lösungsalgorithmen integriert, beim Einsatz von MESA VERDE und NEWEUL mit den Integrationsverfahren der Simulationssprache ACSL [8]. Mit Hilfe einer Kopplung können auch die von MEDYNA erstellten Bewegungsgleichung mit ACSL integriert werden [9].

Gerechnet wurde ein Lastfall, der dem Einfahren in eine Kurve entspricht. Dabei zeigen sich insbesondere für die Aufbau Verschiebung in Vertikalrichtung und für die Sturzwinkel deutliche Unterschiede bei der linearen und nichtlinearen Simulation (vgl. Bild 3), obwohl die Relativwinkel mit max 7.6° noch nicht als groß zu bezeichnen sind.

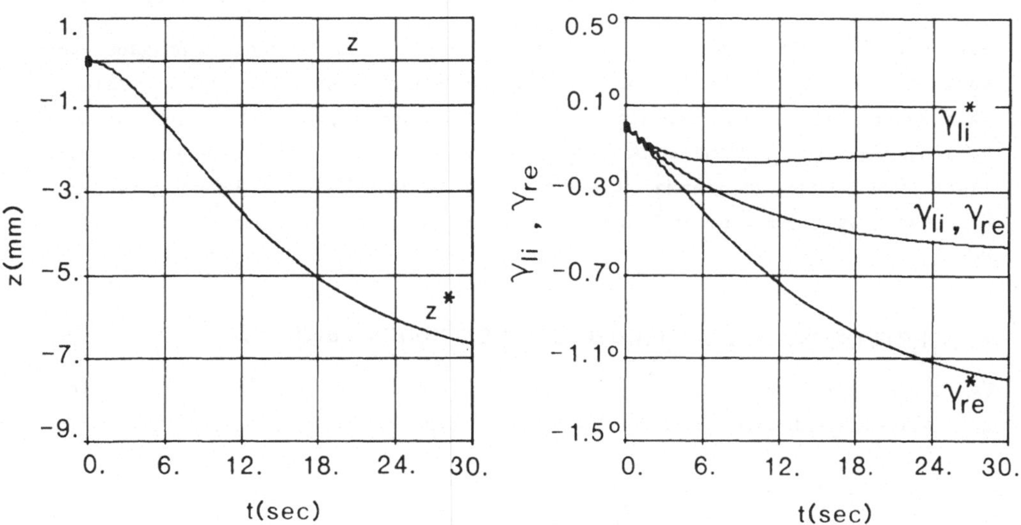


Bild 3.   Zeitverläufe für die vertikale Aufbauverschiebung z und die Sturzwinkel $\gamma_{li}$ und $\gamma_{re}$; die Ergebnisse der nichtlinearen Simulation sind mit einem Stern gekennzeichnet.

Man erkennt, daß die linearen Bewegungsgleichungen die vertikale Aufbau Verschiebung z nicht erfassen und die Sturzwinkel links $\gamma_{li}$ und rechts $\gamma_{re}$ symmetrisch berechnet werden. Bei den Zeitverläufen der anderen Zustandsgrößen und bei den Feder-Dämpfer-Kräften zeigen sich quantitative, aber keine qualitativen Unterschiede. Die Abweichungen liegen zum Zeitpunkt t=30 sec zwischen 2.9 und 10.9% für die Zustandsgrößen und 4.0 und 7.5% für die Federkräfte. Die Ergebnisse für das Modell 1 liegen zwischen denen für den Ansatz 2 und denen von MEDYNA. Dieses Resultat war zu erwarten, da der Ansatz 1 eine Linearisierung von Ansatz 2 darstellt (s.o.). Alle nichtlinearen Programme liefern identische Ergebnisse, jedoch mit sehr unterschiedlichen Rechenzeiten. Diese sind zusammen mit den verwendeten Integrationsalgorithmen in der Tabelle 1 aufgeführt.

Tabelle 1.   Rechenzeiten für die Zeitintegration

| Programm | Integrationsalg. und Integrationsparameter | CPU-Zeit (sec) | Reifen-modell | Rechner |
|---|---|---|---|---|
| ADAMS | GEAR-stiff, Int=0.3 | 135.104 | 1 | GOULD 32/67 |
| MESA VERDE | GEAR, CINT=0.3 | 1.866 | 1 | IBM 3081 |
| MESA VERDE | GEAR | 13.164 | 1 | IBM 3081 |
| MESA VERDE | ADAMS-MOULTON | 15.097 | 1 | IBM 3081 |
| MESA VERDE | RUNGE-KUTTA 4.Ord. h=0.01 | 30.904 | 1 | IBM 3081 |
| MULTIBODY | RUNGE-KUTTA-FEHLBERG h=0.01 | 103.760 | 1 | IBM 3081 |
| MESA VERDE | ADAMS-MOULTON | 15.241 | 2 | IBM 3081 |
| NEWEUL | ADAMS-MOULTON | 5.586 | 2 | SIEMENS 7890F |
| MEDYNA | RUNGE-KUTTA-MERSON | 1.100 | 2 | IBM 3081 |

Sofern in der Tabelle nichts anderes angegeben ist, wurde mit einem Ausgabeinter-
vall von 0.01 sec gerechnet. Man erkennt (bei Berücksichtigung der unterschiedlichen Rechenleistungen), daß die Integration der symbolisch erstellten Bewegungsgleichung weniger Rechenzeit benötigt als die Integration bei Verwendung der numerisch arbeitenden Programme. Die Verarbeitung der linearen Bewegungsgleichung
erfordert natürlich weniger Rechenzeit, da die Systemmatrizen vorab berechnet werden.


## 4. SCHRITTWEISE LINEARISIERUNG DER BEWEGUNGSGLEICHUNGEN

Um die Unterschiede in den Ergebnissen der linearen und nichtlinearen Simulation
zu erklären, werden die mit MESA VERDE erstellten Bew. Gl.

$$A(Y_I)\ \dot{Y}_{II} = B(Y_I,Y_{II},F_i)$$
$$F_i = F_i(r_i)$$
$$r_i = r_i(Y_I,Y_{II})$$

mit:   A, B     Systemmatrizen

$F_i$     Feder-Dämpfer-Kräfte

$r_i$     Feder Vektoren


schrittweise linearisiert. Dazu werden die in $Y_I$ und $Y_{II}$ nichtlinearen Terme der
Matrizen A und B als kleine Größen angenommen und vernachlässigt, indem die Sub-
stitutionen $\cos \alpha_i = 1$, $\sin \alpha_i = \alpha_i$ vorgenommen und alle Terme höherer Ordnung zu
null gesetzt werden. Die Gleichgewichts-Lage wird jedoch noch nicht
berücksichtigt, die Matrizen A und B bleiben also zustandsabhängig. Die Berechnung
der Federvektoren $r_i$ und der Feder-Dämpfer-Kräfte $F_i$ wird nicht geändert, alle
nichtlinearen Terme bleiben erhalten. Die Integration dieser Gleichungen zeigt,
daß alle nichtlinearen Effekte (vertikale Aufbauverschiebung, Sturzwinkel) erfaßt
werden. Für den Zeitpunkt t=30 sec betragen die Abweichungen von der nichtlinearen

Simulation für die Zustandsgrößen max. 1.3%, für die Feder-Dämpfer-Kräfte max. 0.5% und für die Sturzwinkel max. 3.8%. Die Rechenzeit kann im Vergleich zur nichtlinearen Simulation um 25.4% reduziert werden.

Im nächsten Schritt wird in die Matrizen A und B die Gl. Gew. Lage $Y_{IO}$ und $Y_{IIO}$ eingesetzt, so daß die Bewegungsgleichung die folgende Form erhalten:

$$A(Y_{IO})\ \dot{Y}_{II} = B(Y_{IO}, Y_{IIO}, F_i)$$
$$F_i = F_i(r_i)$$
$$r_i = r_i(Y_I, Y_{II})$$

Die Berechnung der Vektoren $r_i$ und der Kräfte $F_i$ bleibt wiederum unverändert. Die Ergebnisse der Integration ändern sich gegenüber dem vorausgegangenen Linearisierungsschritt nicht, die Rechenzeit wird jedoch um 55.9% reduziert (bezogen auf die voll nichtlineare Simulation).

Erst im letzten Schritt wird auch die Berechnung der Feder-Dämpfer-Kräfte und die Feder-Dämpfer-Kinematik linearisiert, indem alle $\cos \alpha_i = 1$, $\sin \alpha_i = \alpha_i$ und Terme höherer Ordnung zu null gesetzt werden. Außerdem ist zu beachten, daß durch das Einsetzen von $r_i$ und $F_i$ nicht wieder Terme der Ordnung 2 oder höher entstehen. Erst mit diesem Schrit liegen die vollständig linearisierten Bewegungsgleichungen vor und man erhält durch Umsortieren:

$$M\ \dot{Y}_{II} + D\ Y_{II} + K\ Y_I = q$$

mit den konstanten Matrizen M, D, K. Die Integration dieser Gleichungen liefert dieselben Ergebnisse wie MEDYNA mit den bereits oben beschriebenen Abweichungen.


## 5. BERECHNUNG DER ZWANGSKRÄFTE

In der Entwicklung von Fahrzeugen ist außer der Dynamik auch der Verlauf der eingeprägten Kräfte und der Zwangskräfte von Interesse, um Anhaltswerte für die Festigkeitsberechnung zu erhalten. Von den verwendeten Programmen berechnen ADAMS und MEDYNA die Zwangskräfte in den Lenkerlagern 1 und 2 (s. Bild 1). Die Werte für den Zeitpunkt t=30 sec sind in der Tabelle 2 aufgelistet. Hierbei treten deutliche Unterschiede zwischen linearer und nichtlinearer Rechnung zu Tage.

Tabelle 2.  Zwangskräfte in den Lenkerlagern 1 und 2 in y und z Richtung

| Programm | $\lambda_{1y}$ | $\lambda_{1z}$ | $\lambda_{2y}$ | $\lambda_{2z}$ |
|---|---|---|---|---|
| ADAMS | 3694.94 | -2564.29 | 4636.52 | 490.68 |
| MEDYNA | 4116.00 | -2547.60 | 4116.00 | 678.44 |

Der Einfluß der Linearisierung der Bewegungsgleichung und der Feder-Dämpfer-Kinematik wurde hier noch nicht untersucht.

Interessant wäre die Berechnung der Zwangskräfte bei der nichtlinearen Simulation außer mit dem Programm ADAMS auch mit einem anderen Programm, bei dem die Bewegungsgleichung auf Zustandsform reduziert werden und die Zwangskräfte erst im Anschluß an die Simulation berechnet werden.

## 6. SCHLUSSBEMERKUNG

Die vorliegende Arbeit zeigt, daß schon bei relativ kleinen Winkeln (hier 7.6°)
der Einsatz linearer Mehrkörper-Formalismen nicht immer ausreichend ist, um alle
Effekte zu beschreiben. Bei dem hier verwendeten Modell ist es jedoch möglich, mit
einer nichtlinearen Feder-Dämpfer Kinematik für die Berechnung der Feder-Dämpfer-
Kräfte das Systemverhalten vollständig zu erfassen (s. Kap 4.), im Gegensatz zur
nichtlinearen Simualtion aber über 50% an Rechenzeit einzusparen.


## 7. LITERATUR

[1]       Pankiewicz, E.
          Anwendung rechnergestützter Verfahren im Kraftfahrzeugbau, eingereichte
          Dissertation, Stuttgart, 1985


[2]       Orlandea, N., Chace, M. A., Calahan, D. A.
          A Sparsity-Oriented Approach to the Dynamic Analysis and Design of Me-
          chanical Systems, Report AFOSR-TR-76-0014, 1976


[3]       Wallrapp, O., Kortüm, W.
          MEDYNA - ein Mehrkörperprogramm zur Analyse und Auslegung der Dynamik
          von spurgeführten Fahrzeugen, VDI-Bericht Nr. 510, 1984


[4]       Wittenburg, J.
          Analytical Methods in mechanical system dynamics, Proc. of the NATO Ad-
          vanced Study Institute on Computer Aided Analysis and Optimization of
          Mechanical System Dynamics, ed. by E. J. Haug, Iowa City, 1983


[5]       Schwertassek, R.
          Der Roberson/Wittenburg-Formalismus und das Programmsystem MULTIBODY
          zur Rechnersimulation von Mehrkörpersystemen, DFVLR-FB 78-08, 1978


[6]       Schiehlen, W. O.
          Dynamics of Complex Multibody Systems, SM-Archievs 9, Martinus Niyhoff
          Publishers, The Hague, 1984


[7]       Wittenburg, J., Wolz, U.
          MESA VERDE - Ein Computerprogramm zur Simulation der nichtlinearen Dyna-
          mik von Vielkörpersystemem, Robotersysteme 1, 1985


[8]       Gauthier, J.S., Mitchell, E.
          Dynamic modelling using the Advanced Continuous Simulation Language
          (ACSL), Proc. First European Cars/Trucks Simulation Symposium, Schlier-
          see, 1984


[9]       Führer, C., Kortüm, W., Wallrapp, O., Bausch-Gall, I.
          MEDYNA - A Simulation Tool for Mechanical Systems and its Interface to
          Simulation Languages, Proc. 11th IMACS World Congress, Oslo, 5.-9. Aug.
          1985

SIMULATIONSMODELLE FÜR DIE UNTERSUCHUNG DES VERKEHRSABLAUFES

IM STRASSENNETZ


Mariusz Kaczmarek

Jarosław Pietrowski

Barbara Wołyńska,  Poznań / Polen


**Zusammenfassung.**  Im Vortrag wurden vier Simulationsmodelle des Straßen-
verkehrs vorgestellt: das modifizierte deterministische Modell TRANSYT
und stochastische Modelle SIEC, SKRZ, TRASIM. Sie werden für die Analyse der Qualität von Algorithmen der Lichtsignalsteuerung verwendet
und sind ein geeignetes Hilfsmittel in der Projektierungsphase. Sie beschreiben den Verkehrsprozeß mit verschiedener Ausführlichkeit und liefern mit gewünschter Genauigkeit Informationen über wesentliche Kenn-
ziffern der Verkehrsqualität für einzelne Knotenpunkte, Straßenzüge ,
und Straßennetze.

**Summary.**  The paper presents four simulation models of the urban
traffic: a modified, deterministic model TRANSYT and stochastic models
SIEC, SKRZ, TRASIM. These models are used in the analysis of efficiency of algorythms of urban traffic control and they are convenient tool
in design. Since they represent the traffic process with different levels of model accuracy they supply, with minutness of detail, the information on basic indexes describing quality of traffic both on single intersections and of arterial traffic and on street networks as
well.


## 1. Einführung

Eine Simulation des Straßenverkehrsablaufes ermöglicht es, wesentli-

che Qualitätskennziffern des Verkehrs ohne Durchführung von meistens

teueren und zeitaufwändigen Felduntersuchungen zu ermitteln. Es ist

insbesondere ein geeignetes Mittel zur Bewertung von Verkehrssteuerungs-

algorithmen in der Projektierungsphase. Die Zeitdauer der Felduntersu-

chungen ist am meisten sehr kurz. Wegen der Zufälligkeit des Verkehrs-

ablaufes besteht die Notwendigkeit der mehrmaligen Wiederholung von

Untersuchungen. Demgegenüber liefert ein gut geeichtes Simulationsmo-

dell schnell und mit erforderlicher Genauigkeit die notwendigen Ergeb-

nisse. Im Vortrag werden vier, in den Forschungsarbeiten der Arbeits-

gruppe für die Straßenverkehrssteuerung des Institutes für Automati-

sierungstechnik der Technischen Universität in Poznań angewendeten

Simulationsprogramme beschrieben. In dem ersten der vorgestellten Si-

mulationsprogramme wurde das ergänzte und modifizierte Verkehrsmodell

des Programmes TRANSYT6 /entwickelt in Transport and Road Research La-

boratory in Großbritannien/ verwendet. Die übrigen Programme /SIEC,

SKRZ, TRASIM/ sind eigene Bearbeitungen.

## 2. Deterministisches Verkehrsmodell - TRANSYT [1]

TRANSYT ist ein Simulationsprogramm auf der Basis eines deterministischen Modells, das eine ständige Wiederholung der Verkehrsbedingungen
in jedem Umlauf der Lichtsignalisierung annimt. Das Straßennetz wird
im Modell durch Knotenpunkte und dazwischen liegende Straßenabschnitte
dargestellt. Es wird vorausgesetzt, daß sämtliche Knotenpunkte in eine
Lichtsignalisierung bzw. in eindeutig bestimmende das Vorfahrtrecht
Verkehrszeichen ausgestattet sind und, daß die Umlaufzeit an allen Knoten dieselbe Länge /bzw. einen halben Wert der Länge/ hat. Fahrzeug-
ankünfte an äußere Netzzufahrten und Abbiegerelationen /ohne Berücksichtigung der Kollision mit Gegenverkehr/ sind gleichmäßig im Umlauf
verteilt. Es gibt keine Fahrzeuge im physikalischen Sinne und die Rechnungen werden mit sog. Verkehrsprofilen durchgeführt, die die Verkehrsstärken in einzelnen Sekunden des Umlaufes wiederspiegeln. Der an die
Haltelinie einer Kreuzung ankommende Verkehrsfluß wird durch das Profil IN repräsentiert. Durch das Profil OUT werden Fahrzeuge vertreten,
die diese Haltelinie verlassen. Das Profil IN an einer Zufahrt im
Straßennetz wird durch die Summation der entsprechenden Anteile der
speisenden OUT-Profile und nach ihrer Dispersion /als Funktion der
Reisezeit entlang eines Abschnittes/ erzeugt. Anhand der Anzahl der
Fahrzeuge, die an eine Zufahrt während der Existenz dort einer Warteschlange ankommen wird die durchschnittliche Anzahl der Halte ermittelt. Durchschnittliche Zeitverluste für einen Straßenabschnitt werden
durch die Summation von zwei Größen berechnet. Die erste Größe entsteht durch die Mittelwertbildung von Warteschlangenlängen in einem
Umlauf, die zweite Größe ist eine Funktion des Sättigungsgrades der
Zufahrt. Für die Einschätzung der Qualität der Verkehrssteuerung wird
eine Gewichtsumme der durchschnittlichen Zeitverluste und der Haltean-
zahl im ganzen Verkehrsnetz gebildet.
Das ursprüngliche Verkehrsmodell wurde modifiziert um die Wiedergabe
des Verkehrsprozesses zu verbessern [5]. Das angewendete geometrische
Dispersionsmodell, das eine zu starke Dispersion des letzten Anteils
einer Fahrzeuggruppe verursachte wurde durch ein rechtwinkliges Modell
ersetzt [4].

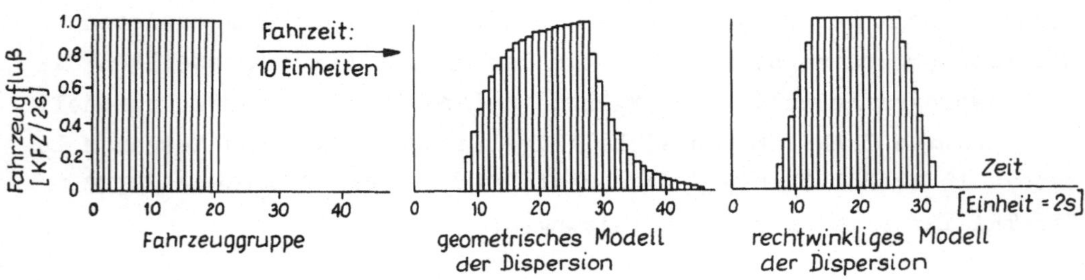

Es wurde ein Problem der Profilbildung in geschlossenen Netzmaschen
gelöst. Bisher wurde eine geschlossene Masche auseinander "geschnit-
ten" und die Fahrzeuge kamen an die Haltelinie eines "durchgeschnit-
tenen" Abschnittes mit konstanter Stärke im ganzen Umlauf an. Diese
Vereinfachung wurde durch eine iterative Bildung des tatsächlichen
Profils eliminiert und dadurch die Genauigkeit des Modells verbessert.
Außerdem wurde das Modell um eine Modifikation der Fahrzeiten infolge
des dynamischen Einflusses der Lichtsignalisierung auf den Verkehrsfluß erweitert. Dies ermöglicht eine getrennte Berücksichtigung der
Zeitverluste an der Haltelinie und der Anfahrzeitverluste.

## 3. Stochastische Verkehrsmodelle

### 3.1. SIEC [2]

Das Straßennetz wird in diesem Modell durch Knotenpunkte und Straßen-
abschitte mit ihrer zusätzlichen Aufteilung in einzelne Verkehrsspuren
/Warteschlangen/ gebildet. Fahrzeuge sind durch ihren aktuellen  Zustand vertreten und die Simulation ist  ereignisorientiert.
Es gibt einen Zustand $s_1$ - der Ankunft von Fahrzeugen in das Netz und
einen Zustand $s_2$ - der Fahrt entlang eines Abschnittes. Sie dauern

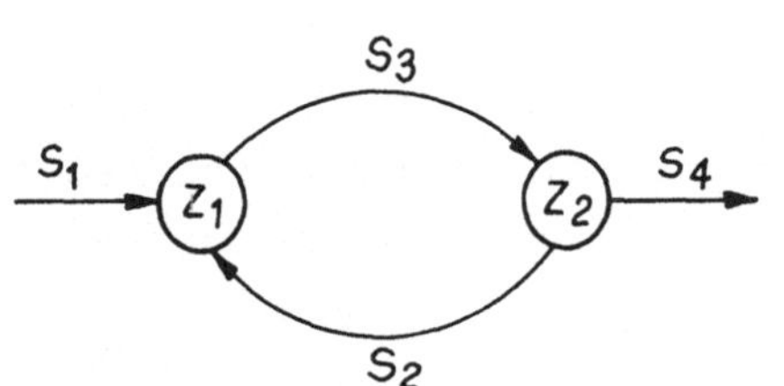


solange, bis das Fahrzeug eine der
Warteschlangen erreicht hat /Ereig-
nis $z_1$/. Das Fahrzeug bleibt dann in
der Warteschlange /Zustand $s_3$/ bis
zum Zeitpunkt, wenn es weiter fahren
kann /Ereignis $z_2$/. In diesem Moment

geht es in den Zustand $s_2$ über bzw. verläßt das Netz /Zustand $s_4$/.
Das Verlassen einer Warteschlange ist unter folgenden Bedingungen möglich: das Grünlicht für jeweilige Richtung, genügend viel Platz im
nächsten Straßenabschnitt und zusätzlich für Linksabbieger bei einer
Kollision mit Gegenverkehr - eine genügend große Zeitlücke zwischen
den Fahrzeugen im feindlichen Verkehrsfluß. Bei der Erfüllung aller
Bedingungen verlassen die Fahrzeuge eine Warteschlange in festen Zeitabständen /2 sek/. Es wurde eine Exponentialverteilung der Zeitinter-
valle zwischen den aufeinanderfolgenden Fahrzeugankünften an äußere
Netzzufahrten und eine rechtwinklige Verteilung der Fahrzeit angenommen.
Das Simulationsprogramm liefert solche Qualitätskennziffern der Verkehrssteuerung, wie: den Mittelwert und die Varianz der Zeitverluste
pro Fahrzeug und die Anzahl der angehaltenen Fahrzeuge bei ihrer Fahrt
durch aufeinanderfolgende Kreuzungen im Straßennetz.

## 3.2. SKRZ [3]

Das Simulationsprogramm SKRZ ermöglicht es, Steuerungsalgorithmen für
einzelne Knotenpunkte zu testen. Das Modell wird durch folgende Eigenschaften beschrieben:

- der Kreuzungsbereich und die Fahrspuren der einzelnen Zufahrten werden in einheitliche Felder eingeteilt,
- die Fahrzeugbewegung wird als das Besetzen und das Verlassen von
  Feldern modelliert,
- Ankünfte an die Kreuzung werden durch Wahrscheinlichkeitsverteilun-
  gen der zeitlichen Abstände zwischen aufeinanderfolgenden Fahrzeugankünften beschrieben,
- es wird nach Fahrzeugtyp /PKW, LKW, Bus/ unterschieden,
- Fahrzeuge verlassen eine Warteschlange mit Sättigungsstärke.

Die Simulation ist ereignisorientiert. Es gibt folgende Zustände:

$s_1$ - das Fahrzeug erreicht eine der Fahrspuren der Kreuzung,

$s_2$ - das Fahrzeug verbleibt in einem der Felder innerhalb der Fahrspur,

$s_3$ - das Fahrzeug befindet sich im letzten Feld der Fahrspur vor der
Haltelinie,

$s_4$ - das Fahrzeug verbleibt in einem der Felder des Kreuzungsbereiches,

$s_5$ - das Fahrzeug verläßt die Kreuzung.

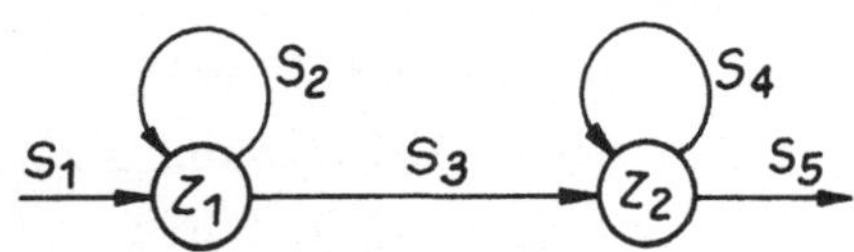


Die Zustandsänderungen werden durch folgende Ereignisse verursacht: $z_1$ - Ankunft
eines Fahrzeuges bzw. Änderung des besetzten Feldes innerhalb der Fahrspur und

$z_2$ - Einfahrt eines Fahrzeuges in den Kreuzungsbereich, bzw. Änderung
des besetzten Feldes innerhalb des Kreuzungsbereiches. Das Programm
liefert den Mittelwert und die Varianz von folgenden Größen: Warteschlangenlängen in jeder Fahrspur, Anzahl der angehaltenen Fahrzeuge
in jeder Fahrspur, Zeitverluste für jede Fahrspur und gesamte Kreuzung.

## 3.3. TRASIM

Das Modell TRASIM liegt mit seiner Ausführlichkeit der Wiedergabe des
Verkehrsprozesses zwischen den beiden Modellen SIEC und SKRZ. Es kann
demzufolge sowohl für Verkehrsanalysen auf einzelnen Knotenpunkten
als auch in kleineren Straßennetzen eingesetzt werden. Das Straßennetz
wird hier in einheitliche Elemente, sog. Segmente, wie z.B. Abschnitte
der freien Bewegung, Bushaltestellen, Fahrspuren auf den Kreuzungszu-
fahrten, u.s.w. zerlegt. Das Kriterium für die Unterscheidung eines
Segmentes ist die Stettigkeit in seinem Bereich der wesentlichen Ver-
kehrsparameter. Es wird nach Fahrzeugtyp unterschieden - die zeitlichen

Abstände zwischen den Ausfahrten aus den Segmenten hängen von den unterschiedlichen Sättigungsstärken für einzelne Fahrzeugarten ab.
Es gibt einen Zustand $s_1$ - das Fahrzeug bewegt sich entlang eines Segmentes, einen Zustand $s_2$ - das Fahrzeug verbleibt in einer Warteschlange und einen Zustand, wenn das Fahrzeug außerhalb des Netzes ist. Die

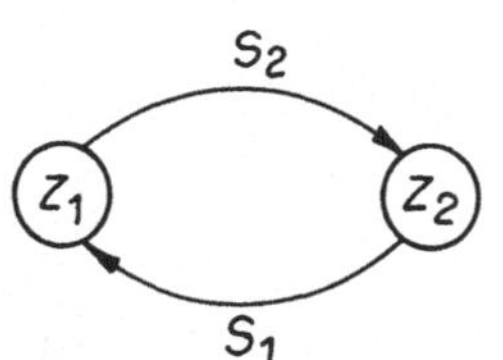


Änderung der Zustände erfolgt mit den Ereignissen $z_1$ /das Erreichen durch das Fahrzeug der Fahrzeit entlang eines Segmentes/ und $z_2$ /die Erfüllung der Bedingungen für das Verlassen des Segmentes/. Die Simulationsergebnisse umfassen: Verkehrsstärken, Zeitverluste und Anzahl der Halte in einzelnen Segmenten, festgelegten Relationen und im gesamten Netz.

## 4. Zusammenfassung

Die Simulationsresultate ermöglichen eine Beurteilung der Qualität von Verkehrssteuerungsalgorithmen, sowohl für das ganze Verkehrssystem als auch für seine einzelnen Fragmente. Die Auswahl eines der Simulationsprogramme hängt von der Größe und der Struktur des zu untersuchenden Verkehrssystems, den Verkehrsbedingungen und dem gewünschten Ausführlichkeitsgrad der Wiedergabe des Verkehrsprozesses ab. Das Einsatzgebiet der einzelnen Simulationsprogramme in Abhängigkeit von der Größe des Verkehrssystems wird in der Tabelle dargestellt:

| | Verkehrssystem | | |
|---|---|---|---|
| | StraBennetz | StraBenzug | Kreuzung |
| Wesentliche Qualitäts-Kennziffern | Zeitverluste DurchlaBfähigkeit | Anzahl der Halte, Zeitverluste | DurchlaBfähigkeit Warteschlangenlänge |
| Simulationsprogramm | TRANSYT        SIEC | TRASIM | SKRZ |

<u>Literaturverzeichnis:</u>


1. Robertson D.I.,Gower P.: User's guide to TRANSYT Version 6, TRRL 255, 1976.
2. Kaczmarek M.: Sieć ulic. In: Symulacja ruchu potoku pojazdów, WKŁ Warszawa 1980.
3. Rakiewicz M.:Skrzyżowania z sygnalizacją świetlną. In: ibid
4. Tracz M.: The prediction of platoon dispersion based on rectangular distribution of journey time. Traff. Eng. and Control 11/1975.
5. Kaczmarek M, Pietrowski J., Wołyńska B.: Modyfikacje modelu ruchu w metodzie TRANSYT. IV Konf. Naukowa IT PW, Warszawa 1985.

# ZUR GLAUBWÜRDIGKEIT EINES SIMULTIONSMODELLES
# FÜR EISENBAHNFAHRTEN


Gerhard Voß, Hannover

Jerzy Kwaśnikowski, Poznań



**Zusammenfassung**. In dem Bericht werden die wichtigsten Probleme besprochen, die mit der Abbildung realer Zugfahrten in einem digitalen Simulationsmodell RSEL verbunden sind. Für Validierung dieses Modells sind einige Meßfahrten ausgeführt worden. Eine Behandlung dieser Zugfahrten ist auch im Bericht dargestellt. Das Modell RSEL ist zwecks Bearbeitung energiesparsamer Fahrweise für Polnische Staatsbahnen vorgesehen.

**Summary**. The paper deals with the basic problems of real train running simulation with a software model RSEL. Some testing journeys of the trains were made for matching this model. Short discussion of these trials is also presented. The RSEL programme is provided for developement of an energy economical mode of train performance for the Polish Railways.


## 1. Einleitung

Genauigkeit der Wiedergabe von Eigenschaften der Gegenstände oder Vorgänge mit Hilfe ihrer Modelle (physikalische, matematische, Simulationsmodelle) ist ein Prüfstein für die Richtigkeit des Modells. Während des Modellierens kommen wesentliche Schwierigkeiten vor, die davon resultieren, daß im allgemeinen alle Eigenschaften weder vom Original noch vom Modell durch die Abbildung erfaßt werden. Das wichtige Problem wird u.a. von Schneider (2) interessant besprochen. Das Vermeiden wesentlicher Fehler ist in dem Bereich nur noch möglich, wenn es eine genaue Erkenntnis der Eigenschaften des Originals sowie der Möglichkeit sie zu modellieren, gibt. Ein anderes wesentliches Problem bilden Möglichkeiten experimentaler Verifikation der Eigenschaften des Originals sowie ihrer Abbildung in einem Modell. Dies ist wichtig in dem Fall, wo die zu modellierenden Gegenstände oder Vorgänge kompliziert sind und die Verifikationsuntersuchungen zwecks Validierung des Modells schwierig durchzuführen sind (z.B. in Hinsicht auf Kosten und/oder Störungen im normalen Betrieb des Objektes). Die Ergebnisse von solchen Untersuchungen lassen sich manchmal sehr schwer ( mal ist es unmöglich) auf ganze Klasse ähnlicher Objekte verallgemeinern.

## 2. Modellbildung der Zugfahrt

Im vorliegenden Bericht wurden einige Probleme dargelegt, denen   man
beim Bilden eines Simulationsmodelles RSEL vom  Zugbewegungsvorgang
begegnet ist. Das Modell wurde zwecks der Durchführung der  fahrdynamischen Berechnungen und Analyse entwickelt und hat  folgende grundsätzliche Eigenschaften:

- Parametern des Wagenzuges ( Anzahl, Masse, Länge ), Parametern  der
Lokomotive und das Streckenprofil ( Neigungen, Bogen ) sind  in  dem
Modell identisch mit den realen;
- grundsätzliche Variablenverläufe des Bewegungsvorganges die  zu
Eingabedaten gehören - wie die Zugkraftkennlinien F über Geschwindigkeit v, F(v), der Motorstromverlauf I(v), der Laufwiderstand R(v) u.a.
werden in dem Modell möglichst am genauesten abgebildet;
- Variablenbegrenzungen, wie die Begrenzung der Zugkraft F(v) mit der
Adhäsionsgrenze $F(\psi)$, die Motorstrombegrenzung $I_{max}$, die Steuerungsbe-
grenzung $u_{max}$, die Zeit- $t_f$ und Geschwindigkeitsbegrenzung $v_{max}$ (nach
dem Fahrplan) und andere werden in dem Modell strengstens befolgt.

Die grundsätzlichen Ergebnisse von simulierten Zugfahrten - die  Trajektorie der Zuggeschwindigkeit v(s), die Fahrzeit $t_p$, der   Energieverbrauch E hängen haupsächlich vom Verlauf der Funktionsdifferenz
F(v) - R(v)  ab.  Deshalb scheint die Genauigkeit ihrer Abbildung  im
Simulationsmodell ein Problem ersten Ranges zu sein.

## 3. Abbildung der Eingabedaten

Die Kennlinien F(v) und der Steuerwert u(t) sowie  ihre Begrenzungen
sind in (1) besprochen worden. Die Kurvenzüge F(v) und  I(v)   können
in Form einer Tabelle oder der Formeln, die die tabellarischen Verläufe F(v) aproximieren, angegeben werden. Die Tabellen F(v) - für  das
Geschwindigkeitsquant $\Delta v = 1$ km/h - können von den Daten  des  Fahrzeugwerkes direkt kodiert werden. Man kann sie auch von den Fahrmotor-
kennlinien mit Berücksichtigung  der Lokparametern generieren.
Das Generieren der Kennlinien F(v) von Daten der Fahrmotoren   macht
eine Analyse der Zugfahrt mit neuentwickelten bzw. modernisierten Lokomotiven möglich. Die Genauigkeit der Abbildung der F(v)- und  I(v)-
Verläufe kann vermindert werden, wenn die Daten des Fahrzeugwerkes
nicht präzis sind oder wenn die Kennlinien bestimmter Lokomotive  mit
den für angegebene Baureihe deklarierten Daten nicht  identisch sind.
Die bislang größten  Schwierigkeiten sind bei der Abbildung der Laufwiderstände R(v) des Wagenzuges  aufgetreten.  Der Widerstandszug
hat die Form eines Polynoms $R(v) = a+bv+cv^2$, wo a, b, c die Konstante sind, die experimental durch die  Versuchsanstalte der Eisenbahnen

bestimmt worden sind. Die Werte der Koeffizienten a, b, c hängen meistens von der Wagenmasse, Anzahl der Radsätze und ihren Lagerarten usw. ab, sie sind aber im nicht ausreichenden Maße je nach den Wagenbaureihen differenziert. Deswegen sind universale Formeln für bestimmten Wagenzug leider nicht genau. Ähnliche Probleme trifft man bei der Bestimmung der Zugkraftbegrenzung mittels der Haftwerte $F(\psi)$.

## 4. Verifikation

Für die Verifikation des Simulationsmodelles RSEL auf Strecken der PKP sind einige Meßfahrten durchgeführt worden. Die Fahrten der schweren Güterzüge - etwa 3500 t Zugmasse + 4000 kW, 160 t Elektrolok - wurden auf einer 170 km langen differenzierten Strecke aufgenommen. Die aufs Papierband registrierten Fahrergebnisse sind abgelesen und in diskrete Form umgewandelt worden. Wegen der Unvollkommenheit der Registrierapparatur sowie der geringen Skala des Satzes gab es viele Schwierigkeiten mit der Interpretation und Ablesung der Meßgrößen.

Zur Simulationsabbildung wurden 3 Abschnitte je ca. 20 km lang gewählt. Die Abb. 1 stellt die v(s)-Trajektorien der realen Fahrten im Vergleich mit den simulierten dar. Eine "Anpassung" der simulierten Fahrten zu denrealen hat man mittels der Iteration durch die Änderung der Eingabedaten gemacht. Insbesondere wurden die Verteilung der Werte zulässigen Motorstromes $I_d(s)$ und die Auslaufabschnitte (antriebslose Fahrt) vorgegeben (1).

Als Kriterien der Ähnlichkeit der simulierten Fahrt mit der realen hat man angenommen:
- identische bzw. angenäherte Fahrzeit,
- angenäherten Verlauf der Geschwindigkeitstrajektorie v(s),
- nachdem die obengenannten Bedingungen erfüllt worden sind, gibt es eine zufriedenstellende Ähnlichkeit, wenn der Energieverbrauch einen angenäherten Wert hat.

Die Simulation ist für 2 verschiedene Formeln für Laufwiderstände - nach COBiRTK (Zentrale Versuchsanstalt der PKP) zu fahrdynamischen Berechnungen auf PKP empfohlen -

$$R(v) = (0.065 + 0.0015\ v)\ m_w + 1.5\ n_a + 0.0008(n + 2.5)\ v^2\ kN,$$

und für die zur ähnlichen Form transformierte Sachs-Formel

$$R(v) = (0.01 + 0.000025\ v^2)\ m_w\ kN$$

durchgeführt worden, wo $m_w$ t - bezeichnet Masse des Wagenzuges, v km h - Fahrgeschwindigkeit, n - Wagenzahl, $n_a$ - Achsenzahl im Zug. Die Sachs-Formel ist deshalb gewählt worden, weil eine Analyse der

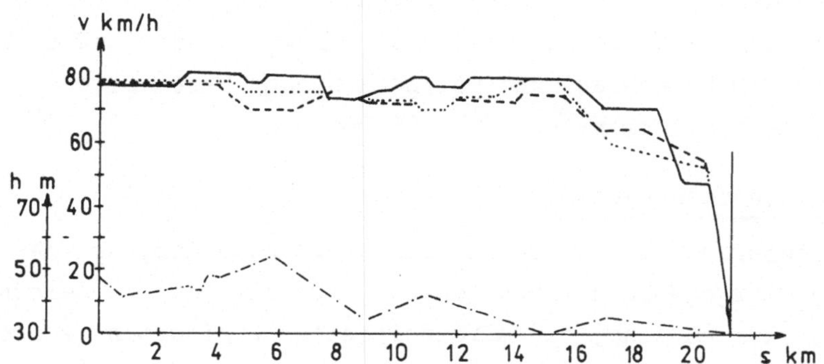


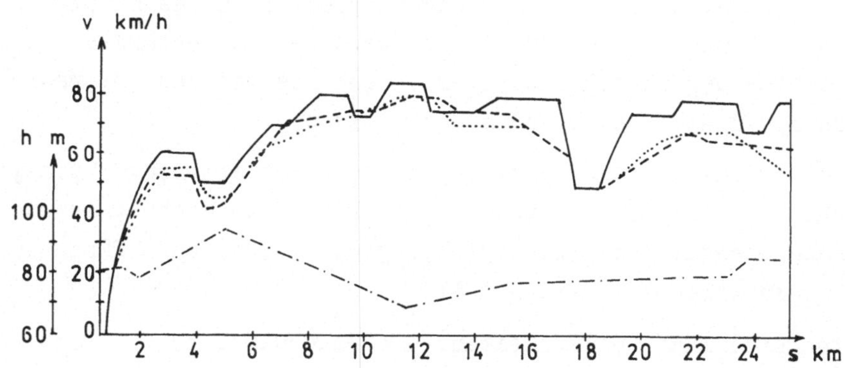


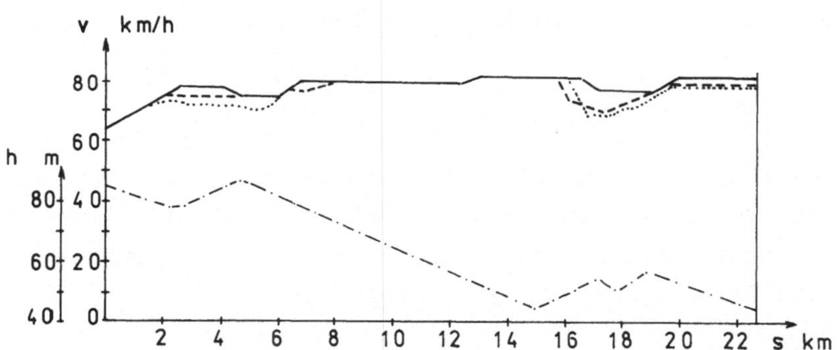


Abb. 1    Geschwindigkeitstrajektorien  v(s)  für

——reale Zugfahrt , ----simulierte nach COBiRTK   und

........nach Sachs.    —·—· Streckenprofil.

Laufwiderstände R(v)  auf einigen Abschnitten registrierten  Zugfahrten , die mittels speziellen Programmes gemacht wurde,  eine  bessere
Annäherung ihrer Ergebnisse und der nach Sachs  berechneten    Werte
bewiesen hat als die nach den  COBiRTK-Formeln.

## 5. Weitere Untersuchungen

Die Vergleichsergebnisse erlauben nicht festzustellen, daß das Modell
RSEL mit den vorgegebenen Eingabedaten,  für die  die    Berechnungen
durchgeführt worden sind, die aufgezeichneten Zugfahrten  ausreichend
glaubwürdig abbildet.
Zur Zeit werden weitere Arbeiten geführt. Sie umfassen Versuche,  die
simulierten Zugfahrten an die realen durch die Verifikation der  Eingabedaten und eventuell der Berechnungsprozeduren des Simulationsmodelles besser anzunähern. Zu diesem Zweck werden fernerhin   weitere
registrierten Zugfahrten analysiert, auch die von den   Personenzügen
und auch mit dieselelektrischen Lokomotiven.

Gleichzeitig  werden  Vorbereitungen  zur  Realisierung   praktischer
( zunächst simulierter ) Zugfahrt  gemacht , wo  schwerwiegend   die
Einführung energiesparsamer Zugführung mit gewählten   Eisenbahnzügen
der PKP berücksichtigt werden soll.

Es bieten sich auch Möglichkeiten, die Glaubwürdigkeit dieses Modelles
durch Berechnungen  und Verifikation  der Eingabedaten    sowie   der
Ergebnisse für Deutsche Bundesbahn nachzuprüfen.  Ende  1984 ist eine
Vortestung des RSEL-Programmes im Institut für Schienenfahrzeuge  der
Universität Hannover durchgeführt worden,  für den  kommenden  Herbst
ist die Fortsetzung der Arbeiten vorgesehen.


## Literatur

(1)  J. Kwaśnikowski - Simulation energiesparender Zugfahrt. Informa-
        tik Berichte Nr.85 (ASIM84-Berichte),1984,Springer,559-563
(2)  B. Schneider - Allgemeine Modelltheorie und Validierung. Informa-
        tik Berichte Nr.85, 1984, Springer, 333-338

# Simulation als Hilfe zur optimalen Prozessfindung

H.-D. Engelmann, H.-H. Erdmann, Dortmund

Zusammenfassung: Es wird eine sicherheitstechnische Betrachtung, wie sie im Rahmen einer Prozeßsynthese erforderlich ist, durchgeführt. Als Beispiel wird die thermische Polymerisation von Styrol ausgewählt. Die Ergebnisse werden sowohl zum Aufbau einer Modelldatenbank wie einer sicherheitstechnischen Wissensbasis im Rahmen eines Expertensystems zur Prozeßsynthese verwendet.

Von der schöpferischen Idee bis zu ihrer industriellen Verwirklichung durch die Inbetriebnahme einer Produktionsanlage führt ein langer oft gewundener Weg, der durch eine Vielzahl von unterschiedlichen Problemstellungen und daraus resultierenden Tätigkeiten gekennzeichnet ist. Die dadurch vermehrte Inanspruchnahme der Planungskapazität auf der einen Seite und die wachsende Verfügbarkeit von Computer-Software auf der anderen Seite haben bereits zur fortschreitenden Automatisierung einzelner Aktivitäten geführt. Die Initiierung und Verknüpfung dieser Aktivitäten ist aber zur Zeit noch allein der Intuition von Ingenieuren und Chemikern überlassen. Der Einzug des Systemdenkens in die chemische Technik hat zwar den Blick dafür geschärft, daß meist eine Vielzahl von Lösungsmöglichkeiten für dasselbe Problem existiert; man muß aber auch erkennen, daß wegen der großen Zahl von beachtenswerten Alternativen eine systematische Bearbeitung und Selektion nur mit umfassender Rechnerunterstützung denkbar ist. So ist es konsequent, wenn sich die weitere Software-Entwicklung nunmehr der Festlegung von geeigneten Verfahrenskonzeptionen, d.h. der Prozeß-Synthese, zuwendet /2/.

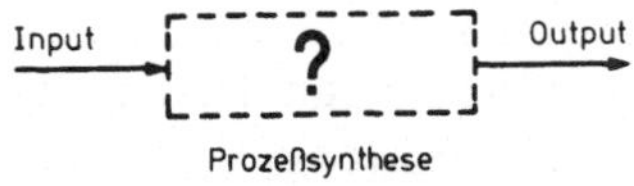



Abb. 1 : Schema der Prozeß-Synthese

Die einzelnen Arbeitsschritte, die bei der Prozeßsynthese zu absolvieren sind, lassen sich in folgende drei Hauptabschnitte einteilen:
1) Die Erzeugung der Prozeßstruktur und der daraus abgeleiteten Grundfließbilder.

In diesem Entwicklungsstadium werden aber nur Entscheidungen über die grundsätzliche Verknüpfung von Reaktionen und Stofftrennungen oder Seperationen getroffen, ohne auf Einzelheiten der Reaktionsführung oder des anzuwendenden Trennprinzips einzugehen. Deshalb schließt sich daraus zunächst

2) die detaillierte Bearbeitung der Prozeßstufen mit Reaktion an, auf deren Grundlage dann

3) die Separationen bearbeitet werden, und zwar sowohl hinsichtlich des anzuwendenden Trennprinzips, wie auch der daraus resultierenden Verschaltung.

Die zwischen den Punkten 2) und 3) bestehenden Wechselwirkungen müssen bei der Synthese beachtet werden        Eine solche Vorgehensweise wird nur im Rahmen eines Expertensystems zu verwirklichen sein, von dem Abb. 2 die grundsätzliche Struktur zeigt /4/.

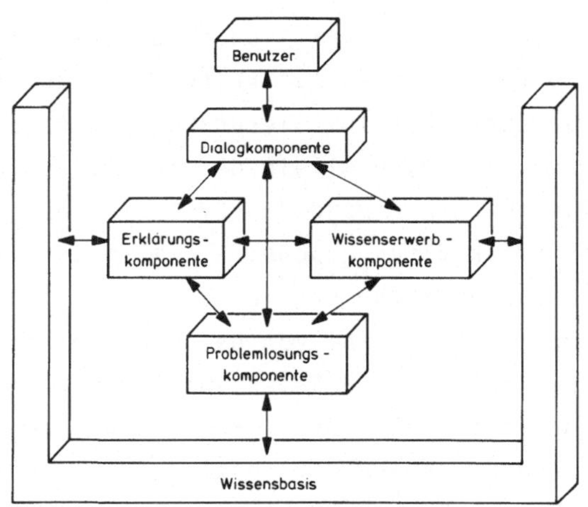


Abb. 2 : Aufbau von Expertensystemen

Neben dem notwendigen methodischen Rüstzeug ist eine interaktive Zusammenarbeit mit umfangreichen und auch je nach Problemstellung austauschbaren Datenbanken als Wissensbasis notwendig, wobei sowohl Methoden wie Wissensinformationen im Dialog mit dem Expertensystem erweitert und modifiziert werden können.

Gerade im Bereich sicherheitstechnischer Fragen, wo eine analytische Lösung nur sehr selten gelingt, ist die abrufbare und mit Erklärungen (Erklärungskomponente) versehene Dokumentatiom von Erfahrungen und Lösungsvorschlägen, die häufig auch noch auf Umwegen wirksam werden, besonders wichtig. Als ein Beispiel für eine Methode des Wissenserwerbes dient die thermische Substanzpolymerisation von Styrol.

Mit zunehmender Größe der Reaktoren wird es schwieriger, die Reaktionswärme abzuführen. Steigt aufgrund von Störungen in der Wärmeabfuhr die Temperatur im Reaktor an, wird die Reaktion beschleunigt. Im ungünstigsten Fall wird die Reaktion unkontrollierbar schnell, so daß es zum Durchgehen des Reaktors kommt. Dieses gleichzeitige Aufschaukeln von Temperatur und Umsatz auf kritische Maximalwerte kann zur thermischen Zersetzung der Edukte und Produkte, bzw. zum Zusetzen des Reaktors führen. Hinzu kommt, daß bei geschlossenen Systemen mit der Temperaturerhöhung meist auch der Druck ansteigt, was gefährlich werden kann. Geeignete Gegenmaßnahmen müssen vorbereitet und im Bedarfsfall eingeleitet werden. Es stellt sich die Frage, ob die Erkennung solcher überkritischen Betriebszustände und die Überprüfung möglicher Gegenmaßnahmen auf ihre Wirksamkeit hin bereits im Rahmen der Prozeßsynthese durchgeführt werden muß, oder ob es ausreichend ist, nach Abschluß der Synthese dieses Problem getrennt zu untersuchen.

Neben der Möglichkeit des Einsatzes betriebsfremder Mittel - wie Stopper und kalte Flüssigkeiten bzw. Gase, die eingedüst werden - besteht die Möglichkeit des Einsatzes    betriebsinterner Mittel, wie:

1. Die vorhandene indirekte Kühlung wird verstärkt. Einschränkend wirken die begrenzte Kühlfläche und die nicht beliebig herabsetzbare Temperatur des Kühlmediums.
2. Im Vergleich zum stationären Zustand wird die Monemerzufuhr erhöht. Der apparative Aufwand ist gering (Puffer - bzw. Vorratsbehälter).

Zur Überprüfung der Möglichkeiten beim Einsatz betriebsinterner Mittel wird der Prozeß im Modell abgebildet. Es wird ein auf chemisch/physikalischen Gesetzmäßigkeiten basierendes mathematisches Modell /3/ erstellt. Nach /1/ gilt bei Betrachtung eines kontinuierlich betriebenen idealen Rührkessels, in dem die Polymerisation nach einer Reaktion erster Ordnung abläuft:

Wärmebilanz:

$$dT/dt = 1/C_p * (n\, \Delta H\, b(1-x) - q(T-T_a) - 1/\tau \int_{T_e}^{T} C_p\, dT)$$

Stoffbilanz:

$$dx/dt = b(1-x) - x/\tau$$

kinetischer Ansatz:

$$b = b_0 \exp(-E/RT)$$

Wärmekapazität:

$$C_p = C_{po} + a\,T$$

mittlere Verweilzeit:

$$\tau = V/\dot{v}$$

| | | |
|---|---|---|
| $V$ = Reaktionsvol. | $a,b,C_0$ = Konstante | $T$ = Temperatur |
| $R$ = Gaskonstante | $t$ = Zeit | $\dot{v}$ = Volumenstrom |
| $C_p$ = Wärmekapazität | $q$ = spez. Wärmeabfuhr | $n$ = Monomerkonz. |
| $T_a$ = Kühltemperatur | $H$ = Reaktionsenthal. | $T_e$ = Eintrittstemp. |
| $b$ = Reaktionsgeschw. | $E$ = Aktivierungsenergie | $x$ = Umsatz |

Wegen der gekoppelten nichtlinearen Differentialgleichung und der
schnellen Variationsmöglichkeit der Parameter, verbunden mit der unmittelbar gekoppelten Darstellung, wird das mathematische Modell auf ein
Analogsystem übertragen.

Bei Störungen der Wärmeabfuhr - durch Ausfall der Monomerenzufuhr und /
oder durch Minderung bzw. Ausfall der Kühlung geht der Reaktor durch.
Das "Zurückholen" bzw. "Abfangen" durch Erhöhung der spezifischen
Wärmeabfuhr wurde von Wittmer /1/ ausführlich untersucht.

Ergänzt werden diese Untersuchungen durch die Simulation des Reaktor-
verhaltens bei Ausfall der Kühlung für einige Minuten (Abb. 3).

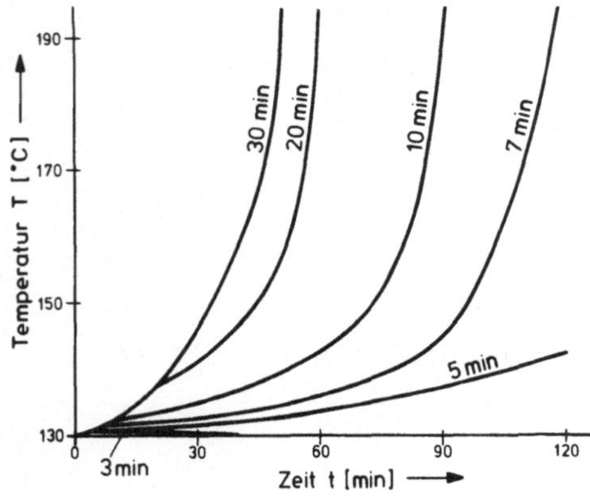


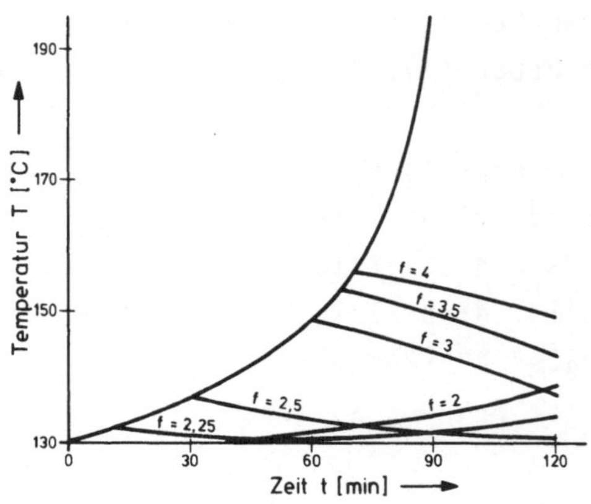


Abb. 3 : Temperatur/Zeit - Kurven
bei Ausfall der Kühlung
für x min

Abb. 4 : Abfangen des Reaktors durch
erhöhte Monumerzufuhr in Abhängigkeit von der Wartezeit

Es kann maximal ein Kühlungsausfall von drei Minuten toleriert werden.
Andernfalls geht der Reaktor auch nach Wiedereinsetzen der Kühlung
durch. Eine wirksame Gegenmaßnahme ist - wie bereits erwähnt - die
Möglichkeit, die Monomerzufuhr zu erhöhen. Rechnerisch ergibt sich,
daß bei völligem Kühlmittelausfall die Monomerzufuhr verdoppelt werden
muß, um die fehlende Wärmeabfuhr zu kompensieren. Alle weiteren Überlegungen basieren auf der Tatsache des totalen Ausfalls des Kühlmittels,
so daß die Monomerzufuhr (f) mindestens verdoppelt wird (f > = 2). Abb. 4
zeigt ein Ergebnis der Simulation. Auf ihr ist abzulesen, wie groß die
Monomerzufuhr mindestens sein muß, damit der Reaktor "abgefangen" werden kann. Parameter ist die Zeitdauer zwischen Kühlmittelausfall (t=0)
und Einschaltung der erhöhten Monomerzufuhr. Bei einer Wartezeit von
30 min bis zur erhöhten Monomerzufuhr muß diese mindestens f = 2,5 betragen. Nach etwa 90 min wird die Ausgangstemperatur von ca. 130° C
erreicht.

Die vermehrte Monomerzufuhr ist eine wirksame Möglichkeit, ein Durchgehen des Reaktors für große Zeitspannen, bis die Kühlung wieder zur
Verfügung steht, zu verhindern. Eine vermehrte Monomerzufuhr ist meistens einfach konstruktiv zu verwirklichen. Sie bietet sich besonders
als Möglichkeit an, andere Maßnahmen zu unterstützen bzw. deren Wirksamkeit zu beschleunigen.

Es zeigt sich, daß die sicherheitstechnischen Betrachtungen von der
eigentlichen Prozeßsynthese losgelöst betrachtet werden können. Neben
der Abspeicherung des auf chemisch/physikalischen Gesetzmäßigkeiten
beruhenden Modelles in der Modelldatenbank, wo zusammen mit anderen
bereits vorhandenen Modellen für künftige derartige Betrachtungen verfügbar ist, dient das Ergebnis dieser Arbeit zur Erweiterung der Wissensbasis und fließt in die Datenbank für Sicherheitstechnik ein.

Literatur:
/1/ P. Wittmer, T. Ankel, H. Romeis: Zum dynamischen Verhalten
    von Polymerisationsreaktionen, CIT 37, Jahrg. 1965 Nr. 4
/2/ Erdmann, H.H., Kussi, J., Simmrock, K.H.: Possibilities and
    Problems of Process Design, Ger.Chem.Eng. 8 (1985) 65 - 74
/3/ Engelmann, H.D./Erdmann, H.H.: Vergleich der verschiedenen
    Methoden der Modellbildung, Inf.-Fachb. 85, Springer 1984
/4/ Raufels, P.: Expertensysteme, Inf.-Fachb. 59, Springer 1982

# DIGITALE SIMULATION DER DYNAMIK GROSSER KREUZSTROMWÄRMEÜBERTRAGER

W. Wiening und H. Rake, Aachen

Zusammenfassung. In der Heizungs-, Lüftungs- und Klimatechnik werden
als aktive Bauelemente Kreuzstromwärmeübertrager eingesetzt. Das dynamische Übertragungsverhalten dieser Systeme wird durch instationäre
Wärmeübertragungsvorgänge bestimmt, deren mathematische Beschreibung zu
drei partiellen Differentialgleichungen für ein kleines Wärmübertra-
gersegment führen. Durch Linearisierung und Transformation in einen
Bildbereich können aus dem partiellen Differentialgleichungssystem
transzendente Übertragungsfunktionen abgeleitet werden, die das Gesamtübertragungsverhalten des Wärmeübertragers beschreiben. Eine Rücktransformation dieser Übertragungsfunktionen in den Zeitbereich ist kaum
möglich, so daß zur digitalen Simulation ein numerisches Integrationsverfahren für die Lösung des partiellen Differentialgleichungssystems
eingesetzt werden muß.

Summary. In heating-, ventilating- and air conditioning systems cross-
flow heat exchangers are used as active components. The dynamic response of these systems is influenced by instationary heat transfer
processes the mathematical analyses of which lead to three partial
differential equations for one heat exchanger element. By linearization
and transformation into a Laplace domain transcendent transfer functions can be deduced from the partial differential equation system
which render the toal dynamic behaviour. An inverse transformation of
these transfer functions into the time domain is almost impossible.
Consequently, a numeric integrating procedure must be used for the
digital simulation of the transient response.

## 1. Einführung

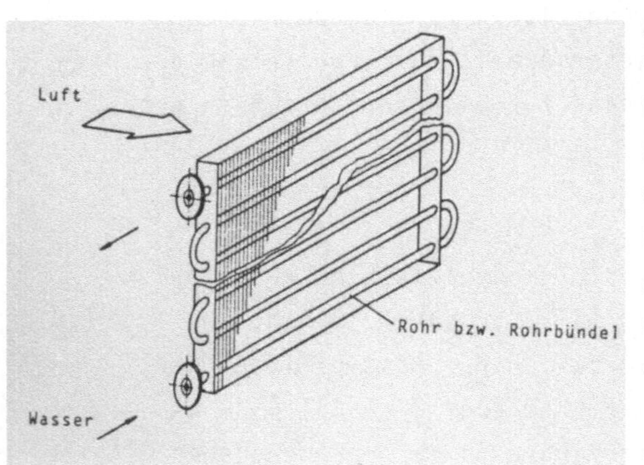


Kreuzstromwärmeübertrager, deren
Aufbau in Bild 1 dargestellt
ist, werden in der Heizungs-,
Lüftungs- und Klimatechnik zum
Heizen und Kühlen von Luft eingesetzt. Aufgrund nichtlinearer
Effekte bei der Wärmeübertragung
zwischen Luft und Wasser ist das
dynamische Übertragungsverhalten
dieser Systeme arbeitspunktab-
hängig. Zur Planung und zum Entwurf von Steuerungs- und Rege-
lungseinrichtungen sind deshalb

mathematische Modelle entwickelt worden, die eine genügend genaue Abschätzung der dynamischen Eigenschaften aus konstruktiven Daten ermöglichen. Diese mathematischen Modelle sind jedoch für eine digitale Simulation des dynamischen Übertragungsverhaltens im Zeitbereich nicht geeignet. Aus diesem Grund wurde eine mathematische Beschreibung entwickelt, mit deren Hilfe sowohl das lineare als auch das nichtlineare Übertragungsverhalten von Kreuzstromwärmeübertragern digital simuliert werden kann.

## 2. Grundlage der mathematischen Modellbildung

Die Vorgänge in Wärmeübertragern sind im allgemeinen als kontinuierliche, zeitvariante Prozesse mit örtlich verteilten Parametern zu beschreiben /I1/. Demzufolge sind zur Entwicklung einer mathematischen Beschreibung für das dynamische Übertragungsverhalten die Wärmebilanzen an einem infinitesimal kleinen Elementarvolumen des Wärmeübertragers aufzustellen, das aus Rohrwand, Wasser und Luft besteht (Bild 2).

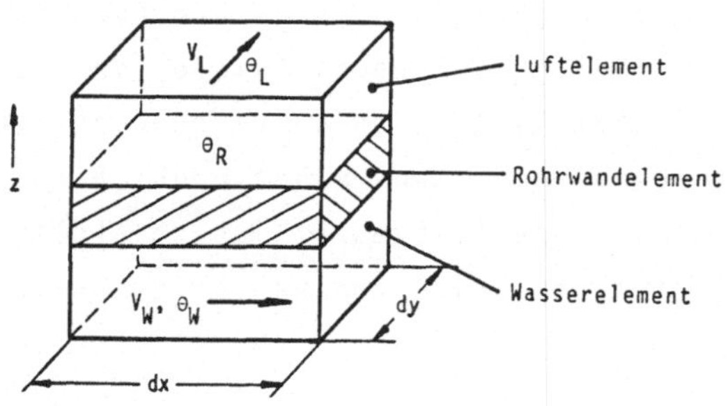


Bild 2: Bezugselement zur Wärmebilanz

Bei der Aufstellung der Wärmebilanzgleichungen für dieses Elementarvolumen wird vorausgesetzt, daß die Rohrwand Wärme an die Luft in z-Richtung mit sehr kleinem Wärmewiderstand leitet, der Wärmestrom durch Wärmeleitung in x- und y-Richtung vernachlässigbar klein ist und die Stoffwerte näherungsweise druck- und temperaturunabhängig sind /B1,S1/. Mit diesen Voraussetzungen liefert die Wärmebilanz folgendes partielles Differentialgleichungssystem:

$$\frac{d\Theta_W}{dt} = -V_W \frac{d\Theta_W}{dx} + \frac{\alpha_W A_W}{M_W C_{PW}} (\Theta_R - \Theta_W) \tag{2.1}$$

$$\frac{d\Theta_R}{dt} = \frac{\alpha_W A_W}{M_R C_{PR}} (\Theta_W - \Theta_R) + \frac{\alpha_L A_L}{M_R C_{PR}} (\Theta_L - \Theta_R) \tag{2.2}$$

$$\frac{d\Theta_L}{dt} = -V_L \frac{d\Theta_L}{dy} + \frac{\alpha_L A_L}{M_L C_{PL}} (\Theta_L - Q_R) \tag{2.3}$$

für das Wasser-, Rohr- und Luftelement. $\Theta_W$, $\Theta_R$ und $\Theta_L$ sind die ort-
und zeitabhängigen Temperaturen der einzelnen Elemente. Dieses Differentialgleichungssystem zeigt, daß das Temperaturübertragungsverhalten
eines Kreuzstromwärmeübertragers linear ist, während bei Änderung der
Strömungsgeschwindigkeiten von Luft $(V_L)$ und Wasser $(V_W)$ das Produkt
der Geschwindigkeiten mit den Luft-, Rohr- und Wassertemperaturen zu
berücksichtigen ist. Demzufolge ist das Übertragungsverhalten von
Kreuzstromwärmeübertragern bezüglich der Änderung von Massenströmen
nicht linear.

3. Mathematisches Modell für die Dynamik von Kreuzstromwärmeübertragern

Zur Entwicklung des mathematischen Modells, mit dessen Hilfe die Dynamik von Wärmeübertragern simuliert werden kann, ist die partielle Ableitung der Wassertemperatur nach der Ortskoordinate x (vgl. Gl. 2.1)
durch einen Differenzenquotienten ersetzt worden. Ferner ist die zeitliche Ableitung der Lufttemperatur (vgl. Gl. 2.3) vernachlässigt und
die daraus resultierende einfache Differentialgleichung der Luft bezüglich der Ortskoordinate y gelöst worden. Das Ergebnis dieser Vereinfachungen ist ein System von Differentialgleichungen 1. Ordnung zur Beschreibung des dynamischen Übertragungsverhaltens eines endlichen
Wärmeübertragersegmentes. Die Koeffizienten dieses Differentialgleichungssystems sind variabel bezüglich der Luft- und Wassergeschwindig-
keiten.

Durch Verschalten der Differentialgleichungen für ein endliches Wärme-
übertragungselement entsprechend der Stromführung für Luft und Wasser
ergibt sich dann das Differentialgleichungssystem 1. Ordnung für das
Gesamtübertragungsverhalten des Wärmeübertragers.

Numerische Untersuchungen im Frequenzbereich haben jedoch gezeigt, daß
dieses Modell die Dynamik von Wärmeübertragern nur ungenau beschreibt.
Dies gilt insbesondere für große Wärmeübertrager, deren Dynamik durch
eine große Transportzeit bestimmt wird. Eine Verbesserung der mathematischen Beschreibung kann durch die Aufteilung des Wärmeübertragungs-
segmentes bezüglich der x-Richtung in ein adiabates und ein nicht-adia-
bates Teilsegment erzielt werden. Die Wärmebilanz für das nicht-adiaba-
te Segment führt wiederum zum Differentialgleichungssystem Gl.(2.1-2.3).
Im Gegensatz dazu sind bei dem adiabaten Teilsegment alle Wärmeübertragungsvorgänge zu vernachlässigen $(\alpha_L = 0 \; \alpha_W = 0)$. Daraus folgt eine wei-

tere Differentialgleichung für das Wasserelement, die allein die Transportvorgänge im adiabaten Teilsegment beschreibt. Mit diesem neuen und verbesserten Modell kann durch numerische Untersuchungen im Frequenzbereich gezeigt werden, daß eine Aufteilung des Wärmeübertragers in 6 Segmente ausreicht, um die Dynamik genügend genau zu beschreiben. Die Transportzeit des Wassers betrug bei dem untersuchten Wärmeübertrager ca. 80 s. In Bild 3 ist ein Ergebnis dieser Untersuchung dargestellt.

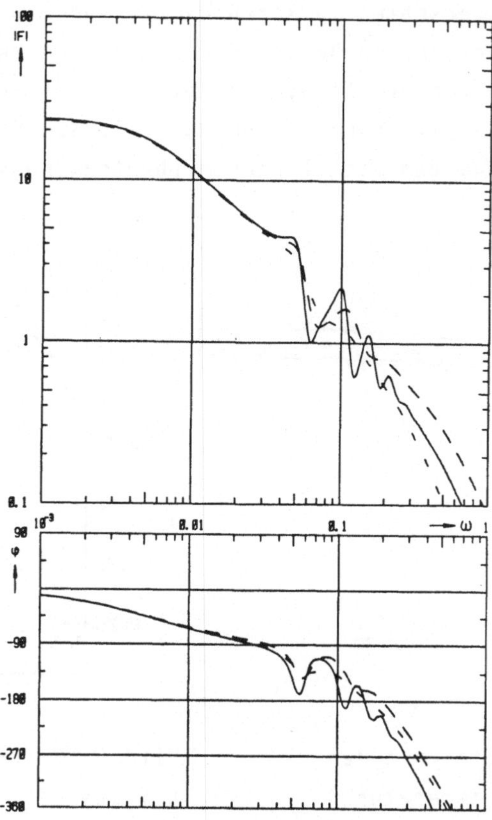


Bild 3: Vergleich des Näherungsmodells mit einem exakten Modell aus
/S1/

4. Ergebnis der digitalen Simulation

Die Koeffizienten des Differentialgleichungssystems sind bezüglich der Variation der Luft- und Wassermassenströme variabel. Aus diesem Grund wurde zur digitalen Simulation des nichtlinearen Übertragungsverhaltens die numerische Integration der Differenialgleichungen mit einem Verfahren nach Runge-Kutta mit automatischer Schrittweitensteuerung eingesetzt. Im Gegensatz dazu konnte das lineare Übertragungsverhalten mit Hilfe der linearen zeitdiskreten Zustandsraumbeschreibung simuliert werden. Dazu wurde das Differentialgleichungssystem bezüglich der Luft-

und Wassermassenströme linearisiert und das Gesamtsystem in eine lineare Zustandsdifferentialgleichung umgeformt.

Die in Bild 4 und Bild 5 dargestellten Sprungantworten der Luftaustrittstemperatur bei sprungförmiger Änderung des Luftmassenstromes (Bild 4) sowie sprungförmiger Änderung des Wassermassenstromes (Bild 5) verdeutlichen den Unterschied zwischen dem linearen und dem nichtlinearen Übertragungsverhalten. In beiden Fällen ist der Endwert der Sprungantwort verschieden. Darüber hinaus ergibt sich bei Änderung des Wassermassenstromes eine Differenz in der Ausgleichszeitkonstanten zwischen dem linearen und dem nichtlinearen Übertragungsverhalten.

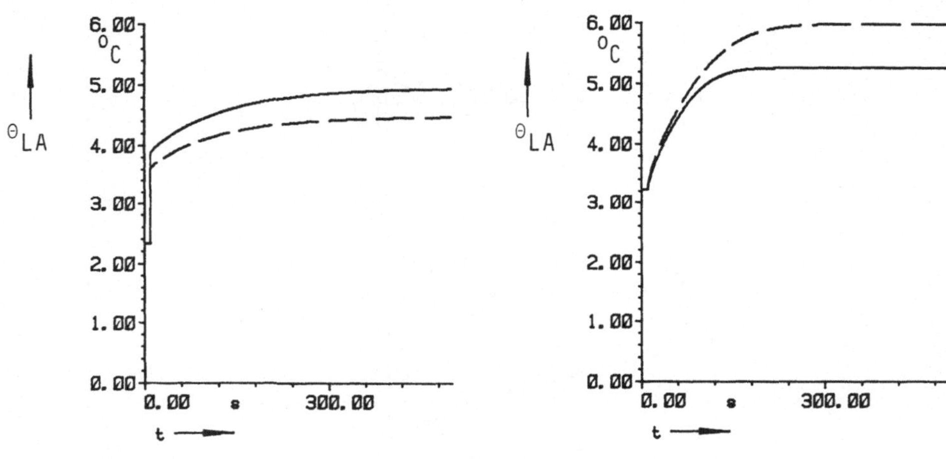

Bild 4: Sprungantwort der
Luftaustrittstemperatur
nicht linear (--); linear (-)

Bild 5: Sprungantwort der
Luftaustrittstemperatur
nicht linear (--); linear (-)


/B1/ Bender, E.: Das dynamische Verhalten von Kreuzstromwärmeaustauschern für Massenstromvariation
Regelungstechnik, 20 (1972) S. 13-20

/I1/ Isermann, R.: Theoretische Analyse der Dynamik industrieller Prozesse (Identifikation II), BI, Mannheim, 1971

/S1/ Schmachtenberg, H.: Zum dynamischen Verhalten großer Kreuzstromwärmeübertrager
Dissertation, TH Aachen 1971

Unterstützung der Prozeßführung im
nuklear-chemischen Bereich durch
den Einsatz der Simulationstechnik


Hubert B. Keller, Karlsruhe


Zusammenfassung: Eine Wiederaufarbeitunganlage entspricht einer kom-
---------------- plexen chemischen Fabrik. Durch die besondere Prozeßproblematik kann mit Hilfe des Einsatzes der Simulationstechnik in
Verbindung mit Prozeßleitsystemen eine optimale Prozeßführung realisiert werden. Der Bericht beschreibt diese Prozeßproblematik und die
Lösungsmöglichkeiten anhand der Simulationstechnik.

Summary: A nuclear fuel reprocessing plant is equal to a complex
-------- chemical factory. Because of the special problems of that
process only the use of simulation techniques in connection with
automation systems guarantees an optimal process guidance. This report
describes these problems and discusses the possible solutions by use of
simulation techniques.


## I. Einleitung

Allgemein evolvieren technische Prozesse zu immer komplexeren Gebilden.
Die zugrundeliegenden natürlich komplexen physikalischen oder chemisch-
physikalischen Wirkungsgefüge müssen infolge erhöhten wirtschaftlichen
Anforderungen genauer berücksichtigt werden, und die Prozeßdynamik wird
dabei aufgrund häufiger Rückführungen noch schlechter durchschaubar.

Diese Problematik liegt auch bei der Wiederaufarbeitung von abge-
brannten Kernbrennstoffen vor, die mit dem bekannten PUREX-Verfahren
(Plutonium-Uran-Extraktion) erfolgt. Mit den dem PUREX-Verfahren angeschlossenen Hilfsprozessen entspricht eine Wiederaufarbeitungsanlage
im Prinzip einer komplexen chemischen Fabrik. Durch die kerntechni-
schen Randbedingungen (Radioaktivität) einerseits und durch die Neben-
wirkungen von beteiligten Stoffen (Spaltprodukte, Prozeßchemikalien)
sind bestimmte Bereiche des Verfahrens chemisch und verfahrenstechnisch
kompliziert (1,5). Innerhalb des Leistungsumfanges der am Markt vorhandenen Prozeßleitsystemen kann die Einhaltung optimaler Betriebsdaten
und damit die Wirtschaftlichkeit dieser technischen Anlage nicht garantiert werden (4). Erst der Einsatz der Simulationstechnik im Bereich
der Prozeßführung ermöglicht in Verbindung mit Prozeßleitsystemen eine
optimale Prozeßführung.


## II. Problematik und Möglichkeiten

### II.1 Forderungen für die Prozeßführung

Die Wirtschaftlichkeit einer Wiederaufarbeitung setzt eine hohe Prozeß-
verfügbarkeit, eine hohe Qualität der Endprodukte und natürlich die
Berücksichtigung von sicherheitstechnischen Belangen voraus. Nur eine
Optimierung der Prozeßführung kann diesen Forderungen gerecht werden.

Voraussetzung hierzu ist aber die Erfüllung der folgenden Bedingungen:

a) die Informationen über den gesamten für die Prozeßführung relevanten
   Prozeßzustand und dessen Dynamik müssen verfügbar sein,

b) Entscheidungsprozesse der Bediener sind durch die Darstellung der
   kausalen Prozeßzusammenhänge (Transparenz von Folgeauswirkungen bei
   Zustandswertabweichungen) informationsmäßig abzusichern und die
   Ausführung von Prozeßeingriffen durch eine umfassende visuelle
   Aufbereitung und Darstellung der Prozeßdaten zu beschleunigen,

c) basierend auf einer Trendanalyse (Gradient) der momentanen Prozeß-
   dynamik ist das Verlassen des zulässigen Betriebsbereiches möglichst
   frühzeitig erkennbar zu machen (Störungsvoraussage), aufgetretene
   Störungen müssen diagnostisch analysiert werden, um Fehlerort und
   -Art zu erkennen und um sofortige Reparaturmaßnahmen mit minimalem
   Aufwand durchführen zu können,

d) das zukünftige Prozeßverhalten und die Auswirkungen von eventuellen
   Eingriffen in das Prozeßgeschehen sollten prognostizierbar sein,
   dies ermöglicht eine umfassende Unterstützung der Prozeßführung
   (Auswahl notwendiger Prozeßeingriffe),

e) den Operateuren ist durch intensive Schulung ein tieferes
   Verständnis (Transparenz) der inneren kausalen Prozeßzusammenhänge
   zu vermitteln.


II.2 Erläuterungen

Zu a)
Eine Optimierung der Prozeßführung setzt die Verfügbarkeit aller pro-
zeßrelevanten Informationen voraus. Im nuklear-chemischen Einsatz-
bereich bestehen jedoch meßtechnische Probleme. Teilweise gibt es
keine Möglichkeiten zur Messung der notwendigen Größen, die prinzipiell
verwendbaren Meßgeräte können aufgrund der extremen Bedingungen nicht
eingesetzt werden (Wartungsfreiheit); wo Meßgeräte zur Verfügung stehen,
sind die entsprechenden Meßpunkte aus sicherheitstechnischen oder
apparativen Gründen nicht zugänglich oder Meßwerte aus dem Analysen-
labor sind um Stunden verzögert verfügbar. Außerdem sollte der
finanzielle Aspekt durch die Genehmigungspflicht einsetzbarer Meßgeräte
nicht unterschätzt werden.
Deshalb sind nicht alle zur Prozeßführung notwendigen Prozeßdaten verfügbar. Der Operateur hat also keine direkte bzw. nur ungenügende
Kenntnis über wesentliche Prozeßbereiche. Die Simulation (digitale)
erlaubt es, die Prozeßzustände und ihre Dynamik nachzubilden. Die zur
Prozeßführung notwendigen Daten können also durch die Simulation erzeugt werden. Dies setzt aber den Einsatz von qualitativ hochwertigen
Modellen voraus, welche den Prozeß exakt beschreiben und Zustandsin-
konsistenzen zwischen Prozeß und Modell ausschließen.

Das chemisch-physikalische Wirkungsgefüge von Teilbereichen des PUREX-
Prozesses ist aufgrund der Abfallprodukte und der Abbauprodukte durch
die strahlenchemische Reaktionen nicht exakt bekannt und eindeutig
beschreibbar. Das mathematische Modell hat möglicherweise qualitative
Fehler (Strukturfehler). Erschwerend kommt hinzu, daß von der gesamten
Anzahl der Modellparameter oft nur wenige exakt berechenbar sind. Im
Prozeß unterliegen einige Parameter Schwankungen infolge nicht oder nur
teilweise modellierbarer Störungen (z. B. Verschmutzungserscheinungen).
Um Konsistenz zwischen Prozeß- und Modellzustand zu erreichen, müssen

deshalb die Werte der meßbaren (vor allem prozeßbestimmenden) Prozeßgrößen in die Simulation einfließen.  Anhand dieser Meßwerte ist das
Modell (Struktur und Parameter) an den aktuellen Prozeßzustand fortlaufend anzupassen.


Bild 1

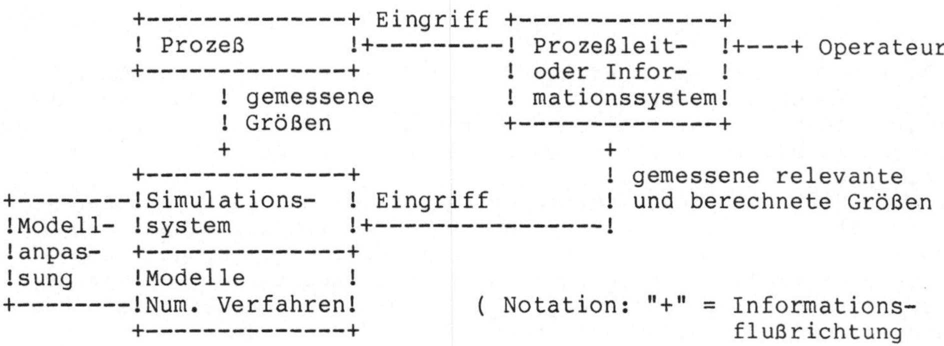

```
        +---------------+ Eingriff +---------------+
        ! Prozeß        !+---------! Prozeßleit-   !+---+ Operateur
        +---------------+          ! oder Infor-   !
                ! gemessene        ! mationssystem!
                ! Größen           +---------------+
                +                          +
        +---------------+                  ! gemessene relevante
+--------!Simulations-   ! Eingriff         ! und berechnete Größen
!Modell- !system         !+----------------!
!anpas-  +---------------+
!sung    !Modelle        !
+--------!Num. Verfahren!          ( Notation: "+" = Informations-
        +---------------+                          flußrichtung
```


Eine Anpassung der Modellstruktur und -Parameter erfordert aber umfangreiche a priori Untersuchungen während der Modellierungsphase zum Festlegen der zu messenden Prozeßgrößen, der anzupassenden Parameter usw.,
sowie Redundanz in den Meßgrößen und den Meßwerten (Meßfehlerkorrek-
tur).  Durch On-Line -Analysen sind die Modellansätze fortlaufend zu
verifizieren.


Zu b)
Das komplexe Wirkungsgefüge des gesamten Prozesses muß dem Bediener
visuell und mit Hilfe einer prozeßkonsistenten Datenbasis transparent
gemacht werden, damit die Entscheidungsprozesse bzgl.  Prozeßeingriffe
beschleunigt und informationsmäßig abgesichert werden.  Die bestehenden
Prozeßleit- bzw.  Prozeßinformationssysteme müssen daher bezüglich
Erfassung, Aufbereitung und Darstellung der Prozeßdaten unter Berücksichtigung des menschlichen Abstraktionsvorganges weiter entwickelt
werden.  Diese Weiterentwicklung erfordert aber vom Datenaufkommen
realitätsnahe Bedingungen.


Bild 2

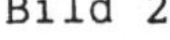
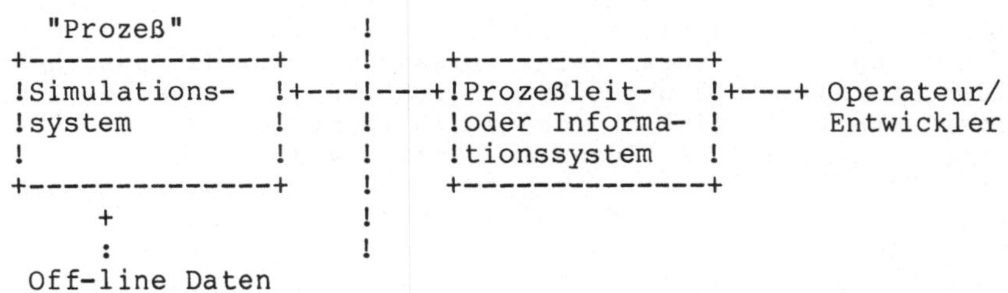

```
            "Prozeß"                !
        +---------------+     !     +---------------+
        !Simulations-   !+---!---+!Prozeßleit-    !+---+ Operateur/
        !system         !   !   !oder Informa-  !      Entwickler
        !               !   !   !tionssystem    !
        +---------------+   !     +---------------+
                +           !
                :           !
        Off-line Daten
```


Eine Kopplung an den Prozeß, um die Semantik von abgeleiteten Reaktionen seitens des Prozeßleitsystems (--> on-line closed-loop expert
systems) oder die durch die Visualisierung der primären und der davon
abgeleiteten Prozeßdaten beim Bediener erzeugten Assoziationen (sie

sind Grundlage für die Auswahl von Prozeßeingriffen) überprüfen zu
können, ist aus sicherheitstechnischen Gründen nur äußerst schlecht
möglich.  Der reale Prozeß darf in keiner Weise beeinflußt werden.
Durch die Simulation des Prozesses können die erforderlichen Daten
erzeugt werden.  Der Datenaustausch (Übergabe von erzeugten Daten,
Übernahme von Eingriffen in den "Prozeß") erfolgt unter prozeßgleichen
zeitlichen Bedingungen.


Zu c)
Durch Analyse der aktuellen Prozeßdaten und ihrer zugehörigen Gradienten ist frühzeitig erkennbar, ob der Prozeß in kritische Betriebs-
oder Zustandsbereiche hineinläuft.  Voraussetzung für diese Analyse ist
allerdings die exakte Kenntnis der Prozeßgrößen in den entsprechenden
Zeitabständen.
Ist der Eintritt von einer Störung erkennbar, so muß eine Prozeßana-
lyse durchgeführt werden, um Fehlerart und -Ort festzustellen.  Abweichungen der Prozeßgrößen aufgrund von Störungsverschleppungen müssen
zurückverfolgt werden.  Prozeßzustände sind grundsätzlich mit Status-
signalen der Stellglieder zu vergleichen, bei Abweichungen müssen Über-
prüfungen im Prozeß jeweils danach und davor durchgeführt werden, um
falsche Signalwerte oder Prozeßwerte zu erkennen (Plausibilitätsprüfung, Einleitung von Reparaturmaßnahmen).

Bild 3

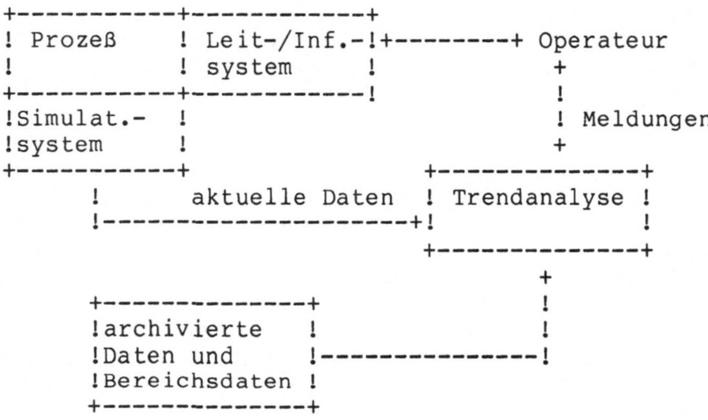

```
+-----------+-----------+
! Prozeß    ! Leit-/Inf.-!+---------+ Operateur
!           ! system    !          +
+-----------+-----------!          !
!Simulat.-  !                      ! Meldungen
!system     !                      +
+-----------+            +--------------+
         !     aktuelle Daten ! Trendanalyse !
         !--------------------+!            !
                              +--------------+
                                     +
         +--------------+            !
         !archivierte   !            !
         !Daten und     !--------------------!
         !Bereichsdaten !
         +--------------+
```

Zu d)
Das zukünftige Prozeßverhalten ausgehend vom aktuellen Zustand und die
Auswirkungen eines Eingriffes des Operateurs in den momentanen Prozeß-
ablauf sollten vorhersehbar sein.  Dies bedeutet, daß ausgehend vom
aktuellen Prozeßzustand unter Berücksichtigung eventueller Eingriffe
das Prozeßverhalten zeitlich voraus simuliert werden muß.  Die Zeitkonstanten des Prozesses liegen im Bereich von Minuten bis zu mehreren
Stunden.  Für eine sinnvolle Prognose dieser Prozeßabläufe muß die
Voraussimulation um den Faktor 30-50 (mind.) schneller als in der Realzeit ablaufen (2).  Der Bediener wird dadurch bei der Auswahl der
richtigen Führungsstrategie unterstützt.  Diese Prognosedaten sind
parallel zu den realen Prozeßdaten darzustellen.  Um eine optimale
Übersicht zu garantieren sind Prognosewerte und aktuelle Prozeßwerte
nicht zu vermischen.  Die prognostizierten Prozeßwerte sind also unter
Verwendung eines zusätzlichen grafischen Systems darzustellen.
Entsprechend der Bedienerhierarchie in einer Warte sind diese Informationen möglicherweise nur dem Schichtführer außerhalb der direkten

Warte zur Verfügung zu stellen.

Bild 4

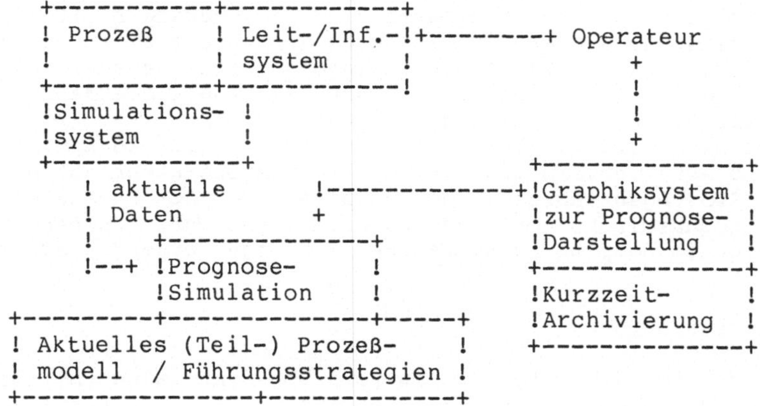

```
        +------------+------------+
        ! Prozeß     ! Leit-/Inf.-!+---------+ Operateur
        !            ! system     !          +
        +------------+------------+!          !
        !Simulations- !           !          !
        !system      !            !          +
        +------------+            !   +--------------+
           ! aktuelle      !------------+!Graphiksystem !
           ! Daten         +            !zur Prognose- !
           !      +--------------+      !Darstellung   !
           !--+ !Prognose-      !       +--------------+
                !Simulation     !       !Kurzzeit-     !
        +--------+--------------+-----+ !Archivierung  !
        ! Aktuelles (Teil-) Prozeß-   ! +--------------+
        ! modell  / Führungsstrategien !
        +------------+------------+
```

Der Operateur sollte dabei die Möglichkeit haben, bestimmte Prozeßbereiche auszuwählen und zurückliegende Prognosewerte ohne einen
erneuten Prognoselauf noch einmal anzuschauen (Prognose = Vorausbe-
rechnung des Prozeßverhaltens bis zu einem (quasi)- stationären
Zustand).  Die Prozeßprognose erlaubt auch das logische Verriegeln von
vom Rechner als falsch erkannten Eingriffen (eventuell auch nur
Warnung), die rechnerseitige Auswahl und der Vorschlag von erforderlichen Eingriffen sowie letztendlich im on-line closed-loop Betrieb der
direkte Prozeßeingriff mit Überwachung durch den Bediener.


Zu e)
Die Führung komplexer technischer Prozesse stellt hohe Anforderungen
vor allem auch an die Operateure.  Ihre Entscheidungsprozesse basieren
teils auf Vorschriften im Handbuch, meist aber auf eigenen Abstraktionen des Prozeßgeschehens, die aber weder nachprüfbar noch umfassend

Bild 5

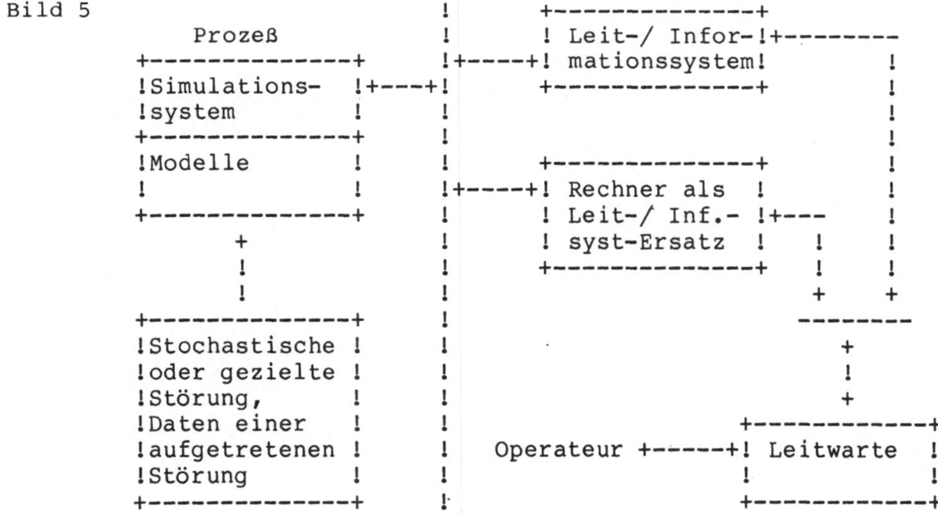

```
                      !       +--------------+
           Prozeß     !       ! Leit-/ Infor-!+---------
        +--------------+      !+----+! mationssystem!        !
        !Simulations- !+---+!      +--------------+          !
        !system      !     !                                 !
        +--------------+   !                                 !
        !Modelle      !    !       +--------------+          !
        !             !    !+----+! Rechner als  !          !
        +--------------+   !       ! Leit-/ Inf.- !+---      !
               +          !       ! syst-Ersatz  !   !      !
               !          !       +--------------+   !      !
               !          !                          +      +
        +--------------+   !                      --------
        !Stochastische !   !                          +
        !oder gezielte !   !                          !
        !Störung,      !   !                          +
        !Daten einer   !   !       +--------------+
        !aufgetretenen !   !  Operateur +-----+! Leitwarte  !
        !Störung       !   !                   !            !
        +--------------+   !                   +--------------+
```

sind.  Zur Absicherung dieser Entscheidungsprozesse ist den Operateuren
ein tieferes Verständnis der Prozeßdynamik zu vermitteln ( Korrektur
bzw.  Erweiterung des operateureigenen abstrahierten Prozeßmodells).

Ein Üben am realen Prozeß ist aus sicherheitstechnischen Gründen absolut ausgeschlossen.  Der Prozeß kann aber auf einem Rechner nachgebildet werden.  Die so erzeugten Daten sind dem Operateur mit Hilfe
eines Prozeßleitsystems oder einem anderen Rechnersystem in einer Leit-
warte unter möglichst realistischen Bedingungen (der menschliche
Abstraktionsvorgang ist zu berücksichtigen --> Modell des menschlichen
Bedieners bzgl. Wissensspeicherung) darzustellen.
Ebenso muß er Eingriffe wie beim realen Prozeß tätigen können.  Um
Situationen zu schaffen, in denen Eingriffe vom Operateur notwendig
sind, können Störungen (kurzzeitige Zustandswert- oder Parameter-
änderungen) stochastisch, von einer höheren Verantwortungsebene gezielt
oder anhand von im Betrieb aufgetretenen Störungen erzeugt werden.


II.3 Zusammenfassung:

Der Einsatz der Simulationstechnik in Form von dynamischen Simulationsstudien hat sich als überaus sinnvoll erwiesen (3).  Die Auswirkungen
von Prozeßverkopplungen konnten besser erkannt und frühzeitig berücksichtigt werden.
Eine optimale Prozeßführung im Sinne der dargestellten Kriterien bei
der obig skizzierten Prozeßproblematik ist nur durch den Einsatz
wissenschaftlicher Methoden möglich.  Dabei kommt der Simulationstechnik eine zentrale Rolle zu.  Die angesprochenen unterschiedlichen
Einsatzbereiche stellen funktionsmäßig hohe Anforderungen an das einzu-
setzende System.  Außerdem kann die Erstellung der notwendigen Prozeß-
modelle aufgrund der Prozeßkomplexität nur durch eine Rechnerunterstützung mit vertretbarem Aufwand durchgeführt werden.
Da die Simulation auch für die Modellierung technischer Prozesse zur
Modellverifikation das wesentliche Instrument darstellt, ist die grund-
legende Forderung zur Erfüllung aller bisher angesprochenen Aspekte der
Einsatz eines Realzeit-Simulationssystems für die Prozeßführung,
welches die rechnerunterstützte Modellierung (ev.  Expertensysteme) von
komplexen technischen Systemen integriert.  Bezüglich der Konzeption
dieses Systems oder der Anwendbarkeit bzw.  der Integrationsmöglichkeit
bisher existierender Programmsysteme sei auf (6) verwiesen.


Literatur:

(1) G. Baumgärtel et al. "Die Wiederaufarbeitung bestrahlter Kernbrenn-
    stoffe - Ein Teilschritt der nuklearen Entsorgung" Vortrag aus
    "Wie sicher ist die Entsorgung", KfK, 1982

(2) W. Bühler "Simulation einer komplexen Chemieanlage am Beispiel der
    Uran-Plutonium Extraktion" Dissertation Universität Karlsruhe, 1980

(3) K.H.Fasol "Erfahrungen mit der Simulation technischer Systeme"
    Interkama 1983, Fb MSR, Springer Berlin, Heidelberg, New York

(4) M. Polke "Prozeßleittechnik für die Chemie - Status und Trends"
    Automatisierungstechnische Praxis Nr.  5, 1985, S.  214-223

(5) K. Schleisik "Nukleare Sicherheit von Wiederaufarbeitungsanlagen"
    Vortrag aus "Wie sicher ist die Entsorgung", KfK, 1982

(6) H. B. Keller, Interner Bericht, KfK-IDT, noch nicht verfügbar

MODELLBILDUNG IM TURBINEN- UND GENERATORBEREICH EINER KRAFTWERKSANLAGE


Helmuth Stahl, Erlangen


## 1. Einleitung

Im Turbinen- und Generatorbereich einer Kraftwerksanlage treten bei bestimmten Netz-
situationen Schwingungsphänomene auf, die von den herkömmlichen Reglern nicht in gewünschter Weise bekämpft werden. Die Ursache ist darin begründet, daß dem Reglerentwurf Streckenmodelle zugrundeliegen, die diese Schwingungscharakteristika nicht erfassen. Stehen dagegen hinreichend genaue Modelle zur Verfügung, lassen sich diese
Mängel durch den Einsatz eines verbesserten Regelungskonzeptes beseitigen.

Im allgemeinen handelt es sich bei den ausführlichen Modellen um nichtlineare
Modelle oder um lineare Modelle hoher Ordnung. Die Forderung nach sehr detaillierten
Modellen bringt deshalb Probleme mit sich. Möchte man nämlich

- leistungsfähige Reglerentwurfsverfahren anwenden, die im Rahmen der
  linearen Regelungstheorie bekannt sind,
- Probleme beim rechnergestützten Reglerentwurf vermeiden,

gilt es, Kompromisse einzugehen. Offensichtlich müssen dabei für nichtlineare
Modelle lineare Ersatzmodelle aufgestellt und gleichzeitig lineare Modelle hoher
Ordnung in ihrer Ordnung reduziert werden. Ziel ist es, ein vereinfachtes Gesamtmodell zu gewinnen, das sich aus linearen Modellen geringer Komplexität zusammen-
setzt. Selbstverständlich haben die hierzu erforderlichen Modellvereinfachungen
unter dem Gesichtspunkt zu erfolgen, daß die wesentlichen Systemeigenschaften
erhalten bleiben.

Im Rahmen dieses Beitrags soll die Anwendung dieser Vorgehensweise auf den Turbinen-
und Generatorbereich, als den dynamisch schnelleren Teil einer Kraftwerksanlage gezeigt werden. Sowohl die Turbine als auch der Generator stellen für sich schwingungs-
fähige Gebilde dar, deren Eigenfrequenzen in einem sehr großen Frequenzbereich von
ca. 0.1 Hz bis 100 Hz liegen. In den folgenden beiden Abschnitten werden deshalb für
diese Anlagenteile sehr detaillierte Modelle vorgestellt, mit denen es möglich ist,
diese Schwingungen zu simulieren. Abschnitt 4 behandelt dann ein Verfahren, welches
über eine Frequenzgangapproximation die Koeffizienten einer analytischen Frequenzgangfunktion erzeugt. Diese analytische Form stellt das lineare Ersatzmodell im
Rahmen der oben erläuterten Modellvereinfachung dar. Die Ergebnisse, die mit dieser
Methode erzielbar sind, werden exemplarisch an einem detaillierten, nichtlinearen
Modell des Synchrongenerators gezeigt.

## 2. Modellierung einer Kraftwerksturbine

Turbinen für Kraftwerksanlagen größerer Leistung bestehen i.a. aus einer Hochdruck-, einer Mitteldruck- und zwei Niederdruckstufen. Diese Teilturbinen und der Generatorläufer sind über eine Welle miteinander verbunden.

Da es sich hierbei um ein System mit verteilten Parametern handelt, wäre eine mathematische Beschreibung mit partiellen Differentialgleichungen erforderlich. Das wesentliche Systemverhalten, insbesondere das Schwingungsverhalten, läßt sich aber auch unter den nachfolgend formulierten Voraussetzungen mit gewöhnlichen, linearen Differentialgleichungen modellieren:

Bild 1:

**Kraftwerksturbine als "Torsionsschwinger"**

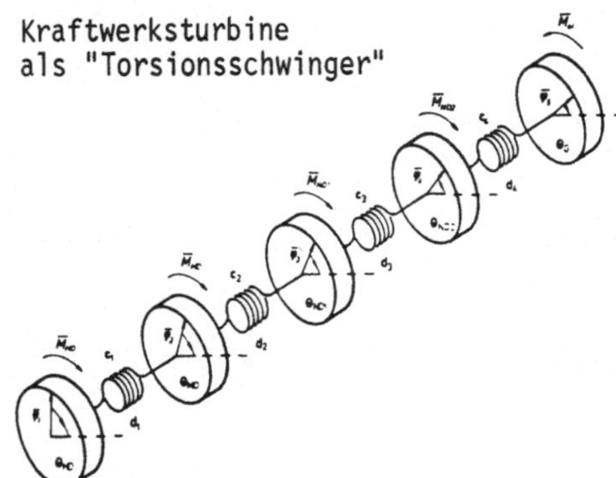

1.) Die Teilturbinen und der Synchrongenerator werden als Massescheiben (konzentrierte Massen!) angesehen mit den Trägheitsmomenten $\theta_{HD}$ für die Hochdruckturbine, $\theta_{MD}$ für den Mitteldruckteil, $\theta_{ND1}$ für den ersten Teil und $\theta_{ND2}$ für den zweiten Teil der Niederdruckturbine und $\theta_{G}$ für den Generator.

2.) Die idealisiert angenommenen Massescheiben seien über eine Welle endlicher Federsteifigkeit miteinander verbunden. Für die einzelnen Federn gelte das HOOKE'sche Federgesetz (Federkonstanten: $c_1$, ..., $c_4$) und die in der Welle auftretenden Dämpfungsmomente seien geschwindigkeitsproportional (Dämpfungsbeiwerte: $d_1$, ..., $d_4$). Lagerreibungsverluste seien vernachlässigbar klein.

Mit diesen Annahmen ergibt sich ein Ersatzsystem wie es in Bild 1 zu sehen ist. Die dynamischen Gleichungen erhält man durch Aufstellen von Momentenbilanzen gemäß:

$$\theta_{HD}\,\frac{d\bar{\omega}_1}{dt} + d_1\bar{\omega}_{D2} + c_1\bar{\Phi}_1 = \bar{M}_{HD}$$

$$\theta_{MD}\,\frac{d\bar{\omega}_2}{dt} + d_2\bar{\omega}_{D2} + c_2\bar{\Phi}_2 = \bar{M}_{MD} + d_1\bar{\omega}_{D1} + c_1\bar{\Phi}_1$$

$$\theta_{ND1}\frac{d\bar{\omega}_3}{dt} + d_3\bar{\omega}_{D2} + c_3\bar{\Phi}_3 = \bar{M}_{ND1} + d_2\bar{\omega}_{D2} + c_2\bar{\Phi}_2 \qquad \text{(Querstrich bedeutet:}$$
$$\text{dimensionsbehaftetes Großsignal)}$$

$$\theta_{ND2}\frac{d\bar{\omega}_4}{dt} + d_4\bar{\omega}_{D2} + c_4\bar{\Phi}_4 = \bar{M}_{ND2} + d_3\bar{\omega}_{D3} + c_3\bar{\Phi}_3$$

$$\theta_{G}\cdot\frac{d\bar{\omega}_5}{dt} + \bar{M}_{el} = d_4\bar{\omega}_{D4} + c_4\bar{\Phi}_4\ ,$$

$$\text{mit} \qquad \frac{d\bar{\varphi}_i}{dt} = \bar{\omega}_i,\ i = 1, ..., 5 \qquad ; \qquad \frac{d\bar{\Phi}_j}{dt} = \bar{\omega}_{DJ} = \bar{\omega}_j - \bar{\omega}_{j+1},\ j = 1, ..., 4$$

Dieses gekoppelte, lineare Differentialgleichungssystem 8. Ordnung modelliert somit die wesentlichen Schwingungsphänomene, die im Turbinenbereich einer Kraftwerksanlage auftreten können. Auf eine Ordnungsreduktion im oben erwähnten Sinn soll an dieser Stelle nicht eingegangen werden.

## 3. Modellierung des Synchrongenerators

Der Ausgangspunkt für eine mathematische Beschreibung der elektrischen Zusammenhänge in einem Synchrongenerator sei das PARK'sche Differentialgleichungssystem /1/. Hier soll dieses umfangreiche Gleichungssystem in Form des Blockschaltbildes 2 dargestellt werden.

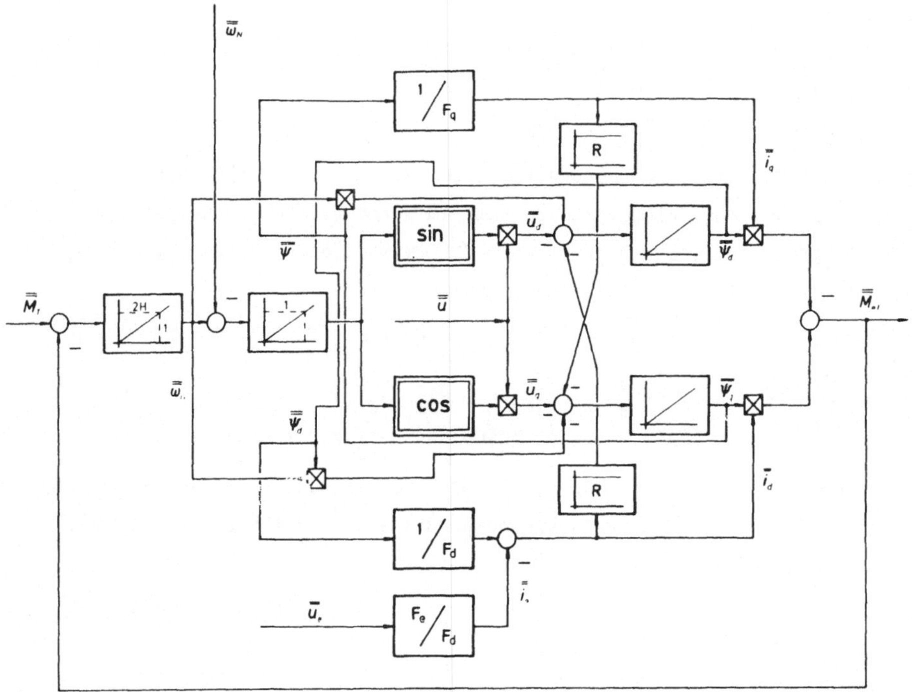


Bild 2: Generatormodell ($\bar{}$ bedeutet: auf den Nennwert bezogenes Signal)

Man erkennt, daß das Ausgangssignal $\bar{\bar{M}}_{el}$ aus den Eingangssignalen $\bar{\bar{M}}_T$ (Turbinenmoment), $\bar{\bar{\omega}}_N$ (Netzfrequenz), $\bar{\bar{u}}_e$ (Erregerspannung) und $\bar{\bar{u}}$ (Netzspannung) hervorgeht. Diese Zusammenhänge sind sowohl linearer als auch nichtlinearer Natur. Es läßt sich zeigen, daß sich das System bzgl. der verschiedenen Ein-/ Ausgangssignalpaarungen quasilinear verhält. D.h. man kann für kleine Auslenkungen aus einem Betriebspunkt die für den Reglerentwurf erforderlichen linearen Ersatzmodelle angeben. Ergebnisse für die Paarungen $\bar{\bar{M}}_T \rightarrow \bar{\bar{M}}_{el}$, $\bar{\bar{\omega}}_N \rightarrow \bar{\bar{M}}_{el}$ sind im nächsten Abschnitt zu finden.


## 4. Methode zur Modellvereinfachung

Die nachfolgend beschriebene Methode zur Modellvereinfachung kann sowohl bei linearen Systemen hoher Ordnung (1) als auch bei nichtlinearen Systemen (2) angewandt werden (Voraussetzung bei nichtlinearen Systemen: quasilineares Verhalten um einen Betriebspunkt). Das Verfahren beruht darauf, daß von dem betrachteten System N diskrete Frequenzgangpunkte

$$(\omega_i, R_{im}, I_{im}), \quad i = 1,\ldots, N \text{ mit } R_{im}, I_{im} - \text{Real-/Imaginärteil des i-ten Punktes}$$
$$\omega_i \quad - \text{zugehörige Kreisfrequenz}$$

vorliegen. Die Frequenzen $\omega_i$ sind dabei so zu wählen, daß der das System charakterisierende Frequenzbereich abgedeckt wird. Die Gewinnung der Wertetripel $(\omega_i, R_{im}, I_{im})$ ist relativ einfach. Bei den Systemen der Gruppe (1) sind sie direkt berechenbar, bei den Systemen der Gruppe (2) gewinnt man sie beispielsweise durch orthogonale Korrelation.

Auf dieser Grundlage ist es jetzt möglich, die Koeffizienten $a_i$, $b_k$ einer Frequenzgangfunktion der Form

$$F(j\omega) = \frac{a_0 + a_1(j\omega) + \ldots + a_m(j\omega)^m}{b_0 + b_1(j\omega) + \ldots + b_n(j\omega)^n} \ , \quad \text{mit} \ m \leq n$$

zu gewinnen /2/. Die Koeffizienten werden so berechnet, daß die Funktion $F(j\omega) = R(\omega) + jI(\omega)$ die vorliegenden Frequenzgangpunkte im betrachteten Frequenzbereich "möglichst gut" approximiert. Durch geschickte Umformung läßt sich zeigen, daß zur Lösung des Problems im Prinzip das Gleichungssystem

$$\underline{M}(\underline{p}) \cdot \underline{p} = \underline{v} \qquad \text{mit} \ \underline{p}^T = [a_0 \ a_1 \ \ldots \ a_m \ b_0 \ b_1 \ \ldots \ b_n]$$
$$\underline{v}^T = [R_{1m} \ I_{1m} \ \ldots \ R_{im} \ I_{im} \ \ldots \ R_{Nm} \ I_{Nm}]$$
$$\underline{M}(\underline{p}) - \text{von } \underline{p} \text{ abhängige Koeffizientenmatrix}$$

iterativ bzgl. dem Parametervektor $\underline{p}$ gelöst werden muß. An dieser Stelle sei erwähnt, daß die bisher bekannten Frequenzgangapproximationsverfahren in diesem Lösungsschema als Spezialfälle enthalten sind.

Die numerische Lösung des Problems erfolgt so, daß der Parametervektor $\underline{p}$ per Algorithmus variiert und dabei das vektorielle Gütefunktional /3/

$$J = \frac{1}{20} \ln \left\{ \sum_{i=1}^{N} \left[ \exp\left(20 \, \frac{e_{Ri}}{c}\right) + \exp\left(20 \, \frac{e_{Ii}}{c}\right) \right] \right\} \ ,$$
$$\text{mit} \ e_{Ri} = \left| R(\omega_i) - R_{im} \right| \ , \quad e_{Ii} = \left| I(\omega_i) - I_{im} \right| \ , \quad c = \underset{i}{\text{Max}} \ \{e_{Ri}, e_{Ii}\}$$
$$\text{(zu Iterationsbeginn)}$$

minimisiert wird.

Die auf diese Weise erzielbaren Ergebnisse seien beispielhaft am Generatormodell aus Abschnitt 3 gezeigt. In Bild 3 sind die BODE-Diagramme der linearen Ersatzmodelle und die zugehörigen Sprungantworten der Übertragungskanäle $\overline{\overline{M}}_T \rightarrow \overline{\overline{M}}_{el}$, $\overline{\omega}_N(\hat{=} \overline{\overline{f}}_N) \rightarrow \overline{\overline{M}}_{el}$ eingetragen. Die Rauten in den BODE-Diagrammen kennzeichnen die durch orthogonale Korrelation gewonnenen Frequenzgangpunkte. Bezüglich der Güte kann gesagt werden, daß Unterschiede zwischen den Originalsprungantworten (nichtlineares Modell) und den Antwortsignalen der linearen Ersatzmodelle nicht feststellbar sind.


Literaturverzeichnis

/1/ Bühler, H.: Theorie geregelter Drehstromantriebe, Bd.1, Birkhäuser-Verl. 1977
/2/ Stahl, H.: Transfer function synthesis ..., Int. J. Control, 1984, pp. 541-550
/3/ Kreisselmeier, G.; Steinhauser, R.: Systemat. Auslegung ..., rt 3, 1979, S. 76-79
/4/ Stahl, H.: Institutsberichte 84/1, 84/2, Inst. f. Regelungst. Univ. Erlangen, 1984

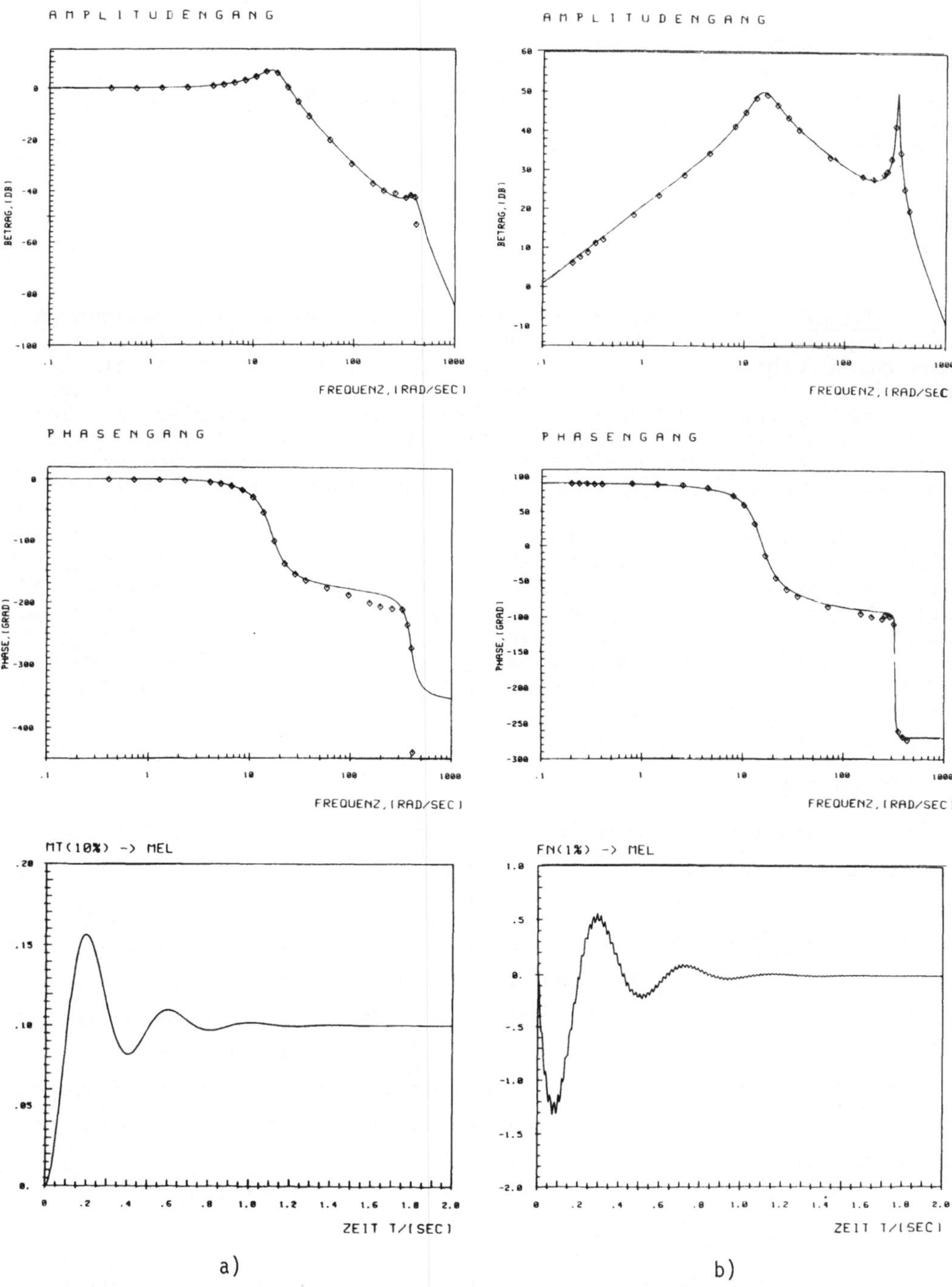

Bild 3: BODE-Diagramme und Sprungantworten um den Betriebspunkt $\overline{\overline{M}}_{To} = 0.6$

a) $M_T \rightarrow M_{e1}$ mit $\dfrac{M_{e1}}{M_T}(j\omega) = \dfrac{261.6 \cdot \left[7.806E5 + 1.827E5\,j\omega\right]}{\left[261.6 + 8.644\,j\omega + (j\omega)^2\right]\left[7.806E5 + 1.573E5\,j\omega + 102.5(j\omega)^2 + (j\omega)^3\right]}$

b) $f_N \rightarrow M_{e1}$ mit $\dfrac{M_{e1}}{f_N}(j\omega) = \dfrac{-j\omega \cdot 261.6 \cdot \left[3.468E9 + 2.139E8\,j\omega + 1.186E6(j\omega)^2\right]}{\left[261.6 + 8.644\,j\omega + (j\omega)^2\right]\left[3.591E8 + 1.746E7\,j\omega + 1.111E5(j\omega)^2 + 167.3(j\omega)^3 + (j\omega)^4\right]}$

# SEMIBATCH DISTILLATION MODELLING AND CONTROL DESIGN


M.Atanasijević, R.Karba, F.Bremšak
Ljubljana, Yugoslavia



Zusamenfassung. In dieser Arbeit ist die Modellierung und Regelung der semicharge Pilotdestillationskolonne dargestellt. Der Zweikomponenten-mischungmehrgrössen prozess wurde durch ein nichtlineares und ein linearisiertes Modell vorgestellt, wobei auch ein lineares Modell reduzierter Ordnung entwickelt wurde. Ein mehrgrössen Ausgangfeedback PI Regler mit Polvargabe wurde für erwöhntes Beispiel entworfen. Die Regelgüte wurde durch die hybride Simulation untersucht, wobei der Prozess auf dem Analog - und der Regler auf dem Digitalrechner realisiert wurden.

Summary. The work deals with the modelling and control of semibatch distillation pilot plant. For the description of such multivariable system the nonlinear and linearized model for two component mixture were used, while the reduced order linear model was developed for control purposes. For the discussed example multivariabile output feedback pole assignment PI controller was designed. Efficacy of developed control is shown through hybrid simulation, where system was realized on analog and controller on digital computer.


## 1.  Introduction

For the separation of components on the basis  of volatility, the different kinds of distillation are used in chemical industry. In the cases of small production and often changing mixture the use of batch distillation is very suitable. In some cases this type of distillation can be improved by the use of semibatch instead of batch rectification. In distinction from batch distillation here the reboiler is continously fed with the same flow as accumulator. The advantage of such distillation is not only the enlarged mass of final product but also constant level of mixture in the reboiler which as a consequence ensures approximately constant vapor flow rate.

## 2.  Rectification Process

The process under consideration consists of reboiler with approximately constant vapor flow rate. A vapor from the reboiler goes up through the column, gives up part of its energy at each plate, and helps the vaporization of the more volatile component. The role of distillation column is to separate the mixture so that distillate flow rate has the prescribed concentration. In the condenser such heat exchanging must be ensured that all vapor will condense, but there is no need of cooling the distillate, because part of liquid is returned to the top of the column as the reflux flow with a temperature which is near to the boiling point. The plant is arranged for rectification at constant quality of distillate, so there is also a reflux distributor which returns one part of liquid from the condenser to the column and the other part is drawn as the top product.

## 3. Reduced linear model of the plant

Distillation column is the plant having multivariable properties which can not be neglected in the process of modelling. The governing equations for the dynamic model can be derived by the application of mass balances under several assumptions. Such plant can be described by the system of nonlinear, time varying, first order differential equations. It was tested by the aid of digital simulation language CSSL-III on CYBER 72 computer. The simulation showed that in spite of mentioned assumptions the accuracy of the model remains sufficient. Because of relatively slow dynamics of the process the linearization is justified, of course only in the near neighbourhood of the chosen working points. The products in the equations of nonlinear model consist of two time-dependent functions and can be linearized as the function of two variables. Using known procedure the corresponding linear model was generated.

Through the study of the plant it was established that a model of input-output behaviour of sensible less order can be obtained by discrete identification /4/. Determination of structure and parameters of reduced model was made by the aid of simulation of previous linearized model, while the model was disturbed with appropriate chosen input signals. The resulting system can be described in well known state space form, where matrices and vectors in our case are as follows:

$$
\underline{\underline{A}} = \begin{bmatrix} -0.4352 & 0.4382 & 0.0172 & -0.0194 \\ -0.1229 & 0.1211 & -0.0092 & 0.0104 \\ -0.1981 & 0.1931 & -0.3431 & 0.3535 \\ -0.1017 & -0.0970 & -0.1698 & 0.1611 \end{bmatrix}
$$

$$
\underline{\underline{B}} = \begin{bmatrix} 0.1259 & -0.0974 \\ 0.1182 & -0.0802 \\ 0.2923 & -0.1168 \\ 0.2198 & -0.0932 \end{bmatrix} \qquad \underline{\underline{C}} = \begin{bmatrix} 1 & 0 & 0 & 0 \\ 0 & 0 & 1 & 0 \end{bmatrix} \tag{1}
$$

$$
\Delta\underline{u}(t) = \begin{bmatrix} \Delta L(t) \\ \Delta V(t) \end{bmatrix} \qquad \Delta\underline{y}(t) = \begin{bmatrix} \Delta y_1(t) \\ \Delta y_2(t) \end{bmatrix}
$$

Here $\Delta$ denotes the difference from steady state, $\Delta y_1(t)$ and $\Delta y_2(t)$ are time responses of less volatile components at the stage under condenser and above reboiler. Expressions in (1) were obtained from the model of nineth order.

## 4. Control design

For the model given in (1) such a regulator was desired that the resulting closed-loop system has a certain number of its poles on the previously prescribed positions. For the synthesis only output-feedback is used because the measurement of all state variables would be too expensive. The approach bases on the equivalence of closed-loop characteristic polynomial of multivariable system and equivalent system with one input and multiple outputs. This results in compensator matrice which is dyadic i.e. has rank equal to one /2/. For the design of such regulator it is necessary to solve only a system of linear algebraic equations. Multivariable PI regulator designed by pole assignment method can shift $2m+\ell-1$ poles to a specified locations (m-number of inputs, $\ell$-number of outputs). Shifting a larger number of poles requires a calculation of nearest possible locations which can be attained. The order of closed-loop system is because of I-part in direct path enlarged to $n+\ell$ (n is the number of states), while P-part of regulator is in the feedback loop (Figure 1). The method is extensively described in /1/. By the aid of interactive program package POLASS /3/, which serves for the computer aided design of seven different types of pole and zero

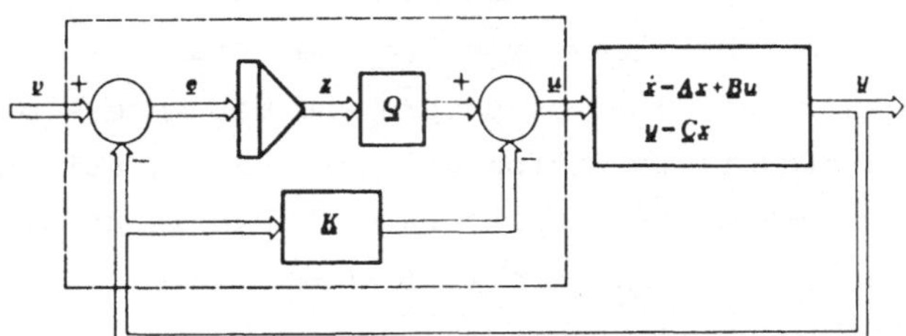


Figure 1.  Block diagram of the descused control

assignment multivariable regulators, the PI regulator for discused system was designed as follows /5/:

$$\underline{K}_p = \begin{bmatrix} 1.3811 & 5.8739 \\ -1.6091 & 5.8423 \end{bmatrix} \qquad \underline{K}_I = \begin{bmatrix} 2.2973 & 1.5900 \\ 0.3842 & 1.4708 \end{bmatrix} \qquad (2)$$

where closed-loop poles have the following values: -0.3654, -0.0656, -0.3699, -0.4612, $-0.2997\pm j0.1998$.

Before realization of chosen control on real system it is very sensible

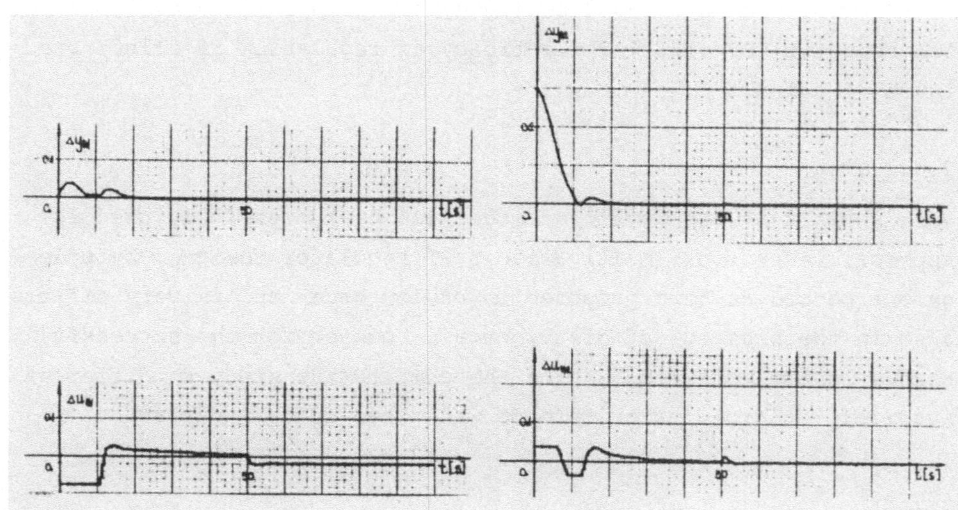

Figure 2.  Closed-loop responses of system excited by initial conditions and step disturbance at t = 50s. Control signals are limited to operative area. Sampling time: T = 0.5s.

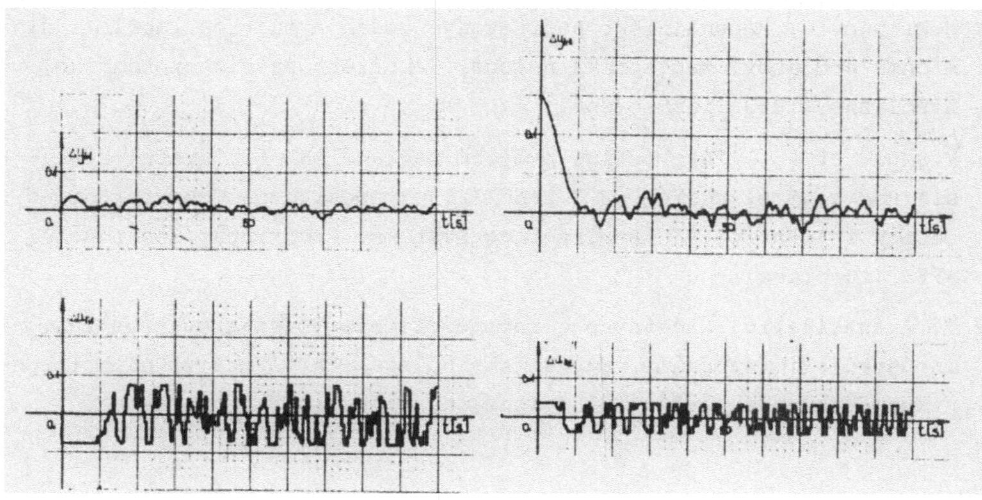

Figure 3.  Closed-loop responses of system excited by initial conditions and step disturbance at t = 50s. Control signals are limited to operative area. Corresponding pseudorendom signal simulates possible measurement noise. Sampling time: T = 0.5s.

to verify the closed-loop behaviour also with hybrid simulation. So the system was realized on EAI-580 analog-hybrid computer and controller on digital computer PDP 11/34. The efficacy of regulation is illustrated in Figures 2 and 3.

## 5. Conclusion

The work shows that the developed model can be successfully used for the appropriate control. Multivariable PI regulator designed by pole assignment method as here proposed is of low order and is very efficient also in the presence of disturbances. However for the successfull and usable control of pilot device the comparative study of different multivariable control design methods will have to be undertaken.

## References


/1/ R.Karba, Sinteza algoritmov za računalniško vodenje multivariabilnih sistemov. Disertacija, Fakulteta za elektrotehniko, Ljubljana 1981 (in Slovene)

/2/ H.Seraji, Design of proportional-plus-integral controllers for multivariable systems, Int.J.Control, Vol. 29, No.1, 1979, 49-63

/3/ M.Milanović, Računalniško načrtovanje vodenja multivariabilnih dinamičnih procesov. Magistrska naloga, Fakulteta za elektrotehniko, Ljubljana, 1983 (in Slovene)

/4/ M.Šega, et al., Interactive program package ANA for system analysis and control design, $3^{rd}$ IFAC/IFIP Symposium on Computer Aided Design in Control and Engineering Systems, Preprints, Copenhagen, 1985 (in press)

/5/ M. Atanasijević, Načrtovanje računalniškega vodenja multivariabilnih industrijskih procesov. Magistrska naloga, Fakulteta za elektrotehniko, Ljubljana, 1984 (in Slovene)

## A MODEL FOR COMBUSTION OF FUEL IN THE BOILER

Jurij Čretnik, Stanko Strmčnik, Borut Zupančič
Ljubljana, Yugoslavia

Summary. In the work theoretical model for combustion of fuel in the boiler is given. The model is nonlinear with variable time delay and is suitable for the cases with too much air and also covers some aspects concerning air deficit. The inputs of the model are norm fuel flow and norm air flow. The outputs of the model are concentrations of the components in the flue gas. The model is suitable for different kinds of fuel with different content of moisture and ash. Indirectly the ratio of $CO_2/CO$ and soot can be set. These two parameters describe the quality of the combustion of fuel in different kinds of the boilers. The model was developed for control design purposes.

Zusammenfassung. Dieser Paper stellt theoretisches Modell der Brennstoffverbrennung bei Industriefeuerungen vor. Das Model ist nicht linear mit veränderlicher Totzeit und ist besonders in Fällen mit Luftüberfluss, sowie auch bei einigen Beispilen der Luftmangel geeignet. Die Eingänge des Modells bilden Normbrennstoffdurchfluss und Normluftdurchtluss, die Ausgänge des Modells sind die Komponentenkonzentrationen im Rauchgas. Das Modell eignet sich für verschiedene Brennstoffarten mit verschiedener Feuchtigkeits und Asche Mengen. Das $CO_2/CO$ Verhältnis und Russ kann indirekt eingestellt werden. Diese zwei Parameter beschreiben die Verbrennungsqualität bei verschiedenen Arten von Feuerräumen. Das Modell wurde für Regelungs Zwecke entwickelt.

## 1. INTRODUCTION

The prices of fuel are increasing from day to day. Therefore there exist a wish to improve the combustion of fuel in every power plant. Except economical and technical aspects of combustion of fuel ecological aspect also exist which become more and more important. With improved control of fuel combustion the concentrations of the noxious gases in the flue gases can be reduced. The losses of the combustion can be reduced in two ways; by reducing the quantity of the not burned fuel and by reducing the quantity of the flue gases. Fig.1 shows aspects of the optimal combustion of fuel.

It is shown in the praxis that optimal ratio of the air and fuel flow (optimal air factor - $\lambda_{op}$) depend on the load of the boiler. This can be clearly seen in Fig.2. Air factor ($\lambda$) is defined as ratio of air flow and stehiometrical required air flow for combustion. Load factor ($\beta$) is defined as ratio of fuel flow and maximal fuel flow.

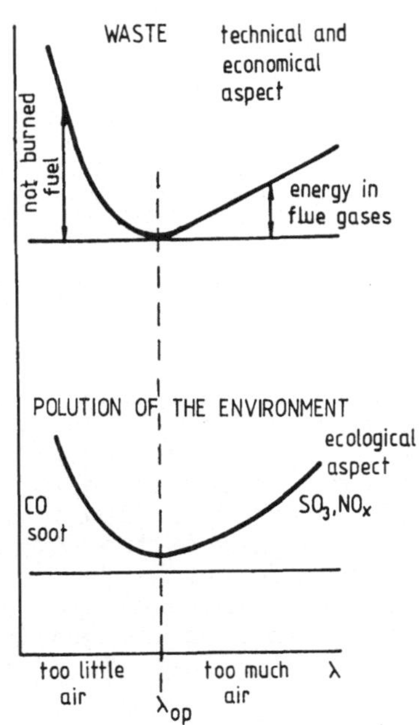


Fig.1. Aspects of the optimal
combustion of fuel

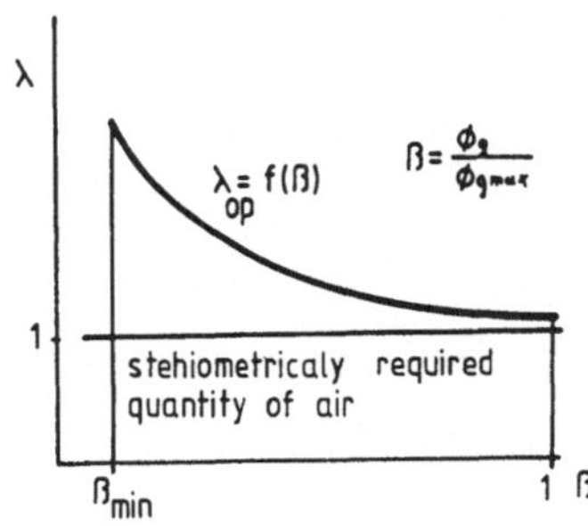


Figure 2.   Optimal air factor in depen-
dence of boiler load – $\beta$

Combustion control isn´t easy task.
There shouldn´t appear some air deficit
in the boiler because of the danger of
an explosion. Economy of the combustion is satisfactory if the air excess is
kept small in spite of the changeable
condition of the combustion. Now this
can be successfully solved with an adaptive controller. Controller obta-
ins information about the oxigen content of flue gases from the $ZrO_2$-
analyzer. In Fig.3 the principle combustion control is shown.

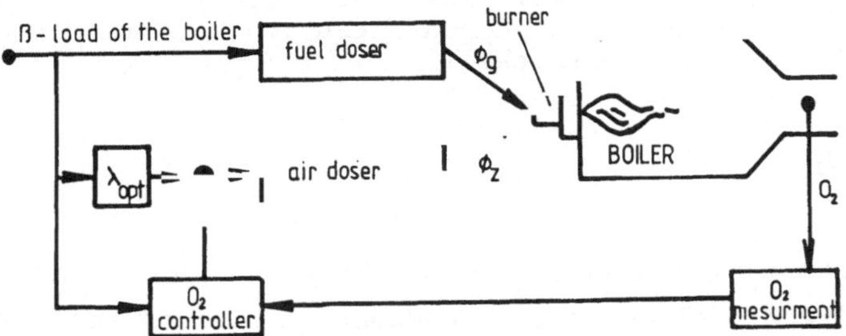


Figure 3. Block scheme for combustion control

## 2.  METHOD OF DEVELOPING MATHEMATICAL MODEL FOR COMBUSTION

Composition of the fuel can be expressed with percentage of carbon (C),
hydrogen (H), oxygen (O), azote (N), sulphur (S), ash (A) and water (W)

$$C + H + O + S + A + W = 100\% \quad . \tag{1}$$

Composition of the air is expressed only with percentage of oxygen ($O_2$)
and azote ($N_2$)

$$21\% + 79\% = 100\% \quad . \tag{2}$$

Moisture in the air is neglected. Following composition of the flue gases is suposed

$$xO_2 + xCO + xCO_2 + xSO_2 + xN_2 + xH_2O = 100\% \quad . \qquad (3)$$

Each term in Eq.3 illustrates volume percent of oxygen, carbon monoxide, carbon dioxide, sulphur dioxide, azote and water. Only the most important components in the flue gases are considered. Fundamental equations of mathematical model are based on stehiometrical chemical reactions of combustion. The latter are supplemented with empirical nonlinear factors m and b. Factors m and b are functions of air factor and illustrate the ratio of $CO_2/CO$ and soot respectively. If under simbol $\emptyset_g^*$ corresponding equivalent of gas flow which arised from fuel in the boiler is considered, the following static balance equation can be assumed

$$\emptyset_g^* + \emptyset_z = \emptyset_{Dp} \quad , \qquad (4)$$

where $\emptyset_z$ is norm  air flow in m3/sek, $\emptyset_{Dp}$ is norm  flue gas flow in m3/sek and $\emptyset_g$ is norm  fuel flow in kg/sek. Dynamical balance equation of the flue gases in the boiler is given in the form

$$d\, V_k/dt = \emptyset_g^* + \emptyset_z - \emptyset_{Dp} \quad , \qquad (5)$$

where $V_k$ is volume of gases in the boiler. Corresponding equivalent of gas flow which arised from fuel is expressed by the relation

$$\emptyset_g^* = \emptyset_g(VD - VO_2) \quad , \qquad (6)$$

where VD is theoretical volume of flue gases arised from 1 kg of fuel, $VO_2$ is theoretical neccessary volume of oxigen for combustion of 1 kg of fuel. Both parameters VD and $VO_2$ are functions of parameters m,b and of composition of the fuel. Corresponding volume balances for separate components of flue gases are:

$$\frac{d}{dt}\, xO_2 = \frac{1}{V_K}\,(21.\emptyset z - 100\ \emptyset g\ VO_2\ -\emptyset Dp\ xO_2) \qquad \frac{d}{dt}\, xH_2O = \frac{1}{V_K}\,(11.117H\ \emptyset g + 1.244W\ \emptyset g - \emptyset Dp\ xH_2O)$$

$$\frac{d}{dt}\, xN_2 = \frac{1}{V_K}\,(79.\emptyset z + 0.8\ N\emptyset g - \emptyset Dp\ xN_2) \qquad \frac{d}{dt}\, xCO_2 = \frac{1}{V_K}\,(m\ b\ 1.853C\ \emptyset g - \emptyset Dp\ xCO_2) \qquad (7)$$

$$\frac{d}{dt}\, xSO_2 = \frac{1}{V_K}\,(0.682S\ \emptyset g - \emptyset Dp\ xSO_2) \qquad \frac{d}{dt}\, xCO = \frac{1}{V_K}\,((1 - m)\ b\ 1.865C\ \emptyset g - \emptyset Dp\ xCO) \quad .$$

Because of the large volume of the boiler it can be supposed that change of $V_k$, because of changes in flow $\emptyset_g, \emptyset_z$ and $\emptyset_{Dp}$ is much faster then the change of concentrations of components of flue gases. Therefore the following assumption can be made

$$d\, V_k/dt = 0 \quad . \qquad (8)$$

$V_k$ is set to be a constant, which depends on the boiler dimensions. Balance of gas flow through the boiler is taken into account in stationary state

$$\emptyset_{Dp} = \emptyset_z + \emptyset_g\,(VD - VO_2) \quad . \qquad (9)$$

Stationary gas flow can be supposed if a momentary burn down of fuel is supposed.

There exist a time delay ($T_z$) in flue gases in the boiler. Time delay is variable and depends on flow of flue gases ($T_z = f(1/\emptyset_{Dp})$). In time delay $T_z$ transport time delay of flue gases in the boiler and response time of $O_2$-analayser are included. The block scheme of developed mathematical model for combustion of fuel in the boiler is shown in Fig.4.

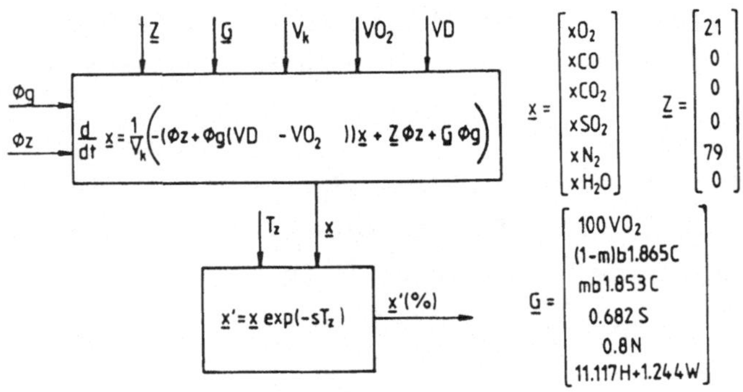

Figure 4. Block scheme of mathematical model for combustion of fuel in the boiler

## 3. MODEL VALIDATION

Theoretically developed model was first simulated with digital simulation language CSSL-III on CYBER 72 computer. Model was then verified by the aid of measurements on the concrete plant - Toplarna Moste in Ljubljana on hotwaterboiler VKL-50. Because the air flow in the boiler can´t be measured, theoretically developed model was completed with the block for air flow as it can be seen in Fig. 5. The inputs in the model were

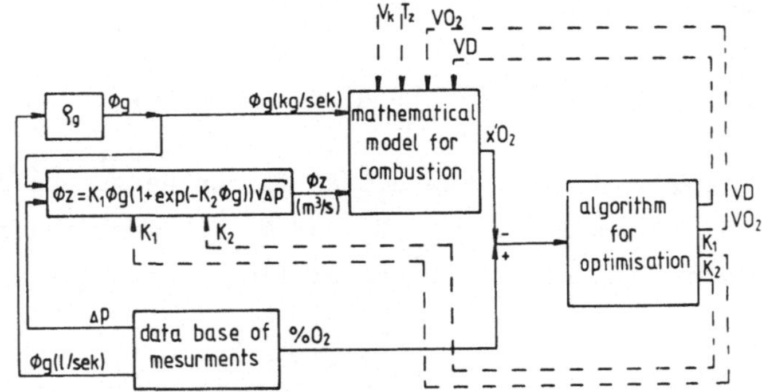

Figure 5. Block scheme for verification of model for combustion

fuel oil flow and air pressure drop between the fan and the boiler. Parameters of combustion were calculated using optimization as it is shown

473

in Fig. 5. Parameters $VO_2$, $VD$, $K_1$, $K_2$, $V_k$, $T_z$ and $\varrho_g$ are supposed to be constant. $\varrho_g$ is the mean value of the density of fuel oil. The measurements of oxygen content of flue gases, the fuel oil flow, air pressure drop and simulated oxygen content of the flue gases with developed model for combustion are shown in Fig.6. Simulation was made on PDP 11/34 computer.

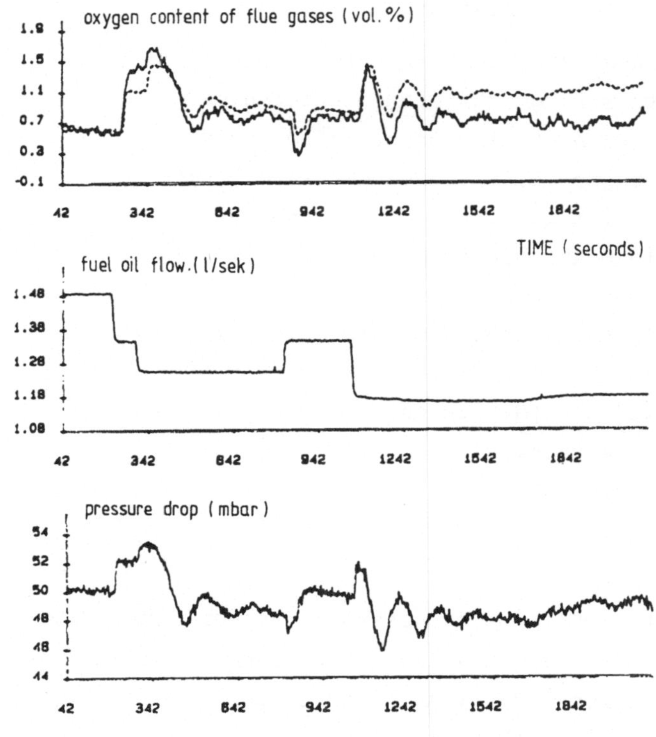


## 4. CONCLUSION

Developed mathematical model for combustion in the boiler in our opinion represents useful tool for further studies of mentioned problems and also concrete controller realization.

Figure 6.   Oxygen content of flue gases

— measurements of oxygen, fuel oil flow and air presure drop

--- simulation with the model for combustion


REFERENCES
1. J.Čretnik,F.Bremšak,S.Strmčnik, Model zgorevanja goriva v industrijskem kurišču, Zbornik radova JUREMA,Vol.1,No.2,pp.277-280,Zagreb 1985 (in Slovene)
2. F.Brandt, Brennstoffe und Verbrennungsrechnung, Vulkan-Verlag, Essen 1981
3. P.Profos, Verminderung des Brennstoffverbrauchs durch Regelung des Abgas-Sauerstoffgehalts bei Indstriefeuerungen, Die Industriefeuerung 22, pp. 49-54, Vulkan-Verlag, Essen 1982
4. K.J.Lehomaki, U.K.J.Kortela,J.J.Luukkanen, New Estimation and control methods for fuel power in peat power plants, 8th Triennial World Congres, Kyoto, Japan 1981
5. U.Kortela, P.Lautala, A new control concept for a coal power plant, 8th Triennial World Congres, Kyoto, Japan 1981

DIE ANWENDUNG DES SIMULATORS GPSS-FORTRAN
ZUR SIMULATION EINES CONTAINER-TERMINALS

Krzysztof AMBORSKI, Maciej KOCIĘCKI
Institut für Regelung und Industrielle Elektronik
Technische Universität Warschau, Warszawa, POLEN

Zusammenfassung

Entwurf eines neuen Container-Terminals oder
Änderungsvorschläge für ein existierendes
Terminal verlangen eine sorgfältige und aufwendige Analyse aller Bedingungen und Ereignisse, die sich im Container-Terminal abspie-
len. Um diese Aufgabe zu erleichtern, verwendet man numerische Simulationen [1]. Da man
ein Container-Terminal als diskreten Prozess
ansehen kann, eignet sich der Simulator GPSS-
-FORTRAN [2] gut für diesen Zweck. An dem vereinfachten Beispiel wird die Anwendung des
Simulators gezeigt.

## 1. EINFÜHRUNG

Die Simulation eines Container-Terminals besteht aus der Simulation
einer Reihe von Ereignissen  - es wird also eine diskrete Simulation
benötigt. Dazu ist die Version 2 des Simulators ausreichend.
GPSS-FORTRAN ist ein Simulationspaket, das im wesentlichen aus einer
Bibliothek von Unterprogrammen besteht und der Simulation diskreter
Prozesse dient. Diese Unterprogramme bilden die Sprachelemente, mit
deren Hilfe der Benutzer sein Modell erstellt. Dank der übersichtlichen
Dokumentation ist es möglich, einfache Modelle sehr schnell mit einem
kleinen Basisset von Sprachelementen zu behandeln.

## 2. ORGANIZATION DES CONTAINER-TERMINALS

Es wird ein Container-Terminal im Binnenland zum Umschlag Schiene-
-Straße betrachtet, es handelt sich im Prinzip um einen speziellen
Güterbahnhof. Die Container werden über große Entfernungen mit der
Bahn zu- und abgeführt. Die Umgebung des Container-Terminals, mit etwa
80 km Radius, als Bedienungsregion bezeichnet, wird mit LKW bedient.

In dieser Bedienungsregion sind die Kunden des Container-Terminals verteilt: Fabriken, Lager usw. Ein typischer Container-Terminal 1 besteht aus folgenden drei Bereichen:

- Kranbereich,
- Lagerbereich,
- Parkplätze.

Die äußeren Attribute des Container-Terminals sind das Bahnnetz und die Bedienungsregion. Der Kranbereich ist mit einem oder mehreren Portalkranen bestückt, die sich auf Kran-Gleisen bewegen. Er umfaßt außerdem Bahngleise, Abstellspuren und Fahrbahnen. Die Bahngleise stellen die Verbindung des Terminals mit dem Bahnnetz her. Die Abstellspuren dienen zum kurzfristigen Abstellen von umzuschlagenden Containern. Die Container können auf den Abstellspuren in mehreren Lagen (bis zu vier) aufeinander gestapelt werden. Die Fahrbahnen für LKW und Terminal-Verladefahrzeuge bilden die Verbindung zwischen dem Terminal und dem Straßennetz. In einem typischen Container-Terminal sind alle Fahrbahnen als Einbahnstraßen eingerichtet. Die Adressierung der Container im Kranbereich ist dreidimensional und umfaßt folgende Angaben:

X - Stellplatznummer,

Y - Abstellspurnummer,

Z - Lagennummer.

Der Leiter des Terminals organisiert Verladung, Lagerung und Transport der Container. Er muß also laufend informiert sein über die Standorte der einzelnen Container, Zu- und Abgänge, Avis von Bahn und Kunden sowie über den Zustand von Verladeeinrichtungen.


## 3. DIE MODELLERSTELLUNG

Das Modell "Container-Terminal" soll zeigen, wie man grundsätzlichen Ereignissen auf dem Container-Terminal mittels GPSS-FORTRAN folgen kann.


### 3.1. Modellbeschreibung

Das Modell "Container-Terminal beschreibt den Kranbereich eines Terminals, welcher 40 Stellplätze (X-Achse) und 12 Spuren (Y-Achse) hat. Davon sind zwei Spuren ausgeschloßen - eine wird als Fahrbahn für LKW, die zweite als Bahngleis verwendet. Die Container dürfen in drei Lagen (Z-Achse) aufeinander gestapelt werden, also besteht die Möglichkeit insgesamt 10 x 40 x 3 = 1200 Container auf den Abstellspuren zu lagern. Alle Container werden durch Portalkran (Facility) bedient. Ankunft und Abfahrt des Zuges sind festgelegt. Die Ankunft des LKW ist stochastisch und wird durch das Unterprogramm ERLANG bestimmt. Es gibt vier mögliche Typen von Transactions:

1.Umordnung eines Containers auf den Abstellspuren,

2.Die Beladung (bzw. Entladung) des Zuges,

3.Die Beladung (bzw. Entladung) des LKW:

    - der LKW hat einen Container mitgebracht, der an einem
bestimmten Platz gestellt werden soll,

    - der LKW hat einen Container mitgebracht, der an einem
beliebigen Platz gestellt werden soll,

    - der LKW soll einen bestimmten Container mitnehmen.

4.Aufdecken des Containers, welcher unter einem (oder zwei) anderen
liegt und zum Transport bestimmt ist. Die oberen Container werden
auf den nächsten freien Platz gestellt.

Für den Portalkran hat jede Transaction zwei Phasen:

    1. Portalkran ist leer und fährt zum Container,

    2. Portalkran fährt mit dem Container.

Die erste Phase darf unterbrochen werden durch eine andere Transaction
mit höherer Priorität. Die zweite Phase darf nicht unterbrochen werden.


3.2. Ausführen der Simulation

Die Simulation des Container-Terminals wurde durch das Programm PLAZA
durchgeführt. Es besteht aus dem Hauptprogramm (dem Rahmen), sieben
kurzen Unterprogrammen (LET, STRX, MIT, CARXY, NEWTX, TRACAR, BREAK)
und Unterprogrammen des Simulators GPSS-FORTRAN.

    LET    berechnet die Schiebevektoren SX,SY und die Zeit, in welcher
der Portalkran die neue Position (X,Y) einnimmt.

    STRX   hilft den Terminalzustand aufzuzeigen.

    MIT    sucht einen freien Platz auf dem Terminal. Die Suche folgt
spiralförmig um einen bestimmten Punkt (X,Y).

    CARXY  bestimmt die Attribute der LKW-Transaction.

    NEWTX  generiert eine neue Transaction, die das "Aufdecken"
ermöglicht.

    TRACAR wählt die nächste Transaction aus der Liste L1 (Abstell-
spuren) oder L2 (Bahn).

    BREAK  nimmt die Attribute der unterbrochenen Transaction zurück.

Das Hauptelement des Modells ist der Portalkran, welcher die einzige
Facility darstellt. Die Transactions werden in drei separate Listen
eingereiht:

    L1 - Umordnung auf den Abstellspuren,

    L2 - Be- und Entladung des Zuges,

    L3 - Be- und Entladung des LKW.

Die höchste Priorität ist L3 zugewiesen, die niedrigste - L1. Die Container aus der Liste L2 werden nur während des Aufenthaltes des Zuges

bedient. Die einzelne Transaction belegt die Facility. Es wurde dabei
berücksichtigt, daß jede Transaction aus zwei Phasen besteht. Die erste
Belegung der Facility - in der erster Phase - wird mittels PREEMP realisiert. Wenn in dieser Zeit eine Transaction mit höheren Priorität zum
Unterprogramm PREEMP kommt, dann wird die gerade ausgeführte Transaction
unterbrochen und in die Warteschlange vor PREEMP eingereiht. Worauf das
Unterprogramm WORK die Fahrt des Portalkranes zum Container realisiert.
Mit CLEAR wird die Facility (also der Portalkran) verlassen und damit
die erste Phase beendet. Sie besteht also aus folgenden drei Aufrufen:

    CALL PREEMP

    CALL WORK

    CALL CLEAR.

Weiter wird geprüft, ob der Container aufgedeckt werden muß. Wenn ja,
dann wird die Transaction in NEWTX modifiziert und das Programm kehrt
zurück zu PREEMP. Wenn nicht, wird die Facility nochmals belegt, diesmal durch das Unterprogramm SEIZE. Dann beginnt die zweite Phase der
Transaction,  welche aus folgenden Aufrufen besteht:

    CALL SEIZE

    CALL ADVANC

    CALL WORK

    CALL ADVANC

    CALL CLEAR

    CALL TERMIN.

Das Unterprogramm ADVANC simuliert das Greifen (bzw. Loslassen) des
Containers, das Unterprogramm WORK simuliert die Fahrt des Portalkranes, diesmal mit dem Container. Mit CLEAR wird die Facility befreit
und mit TERMIN wird die Transaction vernichtet.
Die Simulationszeit wird in drei Fällen modifiziert:

    - eine Unterbrechung (Interruption) ist eingetreten,

    - der Portalkran greift den Container,

    - der Portalkran laßt den Container los.

In solchen Fällen werden die Zeit des neuen Ereignisses und die Schiebevektoren SX,SY berechnet. Im Falle einer Unterbrechung ermöglichen
die Schiebevektoren die Lage des Portalkranes zu bestimmen. Der Termi-
nalzustand wird durch zwei zweidimensionale Tabellen VAT und L5 ständig
überwacht. Die erste ist die Byte-Tabelle 40 x 12  und zeigt die Lagen-
-Belegung von einzelnen XY-Plätzen. Die zweite ist eine Integer-Tabelle
120 x 12, die die Nummern der einzelnen Container auf dem Terminal
enthält.

## 3.3. Ergebnissausgabe

Den Lauf der Simulation kann man auf dem Bildschirm beobachten. Auf dem
Drucker werden die Eingangsdaten (Listen L1, L2, L3, die Zeitgrenze der
Simulation, der Anfangszustand des Terminals, die Ankunft- und Abfahrt-
zeit des Zuges), der Lauf der Simulation und der Endzustand des Terminals samt Tabelle VAT ausgedruckt.

## 4. SCHLUSSBEMERKUNGEN

Die Simulation wurde auf dem Rechner SM-4, der PDP11/40 kompatibel ist,
unter dem Betriebssystem RSX-11M, durchgeführt. Der an der Universität
Erlangen auf der TR440 entwickelte Simulator GPSS-FORTRAN mußte diesem
Rechner angepaßt werden. Die einzelne Aufgabe darf hier höchstens 32 kW
(16-Bit) in Anspruch nehmen. Die Tabellen werden deshalb in einem virtuellen Speicherbereich abgelegt. Bei der Overlay-Struktur entspricht
die Begrenzung (32 kW) dem längsten Zweig. Der Integer-Zahlenbereich in
SM-4 (-2E15, 2E15) ist viel enger als in TR440 (-2E31, 2E31), deshalb
mußten einige Integer-Variablen in Real-Variablen umgesetzt werden. Man
mußte auch die Struktur von GPSS-FORTRAN ein bißchen ändern - statt
eines Set mit 87 Unterprogrammen wurden 61 Sets aufgebaut. Die einzelnen
Rekords wurden von 82 Zeichen auf 72 Zeichen reduziert, dabei sank die
Anzahl der Speicher-Blöcke (â 512 Bytes) von 870 auf 350. Es wurden auch
weitere Beschränkungen eingeführt, es dürfen z.B. maximal 20 Ereignisse,
50 Transactions, 5 Facilities usw. auftreten. Die durchgeführten Test-
aufgaben haben bestätigt, daß GPSS-FORTRAN mit entsprechenden Ergänzungen sich sehr gut für die Simulation eines Container-Terminals eignet.


LITERATUR

[1] K.Amborski - Simulation eines Container-Umschlagplatzes.
            Fördern und heben, Nr 3, 1985.

[2] B.Schmidt  - GPSS-FORTRAN Version 2. Springer Verlag, Berlin-Heidel-
            berg-New York 1978.

[3] J.Szamrej  - Simulationssprache für diskrete Prozessen - GPSS-F.
            Diplomarbeit am Institut für Regelung und Industrielle
            Elektronik, Technische Universität Warschau (Polen) 1984.

# Modellbildung und Simulation von Abwasserreinigungsanlagen

H. Gülich , M. Köhne

Institut für Mechanik und Regelungstechnik
Universität Siegen (GH)
5900 Siegen, Paul-Bonatz-Str. 9-11

Die Bedeutung der Steuerungs- und Regelungstechnik in kommunalen und industriellen Abwasserreinigungsanlagen hat unter den Gesichtspunkten einer besseren Prozeßführung und der Energieeinsparung stark zugenommen. Erste Voraussetzung zur Anwendung moderner Regelungsverfahren ist die Existenz möglichst einfacher mathematischer Modelle, die alle wesentlichen dynamischen Vorgänge des gesamten Abwasserreinigungsprozesses beschreiben.

Im Vortrag werden für diesen Zweck geeignete nichtlineare Modelle vorgestellt, die nicht nur den Stofftransport durch die örtlich ausgedehnten Vorklärbecken berücksichtigen, sondern ebenso die biochemischen Reaktionsvorgänge im Belebungsbecken und den Sedimentationsprozeß im Nachklärbecken erfassen.

Die Modellparameter wurden beispielhaft für das Klärwerk der Stadt Siegen durch Vergleich von Simulationsergebnissen und Messungen bestimmt. Besondere Bedeutung kommt hierbei der gleichzeitigen kontinuierlichen Messung relevanter Prozeßgrößen, wie z.B des biochemischen Sauerstoffbedarfs BSB, im Zulauf und Auslauf einzelner Anlagenteile zu.

Die Simulation des Prozesses und die Optimierung der Modellparameter wurde mit einem schnellen digitalen Optimierungs- und Simulationsprogramm (DOPSI) durchgeführt. Dieses Programm ist modular aufgebaut und benutzt ein direktes Optimierungsverfahren. Die hierbei benötigten wiederholten Simulationen werden mit Assembler-Makros oder im Hybridbetrieb auf einem Analogrechner durchgeführt, um kurze Rechenzeiten zu erreichen.

Die Aussagekraft des vorgestellten Modelles für Abwasserreinigungsanlagen wird abschließend anhand einiger typischer gemessener Zeitverläufe diskutiert.

S I M U L A T I O N   I N   D E R

F E R T I G U N G S T E C H N I K

# Die Simulation unterstützt die Montageplanung

Letters, F., Stuttgart

Das Modell und Programmsystem MOMOS wird am Fraunhoferinstitut für Arbeitswirtschaft und Organisation (IAO), Professor Bullinger, entwickelt.

**Zusammenfassung:** Die Simulation unterstützt die Planung und das Betreiben moderner Montage- und Arbeitssysteme. Der Montage-Modell-Simulator (MOMOS) bildet die Montagesysteme in ein Modellsystem ab. Bevorzugt werden Systeme, in de- nen großvolumige Güter befördert und produziert werden. An einem praktischen Beispiel wird der Weg von der Modellbildung eines bemannten Montagesystems bis zur Darstellung der Ergebnisse einer Simulationsstudie aufgezeigt.


**Summary:** Simulation supports planning and operation of modern assembly- and working-systems. The Assembly-Model-Simulator (MOMOS) models assembly-systems. MOMOS favours systems that transport and assemble spacy products. A practical application shows the way from the designing the model of a manual assembly system to the presentation of the results of one simulationrun.

## 1    Planung von Montagesystemen

Die Planung moderner Montagesysteme stellt hohe Anforderungen an die Unternehmen, da sich sowohl die technischen, ökonomischen und sozialen Umfeldanforderungen als auch die Produktionsaufgaben ändern. Den wechselnden Anforderungen wird durch eine flexibel einsetzbare Planungssystematik, Bild 1 und /1,2/ Rechnung getragen:

1    Die Planung beginnt mit der Analyse der vorhandenen Produkt- und Produktionsdaten sowie der Definition der Aufgabenstellung.

2    Im nächsten Schritt werden die Montagestruktur und die Kapazität geplant /3,4/.

3    Alternative Montagesysteme werden in Form von Prinziplösungen präzisiert.

4    Die Prinziplösungen werden miteinander verglichen und bewertet, um dann die beste Alternative auszuwählen.

5    Das Gesamtsystem wird unter Beachtung von Randbedingungen, z.B. Raumangebot, Personalsituation, Zeitrahmen und Investitionsvolumen optimal geplant.

6    Im Anschluß an die Feinplanung erfolgt die Realisierung des Montagesystems und dessen Inbetriebnahme.


Für einige der Aufgaben, wie z.B. die Erstellung von Vorrangraphen, stehen EDV-Werkzeuge zur Verfügung. Problematisch wird es allerdings dann, wenn die Planungsergebnisse und deren Auswirkungen auf das Gesamtsystem untersucht und bewertet werden sollen. Hier kommt zur Zeit als einziges in der Praxis einsetzbares EDV-Werkzeug die Simulation in Frage.

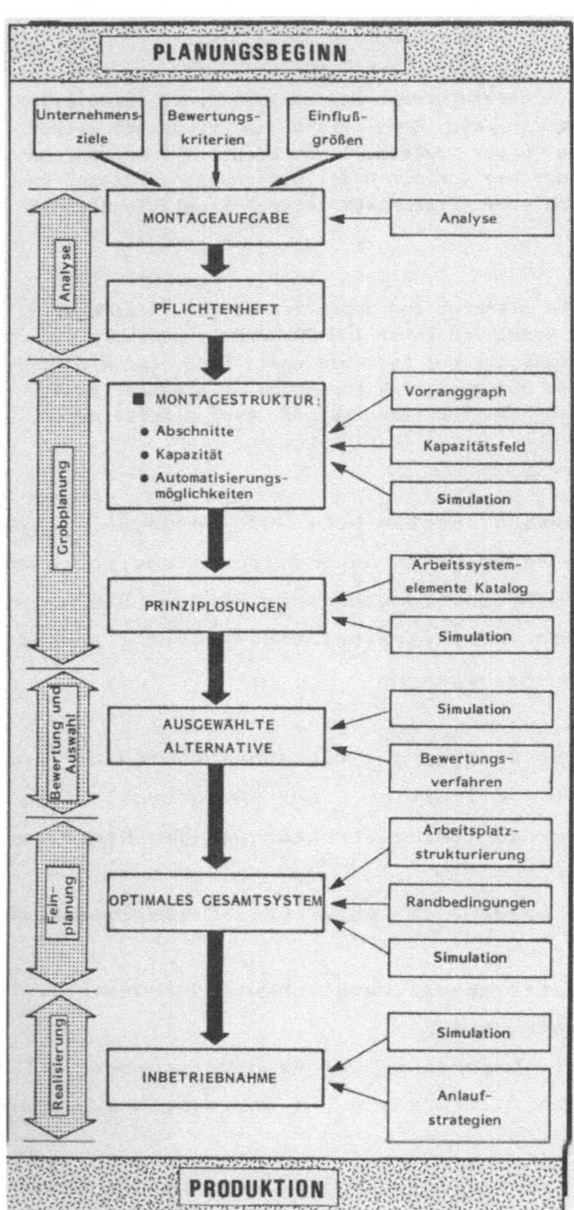



Bild 1:    Planungssystematik

2    Simulation in der Planung

Sobald keine exakten Verfahren zur Bewertung und Überprüfung der Planung vorhanden sind, kann die Simulation eingesetzt werden. Mit ihr können Aussagen über die Funktion und Produktionsleistung eines Systems gemacht werden. Die Daten für die Bewertung werden in Experimenten mit dem Rechner gewonnen. Der Einsatz der Simulation in der Planung erfolgt auf 2 von der Zielrichtung her unterschiedliche    Methoden:

Simulation über einige Monate: Mit der Simulation können unterschiedliche Montagestrukturen, Kapazitäten, Produktionsprogramme und Materialströme untersucht werden /5,6/. Dem Planer werden Entscheidungshilfen zur Auswahl der optimalen Struktur und Kapazität    gegeben. Simulation über einige Tage:    Nach der Vorentscheidung für eine oder mehrere geeignete Strukturen werden detailliertere Simulationen notwendig. Das Zusammenwirken der Elemente des Systems und

die Produktivität werden unter Beachtung physischer Randbedingungen in alternativen Layouts untersucht. In den Simulationen wird der Transport, die Bearbeitung und Pufferung der Werkstücke nachgebildet /7,8,9/. Im Folgenden beschränkt sich der Beitrag auf die Beschreibung der Einsatzmöglichkeiten, der Vorgehensweise und den Erfahrungen mit Simulationssystemen der 2. Gruppe, Bild 2:

485

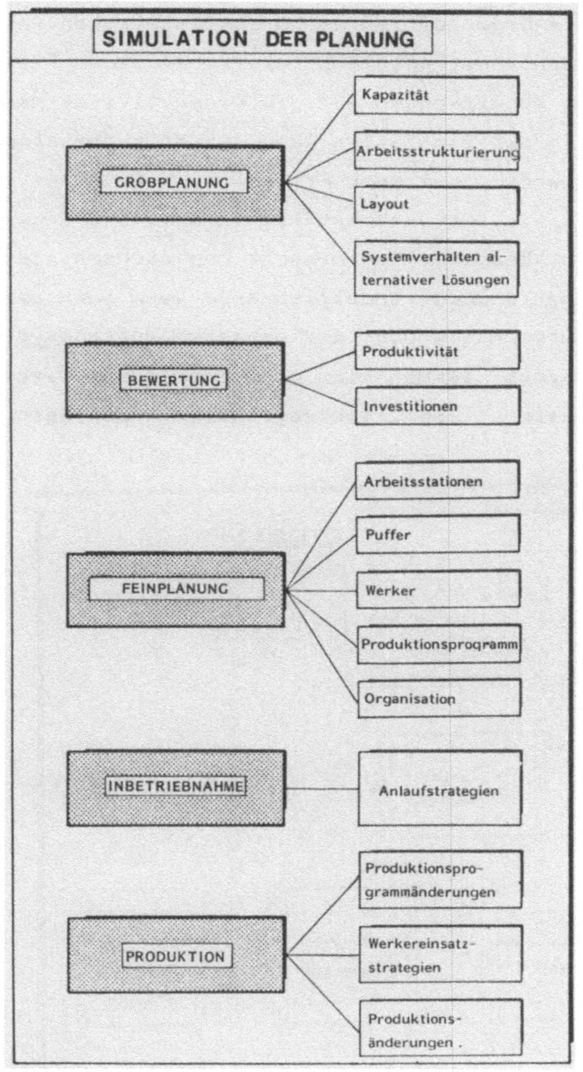



Bild 2:     Simulation in der Planung

In den ersten Simulationen einer Grobplanung können alternative Montagekonzepte, die zumindest in Form von Prinziplösungen detailliert sind, verglichen und analysiert werden. Einige typische Simulationsexperimente untersuchen die Anordnung von Arbeitsstationen und Puffern, sowie die Auslegung der verkettenden Transportsysteme:

<u>Die Simulation erfüllt in dieser Phase 2 Aufgaben:</u>

1 Bevor eine Simulation ausgeführt werden kann, muß die Prinziplösung in ein Modell abgebildet werden. Dieser überwiegend manuell vom Planer durchzuführende Vorgang prüft zunächst die Daten und die Alternative auf ein Mindestmaß an Vollständigkeit und gibt dem Planer während der Modellierung neue Ideen ein, da er die wesentlichen Elemente und Ideen der geplanten Alternative überdenken und präzisieren muß.

2 Die Simulation liefert für alle geplanten Alternativen ein einheitliches Prüfverfahren. Die Ergebnisse, z. B. Produktivität des Montagesystems, eingesetzte Transportmittel, oder benötigte Puffer, können direkt miteinander verglichen werden. Aus den direkt "meßbaren" Ergebnissen können dann die für die Bewertung und Auswahl der Alternativen entscheidenden Daten gewonnen werden. In Form von einfachen Investitions- oder Wirtschaftlichkeitsrechnungen können dann reproduzierbare und gesicherte Entscheidungen getroffen werden.

486

o   Die weitere Planung reicht von der Feinplanung des Gesamtsystems der optimalen Alternative bis zu ihrer Realisierung. Mit der Simulation werden die Puffergrößen, die Organisation der Arbeitsstationen und Puffer, sowie verfeinerte Montagestrukturen, unterschiedliche Produktionsprogramme und deren Auswirkungen auf die Produktivität des Montagesystems untersucht. In der Simulation kann das Montagesystem so detailliert nachgebildet werden, daß auch Fragen wie z.B. Auswirkungen von flexibler Arbeitszeit, Automatenstationen oder Störungen einzelner Elemente des Montagesystems untersucht und nachgebildet werden können. Vor oder während der Inbetriebnahme kann auch das Anlaufverhalten einzelner Abschnitte oder des gesamten Montagesystems untersucht werden. Daraus lassen sich dann Regeln für diese nur schwer überschaubare Realisierungsphase festlegen.

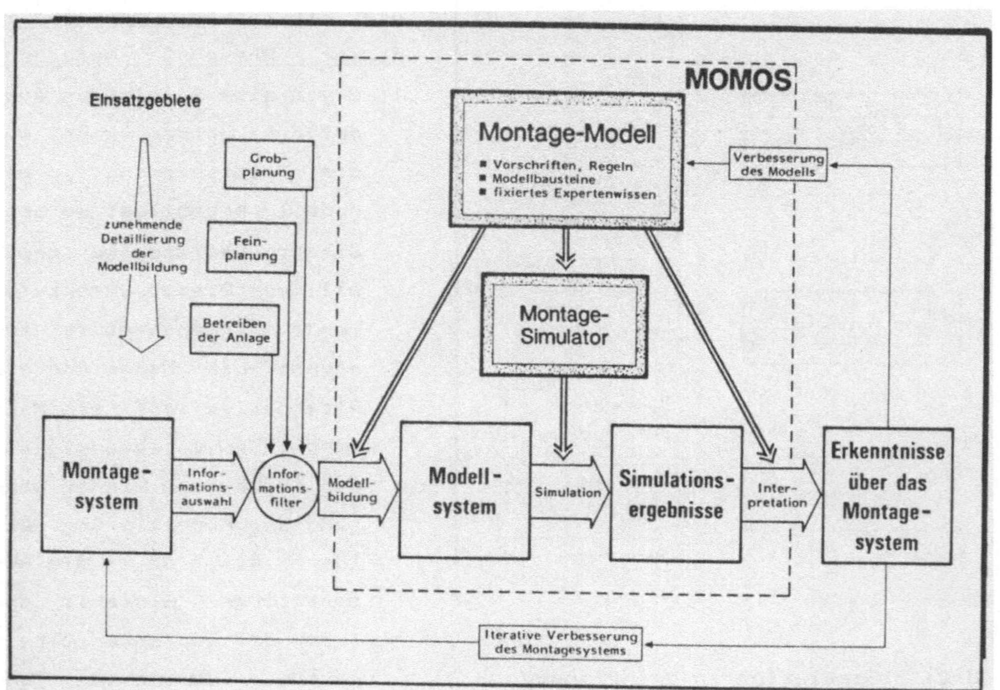


Bild     3:   Gesamtkonzept   des   Montage-Modell-Simulators   MOMOS

o   In der laufenden Produktion können die Auswirkungen von Produktionsprogrammänderungen, verschiedene Personaleinsatzstrategien oder auch Umstellungen im Produktionsprozeß vorab untersucht und teilweise quantifiziert werden.

Um die Möglichkeiten und Grenzen der Simulation verständlich zu machen, wird im Folgenden die Modellbildung und Simulation mit dem Simulationssystem MOMOS, unserem Montage-Modell-Simulator, aufgezeigt /9/.

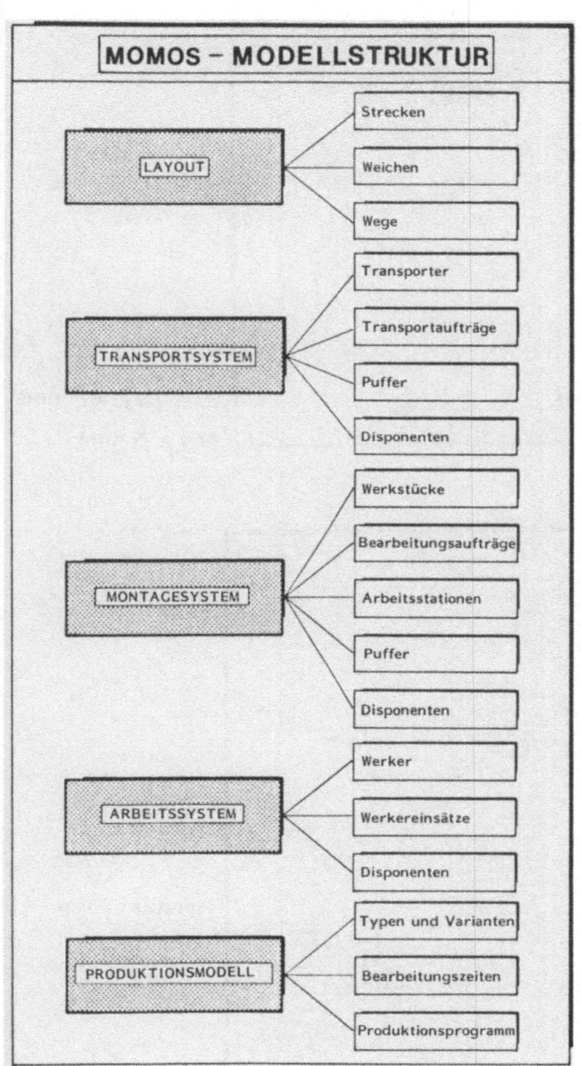



## 3 Vorgehensweise bei der Simulation mit MOMOS

Der Montage-Modell-Simulator (MOMOS) ist ein Simulationswerkzeug. Er eignet sich insbesondere für hybride Anlagen, bei denen der Mensch im Mittelpunkt steht und in einem automatisierten Umfeld arbeitet, z.B. FTS (Fahrerloses Transportsystem) und Handhabungsgeräte in der Montage. MOMOS unterstützt die Unternehmen beim Planen und Betreiben von Montagesystemen. Vor der Simulation werden das Layout, das Produktionsmodell und die Organisationsformen der Montagesysteme in ein abstraktes Montage-Modell abgebildet. Im Modell können das Transportgeschehen und der Produktionsverlauf mit dem Montage-Simulator nachvollzogen werden, Bild 3.

### 3.1 Modellbildung

Das Modell beschreibt den logischen Aufbau realer Montagesysteme sowie die Abläufe in diesen Systemen. Durch eine modulare Abbildung lassen sich stark voneinander abweichende Systeme nachbilden. Konkurrierende Transportsysteme, wie z.B. Plattenband, Hängebahn und FTS können modelliert und kombiniert werden. Die Montage kann in Form von Linien oder auch parallelen Einzelarbeitsplätzen abgebildet werden. Die Werker können einzeln oder in Gruppen arbeiten. Die Steuerung und Organisation kann zentral oder dezentral mit wechselnden Strategien erfolgen. Die Abbildung eines Montagesystems in das Montage-Modell erfolgt in 5 Phasen, in denen zunächst die physische Struktur und dann die Betriebs- und Organisationsformen abgebildet werden, Bild 4. 2 Bilder verdeutlichen die Modellbildung eines Montagelayouts und der vorgegebenen Arbeitsstruktur, Bild 5 und 6, /10/.

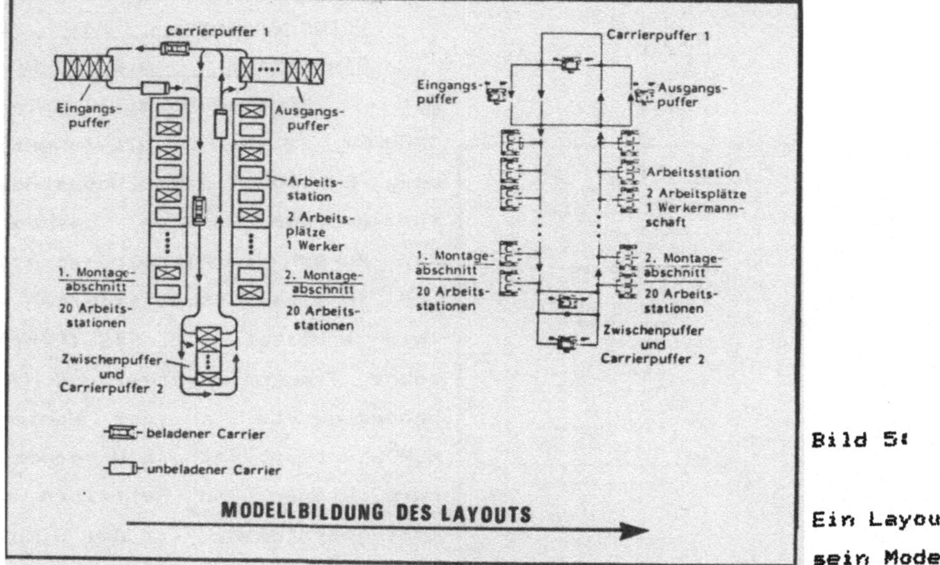



**Bild 5:**

**Ein Layout und sein Modell**

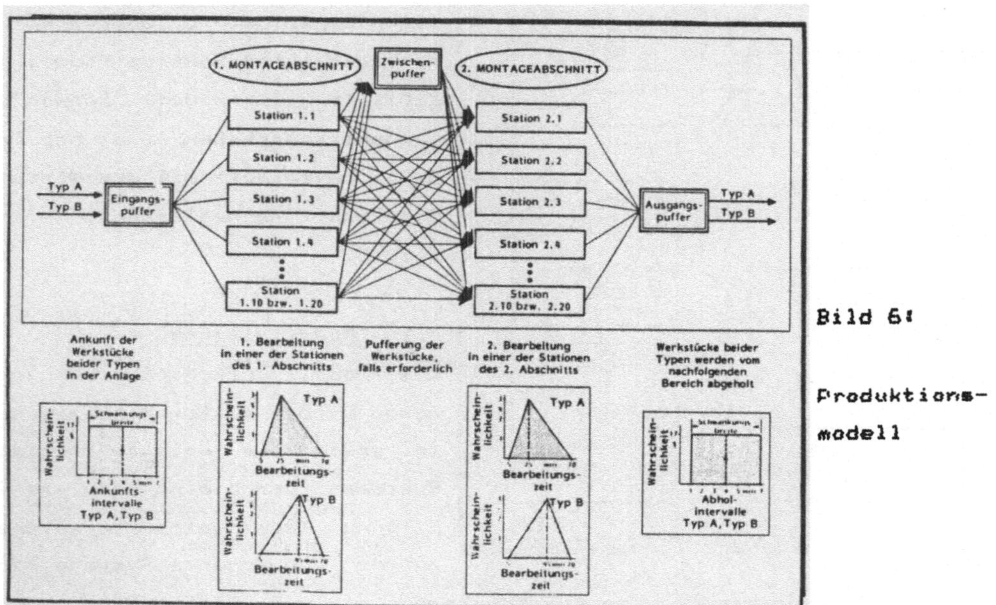



**Bild 6:**

**Produktions-modell**

## 3.2 Simulation und Simulationssystem

Die Simulation "spielt" in einem abstrakten Experiment das Transportgeschehen, den Produktionsprozeß und unterschiedliche Dispositionsstrategien durch. Im Simulator werden anstelle der "echten" Transporter, Werkstücke und Werker Datensätze "bewegt". Das Ergebnis des abstrakten Experiments stellt sich als eine der Realität entsprechende Vielzahl an Daten dar. Die Auswertung dieser Daten ist (leider) nicht eindeutig festgelegt. Sie hängt wesentlich vom Ziel des Anwenders ab, Bild 7.

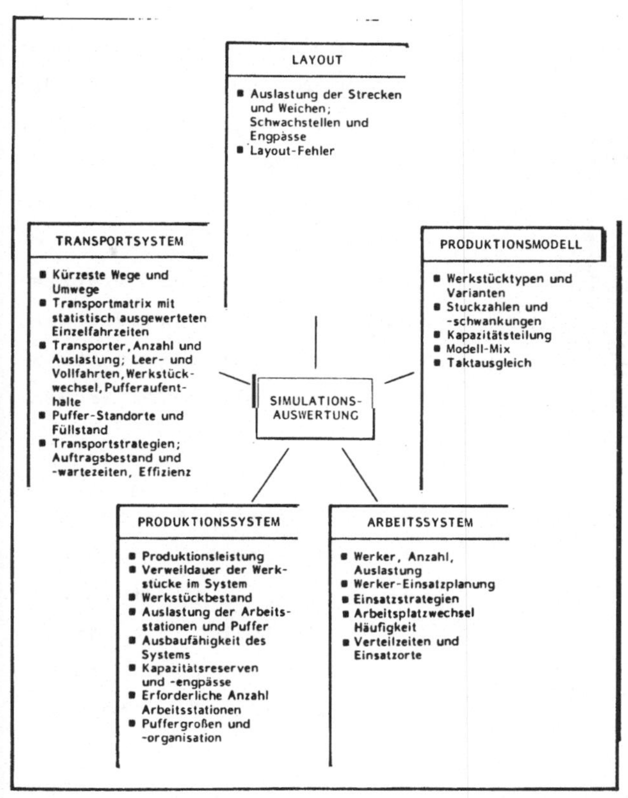

Bild 7: Untersuchungsziele mit MOMOS

Der Anwender beschreibt sein Modellsystem durch Parameter. Anschließend erzeugt MOMOS automatisch ein Simulationsprogramm in SLAM (Simulation Language for Alternative Modeling /11/). Mit diesem wird die interaktive Simulation durchgeführt. Die Daten der Modellsysteme und die umfangreichen Simulationsergebnisse werden vom Simulationssystem verwaltet. Alle Vorgänge während der Simulation können beobachtet werden. Das Modellsystem kann teilweise während der Simulation verändert werden. Der Simulationsverlauf kann durch Änderung einzelner Parameter oder Strategien gesteuert werden. Während der Simulation werden alle Abläufe und Ereignisse in chronologischer Form gespeichert und können auch nach der Simulation wiederholt zu verschiedenen Untersuchungen ausgewertet werden.

## 4.3    Simulationsergebnisse

Nach den Simulationen werden zunächst einige typische Daten ausgewertet, Bild 8. Mit dem Produktionsfortschritt wird die Leistung des Systems summarisch festgehalten. Die Auslastung der Werker und Arbeitsstationen liefert exakte Aussagen über Verluste und Engpässe in der Montage, die mit der Dokumentation der Pufferfüllstände gewichtet werden können. Das Transportsystem kann mit Hilfe des Aktivitätsprofils der Transporter, dem Auftragsbestand und den Reaktionszeiten bewertet werden. Im Rahmen einer Fabrikplanung müssen diese Ergebnisse im Zusammenhang und Vergleich mit weiteren Simulationen untersucht werden. Das jeweilige Optimierungsziel, z.B. minimale Investitions- oder Betriebskosten, entscheidet dann über die Aussagekraft der Einzelergebnisse. Die optimale Auslegung des Montagesystems erfolgt durch Vergleich und Auswertung der ermittelten Simulationsergebnisse. Dies ist jedoch nur ein Teil der

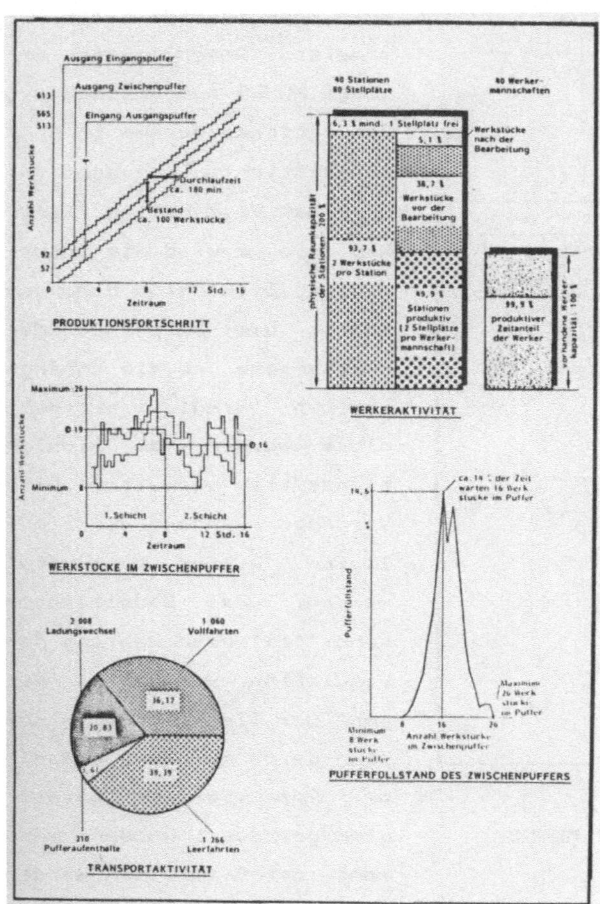

**PRODUKTIONSFORTSCHRITT**

**WERKSTÜCKE IM ZWISCHENPUFFER**

**TRANSPORTAKTIVITÄT**

**WERKERAKTIVITÄT**

**PUFFERFÜLLSTAND DES ZWISCHENPUFFERS**

Bild 8:     Typische Simulationsergebnisse

Aufgaben des Planers. Insbesondere muß ein modernes Montagekonzept mit bestehenden Systemen verglichen werden. Dabei müssen auch Fragen der Materialbereitstellung und Entlohnung geklärt und Randbedingungen (z.B. Platzbedarf, Investitionsvolumen, vor- und nachgelagerte Bereiche usw.) betrachtet werden.

5     Erfahrungen

Zwei Praxisbeispiele bestätigen den Einsatz und Nutzen der Simulation:

o   Pilotstudien zur Konzeption neuer und modular strukturierter Montagesysteme, Bild 9 und /10/.

o   Unterstützung der Planung und des Aufbaus eines modernen und flexiblen Arbeitssystems zur Endmontage von Gabelstaplern, Bild 10.

In beiden Fällen hilft die Simulation bei der Planung bzw. dem Aufbau der Systeme auf 5 Arten:

1   Bereits bei der Entwicklung von Prinziplösungen fördert die Modellbildung die Kreativität des Planers und gibt ihm weitere Ideen ein. Gleichzeitig wird der Planer gezwungen, die Prinzipien mit einer hinreichenden Genauigkeit zu planen, damit die Simulation sinnvolle Aussagen liefert.

2   Die Simulation liefert vergleichbare Daten für die Prinziplösungen und damit zu ihrer Bewertung.

3   Während der Planung der optimalen Gesamtlösung überprüft und integriert die Simulation Systemstrukturen. Insbesondere werden organisatorische Spielräume und notwendige Regeln aufgezeigt.

4   In der Anlaufphase definiert die Simulation Abläufe und organisatorische Regeln für die Inbetriebnahme des Systems.

5   Im laufenden Betrieb werden Produktionsprogrammänderungen und Anpassungen, z.B. Montage eines weiteren Typs, untersucht.

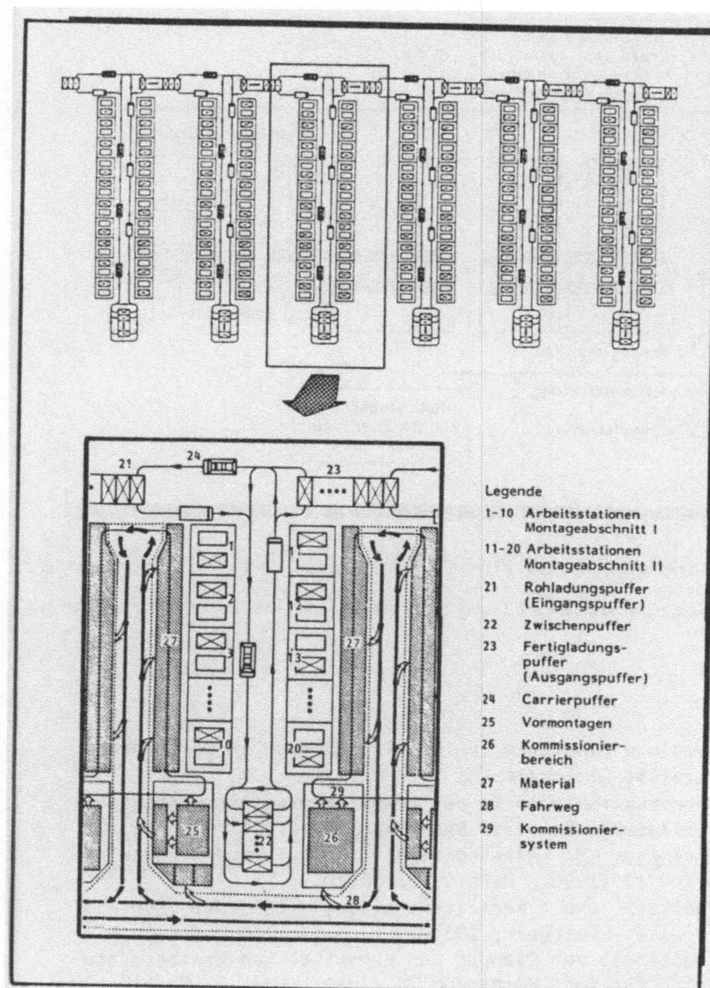

Bild 9:   Prinzip-Layout einer Automobil-End-
          Montage im Boxensystem, unterstützt
          durch ein FTS.



# 6    Zukunft

Um den zunehmend anspruchsvoller werdenden Aufgabenstellungen der Praxis Rechnung tragen zu können, müssen die Simulationssysteme weiter entwickelt werden. Wir beschreiben die Ziele für MOMOS:

o **Modell und Simulator:** Das Montage-Modell wird auf die Beschreibung ganzer Fabriksysteme erweitert um die gesamten Lager-, Fertigungs-, Montage- und Transportabläufe simulieren zu können. Besondere Beachtung finden auch in Zukunft Systeme, bei denen der Mensch im Mittelpunkt steht und in einem automatisierten Umfeld arbeitet.

o **Simulator und Programmsystem:** Die "Intelligenz" des Programmsystems soll erhöht werden, mit dem Ziel, ein Expertensystem zu entwickeln, das den Planer inhaltlich unterstützt, "konzentrierte" Ergebnisse liefert und Optimierungsvorschläge macht /12/.

o **Programmsystem und Hardwareumgebung:** Angestrebt wird eine Einbindung des Programmsystems in eine CIM-Umgebung (Computer-Integrated-Manufacturing) /13/. Die Simulation als Experimentierfeld für EDV-Steuerungssysteme scheint hierbei ein weiteres Einsatzgebiet für Expertensysteme der Zukunft zu werden /14/.

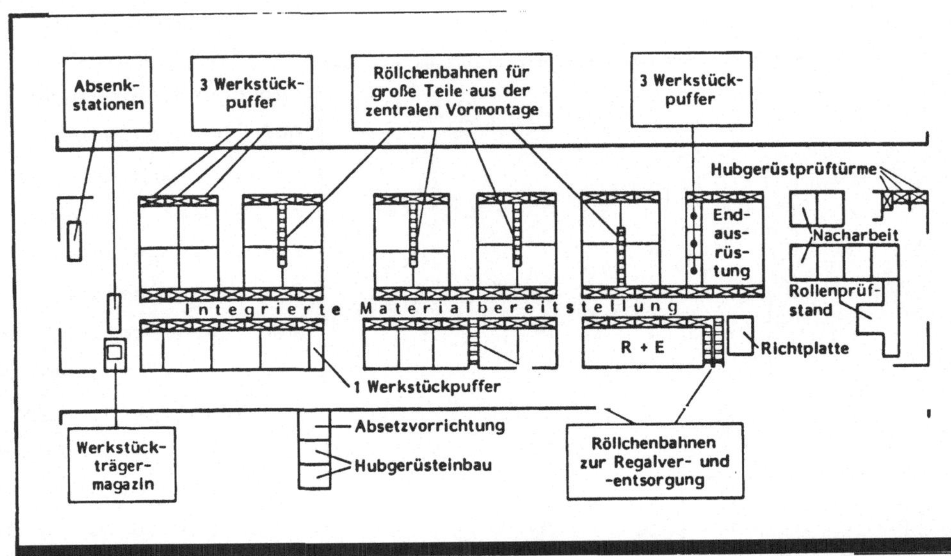



Bild 10: Flexibles Endmontagesystem für Gabelstapler mit FTS und integrierter Materialbereitstellung (Firma Jungheinrich, Hamburg)

## 7 Literatur:


/1/ Metzger, H.  Planung und Bewertung von Arbeitssystemen in der Montage, Dissertation, Universität Stuttgart.

/2/ Bullinger H.-J.  Arbeitsstrukturen in der zukunftsweisenden Produktion, Fachtagung: Der zeitgemäße Betrieb, Bad Soden, Mai 1985, S. 3.1-3.28.

/3/ Warnecke, H. J., Dittmayer, S.  Planungsleitlinien für neue Arbeitsformen in der Montage, AV 17 (1980), Heft 2, S. 35-40

/4/ Dittmayer, S.  Arbeits- und Kapazitätsteilung in der Montage, Dissertation, Universität Stuttgart, 1981.

/5/ Sauer, H. Simulationsmodell zur Planung der Kapazität von Montagesystemen, wt - Zeitschrift für ind. Fertigung 74 (1984), Heft 7, S. 419-422

/6/ Dangelmaier W., Bachers R.  SIMULAP - a simulation system for material flow and warehouse design, Simulation in Manufacturing, März 85, Stratford England S. 151-160.

/7/ Weckerle, E., Scheifele, M., Warschat, J.  Simulation als Hilfsmittel zur Gestaltung von Fertigungs- und Montagesystemen, IAO-Arbeitstagung "Wettbewerbsfähige Arbeitssysteme", November 1983, Böblingen.

/8/ Kuhn, A., Großeschallau, W.  Konzept zur rechnergesteuerten Planung komplexer Materialflußsysteme, VDI-Z 124 (1982), Nr. 7., S. 269-277

/9/ Letters, F.  Vorstellung eines Montage-Modell-Simulators (MOMOS), Informatik Fachbericht 85, Simulationstechnik, Springer Berlin, 1984, S. 231-235.

/10/ Bullinger H.-J., Koether R., Letters F.  Auslegung einer Automobil-Endmontage mit Hilfe der Simulation, ZWF 12/84, S. 607-612.

/11/ Pritsker A. A. B., Pegden C. D.  Introduction to Simulation and SLAM, Halsted Press, John Wiley & Sons, System-Publishing-Corporation, West Lafayette, Indiana

/12/ Raulefs, P.  Expertensysteme, Informatik Fachbericht 59, Künstliche Intelligenz, Springer Verlag Berlin, Heidelberg 1982, S. 61-98.

/13/ Little, A. D.  The Strategic Benefits of Computer-Integrated-Manufacturing, INSEAD, Fontainebleau 1984.

/14/ Szuba, T./  PROLOG as a real time language for process control, Angewandte Informatik 9/84, S. 370-374

SIMULATION : SCHLÜSSEL ZUR OPTIMIERUNG DER BETRIEBS-
MITTELSPEZIFISCHEN AKTIVITÄTEN IM BETRIEB


M. Soliman, G. Reinicke
Institut für Fertigungstechnik (IFW)
Universität Hannover


Zusammenfassung. Die Relevanz einer Optimierung des Betriebsmittel-
wesens in der industriellen Fertigung wird verdeutlicht. Auf die
Entstehunsquellen der Kosten im Betriebsmittelwesen wird eingegangen.
Das Programm BMSIM wird vorgestellt. Dabei werden die Besonderheiten
bei der Simulation von Betriebsmittelkreisläufen im prozeßnahen Bereich, sowie Eingabe, Ausgabe und Funktionsweise des Programms erläutert.


## 1. Kosten im Betriebsmittelwesen

In fertigungstechnischen Betrieben entfallen ein Großteil der Kosten
auf die Betriebsmittel, d.h. Werkzeuge, Spannmittel, Meß und Prüfmit-
tel. Sie binden nicht nur selber Kapital, sondern verursachen noch
weitere Kosten u.a. a) durch ihre Bevorratung, b) durch Transport,
Montage und Aufbereitung, c) durch ihren Einfluß auf den Fertigungs-
prozeß und d) durch ihre unvorhersehbare Nichtverfügbarkeit. Hier
besteht also ein dringender Bedarf nach Rationalisierung. Eine Möglichkeit dazu ist durch die Gestaltung des Betriebsmitteleinsatzes
gegeben.

Einflußmöglichkeiten auf den Betriebsmittelfluß sind u.a. gegeben
durch Änderung der Ablauforganisation des Betriebsmitteleinsatzes. Der
Zusammenhang dieser Maßnahme mit den entstehenden Kosten ist zu komplex, als daß er mit herkömmlichen Methoden bestimmbar wäre. Hier bietet sich die Simulation als ein Verfahren an, das es ermöglicht, trotz
dieser Komplexität, eine Beurteilung der Organisationsalternativen
nach betriebsspezifischen Gesichtspunkten vorzunehmen.


## 2. Besonderheiten des Betriebsmittelflusses

Der prinzipielle Einsatzkreislauf der Betriebsmittel im prozeßnahen
Bereich, in Bild 1 dargestellt, besteht aus den vier Stationen Be-
triebsmittellager, -bereitstellung, -aufbereitung, und Werkstück-

bearbeitung. Die Betriebsmittel durchfließen diese Stationen jeweils nach einem individuellen Fahrplan, in dem die Stationen, die dort auszuführenden Tätigkeiten und das dazu benötigte Personal in logischer Reihenfolge aufgelistet sind. Änderungen des Betriebsmitteleinsatzes bewirken demzufolge Änderungen dieses Fahrplans.

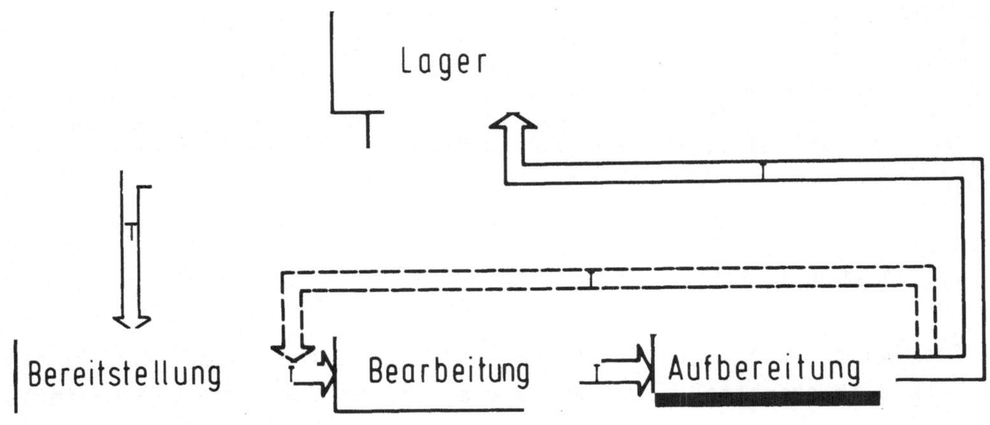


**Bild 1:**  Betriebsmittelkreislauf (T: Transport)

Simulationstechnische Ansätze zur Lösung der verschiedensten fertigungstechnischen Aufgaben in anderen Bereichen der industriellen Fertigung, besonders bei Materialfluß - und Reihenfolgeproblemen, sind in der einschlägigen Literatur reichlich vorhanden.

Folgende betriebsmittelfluß-spezifische Sachverhalte sprechen gegen die Übertragbarkeit dieser Verfahren auf die Abbildung des Betriebsmitteleinsatzes im prozeßnahen Bereich:

- Kreislaufprinzip: wiederholter Einsatz von Betriebsmitteln, die bereits verwendet worden sind,
- durch Verschleiß abnehmende Einsatzfähigkeit der Betriebsmittel,
- die Möglichkeit zur Wiederaufbereitung von Betriebsmitteln,
- unvorhersehbare Störungen, die im Betriebsmittelkreislauf im prozeßnahen Bereich eine gewichtige Rolle spielen, weil sie die Produktivität, die Durchlaufzeiten und durch eventuelle Betriebsmittel-Eilbeschaffungen die Kosten direkt beeinflussen. Eine Erhöhung der Durchlaufzeit kann auch zu Terminverzügen führen.

## 3. Störungen im Kreislauf

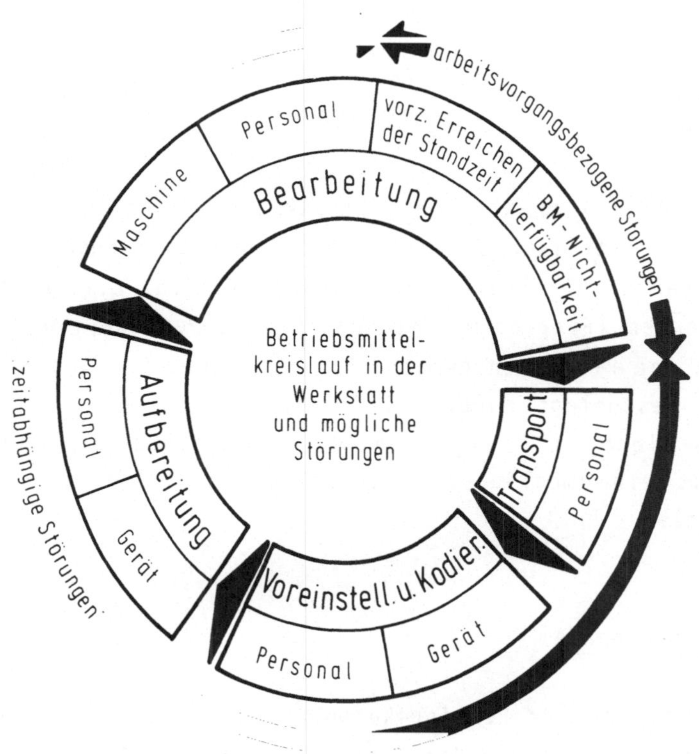


**Bild 2:** Störungen im Betriebsmittelkreislauf

**Bild 2** zeigt die möglichen Störungen, die bei der Bearbeitung eines
Auftrages unvorhersehbar auftreten können. Danach ist zwischen zwei
Störungsarten zu unterscheiden. Die arbeitsvorgangsabhängigen Störungen tauchen an der Bearbeitungsmaschine auf. Sie sind an dem(den) für
die Bearbeitung des Auftrages notwendigen Betriebsmittel(n) und
seinen(ihren) technologischen und geometrischen Eigenschaften gebunden. Im Betriebsmittelkreislauf werden folgende Störungen als arbeits-
abhängig bezeichnet :

- vorzeitiges Erliegen des Betriebsmittels
- Betriebsmittel-Nichtverfügbarkeit

Die zeitabhängigen Störungen hingegen hängen nicht vom Arbeitsvorgang
ab. Sie treten zu einem bestimmten Zeitpunkt in irgendeinem Bereich
des Betriebsmittelflusses auf und stören dadurch den Auftrag, der sich
gerade dort in Bearbeitung befindet. Diese Störungsart umfaßt sowohl

die Personal- als auch die Maschinenausfälle an den verschiedenen Kreislaufstationen.


## 4. Programm BMSIM

Das Programm BMSIM kann als ein zeitdiskretes, stochastisches Simulationsmodell charakterisiert werden. Die Implementierung des Modells erfolgte in der Simulationssprache SIMSCRIPT II.5. Alle wichtigen Betriebskomponenten (Betriebsmittel, Maschinen, Personal) wurden im Modell in Form von Prozessen dargestellt, in denen ihr prozesstypischer "Lebenslauf" festgelegt wurde. Die Kommunikation der Prozesse untereinander geschieht mit Hilfe spezieller Routinen. Die Aufgabe des Programms ist eine möglichst naturgetreue, detailierte Modellierung eines Betriebes.


## 4.1 Simulationseingabe

Nach der Definition der Betriebskomponenten werden noch folgende Informationen zur Darstellung des Betriebes benötigt:
- Angaben über die Parameter eines Betriebes, z.B. über die Anzahl der Maschinen
- Angaben über die Struktur des Betriebes, z.B. Festlegung der Aufgabenbereiche einzelner Personen.
- Eingabe der Organisation der Betriebsmittel, d.h. Festlegung welche Tätigkeiten für einzelne Betriebsmittel ausgeführt werden sollen. Dieses unter Berücksichtigung ihres jeweiligen Zustandes, des geforderten Zustandes und der zu betrachtenden Organisationsalternative.
- Eingabe des zu simulierenden Auftragsspektrums

## 4.2 Simulationsergebnisse

Für die Bewertung einer Organisationsalternative sind in SIMUL folgende Zielkriterien vorgesehen :
(die Berechnung erfolgt jeweils bezogen auf ein Zeitintervall)

### A) Termintreue

Um festzustellen, inwiefern die Auftragsfertigstellungstermine eingehalten werden können, wird in BMSIM für jeden Auftrag der Zeitverzug
berechnet, mit der der Soll-Fertigstellungstermin überschritten wird.
Dann werden die Zeitverzüge über alle in einem Zeitfenster abgew-
ickelten Aufträge zu einem Gesamtzeitverzug summiert. Dieser wird als
ein Maß für die Termintreue bei der simulierten Systemalternative angesehen.

### B) Im Werkzeugfluß verursachte Kosten

In BMSIM werden diese Kosten aus folgenden Anteilen berechnet:

- Transportkosten
- Bereitstellkosten
- Aufbereitungskosten

### C) Auslastung der Kapazitätseinheiten

### D) Investment

Unter Investement wird hier die Summe aller Anschaffungskosten für
die Betriebsmittel und für die in allen Stationen des Betriebsmittelflusses, außer der Station 'Bearbeitung, stehenden Maschinen und Geräte verstanden. Beispiele für solche Maschinen und Geräte sind
Voreinstell-, Kodiergeräte und Nachschleifmaschinen.

**Bild 3** zeigt ein Beispiel der Ausgabemöglichkeiten der Simulationser-
gebisse.

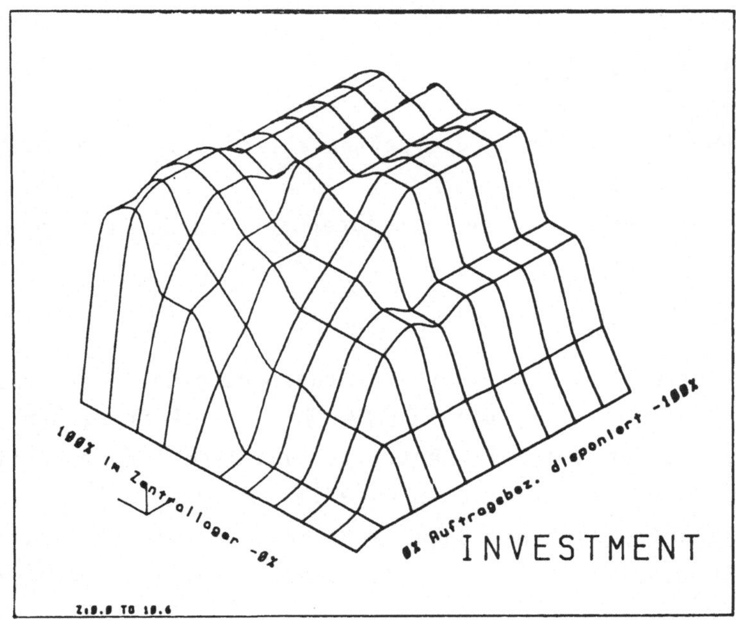



<u>Bild 3</u>:   Ausgabe der Simulationsergebnisse

## 5. Optimierung des Betriebsmitteleinsatzes

Es wurde ein Simulationsmodul gebildet, der, innerhalb eines über-
greifenden Planungssystems, <u>Bild 4</u>, die über eine Optimierungsstrate-
gie definierten Organisationsalternativen des Betriebsmitteleinsatzes
abbildet.

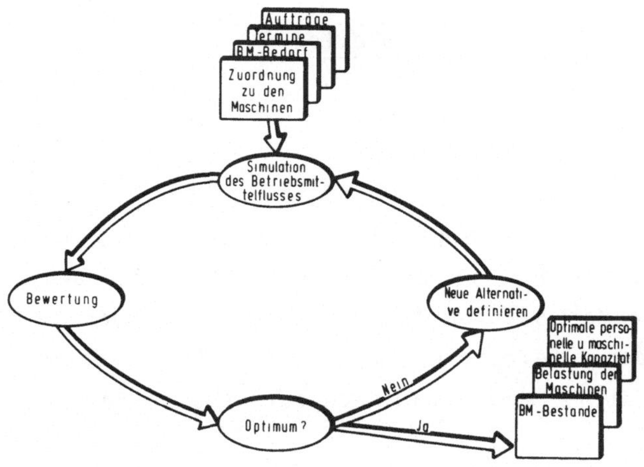



<u>Bild 4</u>:   Prozedur zur Optimierung des Betriebsmitteleinsatzes
            (schematisch)

Anschließend an die Simulation des Zeitverhaltens des Systems werden die Alternativen über einen Bewertungsmodul beurteilt. Zur Bewertung werden mehrere betriebsspezifische Zielsetzungen herangezogen. Die optimale, praxisgerechte Organisationsform wird abschließend ermittelt, der dafür notwendige Betriebsmittelbedarf bestimmt und die dabei entstehende Belastung der verschiedenen Stationen im Kreislauf berechnet.

## 6. Literaturverzeichnis


/1/ Tönshoff, H. K.

Rationelle Organisation des Werkzeugwesens bei spandender Kleinserienfertigung.
Teil 1: Werkzeugplanung
Teil 2: Werkzeugbewirtschaftung
Teil 3: Werkzeugeinsatz
ZwF 78 (1983) 8, 10, und 79 (1984) 1

/2/ Tönshoff, H. K.
M.Soliman

TOOLSIM: A Program for the Simulation of Tool Flow in the Factory
Proceedings of the European Simulation Meeting on "Simulation in Research and Development"
Eger, Hungary, August 1984

/3/ Soliman, M.

Auslegung und Anwendung eines Simulationsmodells zur Struktur- und Parameteroptimierung im Werkzeugfluß
Unveröffentlichter Bericht des Instituts für Fertigungstechnik und Spanende Werkzeugmaschinen Universität Hannover

/4/ Soliman, M.

TOOLOPT. A Programme for the Optimization of Tool Application in the Factory,
Proceedings of the First International Ain Shams University Conference on Production Engineering and Design for Development (PEDD),
Cairo, Egypt, December 1984

# DAS INTEGRIERTE
# MATERIALFLUß-SIMULATIONSSYSTEM
# TRANSIM

Jürgen Sowa, Grenzach-Wyhlen

Zusammenfassung.Der Planer beschreibt ein Materialflußsystem mit TRANSIM sukzessive im Dialog. Hierbei wird er durch ein bereitgestelltes Menue unterstützt. Programmiererfahrung ist nicht erforderlich. Der Detaillierungsgrad des zu simulierenden Systems wird vom Materialflußplaner selbst bestimmt, d.h. TRANSIM kann sowohl in der Grob- als auch in der Feinplanungsphase eingesetzt werden. Für diese Planungsabschnitte stehen die Instrumente TRANSIM-III und TRANSIM-II zur Verfügung.

Summary.The planer describes his material-flow-system by TRANSIM successively in the dialogue. He is supported in this by a ready made menue. No programming experience is required. The material-flow-planer himself determines the degree of detail for the system to be simulated, i.e. TRANSIM can be used both in the rough planning and in the final planning phases. There are the instruments TRANSIM-III and TRANSIM-II available for these planning sections.

## 1. Das integrierte Simulationssystem TRANSIM

In diesem Beitrag wird das integrierte Simulationssystem TRANSIM vorgestellt, das für die Simulation schienengebundener Transportsysteme konzipiert ist. Damit alle Planungsphasen abgedeckt werden können, gliedert sich das System in zwei unabhänhige Simulationssysteme. Für die Grobplanungsphase von Materialflußsystemen ist das Programmsystem TRANSIM-III und für Feinplanung (förder- und steuerungstechnisch) das Programmsystem TRANSIM-II entwickelt worden /1, 2, 3/.

Beide Systeme sind als Dialogsysteme ausgelegt. Die Modellierung und die Simulation erfolgt interaktiv. Der Anwender beschreibt ein Materialflußsystem durch bereitgestellte Bildschirmmasken. Für TRANSIM-III stehen 21 Bildschirmmasken zur Verfügung und für TRANSIM-II 60. Für jede Bildschirmmaske ist eine HELP-Funktion implementiert. Sofern ein Benutzer während des Dialogs zur Maskenbedienung generell bzw. zu den einzelnen Feldern, zusätzliche Informationen benötigt, kann er sich dieser Funktion bedienen. Er erhält dann umfangreiche Informationen.

In den folgenden Abschnitten wird die Modellwelt beider Systeme dargestellt. Auf programmtechnische Details wird nicht eingegangen, da sie den gesteckten Rahmen weit überschreiten würden (vgl. jedoch /1, 3).

## 2. Die Modellwelt von TRANSIM-III

Die Akzeptanz eines Simulationssystems durch den Benutzer (hier Materialflußplaner) wird, neben einer ergonomischen Gestaltung der Bildschirmmasken, wesentlich durch die zugrundegelegte Modellwelt bestimmt. Notwendige Bedingung dafür ist, daß sich die Modellwelt an der Begriffswelt der Planungsingenieure orientiert. In TRANSIM-III wird die Modellwelt in drei Modellierungsebenen gegliedert:

- Fördertechnik (Bausteine und Topologie
- Steuerungsregeln
- Umweltbeschreibungen

## 2.1 Die Modellierungsebene Fördertechnik

Für die Modellierung der Fördertechnik stehen dem Benutzer sechs vordefinierte Bausteintypen zur Auswahl, die nur noch mit den aktuellen Parametern initialisiert werden müssen, vgl. Bild 2-1:

- Quelle, in Quellen werden Objekte (die dynamische Komponente in Materialflußsystemen) erzeugt und in die Topologie eingeschleust.
- Senke, in Senken verlassen die Objekte die Topologie.
- Zusammenführungselement, in Zusammenführungselementen werden mehrere Materialflußströme zu einem Materialflußstrom zusammengeführt.
- Verteilelement, inverse Funktion wie Zusammenführungselement.
- Arbeitsstation, in Arbeitsstationen werden Objekte von einem Objekttyp in einen anderen Objekttyp übergeführt.
- Förderstrecke, eine Förderstrecke verbindet zwei, der zuvor genannten Bausteintypen.

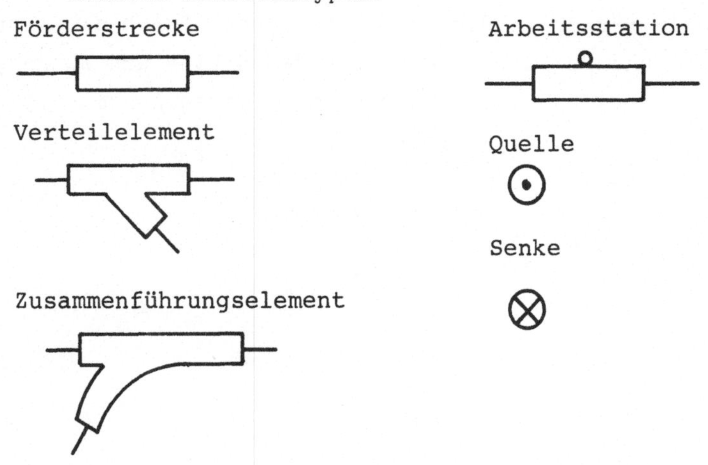


Bild 2-1: Bausteintypen in TRANSIM-III

Der Anwender hat die Möglichkeit, beliebig viele Bausteine zu defi-
nieren. Systemtechnisch ist dabei jeder Baustein eine Inkarnation
der oben aufgeführten Bausteintypen. Jeder Baustein muß nun mit den
nachfolgend beschriebenen aktuellen Parametern initialisiert werden:
- Kapazität, die Kapazität gibt die maximale Anzahl an Objekten an,
        die sich zu einem Zeitpunkt in einem Baustein befinden
        dürfen.
- Transferzeit, die Transferzeit gibt die minimale Zeitdauer an, die
        sich ein Objekt in einem Baustein aufhält.
- Anzahl der
  Ein- und Ausgänge, die Anzahl der Ein- und Ausgänge ist vom Baustein-
        typ abhängig.

| Typ | max(EIN) | min(EIN) | max(AUS) | min(AUS) |
| --- | --- | --- | --- | --- |
| Quelle | 0 | 0 | 1 | 1 |
| Senke | 1 | 1 | 0 | 0 |
| Förderstrecke | 1 | 1 | 1 | 1 |
| Zusammenfüh- rungselement | 4 | 2 | 1 | 1 |
| Verteilelement | 1 | 1 | 4 | 2 |
| Arbeitsstation | 1 | 1 | 1 | 1 |

- Initialbelegung, der Benutzer kann jeden Baustein mit einer Anzahl
        an Objekten vorbelegen, wobei gilt
        $0 \leq$ INITIAL (Baustein) $\leq$ Kapazität (Baustein)

Zu den bisher aufgeführten Parametern muß der Benutzer zusätzlich die
Verbindungen für jeden Baustein definieren. Durch die Nennung der Vor-
gänger- und Nachfolgerbausteine für jeden Ein- und Ausgang wird die
Topologie erzeugt. Das Ergebnis dieser Vorgehensweise ist dann ein
gerichteter Graph, vgl. Bild 2-2.

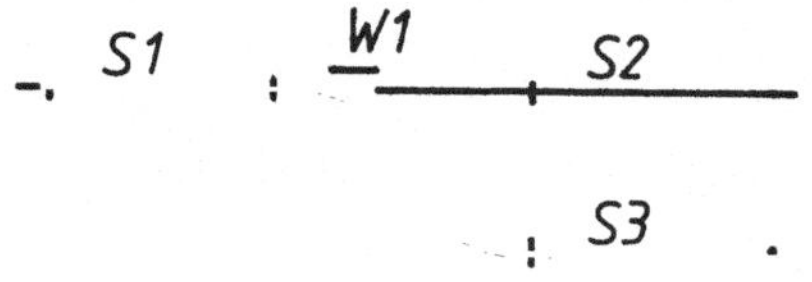

**Eingang:**      S1

**Ausgang 1:**    S2

**Ausgang 2:**    S3

Bild 2-2: Die Verbindungen der Weiche W1

## 2.2 Die Modellierungsebene Steuerungsregeln

Die bisher aufgeführten Parameter sind für alle Bausteintypen gleich.
Für die Typen Verteilelement, Zusammenführungselement müssen zusätzlich die Steuerungsregeln beschrieben werden:

Verteilelement: Für jeden Objekttyp (das System unterscheidet 16 ver-
                 schiedene Objekttypen) Kann in Verteilelementen die
                 prozentuale Verteilung auf die Ausgänge angegeben wer-
                 den, z.B. ein Verteilelement mit 2 Ausgängen:

| Objekttyp | Ausgang 1 | Ausgang 2 | Ausgang 3 | Ausgang 4 |
|-----------|-----------|-----------|-----------|-----------|
| 1 | 30% | 70% | | |
| 2 | | 100% | | |
| 3 | 100% | | | |
| . | | | | |
| . | | | | |
| . | | | | |
| 16 | 80% | 20% | | |

Nach Ablauf der Transferzeit wird der nachfolgende
Bausteine durch eine Zufallszahl bestimmt:
Die Prozentwerte werden in Intervalle aufgelöst, vgl.
obiges Beispiel:

Intervall 1 : 1 .. 30
Intervall 2 : 31 .. 100

Diese Intervalle gelten für den Objekttyp 1. Für alle
anderen Objekttypen ist das Verfahren analog.

- Zusammenfüh-
  rungselement: Bei Zusammenführungselementen ist die steuertechnische
                Voreinstellung das FIFO-Prinzip. Sofern der Benutzer
                dieses Prinzip nicht anwenden will, kann er den je-
                weiligen Eingängen Prioritäten zuordnen.

- Arbeitsstation: Für Arbeitsstationen muß die Bearbeitungszeit, die
                Verfügbarkeit sowie die Dauer von Störungen angege-
                ben werden. Bis auf die Verfügbarkeit (die Verfüg-
                barkeit wird durch einen Prozentwert angegeben) wer-
                den alle übrigen Zeiten durch Umweltbeschreibungen
                definiert. Weiterhin kann der Benutzer festlegen,
                wie sich ein Objekttyp in der Arbeitsstation typ-
                mäßig verändert.

## 2.3 Die Modellierungsebene Umweltbeschreibung

Für die Bausteintypen Quelle und Senke muß, zu den bisher genannten
Parametern, das zeitliche Verhalten definiert werden. Bei Quellen muß
z.B. festgelegt werden, aufgrund welcher mathematischen Verteilung
Objekte erzeugt werden.

Für Senken bedeutet die mathematische Verteilung die Belegungszeit,
d.h. diejenige Zeit, bis die Senke für die Aufnahme des nächsten Objektes bereit ist.

Neben den bisher genannten Fällen, werden Umweltbeschreibungen auch
für die steuerungstechnische Beschreibung von Arbeitsstationen benötigt, vgl. 2.2.

TRANSIM-III stellt für die Beschreibung des Zeitverhaltens folgende
mathematische Funktionen zur Verfügung:

- getaktete Abstände,
- fester Wert,
- Gleichverteilung,
- Normalverteilung
- Exponentialverteilung.

Die Funktionen werden mit den üblichen Parametern aufgerufen.


## 3. Das Simulationssystem TRANSIM-II

Die Ebenen der Modellbildung sind äquivalent zu TRANSIM-III. Jedoch
unterscheidet sich die Abbildungsgenauigkeit - und damit die Güte der
in der Simulation erzielten Ergebnisse - prinzipiell in zwei Punkten:

- das Baugruppentypkonzept und
- das Steuerungskonzept


## 3.1 Das Baugruppentypkonzept

TRANSIM-II kennt keine vordefinierten Bausteintypen /1, 2, 3/. Jeder
Bausteintyp, ob Förderstrecke, Weiche oder Arbeitsstation, muß zuvor
definiert werden. Für die Definition ist eine spezielle Modellwelt
realisiert werden, die auf der Grundlage eines Pfad-Anschluß-Konzepts
basiert. Folgende Ebenen der Typdefinition werden unterschieden:

- die fördertechnische Ebene,
- die steuerungstechnische Ebene und
- das Attribut-Konzept.

Für die Beschreibung der fördertechnischen Ebene wird von der Annahme
ausgegangen, daß jeder Bausteintyp als gerichteter Graph dargestellt
werden kann. Die Knoten dieses Graphen repräsentieren die Ein-/ Ausgänge und die Kanten entsprechend die Pfade zwischen den Ein- und Ausgängen.

Zunächst nennt der Benutzer die Namen aller Ein- und Ausgänge und ob
es sich bei diesem symbolischen Namen um einen Ein- oder Ausgang handelt, vgl. Bild 3-1).

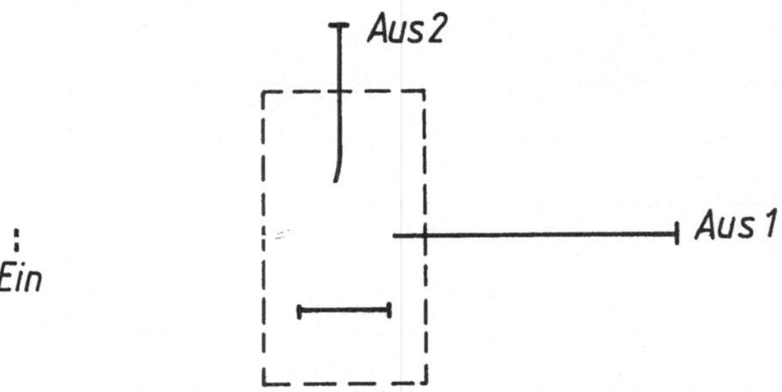


O  Beschreibung der Anschlüsse:    O  Beschreibung der Pfade:

   - durch Eingabe eines Namens       - durch Nennung der Anschlüsse

   - Anschluß Eingang oder Ausgang    Pfad 1 : von "EIN" nach "AUS1"

                                      Pfad 2 : von "EIN" nach "AUS2"


Bild 3-1: Das Pfad- Anschlußkonzept Baugruppentyp

Anschließend erfolgt die Nennung der zwischen den Ein- und Ausgängen
liegenden Pfade, indem die jeweiligen Anschlußname dem System mitge-
teilt werden. Das System überprüft automatisch, daß nicht zwei Ein-
bzw. Ausgänge miteinander verknüpft werden. Nachdem die Pfade defi-
niert sind, müssen noch die Pfadlängen (in mm) angegeben werden. Der
Anwender hat hierfür zwei Möglichkeiten:
- Definition der Pfadlänge durch eine Zahl.
- Definition der Pfadlänge durch Parameter.
In der praktischen Arbeit hat sich die letztere Variante als Standard
durchgesetzt.
Die Beschreibung der Steuerung ist ebenfalls individuell möglich. Als
Beschreibungsmethode ist die Entscheidungstabellentechnik gewählt wor-
den (vgl. Bild 3-2). Jede Entscheidungstabelle gliedert sich in drei
Teile:
- Bedingungsteil,
- Aktionsteil und
- Entscheidungsteil.

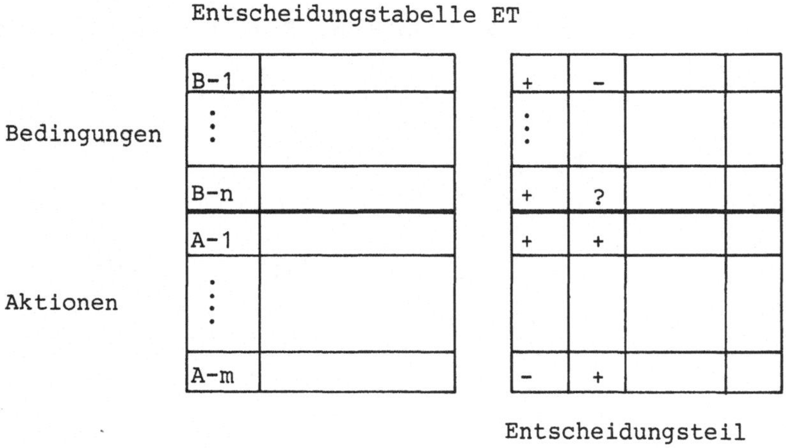

Entscheidungstabelle ET

| Bedingungen | B-1 | | | + | – | | |
| | ⋮ | | | ⋮ | | | |
| | B-n | | | + | ? | | |
| Aktionen | A-1 | | | + | + | | |
| | ⋮ | | | | | | |
| | A-m | | | – | + | | |

Entscheidungsteil

Bild 3-2: Grundaufbau einer Entscheidungstabelle


Für die Beschreibung und Aktionen steht eine spezielle LL (1) - Grammatik zur Verfügung. In Bild 3-3 sind zwei Eintscheidungstabellen dargestellt, die von der Funktion her sicherstellen, das nur jeweils ein Objekt sich gleichzeitig in einem Baustein befinden kann. Alle nicht terminalen Symbole müssen in Anführungszeichen gesetzt sein. Die Symbole +, -, ?, im Entscheidungsteil haben folgende Bedeutung:
- Für Bedingungen: "+" diese Bedingung muß "TRUE" sein,
                   "-" diese Bedingung muß "FALSE" sein,
                   "?" diese Bedingung ist irrelevant.
- Für Aktionen:    "+" diese Aktion wird ausgeführt,
                   "-" diese Aktion wird nicht ausgeführt.
Die Auswertung einer Entscheidungstabelle erfolgt spaltenweise von links nach rechts.
Wie man der Entscheidungstabelle in Bild 3-3 entnehmen kann, sind verschiedene NONTERMINALS verwendet worden, z.B. "ZUSTAND"="belegt". Der Anwender kann beliebig viele Attribute definieren. Die Definition ist vergleichbar mit der Definition von Variablen in Programmiersprachen. Jedes Attribut fungiert als Variable, die Werte aus einem Wertebereich annehmen kann. Für die Definition des Wertebereiches stehen INTEGER, REAL und Aufzähltypen zur Verfügung /4/, z.B. ist das Attribut "Zustand" vom Typ Aufzähl mit dem Wertebereich "belegt", "frei" oder PASCAL-Notation
Zustand: (belegt, frei):

ET : EIN . AN

| Attribut "Zustand" = "belegt" | + | - |
|---|---|---|
| GEBE "EIN" FREI | - | + |
| SETZE "ZUSTAND" AUF "belegt" | - | + |
| SETZE "wartet" AUF "Ja" | + | - |
| SETZE "wartet" AUF "Nein" | - | + |

ET : AUS1. AN

| Attribut "wartet" = "Ja" | + | - |
|---|---|---|
| SETZE "Zustand" AUF "frei" | + | + |
| WERTE "EIN.AN" AUS | + | - |
| GEBE "AUS" FREI | + | + |

Bild 3-3: Entscheidungstabellen für eine Verzweigungsweiche.

In Bild 3-4 ist dargestellt, wann Entscheidungstabellen ausgewertet
werden. Wenn das vordere Rad auf den Anschluß "EIN" trifft, wird die
Entscheidungstabelle "EIN.AN" ausgewertet. Die analoge Vorgehensweise
gilt für die Ausgänge "AUS1" und "AUS2".
An Entscheidungstabellentypen werden unterschieden:

- AN: vorderes Rad trifft auf den Anschluß (Eingang oder Ausgang).
- AB: hinteres Rad trifft auf den Anschluß (Eingang oder Ausgang).
- SONST: Falls nicht alle Bedingungen- und Aktionen in einer ET formu-
         lierbar sind, können zusätzliche ET's definiert werden. Sie
         tragen die Extension SONST. Die Auswertung einer solchen ET
         erfolgt durch die Aktion:
         Wert "... SONST" AUS

Die Auswertung der ET's erfolgt nach dem Prinzip: Eingangs-ET vor Aus-
gangs-ET.

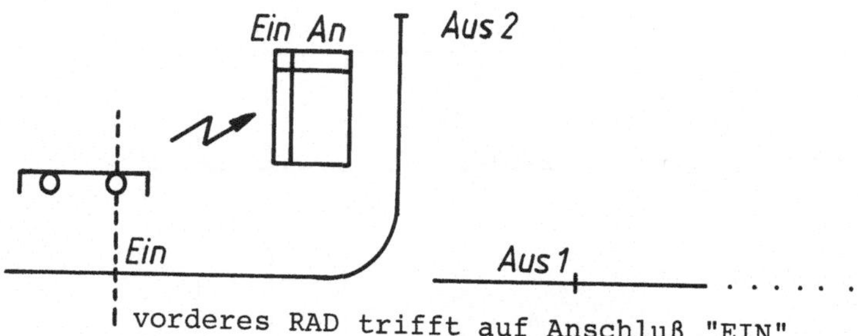


Bild 3-4: Position eines Fahrwerkes für die Auswertung der
ET "EIN.AN".


Sind die Baugruppentypen einmal definiert, können sie in Bibliotheken
abgespeichert werden und dann für die Modellierung neuer Materialflußsysteme wiederverwendet werden.


## 3.2 Das Baugruppenkonzept

Analog wie in TRANSIM-III können auch in TRANSIM-II beliebig viele
Baugruppen definiert werden. Jede Baugruppe ist dabei eine Inkarnation
eines Baugruppentyps. Die Initialisierung der Parameter, die bei dem
Baugruppentyp angegeben worden sind, erfolgt nun spezifisch für jede
Baugruppe. Durch die Technik, eine Baugruppe als Inkarnation eines
Baugruppentyps zu erzeugen, sind natürlich die Attribute an die Bau-
gruppe gebunden.
Die auf der Baugruppentypebene beschriebenen Entscheidungstabellen
werden ebenfalls der Baugruppe zugeordnet. Dadurch ist es möglich,
auf Attribute der Baugruppe Operationen auszuführen. Eine Baugruppe
eines Types kann nie auf Attribute einer anderen Baugruppe des gleichen
Typs zugreifen.
Die Erzeugung der Topologie erfolgt über die Nennung der Anschlußbe-
zeichner:
Verknüpfe "AUS" von Förderstrecke "S1" mit "EIN" von Weiche "W1".


## 3.4 Die Programmgenerierung

Die Umsetzung der Modellbeschreibung in ein Simulationsprogramm, erfolgt durch einen GENERATOR. Aufgabe des Generators ist es, aus der
verbalen Beschreibung der Baugruppen, den Baugruppentypen und der Entscheidungstabellen syntaktisch korrekten PASCAL-CODE zu erzeugen. Z.B.
wird die obige Entscheidungstabelle (vgl. Bild 3-3) übersetzt in:

```pascal
PROCEDURE typ_ein_an (VAR bgr: Baugruppe):

FUNCTION bed_1 : BOOLEAN;
BEGIN
  IF bgr↑.Zustand = belegt THEN
    bed_1:=TRUE
  ELSE
    bed_1:FALSE
END;


PROCEDURE akt_1;
BEGIN
  gen_objekt (bgr↑.first);
END;


PROCEDURE akt_2;
BEGIN
  bgr↑.Zustand:=belegt;
END;


PROCEDURE akt_3;
BEGIN
  bgr↑. wartet:=ja;
END;


PROCEDURE akt_4;
BEGIN
  bgr↑.wartet:=nein;
END

BEGIN (* typ_ein_an*)
  IF  bed_1 THEN
    akt_3
  ELSE
  BEGIN
    IF NOT bed_1 THEN
    BEGIN
      akt_1;
      akt_2;
      akt_4;
    END;
  END;
END (*typ_ein_an*);
```

Das ablauffähige Simulationsprogramm setzt sich dann aus generierten Modulen und Standardmodulen zusammen. Die Programmgröße beträgt minimal 0,4 MB, wenn alle generierten Module einen leeren Rumpf aufweisen. Die maximale Größe ist von dem zu modellierenden Materialflußsystem abhängig.

## 4. Zusammenfassung

Vorgestellt wurden die Simulationssysteme TRANSIM-II und TRANSIM-III. TRANSIM-III ist als kapazitätsorientiertes ereignisgesteuertes Simulationssystem konzipiert. Die Erfahrungen im Umgang mit diesem System haben gezeigt, daß das Handling sehr einfach ist, allerdings auf Kosten der Abbildungsgenauigkeit. Parallele Simulationsstudien mit TRANSIM-II und TRANSIM-III haben ergeben, daß der Abbildungsgrad bei TRANSIM-III (gemessen an den erzielten Ergebnissen) bei ca. 80% gegenüber TRAN-SIM-II liegt. Wenn ein Materiaflußsystem einen Durchsatz von 100 Transporte/Zeit erbringen soll und TRANSIM-III auch diese 100 Transporte bestätigt, kann man davon ausgehen, daß das geplante Materialflußsystem die geforderte Leistung sicher erbringt. Im anderen Fall empfiehlt sich eine genauere Untersuchung mit TRANSIM-II.

Quellen:

/1/ Ludwigs, H.: SIMIS -II - An Environment for Material Flow Systems
Simulation. In: Annual Simulation Symposium,
Tampa, Florida 1983.

/2/ Sowa, J.: Das Simulationssystem SIMIS-II.
In: fördern und heben 7, 1984

/3/ Sowa, J.: Simulationstechnik als nutzbare Planungshilfe.
In: fördern und heben 2, 1985

/4/ Jensen, K.: Wirth, N: PASCAL User Manual and Report.
Springer-Verlag, New York - Heidelberg - Berlin, 1974

Dialogorientierte Simulation von automatisierten
Materialfluss-Systemen


Dipl. Math. Alfons Teriete

Fraunhofer-Institut fuer
Transporttechnik und
Warendistribution

Emil-Figge-Str. 75

4600 Dortmund 50


Die Simulation als Hilfsmittel bei der Planung von
automatisierten Materialfluss-Systemen gewinnt zunehmend an
Bedeutung. Die Systeme werden immer komplexer, so dass
analytische Methoden zur Systembewertung nicht mehr ausreichen.
Hier kann eine Simulation erheblich zur Erhoehung der
Planungssicherheit beitragen. Damit die Simulation sinnvoll in
den Planungsprozess integriert werden kann, muss dem Planer ein
Instrument an die Hand gegeben werden, mit dem er auf einfache
Weise sein System beschreiben kann.


In diesem Beitrag wird ein Simulationssytem vorgestellt, welches
den Aufbau von Modellen im Dialog ermoeglicht. Das Modell wird
wird mit Hilfe von Bausteinen erstellt, welche den in der
Foerdertechnik verwendeten Bauelementen entsprechen. Fuer die
Beschreibung der Steuerung stehen eine Reihe von vorgefertigten
Steuerungsstrategien zur Verfuegung, welche vom Anwender
ausgewaehlt werden koennen. Mit Hilfe dieser Strategien kann ein
grosser Teil der Anforderungen abgedeckt werden. Spezielle,
systembezogene Steuerungsstrategien koennen ueber definierte
Schnittstellen nachtraeglich eingefuegt werden. Dies erfordert
jedoch Programmieraufwand.


Fuer die Bewertung der Ergebnisse werden verschiedene Formen der
graphischen Darstellung angeboten. Diese reichen von einem
Gesamtueberblick der Auslastungen der Bausteine anhand einer
Systemskizze ueber die Belastungsdiagramme einzelner Bausteine
bis zur Darstellung der Objektbewegungen fuer ausgewaehlte
Teilbereiche.

Aufgrund der vielfaeltigen Moeglichkeiten koennen Engpaesse
schnell lokalisiert und die Ursachen hierfuer erforscht werden.
Durch Aenderungen am System kann der Engpass beseitigt und das
Gesamtsystem mit einer neuen Simulation ueberprueft werden.

# REALZEITSTEUERUNG MIT DEM GRAPHISCH-INTERAKTIVEN SIMULATOR SIMFLEX/2

Adolf Reinhardt
Gesamthochschule Kassel

## 1 SIMFLEX/2

SIMFLEX/2 ist ein graphisch-interaktiver Simulator für den Entwurf von Materialflußsystemen und die Steuerung von Modellexperimenten /1/.

Ein Modellexperiment wird mit dem Entwurf eines Anlagen-Layouts vorbereitet (GTS). Die einzelnen Bausteine des Layouts werden aus einer Bibliothek abgerufen, in einem Layoutraster plaziert, mit technischen und steuertechnischen Parametern versehen und zusammen mit einem Experimentplan in einem Dateiensystem abgelegt (Bild 1).

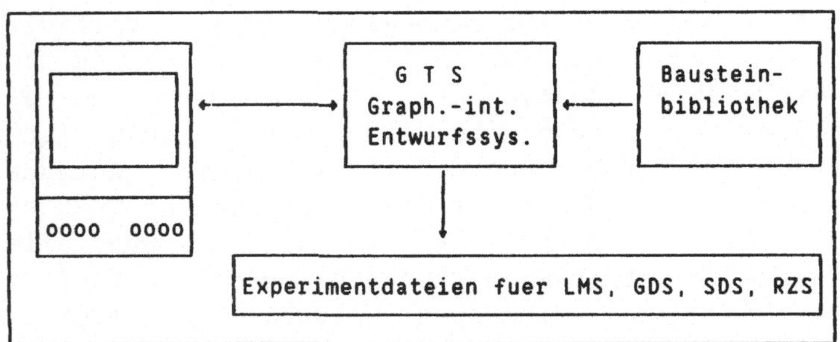


Bild 1. Graphisch-interaktiver Modellentwurf

Für ein interaktives Modellexperiment werden drei Softwaremodule mit unterschiedlichen Modellierungseigenschaften gekoppelt (Bild 2). Auf der Basis der Experimentdateien wird die logische (LMS), graphische (GDS) und statistische (SDS) Struktur eines Anlagenmodells aufgebaut. Der Benutzer beobachtet und steuert den Modellprozeß über zwei Graphikgeräte als quasi reale Prozeßwarte.

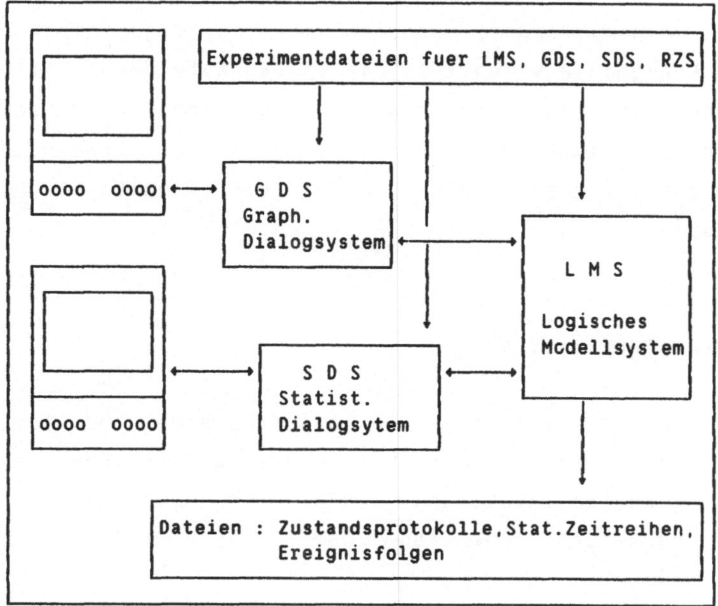

**Bild 2. Graphisch-interaktive Modellexperimente**

## 2 Zeitmechanismus und Prozeßsignale

Die Modelldynamik in SIMFLEX/2 ist ereignisorientiert. Wie bekannt ist,
besteht der Zeitmechanismus aus einem Terminkalender und im Prinzip aus
zwei Kalenderoperationen. Der Terminkalender ist eine geordnete Liste
von Ereignisnotizen. Die Kalenderoperationen dienen zum Einplanen von
Ereignissen und zum Fortschalten auf das nächste, das aktuelle
Ereignis. Über Ereignisprozeduren wird das jeweils aktuelle Ereignis
verarbeitet. Es werden der Modellzustand verändert und Folgeereignisse
eingeplant.

In SIMFLEX/2 wird der Modellzustand bzw. der Zustand eines Bausteins im
logischen, graphischen und statistischen Modellsystem dargestellt. Der
Zustand zeigt eine Aktivität an, die durch ein Anfangsereignis
eingeleitet und ein Endereignis beendet wird. Ist eine reale Anlage
angekoppelt, so wird der Zustand zusätzlich in der Anlage erzeugt. Ein
Anfangsereignis wird als Steuersignal an die Anlage gesendet. Das Ende
der Aktivität wird nun als Signal aus dem Prozeß erwartet. Der

Zeitmechanismus wird dazu um eine Signalliste erweitert. Endereignisse werden nun nicht im Terminkalender, sondern in der Signalliste als erwartete externe Ereignisse verwaltet. Die beiden Kalenderoperationen werden dazu erweitert. Ist ein Prozeß angeschlossen, dann wird sowohl der Terminkalender als auch die Signalliste bearbeitet. Das nächste Ereignis kann dann ein internes Ereignis oder ein Signal bzw. ein externes Ereignis sein.


## 3 Ereignisse und Prozeßaktivitäten

Die Startereignisse für Aktivitäten, die das logische Modellsystem (LMS) an den angeschlossenen Prozeß sendet, werden über einen Softwaremodul zur Realzeitsteuerung (RZS) in Sequenzen von Operationscodes umgesetzt und an das Prozeßinterface (PI) weitergeleitet (Bild 3).

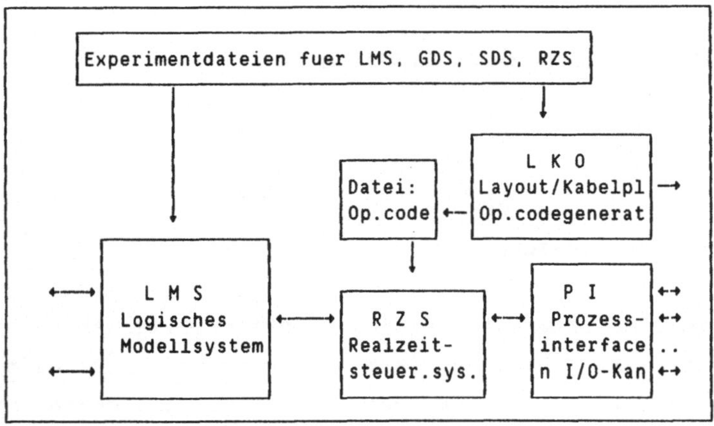


**Bild 3. Graphisch-interaktive Realzeitexperimente**

In den aktuellen Experimenten werden zwei unterschiedliche Prozeßinterfaces eingesetzt. Ein industrielles Interface mit schnellem IEC-Bus-Anschluß, jedoch geringer Intelligenz, und ein in Eigenarbeit entwickeltes programmierbares Interface mit relativ langsamem V24-Anschluß /2/.

An einem Layout-Ausschnitt mit drei Bausteinen soll die Umsetzung von Ereignissen in Prozeßaktivitäten anhand einer Folge von

Palettenbewegungen erläutert werden.

Ein palettiertes Gut wird über einen Staurollenförderer vom Eingangsplatz zum Ausgangsplatz bewegt (FÖRDERN), dort von einer Drehweiche übernommen (AUFNEHMEN), gedreht (DREHEN), von einem bereitstehenden Verteilwagen aufgenommen (AUFNEHMEN) und zu einem Zielpunkt verfahren (FAHREN).

Die Anfangsereignisse A.FÖRDERN, A.AUFNEHMEN, A.DREHEN, A.AUFNEHMEN, A.FAHREN werden an den Realzeitsteuerungsmodul RZS gesendet, die Endereignisse werden von dort als Signal bzw. externe Ereignisse E.FÖRDERN, E.AUFNEHMEN, E.DREHEN, E.AUFNEHMEN, E.FAHREN erwartet.

Im RZS werden die Ereignisse anhand von Tabellen in Sequenzen von Operationscodes für das Prozeßinterface umgesetzt. Ebenfalls anhand von Tabellen werden die Ereignisparameter wie Baustein- und Platznummern in die I/O-Kanalnummern des jeweils eingesetzten Prozeßinterfaces umgesetzt. Die ereignisabhängigen Steuersequenzen können zu Makros zusammengefaßt werden. Im Falle des programmierbaren Interfaces werden die Makros vorab in das Interface geladen. Gesendet wird dann ein Aktivierungscode für das jeweilige Makro. Nach Ablauf der Prozeßaktivität liefert das Prozeßinterface ein Endsignal. Das RZS setzt das Signal in ein Endereignis um und sendet dies an das LMS.


## 4 Realzeitexperimente in Laborumgebung


Der Benutzer hat mit der internen Umsetzung der Ereignisse in Operationscodes wenig zu tun. Er entwirft ein Layout mit dem Entwurfssystem GTS. Für Laborexperimente stehen Bausteintypen in materieller Modelltechnik zur Verfügung. Mit dem Softwaremodul LKO wird eine Hardcopy zum Layout einschließlich des Verkabelungsplanes und einer Datei mit den layoutbezogenen Operationscodesequenzen erstellt (Bild 3). Der Benutzer baut das Materialflußsystem in Modelltechnik auf, verbindet die Bausteine des Layout mit dem Prozeßinterface nach vorgegebenem Verkabelungsplan und startet das Realzeitexperiment /3/. Für den Ablauf des Experimentes müssen Personen für die Einschleusung palettierter Güter und die Instandhaltung der Anlage zur Verfügung stehen.

## 5 Ausblick

Erste Anwendungen des Simulators im industriellen Bereich haben das Konzept in den Phasen des Entwurfs und der strategischen Anlagenanalyse bestätigt. Die Umsetzung der Realzeitexperimente aus der Laborumgebung auf industrielle Anwendungen ist ein nächster Schritt. Die Entwicklung eines intelligenten Bus-Systems oder die Anpassung an industrielle Standards muß anhand technischer und wirtschaftlicher Kriterien entschieden werden.

Das Konzept von SIMFLEX/2 beinhaltet im aktuellen Entwicklungsstand den vollständigen Zyklus vom Entwurf bis zur direkten Steuerung von Materialflußanlagen. Die bisherigen Experimente haben gezeigt, daß die graphisch-interaktiven Eigenschaften des Simulators eine hochwertige Validierungshilfe sind. Wie es scheint, führen die Realzeiteigenschaften zu einer weiteren Qualitätssteigerung der Aussagen über die Modellgültigkeit und damit zu einer erhöhten Akzeptanz der Methode.

## 6 Literatur


1) Reinhardt,A.: Entwurf von Materialflußsystemen und Experimentsteuerung mittels graphisch-interaktiver Simulation, In: (Hrsg. Breitenecker, F./Kleinert, W.) Simulationstechnik, Wien 1984, Informatik-Fachberichte Bd. 85, Springer-Verlag 1984

2) Papengut,U.: Entwicklung einer Hardware-Schnittstelle zur Steuerung von Materialflußsystemen mit SIMFLEX/2, Fachgebiet Produktionssysteme, Gesamthochschule Kassel 1985

3) Eigenbrod,J./Lafery,W./,Ott,W: Entwicklung von Softwaremodulen zur Steuerung modelltechnischer Anlagen mit SIMFLEX/2, Fachgebiet Produktionssysteme, Gesamthochschule Kassel 1985

# Die Ausnutzung der Simulationstechnik zur Untersuchung und die Steuerung der Zuverlässigkeit von Produktionsprozessen im Bauwesen


Oleg Kapliński, Poznań



**Zusammenfassung**. Die Ausdehnung des Begriffs der Zuverlässigkeit eines Produktions-systems, die Annahme der Verteilung einer richtigen Arbeit dieses Systems als eines Zuverlässigkeitsmaβes und die Anwendung eines Ziffernsimulators gab die Grundlage zur Erarbeitung der Methode der Erforschung der Produktionsprozesse. Dabei wurde das Prinzip der Dekomposition und der Synthese von Zuverlässigkeitsstrukturen benutzt. Es wurden Ergebnisse der Experimente an der so genannten Systemsträgheit besprochen. Innerhalb des Problems der Zuverlässigkeitssteuerung wurde die heuristische Regel benutzt.

**Summary**. Elargement of notion of production system reliability, adoption of the distribution of the correct work of the system as a measure of reliability and application of the digital simulator have given the basis for determination of the investigation method of the production processes. At the same time, the rules of the decomposition and the synthesis of the reliability structure have been used. The results of the experiments with so-called system-inertia are given. Heuristic rule has been applied in the problem of reliability control.


## 1. Einführung

Die Notwendigkeit einer anderen Anschauung der Bewertung der Zuverläβigkeit des Produktionssystems im Bauwesen erfolgt u.a. aus folgenden Voraussetzungen:

1/ Es besteht die Notwendigkeit, die Leistung mit der Zuverlässgkeit zu verbinden. Bisherige Stützung auf die Wahrcheinlichkeit der Erhaltung der Realisatiostermine reicht für die praktischen Zwecke nicht aus.

2/ Es treten dabei die analytischen Schwierigkeiten auf. Der Verzicht auf die Bestimmung der genannten Wahrscheinlichkeit und die Anwendung von ausschlieβlich Exponentialverteilungen brachte dazu, daβ es die Notwendigkeit bestand, eine Zahlensimulation der Erscheinungen zu verwenden.

Es wurde auch eine andere Fassung der Störungen eingefürt, der Begriff der Zuverlässigkeit des Produktionssystems wurde erweitert und es wurde eine adere Bewertungsmethode der Zuverlässigkeit benutzt. Als Maβ der Zuverlässigkeit wurde die Zeitverteilung der richtigen Arbeit des Systems angenommen.

## 2. Die Zuverlässigkeitsstruktur der Produktionsprozesse

Anfangs wurden die Forschungen an Produktionsprozessen auf Bauplätzen geführt, später aber wurden mit diesen Forschungen auch die technologischen Prozesse in Vorfertigungswerken umfaβt. Es wurde dabei festgestellt, daβ auβer der durch Havarie der Maschinen und Einrichtungen bedingten Störungen auch solche gibt, die auf die schlechte Funktionsstruktur, organisatorische Faktoren, Absenz, nicht ausreichende Materialversorgung usw. zurückzuführen sind. Es wurde eine groβe Vielfalt von Funktionsstrukturen festgestellt. Es erwies sich aber, daβ die wesentlichen Funktions - und Zuverlässigkeitsmerkmale des Produktionssystems sich in Form von entsprechenden Phasen aussondern lassen und dann durch homomorphische Umgestaltungen können sie auf die Zuverlässigkeitsreihenstruktur zurückgeführt werden.

Man stellte auch fest, daß nur die Arbeitszeitverteilungen und die Störungsverteilungen von mechanischen Einrichtungen der Exponentiellverteilung ähnlich sind. Die Verteilungen des Materialmangels sind dagegen symmetrisch.

Die obengenannten Störungen /und auch der Einfluß der Umgebung/ können als eine selbständige Phase betrachtet werden, die reihenmäßig an die vorher bestimmte Zuverlässigkeitsstruktur angeschlossen werden kann. Die Zeit des Verbleibens der Phase in

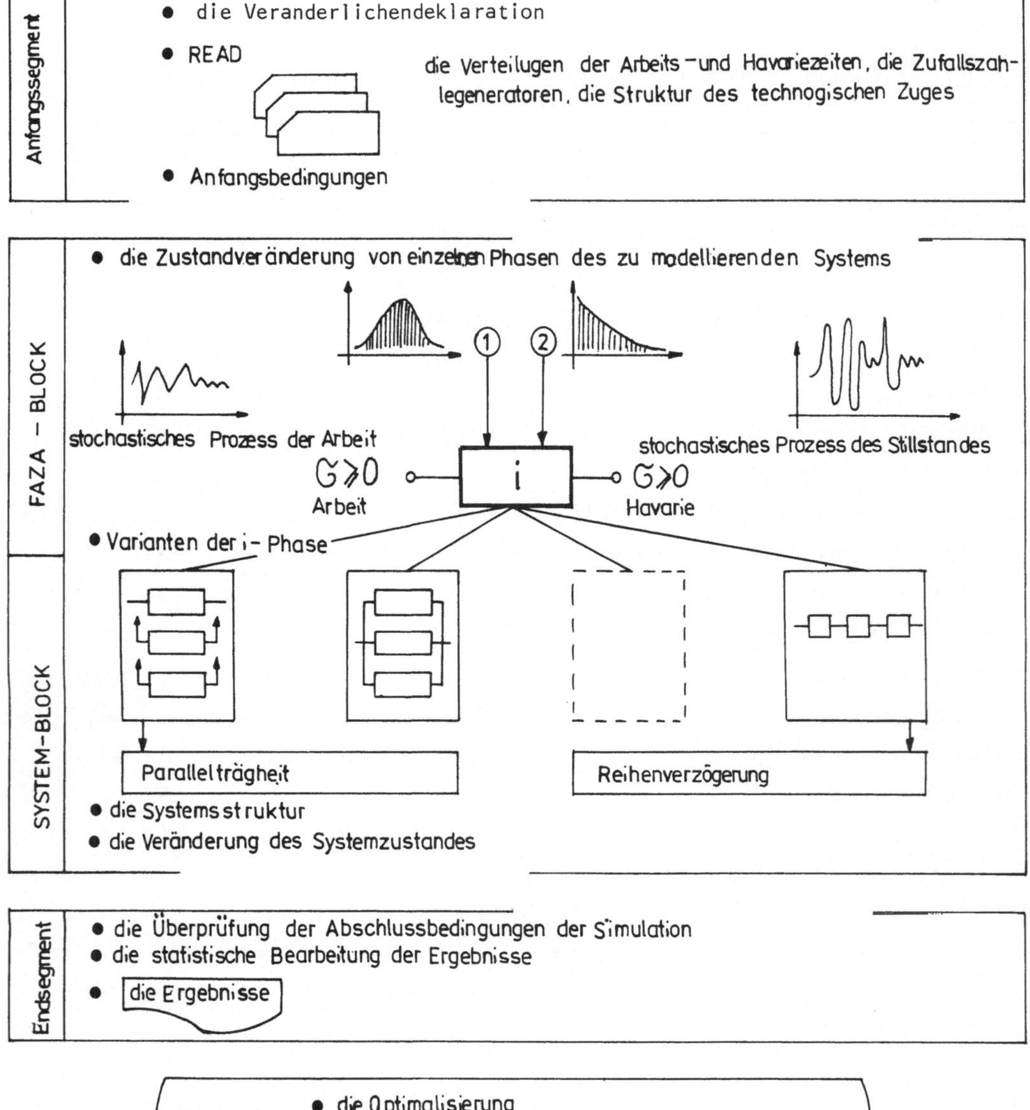


Abb.1. Das Schema des Programms.

einem der zwei Zustände /Arbeit oder Havarie/ kann mit verschiedenen Wahrscheinlich-
keitsfunktionen, dem Histogramm oder dem deterministischen Wert beschrieben werden.
Die Phasen können eine einfache oder eine zusammengesetzte Gestalt besitzen zB.
Reihengestalt, Parallelgestalt, Gestalt mit Reserven, mit Trägheit usw. - wie in
der Abb.1.

## 3. Simulator

Als Forschungsinstrument wird hier das verprogrammierte Modell eines Produktionssy-
stems in Form eines Simulators benutzt. Es ist ein Zweizustandsmodell mit einer
Reihenstruktur. Die Struktur besteht aus 10 oder 20 Phasen /abhängig von dem Pro-
grammwechsel/. Die Zusammensetzbarkeit der Struktur besteht darin, daß in jeder der
Phasen eine andere Struktur auftreten kann. Die Struktur des Programms ist auf die
Erscheinungen der Zustandsveränderung der Phase /erster Block - Abb.1/ und die Er-
scheinungen der Zustandsveränderung des Systems /zweiter Block - Abb.1/ orientiert.
Darüber hinaus wurde in das Modell das Element einer Reihenverzögerung eingeführt.
Das Modell wurde in der Sprache CSL verprogrammiert und auf dem Computer ODRA 1305
betrieben. Das Programm erfordert Speicher 16 k und den empirischen Daten 40 k.
Der Zeitmaßstab 1 : 40 000.

## 4. Analyse der Arbeit von Batterieformen

Als erste Anwendung des Simulators war die Analyse der Arbeit eines Vorfertigungs -
werkes. Das synthetische Zuverlässigkeitsmodell eines Werkes ist im allgemeinen sehr
ausgebaut und die einmalige Analyse seines Ganzen ist wegen der Vielfalt von Elementen /Phasen/ nicht möglich. Es wurde eine Systemdekomposition zum Zwecke der   Forschungen eingeführt. Die Teilschätzungen von Untersystemen könnte man bei weiteren
Berechnungen als die Charakteristik der entsprechenden Phase auf der niedrigeren De-
kompositionsstufe ausnützen.

In der Arbeit einer Abteilung, die Fertigbauelemnte herstellt wie Wände, Keller und
Balkons und die aus u.a. fünf Satzen von Batterieformen besteht, wurde beispielsweise eine Batterieform ausgesondert. Bei deren Arbeit traten drei Arten von Störungen
auf: mechanische Havarie, Mangel an Betonstahl, Umformung. Diese Störungen wurden in
drei nacheinanderfolgenden Phasen dargestellt, wobei wurden, für jede der Phasen,
zwei Informationen in Form von Histogrammen angegeben: über die Zeitdauer der Störung
und die Zeitdauer der richtigen Arbeit der Phase.

Als Ergebnis der Berechnungen mit Hilfe eines Simulators wurden erzielt: Mittelzeiten
der richtigen Arbeit der Phasen und des Systems, Mittelzeiten der Havarie, die   Ge-
samtzeit der Arbeit des Systems, die Havariezeit, der Bereitschaftskoeffizient   und
mannigfaltige statistische Grössen /vgl. [1] und [2] /.

Die aus der Simulation erzielten Ergebnisse bilden die Grundlage zur Bestimmung der
Leistung des Systems /umgerechnet auf die Menge der hergestellten Bauelemente/  und
auch zur Erarbeitung des Systems der Sicherungen, das die Erhöhung der Zuverlässig -

keit der Arbeit des Produktionssystems ermöglicht.
Die Anwendung des Simulators ermöglichte in weiterer Konsequenz eine Durchführung des Vergleichs der
Reservierungsart mit der die Trägheit des Systems
berücksichtgenden Methode.

## 5. Die Trägheit des Systems

Die Trägheit des Systems wird in der Erscheinung
der Fortsetzung der Arbeit, nachdem in einer der
vorangehenden Phasen eine Havarie aufgetreten worden ist, abgebildet. Die Unfähigkeit des Betonwerks
unterbricht zB. die Arbeit der Fertigungslinie erst

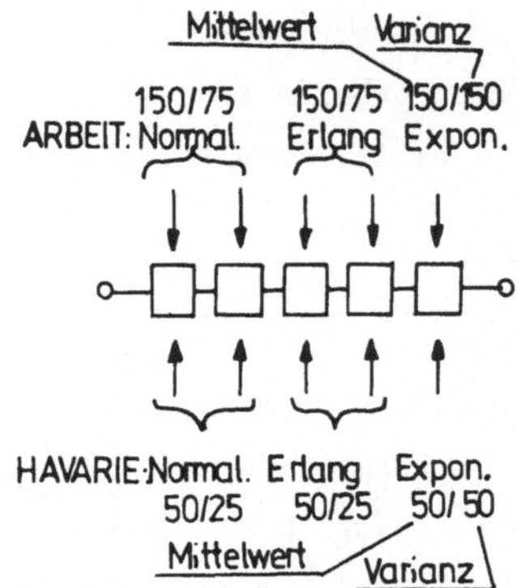


Abb.2. Die Verteilungsarten vom Basissytem.

nach der bestimmten Zeit; die vorher gelieferte Betonmischung erlaubt das Betonele-
ment zu formieren und es weiter nach dem technologischen Prozeß zu bearbeiten.

Um den Auswirkungsmechanismus dieser Erscheinung auf die Leistung des Systems auf -
klären zu können, wurden Experimente mit einem Fünf-Phasen-System /Abb.2/ durchge -
führt. Die Ergebnisse wurden in der Abb.3 zusammengestellt. Die ähnlichen Untersu -
chungen wurden auch im Bereich der Reservierung /Einführung von Parallelelementen/
durchgeführt. Bei dem Vergleich der beiden Methoden der Erhöhung der Zuverlässigkeit
erweist sich, daß die Methode des Systemsträgheit in vielen Fällen gunstiger ist,[3].

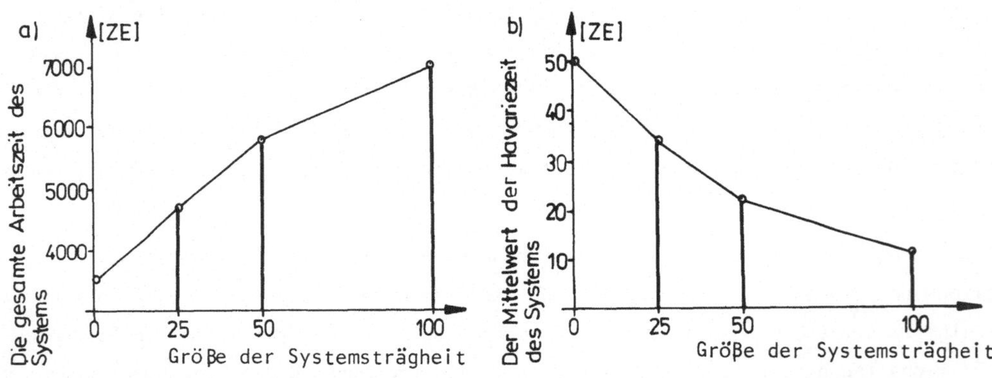


Abb.3.  Der Einfluss der Systemsträgheit auf die Arbeit des Systems /a/
sowie auf die Mittelwerte der Havariezeit des Systems  /b/.

## 6. Die Anwendung der Heuristischen Regel.

Die Frage der Steuerung der Zuverlässigkeit hat viele Aspekte. Am häufigsten wird die
Aufgabe der Steuerung auf die Bestimmung einer solchen $X_i$-Zahl der Reserveelemente
beschränkt, die in der i-ten Phase arbeiten, die das erforderliche Niveau der Zuverlässigkeit bei Mindestkosten der Reservenschaffung versichern. Die so formulierte
Aufgabe wir auf eine Linearprogrammierung, ganze Zahl Programmierung gebracht.

Die GröBe der Steuerungsaufgabe dh. die Menge der möglichen Entscheidungen D wird von
dem Oberlinienprodukt der Steuerungsvariablen $X_i$ bestimmt:

$$D = \prod_{i=1}^{n} d_i \, ,$$

wobei:   $n$ - Phasenzahl,

$d_i$ - die Größtzahl der Elemente in der i-Phase.

Die Durchführung von Simulationsexperimenten für alle Varianten ist aber sehr kostbar und arbeitsbedürftig. Zwecks der Beschleunigung der Erarbeitung einer suboptimalen Lösung wurde deshalb eine folgende Regel angewendet:  Es wird so eine Phase gesucht, die nach der Zufügung von einem Reserveelement einen maximalen Zuwachs der Zuverlässigkeit auf eine Einheit der benötigten Kosten gewährleistet:

$$g_k(X) = \max_{1 \leq i \leq n} g_i(X_i) = \frac{R_i(X_i + 1) - R_i(X_i)}{C_i \, R_i(X_i)} \, ,$$

wobei:   $R_i(X_i)/R_i(X_i+1)$ - die Zuverlässigkeit der Phase vor/nach der Anwendung des Reserveelements,

$\quad k$ - die Numer der Phase, für welche die Funktion $g_i(X_i)$ den Maximalwert erreicht,

$\quad C_i$ - die Kosten von 1. Reserveelement in der i-Phase.

Die Anwendung der obenangeführten heuristischen Regel ist bei den Zuverlässigkeits - reihenstrukturen möglich. Diese Bedingung ist u.a. in selber Struktur des Simulators erfüllt und sie wird auch bei der angenommenen Forschungsmethodik einberücksichtigt.

## 7. Schlußbemerkung

Die oben dargestellte Methodik der Bestimmung der Zuverlässigkeit und der Steuerung kann bei beliebigen Produktionssystemen ausgenützt werden, die der Klasse der Systeme mit Erneuerung entsprechen.

## Literatur

[1] Kapliński O., Efficiency and reliability of the production systems in the stochastic conditions. Proceedings 8 World Congress on Project Management,  INTER-NET 85, Rotterdam 1985.

[2] Borucka, E., Kapliński, O., Simulationsmethode zur Bewertung der Zuverlässigkeit von Produktionsprozessen in Plattenwerken. Wiss. Z. Hochsch. Archit. Bauwes. Weimar, Heft 2, 1982.

[3] Kapliński, O., Borucka, E., Zuverlässigkeit des Systems mit der Systemträgheit und verschiedenen Reservierungsmethoden. 11. Jahrestagung "Grundlagen der Modellierung u. Simulationstechnik", Rostock, 1982.

S I M U L A T I O N   I N   D E R

B E T R I E B S W I R T S C H A F T L I C H E N

A N W E N D U N G

Auswirkungen von Modellverbesserungen bei
stochastischen Systemen

Wolfgang Ettl, Klosterneuburg bei Wien

Zusammenfassung: Zahlreiche  einfache Simulationsmodelle geben nur Erwartungswerte von
prognostizierten Größen an, ohne auf die möglichen Schwankungsbereiche, die durch die
Schiefe der Verteilung bedingt nicht symetrisch sind, einzugehen. Damit ist die Qualität der Modelle meist nicht sehr viel besser als einfachere analytische und meist deterministische Modelle. Wenn als Ergebnis der Simulation eines Systems nicht ein Erwartungswert sondern die Verteilung dieser Variablen angegeben werden kann, wird eine
wesentliche Verbesserung der Aussagen erreicht. Anhand eines Pensionsfonds werden die
bisherigen Verfahren der reinen Prognose der Erwartungswerte der Einnahmen, Ausgaben
und Reserven den durch Simulation errechneten Verteilungsfunktionen dieser Variablen
gegenübergestellt. Die Auswirkungen können folgenschwer sein.

Summary. Many simple models in simulation result only the expectation of the simulated
variables without any remark on the variance or the asymetry caused by the skewness
of the distribution. So the quality of the results of many simulation are the same as
simple analytic and most deterministic models. An enomous improvement can be achieved,
if the results are not only simple expectations but the complete distribution function
of the variables. As an example we computed the payments, premiums,and reserves of a
pension fund. Conventional methods may lead to wrong decisions and a financial desaster.


1. Einführung: Bei konkreten Fragestellungen aus dem Bereich der Unternehmensführung

stellen sich die meisten Entscheidungen in einer wesentlich größeren Komplexität als

bei den meisten technischen Fragestellungen. Deshalb ist ein Lösungsansatz mittels

Simulation oft der einzige Ausweg, will man sich nicht mit simplen deterministischen

Modellen begnügen. Um die Problematik nicht nur theoretisch zu beleuchten soll der

Unterschied zwischen einer einfachen Prognose der Erwartungswerte und der Verteilungs-

funktion der interessanten Variablen an einem Pensionsfonds von ca 3000 Selbststän-

digen erläutert werden, dessen Jahresumsatz rund 40 Mill. DM beträgt.


2.Problemstellung:


Es ist festzustellen, welche Maßnahmen zu trefffen sind, um die Leistungsfähigkeit

des Fonds bezüglich der Pensionen zu gewährleisten ohne exzessive Beitragsveränderun-

gen vorzunehmen. Es wurde sowohl eine Prognose der Verteilungsfunktion der Einnahmen-

-Ausgabenrechnung als auch des Fondsvermögens vorgenommen.

## 3. Modellparameter:

Die relevanten Bezugsgrößen waren die folgenden:

t........Zeitparameter
b(x,e,t)...Betragssatz für einen x-jährigen in % der momentanen Pension bei 100%
   Teilnahme im Jahre t,falls er mit dem Alter e eingetreten ist
b(y,e,t)...Betragssatz für eine y-jährige in % der momentanen Pension bei 100%
   Teilnahme im Jahre t,falls sie mit dem Alter e eingetreten ist
E(t).....Einnahmen in abs. 1000-DM-Beträgen des gesamten Fonds im Jahre t
p(x,t)...Höhe der prozentuellen Pension eines x-jährigen im Jahre t, abhängig von
   der Teilnahme b(x,e,t) in den Jahren seiner aktiven Beitragszeit
A(t).....Ausgaben in abs. 1000 DM-Beträgen des gesamten Fonds im Jahre t
Ma(x,b(x,e,t),t)..Anzahl der aktiven männlichen Mitglieder mit Alter x und Höhe der
   prozentuellen Teilnahme b(x,e,t) im Jahre t
Fa(y,b(y,e,t),t)..Anzahl der aktiven weiblichen Mitglieder mit Alter y und Höhe der
   prozentuellen Teilnahme b(y,e,t) im Jahre t
Pm(x,p(x,t),t)..Anzahl der pensionierten männlichen Mitglieder mit Alter x und Pen-
   sionshöhe p(x,t) in Prozent der Höchstpension im Jahre t
Pw(y,p(y,t),t)..Anzahl der pensionierten weiblichen Mitglieder mit Alter y und Pen-
   sionshöhe p(y,t) in Prozent der Höchstpension im Jahre t
Nm(x,b(x,e,t),t)..Anzahl der neueintretenden aktiven männlichen Mitglieder mit Alter
   x und Höhe der prozentuellen Teilnahme b(x,e,t) im Jahre t
Nw(y,b(y,e,t),t)..Anzahl der neueintretenden aktiven weiblichen Mitglieder mit Alter
   y und Höhe der prozentuellen Teilnahme b(y,e,t) im Jahre t
I(x,p(x,t),t)...Anzahl der invaliden männlichen Mitglieder mit Alter x und Pensionshöhe p(x,t) in Prozent der Höchstpension im Jahre t
I(y,p(y,t),t)...Anzahl der invaliden weiblichen Mitglieder mit Alter y und Pensions-
   höhe p(x,t) in Prozent der Höchstpension im Jahre t
ZI(x,p(x,t),t)..Anzahl der Zugänge an invaliden männlichen Mitglieder mit Alter x
   und Pensionshöhe b(x,e,t) in Prozent der Höchstpension im Jahre t
ZI(y,p(y,t),t)...Anzahl der Zugänge an invaliden weiblichen Mitglieder mit Alter y
   und Pensionshöhe b(y,e,t) in Prozent der Höchstpension im Jahre t
TI(x,p(x,t),t)..Anzahl der Abgänge durch Tod an invaliden männlichen Mitglieder mit
   Alter x und Pensionshöhe p(x,t) in Prozent der Höchstpension im Jahre t
TI(y,p(y,t),t)..Anzahl der Abgänge durch Tod an invaliden weiblichen Mitglieder mit
   Alter y und Pensionshöhe p(y,t) in Prozent der Höchstpension im Jahre t
TA(x,b(x,e,t),t)..Anzahl der Abgänge durch Tod an aktiven männlichen Mitglieder mit
   Alter x und Beitragshöhe b(x,e,t) in Prozent der Höchstpension im Jahre t

TA(y,b(y,e,t),t)..Anzahl der Abgänge durch Tod an aktiven weiblichen Mitglieder mit
       Alter y und Beitragshöhe b(y,e,t) in Prozent der Höchstpension im Jahre t
ZP(x,p(x,t),t)...Anzahl der Zugänge an männlichen Pensionisten mit Alter x und Pen-
       sionshöhe p(x,t) in Prozent der Höchstpension im Jahre t
ZP(y,p(y,t),t)...Anzahl der Zugänge an weiblichen Pensionisten mit Alter y und Pen-
       sionshöhe p(x,t) in Prozent der Höchstpension im Jahre t
TP(x,p(x,t),t)..Anzahl der Abgänge durch Tod an männlichen Pensionisten mit Alter x
       und Pensionshöhe p(x,t) in Prozent der Höchstpension im Jahre t
TP(y,p(y,t),t)..Anzahl der Abgänge durch Tod an weiblichen Pensionisten mit Alter y
       und Pensionshöhe p(x,t) in Prozent der Höchstpension im Jahre t
ZA(x,b(x,e,t),t)..Anzahl der Zugänge an aktiven männlichen Mitglieder mit Alter x
       und Beitragshöhe b(x,e,t) in Prozent der Höchstpension im Jahre t
ZA(y,b(y,e,t),t)...Anzahl der Zugänge an aktiven weiblichen Mitglieder mit Alter y
       und Beitragshöhe b(y,e,t) in Prozent der Höchstpension im Jahre t
W(y,p(y,t),t)...Anzahl der Witwen im Alter y mit Pensionshöhe p(y,t) in Prozent der
       Höchstpension im Jahre t
TW(y,p(y,t),t)..Anzahl der Abgänge durch Tod an Witwen im Alter y mit Pensionshöhe
       p(y,t) in Prozent der Höchstpension im Jahre t
ZW(y,p(y,t),t)...Anzahl der Zugänge an Witwen im Alter y mit Pensionshöhe p(y,t) in
       Prozent der Höchstpension im Jahre t
h(x,y,t)...Wahrscheinlichkeit in t, daß ein beim Tode x-jähriger Aktiver mit einer
       y-jährigen Frau verheiratet ist
i(x,t)....Wahrscheinlichkeit in t, daß ein x-jähriger Aktiver in t invalide wird
i(y,t)....Wahrscheinlichkeit in t, daß eine y-jährige Aktive in  t invalide wird
qa(x,t)...Wahrscheinlichkeit in t, daß ein x-jähriger Aktiver in t verstirbt
qi(x,t)...Wahrscheinlichkeit in t, daß ein x-jähriger Invalider in t verstirbt
qp(x,t)...Wahrscheinlichkeit in t, daß ein x-jähriger Pensionist in t verstirbt
qa(y,t)...Wahrscheinlichkeit in t, daß eine y-jähriger Aktive in t verstirbt
qi(y,t)...Wahrscheinlichkeit in t, daß eine y-jähriger Invalide in t verstirbt
qp(y,t)...Wahrscheinlichkeit in t, daß ein y-jährige Pensionistin in t verstirbt
qw(y,t)...Wahrscheinlichkeit in t, daß ein y-jährige Witwe in t verstirbt
F(t)......Höhe des Reservefonds im Zeitpunkt t
j(t)......Verzinsung der Kapitralanlagen des Fonds F(t) zum Zeitpunkt t


Alle Wahrscheinlichkeiten und die Beitragshöhen b(x,e,t),b(y,e,t),die von den einzelnen Gruppen abhängen, sind stochastische Größen, deren Dichtefunktion, man mit den
ersten drei Momenten beschreiben kann. Die Momente der Wahrscheinlichkeitsverteil-
ungen hängen von der Größe der Gruppe ab. Um von den Momenten der Verteilung für
eine einzelne Person zu der Verteilung einer Gruppe solcher oder ähnlicher Personen
zu kommen, wendet unter Zuhilfenahme des zentralen Grenzwertsatzes eine Chi-quadrat-

approximation (s. P. Hall (1) ) an. Falls die Gruppe aus wenigen Personen besteht, kann man die Verteilung durch rekursive Berechnung der Faltungsintegrale direkt berechnen (s. H.U. Gerber (1) oder W. Ettl (1) ). Eine weitere Möglichkeit ist die Verwendung der schnellen Fouriertransformation (s. J. Bertram (1)).

## 4.Modellgleichungen und Optimierungsaufgabe

Korrekterweise müßte das System mit entsprechenden Markovprozessen und Übergangsintensitäten anstelle von einjährigen Übergangswahrscheinlichkeiten betrachtet werden. Da sich jedoch sowohl in den Ergebnissen als auch in der Struktur keine wesentlichen Unterschiede ergeben, sei es der Einfachheit halber gestattet das vereinfachte Modell zu betrachten. Es ist ohne großen Mehraufwand möglich das allgemeine Modell zu implementieren.

$$Ma(x+1,b(x+1,t)) = Ma(x,b(x,e,t))*(1.-qa(x,t)-ix(x,t)-fp(x,t))+ZA(x+1,b(x+1,t))$$
$$Pm(x+1,p(x+1,t)) = Pm(x,p(x,t))*(1-qp(x,t))+ZP(x,p(x,t))$$
$$I(x+1,p(x+1,t)) = I(x,p(x,t))*(1-qi(x,t))+ZI(x,p(x,t))$$
$$Fa(y+1,b(y+1,t)) = Fa(y,b(y,e,t))*(1.-qa(y,t)-iy(y,t)-fp(y,t))+ZA(y+1,b(y+1,t))$$
$$Pm(y+1,p(y+1,t)) = Pm(y,p(y,t))*(1-qp(y,t))+ZP(y,p(y,t))$$
$$I(y+1,p(y+1,t)) = I(y,b(y,e,t))*(1-qi(y,t))+ZI(y,p(y,t))$$
$$W(y+1,p(y+1,t)) = W(y,p(y,t))*(1-qw(y,t))+ZW(y,p(y,t))$$

$$ZP(x,p(x,t))= Ma(x,b(x,e,t)*(1-qa(x,t)*.5-ix(x,t)*.5)*fp(x+.5,t)*(1-qp(x,t)*.5)$$
$$ZI(x,p(x,t))= Ma(x,b(x,e,t)*(1-qa(x,t)*.5-fp(x,t)*.5)*ix(x+.5,t)*(1-qi(x,t)*.5)$$
$$ZP(y,p(y,t))= Fa(y,b(y,e,t)*(1-qa(y,t)*.5-fp(y,t)*.5)*iy(y+.5,t)*(1-qi(y,t)*.5)$$
$$ZI(y,p(y,t))= Ma(y,b(y,e,t)*(1-qa(y,t)*.5-fp(y,t)*.5)*iy(y+.5,t)*(1-qi(y,t)*.5)$$
$$ZW(y,p(y,t))= \text{Summe über aller x: } Ma(x,b(x,e,t))*qa(x,t)*h(x+.5,y,t)+$$
$$Pm(x,p(x,t))*qp(x,t)*h(x+.5,y,t)+I(x,p(x,t))*qi(x,t)*h(x+.5,y,t)$$

$$E(t) = \text{Summe über alle } x,y,b(x,e,t),b(y,e,t): b(x,e,t)*Ma(x,t)+b(y,e,t)*Ma(y,t)$$
$$A(t) = \text{Summe über alle } x,y,p(x,t),p(y,t):$$
$$p(x,t)*(Pm(x,p(x,t))+I(x,p(x,t)))+p(y,t)*(Pm(y,p(y,t))+I(y,p(y,t)))$$
$$F(t+1) = F(t)*(1+j(t))+(E(t)-A(t))*(1+.5*j(t))$$

Als Optimierungsaufgabe sind folgende Forderungen gestellt:

Es soll garantiert werden, daß der Fonds niemals unter eine bestimmte Sicherheitsreserve fällt. Als Kontrollvariable seien der Beitragssatz und die Pensionshöhe mit gewissen Einschränkungen möglich.

Ferner müssen folgende einschränkende Nebenbedingungen für alle t erfüllt werden:

$0 \leqslant b(x,e,t)$

$0 \leqslant b(x,e,t)-b(x,e,t+1) = \leqslant d*b(x,e,t)$        d:konstant

$0 \leqslant p(x,t)-p(x,t+1) = \leqslant f*p(x,t)$        f:konstant

Die Summe der Veränderungen des Beitragssatzes und die Summe der Veränderungen der Pensionshöhen (jeweils in % ) soll minimal sein.

Die Relation der Beitragssätze in einem Zeitpunkt t soll nach dem Prinzip des Äquivalenzprinzips bestimmt werden.

Es ist sehr leicht einzusehen, daß diese optimale Kontrollproblem eine optimale Lösung hat, wenn die Parameter d und f groß genug gewählt werden können, sodaß sie keine Einschränkung mehr sind. Bei zu kleinen Parametern und zu geringer Anzahl an Mitgliedern kann die Solvenzbedingung an den Fonds nicht erfüllt werden.

## Ergebnisse und Unterschiede zu den bisherigen Methoden:

Mittels der Verteilungsfunktionen der Einnahmen, der Ausgaben und der Reserven, die durch Simulation des skizzierten Systems berechnet werden, können für jeden Zeitpunkt Aussagen über Sicherheit des Fonds, maximalen Finanzbedarf und die Höhe der Reserven getroffen werden. In den früheren Vorgangsweisen wurden weder die stochastischen Elemente des Systems berücksichtigt, noch erhielt man qualitative Aussagen über den Zustand des Fonds. Es wurden lediglich die Erwartungswerte der einzelnen Größen berechnet und diese den Entscheidungen zugrundegelegt. Bei kleiner Mitgliederanzahl des Fonds (unter 1000) und bei langfristigen Betrachtungen bezüglich Schwankungen des Neuzuganges an Mitgliedern können nach den bisherigen Verfahren wesentliche Fehleinschätzungen eintreten, die mittels der hier verwendeten Simulation vermieden werden. Es werden somit Fehlplanungen, die schwerwiegende Auswirkungen haben soweit als möglich verhindert. Die Sicherheit des Fonds kann durch verschieden Maßnahmen im Fonds, wie zB. rechtzeitige gleichmäßige Beitragsanhebung oder Leistungsherabsetzung oder Versicherungsschutz von außen, bei geringerem Finanzmitteleinsatz beträchtlich erhöht werden.

J. Bertram (1) : Numerische Berechnungen von Gesamtschadenverteilungen, Blätter der Deut. Gesell. f. Versicherungsmathematik, XV, S. 175- 194

W. Ettl (1): Numerische Berechnungen von Gesamtschadensverteilungen mittels der Methode der Laplacetransformation, in Vorbereitung

H.U. Gerber (1): On the numerical evaluation of the distribution of aggregate claims and its stop-loss, Insurance: Mathematics and Economics, 1, p.13 - 18

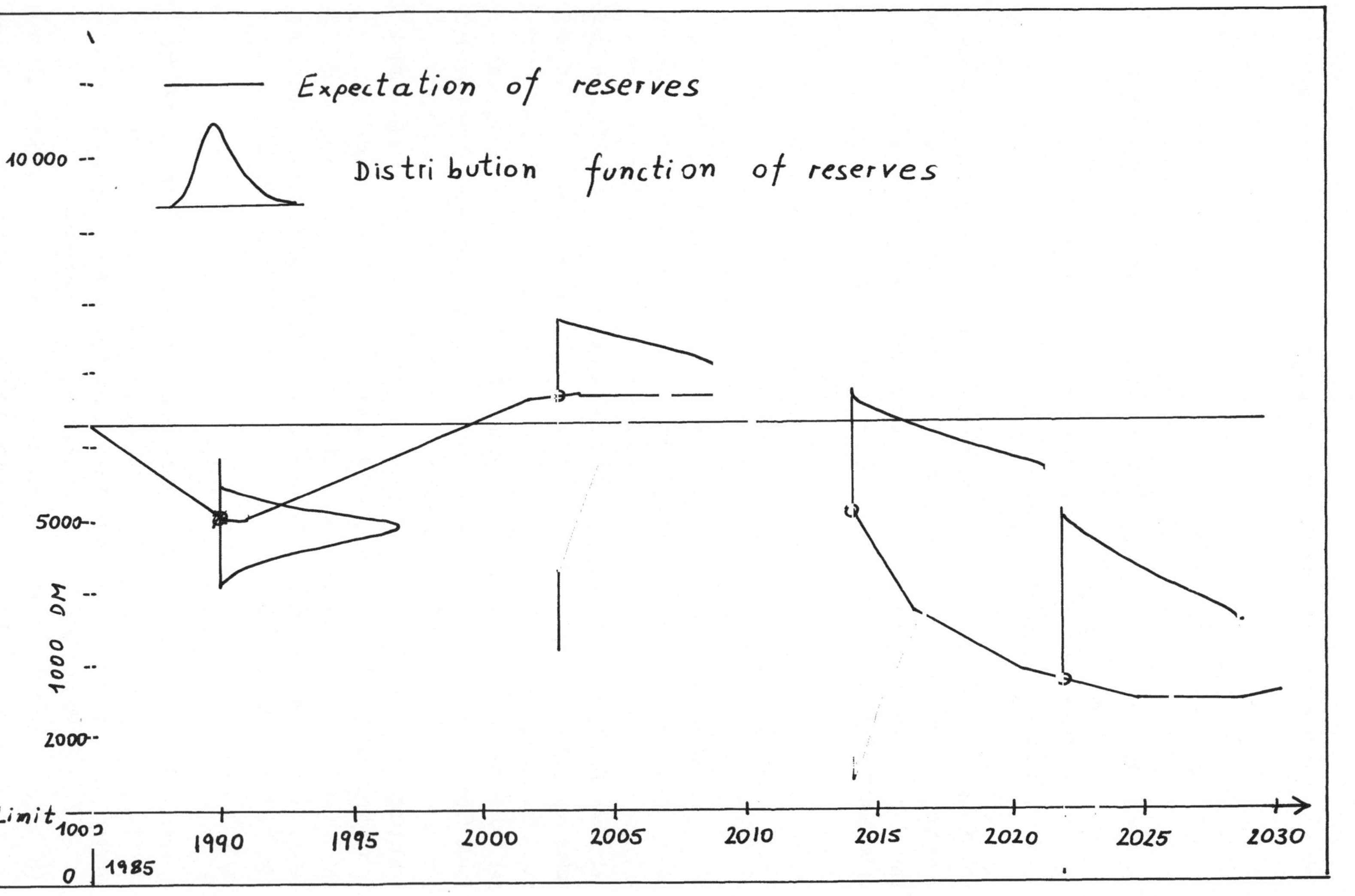

Expectation of reserves
Distribution function of reserves
10 000
5000
2000
1000 DM
Limit
0
1985
1990
1995
2000
2005
2010
2015
2020
2025
2030

# Finanzielle Auswirkungen von Änderungen eines Pensionssystems auf eine Pensionskasse

Wolfgang Ettl, Klosterneuburg bei Wien

Zusammenfassung: Prognosen über die Finanzentwicklung von Pensionskassen sind sehr komplex. Falls Änderungen im Beitrags- und Leistungsrecht durchgeführt werden sollen, sind sie jedoch unbedingt notwendig. Durch die Vielzahl der Parameter wurden bislang nur Variantenrechnungen durchgeführt, ohne das Problem von Schwankungen, Liquidität, und Optimalität zufriedenstellend gelöst zu haben. Es ist aus obigen Gründen notwendig nicht nur eine optimale Lösung zu finden, sondern auch deren Stabiltät hinsichtlich einer Vielzahl von Parametern zu überprüfen und die Verteilungsfunktion der Lösung als Grundlage der Entscheidung zu verwenden. Eine Vernachlässigung der gegenseitigen Koppelung der Variablen kann zu schweren Fehlentscheidungen führen.

Summary. Developements of the financial balance of pension funds are in any case very compilcated questions. If the management of the fund is planning some changes of premiums and/or payments, such calulation are necessary. Due to the lot of variables and parameters changing over time only a lot of variants of the planned changes were done. The question of liquidity and optimality of the solution for the structure of the fund were not solved in an appropiate manner. It is very important to consider not only the optimality of the solution but also the stability. For the management the distribution function of the variables they are interested in should be the basis for their decision.

1.Einleitung: Prognosen über die Entwicklung des finanziellen Status von Pensionsversicherungssytemen sind immer mit sehr großen Fragezeichen zu versehen. Die betroffenen Personen verändern ihre Verhaltensweisen in Abhängigkeit vom Pensionssystem in meist unvorhersehbarer Weise, daß Modellbeschreibungen schon sehr oft in die Irre geführt haben. Eine Möglichkeit diese Gefahren auszuschließen besteht darin, das System stabil gegenüber solchen Verhaltensänderungen zu machen. Mittels Simulation sollen Lösungsvorschläge erarbeitet werden, die diese Stabiltät aufweisen. Im konkreten  wurde für eine Pensionskasse das Problem der vorzeitigen Pension (Frührente) gelöst. Als Bedingung wurde verlangt, daß die Liquidität der Kasse nicht beeinträchtigt wird und das Prinzip der Gerechtigkeit in Form des horizontalen Äquivalenzprinzips soweit alks möglich gewahrt bleibt.

Eine Pensionskasse nach dem Umlageverfahren, die derzeit ihren Mitgliedern Freizügigkeit in bestimmten Grenzen hinsichtlich der Beitragshöhe (mit der Folge der Durchrechnung für die Pension) gewährt, möchte vom derzeitigen Endalter 70 auf das Pensionsalter 65 herabsetzen. Die Bedingung lautet, daß die derzeit kostendeckenden Beiträge nur eingeschränkt wachsen dürfen und daß alle bald in den Genuß der früheren Rente kommen.

## 2. Stabiltät des Lösungsansatzes:

Aus analytischen Überlegungen für einen großen Bestand im Beharrungszustand kann man einen vernünftigen Startwert für die Lösung finden (s. W. Gysin (1)). Da jedoch in einem analytischem Modell weder die Größe der Pensionskasse noch die spezielle Struktur eingeht, sind Modifikation der Lösungsansätze notwendig. Ferner muß die Liquiditätsbedingung erfüllt sein, daß ein Mindestreservefonds immer vorhanden sein muß. Die Probleme sind ferner daurch verschärft, als es für die bisherigen Mitglieder nicht zwingend sein soll, schon früher als mit dem bisherigen Endalter 70 die Pension zu beanspruchen. Es darf daher keine starke Benachteiligung derer, die bis 70 aktiv bleiben, geben.

Es wurde ein simpler Ansatz gewählt, der einerseits vom versicherungsmathematischen Grundsatz der Äquivalenz von Leistungen und Beiträgen ausgeht aber auch andererseits so einfach ist, daß er sowohl leicht administrierbar ist als auch von allen Mitgliedern verstanden wird. Die Änderung wurde in der Delegiertenversammlung beschlossen und mußte daher allgemein verständlich sein. Eine genaue Analyse der versicherungsmathematischen Berechnungen für den Großbestand im Berharrungszustand ist in W. Ettl (1) zu finden.

Es wurde folgender Ansatz gewählt:

    e.......Beitrittsalter
    x.......Momentanes Alter ( x = e )
    p(alt)..bisheriges Alter beim Pensionsbeginn
    p(neu)..neues niedrigeres Alter beimPensionsbeginn
    p(x,e)...neues Pensionsalter für konkrete Person mit Eintrittsalter e und momentanem Alter x am Umstellungsstichtag

    p = p(alt) - (p(neu)-x)/(p(neu)-e))*(p(alt)-p(neu))

Neueintretende erreichen somit immer das neue niedrigere Pensionsalter. Die Reduktion des Pensionsalter hängt deshalb vom Eintrittsalter ab, weil die Beiträge mit steigendem Eintrittsalter zunehmen.Bei längerem Verbleib als nach obiger Berechnung notwendig wäre, entfällt die Beitragspflicht, allerdings fallen keine Leistungen an. Diese Benachteiligung wurde aus geschäftspolitischen Gründen gewählt.

Es wurde nun für die konkrete Pensionskasse unter der Annahme, daß keine Mitglieder über ihr errechnetes Pensionsalter hinaus aktiv bleiben, die Einnahmen-Ausgabenrechnung sowie die Liquiditätsentwicklung simuliert, wobei auf die spezielle Struktur der Alters- , Beitrags- und Leistungsverteilung der Pensionskasse Rücksicht genommen wur-

de. Als Modell der Pensionskasse wurde ein in diesem Tagungsband vorgestellter Bei
trag von W. Ettl, "Auswirkungen von Modellverbesserungen bei stochastischen Systemen"
verwendet.


## 3.Ergebnisse:

Bei Verwendung obiger Formel für das herabgesetzte Pensionsalter ist die Entwicklung
der Pensionskasse im Vergleich zum unveränderten bisherigem Pensionsalter mit kleinen
Beitragserhöhungen bei großer Sicherheit hinsichtlich der Liquidität gut abgesichert.
Kritisch bis unlösbar ist die Lage der Pensionskasse, wenn die Altersherabsetzung
durch eine Kürzung der ausbezahlten Pension finanziert werden soll. Da im schlech-
testen Fall 5 Beitragsjahre wegfallen und gleichzeitig 5 Pensionsjahre hinzukommen
ist eine Finanzierung auf diesem Wege mit hohen Vorfinanzierungskosten verbunden und
damit für kleine Kassen praktisch undurchführbar. Nur große Altersversorgungssysteme
wie die staatlich organisierte Rentenversicherungen hatten bisher die Möglichkeit solche Vorfinanzierungen über Beitragserhöhungen oder Kredite aus Steuermitteln zu leis-
ten. Das Ergebnis, daß die Zeitverschiebung zwischen fehlenden Beitragseinnahmen und
reduzierten Leistungen bei limitierten Kreditrahmen wesentlich ist, sollte Befürwor-
tern des reinen Äquivalenzprinzips zu denken geben.

Mittels Simulationsverfahren kann der Finanzbedarf mit seiner Verteilungsfunktion angegeben werden. Eine Entscheidung über die Durchführung der wesentlichen Eckdaten
eines solchen Pensionssystems ist somit möglich. Parallelberechnungen, die ohne Simulationsverfahren und ohne Berücksichtigung der Größe der Pensionskasse durchgeführt
wurden, haben die Entscheidungssituation verzerrt dargestellt. Ein Verzicht auf das
Mittel der Simulation wäre folgenschwer.


Literatur:

W. Ettl (1) : Herabsetzung des Pensionsbeginns bei Vorsorgeeinrichtungen mit Umlage-
charakter, in Vorbereitung.
W. Gysin (1): Zur Berechnung des individuellen Deckungskapitals bei Vorsorgeeinrichtungen mit Einheitsbeiträgen,Blätter der Deut. Gesellschaft für
Versicherungsmathematik,XIV, S. 683-695


Vergleich der klassischen Methode ohne Simulation (Bild 1) mit den Schaubildern nach
obigem Modell mittels stochastischer Simulation (auszugsweise) Bild 2- Bild  4.

Pensionsalter 70       Zinsen auf Guthaben: Anpassung nach ASVG + 2% p.a.

| Jahr | | | | | | | | | | |
|---|---|---|---|---|---|---|---|---|---|---|
| 1986 | 1987 | 1988 | 1989 | 1990 | 1991 | 1992 | 1993 | 1994 | 1995 | 1996 |
| Proz. Erh. pa. | | | | | | | | | | |
| .704 | .704 | .704 | .704 | .704 | .704 | .704 | .704 | .704 | .704 | .704 |
| Jahresergebnis | | | | | | | | | | |
| -9015.4 | -1017.6 | 6890.4 | 12567.6 | 17610.3 | 18963.6 | 19996.7 | 19059.6 | 16682.6 | 12671.1 | 7891.0 |
| Kumul. Jahreserg. | | | | | | | | | | |
| -9015.4 | -10032.9 | -3142.5 | 9613.6 | 27768.4 | 47666.6 | 69016.5 | 89837.6 | 108650.6 | 123748.1 | 134271.9 |

| | | | | Jahr | | | | | | |
|---|---|---|---|---|---|---|---|---|---|---|
| 1997 | 1998 | 1999 | 2000 | 2001 | 2002 | 2003 | 2004 | 2005 | 2006 | 2007 |
| | | | | Proz. Erh. pa. | | | | | | |
| .704 | .704 | .704 | .704 | .704 | .704 | .704 | .704 | .704 | .704 | .704 |
| | | | | Jahresergebnis | | | | | | |
| 6777.1 | 3198.8 | 4429.9 | 3732.3 | 1346.8 | -1938.5 | -3353.8 | -3299.5 | -329.5 | 711.3 | 1834.7 |
| | | | | Kumul. Jahreserg. | | | | | | |
| 143870.0 | 150010.1 | 157528.8 | 164486.3 | 169149.8 | 170555.5 | 170545.7 | 170591.1 | 173666.9 | 177865.7 | 183294.5 |

| | | | | | | | | | Jahr | |
|---|---|---|---|---|---|---|---|---|---|---|
| 2008 | 2009 | 2010 | 2011 | 2012 | 2013 | 2014 | 2015 | 2016 | 2017 | 2018 |
| | | | | | | | | | Proz. Erh. pa. | |
| .704 | .704 | .704 | .704 | .704 | .704 | .704 | .704 | .704 | .704 | .704 |
| | | | | | | | | | Jahresergebnis | |
| 4824.7 | 6473.1 | 4468.3 | -2676.1 | -9148.1 | -13096.4 | -13892.0 | -17834.0 | -21325.0 | -18222.7 | -20982.3 |
| | | | | | | | | | Kumul. Jahreserg. | |
| 191881.6 | 202321.7 | 210925.9 | 212414.7 | 207331.9 | 198120.2 | 187912.8 | 173480.4 | 155198.5 | 139715.3 | 121107.7 |

| 2019 | 2020 | 2021 | 2022 | 2023 | 2024 | 2025 | 2026 | 2027 | 2028 | 2029 |
|---|---|---|---|---|---|---|---|---|---|---|
| .704 | .704 | .704 | .704 | .704 | .704 | .704 | .704 | .704 | .704 | .704 |
| -20444.7 | -18545.1 | -17332.1 | -15609.2 | -13996.4 | -11767.5 | -10026.8 | -8196.3 | -6158.9 | -4024.5 | -1872.9 |
| 102676.2 | 85813.7 | 69851.2 | 55326.9 | 42157.1 | 30997.5 | 21390.0 | 13457.7 | 7444.7 | 3488.6 | 1648.0 |

| 2030 |
|---|
| .704 |
| 276.8 |
| 1963.3 |

*BILD 1*

Bild 1: Verteilung der Einnahmen für ausgewählte Jahre, wobei der Mittelwert aus
Bild 1 der deterministischen Methode eingezeichnet wurde

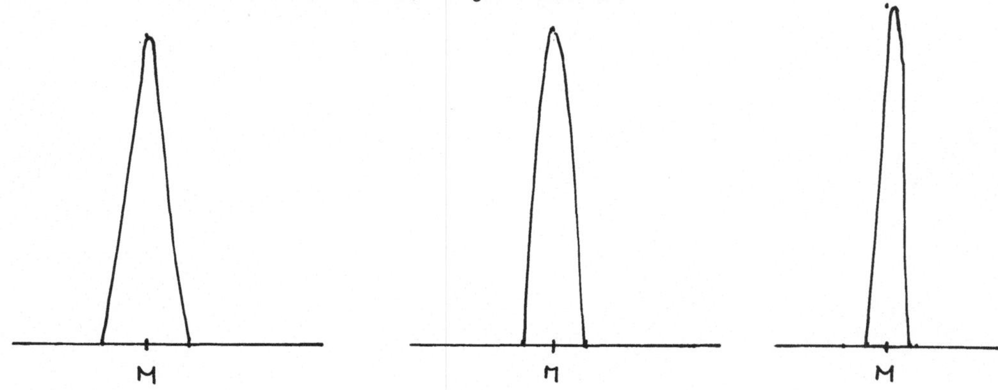

Bild 3: Verteilung der Ausgaben für ausgewählte Jahre, wobei der Mittelwert aus
Bild 1 der deterministischen Methode eingezeichnet wurde.

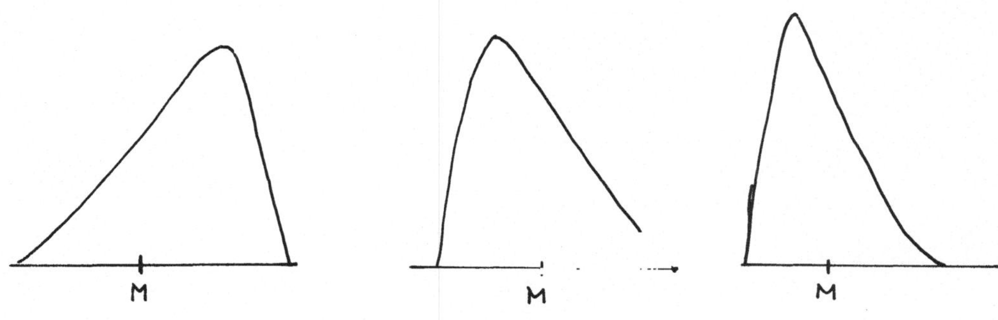

Bild 4: Verteilung des Reservefonds für ausgewählte Jahre, wobei der Mittelwert aus
Bild 1 der deterministischen Methode eingezeichnet wurde

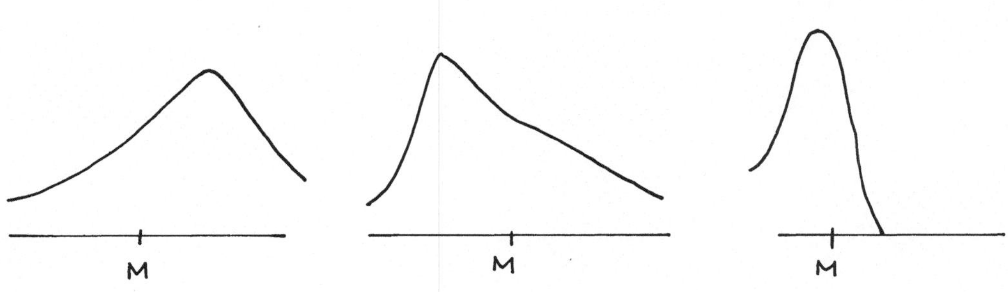

Amborski, Krzystof Dr.-Ing. TU  Warschau z.Zt. TH Darmstadt Inst. für Regelungst.
         Schloßgraben,  D-6100  Darmstadt

Ameling, Walter Prof. Dr.-Ing.  Institut für Allgemeine Elektrotechnik und Daten-
         verarbeitungssysteme RWTH Aachen, Schinkelstr. 2  D-5100  Aachen

Bausch-Gall, Ingrid Dr. rer. nat. Wohlfahrstr. 20  D-8000 München 45

Behrens, Michael Dipl.-Ing. Institut für Allgemeine Elektrotechnik und Datenver-
         arbeitungssysteme RWTH Aachen, Schinkelstr. 2,  D-5100  Aachen

Bell, Robert K.  Marloffsteinerstr. 14   D-8525  Uttenreuth

Bentz, Jerry L. Mgr. Adv. Eng.  McDonnell Douglas Electronics Comp. P.O.Box 426
         Dept. 0046  St. Charles, MO, 63302  USA

Braun, Hans Dr.-Ing.  Institut für Meß und Regelungstechnik Univ. Karlsruhe
         Richard-Willstätter-Allee,  D-7500  Karlsruhe

Breitenecker, Felix Priv. Doz. Dr.rer.nat.  Inst. für Technische Mathematik TU
         Wiedener Hauptstr. 6-10  A - 1040  Wien

Buse, Monika Dipl.-Math.  Inst. für Med. Informatik und Biomathematik, Ruhr Univ.
         Universitätsstr. 150   D-4630  Bochum

Cretnik, J. Dr.Inst. St. Stefan der Univ. Ljubljana, Jamova 39,  YU - 61000 Ljublana

Diekmann, Klaus Dr.-Ing. Lehrstuhl für Meß und Regelungstechnik, Ruhr Univ. Post-
         fach 102148,  D-4630  Bochum

Egger, Franz Dipl.-Ing.  Siemens AG, Otto-Hahn-Ring 6, D-8000  München 83

Engelmann, Hans-Dietrich Priv. Doz. Dr.-Ing. FB Chemietechnik, Univ. Dortmund
         Postfach 500500, D-4600  Dortmund

Eschenbacher, Peter Dipl.-Ing. IMMD IV, Univ. Erlangen, Martensstr. 3, D-8520
         Erlangen

Ettl, Wolfgang Dr. Inst. für Versicherungsmathematik TU Wien, Wiedener Haupstr. 6-10
         A - 1040  Wien

Fischer, Kristian Dipl.-Inf. Universität Passau, Innstr. 27  D-8390  Passau

Fuss, Hans Dr. GMD-F1  Postfach 1240   D-5205 St. Augustin

Gabriel, Wilfried Dr.rer.nat. Max-Planck-Inst. für Limnologie, Postfach 165
         D-2320  Plön

Galke, Lioba  Goetheweg 3   D-5630  Remscheid 11

Giersch, Christoph Priv. Doz. Dr.rer.nat.   Botanisches Inst. Univ. Düsseldorf
         Universitätsstr. 2  D-4000  Düsseldorf

Gilg, Albert Dr.rer.nat. Siemens AG  Otto-Hahn-Ring 6, D-8000  München 83

Gottwald, Björn A. Prof. Dr.rer.nat.  Fakultät für Biologie Universität Freiburg
         Schänzlestr. 1  D-7800  Freiburg

Gräff, Martin  Inst. für techn Mathematik TU Wien, Wiedener hauptstr. 6-10
         A - 1040  Wien

Gülich, H. Dipl.-Ing.  Inst. für Mechanik und Regelungstechnik Univ. Siegen
         Paul-Bonatz-Str. 9-11   D-5900  Siegen

Halin, Jürgen Priv. Doz. Dr.-Ing.  Inst. für Energietechnik ETH Zürich  Clausius-
         str. 33   CH - 8092  Zürich

Hass, W. D. Dipl.-Ing.  Lufthansa Frankfurt Abtlg. Flusimulation  D-6000 Frankfurt

Havranek, William A. C.Eng.  Rapid Data Ltd. Crescent House, Crescent Road, Wor-
         thing, BN 115RW, England

Heller, Moshe R. Control Data GmbH,  Berg-am-Laim-Str. 47   D-8000  München 80

Hoffmann, Oskar Dr. Neurochirurg. Univ. Klinik, Klinikstr. 29  D-6300  Gießen

Ilic, Z. V. Electronic Associates, Inc. West Long Branch, N.J. 07764 USA

Karba, Rihard Dr.  Univ. Ljubljanni Fakulteta za elektrotehniko, YU 61001
        Ljubljana, Trzaska 25

Kaplinski, Oleg Dr.  Politechnika Poznanska  PL-60965  Poznan

Khakzar, H. Kanalstr. 38  D-7300  Esslingen

Keller, H. B. Dipl.-Ing.  Kernforschungszentrum Karlsruhe  Inst. für Datenverarb.
        Postfach 3640   D-7500  Karlsruhe

Kodweiß, Reinhard Dipl.-Math.   Dornier GmbH  Abtlg. Flugsimulation, Postfach
        D-7990  Friedrichshafen

Kohel, Karl  Inst. für Informatik  Univ. Linz, Altenbergerstr. 69  A - 4040 Linz

Köhne, Manfred Prof. Dr. Univ. Siegen  Paul-Bonatz-Str. 9 D-5900  Siegen

Krechel-Mohr, K. J.  Kehrstr. 6   D-5444  Polch

Küspert, Klaus Dr.  IBM Wissenschaftszentrum, Tiergartenstr. 15  D-6900 Heidelberg

Kwasnikowski J.  Os Kraju Rad 9m14   PL - 61 674  Poznan

Langer, Klaus-Jürgen Dipl.-Inf.  IMMD IV Univ. Martensstr. 3  D-8520  Erlangen

Letters, Fritz  Zollernweg 1   D-7022  Lei-Leinfelden 1

Liedtke, Rolf-Peter  Forschungszentrum Informatik, Haid-und-Neu-Str. 10-14
        D-7500  Karlsruhe

Lunderstädt, Reinhardt  Prof. Dr.-Ing.  Univ. der Bundeswehr Hamburg, Institut für
        Automatisierungstechnik   Holstenhofweg 85   D-2000  Hamburg 70

Mansour, M. Prof. Dr.  Inst. für Automation und ind. Elektronik  ETH Zürich
        Physikstr. 3   CH - 8092  Zürich

Maschtera, Ulrike Inst. für Automatik  Univ. Linz  Altenbergerstr. 69  A-4040  Linz

Matko, Drago Dr. Faculty of Electrical Engng.  Univ. Ljubljani,  YU 61000 Ljubljana

Möller, Dietmar P.F. Dr.-Ing.  Physiolog. Inst. Univ. Mainz  Saarstr. 21
        D-6500  Mainz

Mündemann, Friedhelm  Dipl.-Inf. Univ. der Bundeswehr  Werner Heisenberg Weg 39
        D-8014  Neubiberg

Munser, Hans-Joachim  Dipl.-Ing.  Flugsimulation Dornier GmbH, Postfach 1420
        D-7990  Friedrichshafen

Nagel, Sabine  Dipl.-Inf. IMMD IV Univ.  Martensstr. 3  D-8520  Erlangen

Pösinger, Heribert  Dipl.-Ing. Inst. für Elektro- und Biomed.  Technik TU Graz
        Inffeldgasse 18  A - 8010  Graz

Rake, Heirich  Prof. Dr.-Ing.  Inst. für Regelungstechnik RWTH Aachen, Steinbacher-
        str. 54  D-5400  Aachen

Ray, Wayne R.  Control Data Corporation, Minneapolis, MN 55440  USA

Regen, Franz  Dipl.-Inf. Institut für Allgemeine Elektrotechnik und Datenverarbei-
        tungssysteme  RWTH Aachen, Schinkelstr. 2  D-5100  Aachen

Reinhardt, A.  Prof.  GH-Kassel, Fachgebiet Produktiossysteme, Mönchenergstr. 7
        D-3500  Kassel

Reinicke, Gottfried  Inst. für Fertigungstechnik Univ. Hannover  Schloßwenderstr. 5
        D-3000  Hannover

Renn, Walter Dr.  Med. Klinik Univ. Tübingen  Otfried Müller Str. 19  D-74 Tübingen

Richter, Otto, Prof. Dr. Abtlg. Angewandte Statistik Univ. Bonn, Mecken-
        heimer Allee 174   D-5300  Bonn

Schabach, R.  Prof. Dr.  Inst. für Numerische Mathematik Univ. Göttingen, Lotzestr.
        16-18   D-3400  Göttingen

Schloeder, Johannes  Inst. für Angewandte Math. SFB 72  Wegelerstr. 6  D- 53 Bonn

Schmidt, Bernd Prof. Dr.rer.nat.   Inst. für Math. Masch. IV Univ. Erlangen
        Martensstr. 3  D-8520  Erlangen

Schneider, Berthold  Prof. Dr.  Med. Hochschule Hannover  Inst. für Biometrie
        KOntstanty-Gutschow-Str.  D-3000 Hannover

Schöne, Arnim  Prof. Dr.-Ing. Lehrstuhl Meß-Steuer- und Regelungstechnik Univ.
        FB Produktionstechnik, Postfach 330440    D-2800  Bremen

Shorrock, David  Rediffusion Simulation Inc. USA

Schütz, Georg Dipl.-Ing. Lufthansa Frankfurt  Abtlg. Flugsimulator D-6000 Frankfurt

Senger, Karl Heinz  Dipl.-Ing. DFVLR Inst. für Dynamik der Flugsysteme  D-8031
        Weßling

Sowa, Jürgen  Dipl.-Inf. Translift GmbH, Salzwerkstr. 3   D-7889 Grenzach-Whylen 2

Stahl, H.  Dipl.-Ing. Inst. für Regelungsetchnik  Univ.  Cauerstr. 7 D-8520 Erlangen

Sturm, Karl-Heinz Dr.  VDP Berlin, Seestr. 13   D-1000 Berlin 65

Tavangarian, D. Dr. FB 20 Univ. Frankfurt, Dantestr. 5  D-6000 Frankfurt

Teriete, Alfons  Fraunhofer Inst., Emil-Figge-Str. 75  D-4600  Dortmund

Tettweiler, Wilfried  Regenstr. 19   D-8032  Gräfeling

Trier, Reinhold Dipl.-Phys.   M.A.N. Abtlg. ZOT3  Postfach 8500  D-85  Nürnberg 44

Winkler, Peter  Dipl.-Phys.   PSI  Heilbronnerstr. 10 D-1000  Berlin 31

Band 66: Applications and Theory of Petri Nets. Proceedings, 1982. Edited by G. Rozenberg. VI, 315 pages. 1983.

Band 67: Data Networks with Satellites. GI/NTG Working Conference, Cologne, September 1982. Edited by J. Majus and O. Spaniol. VI, 251 pages. 1983.

Band 68: B. Kutzler, F. Lichtenberger, Bibliography on Abstract Data Types. V, 194 Seiten. 1983.

Band 69: Betrieb von DN-Systemen in der Zukunft. GI-Fachgespräch, Tübingen, März 1983. Herausgegeben von M. A. Graef. VIII, 343 Seiten. 1983.

Band 70: W. E. Fischer, Datenbanksystem für CAD-Arbeitsplätze. VII, 222 Seiten. 1983.

Band 71: First European Simulation Congress ESC 83. Proceedings, 1983. Edited by W. Ameling. XII, 653 pages. 1983.

Band 72: Sprachen für Datenbanken. GI-Jahrestagung, Hamburg, Oktober 1983. Herausgegeben von J. W. Schmidt. VII, 237 Seiten. 1983.

Band 73: GI-13. Jahrestagung, Hamburg, Oktober 1983. Proceedings. Herausgegeben von J. Kupka. VIII, 502 Seiten. 1983.

Band 74: Requirements Engineering. Arbeitstagung der GI, 1983. Herausgegeben von G. Hommel und D. Krönig. VIII, 247 Seiten. 1983.

Band 75: K. R. Dittrich, Ein universelles Konzept zum flexiblen Informationsschutz in und mit Rechensystemen. VIII, 246 pages. 1983.

Band 76: GWAI-83. German Workshop on Artifical Intelligence. September 1983. Herausgegeben von B. Neumann. VI, 240 Seiten. 1983.

Band 77: Programmiersprachen und Programmentwicklung. 8. Fachtagung der GI, Zürich, März 1984. Herausgegeben von U. Ammann. VIII, 239 Seiten. 1984.

Band 78: Architektur und Betrieb von Rechensystemen. 8. GI-NTG-Fachtagung, Karlsruhe, März 1984. Herausgegeben von H. Wettstein. IX, 391 Seiten. 1984.

Band 79: Programmierumgebungen: Entwicklungswerkzeuge und Programmiersprachen. Herausgegeben von W. Sammer und W. Remmele. VIII, 236 Seiten. 1984.

Band 80: Neue Informationstechnologien und Verwaltung. Pro ceedings, 1983. Herausgegeben von R. Traunmüller, H. Fiedler, K. Grimmer und H. Reinermann. XI, 402 Seiten. 1984.

Band 81: Koordinaten von Informationen. Proceedings, 1983. Herausgegeben von R. Kuhlen. VI, 366 Seiten. 1984.

Band 82: A. Bode, Mikroarchitekturen und Mikroprogrammierung: Formale Beschreibung und Optimierung, 6, 1-277 Seiten. 1984.

Band 83: Software-Fehlertoleranz und -Zuverlässigkeit. Herausgegeben von F. Belli, S. Pfleger und M. Seifert. VII, 297 Seiten. 1984.

Band 84: Fehlertolerierende Rechensysteme. 2. GI/NTG/GMR-Fachtagung, Bonn 1984. Herausgegeben von K.-E. Großpietsch und M. Dal Cin. X, 433 Seiten. 1984.

Band 85: Simulationstechnik. Proceedings, 1984. Herausgegeben von F. Breitenecker und W. Kleinert. XII, 676 Seiten. 1984.

Band 86: Prozeßrechner 1984. 4. GI/GMR/KfK-Fachtagung, Karlsruhe, September 1984. Herausgegeben von H. Trauboth und A. Jaeschke. XII, 710 Seiten. 1984.

Band 87: Musterkennung 1984. Proceedings, 1984. Herausgegeben von W. Kropatsch. IX, 351 Seiten. 1984.

Band 88: GI-14. Jahrestagung. Braunschweig. Oktober 1984. Proceedings. Herausgegeben von H.-D. Ehrich. IX, 451 Seiten. 1984.

Band 89: Fachgespräche auf der 14. GI-Jahrestagung. Braunschweig, Oktober 1984. Herausgegeben von H.-D. Ehrich. V, 267 Seiten. 1984.

Band 90: Informatik als Herausforderung an Schule und Ausbildung. GI-Fachtagung, Berlin, Oktober 1984. Herausgegeben von W. Arlt und K. Haefner. X, 416 Seiten. 1984.

Band 91: H. Stoyan, Maschinen-unabhängige Code-Erzeugung als semantikerhaltende beweisbare Programmtransformation. IV, 365 Seiten. 1984.

Band 92: offene Multifunktionale Büroarbeitsplätze. Proceedings, 1984. Herausgegeben von F. Krückeberg, S. Schindler und O. Spaniol. VI, 335 Seiten. 1985.

Band 93: Künstliche Intelligenz. Frühjahrsschule Dassel, März 1984. Herausgegeben von C. Habel. VII, 320 Seiten. 1985.

Band 94: Datenbank-Systeme für Büro, Technik und Wirtschaft. Proceedings, 1985. Herausgegeben von A. Blaser und P. Pistor. X, 3 519 Seiten. 1985.

Band 95: Kommunikation in Verteilten Systemen I. GI-NTG-Fachtagung, Karlsruhe, März 1985. Herausgegeben von D. Heger, G. Krüger, O. Spaniol und W. Zorn. IX, 691 Seiten. 1985.

Band 96: Organisation und Betrieb der Informationsverarbeitung. Proceedings, 1985. Herausgegeben von W. Dirlewanger. XI, 261 Seiten. 1985.

Band 97: H. Willmer, Systematische Software- Qualitätssicherung anhand von Qualitäts- und Produktmodellen. VII, 162 Seiten . 1985.

Band 98: Öffentliche Verwaltung und Informationstechnik. Neue Möglichkeiten, neue Probleme, neue Perspektiven. Proceedings, 1984. Herausgegeben von H. Reinermann, H. Fiedler, K. Grimmer, K. Lenk und R. Traunmüller. X, 396 Seiten. 1985.

Band 99: K. Küspert, Fehlererkennung und Fehlerbehandlung in Speicherungsstrukturen von Datenbanksystemen. IX, 294 Seiten. 1985.

Band 100: W. Lamersdorf, Semantische Repräsentation komplexer Objektstrukturen. IX, 187 Seiten. 1985.

Band 101: J. Koch, Relationale Anfragen. VIII, 147 Seiten. 1985.

Band 102: H.-J. Appelrath, Von Datenbanken zu Expertensystemen. VI, 159 Seiten. 1985.

Band 103: GWAI-84. 8th German Workshop on Artifical Intelligence. Wingst/Stade, October 1984. Edited by J. Laubsch. VIII, 282 Seiten. 1985.

Band 104: G. Sagerer, Darstellung und Nutzung von Expertenwissen für ein Bildanalysesystem. XIII, 270 Seiten. 1985.

Band 105: G. E. Maier, Exceptionbehandlung und Synchronisation. IV, 359 Seiten. 1985.

Band 106: Österreichische Artifical Intelligence Tagung. Wien, September 1985. Herausgegeben von H. Trost und J. Retti. VIII, 211 Seiten. 1985.

Band 107: Mustererkennung 1985. Proceedings, 1985. Herausgegeben von H. Niemann. XIII, 338 Seiten. 1985.

Band 108: GI/OCG/ÖGJ-Jahrestagung 1985. Wien, September 1985. Herausgegeben von H. R. Hansen. XVII, 1086 Seiten. 1985.

Band 109: Simulationstechnik. Proceedings, 1985. Herausgegeben von D. P. F. Möller. XIV, 539 Seiten. 1985.